DATE			

THE CELTIC PEOPLES
AND RENAISSANCE EUROPE

THE CELTIC PEOPLES
AND RENAISSANCE EUROPE

A Study of the Celtic and Spanish Influences on Elizabethan History

By
DAVID MATHEW

With an Introduction by
CHRISTOPHER DAWSON

PHAETON PRESS

NEW YORK

1974

Originally Published 1933
Reprinted 1974

Published by Arrangement
With Sheed & Ward

Published Jointly by Paul P. Appel and Phaeton Press

Library of Congress Cataloging in Publication Data

Mathew, David, Abp., 1902-
    The Celtic peoples and Renaissance Europe.

    Reprint of the 1933 ed. published by Sheed & Ward,
London.
    1. Great Britain--History--Elizabeth, 1558-1603.
2. Church and state in Great Britain. 3. Catholic
Church in Great Britain. 4. Celts. 5. Great Britain
--Relations (general) with Spain. 6. Spain--Relations
(general) with Great Britain. I. Title.
DA356.M3 1974   942.05'5   70-162497
ISBN 0-911858-27-X

TO
GERVASE MATHEW

FOREWORD

THIS study of the Celtic and Spanish influences on Elizabethan history bears at every point the impress of my brother Gervase without whom it would never have been either completed or begun. For the encouragement in its earlier stages I must record my deep gratitude to the late Master of Balliol and to the late Professor H. W. C. Davis, who gave his approval to a first portion of the draft during his brief tenure of the Oxford Chair; while I owe to the wise teaching of these two men the great happiness of an objective and calm historical labour. A similar gratitude for a constant interest in the progress of this book is due to Mr. K. N. Bell of Balliol and to Professor William Rees of University College, Cardiff, whose aid in all that concerns the presentation of the Welsh section of the work has been invaluable. I am also very grateful to Mr. Christopher Dawson for his kindness in consenting to write an introduction.

It is essential to explain the system of references and footnotes. These are not intended to elucidate the text, a work which it is to be hoped would prove superfluous, but rather to amplify and substantiate certain detail and to suggest side issues for research. Under these circumstances it can hardly be argued that such notes act as an irritant or impede the narrative, since those who have no taste for these slow branch lines of historical detail are not compelled to abandon the express.

On the other hand it appears an obvious duty to indicate the sources for all *verbatim* quotations and, in the many questions of intricate and changing policy which are involved, the matter of dating letters is important. The series of State Papers and the various private collections of sixteenth-century manuscripts, which contain so much of the extant data concerning the political and social life of the period, lend themselves easily to this treatment.

From the nature of the case the subject of this study, the change in the structure of life in Britain and the political influence of the Celtic fringes upon the new England, bases itself principally upon this type of document. It is likewise in the light of these personal memoranda that the effect of the religious changes and the conflicting cultural standards can best be viewed. The fading of the old conceptions, the lingering effect of the mediæval background, the altered attitude to Spain are here reflected. Spain itself in the comparative stability of the national outlook and policy provides a rough index of the changes in England; while the persistent strength of the anti-Spanish sentiment and its rapid growth can only be understood in the light of the relations between Spain and those Celtic countries which were bound with enthusiasm or reluctance to the Tudor rule. With Spain is bound up not only one facet of the Tridentine outlook, but also that new European military tradition, which the survivors of the Flight of the Wild Geese were so fittingly to close. In England the Continental influences, suffering a sea change, appear most clearly in the profoundly secular-minded Court of Elizabeth, where a gulf had widened between the insular traditions of the squirearchy and the atmosphere of a transient overwrought culture in the highest strata of the nation's social life. To all these influences English and Continental the vague term Renaissance can apply, suggesting the antithesis of Mediævalism, while against them stand the alien Celtic nations with their weakening and pre-Mediæval system of life. It is in fact in some measure a psychological problem which is presented by alterations of standpoint, as gradual as they were profound and complete. The last influences of feudalism in the North, the reactions which were set up by the changes in Wales and Ireland and among the Highland Scots only reveal more clearly the new and strong centripetal forces. The old Celtic tides drew out; it was the victory of a changed England.

DAVID MATHEW.

Cardiff, November 1932.

CONTENTS

APPENDIX OF DOCUMENTS

ILLUSTRATIONS

xi

GRATEFUL acknowledgment of a very courteous assistance is due to the Librarians at the Record Office, the British Museum and the Bodleian, at Trinity College, Dublin, the National Library of Wales at Aberystwyth, the Cardiff Library, the Colleges at Valladolid and the Archives at Simancas. The Editors of the *English Historical Review,* the *Bulletin of Celtic Studies,* and the *Dublin Review* have kindly given permission to reprint two studies and a number of documents which have appeared in their pages. Acknowledgment is also due to the Trustees of the British Museum and the National Museum of Wales and to the Curators of the Prado for permission to reproduce pictures and engravings in their possession.

INTRODUCTION

It is notoriously difficult for an historian to rise above national prejudices and national sympathies and to write the history of a people in a purely objective spirit. But there is a still harder task of which history is only just becoming conscious, and that is the task of transcending the limits of a particular culture. In the past, history has been *intracultural*, and the historian has passively accepted the cultural forms and values that are peculiar to his own civilization. He has identified his own tradition of culture with civilization in the absolute sense and has tended to treat all other traditions as barbaric or naturally inferior. There is no great harm in this when the historian is dealing with a society which is culturally uniform and which belongs wholly to his own civilized world, but it is a very different matter when he has to face the more complex conditions that exist in societies that lie on the border line between two different cultures or that are themselves in a state of cultural transition. Here he fails not only to do justice to one of the protagonists in the historical drama, but even to perceive that any drama is taking place. He is like those early European travellers who discovered new lands and who saw in their strange and ancient civilizations nothing more than ' the beastly devices of the heathen.'

We have a classical example of this at our very doors in the case of the Celtic peoples. For the latter possessed an entirely different tradition of culture to that of the other peoples of Western Europe, and it is impossible to understand their history or their literature or their social life, if we see them through ' European ' eyes or judge them by ' European ' standards. They belonged to an older world that had not known the Roman legions and the Roman city and the Roman law. When Rome fell, the free Celtic peoples were in much the same position as the free Germans whom they helped to convert to Christianity, but while the Germans were subjected to a process of intensive discipline and organization under the Carolingian empire and the mediæval church, the Celtic peoples at least in Ireland and Western Scotland

xiii

turned back to their old traditions and gradually drifted further away from the common tradition of Western culture. Thus Irish history follows a reverse direction to that of the rest of Europe. When Continental culture was at its lowest ebb, Ireland was a great centre of Christian culture and even of classical studies, and when the rest of Europe was schooling itself for the coming of the Renaissance, Celtic culture found its typical expression in the Ossianic poems with their deliberate exaltation of pagan and barbaric ideals. Strictly speaking, Celtic culture outside Wales had no Middle Ages. It passed directly and without transition from the heroic atmosphere of the pre-classical Celtic warrior culture to the hard practical world of Renaissance statecraft—the world of Machiavelli and Granvelle and the Cecils. Already in the mediæval centuries the clash of culture was sharp enough, as we see from the Anglo-Norman historians and the Anglo-Irish legislation, but the conflict was limited by the looseness of texture of the mediæval state and by the adaptability of feudal society to regional conditions. The international Norman warrior class could attach itself like a parasite to the Celtic tribal society as it did with the Oriental and Byzantine societies of Sicily and Syria and Greece. But there was no room for such compromises between the ancient Celtic society and the new Renaissance state. No sociological contact was possible between the Tudor courtier with his mind attuned to all the subtleties of political intrigue and to all the refinements of Renaissance culture, and the Gaelic chieftain who still reckoned his wealth in cattle and his renown by the praises of his hereditary bards, while between the new national middle class who provided the personnel of Tudor administration and the long-haired saffron-clad swordsmen and retainers the gulf was wider still.

These contrasts are recognized in a general way by every modern historian. But it is a very different matter to bring home to the modern reader the tragic realities of this process of cultural conflict and change. The historian who concentrates his attention on concrete individual personalities and events that are the raw material of history tends to lose sight of the deeper spiritual forces that make history intelligible to us, while the writer who attempts, in the Hegelian fashion, to trace in history the progressive realization of an idea is apt to make history rational at the expense of historical reality. One often has an uneasy feeling in reading this kind of history that the victorious party cannot

INTRODUCTION

have been as right as all that and that there is more to be said for the defeated than the historians usually realize. It is rare to find an historian like Father David Mathew who makes us see the past not only from the point of view of the statesmen and rulers who ' made history,' but also with the eyes of those at whose expense history was made. He has abandoned the false simplication that follows from the adoption of a unitary national point of view, and shows how the same events present an entirely different appearance when they are viewed from different social angles and incorporated into different social patterns. In this way he follows the different elements in sixteenth-century culture down to their roots in the regional life of the country-side and the characteristic social types that it produced. Each such type—the English courtier and the Welsh squire, the Italian cardinal and the Tudor country priest, the Spanish noble and the Irish chief, the oarsman of the Western Islands and the Cornish pirate, has its own social tradition and its own spiritual world. They are to be seen not as picturesque figures in an historical pageant, but as the representatives and vehicles of social traditions which are also spiritual forces. And it is only when we have grasped the complex process of cultural and religious change set up by the interaction of these forces and traditions that we can understand the true significance of the great historical crisis which determined the fate of the Celtic peoples in the sixteenth century.

CHRISTOPHER DAWSON.

CHAPTER I

THE DEATH OF QUEEN MARY

A survey of the state of affairs at the moment of Queen Mary's death, when the personal union between the Crowns of Spain and England was severed, will indicate the strength of the idea of the Spanish Alliance. This was bound up with the support which the old Catholic section had received from the Emperor, as the protector of Catherine of Aragon's child. For the same reason, only that section of English life which was in contact with the Queen and personally concerned in her quarrel need, at this time, be considered, the great lords of the Court and the Household.

In its inner circles this was a dying Court, for the Queen chose to surround herself with the elderly members of her Household, who had shared the years of her ' restraint,' and the few survivors of her mother's friends. Lady Exeter and the Dowager Duchess of Norfolk thus represented the old feudal element of Courtenay and Stafford, conservative, unyielding, embittered by suffering. By the end of the reign this element had vanished, while the northern feudalism of Percy, Neville and Dacre, which derived from the same parent stock, was to be destroyed ten years later in the Northern Revolt. In the group below, the new official peers, Paulet, Paget and Rich, were of too pliant a temper to support any policy which had gone out of favour, so that the old remedy of official Catholicism and alliance with Spain was left without any serious upholders among the lay peers in the Lords. Even when the new lords were Catholic, their heredity was not of the temper to withstand persecution and, as a result of the thirty years changes, it was with complete indifference and tedium that the bulk of the courtiers regarded religious affairs. The serious support for the Church among the Court circles came from a quite different ' milieu,' the group of the wealthy squires who held Household appointments. By contrast their interests lay, not in the capital, but in the country, in the wool trade and markets, manorial rights, enclosures, good dowries and the purchase of land. The presentation to their livings, the maintenance of chantries and foundation Masses attached them to the Catholicism of the soil, while their leaders had been connected with the Princess Mary's Household and had supported her in the religious struggles of her brother's reign. They were connected by relationship and a long tradition of Household service, and it was this group that provided that nucleus of Dormers, Throckmortons, Waldegraves and Bedingfields, the future leaders of the Catholic squires. The careers of two men are considered in detail, as contrasting the older more impassive attachment to the Ancient Religion with the more energetic and resourceful temper of the Queen's younger adherents. Sir Henry Jerningham represents the first group and Sir Thomas Cornwallis the second. It was a mark of all these men that the Queen's death was a personal tragedy and closed their official careers. Their sympathies were Spanish to the extent that they had supported Queen Catherine and her daughter and thus looked to the Emperor, while they had come to think of their enemies Anne Boleyn and the Edwardian Governments as politically French. Yet this sympathy for Spain against France was a mere political sentiment, which they maintained in retirement. It did not survive them and was not shared by their friends in the country, and was in fact only found in the case of those squires whose experience of official life was co-terminous with the Spanish period at Court.

The copious detail of the survey, which occupies the first two chapters of this volume, is intended to provide an impression of the state of the life of the country at the time of the changes. The mass of information concentrated upon a few individuals and families and small tracts of the country has been selected with a view to illuminating by such examples the condition of the whole. In the Celtic areas on the circumference of the Tudor system very different reactions were set up, but these cannot be seen in their perspective until the conditions at the centre have been considered.

On the feast of St. Hugh of Lincoln, the 17th November, 1558, the reigning Queen Mary of England, France and Ireland, Queen of Spain, the Sicilies and Jerusalem, Archduchess of Austria, Duchess of Burgundy, Milan and Brabant, Countess of Flanders, Hapsburg and Tyrol died in St. James' Palace at about seven in the morning as her chaplain gave the blessing after the Communion in the Mass. Shortly after Vespers in the afternoon of that same day, across the river at Lambeth, the death took place of Reginald Pole, Cardinal Priest of the title of St. Mary in Cosmedin, Archbishop of Canterbury and Legate of the Apostolic See. For thirty days the Queen lay in state in the Chapel Royal at St. James' and the Cardinal in the great hall of Lambeth Palace. In the capital and at the Charterhouse of Jesus of Bethlehem at Sheen there could be Vespers of the Dead on St. Hugh's feast and on the following days Requiem Masses for the Queen in all the cathedrals of her kingdom, sung at the same time by Bishop Tunstall at Durham and by King Philip's Minister, Bishop de Gran-velle of Arras. Later as the messengers went South this was echoed at Naples by the Spanish Cardinal Viceroy d'Albuquerque and in Spain by the Cardinals of Pamplona, Burgos and Valencia, by Arch-bishop Carranza of Toledo in the last days of his security and by the great Las Casas blind and very aged, but still battling for the natives with the Council of the Indies at Seville. As the despatches were sent forward again from Brussels, they reached the Chapter of Besançon, the Vicar Capitular of Milan, the Cardinals of Capua, Acerenza, Manfredonia and Messina and, with the sailing of the Indian Fleet, the Archbishop in Mexico. All these prelates, with eleven Cardinals among them, were the Queen's subjects. There

2

was Mass for the Cardinal of Canterbury throughout his diocese and a great Requiem in Rome before all the Sacred College. Finally on the 14th December the body of the Cardinal was buried in St. Thomas' Chapel in Canterbury Cathedral, and the preceding day there had been the Queen's funeral in the Abbey with the Archbishop of York pontificating and a sermon from the Bishop of Winchester and the last procession of the monks of Westminster. Thus, on the eve of the feast of St. Damasus, the Queen's obsequies, the most elaborate that any English sovereign was destined to receive, were at length completed. The piety of all her clergy was satisfied and after thirty days the sovereign was buried, and they were wise in so magnificent a burial, for the sovereignty of the Catholic Church in England went down into the tomb.

The reign had been undeviatingly Catholic. The House of Lords had carried the restoration of the Pope's authority without one dissentient vote and, upholding everywhere this framework of the Catholic life, there had been the Queen's friends, the survivors of her mother's Court, bound to the Church with a devotion, profound and stiff and bitter. In the twenty years of her confinement, the Queen had never known her contemporaries, while her friends were the elderly members of her household and the still older companions of Queen Catherine, the Maids of Honour of forty years before. It was in its inner circles in very truth a dying Court. The Queen's closest friend was her cousin, Lady Exeter, who had been intimate with her mother and had lived at the Court at Windsor where Lord Exeter had been Constable in the fifteen-twenties, that time of peace. But King Henry had widowed her and she was now growing old with a calm and intense remembrance of her fortunate youth : meanwhile she slept in the royal bedchamber and the Queen cherished her greatly on account of her imprisonment and her sufferings. Such memories were the thin life blood of the great old-fashioned households and in particular of the heavy outworn pomp of Norfolk House at Lambeth, where there rested the flotsam and jetsam of several generations of ancient Howard ladies. These were headed by the Dowager Duchess, who had been another friend of Catherine of Aragon and had once sent her a letter concealed in an orange in the difficult days of 1530. She was a harsh, firm woman of sixty-four, a daughter of the Duke of Buckingham and entirely free from any suspicion of complaisance, either in the despoiling of the monasteries or the royal divorce, for she had separated from her husband thirty years before.[1] In the same house, presiding over a crowd of relatives and dependants, the remnants of the establishment of an earlier Duchess, were the Dowagers of Oxford and Bridgwater, who had lived there for twenty years keeping fast in the old ways. Their mother the widow of the second Duke had always worn the head-dress and kirtle of Henry VII's time and kept up the ancient, long devotions and only increased the number of her chaplains when the monasteries were suppressed. The third Duke had quarrelled with both these establishments, because they were so unworldly, and in the fierce struggle between the boy's mother, aunt, grandmother and step-great-aunts for the religious education of the young Duke they had been routed. The Duke had a more accessible town house near St. Katherine's and did not disturb them, while the dowagers, impervious to change, remained in the rambling warren of old Norfolk House by the fields of Lambeth Marsh, going down in their roughly swung horse litters, surrounded by a cloud of servants, to find a great mass of dependants at Horsham St. Faith and Redbourne,[2] where the Duchesses maintained the dispersed nuns of the countryside in their employ.

Meanwhile at Holywell near Shoreditch, the Dowager Duchess' sister, old Lady Westmoreland, kept up an antiquated state and lived equally apart from current politics; for she had quarrelled with her son, Lord Westmoreland. He had attempted to rob her when in an urgent need of money and had been barely able, even with Northumberland's assistance, to explain away an attempt to carry off the royal treasure, which had been collected at Middleham for the Wardens of the March. Also he was unfortunately not at all religious, and the piety of her nine daughters could not atone to Lady Westmoreland for such a lapse. The Queen derived much comfort from these friends, whose slow and faithful minds still held firm to those ideas which they had absorbed in the days of those cumbrous, regal progresses when the sisters and their cousins had been carried forward to the Court surrounded by a press of retainers and baggage wagons, with

---

[1] 'Mine ungracious mother-in-law,' wrote the Duke of Norfolk to King Henry in December, 1541, 'mine unhappy brother and his wife with mine lewd sister of Brydgewater . . . committed to the Tower,' a reference sufficient to show how remote these Howard ladies were from the mild court standards. *Letters and Papers, Henry VIII*, xvi, p. 677.

[2] Many details of the Dowager Duchess' households are contained in her examinations on the fall of Queen Catherine Howard. *Ibid*, pp. 650–684.

all the tapestries and household stuffs, on their way from Thornbury Castle to the Manor of the Rose. It was the end of feudalism in its decrepitude, the heralds, the chaplains, the army almost, of the most puissant Duke of Buckingham blocking the London road.[1]

Joined with this group were Lady Arundel, who was a kind of aunt, for she had been the last wife of the Duchess' uncle, old Lord Sussex, and two elderly peers, the second Earl of Sussex, who was Lady Arundel's stepson, and Lord Bath. They lived down in the country at Woodham Walters and Tawstock and had taken no part in public affairs until they had ridden up from their estates to join Queen Mary. These ancient households of.Courtenay, Stafford and Bourchier were all conservative, profound and unyielding, reverencing and upholding that Catholic Throne, which they did not survive. In the Tudor order they were remote on the pinnacles of that fantastic mountain and they passed like the snow.

There was an extreme contrast between these ancients and the qualities of the second group, the tenacious, possessive, shrewdness of the northern Earls. These were north country and Catholic, quite untouched by the Reformation, an alien and southern thing. A network of cousinships enmeshed them, but above the others and bearing down upon his sons-in-law and nephews rose the impressive personality of Lord Dacre of the North. He was a man of fifty, with a chain of estates behind the Border and an unrivalled understanding of cattle driving and the management of Border thieves, a great official also, for the Wardenship of the Western Marches had come to him and he had a valuable power of intercession with the King.[2] In religion he was a sound Catholic with two chaplains at Naworth and another at Kirkoswald and a chapel in his house at Greystoke.[3] He was extremely wealthy, for many of the horse dealers were his agents,

---

[1] A Household Book of Edward Duke of Buckingham kept up from 5th November, 1508, until 22nd March following describes these progresses of their childhood. The journey from Thornbury to London lasted four days and the Duke travelled with twenty gentlemen in attendance. The gathering at Epiphany of 459 persons, 134 being gentry, indicates the feudal crowds which surrounded them, while the religious aspect is seen in the hermit that the Duke still maintained. Cal. Bagot MSS. Report iv, Appendix, p. 327.

[2] Chapuys declared that he was a friend of Catherine of Aragon and of the Princess Mary and maintained their cause. An evidence of his great power with the north countrymen is provided by Sir W. Musgrave's letter to Cromwell, ' As soon as they shall see him go down they will cry " Crucifige," for the country has been so overlaid with him that they thought here (Cumberland) there was no other King.' Letters and Papers, Henry VIII, vii, p. 313.

[3] The details of the altar furniture from Kirkoswald and of the elaborate painting of the Crucifixion ordered by old Lord Dacres for his oratory at Naworth in 1514 indicate the care lavished on these chapels in the North. Household Books of Naworth, pp. lxxi–iii, Surtees Society.

and he was especially, although fluctuatingly, rich in cattle; since he had men all along the Western Border and cattle could be driven at night East into the safety of Northumberland between Bewcastle Fells. His uncle, old Sir Christopher Dacre, helped him with his great experience of the Border, and his brother, the Bastard of Lanercost, was his agent, going to places where it was not suitable for the Warden to be seen.

Lord Dacre was a man of strong and downright character, tempered by resource. As a result of a difference of opinion with Sir William Musgrave, one of his subordinates and Governor of Carlisle, he was said to have arranged with the Scots for an attack in force on Musgrave's camp at a time when his own troops hurrying to their relief would not be able to arrive in time to prevent the massacre that would ensue. He was arrested and sent to London in May, 1534; but at his trial the peers decided that there was not a shred of truth in the accusations against the noble lord, since the charges were made by base Scotsmen of mean condition. He was honourably acquitted and was not employed again.

Lord Dacre had never lived regularly in London, only taking a house occasionally in Carlisle Rents,[1] and he now devoted himself to the management of the northern leaders, ruling by force of character his timid delicate son-in-law, Lord Cumberland, who had been brought back to strict Catholicism by Anne Dacre, his nephew, Lord Scrope, and his single-minded young cousin, Sir Thomas Percy, known as Simple Tom, to whom the earldom of Northumberland [2] was restored. On the Queen's accession he became Warden again, and his son, Sir Thomas, sat for the county, while the East Marches were given to his brother-in-law, Wharton. Marian Catholicism was firmly entrenched in the North with Lord Dacre victorious.

In close connection with Dacre were his cousin, Lord Derby, who was an unofficial viceroy in Lancashire, and his brother-in-law, Lord Shrewsbury, who represented the Government as President of the Council of the North. These men, after absorbing a great acreage of monastic land in their carefree and profitable youth, had turned

---

[1] Carlisle Rents seem to have belonged to the Bishop of Carlisle, whose town house stood just west of the Savoy. Clifford's Inn and the old Scrope's Inn near Paul's Wharf appear to have been the only houses permanently occupied by northern families. Stowe's *Survey*.

[2] The memory still lingered of the princely devotion of the fifth Earl, who died in 1527 and had maintained eleven chaplains and a Dean of the Chapel. Household Book of the Earl of Northumberland.

seriously to religion in middle age, instigated by their second wives, devout women from those buried Derbyshire manors to which the religious changes had never come. Lady Derby was particularly staunch, a Barlow of the family of Ambrose Barlow the martyr. Both ladies were friends of the Queen and their influence was all the stronger, because, after years of arranged political marriages, their husbands could lavish only too much affection on the wives of their choice. So, for the moment, the North was Catholic [1]; but in the case of these earls the influence of their wives implied a feud with their sons and neither Lord Stanley, nor Lord Talbot followed their step-mother's religion, and before the Queen's death Lady Shrewsbury was dead and Lady Derby was dying.

After these allies had left them, the Dacres still kept up an uneasy magnificence, careless alike of the source of their income and the amount of their spending, until all these armed retainers at Naworth and Greystoke proved their undoing. Old Lord Dacre died and his son Leonard ruined his house by plunging his tenants into the hopeless flurry of the Northern Revolt. In 1569, only ten years after the Queen died, the Catholic leadership in the North was broken, for although the power of the ancient Staffords and Bourchiers had been allowed to crumble away, this was demolished.

Below these two groups, there came the old-fashioned Catholics among the lesser peers, who had been rather Queen Catherine's pages than her friends, like old Lord Morley, who was eighty and had visited the Queen in prison at Hunsdon, and Lord Chandos, the Governor of the Tower, men who remembered the coronation of 1509 and were middle aged before the troubles. The case of Lord Delawarr was typical. He was a peer whose wealth was derived entirely from land, a magnate immersed in the rural life of his county, Sussex, a Catholic who took no part in politics. At Court he was *persona grata* and had received the Garter in old age and the Bath in his youth, sixty-five years before. At the time of the suppression of the monasteries he had asked that Boxgrave Priory might be spared as the burial place of his family, but finding that his efforts were

---

[1] The voting of the following northern peers against Government measures which were bound to pass and when they could easily have abstained shows their attachment to Rome. Lords Derby and Dacre voted against the Book of Common Prayer in 1549, and Lord Wharton also opposed it. Lord Shrewsbury voted against the Act of Supremacy in 1559, and Lords Northumberland, Neville, Dacre and Monteagle, a satellite Stanley, voted against an Act for approving the title of the Elizabethan Episcopate in 1566.

useless he had taken under his charge, with a faintly uneasy conscience, both that house and Wherwell Abbey lest they should fall into impious hands.[1] At this time he was occupied in building a mortuary chapel for himself at Broadwater. His wife was dead and his nephew, William, whom he had adopted, was an impossible person to live with, an impatient, high-spirited boy, who put poison into his food.[2] He was lonely and very old. Queen Mary had made him a Privy Councillor and Lord Lieutenant of Sussex; but, although this appointment might give the Queen an illusion of unchanging stability, it was clear that Catholicism could not survive through such veterans.

For these first three groups the Queen had approval and confidence, but to the next section she was bound by a pure gratitude untempered either by affection or respect. These were the new peers who, having passed a lifetime in the service of the Crown without ever losing the royal favour, possessed an unrivalled experience of the affairs of State, men like the first Marquis of Winchester, the first Lord North of Kirtling, the first Lord Paget of Beaudesert. They had turned back to religion in their old age and had all performed very real services to the Queen, although their methods varied. A certain malleable and pliant character had been induced by a daily realization of the strength of Tudor power. Their conception of the State had also led them to support each successive lawful ruler, while the changes of the time had bred indifferentism in such spirits. It is to be noted that, as far as contemporaries were concerned, Rich alone enjoyed an evil reputation. Yet, in this common Erastian outlook, temperament played its part and there was a strange contrast between Lord Rich, who favoured early decisive movements, and Lord Paget, who seemed to believe that the value of each of his moves was increased by delay. Rich had had the resource to provide evidence against Sir Thomas More which was essential to the Crown. He had managed all the financial side of Cromwell's transactions in monastic land and had been so completely in his confidence that his unhesitating evidence at his trial was con-

---

[1] A great deal of the conservative and Catholic attitude to the changes is condensed in the following letter. On 25th March, 1536, Lord Delawarr had written to Cromwell begging that the house of Boxgrave, of which he was founder, might be spared, as many of his ancestors and his wife's mother lay there. If the King would not forbear to suppress it, he might translate it into a college; otherwise he begs that he may have the farm. Cromwell would be well recompensed for his pains. Letters and Papers, Henry VIII, x, p. 216. When disentangled, this is an interesting sequence of thought.
[2] State Papers, Dom. Eliz. iii, 39 contains papers dealing with the results of this case.

clusive. The Crown also obtained through his means very damaging information in the cases of Wriothesley and Gardiner, and at the moment when Protector Somerset was falling he had the courage to take the Great Seal to Northumberland.[1] Later he succeeded in proclaiming Queen Mary in Essex. In the case of Lord Paget, however, a slow prudence was the predominant quality, and instead of abandoning the Protector, like Rich, he had remained with him as one of his strongest apparent supporters, so that he could thus best assist at his capture. 'We must not think that Heaven is here,' he wrote with piety to Sir William Petre at this time.

Nevertheless, although these men had a claim on the Queen's gratitude, she could hardly be expected to forget their previous treatment and Lord Winchester's post as her gaoler might have been remembered to his misfortune. For an understanding of the Court life of this period it is worth pausing for a moment to consider the marks of honour which his sovereigns granted to this forerunner of the Erastian [2] peers. Sir William Paulet, first Marquis of Winchester, first Earl of Wiltshire and first Baron St. John of Basing in the County of Southampton, stood far above his companions, for he had proceeded calmly relying on a very just perception of affairs. Mr. Paulet had been an easy-going conservative squire before he turned serious, but Sir William was a most prudent official of Henry VIII and Lord St. John was a friend of Somerset, a friendship which remained unimpaired until the day that Lord Wiltshire became an intimate of Northumberland. It was to Lord Winchester's credit that he extricated himself from this intimacy, as also from his entanglement under Lady Jane Grey, and passed on in prosperity. It cannot be denied that continued service of the English Kingship gave, under one aspect, a complete consistency to this career. When not long past his seventieth year, Lord Winchester turned to religion, as his colleagues had done, but the late conversion of these leaders [3] could hardly be expected to

---

[1] All considered it is not surprising that More should have stated of Rich at his trial that 'yourself can well tell you were always esteemed very light of your tongue . . . and not of any commendable fame.' Cresacre More's *Life of Sir T. More*, p. 263.

[2] The claim of Knox to have denounced Winchester in a sermon in 1553 is interesting. ' And Shebna,' he is said to have declared, ' was unto good King Ezekias sometime Comptroller, sometime Secretary and last of all Treasurer. . . . No, Sobna was a crafty fox, and could show . . . a fair countenance to the King.' The quotation in Strype's *Memorials*, II, ii, p. 71, shows at any rate how anti-pathetic was this Erastian quality to the mind of Geneva.

[3] From among this group Lords Winchester, North and Rich voted against the Act of Uniformity and Lord Cromwell against the Act of approving the title of the Elizabethan bishops.

affect their children's opinions. Even when these were Catholic, their heredity was not of the temper to withstand persecution.[1]

Around these men there moved the great mass of the courtiers, who followed the prevailing custom, but were utterly uninterested in religious affairs. In any case their habits of life and the irregular and elaborate establishments, which so many maintained, must have prevented a very large number from receiving the Sacraments. It was with a complete indifference and tedium that they regarded the struggle and since the Catholic groups, which have been described, were vanishing as the Queen's councillors died, it was obviously that it was only from an entirely different *milieu* that the Church could hope for support.

*   *   *   *   *

Under the Tudors the Household appointments were governed by a family arrangement, so that these posts were passed to and fro among a small number of wealthy squires in the home counties who were closely related. They were not the Queen's friends, but her servants, following their mistress with a personal loyalty, and it was this quality which brought them also to the defence of the Church. Although few of them lived very far from London, they were quite apart from the world of the Court, since their chief interests were centred in the management and increase of their property and they were prosperous, for there was a good profit in wool and they had had luck with enclosures. In Queen Mary's case, the majority of her officers came from East Anglia, which was partly the cause of her ride into Kenninghall on her brother's death to raise her standard in Norfolk. They were

[1] The second, fourth and fifth Marquises of Winchester and Lord Giles and Lord Chideock Paulet, the second Earl of Southampton, the second and third Lords Paget and the second Lord Cromwell seem to have been the only supporters of the Catholic Church which these families provided. Votes in the House of Lords and Recusant Rolls.

Catholics, too obscure to suffer persecution under King Henry, but influential enough in their countryside to maintain their own chaplains, country squires, with all their wealth in land and wives with substantial dowries, also in land, and large families, very domestic. All these things and a deep attachment to the rural church, the chantries and chapels of the Catholicism of the soil, caused them to keep up their practice and also that regular use of the Sacraments, which the world of the Court had so largely abandoned.

Two men summed up in their lives the characteristics of this class, the one representing the passing tradition of the old generation and the other the more enterprising keener outlook of the younger squires. Sir Henry Jerningham, the elder of these men, was brought up in his father's manor house at Somerleyton in the valley of the Waveney, a second son. He came of a family long settled in Suffolk, which held all the land down the left bank of the Waveney to Breydon Water, as well as some manors in Mid-Suffolk, which had come through a Bedingfield marriage. Their farm produce was sent to the fairs at Norwich or to the market in Blue Boar Lane in Lowestoft, where the family possessed manorial rights. The presentation to several livings was in their gift, including that of Somerleyton, the church of their burial. It was all perfectly self-contained.[1] Henry Jerningham's own inheritance was good, a house at Huntingfield and another at Wingfield, twenty miles further up the Waveney Valley; but, as a younger son, he was expected to make his way at Court like his Uncle Richard had done. Fortunately he had influence there, since his step-father, Sir William Kingston, was Constable at the Tower and his aunt, Lady Jerningham, a devout Catholic, had married Lord Bedford. Meanwhile a suitable marriage was arranged for him and his cousin Frances Baynham was brought up from Gloucestershire. Her dowry, a substantial one for her station, consisted of the reversion of Sir Anthony Kingston's estates and the manor of Bedingfield, which adjoined the outlying Jerningham land at Horham and was six miles south of Wingfield along the Stow-market road. This was a definite and careful accretion to his standing

---

[1] This estate of eleven manors was so self-contained that the elder son, Sir John, rarely left it. He was a substantial Catholic squire, chiefly interested in acclimatizing the firs at Somerleyton and Herringfleet, which had just been introduced into England. In the church there was the tomb of Sir Thomas, the patriarch of the family, and his wife, an Appleyard, a surname so redolent of the soil, with an inscription, 'Jesu Christ both God and Man save thy servant Jernegan.' Camden's and Fuller's *Journeys*.

and worth in the shire. Later, he received a royal grant of the manor of Costessey near Norwich, where he moved in 1547, and he had connections with the Lady Mary's household, for his cousin, Edward Waldegrave, was Master of the Wardrobe and six years later he was the very first to join her when her standard was raised. Marching through the Jerningham villages and raising his brother's tenantry, as he passed on the way, he seized Yarmouth for Queen Mary and was made Captain of the Guard and Vice-Chamberlain. In 1557, being already a Privy Councillor, he became Master of the Horse, a great promotion, which gave him the leadership of the permanent officials at the Court.[1]

As he rode from Costessey to London he passed from manor to manor owned by this Catholic group, so that he could dine the first day at East Harling with Sir Thomas Lovell, whose brother Gregory was the Queen's Cofferer, or perhaps push ten miles farther on in the evening to sleep with his cousin, Mrs. Rookwood, at Euston and then dine with Lady Bath at Hengrave Hall, the vast place which Sir Thomas Kitson had left her; but this house was perhaps more within the Cornwallis' circle. After riding through Bury in the afternoon, he could spend the night at Borley with his cousin Waldegrave, now Sir Edward and Chancellor of the Duchy. Setting out again towards London, he could make a second break at this same cousin's house at Navestock, within the jurisdiction of Epping Forest, which together with the County Seat was also in Waldegrave's control; or he could ride across country [2] from Borley to Great Hallingbury to visit old Lord Morley and then enter London along the northern road.

When his route lay further to the east, Sir Henry would cross the Waveney at Syleham Bridge, where old Sir Robert Rochester, the Comptroller of the Household had his land, and then sleep at his own house at Bedingfield. On occasion he might call on Sir Thomas Holland, the Duke's agent, at Framlingham about disputes; for the Norfolk estates, doubled by the monastic lands, were scattered all

---

[1] A letter from the Privy Council to Sir Henry Jerningham in 1553 indicates his intimate relations, 'the oftener he writes the more pleasure he will give to the Queen.' Cal. Stafford MSS. Report 10, ii, p. 158.

[2] There was perhaps less movement on purely social occasions in East Anglia than in the lonelier manors of the North. A contemporary correspondence throws light on the habits of a Yorkshire family of similar standing. 'And whensoever ye come,' Sir Henry Saville wrote to his Cousin Plumpton on 5th March, 1546, 'bring bowes and grayhoundes, a polard is swet now and I love it best now at this season. Ye shall come no time wrong, fence time then other.' Plumpton Correspondence, p. 231.

over East Anglia and the old Duchess' dower lands at Horsham bounded Costessey on the north. Riding south through Ipswich, he could stay with some poor relations, the Mannocks at Gifford's Hall in Stoke by Nayland across the Stour, and then take the London road, breaking the journey to dine with the Secretary of State at Writtle in those elaborately rural surroundings which were the affectation of Sir William Petre's age.

If he went to join the Court at Windsor, he would ride west from Costessey, dine with his son-in-law, Sir Thomas Southwell, at Wood Rising and sleep at Oxburgh [1] with his cousin, Sir Henry Bedingfield, County Member and Constable of the Tower, a sound Catholic in the middle 'forties. Then, turning south through Cambridgeshire and along the northern side of the Chilterns, he would go past house after house, Lanwade, Sawston, Eaton Bray, all belonging to this cousinship of slow-moving Catholic squires, until he reached Buckinghamshire at Wing, where the Dormers clustered. Sir William Dormer, whose daughter Jane, afterwards Duchess of Feria, was the Queen's favourite Maid of Honour, had always succeeded in keeping in the parish a staunch priest, Dom John Holyman, one of the Reading Benedictines, who survived to be the last Catholic Bishop of Bristol. Halfway between Wing and Windsor stood Lord Windsor's house at Bradenham and then, within easy reach of the Castle, Stoke Poges, where Sir Edmund Windsor lived, and Denham Place, which belonged to Sir Edmund Peckham, who sat for the county.

All these men represented the elder generation and were immovable in their attachment to the Throne and the Altar, loyalties which their imagination conceived as inseparable. They were touched with a certain slowness,[2] which enabled them to pass calmly through jealousies ; for their real interests were not in London at all, but in the country, in the gradual increase of their property, in the wool prices and the harvests. The old monastic life appealed to them, and Sir John Gage, Lord Chamberlain of the Household, was said to have decided to join the Carthusians with the consent of his wife, shortly before the fall of the monasteries, as his children were already grown

---

[1] A sidelight is thrown on the regular communication by an inventory of goods at Oxburgh, taken on 27th November, 1598, in which mention is made of ' two posts' rooms.' Cal. Stafford MSS., p. 162.

[2] A letter from Sir Henry Jerningham to the Council suggests this quality. ' A sea coast,' he wrote on 4th April, 1558, ' is most necessary to be foreseen. I have viewed some parts and will peruse the rest.' Cal. S.P. Dom. Add., 1547-65, p. 471.

up and the times were evil. Again the last Abbess of Denny lived with her Throckmorton nephews and great-nephews at Coughton and Elizabeth Shelley, Abbess of St. Mary's at Winchester, returned to the shelter of her family at Michelgrove.

These monastic sympathies only increased the dignified reserve of the older squires, when they were removed from their posts after the Queen had died and the State Religion was changed ; but there is a pleasant contrast between the almost impassive fidelity of Sir Henry Jerningham and the genial activity of his nephew, Sir Thomas Cornwallis. They came from the same part of the country, as the latter's home at Brome was also in the Waveney Valley, and Wingfield lay just across the water meadows to the east. There was a similarity, too, in their official careers. Before the Queen's death, Sir Thomas had passed through the Treasurership of Calais to be Comptroller of the Household, and he was also a Privy Councillor and sat for the County, but it was later that the contrast appeared between his own enterprise and his colleagues' retirement, for he was not yet forty when all these public careers were broken.

He soon became the leader [1] of the East Anglian Catholics, especially after Waldegrave was arrested, and he arranged the organization of priests and later, when the persecution began, tried to ward off the attack through his influence with the Bishop's Chancellor at Norwich. Then he smuggled his secretary over to France to become a monk, when this was forbidden, and built hiding-places and secret chapels and welcomed the seminary priests with enthusiasm. He was always employed on Catholic business riding about the county, enterprising and genial.

When the Queen died, it was the members of her household who were the chief support of the religion to which she had devoted her life. Her personal friends seldom survived her, and it was from the squires that the strength and energy came to build up her religion again. Slow and tenacious, bound to the soil, the revived Catholic life sprang afresh from the acorns self-sown by the Royal Oak in its fall.

[1] A list of the principal Catholic Recusants in March, 1588, begins with these names : Sir Thomas Cornewallis, Sir John Arundell, Sir Thomas Tresham, Sir William Catesby, Sir Thomas Fitzherbert, Sir John Southworth, Sir Thomas Jarrett, Sir George Peckham, Sir John Cotton, Sir Thomas Kitson, Sir Alexander Culpepper, all men among the rich landed squires. Lansdowne MSS. Burghley Papers, lvi, p. 163, printed in *Catholic Record Society*, Miscellanea, xii, p. 120

CHAPTER II

THE ACTION OF THE MARIAN PRIESTS

A consideration of the position of the parochial clergy is essential to any understanding of the history of the Anglican Settlement. The importance of the village unit, the dependence of the priest upon the squire who had granted him the appointment, the gulf between the parochial clergy and the Episcopate are all factors which contribute to the division of policy, which became clear in 1559, between the country priests and the bishops. The rarity of Visitations, the long absence of bishops from their sees upon official and diplomatic journeys, the system of promotion, the mere physical distances in the great dioceses all tended to make the separation complete between the country rector and his diocesan. The bishops were for the great part, humanist, subtle, very intelligent and, if possible, too well informed ; while the priests in the country were ignorant of all political change. Thus, in the quarrel with Rome, the bishops had at first drawn on their knowledge of history, comparing the dispute to the Interdict under Innocent III or the old Investitures quarrel and balancing the King's known abhorence of heresy with his individual views on Church Government. They had a certain cold admiration for Bishop Fisher and Sir T. More, but, they disliked intensely the Pilgrims of Grace and were convinced that no good could arise from a *Jacquerie*. Under Edward VI they could console themselves with the thought that the evils were temporary, but after the brief Catholic success under Mary the weight of testimony convinced them at last and persuaded them that the Anglican Settlement involved an attack on the Mass they firmly opposed it. But the country priests were hardly affected by these national quarrels, while the conservative, tradition-loving squires were all powerful. Cranmer as a Lutheran meant little to them, for they had never seen the Archbishop of Canterbury and could not imagine a Lutheran, but they knew the rooted loyalty to the Church of their own people, the legacies for Masses for the dead and the devotion to the Wounds of Christ and to the Saints, the constant use of the Rosary and the fervent prayers of the harvest Collects. Up till now they had always followed their leaders the distant bishops, whose minds they did not understand, and they had expected submission ; but when the bishops refused most of the rural clergy, following the nearer influence of squires, submitted again. Both priests and people had felt the influence of the long Schism and the notion of the priest as a State functionary was so strong that it did not seem unreasonable that the priest should remain, consenting to read the Anglican service occasionally and saying Mass in private till good times should return. Yet this system of nominal acceptance of the new order by the Marian priests was bound to prove fatal in time to Catholicism, as is shown in two instances where the squires made an especial effort to protect that religion. In the one case, that of the estates in South Norfolk centring about the property of the Lovells of East Harling, the attempt broke down after the death of Sir Thomas Lovell and in the other the effort of the absentee Catholic landlords to maintain Marian priests in the livings that they controlled in the hundred of Newport in Buckinghamshire was also a failure. It was at best a policy of preventive measures, the effort, unsuccessful in the end, to keep the Marian priests

15

in their place, for there was no chance of obtaining a Catholic when a new appointment was made. In addition, wherever a living or curacy had been in the gift of the monasteries the opportunity of maintaining the parish in Catholic hands vanished, for the appointments were in the hands of the Crown ; while at the best all that the Conservative squires with their confused intentions could hope for was a form of schismatic Catholicism, such as had prevailed under Henry VIII. The occasional conformity that was practised was undermining the Faith of the children and the Church could not survive on such terms.

In the North and especially in Lancashire a different system was practised for the squires and the clergy defied the Crown from the outset and gained success through defiance as the state of Ribblesdale now makes clear. The influence of the bishops was here still more remote, but the power of the squires had gained in proportion and the undeveloped state of the parishes, where the curates of moorland villages would often depend on the priest of some neighbouring town, gave a prestige to the elder clergy in the less accessible parts. James Hargreaves, Vicar of Blackburn, who with ten of his priests refused the oath of supremacy, and Sir John Southworth of Samlesbury, the chief supporter of the dispossessed priests, are typical of the independent spirit which was found through the North. This hard and stubborn self-reliance of the Northern Catholics is in marked contrast to the milder outlook of the squires in Southern England always eager to meet the Government, to pacify and to placate.

A survey of this nature is essential to the understanding of the Spanish and Celtic influences, for the manner in which these forces impinged upon English affairs was the result of the divergent reactions which the religious changes set up. The hostile contact and friction turned to a large extent on the new more centralized policy, the expanding national sentiment and the change in religion.

At the accession of Elizabeth it must have seemed to those Englishmen who had passed nearly the whole of their lives under the varying forms of the Henrican system that a certain measure of control of parochial life was essential, if the Catholics were to continue to exist as an organized body. Within the village life the parish boundaries marked the recognized limits and in those slow countrysides not only the labourers and the squires, but also the spiritual pastors were in a sense rooted. In all the material aspects of life there was little difference between the country priest and the farmer ; both of them showing a dumb and confused hostility to the towns, both ignorant of politics, familiar only with their own fields and the two next parishes and the market, and recognizing but one force above them, the increasing weight of the squire. In a great many cases it was this same squire who chose both his priest and his tenants, giving the parish to the son of a farmer on some neighbouring manor and maintaining him there till he died ; so that the priest and the steward and the bailiff and the woodreeve of a manor would all grow old together, rooted and unchanging as trees. This state of affairs still exists in certain small enclaves in Italy, where the parish priests are bound to a lifetime of service in the remote churches of the hills, tied to their countryside and as closely identified with the seasons and the soil as are their fathers and brothers, bounded by the same material interests, the sparse vines, the olive yield, the sheep.

There was a profound gulf between such parochial clergy and the bishops, the Tudor parish priests immovable, unaffected by change, and the episcopate, only too sensitive to the light winds of the Court. The episcopal curia in England had a delicate appreciation of public affairs, the fruit of a humanist-trained sometimes over subtle intelligence playing on information both detailed and accurate, while everything was discussed and over discussed as their more fortunate members were carried forward on their leisured careers. Here there was no stagnation, for all were gently in movement, since each promotion was followed by a quiet ripple of changes, which led from the Court of Arches or from those welcoming abbeys to which the King returned from deer, upwards to a deanery with employment at Court or in France. The next stage brought a mitre and embassies further afield, until like a consolation peerage came the final reward, the passing of the last of summer in the drone and haze of the Close at Lincoln or some rich sleep-laden see. Not only the age and inclination of the great prelates, but even the mere distances in the cumbrous dioceses, which Henry VIII had inherited, made any thoroughgoing visitation impossible. The see of York stretched right across England to the coast parishes in Cumberland and then southwards to the border of Leicestershire beyond the Trent. The neighbouring diocese of Lincoln extended from the Humber to the Thames Valley, so that the parishes between Wychwood Forest and the Cotswolds beyond the Evenlode were more than a hundred miles away from their cathedral city over the lost and untracked bye-roads across the shires.[1] But far more important than the distance which separated the Bishop and his curia from the remote parish clergy was the immense divergence of standpoint from which public happenings were judged.

---

[1] The diocesan organization in the essential matter of ordinations was carefully considered, as is shown by the detailed titles for the ordination held by John, Bishop of Negropont in the conventual church of the Friars Preachers at York on 14th June, 1511; the phrase, ' ad titulum domus monialium villæ Novi Castri super Tynam per literas dimissorias ' has a very modern ring. Register of Cardinal Bainbridge, Surtees Society, pp. 361–367.

When the King quarrelled with Rome the prelates drew on their wide knowledge of human affairs. This was, so they reasoned, a case of interdict, a purely personal difficulty like the affair of Innocent III and Philip Augustus with a touch, too, of the old Investitures quarrel; meanwhile they could use the clause ' as far as the law of God will allow ' to the oath of Supremacy, and it was clear that the King was a firm opponent of heresy and these troubles would pass. They had a certain cold admiration for the Bishop of Rochester and Lord Chancellor More, but they disliked intensely the Pilgrims of Grace and their leaders, old Lord Darcy shouting and clanking about in his old-fashioned armour in the quiet of the Archbishop's palace at Cawood, and the armed peasants in this and the later revolts ; for the Church could never be saved by a *Jacquerie*. Under Edward VI, affairs became difficult, but Protector Somerset only lasted three years, and it seemed unlikely that Northumberland's rule would last longer, and the Acts were not the King's, but his Councillors'. Still it was a doubtful question with Archbishop Cranmer clearly a Lutheran, and in the disputes there was an opposition again, Bishops Tunstall and Gardiner ; they were deprived and their attitude was very praise-worthy no doubt, but at the same time it was perfectly clear that politically the Bishop of Winchester had been sailing too close to the wind ; so the Episcopate waited in hope. There was no strength in the young King, and they felt confident that in a few years England would be Catholic again and in this they were right. The bishops admired martyrdom and they did not refuse it, but in their too clear perception of material affairs they failed to find any reason why they should be martyrs themselves. But after the brief Catholic success under Mary their hesitation was at length overborne by the obvious purpose of the Anglican Settlement to destroy the Mass and Catho-licism and so they opposed it. An overwhelming accumulation of data had been needed to persuade men so dependent on their sovereign to oppose her at last and after this effort they ended their days under a mild form of confinement in melancholy clear-sighted peace.

There was nothing more alien to the country priests than such cumulative labyrinthine reasoning, a Renaissance balancing of impon-derable political chances, while their own minds were as sure and as calm as the harvest. The remote quarrels of the Court affected them little, and the first disturbance which touched them was the fall of the monasteries. Undoubtedly they disliked the destruction of these houses of prayer, but the indignation could not last for ever and the sympathy cooled under the stress of so many monks cast adrift on the countryside, for these were often received as chaplains by the squires and now served those private chapels which had formerly belonged of right to the parish.[1] It was a dislocation and an interference with their jurisdiction which touched the country priests much more nearly than vague rumours of national quarrels. Later for similar reasons the destruction of the chantries was a serious blow, and then came the Prayer Books of Edward VI, but it is very doubtful how far these were enforced in remote parishes, where nothing that happened in London could weigh as against the preferences of some heavy conservative squire. The Mass was preserved intact everywhere until 1549, and the rapidity of its restoration in 1553 would seem to show its destruction was partial. In all these matters the clergy remained passive and followed the bishops and so far every doubtful case had ended in submission and they could well believe that no serious harm could come to God's Church from these tea-cup storms in the capital. Besides all these disputes came to them merely by hearsay. Thus it was said that the Archbishop of Canterbury was a Lutheran; but they had never seen the Archbishop and they could not imagine a Lutheran and this counted as nothing when compared to the rooted loyalty to the Church of their own people, the legacies for Masses for the dead and the devotion to the Wounds of Christ and to the Saints [2] and the constant use of the Rosary, with the union of Church and people in the Collects for fair weather for the crops and for rain.

After Queen Mary died there were rumours of changes, but all through that wet winter of 1558 nothing came and the great epidemic of Christmas drove them out of men's minds. Then in the spring there was the opposition of the Episcopate and finally the order for

---

[1] An interesting light is thrown on the subsequent lives of the monks of the suppressed Priory of St. Milburg by the 'Register of Sir Thomas Butler, Vicar of Much Wenlock in Shropshire,' which extends from 26th November, 1538, till 20th September, 1562, and is printed in *Cambrian Journal*, iv, pp. 81–98. The case seems typical. An entry Monday, 25th December, 1547, runs 'departed and died in the manor house or place of Madeley, Sir John Baily, clerke, the last Prior of Monks that was in the monasterie of Much Wenlock. *Ibid.*, p. 91.

[2] Henry Machyn's *Diary*, pp. 150–191, *passim*, provides many instances of devotion paid to the saints at funerals in London, and although the almost aggressive display of Catholicism, which the Dudleys arranged at the funeral of the Duchess of Northumberland in 1555 may have had a political significance, this cannot be said of the other burials, some of which, including the funerals of Lady Winchester and Lady Oxford, where four banners of saints were carried, took place as late as the reign of Elizabeth.

the abolition of the Mass before the Nativity of St. John and the deprivation of every bishop in England. There was only the time between the spring sowing and the hay-making for the priests to make their decision.

During more than twenty years of trouble the country priests had solved every point of conscience by submission, and so far the Episcopate had taken the lead in acceptance of the royal commands; but now they refused. They were followed in this refusal by the bulk of the Episcopal Curia and by a great many clergy in the towns, where the issue was clear cut; but the greater part of the country priests, who had known nothing of the long hesitation of the bishops, broke away and submitted again. This action can be best understood in reference to the rural unit and the power of the squire. The fidelity to the Church and to the framework of the Catholic life, which the majority of this class possessed, might have produced a despondency had it not been tempered by a profound loyalty and pride in the dynasty and an increasing material prosperity as a result of which they saw the whole situation *couleur de rose* and were able to devise a happy expedient for these dangerous times. Both priests and people had felt the influence of the long Henrican Schism and the notion of the priest as a State functionary was so strong that it did not seem unreasonable that the priest should remain and consent to read the Anglican service, while saying Mass in private till good times should return. Besides, in a remote part of the country with a Catholic squire it was not necessary to read the Anglican service very often; for so many of the clergy were non-resident and all that was required in the early years was the removal of the Catholic symbols from the churches and the abolition of the public celebration of Mass.[1]

It was this system of nominal acceptance of the new *régime* by the Marian priests in the country that satisfied the great Catholic body among the squires; but it was a system which was bound to prove fatal in time to the religion which it was designed to protect. Two

[1] The changes at Ludlow can be followed in the Churchwardens' Accounts for 1558-9, 'Payd for ij li of candles to hange in the churche on Christmas day in the morninge; to the pavyor for beinge at the makynge of the pascelle (candle); to Thomas Season for makynge of the sepulcur and for takyng ytt down. Payd upon Corpus Christi day for pynes and poyntes to dresse the canapie.' This is the last Catholic entry. Then ' payd the xx day of June for ij pieces of tymber to set by the comunyon table. Payd xxvj day of September for takynge down the rowde (rood); for iij bushells of lyme to plaster the walls where the autors was; for iiij dayes work takynge down the auters (altars).' Churchwardens' Accounts of Ludlow, 1540-1603, Camden Society, pp. 92-94.

examples of the working of this plan, one among the lesser gentry of South Norfolk and the other among the rich proprietors in Buckinghamshire show in themselves the general trend of the movement, while a third instance, the method adopted for maintaining Catholicism by the squires of the Ribble Valley, shows the alternative system, which alone contained the elements of success and which came in time to prevail.

At the moment cf the Elizabethan Settlement the manor of East Harling in South Norfolk, close to the fields where the Waveney rises, was held by Sir Thomas Lovell, an elderly Catholic squire, who lived there with his wife Elizabeth, a daughter of old Sir Philip Paris of Little Linton, and their eleven children. The eldest son, Thomas, was married to a Huddlestone of Sawston in the next county and spent all his life with his six brothers managing the small estate remote from affairs. The advowson of East Harling belonged to them and, in the last year of Queen Mary, Sir Thomas had provided a zealous priest for the parish, so that the Catholicism of the district was well maintained. After Sir Thomas' death in 1567, his son continued the system. They were an old-fashioned family with a moderate but sufficient income, Thomas Lovell's lands bringing him in £400 a year, while his mother, Lady Lovell, had dower lands worth £100 a year, as had his mother-in-law, Lady Huddlestone. Both these old ladies lived with him at Harling, with his children and all his unmarried brothers. They were surrounded by relatives who spent all their time on their manors with an occasional ride into Norwich as their greatest adventure, men whose incomes were not large,[1] but whose expenses were exceedingly small, so that they had at all times contentment and in a good year prosperity. Also their intense concentration on the parochial affairs of their manors made their influence on local religion the stronger. Ten miles from Harling at Merton there was a Catholic centre in the small parish which belonged to Lovell's brother-in-law, Robert de Grey, and that was half-way to Uncle Audley's house at Pagrave Magna. Farther north again, there was another little Catholic parish belonging to the Norfolk

[1] The Lovells' income would have corresponded to a modern income of about £6,500 a year, while Mr. de Grey and Mr. F. Paris, who had £200 a year in Elizabethan money would have had the value of £2,200 and Mr. Audley £1,100 a year. But while the Lovells had certain considerable expenses in regard to the office of sheriff and occasional visits to Court, their relations were free from this, nor were there any educational expenses as the de Greys and Paris would be brought up at home by their priest.

branch of the Paris', where Cousin Ferdinando kept a Marian priest. The de Greys in particular had been a rather clerical family, as Robert's uncle, Thomas de Grey, although the eldest son, had passed the estate to his brother and became a priest after the death of his wife, living on the estate and saying Mass in the chapel for forty-one years, until he died in the middle of the reign of Queen Mary. In all these parishes there were thus Catholic families and children, for these men were recusants brought up by the Marian priests in isolated Catholic 'islands,' knowing no other religion and becoming strict in their practice when the persecution began. The rooted Catholicism of these priests is shown in the fact that the leaders of their flocks all accepted the Papal Decrees and appear in the Recusant Lists of 1577 and the following years. But the attempt to maintain Catholicism by such Marian priests could only be a temporary measure, and the first blow was the deprivation of Mr. Moore, of East Harling, in 1568, after the death of his protector, Sir Thomas,[1] and the disappearance of the others soon followed.

An attempt to solve the problem along similar lines was made by the wealthy Catholic owners of advowsons and a consideration of the condition of the parishes in the hundred of Newport in Buckinghamshire, which lay along both banks of the upper reaches of the Great Ouse, will explain the measure of success of this system. This was a country of rich manors, often in the gift of the Crown, and of wide estates belonging to great families, who administered them through stewards and had acquired them through some service at Court. And in this connection it is a curious fact that the districts where the Catholic influence was weakest were precisely those great monastic estates, where the abbeys had held the lordship of the manor as well as the presentation of the living and those small parishes where the hospitals and priories appointed curates and drew an income from the tithes. The hundred of Newport had lived under the distant shadow of St. Albans and Sion Abbey also held livings, but after the Dissolution there could be no Catholic influence where parishes fell to the gift of the Crown.[2]

[1] In contrast to East Harling, the manor and living of West Harling belonged to a rising egal family of strong Protestant complexion, represented by Sir Bassingbourne Gawdy and his son Framlingham. They bore as their arms ' a tortoise passant argent,' and as their crest ' on a wreath argent and gules a chapeau turned up ermine.' Cal. Gawdy MSS., *passim*.
[2] Thus the Catholic influence was neutralized at Costessey and Oxburgh where the churches had been controlled by St. Giles' Hospital at Norwich and West Dereham Abbey.

THE ACTION OF THE MARIAN PRIESTS

An instance of such change is shown in the case of the Throckmortons of Coughton; for in this part of the Great Ouse valley the chief centre for Catholics was Weston Underwood House, where the Throckmortons, who drew considerable income from their lands about Olney, stayed on their way from the Court into Warwickshire. This manor, their secondary property, was sometimes used as a dower house, but more often as the establishment for the eldest son on his marriage. But, although Coughton was Catholic, here Weston Underwood was a curacy under Olney and both churches had belonged to the Abbess of Sion, so that there was no hope of local influence on the royal nominee. Yet, on the other hand, Broughton by Crawley Brook and Moulsoe, two miles to the north, and Crawley, three miles farther on towards Bedfordshire, were all in the hands of the Catholics. To the last parish, an outlying manor of the great Dormer estates by Ethorp and Wing, Sir Robert had sent his cousin, Walter Dormer, a scholarly dependent of that wide Catholic clan, while Moulsoe was an offshoot of the Mordaunt influence at Turvey across the Bedfordshire border, and Broughton belonged to Lord Winchester, the fruit of speculation at Court. These great men, living away from the district, made some attempt to maintain their parishes Catholic; but by 1568 the Marian priests had vanished and they gave up the effort. As Catholics they did not present again, Lord Mordaunt leaving this to an Anglican cousin; for Sir Robert Dormer's last cast had proved a misfortune, as he had given Crawley to Garbrand Herks, a young scholar from Oxford, who, contrary to all reports, turned out a Puritan. Such affairs could not be arranged from a distance, nor was it easy for the farmers to remain Catholic without the support of a resident squire. Although Middleton Keynes and Adstock and Bradwell, which belonged to the Anglican Longuevilles, were in the hands of most zealous Marian priests, who were later deprived for their Popery, Catholicism could not survive without leaders. Even when there were leaders the Old Religion could not subsist on this system, for one deprivation would ruin the Church in a parish, since under Elizabeth there was at best the hope of maintaining a priest and never of gaining a Catholic appointment. Finally, it was the Catholics themselves who brought this state of affairs to an end, since year by year the old Marian priests were becoming decrepit and of course they could not be replaced; while the occasional conformity, which so many Catholics practised, was under-mining the faith of their children. Drastic measures were essential and the excommunication of the Queen and the setting up of the seminaries abroad was an unavoidable challenge, if Catholicism in England was to be rescued from a drying up at the roots and a withering death.

Now in Lancashire a different system was practised, for the strong hard independence of the squires and yeomen in the North coloured their outlook on religious affairs. The development of Catholic life in Ribblesdale throws light on their theory, and, unlike the efforts of the southern squires, this attempt was successful, for they opposed the Crown from the outset and their religion survived. The country priests, too, were even more remote from the Episcopate than those in the South and until 1541 the Ribble formed the boundary line between the sees of Lichfield and York. As a result there was almost no connection between the Court prelate in the Midlands and the priests along Ribblesdale ; nor was this remedied by the erection of the Henrican see of Chester, for the strong Catholicism of the country-side, which gloried in the protection of the martyred Abbot of Whalley, made close contact impossible. But, if the power of the Bishops was negligible, the influence of the squires was profound and to this was added the prestige of the elder priests which was caused by the undeveloped state of the parishes. In that wild country the fully independent rectories of the South had not developed, so that in these moorland villages the priest would most often be a curate having a vague dependence on the vicar of some neighbouring town. At the same time the influence of the landowners was increased by the inde-pendent but strong support of the farmers, based on a feudalism not long vanished, and all were bound together by a suspicion and con-tempt for any change in Government or taxation or religion that came north into Ribblesdale along the London road. The Catholic squires in the South admired and favoured and supported the Government and wished it were Catholic, but in the North they did not support it at all.

At the Elizabethan Settlement not only James Hargreaves, Vicar of Blackburn, but also all the ten priests, who served Ribbesdale South of the river in dependence upon him, refused the oath of supremacy [1]

---

[1] It is curious that, since in the North the country priests came to the same conclusion as the bishops as to the necessity of refusing the oath, this brought a contact which nothing else could

and organized for resistance with the help of the squires. Although all were united, Sir John Southworth, a middle-aged landowner of great weight in the County, could perhaps be considered their leader in arranging Masses in secret ; for he kept a household of forty persons, all Catholics, in his new hall at Samlesbury. This made the arrangements quite simple and Mass could sometimes be said even in the great house in safety ; but also more often in the chapel of the Lower Hall in the orchards down by the river and later at the lodge in the park, where Thomas Southworth the eldest of the seven sons made his home or, in difficult times, in a secret place, the outhouse of a tenant. Meanwhile, in moments of danger, the priests could still find safety without leaving the Southworths, going from the Ribble Valley eastwards across the moor to find refuge in some shepherd's hut by Mellor or moving south across the Darwen to the neighbouring estate. There Sir John's cousin, young Mr. Hoghton, provided a shelter on his farms or in his old manor house at the Bottoms, away from Hoghton Tower with its dangerous splendour. Besides, all the fields and moors for some miles along the Ribble and down south far beyond the Darwen belonged to these two families, a matter of 30,000 acres under their ownership,[1] and with the still lingering feudalism to aid them, the priests could go fearlessly in such a district. Even had there been hopes of betrayal, the speech of the shepherds could be barely made out by pursuivants from London. The smaller squires were also determined and, if there was search in the neighbourhood, a refuge could be found six miles farther up the Ribble Valley at Salesbury, an old timbered house under the hanging woods by the river. Here Sir John's second daughter lived with her father-in-law, old Mr. Talbot, who had an estate of about 500 acres and would pass the priests south to the Wilpshire Moor or in times of stress send them north to the families about Stonyhurst, who would lead

have achieved, so that in later years Bishop Goldwell, living at San Silvestro on Monte Cavallo, was the chief supporter of the Lancashire men who went abroad for the priesthood. The Bishop had all the breadth of view of the reforming Cardinals of Trent and an elegant Latin phrasing and a balanced understanding of politics, but the new priests had come straight from the ploughing, from the birthright of a strong farmer's son, hardly following the speech even of London. The Bishop considered the application of the Pauline Privilege to the Indians in Mexico and the dangers of the Nagasaki Missions, but all their thoughts were bounded by the Pennine Wall, dark against the morning and the sunsets on the peace of the Irish Sea.

[1] Sir John Southworth owned 14,000 acres and held the lordship of seven manors, while Mr. Hoghton had a rather greater estate which he managed, from 1569–1580, for his elder brother Thomas Hoghton, an exile in Liège for his Faith. According to the will of the second Thomas Hoghton, this family held at least 16,600 acres in 1589.

them north again through the Trough of Bowland to some secure
hiding place among the fells. And then, free from the district
altogether, they could come down in safety to Claughton and, if the
hunt was not up in that part of the County, they could give the
Sacraments in the Lune Valley and in the farm houses along the Sands.
Their strength lay in this that the rest of Lancashire was as Catholic
as Ribblesdale, and it was the independence [1] of these men that made
them successful.

In the intricate society of the South the greater squires depended
on the peers and both were affected by the Court and the great lords
of the Council, for they were all in some sense bound up with the
Tudor system and the landed prosperity. The Throckmortons and
Jerninghams might secretly pray for religious deliverance, but they
would never have denied that in all material aspects it was a fortunate
and prosperous reign. But across Lancashire lay the bones of the old
bare feudal skeleton, just the remnants of that giant, a bone here and
there on the wild heaths under the wind. Thus the tenants held by a
feudal instinct to the squires and the yeomen followed, but everyone
was independent with that sturdy Lancashire freedom, the squires
independent among themselves and all again free from the great
lords. There was one point, however, of union, attachment to all
things Lancastrian, the Mass in the windswept churches and the local
customs and the feasts and a universal distrust of the South. The
ancient Church was secure as long as it was from the South that there
came the Protestant wind. Finally, their whole natures impelled them
to oppose, when the southern Catholics wished to placate.

In the home counties the Catholic squires had relations with the
more tolerant Anglican bishops and in that criss-cross of dovetailed
self-interest they often possessed the means of knowing the intimate
mind of opponents, and it was easier too in the South to be impressed
by the increasing material greatness of England. Thus the eighteenth century only gave strength to the Cisalpines, who were a
Tudor inheritance ; but a subtle appreciation of worldly forces, a
desire for agreement even at the cost of some compromise with their
Protestant neighbours, all this Cisalpine slightly Gallican temper was

---

[1] The will made by Sir John Southworth in September, 1595, shows his determined Catholicism. Lancashire and Cheshire Wills, Chetham Society, ii, pp. 160–161. The only act of
' complaisance ' which is recorded of him was an attendance at a Protestant sermon at Latham,
when a guest of Lord Derby in January, 1590. Derby Household Books, p. 58.

scorned in the North. This is seen in the attitude to the Crown forces, where there is a contrast between an understanding and perhaps too complaisant respect and the north country's blunt opposition. For instance, the Earl of Leicester, who through his great offices represented in many districts the power of the Crown, stood throughout the South and the Midlands in the highest rank of the Government lords. Now in this case the profound ambition and the motives which led him to support the extreme Protestants would be well understood, and he would be recognized as an opponent, a man who failing some heavy inducement in a particular case would support and enforce all the laws against Catholics. But, on the other hand, old Sir Edward Gage at Firle under the Downs and his brother at Bentley and Mrs. Gage of the Moate and his other relations, scattered through the Sussex Weald and in Kent, and his nephew, Lord Montague, away west at Cowdray, would never forget that they could call cousin with him through their mothers. Again Sir Henry Jerningham and the Bedingfields would also be at pains to remember the friendship of the Earl's father-in-law, Sir John Robsart, although this was a sore subject with Leicester, and their meetings with Lord Robert at Stanfield when they rode across country to visit that hospitable knight. And then, as with every great officer of State, the southern squires would have been involved in a network of minor favours and gifts, invitations to the feasts at Kenilworth, dinners at Leicester House, not at the gentlemen's table only, but a rarer privilege being bidden sometimes to My Lord's own table in the palace he was building in the Strand. For all those who ever rode to Court, even among the Catholics, were in some sense influenced by that gay prosperity which a multitude of causes was heaping upon the landed class and their personal preferences and their regrets would be tempered by an appreciation of the magnificence of Leicester's achievement, his riches and his power, in what was, for the fortunate, so glorious a reign.

This wide faculty of appreciation, which we find most marked in the Catholic devotion to the Royal Stuarts and even surviving them in the support which Frederick, Prince of Wales received from Norfolk House and in the magnificent entertainments for George III at Lulworth and at Thorndon, was a quality which the southern Catholic gentry never lost, though it was an ill equipment for so fierce a struggle. In the North this was not understood, and a hard stubbornness and opposition was shown, so that while the southern squires survived each with only a tiny Catholic ' island,' the religious faith of Lancashire was preserved, unyielding and solid, a Catholic block.

In contrast to Leicester's position we have the relations between the Lancashire squires and their Lord Lieutenant. Henry, Earl of Derby, was a strong Elizabethan, profoundly loyal to the Crown, who had been brought up at the Court of Edward VI and retained all his life the conviction that he received there that the Catholic religion could not be true.[1] A similar development in the mind of his companion the great Earl of Ormonde was in its effect on Ireland one of the more lasting results of that ephemeral reign. Now, towards Lord Derby the squires of the North showed complete independence. There was nothing of Leicester's vast assemblage of dependent friends and supporters and clients. Although Lord Derby had his own tenants [2] and the Crown officials and the not very numerous body of Anglican Lancashire squires, all the rest stood aloof and when he rode through the County as the Man of the South they opposed him. Thus the Church could not be destroyed by a slow infiltration, and there were men to send abroad to the seminaries, since the priests could ride for days through the North without lacking a shelter. After three centuries the results of these policies became clear, for, while to the Catholics the southern shires seem to stand forever white for the harvest, in Lancashire their hold remained firm.

[1] Lord Derby's case affords an instance of the religious division in families, for while his sons were Protestant, his wife, Lady Margaret Clifford, from whom he was separated, was a Catholic, as was his brother Sir Thomas Stanley of Winswick. His sisters, the daughters of his devout step-mother, Margaret, Countess of Derby *née* Barlow, were Catholics also, as were his brothers-in-law, Lords Stafford and Morley, Sir John Arundell and Sir Nicholas Pointz.

[2] Nevertheless, as late as 1590, there were 140 servants at Knowsley. Derby Household Books, p. 88.

THE WELSH SCENE

A BRIEF sketch of the situation in Wales, grouped under the three heads of the physical aspect of the country and the religious and civil administration, is necessary for an understanding of the Elizabethan changes. The country was divided into three well-defined regions; Northern coast lands, easy of access from Chester, served by the adequate road to Cærnarvon along which the Irish traffic passed, well provided with market towns as trading centres; the area of South Wales which also formed a coastal strip, connecting the Vale of Glamorgan and Gower with the southern part of Carmarthenshire and that ' English ' county Pembroke; and lastly the mountainous forest region of the central ' massif.' Geographically the coast lands of South Wales formed a counterpart to the three northern counties, served by good roads, and, on the whole, well ordered and peaceable. The early conquest of Glamorgan, like the later, but complete, administrative system of Cærnarvon, had greatly modified the habits of the people. Farther west, Carmarthen, as the seat of the Chief Justice of South Wales, extended the influence of the central Government into a less settled district, and Pembrokeshire, aided by the considerable traffic, particularly in merchandise, between Milford, Haverford and Tenby and the Southern Irish and Breton ports, reproduced the characteristics of an English shire. Nearly all the lines of communication in Wales ran East and West, feeding on their way those harbours, which the sea-borne trade would also come to help.

Except in the Vale of Glamorgan, the woods came close down towards the sea coast, as in the case of those five long woods above the English road, the fragments of that great forest which had formed the watershed of Usk and Wye. It was these stretches of wood and moor which rendered communication dangerous and difficult, for even the old track to Brecon, called in Elizabethan times the Kevenfford, which ran through the forest ot Glyn Cynon and passed into Brecknock at Llechryd, was not safe from the outlaws from the seaport towns, who had found a refuge in these hills. The commercial prosperity of the country came in by the coastal roads and by the sea, and thus Cardiff was described by George Owen of Henllys as ' the fairest town in Wales, but not the wealthiest,' and Swansea as ' a pretty town and good, much frequented by shipping'; but the hill country was almost unsubdued. Similarly in the North it was the seaport towns of Conway, Cærnarvon and Beaumaris on which the prosperity of that coast depended, although the old administrative and ecclesiastical centres of Denbigh, Bangor and St. Asaph contributed to the ordered stability of northern life.

At this period the old fortified strongholds were already in decay, Pembroke was in ruins and the outer towers of Harlech, roofless. In Monmouthshire Abergavenny was in the mid-sixteenth century the most thriving town, while in the western shires Carmarthen was something of a social centre, for the Bishop of St. David's lived just outside at Abergwili and the Devereux kept a town house there where the first Earl of Essex had been born. The comparative wealth of the three northern counties and of Pembroke, Carmarthen and Glamorgan is indicated by the varied obligations of providing soldiers which the muster rolls reveal. The poverty of Central Wales was the result of the nature of the country, for sheep pastures, alternating with the forest land, covered the greater part of the region, although much of this area, the forest of Radnor, for instance, a great tract of moor and sheep walk, was forest only in the legal sense. The absence of any Anglicized authority in these districts was very notable ; for the attainder of of the Duke of Buckingham in 1521 had brought the forest of Brecknock to the Crown and the death of the last Lord Grey de Powis in 1552 had removed the influence, already long decrepit, of the solitary survivor of the feudal English families in Mid-Wales. There was thus no intermediate influence and interest between the Crown, as represented by the Council of the Marches and the official families carried in its train, and the dying influence of the old Welsh lords.

A complete contrast existed between the patriarchal customs of the centre of Wales and that well ordered system of local gentry and justice and officials which prevailed in North Wales and the South. The contrast, too, in such details as the style of building was marked ; for the coastal regions were subject in these matters to the influence of the standards of Bristol or Chester, although most of the greater houses, especially those in Denbigh and Flint, were only to receive their familiar Elizabethan form in the generation which followed. The House of Dynevor perhaps best represents, in its Tudor detail, a phase midway between the style of building of the Welsh in the hills and that of the more Anglicized lowlands. Rather over twenty years earlier, the great hall, gallery and dungeon had all been restored and the manor house at Abermarlais had been moated and paled and a dais in the great hall had been added. In this connection it is of note that, as far as can be gathered, all the buildings of the Abbey of Strata Marcella, with the exception of the monastery church, were of wood.

Throughout Wales the prestige of the Tudor dynasty stood high, the seventy years of their strong rule, the attentions which these sovereigns and especially Henry VIII had lavished upon their native country and the peculiar possessive attitude, which all Welshmen took up towards the scions of Ednyfed Vychan's stock, gave them a position, strong and unassailed. In every question of religious change, this quality of Welsh loyalty towards the Tudors has a high importance, for no Welshman proposed to attack or to desert his native sovereign. Among subjects there were two families, whose leaders held great influence in Wales, the Herberts and the Devereux, both from the South. At the accession of Elizabeth, William Herbert, Earl of Pembroke was undoubtedly the spokesman of the Welsh, marked out by his prestige among the Council, his ability and long service, while in Wales his marked preference for his native tongue had made him a figure almost legendary. Nevertheless, with the acquisition of Wilton Abbey, the centre of gravity of his family was moving towards South England out of Wales, while the March lands of the old Pembrokes about the key stronghold of Raglan had passed to his cousins the Somersets, Earls of Worcester, who were themselves too weak to sway much power. In Carmarthen, the Devereux, now Viscounts Hereford and soon to be Earls of Essex, had built up a considerable position, mainly within the framework of official power, while the character of Walter Devereux, their chief, gave them an influence, which their wealth alone would not command. Erastian in religion, political supporters of the new hierarchy, they yet failed to commend themselves to the Queen, and, in this early period of the reign, Lord Essex appears as the spokesman of the discontented Anglicized Welsh squires on the occasions when they wished to bring before the Government complaints against official servants of the Crown. The Earl of Leicester, who was later to be so disturbing a figure in Welsh politics, when his claims in Denbigh and on the forest rights of Snowdon brought him into permanent conflict with the squires, had not yet appeared upon the scene. These were the only leaders who by virtue of their position stood apart from the official Government machine, which the old Welsh detested, but the new generation used.

Sixteen years before, by the Act of Union of 1542, the constitution of the Council for Wales and the Marches had been definitively set up, after the *régime* of experimental labour under that great administrator Bishop Lee. It was this Council with its headquarters and court and officials, its presidential seat at Ludlow and its jurisdiction over seventeen counties, including the four counties towards Wales, that impressed itself upon the Welsh as the chief instrument of Government. The sheriffs and justices of the peace were nominated by this Council, which acted both as a criminal and civil court, having responsibility for the general order of the shires, but it was not in fact a supreme tribunal, and the rights of the Privy Council to independent or concurrent action were often used. The winter of 1559 saw an increase of the prestige of the Council of the Marches, through the appointment of Sir Henry Sidney as President, with Sir Hugh Paulet and nineteen other nominated Councillors as his assistants. His immediate predecessor Lord Williams of Thame had died at Ludlow on 14th October, 1559, only eight months after the Queen had appointed him to succeed Bishop Bourne of Bath and Wells, whose firm Catholicism was distasteful to her. The Bishop had himself only received this high promotion on 29th October, 1558, less than three weeks before Queen Mary died, and Sir Henry's long and uninterrupted rule of twenty-seven years was to form a contrast to these hurried months.

The brigandage, which had been the most pressing social problem of the preceding generation, had been in great measure broken by the seven years severity of Bishop Lee and the new system of government now in force. The statement of Serjeant Puleston, dating from thirty years before, that ' the gentlemen of the said County of Merioneth were the maintainers and comforters of the same mis-doers ' was no longer accurate, while the thieving had been much diminished by the steps taken to prevent the re-sale of stolen cattle. Nevertheless, it was only three years since the murder of Baron Lewis Owen on his way to the circuit at Rhayader by a band of robbers, who had lain in ambush in the thick oak woods of Llansaintffraid Cwmdauddwr. It is to this period also that the episodes belong, which Lord Herbert of Cherbury has related, concerning Sir Edward Herbert's struggles with the outlaws and thieves of Montgomeryshire and in particular that contest with robbers armed with arrows outside an ale-house near Llandinam, which throws so vivid a light upon the customs of the time. Yet, by the reign of Elizabeth, these had become mere isolated quarrels and an account of the sup-pression of brigandage in Kinleth and Mochnant, some twenty years earlier, shows that, as places of refuge, the sanctuaries had even then lost their authority, except in cases of the chance medley and killing.

On the religious side it was now nearly a quarter of a century since the peaceful possession of the Catholic Religion by the Welsh people had been first disturbed. As a result of the suppression [1] of the monasteries, whose communities had assisted the parochial administration to a great degree, there was a situation of much con-fusion, not made clearer by the impropriation by the squires of those tithes which the religious houses had possessed. Attachment to the Old Religion was still universal, as the Bardic literature can show, and particularly to the Church in its popular aspect, the veneration of shrines. The Cistercians, who were the only monastic order well represented in the country, had been popular and the con-tinuance of legacies would seem to show that this favour was shared by the Friars, the Dominicans and Franciscans in the towns. At the same time there is no doubt that in some monasteries the rigour of Cistercian discipline had been much relaxed

---

[1] The effects of this measure are discussed in detail in the appendix.

and the appointments of abbots too much influenced by the local gentry, had been at times most unfortunate in effect. The general attachment of the people to the Old Religion, even in such an ' English ' district as Pembroke, is shown by the phrase of Bishop Ferrar of St. David's, in a letter of 1549 to the Council. ' The country round St. David's,' wrote the Bishop, ' is as Bethel and Dan and a seat of horrible blasphemy and the inveterate siege of the superstition of Wales.' These words indicate how deeply the Bishop's attack on the old observances was resented. Yet it was among the people that the devotion to the Catholic doctrines was strong, for the policies of Henry VIII and the Protectors had bred an indifference in the wealthier classes. The constant contact with England had produced a great effect on the outlook of the Anglicized families, which the accommodating temper of many of the parochial clergy did much to encourage. This was in particular the case in those districts, where the living was in the hands of the squires who were accustomed to appoint their kinsmen to the charge of the parish. But it is not possible in this space to indicate more precisely the confused and intricate religious situation.

As regards the official hierarchy of the Church, the death of Queen Mary had surprised the episcopate in the midst of changes. The leader of the Welsh Bishops was Dr. Henry Morgan, who held the see of St. David's, the largest and wealthiest of the bishoprics, with an annual revenue more than double that possessed by any of the three smaller sees. The see of Llandaff was occupied by Bishop Kitchin, a prelate now over eighty years of age, who had been the last Benedictine Abbot of Eynsham. Bangor had been vacant since the death of Bishop Glyn in the preceding May; but the Queen had contemplated a rearrangement of appointments, and at the time of her death Dr. Morys Clynog had been nominated to the see of Bangor, Bishop Goldwell of St. Asaph had been transferred to Oxford and Dr. Woods had been designated in his place. These transfers were not completed and, while the Bishop of Llandaff gave in a passive acceptance of the New Order, the Bishops of St. David's and St. Asaph and the Bishops elect of St. Asaph and Bangor were deprived for their loyalty to Rome.

The accession of Elizabeth found Wales under a state of comparatively ordered government, with the material prosperity of the coastal regions rapidly increasing and the central lands quieter and more peaceful, under a measure of control. Throughout the country, both among the Anglicized and the completely Celtic sections, there was a profound loyalty to the dynasty and a pride in the rulers whom the Welsh nation had produced.

CHAPTER III

THE ACCEPTANCE OF THE NEW ORDER

After the preliminary survey of conditions in England, which alone can explain the intentions of the English rulers of Wales, we come to consider the first effects of the New Order in Wales, and the reactions which this had set up. It is along the Northern Road from Holyhead to Chester that these contrasts are best studied, for here the old Welsh in the hills met all that line of traffic which the English policy in Ireland sent out along this coast. A similar but less striking contrast could be observed in Southern Wales, but there the long ordered civil administration had made English methods more familiar. In Central Wales the Welsh were so remote and the power of Government penetration was so hindered that the conditions there require a separate study.

The development of the religious changes in North Wales was conditioned by the close dependence of the wealthier squires upon the workings of the administrative machine, now long established. It was this organization, existing since Edward I's conquest, but now gaining in importance from the aggressive Tudor policy in Ireland, which gave to the squires their local influence and their more ample livelihood and which assured an occupation for their sons. It was this ultimate dependence upon London, which their offices and the constant contact of the Irish Road involved, that led the greater gentry, first to gather in the lands of the former monasteries and then to accept such changes as the English Government might dictate. A brief study of the effect of these new changes on three families, the Bulkeleys in Anglesea, the Wynnes in Caernarvon and the Salusburys in Denbigh will make this situation clear. Above them there was the shadow of Leicester, below them the constant pressure of the rising Anglicized families and neglected in the background the old Welsh stocks in the hills. For the laity the three Sir Richard Bulkeleys cover the whole extent of the changes, men too distant from London to play a prominent part and yet urgent to win the favour of the changing line of the favourites. On the ecclesiastical side the changes can be seen in the life of their kinsman Thomas Bulkeley, a priest who for thirty years from 1533 till 1570 was an Anglesea rector. It is seen how imperceptibly, as far as the gentry were concerned, these changes developed, aided by their firm determination always to follow the Crown. At the same time the details of the Irish Road provide an introduction to the new settlement of Ireland ; for a new Viceroy, for Perrot or Essex, the hospitality of the Bulkeleys and the other North Welsh squires would be the first stage in any Irish journey. This perpetual stream of official traffic therefore only served to emphasize the dependence of the leaders of North Wales upon the Crown.

In an age of strong monarchy, superimposed upon a basis of feudal feeling and expression, it is difficult to exaggerate the attraction which such a centre of power must exercise on remote peoples, acutely conscious of their national spirit and of the links that bind them to the sun of this glory. Such was the situation in Wales throughout the time of the Tudors, the Welsh people only under-standing vaguely the position and power of that sovereign whose distant reflection was a glory to the race of the Cymri. The succession, too, in their eyes was utterly Welsh, Henry VII, Henry VIII, Edward VI, Mary and now Elizabeth ; but beyond these there was only a vague crowd of foreigners, English and Scots. It would be an error therefore to minimise in the least the attachment, undeviating and loyal, which was given through Wales to this Queen, the last of Welsh sovereigns. It is needless to say that Elizabeth was hardly so conscious of her Welsh characteristics as were her subjects in Wales ; but this did not make the image of the Queen of the Cymri less strong.

The opening chapters, providing the setting in England, suggest the form which the Government wished that the New Order in Wales should assume and, if the first reactions to these desires are to be studied, the best vantage point is that meeting place of the nations along the northern road. The South of Wales, Carmarthen and Pembroke and the roads West through Glamorgan provide also a line of contact with the English, the long established civil administra-tion, the way that the officials must take for Southern Ireland, the proximity of the merchant town of Bristol, the easy journey to the western ports. But, for the present purpose, the northern coast line can show in sharper contrast the old Wales and the new administra-tion, the Elizabethan soldiers on the road. Here the reactions were more immediate and clear than in the South, where the volume cer-tainly of English official traffic was much less and where the power of the old Welsh was not so close.

There are few contrasts in the Elizabethan period which are more remarkable than that deep fissure, which even the most cursory study of the documents makes plain, that divided the life of North Wales from the outlook of the Welsh further south in the mountains. In the case of the old Welsh there was a suspicion and a retreat from all things English, a fear of Ludlow and of the Court of the Marches and a great desire to preserve, if only for a generation, their ancestral customs and language. The squires of Mid-Wales could never forget that they came of a glorious ancestry and from a line of magnificent

34

lords and this surely counted for more than all else ; but such a belief needed a buttress and they always took refuge in the fantastic tower of their dreams, where the changing shapes of their forefathers' legends crowded their vision. This had stood to them in the place of the material wealth, which they had no means to attain, and they were determined to avoid every contact that might roughly destroy it.

In North Wales, on the other hand, Chester was regarded as a friend not as an enemy, for the whole civilization rested on a quite different basis, and it was in great measure the trade route into Ireland, which had been the instrument of such a change. For there came every year along the road from Holyhead to Chester a great volume of traffic, the merchant trade to Dublin, the Irish lords coming to London on ceremonial visits, the commanding officers and officials passing at the whim of the English Council backwards and forwards to their posts in Ireland, and then a great stream of soldiers, young officers on their way to their first service, the troops despatched for some progressive policy and then all the followers of the camp. Meanwhile every few years there would come the progress of a new Lord Deputy taxing, with the splendid hospitality that taste demanded, the last resources of the richer squires. It was a lesson in politics and in every courtly usage to send such a host upon its journey, and it was a testing in diplomacy to welcome in the proper measure the powerful viceroys suffering varying stages of disgrace in their recall.

For the greater part of the year the traffic flowed along the coast roads from Chester, bringing prosperity and the knowledge of current matters to the villages on Deeside beyond Flint, to the inland towns of Rhuddlan and St. Asaph and to all those manors on the road to Conway between the mountains and the sea. Beaumaris and Bangor were stages on almost every journey and a vessel could be obtained at either port, thus avoiding the lonely moorland ride to Holyhead. In the summer a well-armed party could take the mountain road through Llanrwst and Pentre Veolas, which came down to Upper Deeside beyond Valle Crucis and went forward as a valley high road through Llangollen to Shrewsbury and the March. But this route, which was to become the celebrated posting road of the eighteenth century, was at this period hardly practicable in winter, and was at all times dangerous to an unprotected party on account of the robbers near Yspytty Ifan and from beyond Bettws-y-coed in the hills.

Farther south, too, there was all the tangled country of the brigands of Mochnant, while in the west the influences which the travellers had brought into the country abruptly halted, for Anglesea was primitive, with a wild ancestral life unknown to Flint and Denbigh, and beyond Caernarvon all roads ceased. We find echoes in Sir John Wynn's writings of the savage condition of the outer clans on the barren coasts of Eifionydd and Lleyn; but this control only threw into relief the life of the prosperous and long wealthy families of the great manors in the North. A stream of wealth passed by them comparable to that which flowed through the Home Counties and along the high roads into Scotland and only inferior to that cosmopolitan traffic, which moved southwards out of London to Dover and the sea. In fact many a manor house in the remoter Midlands and nearly all the houses in the North were far further removed from contact with affairs. It was a common matter to find officials, with all that exaggerated air of London that Dublin Castle then affected, waiting with Sir Richard Bulkeley at Beaumaris for the coming of the Irish packet or staying at the new Hall, which Sir John Salusbury had just completed, at Lleweny, until the bad weather should break upon the hills.

This was not a mere question of the Tudor Government in Ireland, since during nearly four centuries wealth had flowed along that coast in the wake of the royal armies, and it was here that the imported customs had found a root. Monasteries and the more important canonries and prebends all clustered in the North, while within a range of thirty miles there lay the Cathedral cities of St. Asaph and Bangor, which controlled half the dioceses and the most settled portion of the organized Church wealth throughout Wales. This was a form of income that the wealthier families had diverted at the source, just as they had obtained control of the local administration and of the various offices beneath the Crown. The livings were richer than in the South and in many cases the rectorships, sometimes lay and sometimes clerical, were held by the dominant families among the squires, whose influence thus saturated every section of the calm movement of the public life.

The development of the religious changes in North Wales was conditioned by the close dependence of the wealthier squires upon the workings of the administrative machine, for it was this that gave them their local influence and their more ample livelihood and which assured an occupation for their sons. This connection became closer when the suppression of the monasteries led to the absorption of the monastic land by the greater gentry, who found in the Elizabethan Settlement their testing time. No personal attachment to the New Religion [1] was involved, but it was now over twenty years, back in their father's time, since they had lost experience of the unbroken fullness of the Catholic life, and it was clear at any rate that the machinery of Government, which depended on the will of London, would not fail. There was, too, a superficial resemblance between the new system and the old, for there was no change either in the method of preferment or in the emoluments, when the basic principles shifted. There were of course many refusals of the Anglican settlement among the clergy and the less prosperous laity, but as a body the richer squires gave in their acceptance. It is this acceptance and the motives prompting it that colour the situation in North Wales during the whole of the reign.

The squires had taken a definite stand, which their children endorsed, and the few disturbances of the period were merely the last movements of the Catholicism in their families, first latent, then dying. It was a time of material prosperity, which precedes disappointment, and they set a pace in expenditure, which their sons were not able to follow. They had an enlightened understanding of the opportunities that the Queen's reign provided and they were hopeful of seizing them, for all the Crown lands in the *hinterland* were before them and the very struggles which they maintained against the new grantee, Leicester, gave a chance to their prospects. The Queen had already made these great grants to her favourite and it seemed not impossible that later her loyal Welsh subjects might gain them, for all the moves of the Court were brought to them by the travellers to Ireland and as they regarded their adversary Leicester, now childless and aged, they could build day dreams on his death. There was more than a touch in all this of the spirit that had urged these squires forth on their mercantile ventures and which had proved the death

---

[1] Instances chosen at random from among the ' conforming ' members of the greater families are Sir Richard Bulkeley's abstention from the Anglican communion during sixteen years (see later), the Catholic emblems which Sir Richard Clough put up at Bachegraig and his attachment to his knighthood of the Holy Sepulchre, which prudence led him to conceal, and the IHS and other Catholic symbols, which Robert Wynne of Gwydir erected at Plas Mawr as late as 1585. No considerable evidence of zeal for the Reformation is recorded of this first generation of nominal Protestant squires.

blow of chivalry and it was in truth the keenness of these material desires, which caused their frustration. There were too many 'first families,' and the land could never support them in greatness, and then, when Elizabeth died, the succession passed to the Stuarts, a race which with all its lavishness seldom provided a fortune for a family from Wales.

Among these greater squires there were three families predominant, the Bulkeleys in Anglesea, the Wynnes in Caernarvon and the Salusburys in Denbigh, stocks which by their lands and alliance had secured a paramount place in their counties. They were not merely single families, but the chiefs of a wide range of cousins and with a strong array of supporters. Thus the Bulkeleys of Beaumaris had their younger branches at Porthaml and Gronant and the influence of their uncle the Bishop, while the Salusburys of Lleweni had the office of Chamberlain as an asset and their cousins in Denbigh town and in the mountains at Rug and a whole host of officials in the town life of Deeside. Then to the west were the Wynnes with their power in the hill lands, for however Anglicized Gwydir might be, they could always rely on the strength of a clanship. Across this background there fell the shadow of Leicester, whose agents were always endeavouring to extend the rights of his Forest of Snowdon, which led to his dual *rôle* of oppressor and patron. This remote and great power, always exercised from a distance, brought the richer squires into harmony and helped to establish their place as leaders of a class threatened by an alien and irresponsible influence, which it needed all their efforts to curb.

In this network of interests the figures of the chiefs become clear, closely allied by marriage and gaining a place in the countryside, which their personality rather than their wealth had procured them. For immediately beneath these families there was a host of others, Conways, Pennants, Cadwgans, Mostyns and Thelwalls, who must not be driven but led, for they were now 'English' and prosperous, and if their leaders would not serve the Government they were prepared to step into their place. And then below these again were the Welshry, the old families of Lleyn and the Anglesea tribes and the squires with the poor lands in the hills, Welsh-speaking, vociferous, loud over the ale, shocking with their boasting the more restrained minds of the Anglicized squires. It was somewhere in this strata that there was found

Map of the coast of North Wales and Anglesea.

The houses of the Welsh squires referred to in the text are indicated thus ⊟

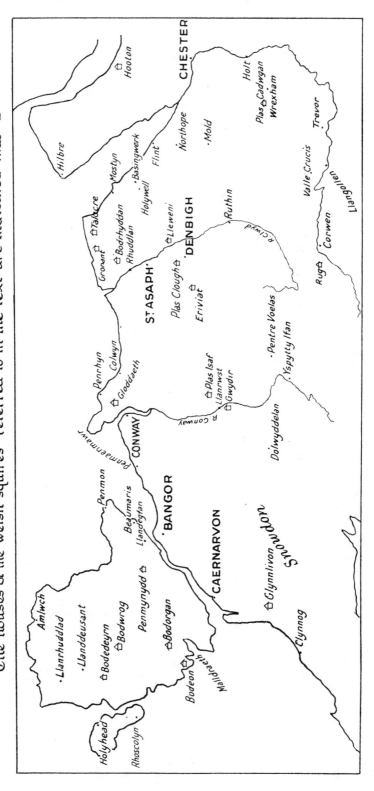

the lost family of the Penmynydd Tudors, retaining the name of a property long since divided, impoverished and wraith-like dependents. They were so feckless and poor that, after 1575, not even their name could procure them a sheriff, and the fact that through their now weakened stock all these loud ignorant squirelings could boast of the blood of the Tudors did not make the great families more prepared to accept them.

This was in deep contrast both to the strong class of yeomen, attaching themselves to the more settled and prosperous element, and to the firm burgess group, who served the needs of the travellers and had often been set up in the town properties of Salusburys or Bulkeleys who had given them this opportunity of a living in commerce when they were boys on their distant farms in the country. The leaders were thus provided with a body of constant support, and this was always increasing from the ranks of those who demanded a settled commerce and policing.

Then at the very bottom of the social ladder, yet welding all things together, there was the opposing spirit of taverns, the Welsh ale-house [1] on the moorland track and the new-built inn of the town. In the remote parts the shepherds foregathered and drank confusion to Master Bwlkli and his extortions, muttered words sweet to the hearing of the old ' Esgwier,' who after the labours of lambing time would sit in a high seat taking a draught with his freemen. Then their sympathies would respond in unison to the words of the bards and the old tales of the Secrets, of the head of ' Bendigeituran ' in the great white tower in London and of the finding of that place of refuge where the bones of Vortimer the Blessed lay concealed.[2] And when these songs were ended the shepherds would return to the night watchings, while the old ' Esgwier ' rode away on his fine great horse with a saddle to the home where his sons lay waiting in his bed. It is hardly surprising that these figures from the underworld of the Welsh fringes should have become faded and powerless before the precise force of the law.

In the town inns on the contrary there was a stream of organized

---

[1] It is noteworthy that in South Wales the ale-houses were regarded as strongholds of the Old Religion ; an instance of this opinion is provided in the Dream of Thomas Llywelyn of Rhygos. *Y Tafarn yn traethu*, a mid-Elizabethan poem in the form of a controversy between the newly Protestant church building and the Tavern. Printed by Chancellor L. J. Hopkin James in *Hen Gwndidau*, p. 87.

[2] *The Three Good Secrets of the Isle of Britain*, Harleian MS. 4181.

39

bustle, especially when the forces for Ireland were once more upon the march. Rooms were often needed for the minor officials and the merchants' clerks from Dublin, who would always wish for house space of an honest burgess fashion, and then, when the Deputy or the Presidents passed, the swashbucklers would come and all the tawdry fine swordsmen who had failed to gain entrance to Lleweni in the train of their masters. Here there was need for accuracy and a quick wit and courage, while these again led on to a fortune and influence provided that inn-keepers could depend on their patron. It was no wonder therefore that this Irish traffic spilled prosperity over the country and this was encouraged by the zest with which the greater families had promoted mercantile ventures. There was a mutual co-operation between the greater squires and those towns, which the old Welsh avoided, while the system of dependence on the lords, whom forefathers had served, gave the Bulkeleys and Salusburys a power in these centres. A burgess of Denbigh or Bangor was so often a son or grandson of their tenants, who had been brought up in the hillside cottages in a state scarce removed from villeinage in Henry VII's day. As in all mainly agricultural districts, it was always a question not of the town gaining on the country, but of the owners of the countryside encroaching and spreading their influence across the towns. It is a consequence of such concentrated power that the life of North Wales can most easily be studied in the history of these leaders, like Sir John Salusbury of Lleweni and the third Sir Richard Bulkeley, who held in doubtful equilibrium the balance in the North.

It was in 1578 that old Sir John Salusbury, the Chamberlain of North Wales and the firm driving petrel of so many storms, died in the last of the winter, leaving Lleweni to a child. There was a will, troublesome to his family and the source of many feuds, by which the Earl of Leicester was appointed a guardian in order to remove the influence of Maurice Wynne, who was the young Thomas Salusbury's step-father.[1] But this was not the only cross-current, for, while Leicester ' sought to compasse ' the estate, there had been a revolt of the indignant cousins, ' Mr. Salusbury of Rugge, Mr. Thomas Salusbury of Denbigh . . . and that crewe,' [2] which broke the solidarity of

---

[1] For a description of the Salusburys under Elizabeth see *Katheryn of Berain*, by John Ballinger, published in *Y Cymmrodor*, 1929, pp. 3–25.
[2] *Ibid.*, pp. 17–18 from letters in Lleweni MSS. Details of house property owned by the Salusburys of Lleweni in the town of Flint are set out in Cal. Coleman Deeds, p. 349.

the stock. But the misfortunes of Lleweni increased the prosperity of Beaumaris and this distress of the chief rival brought Sir Richard Bulkeley to a position of supremacy, which his adversaries were never able to displace.

Sir Richard came of a family sprung originally from Cheshire, where the Bulkeleys still retained estates, and something of the English spirit remained in all their dealings, for, while they made predominantly Welsh marriages for their daughters, they turned to England for the marriages of their sons. This was in a certain measure the cause of their strength, for although they had struck deep root in Wales through their alliance these repeated connections with England kept up a link with the Court [1] families, whom their Welsh relatives were hardly able to approach. These points come again into the problem of communications, since in the variations which it contains there is no episode that can compare with the development of the Bulkeleys for the light that is thrown upon the influence of the constant line of traffic. More than any other squires along that coastline they built their fortune on the Irish road.

This fortune had already grown during three generations before it enabled the third Sir Richard to attain to power. An understanding of the method of this growth can alone explain the religious attitude of the Bulkeleys and the predominant place that they attained. It had begun with the first Sir Richard Bulkeley, who was caught by the storm of the schism, when he was already well advanced in years. A commercial fortune had been his first success,[2] and this had led on to a slow official career of the type that a prosperous country gentleman could with reasonable facility enjoy. His connections with London had brought him into contact with Wolsey, and his whole later history provides an instance of the inability of an ageing man to adapt himself to the new *tempo*, to the more rapid movement of events. It was the holding of Beaumaris that brought him the news from London, but it was his tragedy that the news was late. In religion he was a Catholic by habit and long use and he died when the conviction had

[1] Letters and Papers of Henry VIII, *passim*, for the correspondence of the family and especially that of Sir Richard Bulkeley the first.

[2] As instance of the rapid development of his sea-borne trade there are details of the following ships owned by his family, the *Mary de Beaumaris* with a cargo of Gascony wine, Spanish iron and fardels of canvas and the *Mawdeleyne de Caernarvon* with a cargo of Gascony wine, both ships trading to their home ports in 1531. The Midletons had been interested in the Gascony wine trade to Beaumaris as early as 1518. Details are given in *Commercial History*, 1301–1547, by Edward A. Lewis, printed in *Y Cymmrodor*, 1913, pp. 86.

been borne in upon his countrymen, by the enforcement of the King's Six Articles, that England would end upon the Roman side. But the suppression of the monasteries provided him with an opportunity for the final establishment of his family and the rather chequered course of his career was the result not of uncertainty in the motive, but of imprudence in the choice of means. He had had some difficulty in repelling the accusation of complicity in the plot of his nephew, Sir Rhys Griffith,[1] which the Government was anxious to magnify, and having decided to bid for Anne Boleyn's support he had joined with Henry Norris and his cousin, William Brereton, both ' inward gentlemen ' of the Court. At the same time a steady flow of compliments and subsidies went out to Thomas Cromwell,[2] but in the remoteness of Beaumaris he could not see the impossibility of such double harness. In return during three years a corresponding stream of reward came slowly, the survivorship of the chief royal office of Chamberlain of North Wales and the control of the fort at Beaumaris, for which he had to wait, in spite of a long campaign of patient slander, until Sir Roland Vyleville died.[3] Then to Sir Richard's surprise there came the fall of Anne Boleyn and the execution of Brereton and Norris and his reputation was shattered.

It needed a drawn-out campaign to reconcile Cromwell again, although in this he had the assistance of his sister, the Abbess of Godstow,[4] and he had to continue more slowly his plans for absorbing the neighbouring monasteries. In addition, he had always to fight against the old lords of the country, the Griffiths of Penrhyn and their cousins, the Glynns of Glynllivon and especially their leader, Dr. Glynn,[5] the Archdeacon of Anglesea, whom he always hoped to

---

[1] For the charges against Lady Bulkeley's servants see Letters and Papers of Henry VIII, 1531–1532, p. 347.

[2] Sir Richard asking Cromwell for a benefice for his ' brother John, a priest well seen in Divinity,' offered £20 down and one-third of the value of the benefice yearly. In 1535 he began a life payment of ' £20 in a poor token, which I intend to continue yearly ' and also sent ' a bag which my old master the Cardinal ware and gave me.' *Ibid.*, 1533, p. 82, and 1535, i, p. 292.

[3] Dame Agnes Vyleville annoyed Bulkeley by retaining part of the ordnance of Beaumaris, the end of a long feud in which he had always maintained that Sir Roland was outside the King's peace for a murder. Letters and Papers of Henry VIII, 1534, p. 328.

[4] Sir Richard wrote to Cromwell of all ' the salt tears ' he had shed at the thought of his displeasure, but his sister, Katherine Bulkeley, was able to placate him more effectually by the offer of the valuable stewardship of Godstow and the gift of ' the usual fee.' *Ibid.*, 1536–1538, *passim.*

[5] A letter to Cromwell against the Glynns states, ' they play with me scogan, because they know that I have special good matter to lay to their charges. My only hope is in you and Mr. Norris.' Letters and Papers, 1535, i, p. 363. They were also rival competitors with their ally Dr. Elys Price for the Priory of Penmon.

discover in some 'papisticall' speech. It was anxious work, too, reminding Cromwell of all his embarrassments,[1] but the long-delayed reward came at last, ecclesiastical land for himself and a voice in preferment.[2] He was thus able to establish his brothers and give help to his cousin Arthur, from the Court of the Arches, who was later Bishop of Bangor. Then Cromwell fell and all question of his promotion had passed. His son, Sir Richard Bulkeley the second, was a less decided character and overshadowed in his country by the turbulent Sir John Salusbury, who obtained his father's post as the Chamberlain; but the power of the family was firm. Still these gradually gathered increases had raised them now far above the poor squires and, once the Chamberlain Salusbury was dead, Sir Richard Bulkeley the third was the unquestioned leader.

In spite of all these relations with the Court it is nevertheless clear that there was a deep cleavage between the English courtiers and even the most Anglicized squires; for the Bulkeleys occupied a midway position between the rich London gentlemen and the Welsh in the mountains. In dealing with the Court they suffered from a fundamental lack of understanding, since if they knew of the actual course of events they were still at a loss to explain their significance. Thus in an effort to placate Cromwell, who then possessed an Europe-wide power, Abbess Katherine of Godstow would send up 'two Banbury cheeses' and 'a dish of old apples,' while her brother, Sir Richard, would scrape together a paltry 25 marks;[3] but for Cromwell the only value in this lay in the fact that the Bulkeleys were prepared to pretend that they thought him a gentleman. Similarly time and again the third Sir Richard Bulkeley was mystified by the Court, for the travellers to Ireland could mitigate, but they could not radically alter the remoteness of Beaumaris. From the spring until late in the autumn Sir Richard might sit sipping sweet wine with his guests, but there were always the long silent intervals, and those months in the winter when Beaumaris was as deserted as the poorest squire's farm, alone with the mists under Snowdon, solitary and lashed by the rain.

[1] Sir Richard owed 600 marks to Lord Beauchamp, later Protector Somerset, and 200 marks to Cromwell, which he hoped to repay with the proceeds of Llanvaes and Penmon, religious houses for which he petitioned. *Ibid.*, 1537, p. 290, and 1538, ii, p. 371.

[2] The resilient character of the religious outlook of the family is shown in the letter sent to Cromwell by the Abbess of Godstow. 'Be assured there is neither Pope, Purgatory, image nor pilgrimage, nor praying to dead saints used amongst us.' *Ibid.*, 1538, ii, p. 378.

[3] Letters and Papers of Henry VIII, 1536, p. 227; 1537, ii, p. 531; and 1538, p. 465, for these three gifts.

THE CELTIC PEOPLES & RENAISSANCE EUROPE

Sir Richard Bulkeley the third was born in 1533,[1] the eldest of seventeen children.[2] From the beginning of Elizabeth's reign, when he became Constable of Beaumaris, he assumed the leadership of his family in the place of his invalid father, who had sat as M.P. for Anglesea in the Parliaments of Philip and Mary, to whom Lady Bulkeley had been Maid of Honour. Towards the new Queen Elizabeth, who was exactly his age, he always kept up that somewhat romantic loyalty, which the prosperous squires always gave to the Tudors.

His ancestors had borne the doubts and the burden, and he had entered into their labours, for every year now brought an increase of commerce, while all the countryside flourished through the steadily growing traffic to Ireland. He was able to complete his fine house the Cwrtmawr, and he early showed himself as a leader of freedom. Leicester gave him this opportunity with his pretensions to the Anglesea freeholds, and Sir Richard fought him successfully and the victory had marked him out for a leader. Sir John Salusbury of Lleweni the Chamberlain had temporized in the matter of Leicester, unwilling in his old age to offend such a patron and this had lost him support, while the other powerful family the Wynns were in a period of weakness, for Maurice Wynn, who had married a Bulkeley, was ' a man who had no following among the men of that country.' [3] Then there was a complicated series of feuds between the Salusburys and Wynns, which only increased when Sir John Salusbury died and Sir Richard was dominant.

He was now forty-five and a knight, with that mild court favour that the Queen reserved for the gallant and loyal and rich, while in his country there were none to gainsay him. These were his prosperous years [4] as he rode through North Wales with two lacqueys running beside his great horse and twenty proper and tall men to attend him. He had made two well thought-out marriages, first with

---

[1] This date is accepted by the writer in the D.N.B., but the otherwise careful pedigree in Ormerod, *History of Cheshire*, iii, p. 628, gives the impossibly late year of 1551, while Erewaker suggests ' about 1529,' *History of East Cheshire*, i, p. 181. In a reference to ages, taken from Inquist. post mortem, Ormerod confuses Sir Richard with his father.

[2] Lewys Dwnn, *Visitations*, ii, p. 134.

[3] Sir John Wynn, *History of the Gwydir Family.*

[4] His subordinate offices are mentioned in a letter of 1565, ' the holder of Beaumaris Castle has always been Mayor of the town and customer of the haven and has the prisage of all cargoes of wine.' Cal. Wynn Papers, p. 5. Details of official payments are given in Sir John Dodridge's *History of the Ancient and Modern Estate of the Principality of Wales*, published in 1630.

Mistress Damport from Cheshire, a lady of unimpeachable family, and then with the Lord Borough's daughter, and all his affairs went with smoothness in that time when on every hand the material fortune of England was rising. There was a pleasure, too, in his sense of civilized power, in the venison that he could provide for his friends and in the red and fallow deer in his parks and especially in those Spanish wines, in which he so consciously followed the fashion. He, who was so unsophisticated at Court, had the ' flair ' of a merchant to place his commodity and nowhere else would the great lords find their new tastes expected. Besides that sense of courtliness, which his age so valued, could be seldom cultivated with greater profit than in the preparation for those gradual changes of the palate, which rendered unacceptable those sweet French wines of Anjou, which the old King Henry loved. It was likewise a balm to his just sense of importance, the knowledge that these pleasures were meaningless to those who lived near him, for it ministers to the self-respect of the English to live among strangers. This Sir Richard experienced clearly as he rode ' fair of complexion and tall, temperate in diet, not drinking of healths,' [1] while around him were the low, dark men with their imaginations soaring from the old songs and the ale.

Perhaps the words of Sir John Wynn of Gwydir, his nephew and friend, bear out most clearly all that he turned to in his fortune. ' Yet a great temporall blessinge yt is and a great hart's ease to a man to finde that he is well dissended and a greater greef it is for upstarts and gent of the first head to looke into their dissents.' [2] Few passages could describe so closely where Sir Richard sought his pleasures and where his heart had found its ease.

It is natural at this point to consider Sir Richard Bulkeley's religion. His attitude was one of slight Catholic preferences on a background of deep and very consciously cultured indifference ; for in his father's generation the Catholic influences in his family had weakened and in his own day they died. Sir Richard the second had held a watered Catholicism, which never permitted his conscience to disagree with the Crown, and under Edward VI he was attached to that so-called Catholic influence, which supported Northumberland against Somer-

---

[1] This actual description, which is, however, borne out in general by the State Papers and the Acts of the Privy Council, appears in an appendix to Pennant's *Tours in Wales* (1784), ii, p. 479, quoted without reference.
[2] Sir John Wynn, *History of Gwydir*, p. 37.

set. Then under Queen Mary he had been entirely at ease, and his old age was passed in a moderate contentment in the earlier and unpersecuting years of Elizabeth. His son, Sir Richard the third, had been brought up in the last period of King Henry, when the monasteries had gone, but the Mass remained strongly protected in an atmosphere where the less ascetic priests were in fashion, conservative, prosperous, sufficiently celibate, very loyal to the King. This was the quietened religious sense of those years, when the custom continued, while the old system faded, entrusted to men, who depended on the heavy Cæsarian piety and were fully ready to render to Cæsar all things that the royal conscience required.

Such was the nature of the churchman, the uncle of Beaumaris, Thomas Bulkeley, Rector of Llanddeusant, a man who always remained to his family the fine civilian of the time of his studies at Cambridge; but now he gradually rusted from system to system, retaining always a store of theological proverbs and quips in the homely and rustic Latin, which the years had still left him. He was a man of sound judgment to whom religion was pleasant as he read in his great Book of the Mass, with the arms of his family wrought fine on the cover, and he was never unconscious of the gulf that divided him from the yeomen, like those voluble, pen-scratching priests at St. Asaph and Bangor with their too hot divinity. It was all very well for Owen Lewis or Clynog to go to the Continent, but one could hardly expect a Bulkeley to seek bread at other men's doors, so he regretfully laid aside for the second time, as the Queen had ordered, the heavy worked cope embroidered with the silver bull's head and the sacring bell stamped with the device of his family. This was the mellow influence over all that generation in childhood and he set the tone for all the lesser men in the island, like Sir Lewis ap John, the Bulkeley family priest at Llandegfan, on whom the Beaumaris chapel depended.[1] Besides, in his compliant old age, Thomas Bulkeley could look out on the lands of the rectories of Llangefni and Llanrhuddlad, which he had annexed to his own, and if in those last heavy

---

[1] For personal details of Thomas Bulkeley see the Letters and Papers of Henry VIII, *passim*, and for certain sidelights the will of Bishop Arthur Bulkeley of Bangor, who left to him ' the paraphrases of Erasmus in Latin . . . noted in my own hand.' Mathew Parker MSS. Corpus Christi College, Cambridge, Miscell. 4, contains the report of Bishop Meyrick, which refers to his residence ' at Llanrhuddlad (where he) keepeth a good house.' Browne Willis, *Survey of Bangor*, pp. 256–259 contains some details.

summers the Angelus and the Sanctus bells were silent, there still remained, through those low sounds of gathered harvest, the slow unfailing grinding of the tithes.[1]

There was no question here of any zeal for Reform, nor was there any conscious denial of old custom. Indeed, their sentiment was strongly opposed to that clerical marriage, which had led to the temporary exile of their less prudent English brethren, when the Catholicism of Queen Mary had returned. These good lands in Anglesea could support a bachelor, but not a family,[2] and it was difficult to propose to any man of standing that his daughter should accept this doubtful rank. Besides in their later years these clergy felt the need of a certain dignity, which their reverend bearing as they rode heavily from marriage feast to funeral made seemly, and they could not accept the prospect of a life tie with some old woman of no fortune. They could not understand this affirmation of illicit ties, for if in his youth a man had pleasured himself in the white farm houses, this was not a matter for remembrance when he sat grave in the seat of honour interpreting the parchments, which re-aligned the estate for some rich squire's daughter, the reluctant division of the manor and the slow surrender of the grange. If the new doctrines made no headway while such men remained, entrenched and stolid in the glebe lands, it is not surprising that the Catholic Faith in Anglesea should wither and that before they vanished it should die.

It was to this atmosphere that Sir Richard Bulkeley was accustomed from his childhood until he was close on forty and such interest in religion as he possessed never fully attuned his mind to greater change.[3] Thus when the old priests of his youth had died he no

---

[1] Although there were no 'active preachers' in Anglesea in 1561 the Marian rectors in the island showed a profound attachment to the soil as the following list of tenures indicates. Thomas Bulkeley LL.B., was Rector of Llanddeusant, 1543–1579, also of Llangefni and Llanrhuddlad, Humphrey ap Richard was at Llanbeulan, 1548–1587, Lewis ap John at Llandegfan 1555–1573, Reynold ap Griffith at Llandyfrydog, 1550–1569, Thomas Jones at Llangadwaladr 1554–1572, John Rowland at Hen Eglwys, 1558–1578, Lewis ap Evan at Llanidan, 1554–1579, Robert ap Hugh at Newborough, 1554–1596, Hugh Powel at Rhoscolyn, 1558–1583, and David Moythe at Llanfair Pwll Gwyngyll, 1543–1583. In addition Llantrisant was held from 1556–1577 by the permanent absentee, Dr. Yale. In 1566 Bishop Robinson complained of 'the images and altars still undefaced,' but they were Catholics by preference, not by conviction.

[2] The Commonplace Book of the Vicar of Llan Gelynin, Cwrtmawr MS., 18, gives a basis of comparison.

[3] His position equivocal, but then not rare, led to his inclusion among the 'Catholics' in the list prepared by a Scottish agent in 1574, although he had never absented himself from Anglican attendance. In a list of 'seven justices of peace not known to be of any religion and therefore suspected to be Papists,' the names of Sir Rowland Stanley and Sir Richard Bulkeley appear. Cal. S.P. Dom. Add., 1580–1625, p. 35.

longer cared to receive the ministrations of this new race of married clerks, with whom socially he felt so ill at ease. It was in him a mark of conservatism and perhaps the last flickering of his Catholic spirit, which within ten years was dead; for life was full of interests, and these disputes were hardly worthy of a man of fashion. Meanwhile the family living must be filled, so Llandegfan passed for nearly half a century to Sir Richard's brothers and the Oxford of the late Elizabethans provided a definite religious outlook, which Beaumaris neither defended nor denied. Without any other effort or assistance, time unaided would have carried the Bulkeleys outside the Catholic Church.

This gradual slipping from the moorings of Catholic practice and dogma was typical of all those great families, who were determined that under no circumstances would they defy the Crown. At Lleweni the Salusburys went through the self-same course, the gradual loosening and then the abandonment of the old custom, with the same ancient clergy presiding unwillingly at these changes that they would not themselves agree to engineer. In this case Thomas Bulkeley's place was taken by Robert Salusbury, who was Rector of Llanrwst from 1537 till 1573 without a break,[1] a man who lived at the western frontier of the family interest, where the tracks rise southwards into the hills, ' a forest, rough and spacious . . . and all over growen with woods, for . . . green grass grew on the market place in Llanroost called Brin y Botten, and the deer fled in the church yard of Llanroost.' [2] Under the soporific calm of that quiet influence the memory of the Old Religion fell asleep, and when Sir Richard Bulkeley went forward in acceptance of the new worship he was followed by his brother-in-law Wynn of Gwydir and by the matriarch of the Salusburys, the famous Katheryn of Berain.

This celebrated lady, who was two years Sir Richard's junior, pursued the same line of movement, which the different phases of her four husbands had made more clear. Her first marriage in Queen Mary's time was with Thomas Salusbury of Lleweni, a young man, Catholic and loyal, with the reserved Sacrament on his altar and with a chaplain to intone the dirges for his kin. And then there came her three brief years of union with Sir Richard Clough, that merchant

---

[1] From a list printed in David Thomas' *History of St. Asaph*, p. 604.
[2] Sir John Wynn, *History of the Gwydir Family*, pp. 52–53.

with a great fortune and old, who built for her the Dutch house of Bachegraig, a man who disguised under a surface acceptance of the new order a deep attachment to the ancient ways. Then quite suddenly her second husband had died alone in Hamburg in the hot weather of 1570, in one of those tall narrow houses, the well-ordered legacy of the Hansa League. To the dying man it was the earlier memories that were returning, Palestine, the Cross of the Sepulchre and the crowds, and yet more clearly his boyhood days at Chester, a chorister singing in the Abbey as the Black Monks came slowly up the choir. But the brief and very eligible widowhood that Katheryn now enjoyed was ended by a journey from Bachegraig to Gwydir to become the wife of that weak and careful man whom this new family suffered as its head. Maurice Wynn, frugal, querulous and solemn, was of the younger generation to whom King Henry's Mass was a memory, now dead, which he had replaced by a support for newer things. There was in him the quality that was to become the separating mark of the Parliamentarian landlords, that Puritanism of the spirit, a distaste for roystering, a lack of ease in the company of men.[1] But in 1580 Katheryn was delivered into her third widowhood and with the character of her last husband, Edward Thelwall, the cycle of these changes is complete.

In this fourth marriage she had chosen a man much younger than herself and one brought up from childhood in that Elizabethan spirit in which the religious questionings had ceased. Mr. Thelwall had all the realistic outlook and the acuteness of perception, which marked the Tudor lawyer caste from which he sprang, shadowed with that restrained and prudent scepticism of the Temple, while in the background there was his father's office as Vice-Justice of the Court at Chester, and, in contrast to the dull squires' houses, the lighter, the more *mondain* circuit talk. Thus in her last years Katheryn of Berain had passed from those first religious struggles, slowly from state to state, until the memory of the earlier times had vanished. And this is the fate for which the portrait at Llewesog prepares us, for it brings out clearly the dignity of her carriage with the wide serene brow and the bearing, calm and steady, and the slightly tightened lips. She continued on her course, keeping always before her the cares of her house-

---

[1] Calendar of Wynn Papers, pp. 13–17. Llanstephan MS., 179b, and the writings of Sir John Wynn combine to produce this impression.

hold and the duties of her rank, while in time the Old Religion fell away from her almost imperceptibly in her labours, as she divided up her property and supervised her bailiffs, intent on the preservation of the land.[1]

As far as religion was concerned these Salusburys and Bulkeleys confined themselves to a mere passive preference and, in this time of struggle, such weak emotion expired. It is not the attack of enemies so much as the indifference of friends that has caused the destruction of apparently well-founded systems and this, which is most clear in the history of monarchy, is shown also in the matters of faith. Only an ardent and vehement faith, like that of the Lancashire squires, could save the Catholic position and the acceptance of the new system proved all the more deadly since it was a failure of natural supporters. When the Salusburys, on whom the Denbigh Carmelites had always depended, and the Bulkeleys, with their great ecclesiastical interest, abandoned the Church the lesser men could only with difficulty continue the struggle. Besides, every one in the North was affected by the news of the couriers from London, and in addition there had been a surfeit of controversy about the Six Articles and the Prayer Books and now they were resting. By 1586, at the end of the first period of the reign, Sir Richard Bulkeley and his friends had passed nearly thirty years of such acquiescence, so that the old beliefs and customs were dying, while around them the whole countryside prospered materially and the crowds on the Irish road daily increased. In the next generation such a materialist outlook produced a reaction, but it is remarkable how powerfully these first squires were affected by the English custom and fashion and the shifting vista of gain. It is perhaps a tendency for the people of a barren and unprofitable country to accept very readily the vaguer suggestions of economic advantage and certainly in this temptation the Welsh have suffered their share. They have struck their tents and rooted up every settled habit of life for the sake of this mirage, as in the later exodus to the mines, when the fields were abandoned. But even now, when these fevers are passed, it is difficult to decide whether Welsh gold exists, save as an illusion.

[1] The evidence of the Wynn Papers shows her as careful and not without a certain feminine dependence of character, a great contrast to those legends which describe her as burying her poisoned husband in the orchard at Berain. It is clear that there has been attributed to her, since before the days of Pennant, the old legend of the lady with the four husbands, whose ritual questions and answers can be found exactly repeated in the account of Lady Penelope Darcy in the *History of Dorset*. This legend of the four Dorset husbands, which is the basic type of the cycle, goes back to the reign of Charles I and has been given a literary form by Thomas Hardy.

CHAPTER IV

THE CHARACTER OF THE RELIGIOUS TRANSITION

After considering in the previous chapter the nature and development of the first religious changes in Wales, we come to a more general view of the manner in which these were completed. The earlier changes before 1570 have now been described, and it is rather a question of the formation of that opinion which was, in the succeeding generation, to make the Welsh squires sound Churchmen and Royalists. Similarly in England the first Elizabethan laws have been considered and the two systems which the Catholics adopted with regard to the Marian priests. Here it is the effect of the Papal action upon the mind of the squires that is dealt with, the reactions produced by the Bull of Excommunication against Queen Elizabeth, by the strong Catholic attitude and the Marian priests. Appearing in every aspect of the whole situation there is that great strength of the Crown, which has already been noted, the firm hold of the Tudors. Such endeavours as the Babington Plot, which had so many repercussions in Wales, thus falls into its own insignificant place. A great part is played by the rapid development of the new doctrine of kingship, which in measure filled the place of religion in a de-Catholicized world. The attitude of Pope Pius V, concerned for the spiritual re-conquest of England, was based to some extent on a misconception of the degree to which the Catholic outlook of the squires remained constant. The old loyalties, feudal and Catholic, which are last seen in the Northern Revolt, were credited without any foundation to all those squires in the South who could be conceived as possessing a sympathy for the Ancient Religion. But in the South there was no response to the Pope and each year the Old Church became weaker, a weakness which can most clearly be traced among those squires in North Wales who were anxious to follow in all things the suggestions of London.

It was at this point that the earliest seminary priests came to England. With rare exceptions, like John Bennett the martyr, they were unable to penetrate into Wales, as the work in England was pressing, but the increasing desire which the Welsh squires possessed for the life of the capital brought their elder sons into the sphere of this influence. Continuing the history of the development of the three North Welsh families of Bulkeley, Salusbury and Wynn, it is seen that it was in London that the first serious effects of the Catholic reaction were felt in the conversion of young Thomas Salusbury and his friend Edward Jones. Their friendship with Babington, the plot for releasing the Queen of Scots and the arrest and trial of the conspirators all provide evidence of the strength of the Government. In contrast to Salusbury's return to Catholicism, there is the significant episode of Sir Richard Bulkeley's decision to abandon finally his old Catholic preferences and to accept the Established Religion. The influences of Leicester and Burghley, diverse but both favouring submission, that fear of the loss of their property which the Babington prosecutions aroused, and finally the religious tests for all civil preferment decided the issue. In those sections of North Wales, where the English influence extended, the Catholic squires were reduced to a tiny minority, like the Mostyns of Talacre and the Wynns of Melai, and with the submission of Sir Richard Bulkeley, the fortunes of whose family have now been traced since the old Catholic days, the Ancient Religion had lost the support of the squires.

THE CELTIC PEOPLES & RENAISSANCE EUROPE

It would seem a very difficult problem to explain the transition from the Catholic squirearchy, which had conformed and bent before its dynastic faith in the Tudors, to that solid phalanx of the Cavalier body, sound Churchmen and Royalist. Yet a bare half century divided these phases in each family's development; for all the squires who were living in 1570 had experienced, and most had welcomed, the Catholic life under Mary, while by 1620 all the older generation of Royalists, who had been most of them born, like Charles I, at the turn of the century, were already men. These were the grandsons of the squires who had followed the policy of the acceptance, those whose Catholic beliefs had already been weakened by successive submissions, as the career of the three Richard Bulkeleys makes clear. It would seem that the most probable explanation of this completely achieved transition is the abrupt rise into favour of that new doctrine of kingship, which came to saturate the mind of the squires.

As the old idea of the Church was weakened, this Tudor theory of kingship increasingly filled the place and borrowed the phrase of religion, working through the still Christian trend of the de-Catholicized mind of that century. In this aspect it was one of the struggles of Nationalism with Rome, the increasing, unrestrained veneration of those national symbols, which, whether or not they are monarchical as under the Tudors, are found in eventual conflict with the Catholic conception of the teaching of Christ. It follows that the worst service, that was done to the Catholics in England and Wales, was the identification of some of their body with active opposition to the kingship, which stood for the national unity that had lately come to prevail.

As a means to explain the general trend in the country, it would be perhaps preferable to consider one area, the seaboard strip of North Wales, and to return, after considering the general effects of the chief movements in the struggle, to the history of those families, the Bulkeleys and Salusburys, whose development has already been traced. This is the more appropriate on account of their close connection with the Babington Plot, which first moved public opinion in the direction of a hatred of Rome, and because the life of Sir Richard Bulkeley the third covers the whole of the period. He had been born in 1533, and had experienced in his youth the full Catholic time under

Mary, while he survived till 1622, nearly the end of the reign of King James, when the mind of the Cavalier squires was first forming. In this process of increasing estrangement from Rome there was always in waiting that theory of the claims of the kingship, which leading to Divine Right and Passive Resistance, would so soon dominate the great land-owning class. The reactions towards Rome only emphasized, for the majority, the strength of this Royalist doctrine and when a vacuum was created, by the weakening hold of the Catholic Religion, it was speedily filled by the new idea of the national kingship, which gave vitality to the various institutions of the State Church by which it had been clothed. In this sense the marriage of Queen Mary with Philip of Spain was the last action of an international policy to support the Throne and the Altar, both independent, that concept of the temporal and spiritual powers each supreme in its sphere. But when the Altar was cast down all equality was over and in the seventeenth century no Englishman would hesitate as to the relation of the Communion Table with the Crown.

The slow destruction of the practice of Catholicism in North Wales had proceeded very far before any appreciable reaction could set in, for the point of view that the Crown adopted was mirrored in the actions of the squires. The apparent tolerance of private Catholic practice, which seemed to mark the first ten years of the Queen's reign, was changed into severity after the Northern Rising and then gradually deepened into that tyranny, which marked the last laws against the priests. All this time the great body of the squires, who had accepted the new religious changes, followed with a constant loyalty in the wake of all these moods, reflecting at each new step the shifting spirit of the legislation of the Crown. Two explanations, one political and one religious, will cover the twofold nature of this change ; nor should this seem surprising, for it was on the first acceptance, the destruction of the Altar, that all depended and in this the subsequent changes were contained.

On the political side the nationalist sentiment, which desired a wider freedom, came into conflict with the old Catholic claims, put forward with fresh vigour by the new Tridentine force, and in this question the excommunication of the Queen and the deposing power, which this implied, brought into the controversy those notes of bitterness that it had lacked. For hitherto the party which had obtained all the monastic land and controlled the churches could afford a certain objective calm in its remarks. It was early seen that this bull of excommunication, *Regnans in Excelsis*, would become the strongest card that the English Government could play, and it was a matter of very great importance to bring every political attempt within its scope. It is necessary to avoid underestimating the effect of this constant propaganda in North Wales, the suggestions that came up with the couriers from London that every attempt and movement against the Queen was the immediate and direct effect of Papal words. Thus the broad outlines of Continental policy, the massacre of St. Bartholomew, the murder of William of Orange, and the firm growth of the League were all used to arouse in the English mind a disquiet in the face of Roman power. It was not that the idea of the return of Rome was unusual, for this was what the squires had peacefully voted for barely twenty years before; but it was that sense, which was forced upon their minds, of a Church which would rest unsatisfied until she had obtained the blood of the Queen.

Since they aimed at the complete destruction of the Catholic Religion it was necessary for the Government to check the inflow of priests, and the introduction of the penalties for treason was designed to secure this; but the Government was powerfully aided by the plots of the laymen. In the mind of the period a peculiar solemnity attached to the exaction of these barbarous penalties, quartering, disembowelling and castration, from gentlemen of position, and this provided a line of argument to cause from effect, which in time hardened and turned the national conscience from calm allegiance to Rome into hatred. It was a slow progress from the execution of Felton for pinning the Bull against the Queen to the gatehouse at Fulham until the death of the last layman in the Titus Oates 'Plot,' and after every series of deaths the public opinion grew harder. These men were laymen, not priests, and there was nothing sacramental in their action and whether their deaths were just, as with Babington, or a flagrant injustice, like the judicial murder of the innocent Popish Plot victims, was a point beyond the power of the unenlightened contemporary opinion to fathom. What men saw was the unexampled torture inflicted on gentlemen of substance and rank, and if their sufferings were so fierce and exemplary, how terrible must have been their crimes? To this the Crown had always one answer, that they had drawn their swords against the life of their Sovereign and that they did this at the express command of the Pope.

Everything came back to this, all the conspiracies with which the career of a successful and despotic sovereign was strewn; while Burghley and Walsingham made their position stronger and firmer, as every few years they succeeded in rescuing and preserving the life of their ruler. Throckmorton, Babington, Williams and Lopez and all the plots and conversations, unknown and abortive, came back once again to this 'motif,' just as did every method of killing, by the sword, by sweet draughts, by fireballs and by the poisoning of the Queen's saddle pommel, while at the root of the evil the Government always made clear the form of the Pope and the Papal gold and the agents. Finally as a climax there came the Gunpowder Plot, and after the explosion, that then shook the mind of the people, the memory of the nine centuries of the long and benevolent rule of the Popes over England had vanished.

To us there is often something unreal in the bitterness of the estrangement that followed, but, keeping still to the political side of the question, a great gulf had opened when the ordinary lines of communication were broken. Until the last breach with Rome there was constant contact through the ambassadors and bishops and all the trains of clerics and servants that such high journeys involved, and quite apart from this knowledge there was the vaguer news of the pilgrims, who kneeling at the Confession, where the Apostle lay buried, could see the Papal procession move through in its glory. It was the starvation of intercourse that gave rise to the phantasy and to the flickering of those monstrous forms, shadows of a reality which to the average Englishman had become hardly less remote than the Lama. It is hardly conceivable that Giant Pope could have appeared either earlier or later.

On the religious side also there was something that made the mind of the squires of the acceptance harden at this Bull of the Pope's. However indifferent, they had been accustomed all through Henry VIII's reign and under Queen Mary to the sacramental cleansing of their soul in the Shriving. This was the custom, handed down from their ancestors, that on the solemn occasions they should follow this way of repentance and even the most careless would have certain moments, as for instance when they abandoned their mistresses on their marriage, when this Sacrament would set its seal on their lives, as they knelt beside the priest's chair in the chaplain's room in their manors. It was no easy matter either to replace or forget the hope that they had received there of God's ultimate mercy on their turbulent lives, but now every question of Shriving was over. Careless as they were, these squires had been brought up under the system when this penance was the inevitable prelude for death and now they were without it. In the confused mists of those times there was need for self-justification and those who had used the old ways accepted the Pope's Bull as that proof, for which they were seeking, that patriotism could not permit them to follow so extreme a religion. Now once their conscience was disposed in this fashion their drift away from the Old Religion was rapid, for each new act that the Government could ascribe to the Pope was an additional reason, after the event, for abandoning his allegiance. It was pleasant to them, too, to realize, as they became more and more prosperous, that all along they had been right.

Thus such influences conspired to produce a bitterness towards Rome in the families of these once Catholic squires. Not that they troubled themselves in this matter, but when it came into their mind and some fresh legislation was passed they were quite prepared to support it. As they sat honest at home they would picture the Pope as inspired by a stealthy hatred of England, a constant fomenter of troubles and audaciously attacking the Queen in the seat of her kingdom. And this was an inevitable change for it is always most difficult to preserve our charity in dealing with those whom we have abandoned and who still oppose us. Yet there was a deep contrast between the Government propaganda of the Pope and his policy, with its tortuous and intricate aims, the tangible evidence for which were the poisoned perfumes and the dags, and the sober reality. It is as if in 1559 a fog had come down, obliterating from sight and confusing the memory. Accurate bearings were out of the question and it was only in after ages, when the sea had blown clear, that it was possible to find the Barque of Peter again, how solid and calm and familiar, with the heavy lines and the rigging, and how different from that wrathful phantom that the closing mists had called forth.

The Bull, *Regnans in Excelsis*, was issued on 25th February, 1570, the feast of St. Mathias, which fell that year on the Friday of the third week in Lent. The Pope Pius V had held a Court of Enquiry into the affairs of England in the first week of the fast and the evidence against the Queen had been most clear. The details of the destruction of the hierarchy and of the Queen's establishment of heresy had made a great impression on the active and direct mind of the Pontiff, who retained a mental outlook of extreme simplicity, which increasing age served only to refine. His councillors were few, for the Sacred College and the Ambassadorial suites were kept somewhat remote from this severe figure, but the Pope had during twelve days, since the inquiry was ended, brought the matter into the forefront of his prayer and offered it in the celebration of the Mass. Yet to the Pope, emaciated, drawn, self-starved in the isolated apartments of the Vatican that he had chosen, this was an affair translucently simple, for the Queen was an open avowed heretic and she had broken her solemn promise and all that was necessary was this Bull, which should bring back his scattered children to the Faith. There was no question whatever, all the pious English gentlemen had assured him that the misguided nation would return quickly with joy. It needed only that call, which as the *Pastor Gregis* he was bound to give, and they would come back to their Father, as the sheep had answered to him as a boy, when he had had the charge of flocks on those last long folds of the Apennines of Voghera, which dip east of Alessandria to the plain. This was a matter for God and not for the Cardinals, and there was no need for consultation,[1] but after the recitation of the Rosary, which he never allowed himself to omit, he summoned his secretary, the reserved, the silent Rusticucci, and signed the document which freed the English race. In the afternoons of Lent he was accustomed to go through the olives on the Aventine to Santa Sabina, a house of his own Dominicans which had at one time been his home, and in the first light airs of the Roman spring he had profound contentment, for he had a gaiety which went with his direct simplicity and he had endeavoured to guard the freedom of the Church and to fulfil God's Holy Will.

His mind was clear from all thought of policy. He had not consulted, he had in fact offended, the King of Spain about this matter and still less was there any thought of France or of the importunate

[1] The evidence of Tiepolo quoted by Pastor, *History of the Popes*, xvii, pp. 80–81, indicates the Pope's dislike of any consultation and the concealment of the Bull from the King of Spain would suggest an extreme probability that the Spanish Cardinals were not given his confidence.

Ambassadors of the Powers. The Queen of Scotland he regarded as hardly better than Elizabeth with the painful memory of that wanton Bothwell marriage. It was a question of the English and of their once vivid Faith. The Pope was uncertain whether the rising of the northern earls had failed,[1] but what the English Catholics needed was encouragement, that freedom in conscience from obedience. Before him lay the Dominican priory with the last of the February sun upon its windows and on the calm of the red tiles on the floor of the refectory and on the long and empty tables. If only this simplicity in God's service could be restored and when, above the noise of the ox carts on the cobbles, there came the sound of the 'Ave Maria,' rising from the church steeples of the faithful city it surely could not seem impossible to reconcile Religion and the World.

In England Religion, in the technical sense of the great orders to which the Pope's soul was bound, had been absorbed and swallowed wholesale by the squires and such an idea of a peace between Religion and the World was as meaningless as that between consumer and consumed. Besides, however Catholic-minded were the sons of the men who had established themselves on the monasteries the monastic side of the Church was the very last they wished stressed. Besides Pope Pius V was a friar of the old stern rigorous observance and he had tramped from house to house in his province with his bread in his wallet in that exact and scrupulous poverty in which the welcoming sun of his country allowed his brethren to mirror the exact ways of the founder. To the old Marian priest, who had perhaps slipped into conformity, such a figure seemed menacing and disturbing with his solitary and absorbed attention to the simple service of God. But in England the outlook of the old priests was in contrast, for they were men whom the strainer of Henrican conformity had drained of their fervour. Instead they possessed considered worldly experience and the wisdom of compromise and with them the old memory of the Schism still lingered. Ease of conscience and freedom from allegiance were fine terms in the Vatican with the halberdiers and the Swiss, but in plain English what did they come to? The path of justice when the

---

[1] The Pope's letter to the Northern Earls, written on 20th February, five days before the publication of the Bull, expresses anxiety, and although Northumberland's letter of 8th November only reached Rome on 16th February, there were special reasons for this delay. Advices in Italian were sent to the Pope from Antwerp at regular intervals, and while those despatched on 14th and 15th January contain reports of the defeat of the rebels, this is more forcibly described in the letter of 28th January. Cal. S.P. Rome, 1558–1571, pp. 321–328.

Northern Rising had ended was answer enough and now, since the squire was good living and loved the old ways, the priest was respected and he could say Mass in privacy and there was still a recognized status and the perquisites and the game. And if they should take the Pope at his word all this good calm would be shattered, uselessly and quite without need and they would die on the gallows. It is noticeable that on this subject neutrality could not be obtained and all those who did not follow the Pope came in time to oppose him.

Regarded in the political effects of its action this excommunication was the last of the feudal bulls of the Papacy, just as the last action in England, which the feudal spirit inspired, was that Northern Rising which led to the death of the Percy. On no subsequent occasion did the Pope ever excommunicate a non-Catholic head of the State. But in Rome it was impossible to make clear the difference of outlook in England between the northern lords and the southern. The Pope had before him the thought of Northumberland, anxious and troubled in conscience, direct and used to those wide feudal spaces, as he knelt on the stones in the hour of that brief triumph at Durham to adore that Sacred Host, which through the Divine Mercy could be raised again by his efforts. These were the simple-minded children of Faith to whom the Pope's words were addressed, and he read this frame of mind even into the most guarded protestations of loyalty and into Ridolfi's confident lists.

Yet there was no real contact between the careful lords in the South and this last feudal survival and in this matter also the squires followed their leaders. Two years later Simple Tom died under the headsman at York and the crowd groaned at the sight of the blood of the Percy. This was in a line with the Pope's ideas, and he imagined that these were the sentiments of the thirty peers of the realm, who figured on the lists sent to the Vatican as ' undoubtedly Catholic.' But these were men whom the Renaissance had touched before the Counter-Reformation could reach them and they were hardly disposed in their later years to follow the Pope's call, which might end in a martyrdom and would belie all those calculations on which the ordering of their lives had been based. It was possible, too, for them to retain their convictions without recourse to such measures and their wealth was still drawn from a soil, from which they would never consent to be severed. Besides, the logic of an abstract reasoning is more usually translated to action by minds either detached and enthusiastic or simple and these were characteristics quite foreign to the Courts of the Tudors.

When the news of the Queen's excommunication reached the great Catholic lords, they recoiled from such a suggestion as the freedom from their allegiance, and as they gazed over their widened and compact estates, past those monastic granges which had now fallen within their domain and over those tracts whose administration ran simpler now that the friction between religious and lay lords was over, there was a movement of distaste as they thought of the Pope's logic, unchanged and persistent. For after all with patience, religious questions might turn and meanwhile they had all they required. In this state they continued, until they died in their age in their county with a Catholic priest, brought across country, beside them to give the Sacred Anointing and the silver vessels from the old chapel taken out from their presses. Down below in the room where the business was done the bailiffs of the estate would receive the vicar with courtesy, and after a glass of the wine, kept for the more ordinary guests, he would ride home through the lanes on his cob from the visit of ceremony. At the funeral, too, there would be accommodation and reason and, after they had had all the prayers for the dead by the tapers in the seclusion of the great manor, the priest would depart once again and the body would be buried in the tomb of the family with that service which the Queen had prescribed. There the whole countryside would be present and the rural life in its most prosperous aspect would go forward in calm and the trees that the old peer had planted would form avenues for his son. It is not surprising that those who had so admirably fitted in their lives with their fellows would not find any response to the reasoning of the Papal solitary alone with his God. But the Pope looked to the future, and there would seem little doubt that, without the explicit command to refuse the title of Head of the Church to Elizabeth and to abstain from all Anglican worship, the Catholic Church in England and Wales would have perished. There was not the result that Rome expected, but a rapid and deepening hostility and only a remnant was saved, yet unless this action had been taken is it not likely that this remainder, too, would have died ?

Since the immediate effect of this Bull was so slight, as far as the question of rallying the Catholics was concerned, the ripples of this controversy would hardly have spread into Wales. When a response

THE CHARACTER OF THE RELIGIOUS TRANSITION

from even acknowledged Catholics was lacking, it is not to be expected that in Wales it would have had any effect on the conduct of those who, like the Bulkeleys and Salusburys, had already conformed, however Catholic they might remain in their sympathies. In its first launching the Bull then was a failure, except in so far as it strengthened the open avowed Catholics of Lancashire and those small islands of Catholics, scattered through the whole country, who would now be permanently emboldened to refuse to attend the Queen's service. As for the bulk of the nation, now indifferent and once Catholic, it greeted the Bull with that irritation deepening to anger with Rome, which was so soon to set the English on an unreturning path of estrangement.

Nevertheless, this firm Papal standpoint was ultimately the cause of the Catholic survival, for if the faithful were to be strictly forbidden to attend the Anglican service they must have their own priests and the Catholic colleges were founded to supply a need, which the rapid extinction of the Marian clergy had rendered acute. Besides the way in which the Pope's Bull was received showed that the existing priests were in need of a stiffening [1] and, if the Tridentine spirit could not penetrate into England with the words of the Pope, it must come through the missionary priests.

But, as the years passed, Wales was only remotely affected, for the priests landing in England had so much work in that country before they could even consider penetrating so far to the West. The capture of John Bennet, one of the new Douai priests, as he was trudging past Sir Thomas Mostyn's house at Gloddaeth in the summer of 1582 is one of the earliest indications that we possess of their efforts, and it would seem not unreasonable to suppose that the arrest of the Recusant schoolmasters, William Griffiths of Caernarvon and Richard Gwyn of Iswyd, was connected with the arrival of the first new priests in the country. These also are the circles, the yeomen rising to gentry, who would be first affected by the secret return from

---

[1] This is borne out by a reference to the Catholic leader, Lord Montague. 'If . . . he went to hereticall churches, it was not so much to be imputed to him as to his priest, a learned and pious man indeed, but too fearfull, who supposing it expedient something to give to the tyme, durst not determine such a fact to be sinne.' *Life of the Lady Magdalen, Viscomtesse Montague,* p. 11, a work published by R. Smith in 1627.
A type of the great Southern families, whose transition has just been described, is provided by the Paulets, Marquises of Winchester. Their high official connections, the lawsuits and family feuds are seen against the strict Recusancy of Lord Chideock and Lady Giles Paulet. Cal. S.P. Dom., *passim.* A certain light on the attitude of the third Marquis is thrown by the correspondence in Series 2, Legajo 6. Valladolid MSS.

abroad of old Bennet of Brincanellan's son. It was among this section, the old Welsh still untouched by the Court, that the missionaries achieved their success; but the long duration of imprisonment, the five years that elapsed before Gwyn's execution in October, 1584, would seem to indicate that the rich conforming squires were not greatly alarmed by these events. And then, while the slow efforts of the missionary priests were continued, there broke out the first of the chain of Catholic conspiracies, exploding into the midst of that wealthy circle in Wales, who had so far accomplished the changes with such ease and complaisance.

After twenty years, during which the drift from Rome was continuous, the first reaction began to make itself felt, and, in so far as it was based on a solid conviction, this was the result of the early labours of the missionary priests. Thus the activities of Babington and of all the young men who supported the new Catholic clergy and gave shelter to priests were in the first place the result of such efforts. But in the case of Babington and his friends another force, quite divorced from religion, entered into their lives, and if Campion had disposed them to prayer it was through the Queen of Scotland that they were brought to the scaffold. Here we have the influence that created conspirators, and how very much simpler the situation would have been for the Catholics if there had never been any choice except between Elizabeth and Philip II. But at Tutbury and later at Chartley there remained, closely guarded, a prisoner with a pretence of honourable confinement, that desolate and beautiful Queen. It was not that the Queen of Scots would influence men in a return to Catholicism, but that for those younger men who returned to the ancient allegiance she was the supreme symbol of their stricken and unfortunate Faith. This became more vivid after the execution of Campion and the enforcement of the Recusancy laws had brought home to them the bitterness of their sufferings, which in royal patience she shared and surpassed.

Meanwhile the priests went to and fro quietly and the elder Catholics returned to a stricter practice, while in North Wales there was little effect, and as far as the squires were concerned all might have passed peacefully. The gulf was not yet deep which divided Sir Richard Bulkeley from Sir Thomas Gerard or any of his Recusant cousins, and they were all profoundly loyal to Elizabeth; but the opposition of the younger men, impatient of their fathers, was anxious to attach itself to a standard. If the Queen of Scots had been Protestant, it seems most probable that the conspiracies would have occurred just the same, aiming at a change of *régime*, not a change of religion. The same excitement, which drew those of the English seamen who were both romantic and mercenary to the coasts of the Indies, affected the idle young blades of the Court at the thought of the park walls at Chartley. The fascination and all the elaborate staging of this Tragedy Queen, with her secretaries and her women, moved them profoundly; for the Elizabethans were always responsive to the somewhat obvious pathos of her cruel situation, which would seem, to a later age, a little heavily charged with the sword hilt protestations of loyalty of her too numerous and passionate friends. And if Queen Mary had been opposed to the Catholics, so long as she retained her charm and that fragile dignity and, what was to the boyish mind of her followers, her wonderful past, these plots would probably still have arisen and Babington, whose passionate devotion could hardly have been quenched by religion, would now be remembered as her most unfortunate servant. Yet in such a case the Babington Plot would have had just that historical significance of the affair of Cinq Mars, a harmless insignificant firework, instead of being the first of the candles thrown into the powder of the anti-Catholic feeling in England.

It was in the early August of 1586 that the peace of the North Welsh houses was first disturbed. At Beaumaris and at Lleweni, where the young master had now gone to London, they had never been greatly troubled by the Queen of Scotland's affairs. It is true that both Sir Richard Bulkeley and the old Sir John Salusbury, now dead, had appeared in those sanguine lists, which her supporters compiled, as well affected to her cause; but so also did all the more or less Catholic-minded squires throughout the whole country and no one in Wales would wish to replace a Welsh Queen by a Scots one. The devotion of a party of young courtiers to her cause was not a fact that would reach them, for the outer fringes of politics were unaware of this trend, which remained one of those happy secrets which it was the Government's consolation to guard. To a man like Sir Richard this attachment, like many of the other customs of the young men in London, would have seemed unpleasant and rather absurd. The Queen must be nearer fifty than forty by now and she had had an interesting history, which quite brought back old times, when poor Maurice Wynn and old Sir John, who was still hearty then, had sat in the evenings at Beaumaris discussing her case over the wine. Even now he could recall the honest and forthright humour of some of the episodes, Châtelard, her French poet found twice under her bed and her husband running in his nightshirt through the bushes when his house had exploded. And while all this was happening, her present maudlin admirers, who did not know how to treat a fine woman, were falling about in the nursery.

While these episodes seemed so remote, it would appear most unlikely that any suspicion of danger reached Wales, for Babington's mercurial temperament led to the rapid change and evolution of plans, and the associations which ended in treason had begun under the shadow of Leicester House in the meetings of those who were gentlemen of the ante-chamber to its powerful and Puritan lord. There young Thomas Salusbury, the owner of Lleweni, had gone after he had abandoned the tedious county politics and all the disputes on inheritance, which had followed his forced marriage, aged ten to his step-father's daughter.[1] After a period at Oxford, where he had kept terms at Trinity College, he had entered the service of his guardian, Lord Leicester, and there his relations left him in security. He was at this time twenty-two, reconciled with his wife who had recently borne him a daughter and popular in his county, with a short and bushy black beard, which satisfied his early virility, a carefully proportioned side whisker, that argued his acquaintance with fashion, and finally a new jewel swung from an ear-ring,[2] the mark of an exquisite. It seemed in that summer that his popularity was ever increasing, for he was frequently to be seen in those taverns, where the courtiers most resorted, and in the long evenings in the promenading in the fields at St. Giles' and always the centre of a gathering,

---

[1] Details from the Memoranda Book of Maurice Wynn of Gwydir, Llanstephan MS. 179b, and from correspondence in Calandar of Wynn Papers, pp. 11–20. The settlement was arranged on 8th October, 1574, and in 1576 Katheryn of Berain, writing to her step-son, John Wynn, about the arrest of one of her servants, stated, ' my poor son little Thomas Salusbury will be filled with great perplexity, for he was his father's man and his and one that he loved tenderly.' Cal. Wynn Papers, p. 15. All these letters show the misery and feuds that arose from this marriage.

[2] These various details of dress confirm the authenticity of the Lleweni portrait described by Pennant, *Tours*, ii, p. 29, while the identity would seem fully established in the case of this family, where only the heads of the house could afford to be painted. *Cf.* the undoubted portrait of Sir John Salusbury the Strong.

Vera effigies Clariss Do^m Iohãis Wynn de Gwedir in
Com Carnarvon Equitis et Baronetti &c.
Obijt primo die Martij 1626. Ætat: 55

SIR JOHN WYNN
From an engraving by Robert Vaughan in the National Museum of Wales.

a group of the younger courtiers, prosperous and admiring. There were already some aspects in this wide friendship which failed to recommend themselves to Sir Richard and the older squires in North Wales, that affection, so heavily and warmly romantic, which rang a little doubtful in his seniors' unjewelled ears. Yet, nevertheless, it would seem a question of folly and never of danger, for even those who could make out the first links of this cherished affection could not see the end of the chain.

On their outer fringe stood Edward Jones of Plas Cadwgan, a young Welsh squire of means, who had been recommended to Leicester by his father, a Master of the Wardrobe at Court. He was a friend and devoted admirer of Salusbury, a standpoint which seemed perfectly reasonable; but Salusbury had no eyes for him, but only for Babington, who must have possessed a fascination which we have now no means to explain. Chidiock Tichborne again centred his whole life upon Babington, as did to a less marked degree John Travers and Abington and such a resolute young soldier as Savage.[1] It was the tragedy of this friendship that Anthony Babington could not return their affection; but he was himself absorbed by an interest far beyond him and his devoted and unreckoning passion brought them all to their death.

This devotion to the Queen of Scots would seem to have been the driving force of the movement and, if Ballard was the first to broach this plan of conspiracy, it was Anthony Babington's fervour which could alone carry it through to an issue. He saw it always in the light of an organized warfare with his companions fighting in London, choice swordsmen and gallant; yet this was but a background to his action as he set off on the road for the North to release his own Queen and to avenge all those insults and wrongs that she had suffered for years. It was in the Queen of Scotland that he could see the true type of some pale, yet unvirginal, martyr and as he felt for his hilt there was the full joy of that combat with the heavy and Puritan Paulet, her gaoler. Then alone could he offer to his peerless and incomparable mistress, a worthy gift, the Crown. Here there was a

---

[1] At the same time Babington's large income, stated to have exceeded £1,000 a year of Elizabethan money, and his fine house in the Barbican, beside Lord Willoughby's garden, gave him a natural leadership among the young men who for the most part could only afford to return his hospitality at one of the taverns like the *Rose* outside Temple Bar. Cal. S.P. Scottish, 1585–86, pp. 395, 603-4.

great contrast with the attitude of the late Elizabethans, calculating and civilized; but however splendid and worldly he might seem to Tom Salusbury there was always much of the simplicity of the rustic in Babington. It is not now possible to determine in what degree he shared his plans with his supporters, but it seems that there were only those four summer months from April to August [1] during which the affair could take shape, while Babington was employed dropping hints of the confidence and trust he reposed in these men, who were delighted to find how greatly they were esteemed by their leader.

The Catholicism of this group was conscientious and rooted, but for the most part it was recent and there was in it something of that revolt from their fathers' opinions, a riot of independence which they knew could not be approved. Even Anthony Babington had not always been a Recusant and Edward Jones came of a profoundly Erastian family, while in the case of Thomas Salusbury there was probably a certain conscious reaction against his careful brother-in-law Wynn and those prim uncles from the Court of the Arches. In Salusbury's case a misconception as to his age [2] has given a false idea of maturity, but at twenty-one it would seem that his new religion was secret, something cherished, an effect of his wonderful new London life. It was not yet applied in practice to the world of Lleweni,[3] and it is just this secrecy which would have helped to lull Sir Richard and Thomas' mother to a sense of security. This will go far to explain that sense of the utterly unexpected with which this disaster broke upon those great Welsh families, whose worldly prudence had hitherto proved the backbone of prosperity.

This element of surprise comes out clearly in the deposition of Edward Jones at his trial.[4] ' I heard that night he (Salusbury),' this later statement begins, ' would be at my house and indeed he came thither about twelve of the clock and the door being opened him, as he was very familiar with me, he came running up to my bedside with a candle in his hand, which he took from one of my men, saluting me with these words. "Ned Jones how dost thou?" "Ah Tom,"

---

[1] All the evidence at the trial supports this short period of preparation. See State Trials, i, pp. 1130–60, as do the State Paper reports.

[2] The writer in the DNB gives his birth as approximately 1555, but the date of his matriculation at Oxford is given 29th January, 1579–80 in Foster's *Alumni*, and his age was sixteen at the time. See Ballinger, *op. cit.*, for further evidence.

[3] The entire absence of any reference to his Catholicism in the Wynn Papers would tend to confirm this view.

[4] State Trials, i, p. 1160.

said I, " Art thou one of them that would have killed the Queen." '
This was in August when the Government had arrested Ballard and
was closing in on the other conspirators. Jones, who always asserted
that his knowledge of the whole plan was vague and confused, gave
him a cloak and set him off towards Wales. It is difficult to see what
else he could have done, when their brief life of fashion had come to
this shipwreck ; for, as we can see from the words of his statement,
Salusbury was in desperate need. ' I confess this . . . my case was
hard and lamentable either to betray my dearest friend, whom I
loved as myself and to discover Thomas Salisbury the best man in
my country of whom I alone made choice.' ¹ It is in particular in this
case that we see the effects of Babington plunging ; ² for all the correspondence and secrets and Gilbert Gifford's inexplicable character were
hidden from the sight of Ned Jones, who only saw Salusbury in danger,
the man who had so generously accepted his friendship. As Jones
stated before his death, ' Only Thomas Salisburie motioned unto me
the delivery of the Queen of Scots desiring my aid and I told him it
was Babington's high mind only and prayed him to refrain his company. At last when he urged me I said, " Well, Tom, thou maiest
commainde me anie thinge." Herein I have offended Her Majesty and
I beseech her to forgive me. . . . And when Salisburie came to my
countrie I kept house anew, having kept no house before, only to keep
Thos Salisburie at home, meaning to bring him from his gadding life and
make him lead a settled life. Also because myself would live quietly I
made means to Mr. Secretary that I might have conference because I
would not be obstinate. . . . I confess that I concealed these treasons."³

Thus Jones with his slow-witted loyalty was arrested in London,⁴
while Salusbury in escaping, rode through to the North past the tired
City watchmen, who had been warned to arrest him.⁵ In the great

¹ *Ibid.*, i, p. 1152.
² Babington's tribute under examination stands in his favour, ' Mr. Salisbury (was) holden
for a man very much beloved in his countrie and one of whom there is amongst them a universall
great good opinion . . . , himself a comely personage, valiant, and extreme lover of his nation.'
He also asserted that Salusbury maintained the cause of his countrymen against Leicester's
oppression and that he was unwilling to do the Queen any violence. Yelverton MSS., ff, 218–23.
Printed by the Scottish History Society, 1922, p. 87, *passim*.
³ An account of his trial and death is contained in Harleian MS. 290.
⁴ By his will, the elder Edward Jones appears to have left his son a London house in Cornhill
when he died at Cadwgan on 23rd January, 1581.
⁵ On 10th August, 1586, Lord Burghley wrote to Walsingham of the stupidity of the
watchmen who said they would know the young men ' by intelligence of their favour,' for
' marry one hath a hooked nose.' He complained of the negligence of the justices in appointing
such silly men. Cal. S.P. Dom., 1581–90, p. 344.

F 2

houses in North Wales there was consternation at this disaster, as the couriers rode up to their gates with news of the panic in London.[1] Sir Richard Bulkeley and Mr. Thelwall, who was now Thomas' stepfather, had acted so prudently and now these fooleries of the Court had suddenly changed into treason, while the thought of the young Thomas riding home to his own people only heightened the danger. There was very little possibility of his final escape, and instead of trying to flee from the country, he was riding back to Lleweni to involve all his countrymen in his treason and folly. This was the end of that patient accumulation of centuries and it brings home the truth of the saying that when these distant country squires mingled in the affairs of the capital they were playing with fire, with a danger which in their inexperience of the world of London they could only rarely control. If Sir Richard who always seems to have retained a dress unchanged by the fashion, the round breeches and the thick bombast doublets,[2] could only have avoided this danger, refraining from his quarrel with Leicester and not yielding to the temptation to encourage his young kinsmen to seek a fortune at Court, nothing could have arisen to prevent his continued prosperity. As it was, they were all endangered by this unconsidered ambition.

But the Elizabethan political scene at this moment is not completed by these disturbances in North Wales and the certainty that the conspirators had of their death and the rising anger of public opinion against them without reference to the calm and untroubled peace of Lord Burghley. There had been moments, increasing in frequency with his age, when the old statesman was doubtful and hesitant, but now that he had had the threads of the conspiracy so long in his hands he felt clear from all danger. For the Government had dealt with that side of the plot that was beyond Babington's talent and which his simpler supporters had never suspected and it was the discovery of Gilbert Gifford that enabled them to lie calm. He was one of the strangest of the lesser men of his period, certainly not a debauchee who had turned against his religion, for he became a spy first when he

---

[1] Great excitement was caused by the discovery of ' three Irishmen in a bed and three sprigs of palm with crosses bound on them in Mr. Waferer's house on 13th August. Cal. S.P. Dom., 1581–90, p. 345.
[2] These details as to the round breeches and the ' bombast doublets, very gallant and rich,' appear in the account of Sir Richard Bulkeley in an Appendix to Pennant's *Tours*, ii, p 479

was little more than a boy out in Rome. And all the while he was progressing to the priesthood, which the Archbishop of Rheims was to confer, ignorant that the ordinand had been responsible for the death of his friends. There was nothing of the common informer about him, for he was a boy, undisciplined, but everywhere trusted and a younger son of that ancient and staunch family at Chillington. No evidence has yet come to light as to what it was that caused him to change from that life of the zealous squire's son, hot for the ancient religion. It would perhaps seem that, after the injured feelings and vanity that may have led him to consider the first post as an agent, he succumbed to that Levantine pleasure in the continuous and unravelling skill of an undiscovered deception. He went on from triumph to triumph never suspected; but his skill was such that after the Babington conspiracy the Government refused to use him again. Among all those who hung upon the fringes of the Church testing for the philosopher's stone or the great elixir, it would appear that here at last there was a shadow of success; for Gilbert Gifford was the farthest trusted of Lord Burghley's many agents and attained also to that priesthood, which in a time when men were specially tested, was the supreme mark of confidence that the Old Religion could bestow. It is to the great credit of Lord Burghley that, for three years before Babington began to construct his garden of paradise, he possessed the serpent which would cause his fall.

While all these arrangements slowly matured, the Lord Treasurer could rest with the knowledge that with every fresh post public opinion was strengthening behind him and these were the fortunate proofs that Her Majesty's present counsellors would remain at her side till the end. At Court there was the first movement of the vultures slowly circling, the voyagers of the Indies, who could now grasp an easier prize ;[1] but in his last years Lord Burghley was far from such concern. The fate of Dethick or Lleweni did not affect him, but he could now watch the gradual unfolding of his policy, while with each year its success seemed more assured. No one could have wished more for the health of the Queen's Majesty than Sir Richard Bulkeley, but this episode only shows the remoteness from affairs of even the most prosperous among the Welsh. The Cecils, with their

---

[1] Sir Walter Raleigh obtained Babington's lands at Dethick, while it was said that Frobisher was to have Abington's. Cal. S.P. Dom., 1581–90, p. 356.

touch on all affairs, could move with safety [1] through changes which the turbulent, plunging squires could not foresee. Yet if Thomas Salusbury was ignorant of the main purposes of the plot that caused his death, so also Sir Richard Bulkeley, in spite of his calm prudence and desire for accommodation, was unable to avoid the errors which check-mated his career. When one lived so remote from the Court centre, the only prudent course in regard to London politics was to abstain.

It was only very gradually that the complications produced by this conspiracy were unfolded. After an eddy of rumours [2] it was known that Thomas Salusbury had been taken to Chester and then followed the uncertain time of the trial and on 21st September Babington and all his friends were executed together. As the result of a great effort by a local jury [3] it was found that an old entail preserved Thomas' estate for his family and the Salusburys and Bulkeleys settled down to obliterate all the memories of him who had been called ' the Pope's white son.' [4] Thus the first effect of this conspiracy was a firm movement away from the memory of the few Catholic survivals. Katheryn of Berain, the boy's mother, had reached her last stage, the period of Edward Thelwall, her fourth and most Anglican husband, and Sir Richard Bulkeley sacrificed to the needs of the times the last traces of what had become a most dangerous sentiment. Religion was a support of the Crown and should assist a man to uphold, not to undermine, the position of Princes. He would bestir himself too in the apprehension of Recusants and might even go to the Sacrament, if the Queen should come to regard such an act as a sign of his loyalty. It had required such an effort to save Lleweni from the effect of Tom's folly and none of the old priests, who had lived through the changes, could give countenance to these plotters ; men who would gamble away in an evening all the good lands, which their

---

[1] At the time when opinion was in a ferment over the plot Burghley, who knew his security, was grieved at not obtaining the lieutenantcy of Hertfordshire since he was ' no new planted or new feathered gentleman ' and, while the world was still speculating about the execution of the conspirators, Burghley was concerned with the reversion of the office of ' Keeper of the Lions, Lionesses and Leopards in the Tower of London and a yard for burying them in when they shall die.' Cal. S.P. Dom., 1581–90, pp. 352–6.

[2] For instance, Thomas Screven wrote from London on 19th August to the Earl of Rutland at Walthamstow. ' It is advertised from Sir John Savage that Salusbury shortly after his late escape was taken within two myles of the place where he escaped.' Calendar of Rutland MSS., i, p. 204.

[3] Calendar of Wynn Papers No. 1387

[4] According to an information in the State Papers on the Babington group, ' they are the Pope's white sons for divers pieces of services which they do against this realm.' This is quoted in Foley, *Records of the Society of Jesus*, i, p. 205.

fathers had taken centuries to gather. Sir Richard Bulkeley had never seen these new priests, but they had suffered for treason, and the foreigners must have tampered with them while they were away. For in the mind of the squires the retrospective effect of the Babington Plot could be traced back to Campion, since the Government, preaching to the already converted, always maintained that the Pope's white sons were the spiritual children of those who had bound themselves to the Holy See by that especial and solemn last vow of fidelity.

There was such a great contrast between old Thomas Bulkeley wandering through his great book from service to service and this new man, the Jesuit Campion, so witty and brilliant. These are not qualities to which a slow squirearchy would respond, and it became fatally easy to believe that the new priests were up to some mischief and always behind this there was the distrust and dislike of the young men at the Court, so unlike to their fathers. If Henry Babington had lived Anthony would never have come to this trouble and they would all have been spared.[1] It is always simpler, especially for those whose thoughts follow a slow and monotonous round, to ascribe every ill to one object, and in this way the old squires used the notion of the new Jesuits and seminary priests, first to explain these conspiracies that they detested and then to excuse to themselves the last destruction of the Catholic Faith in their conscience. Many of course had neither any recollection, nor any attachment to the ancient religion and were in no need of such opiate, but it was in 1586–7 that those who had been gradually drifting away from the Church abandoned her finally. The new priests came over from France preaching in the identical words, which had formed for centuries the English religion ; but the metal which had been poured as the Queen had required was now hardened and they could not break that mould into which the newly established State Church had settled.[2]

---

[1] In contrast to Anthony Babington's outlook we can see the standpoint of his father ' inclined to papistrie,' but outwardly conforming. Sir Miles Whitworth the priest at Dethick had taken the oaths under Elizabeth, as had Anthony's uncle Francis Babington, who continued to live at Aston as chaplain to his brother-in-law Lord Darcy. Rutland MSS., i, p. 80.

[2] The right of presentation to livings and the lay possession of tithes played their part in anchoring the squires. The tithes held by the Salusburys of Bachegraig are mentioned in a marriage covenant of 1599. Cal. Hawarden Deeds, p. 42. On 12th April, 1579, a grant was made in perpetuity to Sir Christopher Hatton of ' the collegiate church, the college and precentory of Llandewy Brevy, the site of the said college, the prebend of Llanwayre Cledogre and the right of patronage,' while the grantee was to find the stipends of the incumbents. Cal. Crosswood Deeds, p. 16. This was truly a very intimate connection with the Church for ' that mere vegetable of the Court that sprang up at night and sank at his noon.' Naunton on Hatton, *Fragmenta Regalia*, p. 44.

The work of the missionary priests was to consolidate rather than to recover and to give strength to those squires, so numerous in the North and above all in Lancashire, who had always been faithful. But in Wales and the South of England it can be easily seen how large a proportion had passed permanently beyond any reach of their influence. In Worcestershire, for an instance, the Catholics were strong and the Recusant lists seem complete. Nevertheless, a very great discrepancy will be discovered between the number of Catholic families, even including those in which only the wife was a Recusant, and the total number of gentry, which the list of the Visitations provide. Yet just as it was among the remote and home-keeping squires that the Old Religion was strong, so also it was inevitably weakest among those who, like the Bulkeleys and Salusburys, still based their hopes on the Court. This was a difficulty which arose again in another way in North Wales. It was easy for Catholicism to be practised in secret in a house on the remote fields below the Cotswolds or on some lost manor in the Fen, but all the Anglicized families along the coast of North Wales lived out in the open, near the magistrates and the bishops and always close to the high road which ran through that country. Besides the new ardour which the plots had aroused in the minds of those who were now anxious to give proof of their loyalty had raised determined opponents against the missionary priests from among those whom they had grown to consider as lukewarm and unvigilant friends. Thus Sir Richard Bulkeley was aroused by the miseries of the Babington Plot to an ardour of zeal, and it is strange that it should have been reserved for this half-Catholic to secure the arrest and conviction of the first of the priests to die in Wales for the sake of religion.

It was unfortunate for Sir Richard that one of the remote effects of the Babington Plot was to stir the anger of Leicester, who had been absent for the whole of the year, commanding the forces of the States General in Holland. In this case Leicester was aware that Burghley and Walsingham had stolen a march on him, and this was the more unfortunate in that several of the conspirators had belonged to his service. But, if he had missed the good fortune of discovering a lethal conspiracy, he was able to prove his devotion to Her Majesty's service by his vehement demands for the execution of her cousin of Scotland and by harrying the friends of that Queen's now executed supporters.

Sir Richard Bulkeley had the double disfavour of a long-seated personal enmity, dating from his opposition to the extension of Leicester's Forest of Snowdon, and of the responsibility for the whole Salusbury group, who, after Leicester had greatly befriended them, had returned evil for good by compromising the name of their patron when they fell into treason.

In 1587 Leicester returned and in due course the charges against Sir Richard drifted into the Council, formulated by Lewis Meyrick and Owen Wood of Rhosmor. In the first place he was merely charged with dishonesty in assessing the musters,[1] but later they became more particular, asserting that ' the said Sir Richard should have secret conference with Salysburie one of the late traytours and that, about the tyme of the conspiracie of the said Salysburie and others his complices, Sir Richard should repair into the deserte of mountaignes of Snoden and lodge at a dayry howse, where there were meetings of divers gentlemen.' Then ' amongst other thinges Sir Richard was personallie charged not to frequent the Churche duly and in soche sorte as one well affected in religion would doe and that he had not receaved the Communyon for the space of xvj yeres.' [2] It would certainly seem that the truth of these second charges undermined Sir Richard's position, although he attempted to counter them by a spirited attack on Bishop Meyrick of Sodor and Man, who was his adversary's kinsman. He asserted that the Bishop had never attended Divine Service during his stay in the island,[3] but the prelate obtained a testimonial certificate from the Archbishop of Canterbury and Sir Richard's enemies made a third attack on him, a charge of the unlawful imprisonment of Hugh Griffiths, a freeholder of seventy years.[4] Leicester had died while this was in progress,[5] but it had become a Star Chamber case and as late as 1591 Sir Richard was confined to his house by an order of that court. Any further important official appointment was now out of the question, and the closing of this career, of which Salusbury's treason had been a part cause, is merely another instance of the unwisdom of an inexperienced dabbling in the

---

[1] Acts of the Privy Council, 1586–87, pp. 375 and 534.
[2] Acts of the Privy Council, 1588, pp. 23–4.
[3] Ibid., 1588, p. 245.
[4] Ibid., p. 310.
[5] The second charges against Sir Richard were issued on 9th April, 1588, and the counter-charge against Bishop Meyrick on 18th August. Lord Leicester died suddenly at Cornbury on 4th September, while riding to Kenilworth.

affairs of the nation. Sir Richard had no powerful friendship with Burghley or Walsingham, and he possessed no influence to rely on in case his defence of the liberties of Caernarvon and Anglesea in his contest with Leicester [1] should chance to rouse that great man. He was in that weakest of positions, a badly informed opportunist, and Leicester's slow and implacable anger [2] found him out in the end.

In his later years [3] Sir Richard was determined not to give to his political enemies any chance of attacking again, and decade by decade all his memory of his former standpoint was fading. The new solid squires of the country had no recollection of the ancient religion, and it is clear in the writings of his nephew John Wynn how easily the phrases of ' God's Word ' and the ' preaching ' now rose to the surface. Besides, with the coming of James I and after the Hampton Court Conference, it became almost fashionable to champion the Elizabethan religion, which the courtiers of the old Queen had accepted so carelessly. In addition, the greatly increased respect of the new King for the bishops had enabled them on their side to deepen their profound veneration for kingship and all this change filtered slowly down through the country. Now the old priests of Sir Richard's childhood were a memory, long since departed, and the system of advowsons had created a new race of clergy, who acted as an intermediate authority between the squire and their flock. It was true that certain families had retained the ancient religion like the Wynnes of Melai and the Mostyns of Talacre and the Conways out at Bodrhyddan, but to the average squire in the North these seemed old-fashioned and the new clergy had grown so useful and had so rapidly discovered their place.

[1] It seems probable that the reconciliation feast with Leicester was apocryphal. Sir Richard ' was bidden to dinner, but did not eat or drink nothing, save what he saw the Earl (of Leicester) taste, remembering Sir Nic. Throckmorton who was said to have received a fig at his table.' It would seem that this was a sixteenth-century legend, which *Leicester's Commonwealth* had thrown up.

[2] A letter of Dr. Elis Price to the Earl of Leicester, dated 31st March (1588 ?) concludes, 'consider my good Lord that " mora trahit periculum," ' a needless warning. Cal. Montagu of Beaulieu MSS., p. 20.

[3] When over seventy Sir Richard disinherited his eldest son, who had married a cottager's daughter, and his remaining years were troubled by lawsuits. His end was unhappy, and Thomas Cheadle, who subsequently married Lady Bulkeley, was charged with poisoning him with her aid. Fortunately, ' there had been much kindness between Chedle and William Brunoge, the foreman of the jury in Anglesey, who assured Chedle that he would be his firm friend in that business,' and this led to an acquittal. Thirteen years later the matter was closed through the influence of the Justice, Sir P. Mutton, and in this Court it was considered ' probable that Sir Richard died of poison, but not infallibly to convince.' Prytherch, a servant who used to prepare tobacco for him, ' reported that he had poisoned him.' Cal. S.P. Dom. Add., 1580–1625, pp. 640–1, and 1634–35, pp. 194 and 241, and Cal. Wynn Papers.

THE CHARACTER OF THE RELIGIOUS TRANSITION

It was the Conservatives under Henry VIII and Mary whose descendants again formed the backbone of Conservatism under the Stuarts. The Puritan line of descent was quite different, coming from the prosperous townsmen and from some of the almost commercialized squires in East Anglia. But the great body of the Royalist squires were of those whose families had slowly, almost imperceptibly, drifted out of a Church, which had ceased to be that ark of temporal and spiritual safety, which they had known for hundreds of years. They had that fixed determination not to endanger their familiar lands and the framework of their lives and from father to son there had come that heritage, which it was surely a pious duty to garner. Besides, at the time when Sir Richard's life was closing, there was great prosperity and unbroken peace and in the good order of the law and of the Established Church and in the slow movement of administration over the heavy tranquil fields, even the least perceptive of the squires could see reflected the truth that the King can do no wrong.

CHAPTER V
THE WELSH EXILES ABROAD

In the two preceding chapters the effect of English influence on Wales has been considered, that pressure which the Government was able to exert upon the North Wales squires to induce them to enter the political service of the new administration and to accept the Established English Church. The position of the Welsh squires in the hills has been touched on, and it is their outlook that is now studied at greater length. In this case it was the clergy who made vocal the standpoint of the old Welsh-speaking gentry. The Catholic exiles from St. Asaph and Bangor, men like Bishop Owen Lewis and Morys Clynog, stand forth in sharp contrast to the old conforming clergy, priests who like Thomas Bulkeley were often bound up in their fortune with the rich Anglicized squires. This fervent group, which has been referred to in passing in the earlier chapters, is here seen in detail, the movement from Oxford, the establishment at Douai and, above all, the friendship of Lewis and Allen. Yet their very existence poses the question how was it that the Catholic religion, so deep-rooted in Wales and so strong, died out in that country ? It is here to be noted that the defeat of the Catholic Church in Wales was not, as in Scotland, the result of the victory of some powerful faction, but rather a surrender forced by a long encirclement and slow starvation. The Welsh were not lacking in leaders, but what failed was the output of priests ; for the organization of the Catholic Church in a country stands or falls by the quality and number of the priests for the home mission that its people provide and a consideration of the life of Bishop Lewis, who was the most active leader of the Welsh Catholics, may help to explain how this vital element failed. The following study is an attempt to suggest an explanation of one aspect of the question, that utterly alien speech and background and temper of mind, which divided the Welsh from all the non-Celtic countries. It was not a question so much of an absence of endeavour and sympathy on the part of the English, as of the presence of a barrier, that lack of all understanding which they could not avoid. This aspect of the Welsh background is one that English writers have in general neglected, but by considering the Catholic leader, as seen against the life of his time, it may be possible to trace some of the forces which caused the old religious life of the Welsh to founder.

This divergence of temperament and outlook is first seen in the College at Douai and then disastrously in the fall of the first administration of the English College at Rome and again when the Welsh were confronted with a great Tridentine ecclesiastical court in the household of St. Charles Borromeo at Milan. In this last instance the contrast is clear between the mediæval spirit of the old Welsh and the careful bustle of Trent. All the Welshmen had come there, at one time or another, Bishop Goldwell, Morys Clynog, Owen Lewis, Griffith Roberts and the spiritual ties which bound them to their patron St. Charles only emphasize the failure of the effort to assist their own country. Owen Lewis for instance was Vicar-General in Milan, acting for the Bishop in all that business that did not need the exercise of the ordaining and consecrating episcopal power. Through this

76

office he became one moral person with his prelate, capable of performing in his name all those actions which the Bishop's will and the Canon Law of the Church would allow. Yet his success in all these complex duties only throws into clearer relief the failure of Bishop Lewis to organize a priesthood for his country.

Turning to the relations between the Welshmen and the other exiles on the political side, we find this same separation of the remote Celtic mind. Yet in the lists of the time the Welsh are always found bracketed with the Scottish and anti-Spanish party abroad. A consideration of the motives of the leaders of this group, the Pagets, is necessary here, and it would seem that patriotism towards England and Wales was the link to unite them. Apart from the rash statements of the excitement of the days when the Armada was sailing, the utterances of both these groups seem to show a belief in the fundamental soundness of outlook of their own native countries. Thus, if only their consciences were left free, both the English supporters of the Scottish party and the various Welshmen abroad would willingly return to their homes ; but the Jesuit and Spanish party, whose members had not the same memories of the old Catholic days, demanded a radical change in the structure of politics. Still, even so, these vague sympathies and antagonisms left the Welshmen far apart from all others. The tradition of the Jesuits continued unbroken and the Pagets were at the head of that line from which the Cisalpine temper in the Catholic squires derived, but the Welsh priests left no succession.

A SENSE of deep unchanging isolation has always divided the untrammelled Celtic spirit from the calmer peoples of the Eastern fields, and in no aspect of life is this more marked than in the practice of religion, where the patriarchal custom of the Celtic gatherings contrasted with the complex and settled English ways. For across the stretches of Wales, open and bare of enclosures, there was the day's work for the Welshmen in the grudging and rock-sown soil and the pastures, and in the evenings the ale at the rough-fashioned tables, with the singing of the long monotonous legends of Gwynedd and Powys, against the wind rising in gusts through the valleys. In the background there were all the complicated duties and bonds of the kinship and above them the protection of Lord Michael the Angel and the holy host of the saints. Llanvihangel, Llanvihangel how constantly is this name of St. Michael repeated across the empty and desolate spaces ? It was a life with a pattern, simple and broad, and with an almost migratory instinct in the ebb and flow of the pilgrims, while the reverend elders lamented the last carving up of the shire ground. Even yet, the ancestral and almost mythical divisions still lingered and all the men would now gather from the old lands of Gwerthrynion and Elfael to honour the saints in the calm nights, as the torches wavered.[1] It was this essential remoteness of the Celtic life which rendered assistance impossible, for Welsh priests, and these were denied her, could alone keep the allegiance of Wales. There were few subordinates, although there were leaders, and in the gradual failure of these men there is marked the doom of the Old Church in their country ; for while Owen Lewis, for instance, had contacts with the English and Romans and French, his career only served to confirm how deep was the cleavage. For, although he possessed a theologian's equipment, Dr. Lewis had the fundamental simplicity of the Cymric Middle Ages and, in his failing efforts for his country, he went down before the complex modern world. There were three stages in his endeavour to sustain the fading religion of his people, which each correspond to the scenes of his thirty years' exile, Douai and Rome and Milan, the check, the defeat and in the end the frustration.

Although he had lived among them so long, Dr. Lewis could never really understand the point of view of the English, for he had gone to Winchester late and he was already past twenty before he reached Oxford and then he had been obliged to cross over to France to avoid the Queen's new religion. There had come with him from the University some other Catholics, Dr. Allen and his personal following, as well as the stray Catholic Welshmen who made Oxford their home. They were received at Douai and welcomed, but this beginning of exile was perhaps hardly auspicious for Wales, for it is of capital importance, the divergence of intention and hope between Lewis and Allen. A plan, which they both supported, was the setting up of a college to supply their nations with priests and they were suitable leaders, since their devotion to the Holy See was unquestioned and their external peace was not broken, but it was impossible for one type of college to provide both for England and Wales. For behind Allen there was all the long-established and careful tradition of the church life of England, ordered, selective, efficient ; but the Welsh priests were as free and untethered as the sheep on their mountains.

In those early days of discussion at the table at Douai, the situation became outlined so clear, William Allen at the head, with the Canon's

---

[1] For the survival of Catholic pilgrimages during and after the Reformation period, see British Museum Add. MSS. 814, 972 and *Ode to the Four Brothers* in Llyfr Ceniarth, British Museum Add. MSS., 14,948 and 14,989, *Ode to the Choir of Heaven* and Llanstephan MSS 47, f. 809 and 164, f. 166.

stall in York Minster and the Principalship to give him authority and that manner, courteous and grave, as he put forward his detail. There was so much support that he could count on from the strong farmers and squires all over Lancashire and the whole of the North, in fact, was so Catholic. And then he would speak of what he had heard up at Rossall, with before his mind always the simple map of the Fylde, every farm and its owner known to him and their spirit of Faith. Thus it was not easy for him to consider in detail the question of training the Welsh, although that was a matter that Mr. Lewis and old Mr. Precentor Phillips were always discussing, until the latter went wandering off into one of those philosophic and would-be humorous tangles, which had earned him the name at Oxford of Morgan the Sophister. Yet Dr. Allen was most anxious that Mr. Lewis should not be discouraged.

In every other matter, except the preservation of Wales, there was no tendency to discourage Owen Lewis at all. His work was successful in the theological faculty at Douai, but his rewards were also considerable, the chair of Canon Law, which had just been created, and a Canon's stall at Cambrai, to eke out the inadequate stipend, and finally, when his legal powers were well tested, the important post of Archdeacon of Hainault. He was valued as a very sound canonist and his preference for conversing in Latin, fluent if not very elegant, was welcome to the Low Country priests. It is this external success which is admitted and grasped, but it is sometimes forgotten that all the while he was halting in the Western languages and spoke Latin better than English and looked steadily back to the Welsh. So although he had a theologian's and a canonist's knowledge, how great was the contrast with his fellow professors. They had behind them the solid and burgher inheritance of the Low Country cities, with the memory of the votive lamps in their own guild chapel and all that ease in the quiet sunlight that fell on the chests and the Memling linen. This was an inheritance that was still their possession, a life that continued beside their theology.

But Lewis was a wanderer, neither at home in England, nor France, an exile alone with the memories of his wide and solitary country, the tide making and the heavy sea upon Malldraeth, the rain beating uneven on the new and the old thatching, and the warmed ale and the song. And now he was far from Anglesea and his life was passed in the worn discussions of the schools and the long wearied law cases with the feudal lord and the Crown about the tolls and dues of the Lord Bishop, which were contested by His Catholic Majesty for his County of Hainault. Yet this could assist so little in the desire of his life the restoration of the old worship in Wales, where he could remember so well the feast day at Llangadwaladr,[1] with the heavy carts lurching across the rough tracks of the island and the gathering at the altar of all the prime men of his country and, in the high seat by the chancel, the old and white bearded ' Esgwier,' dozing at the thought of the roast that his bounty provided, while the haze drifted from the fine chimney with which he had replaced the smoke vent at the House of Bodorgan.

It was abundantly clear that nothing would be done for the Welsh in these first beginnings at Douai ; but as Dr. Lewis' external career developed, it always seemed possible that some opportunity to aid his countrymen might develop. Then by a good chance he was summoned to Rome on a law suit for the Chapter of Cambrai, and, attracting a favourable notice, was made Refendarius of the *Segnature*. Meanwhile, the plans of Dr. Allen and his advisers for the training of priests were developing, first the College at Douai, the move to Rheims and then Rome, while fortune suddenly gave the control of the new Roman house to the Welshmen. How impossible it was for the old free Celtic temperament to adapt itself to the needs of the English or the new Tridentine Italians, and it is easiest to survey the disaster from that Ash Wednesday morning of 1579 when the administration of the English College had fallen in ruins.

The situation was perfectly simple, for all the English students, thirty-three out of forty, had left in a body and the clamour of their going was only just dying away through the streets of the city. Monsignor Owen, as he was now known since his papal appointment, was left alone in the College, with the ancient and garrulous rector, Dr. Morys Clynog, some seven Welsh students, who were mainly relations, and the admirable and courteous Fathers of the Society, who had been brought in to teach the just vanished apostles. It had all been the fault of old Bishop Goldwell, that excellent and benevolent man, who, like the eternal prelates of Rome, would from time to time

---

[1] The state of Anglesea is described in Williams Add. MSS. 184d at Aberystwyth, while a contemporary account of the local customs is to be found in Sir John Wynn's *Historie of Gwydyr*.

come down to dinner. He had been mainly responsible for the appointment of Morys Clynog, which, as far as Owen could make out, would seem to have been the root of the trouble. For Dr. Maurice, as he was called, was one of the old school of clergy, irreproachable in his morals, but perfectly untouched by the new Tridentine reforms. Like Goldwell, he had belonged to the late Cardinal Pole's household, and had been Dean of Croydon, while, at the moment of Queen Mary's death, he was Bishop elect of Bangor; but it is significant that no Pope felt impelled to confirm him or to offer him some other see. Of course, he had hardly kept up his learning,[1] and he certainly was not a preacher, but he had been Warden of the old-fashioned Hospice and he was clearly the man on the spot. Owen Lewis felt bound to support him and certainly, as Allen had said,[2] he was very ' honest and friendly,' and then they shared the same background, for Owen knew his village so well, Clynnog where the hill tracks out of Lleyn past Llanaelhaiarn dip down from the moors to the Anglesea waters. But Dr. Clynog had no gifts of management and this was the immediate reason for the refusal of duty, which the English students had made. As to the Fathers of the Society, who were now in the house, they formed an element quite apart from Owen's previous knowledge; but they were religious men and were doing a wonderful work, which His Holiness often attested; while in the case of the English boys he could not understand them at all.

To Fr. Alfonso Agazzari, the senior of the three Jesuit teachers, the situation was clearer. It had been his privilege to receive, while quite young, the call to leave his good Sienese home and to enter holy religion and now he had been instructed by his superiors to assist in forming the characters of these youths who were destined to be the new apostles of England. He had already acquaintance with Fr. Parsons, that excellent English religious with his apt Scriptural quotations and his truly Catholic ideals and the careful *bonhomie* that made recreation so pleasant. As for Dr. Maurice the Rector, he was a worthy old man, but somewhat lacking in that control which a

---

[1] According to a report of Owen Lewis, ' the chaplains (of the English Hospice) although pious were old and not addicted to studies of any kind.' Vatican MS. 3494. Dr. Clynog was then among their number.

[2] Letter from Dr. Allen at Paris to Dr. Lewis, dated 12th May, 1579 and printed in Tierney-Dodd, ii, p. 366.

priest should possess and for him to shout ' abire in malam crucem ' [1] at the students was hardly a dignified ending for this regrettable squabble. With regard to the wish of the students to have one of ours as their ruler, that was of no value at all, for Fr. Agazzari had no desire save that the Glory of God should increase under the guidance of the Holy Father, who was the custodian of the good of the Church. At last, after all these days of dispute, he could prepare the points of his meditation more carefully, undisturbed by the high noise of the wrangling and good would thus come out of evil.

Upstairs on the ' piano nobile ' the Rector was also enjoying a moment of freedom, while he could view with more equanimity these disturbing events, as the wine from his own vineyard on the Via Aurelia sank down in his glasses. He was still as ' honest ' as ever, but he had grown increasingly ' friendly ' with age. Beside him was his nephew, young Morgan, and the Monsignor's nephew, Hugh Griffith, who had leaped in the College Hall, shouting, ' Who now but a Welshman,' a gallant boy, but tempestuous, and then there was Lewis Hughes, the Monsignor's cousin, with his sharp North Welsh wit, and Meredith, that man, strong and determined, who had raised his knife at the English and was making such a fine attempt to begin to learn Latin. The English had accused the Rector of favouring the Welsh and of bringing in ignorant students, but surely he had only done what a nobly descended Christian should do ? It was an honour that his elder brother, the head of his line, should send out his son to his care to learn to offer the Sacrifice and to call down on the fields of his people the blessings of the saints of his race. Nothing could be more clear than his obvious duty to share with his kinsmen the last crust of the Hobnails, as the English were so justly called, and now the talk could run freely at last on the stock of Collwyn ap Tangno and the saints of the high lords of Gwynedd.

Dr. Owen Lewis often made mistakes about people and he had supported the adventurer Stukeley, for instance, yet there were moments when no one could fail to see the coming disaster. That very afternoon the Pope, returning from Santa Sabina, the first

---

[1] According to the account sent by Mr. Haddock at Rome to Dr. Parsons, dated 9th March, 1579. The version given by the spy Anthony Munday in *Englishe Romayne Life*, Harl. Misc. vii, although quite unreliable, is very diverting. ' And many nightes he (the Rector) must have the Welshmen in his chamber, where they must be merry at good cheer : wee glad to sit in our studies and have an ill supper.'

Station at the opening of Lent, had been pressed to make a decision. There had been mismanagement and the chance for Wales had vanished and Owen Lewis rode away from Rome. Although his departure was neither immediate nor final, for he did not leave for Milan until June, 1580, this was the moment at which his active concern with the government of the English College and with the supply of priests ceased. He was still staying at the College when, through no efforts of the Society, Fr. Agazzari was appointed to take Dr. Maurice's place [1] and to rule the now returned English, and he lived in Rome again [2] after the death of St. Charles Borromeo and during his tenure of the Calabrian see of Cassano. But in the last years of Dr. Lewis' life, from his appointment to the Bishopric in 1588 until his death at Rome at the age of sixty-two, in 1594, he had no real share in the furthering of religion in Wales, since his previous efforts had failed and the outbreak of war between England and Spain made him still farther remote from his country. Yet, if there was no real contact between the English and Welsh, the direct needs of the Catholics in Wales also failed to impress that careful and sagacious temper of mind with which the decisions of Trent had marked the new rulers. For Owen Lewis, prosecuting his upward career, became Vicar-General to St. Charles Borromeo at Milan and one of his family, and in this phase of his life it is clear how his hopes for Wales were frustrated, caught and swept aside by the Europe-wide movement of that Cardinal's affairs, as he faltered, a mediæval survival, beside the strength and the pressure of the great Tridentine machine.

At Douai there had been a small college with the talk at the table dominated by Morgan the Sophister under the pregnant silence of Allen, with his grave and courteous smile, while in the hurly-burly at Rome there were just a few English and Welshmen and Jesuit Fathers, but at Milan there was that vast princely household, which the Reforms of Trent had not decreased, but had chastened, with all the business of State. The picture which Giovanni Pietro Giussano, who was one of the Cardinal's chaplains, has drawn us can provide an idea of that seething ecclesiastical tide upon which Dr. Owen

[1] As an instance of purely external support for the Jesuit appointment Dr. Allen had written that ' it was so honest a thing for the students to have the fathers for their governors.' Knox, *Records*, ii, p. 78.
[2] According to a letter written by Thomas Morgan to the Queen of Scots on 5th January, 1586, ' Dr. Lewes is advanced to a place of honour in Rome by his holiness' favour borne to the said Lewes.' Cal. S.P. Scottish, 1584-5. p. 529.

Lewis was carried. For a household of over a hundred surrounded the Cardinal, all grouped in a well-balanced hierarchy under the Præpositus, Antionio Seneca. It was so easy amid such movement to be lost in that crowd, with the Vicar and the twelve Chamberlains under him, all priests and doctors, and the Economus and below him the Almoners and the Stewards and the Prefects of the Guest Chambers with their subordinate staffs, in addition to the continual ebb and flow of the three hundred guests in the month.[1] And then there was the endless arrival of messengers from the princes, the result of the awe, and almost the fear, in which the Lord Cardinal was held, as the holy man of his century, as the great Thaumaturgus, who could pierce on its under side that curious astrological fear, which was the weakest point in the system of Catherine de Medici and her perverted, Italianate sons. Even the Elector Augustus of Saxony, of the straitest sect of the Lutherans, sought his counsel and princes, like Emmanuel Philibert, wooed him with relics, an unending stream of petition, which makes it clear that the claim of the Welsh to assistance could not fail to be swept under the weight of these burdens. While in the more immediate circle of the Cardinal there was the Auditor-General to be faced, Monsignor Bernardine Morra, ' a prelate of great prudence and care,' and the young and serious Oblates and that experienced Father of the Society, Achille Gagliardi. Beyond these, the Monitors of His Eminence, were the ' Discreets ' of the Confraternity, and by contrast up in the Mesolcina, that legacy from an earlier age the sorcerer Quattrini, whilst, as a constant factor, the Civil Power strained into opposition, with the Governor Don Carlos of Aragon on his dais, below the choir of the Duomo, to represent the uneasy rights of Spain. And then at this hub of the new revival, where the Catholic travellers came streaming from the North, there was the entry of the soldiers of the train of the Most Illustrious Andreas Bathori and all the Embassy of the ' Respublica Poloniæ,' the kettledrums upon the eastern road.[2] Calm in the maelstrom, unaffected at its still, unmoving centre, was the figure of the Cardinal, St. Charles.

His is a character strange and elusive and, at the centre of a company whose motives we can understand so clearly, suddenly disin-

---

[1] Giussano, *Vita di San Carlo*, Book viii, c. 26.
[2] Giussano, *op. cit.*, viii, c. 26. Andreas Bathori with Pan Alexander Nevski stayed in the Cardinal's palace with fifty of their retinue.

terested and remote. It is a most interesting problem to attempt to reconstruct the attitude of St. Charles towards the Welsh. His influence in politics greatly exceeded his interest, which was dominated by that benevolence, impersonal and quite universal, which was, as it were, the distillation of his zeal for the service of God. It was an unforgettable impression, the slightly bent form of the Cardinal, the almost Cyrano nose, the sunk cheeks carefully shaven, the eyes, blue under the half-closed eyelids, as His Eminence would enter quietly with that hesitant, dragging step that erysipelas had brought him. Nor did this constraint decrease as he spoke, with his low voice scarcely audible,[1] the hands cold even in summer from the insufficient circulation,[2] with in his manner that studied avoidance of gesture and absence of laughter, and accompanying every movement that careful and so impersonal smile, almost continuous. Before his mind there was always the subjects of the spiritual reading and of those set retreats he valued so greatly, and over all his days was a sameness, the bare, solitary meals in the centre of this magnificent household, the thin bread soup, the dish of lupines and then at night the folding bedstead and the hair shirt, carefully mended. It is difficult to see what contact the spirit of the mediæval Welsh in Dr. Lewis could make with this outlook, besides his reports as Vicar-General; for the material background of the Cardinal's life had this same definiteness and precision, the formal Borromean garden at Isola Bella he had abandoned with the careful range of statues in the ilex and the stone. Yet what could be in greater contrast to the noisy ale-warmed farmers and their loud, uncertain singing and the waters under Malldraeth and the freedom of the Welsh.

Owen Lewis' practical hopes were quite abandoned; yet he had a deep affection for the Cardinal who in his turn had a devotion for the Welsh and Bishop Goldwell had been his Vicar-General, and he had kept, as his confessor for fifteen years, the Canon Theologian, Griffith Roberts, the author of Drych Cristionogawl. But, in his profoundly Christo-centric life, it was not any accidental friendship which drew the Cardinal's attention to these men, for he honoured them as representing the suffering members of Christ's mystical body. In the calm

---

[1] Depositions of Fr. Achille Gagliardi, S.J., at the Process of Canonization from which the other physical detail is largely drawn.   Giussano, op. cit., vii, cc. 17–8.
[2] Evidence of Fr. Panigarola at the Process.

of his withdrawn existence, in the six hours, which he would spend in preparing for his Mass, he would think of how the Holy Sacrifice was reviled and of all the altars cast down and it was as Confessors, as those who had endeavoured to keep unsullied the seamless garment of Christ, that he honoured the Welsh. This was a line of reasoning which Canon Roberts and Dr. Lewis could follow, but it did not assist them; for it had no contact with practical matters. To the Cardinal it was clear that the Divine Will had called him to the See of Milan and the world was in the Holy Father's care, but he would assist them with his prayers.

For four years Dr. Lewis served the Cardinal, a time of strong and mutual personal devotion and yet, in human terms, so ineffective; and then on 3rd November, 1584, there came the breaking of this partnership, a scene typical in its contrast between the strong new age and the old Wales sinking. A great horde surrounded the dying Cardinal, lying ill of a tertian fever, which incapacitated him from mental prayer, on a pallet bed and ashes in one of the great public halls of the palace, called from the paintings of Gethsemane and the Passion, the audience chamber of the Cross. Kneeling in the privileged place beside the pillow were Count Jacob Hannibal d'Altaemps and Renato Borromeo, the courtier kinsmen, stiff and worldly, from the Escorial, accustomed to the ' decor ' of princely deaths, and behind them the Major Duomo and the household and the Archpriest and the Canons, and over all the sound of the high reading of the Passion and the noise of lamentation and outside the crowds of Milan surging against the halberds of the guard. It was a great room, crowded and draughty, with the fires on the hearth-stones roaring and lighting up the black liveries of the Cardinal's servants and the frescoed ceiling and the high, bare white walls, which in the plague of '76 had been stripped of their hangings. Through the evening Owen Lewis knelt supporting the Cardinal, while the cold wind from the glaciers came down, when the sun had set, over the city and the draughts played over the flooring, and all the time, except for the lull as the Duke of Terranova came with his Switzers, there was the noise of the discreet surging of priests, and behind them the packed humanity and the great fires and the heat; but the failing eyes of the Cardinal saw only the Crucifix. The Welsh, having failed to establish a centre for the training of priests, had now lost their protector. About these exiles

S. CAROLVS BOROMÆVS. CARD. ARCHIEP. MEDIOLAN.
natus 2. Octob. obijt 4. Nouemb. 1584. canon. 1. Nou. 1610.
Quasi stella matutina in medio nebulæ: et quasi luna plena in diebus suis lucet: et quasi sol refulgens, sic ille effulsit in templo Dei. Ecclesiastici 50.

ST. CHARLES BORROMEO
From an engraving in the British Museum.

the Tridentine movement of renewal still gathered in strength and the tide of the Catholic Religion slowly returned over the reaches lying abandoned, but not to Welsh Wales.

It was a mark of the inextricably mingled policies of the late sixteenth century that the division between lay and clerical life had become so vague and confused. For, on the one hand, nearly all ecclesiastics, who were free from the vows of religion, felt the necessity for taking their share in the social life of the time, and, on the other, even the most licentious of swordsmen could not embark on expeditions for plunder until they had labelled themselves as defenders of the New Learning or Rome. This theocratic suggestion, the close dependence on spiritual forces, in which all were deeply concerned, colours in every detail the whole life of the period and, where the strength of the old religion had fallen, the growth of the royal Divine Right was now seeded. For this reason the Welsh Catholic exiles abroad could not fail to suffer close contact with politics and, after being drawn into the stream, to be swept away on one or other of the currents, which the religious changes had loosed. In this connection the most curious fact is the wholehearted support, which the Welsh exiles, almost without exception, came in time to provide for the so-called Scottish and anti-Spanish party in Europe. Yet, after all, when the excited fever before the Armada's sailing had died down, a mental disturbance in which all the exiles were in some measure concerned, one question rose dominant and clear, the attitude to be taken up towards the home country. There were three sections, the Jesuits and their lay supporters, then the laymen, like the Pagets, and lastly the Welsh, and it was this question that ranged the Welsh priests with those very well-bred, but extremely discontented English gentlemen, with whom their interests were else so unavoidably few.

But before considering these diverging policies a reference should be made to that charge of continued and double treachery under which the Pagets have fallen,[1] for a study of the sincerity of their action is essential to an understanding of the line that the Welsh exiles took up. One point makes it most difficult to accept the accusation of treachery, the fact that at any moment Charles Paget and his brother could have returned to their country if they had been pre-

---

[1] The article on Charles Paget in the D.N.B., vol. xliii, p. 48, provides a succinct statement of this charge.

pared to accept the newly Established Religion; but on this point they were always most firm. Every offer that they made to the Queen from their French exile contained the proviso, ' saving the freedom of their conscience,'[1] and this alone would tend to prove their sincerity. Except in the fever of the Armada excitement, the brothers would always seem to have maintained the same attitude, that readiness to assist the Queen with a little secret service work, which to the taste of the time would seem laudable, combined with that urgent desire to return, if only in conscience it was possible, to the country life of the shires. And in the Welshmen this desire found an echo; for, behind all the disillusion and tiredness that the twenty years exile had brought, there was their own Welsh patriotism resurgent,[2] that wish that they only felt the more keenly for the fields of their home, as the serious chance of return faded further and further.

It was so different for Father Parsons, for instance, with those bitter memories, which converts sometimes possess, for he had before him the thought of those last sullen meals at Balliol, when the plans for his dismissal were ready, nor were his earlier experiences pleasant, Stogursey with its harsh poor school and the crowded home at Stowey. Besides, it was hardly much comfort with his later ideas to remember the aid he had been given by Magister Hayward, that benevolent and time-serving priest. How clear it was, as he thought of the Church established by law, that a new heaven and a new earth would be required before the Catholic religion could settle again in a country where every manor and parish must be purged of the dross of its sacrilege. But it was here that a contrast was found again between the new Jesuit priests and the Welshmen, for the latter came of an older race, who could remember the good times of peace. Thus they knew the contentment of the Catholic life of old Gwynedd and the homely devotions at shrines, and they remembered the sound of the Sanctus bell ringing as the light would filter through the high and narrow window spaces of the little churches and the wax falling from the slanting candle, and those calm, vague, haphazard hours of Mass.

[1] Thus Charles Paget wrote to the Queen from Paris on 5th April, 1582, ' By most humble petition I desire your gracious favour and liberty of conscience in religion which will procure my return . . . to spend my life at your command.' Cal. S.P. Dom. Add., 1580–1625, p. 77.
[2] As an instance of the strength of this sentiment, there is the statement attributed to Dr. Lewis, who is asserted to have said to the Scottish Bishop of Ross, ' My lord, let us stick together, for we are the old and true inhabiters of the isle of Brittany. These others be but usurpers and mere possessors.' S.P. Dom., cclii, 10, and Knox, *Records*, ii, p. 82.

THE WELSH EXILES ABROAD

In the years of their exile, in Milan, Rome or Flanders, the Welsh priests could recall so well these details, which the new English clergy missed. They could see it with the light of yesterday most clearly, the rain drifting upon Caernarvon and the boy stumbling with a lanthorn, as the priest rode slowly up the sheep track with the Blessed Oil and the Holy Sacrament for some shepherd people who lay dying in a cabin in the hills. And then there came the thought of the return journey down again into the valley under the familiar stars of that cold and northern heaven, while the tracks yielded water-soaked. This was the vision of the arduous and calm years of their priesthood. Yet Robert Parsons was too young to have knowledge of the Catholic life of his country, but only the recollection of how his masters had treated him at Stogursey and at Taunton, when he was still a swarthy boy, and of that evening at Balliol, the Fellows' Meeting and the oak door carefully closing, as they debated on his end. When we consider this contrast, it can seem hardly surprising that there arose this conflict among the exiles or that the Welshmen should have so much desired their country, if only their consciences were left free.

Yet in spite of their remoteness from affairs, the Welsh priests were inevitably drawn into the struggle of the long forty year, ' Question of England,' which was the form in which the difficulties of the islands of Britain appeared as they took shape before the minds of the Pontiffs. But this first Tridentine period in Europe was an age when every detail of international life was docketed and reduced to a system and in consequence the Welsh were included with the English squires in the same political orbit. It is therefore worth noting the contrast between these men of the world and the Welsh clerics, as well as the rather casual encounter which had brought them together. The gulf, and it was certainly wide, was bridged by Mr. Thomas Morgan, a Catholic Welshman from Monmouthshire apparently of the Machen family, who lived in the Faubourg St. Michel as the busiest of the Parisian agents of the imprisoned Queen of the Scots. As a Welshman from the southern extreme of the Marches, who had been still a boy at the time of the changes, he had little real contact with the elderly priests from St. Asaph and Bangor, only just sufficient to enable him to act as a link with the cold and stiff English. The actual introductions also would seem to have been effected, not very happily, by this same voluble Morgan ; for Charles Arundell and the Pagets, gentlemen of a somewhat conscious good breeding,[1] whose minds were happily quite unaffected by any literary tastes, which might have led them into socially questionable circles, had nothing to induce them to venture beyond the society of their equals in rank. As to Mr. Morgan they appraised him at an accurate value, for the Pagets could remember their journeys to Tutbury, to the great hunting parties that my Lord of Shrewsbury had given and in those days Mr. Morgan had the place of a servant. Besides these Welshmen were priests, and this made it necessary for Mr. Morgan to explain, after that dissertation on the status of his own family which was always so galling, that, although his clerical friends were of a sufficient lineage, they did not enjoy his advantages in the land of their birth. Then again their dreams of a Wales restored once more to the Faith made them remote, for it was not because of any desire to re-establish a theocracy in hither Snowdon that the Pagets found themselves abroad. Yet, in spite of this far differing approach, it was this one idea of their exile which bound them together, since they both wished to return and they believed in their country ; but here again their attitude towards England and Wales were in contrast.

In the case of the Welshmen, whom a spiritual cause had driven away from their homes, it was a hunger for the soul of the people, a desire that the flame of the ancient Faith of the Cymri would re-kindle the sanctuary lights of those altars which now only survived in the hearts of the people. In the most difficult hours of the long trek of their exile they had always this hope to sustain them and just as Cardinal Allen, even to the hour of his death-bed, believed that the time of deliverance was already at hand, so also did the Welshmen scattered at Paris and Cambrai and Milan imagine that their country would be restored to the Universal Church, its inheritance, which through God's mercy would vanquish the worldliness of their rulers. Surely it seemed to them, as in their exile they attempted to follow in the footsteps of Christ, the memory of the myriad saints of their nation, now before the Throne of All Grace, would serve to keep their countrymen loyal and so for the highest, most spiritual reasons they were opposed to any invasion. The Pagets also were opposed to

---

[1] An independent witness to the decorum of their manner is contained in a letter written in April, 1582, to Lord Northumberland by his son in Paris. 'Mr. Paget,' Lord Percy wrote, ' has always carried himself dutifully (his private opinion in religion I speak not of) or I would not entertain his company.' Cal. S.P. Dom. Add., 1580–1625, p. 55.

a foreign invasion, partly from considerations of practical politics and partly because of a lingering patriotism which could never desert them, but the motives which led the two parties to such a conclusion could hardly have been more divergent.

In the case of the Pagets it was a very material cause which had led to their exile, so that reasons equally terrene were at work to draw them back home. Indiscretion in their communications with the Scottish Queen's agents had been the cause of their flight, a too great reliance on the secrecy of that great household at Petworth as they discussed affairs of State in the evenings with the new Earl of Northumberland. Lord Paget and his brother were men of the world and by religion Catholics, maintaining practices of devotion with that moderation which fashion prescribed, while it seemed such a little matter that separated them from their country and they were careful of their company in the midst of the rabble. With Mr. Fitzherbert and Mr. Gifford they were sufficiently friendly, for they were gentlemen of position and in a remote degree neighbours. Yet with the commonplace exiles and the young ' Spanish ' priests, with their book learning and their jargon from Oxford, they would have nothing to do ; for it was clear to them that the core of England was sound as the oaks under Cannock. It was this that always brought their thoughts back again, the remembrance of their father's wealth and the splendours of Beaudesert, and as they sat in their hot lodgings, above the continual noise that the stones sent up in Paris, they remembered the open and wide space of their heritage. Yet few shared fully their desire-laden knowledge of England and to them Beaudesert was the great work of their father, the Chancellor, as it stood in the high hollow of those quick tumbled ridges of moor, which seem thrusting back under the trees of the forest. Above rose the Cannock Chase with that constant wind on the moorland, which at Gentleshaw would bend the high leaves of the beeches, but it would never come to disturb the ' arras ' in Paris. And then, from the great entrance, how the rich lands fell southward, the hay-fields and then the corn falling below them, the sun pricking the western spires of Lichfield and, in the foreground, the trees that screened Farewell.

It was a far cry from Beaudesert to the mountains of Gwynedd ; but the bond was sufficiently strong to keep the Welsh priests and the English laymen in sympathy ; while as for the opposing party, the

Spanish faction, which the Jesuits supported, their outlook was radically different. There was an aspect perhaps in which they were more close to reality and it was not that they did not possess an ardent desire for their country, but it was for an England transformed. They had perhaps a clearer realization of the magnitude of their task, and they were for most part guided by men who had schooled themselves to indifference to the accidents of their life, an indifference which did not prevent them from adopting a very vigorous manner when they considered that their principles were at stake. To Robert Parsons, for instance, all that was understood by a home was contained in the *Gesu* at Rome with its community, and the long corridors and the Fathers pacing and waiting for the bell for the devotions held in common, and all the carefully controlled energy of that so recollected life. Outside in the depths of the vicolo, below the new pattern iron guards of the windows, the wine carts would pass from the ' Castelli,' bumping up through the Botteghe Oscure from Santa Caterina ai Funari, past the taxing masters of the Gaetani, with the street sounds from the Larga Argentina floating strident in their rear. But the Fathers were detached from any too close earthly contacts,[1] kneeling motionless, stiff in their black cassocks, while from beneath them rose confusion and the noises of the rough wheels grating on the cobbles and the Bacchic Roman curses and the whips.

The tradition of the Jesuits has continued unbroken and the Pagets were also at the head of a great line, that Cisalpine temper in the Catholic squires ; but in political action the Welsh priests have left no succession,[2] for they had the inheritance of the Catholic Ages, but in Wales they left no heirs.

---

[1] *Cf.* Letter from Charles Paget to Sir Henry Cobham, dated at Paris, 23rd October, 1582, ' I would go to Rouen as it will agree better with me and there I may drink English beer.' Cal. S.P. Dom. Add., 1580–1625, p. 78.

[2] The register of the English College at Valladolid throws light on the proportion of Welsh to English students in that house at the close of the century. Out of a total of 219 men entering the house between 1589 and 1603 there were eleven natives of Wales, nearly all from the dioceses of St. Asaph and Bangor. Only one, Humphrey Turberville, came from Glamorgan. One entry is somewhat pathetic. ' Joannes Benettus . . . excepit catholicum Regem Philipum Lingua Walica quando inuisit hoc collegium.' Registers of Valladolid, C.R.S., vol. xxx pp. 10–78.

THE EUROPEAN SCENE

IN the earlier chapters the failure of the pacific Spanish influence, consequent upon the change of policy at Elizabeth's accession, has been considered a failure which the break with Catholicism rendered inevitable. The first portion of the succeeding studies, dealing with the reactions set up in Wales by these changes, has also concerned a situation in which aggressive political action by the foreign Powers had little part; while the chapter on Archbishop Creagh shows those early contacts abroad, not political but religious, which the attempt to maintain the Old Religion set up. The Papacy is therefore the only power outside England whose actions have so far been considered. At this point the use of the terms 'political' and 'religious' with regard to purposes and methods of action should be made perfectly clear. By political action is understood every method of policy which has for its object the material welfare of the State; by religious action any course which is dictated by a desire for spiritual freedom or supremacy. The further question as to the occasions on which political results flowed from specific forms of religious action must be considered separately in each different instance, bearing in mind the special position in the thought of sixteenth-century Europe which the Papacy held. In the later chapters the hesitant Spanish policy with regard to England and Ireland is examined in detail with especial reference to the Celtic movements which the Elizabethan system provoked; but France, the remaining great Western Power, succeeded in keeping politically altogether aloof. In the chapter which follows, on the Spanish Project in Scotland, the Northern Rising of 1569, and the subsequent flight of the rebels, first into Scotland and then to the Spanish Low Countries, are seen to arouse for the first time the hostility of King Philip, an enmity, political and aggressive and carrying with it (as the previous diplomatic passes had not carried) the seeds of war. The system of piracy and in particular Hawkins' attack on San Juan de Ulloa had brought in the element of anti-English feeling in Spain and until the end of the reign the Anglo-Spanish complications must be considered overshadowing each movement. So far these studies have been concerned chiefly with the Tudor dominions and Rome; but as the political situation between Elizabeth and Philip II becomes so complex and tense, it is necessary to refer briefly to France and to offer some explanation as to why her political rulers remained so unconcerned by those Celtic movements so close to her shores.

It will appear later how completely the Spaniards failed to grasp even the most necessary data about Irish affairs. The gulf between the civilizations was too wide to be bridged. This same difficulty would have occurred had there been any French intervention; but the political situation made this impossible. Throughout the period the hostility and fear of Spain kept England and France in a state of shifting alliance, which grew hot and lukewarm and cold, but never even in moments of strain could be said to veer towards war. This proved sufficient to quell any tendency to embark on an Irish adventure. Again England and Spain both possessed in their outlying territories, in Ireland and the Low Countries respectively, large groups differing in their language and customs from their sovereigns and governors and anxious, for various motives, to receive foreign aid. In both these distant provinces the Catholic Church was the storm centre, acting by repulsion upon the leaders in the Netherlands and by attraction upon the Irish chiefs. Both

93

THE CELTIC PEOPLES & RENAISSANCE EUROPE

Elizabeth and Philip II gave aid, in the period we are about to consider, to the rebels attacking their rivals. The aid varied greatly both in duration and in degree ; but in a measure it cancelled out when the policies were considered in London and Madrid. France, however, although the desire might be strong, could never risk for a moment this by-play in Ireland. Her own political problem, that state within the state which the Huguenots under Coligny were forming, would never allow her this freedom. If England should tamper seriously with the anti-Catholic faction in France, these intrigues and the possible support of an army would constitute a threat to the Valois, which none of the ru'ers in Paris were ever prepared to incur. This will serve to explain why France always inclined to welcome the calm Catholic exiles ; for those who were the most likely to be involved in political action avoided, when possible, a prolonged stay in a country whose rulers were always friendly to the established order in England.

The position of the supporters of Guise, conservative, Catholic, somewhat pro-Spanish, indicates the different policy which might have been expected had they been victorious. It was in the territory controlled by the Guises and their cousins the Dukes of Lorraine that the most militant of the English Catholic organizations in France were located. Even so, the peculiar links which bound Ireland to Spain were not here repeated. The age-long policy of support for Scotland, intensified by the fact that the Queen Mother of Scotland was from Lorraine, had cast their minds upon reasoned schemes of opposition. Even had the Guises managed to seize control of the royal power in France, it seems certain that their part in an attack on England would concentrate upon some Scottish plan.

Another factor militated against an Irish contact. To the Celtic chiefs with their lofty notions of sovereignty there was nothing derogatory in accepting the friendship of the high King of Spain. They knew vaguely of the great monarchies which were now held under his rule and he was the son of the Emperor, the temporal head of the Universe. With such claims the King of France could not compete, and ' Duc Guiber,' as they called Guise, was but a vassal. In addition there was a Spanish quality, military and somewhat primitive, which made the beginnings of relations easier between the exiled Irish lords and those soldiers whose fathers had found the Americas and made, under Cortes and Pizarro, that hard riding conquest. The Irish ecclesiastics, who were the messengers of their chiefs, found matters less easy in Paris, where Government circles had a somewhat cynical regard for the Church, than in the strict Madrid court with the King austerely paying to even the most unwelcome prelate the honours of his rank. Political considerations apart, there was little chance of sympathy for the Irish in the somewhat morbid and Italianate Valois circles or, even had it been Catholic, at the sophisticated court of Navarre.

This sophistication was a mark of the polite France of the period. In Spain the former political and military conceptions lingered, and it was just because the Spanish ideals were anchored in the old united Christendom that the Irish might there obtain support. France, as far as mere modernity was concerned, was in the vanguard of the social life and the political theory of Europe. It is an arguable proposition that the dominating factor in the Hispano-Celtic movement was this difference in outlook, so that, while in these matters France and the English Government were together, the thought of Spain was fifty years behind. The contrast in social organization made it impossible for the exiles from Ireland to find that place in French life which they could acquire under the wider and freer system of the great Spanish families. A *bourgeois* prosperity, the presence of the *noblesse de la robe*, the careful gradations of social order, a somewhat thrifty outlook on the future, had made of the social life of France a pyramid, compact and national and self-contained.

THE EUROPEAN SCENE

There was little curiosity in France as to affairs in foreign countries, and especially among those Celtic races, so remote from the Renaissance traditions which, since the days of Francis I, were bound up closely with the influential and cultured life of the nation. More than ever in these days of Civil War was the French life turning inward ; each Power demarked and nicely ordered. The building of the *chateaux* of this period, the new laying out of gardens, the organization of estates had done something to render the French *noblesse* of the time perceptive, cultivated, yet immobile. The Colonial tradition, so strong in Spain, which would lead the Spanish soldiers to seek adventure, had not yet touched them. In ecclesiastical circles the Irish prelates could likewise find no home. Archbishop Beaton, the Scots Queen's Ambassador, himself a royal official as Treasurer of the Queen's Endowments in Touraine and Prior *in commendam* in Poitou, could find a place, but no one who could fit less well into the system. The already slightly Gallican tendencies of the Episcopate cast a veil upon their sympathies with wandering bishops. To such as Richard Creagh the great French bishops with their elaborate and well-ordered households, the graded ecclesiastics, the careful training of *enfants d'honneur* would seem unattainably remote. The Tridentine households in Italy could mitigate this difference, but not the national system of the French.

The symbol of this distinction was that Court of France over which Catherine de Medici so long presided. It was re-fashioned, maintained and guided by her influence and her spirit was impressed upon it deeply, whether in the mere detail of organization, as in the three hundred ladies whom she kept to serve her, or the operations which her taste had fashioned, the buildings and the careful rock-built gardens and the water fountains, or in the intentions which led her policies throughout her life. The range of her clear and sceptical intelligence, intuitive and rapid, the antipathy which she felt from childhood for the cumbersome processes of the official Spanish mind, the pleasure in an intricate deft balance had left their mark upon her servants. Few ministers have had a more definite desire to keep clear of petty foreign complication than have her chosen statesmen the *politiques*. Her constant progresses and that pre-occupation with the political perils from the right and left, from which her sons throughout her long rule (from 1560–1589) were never free, kept her busied with affairs of the interior. With these characteristics and the necessity of friendship with Elizabeth it is not surprising that her Court was closed to any suggestions of an Irish venture.

The knight errant blood of Maximilian, the Crusading memories of Castilian kings had brought into the traditions of the Spanish Crown an element almost Quixotic and in so far helpful to the Celtic claims. The inheritance of Catherine de Medici, that hereditary interest in commerce, the careful management of her own great dowry, the element of prudence in her expenses, for instance, the exact and competent knowledge of her store of pearls, her pleasure in the theatre, her delight in comedies and tragi-comedies, that reasonable literary understanding, all combined to make her far remote from such adventure. The work of Brantôme, when he deals with those details in regard to which he can be considered accurate, in itself explains this fully. This is perhaps sufficient to indicate why, although the Irish had support in Rome and Spain, there was never any question of serious sympathy or assistance for the Celtic movements out of France.

CHAPTER VI

THE SPANISH PROJECT IN SCOTLAND

The various plans to aid the Scots which are here considered have a direct bearing on Elizabethan history, as the English rebels of the Northern Rising, who had just escaped northwards across the Border, were the pivot upon which the project turned. Scotland had been up to this time within the French political orbit and only in temporary alliance with England when the anti-French party held power. The Queen's party was French, and even more dependent on France since the Queen's deposition, for now that she was a prisoner in England the only funds they could rely on were her revenues as a Queen Dowager. Ever since the days of her own French upbringing and her first marriage to Francis II, all Queen Mary's personal intimates had ties with that country. The machinery of diplomatic representation, maintained till her death in 1587, is here examined and the bases on which it reposed, her own revenues from Touraine and the ecclesiastical benefices which her envoys, who were nearly all prelates, could acquire when abroad. The Scottish party among the English Catholics abroad was one of the results of the work of her foreign ambassadors.

The Highland Catholics who had not received friendship from Mary were therefore perfectly ready to look towards Spain, a tendency which was more marked after the Easter of 1570 when the English leaders, Lord Westmoreland and Lady Northumberland, had found their way to the North. A discussion of the designs of the northern leaders, Huntly and Atholl, and also the more complicated aims of Argyll shows that independence of the Southrons, practical but not theoretical, was the goal that they aimed at. That no invasion of Spaniards ever took place was mainly due to Secretary Maitland of Lethington. This man who was Atholl's intimate and had been Queen Mary's minister was determined on peace. The great central party in Scotland, the Hamiltons, compromised in the murder of the Regent Moray, was anxious for safety from his Calvinist friends. By a system of compromise Huntly was persuaded to forego the hope of Spain's intervention, the English exiles were shipped to the Netherlands and the Spanish project collapsed. Lethington had prevented a blazing torch being cast on the inflammable Highlands.

THE affairs of a country so remote from the movement of European political thought, as was sixteenth-century Scotland, could not have been regarded with any close care by the great Powers in their policy. Just as the Scandinavian Kingdoms only impinged upon the general trend throughout Europe by their influence on the rule of the Empire, so also Scotland was regarded as within the orbit of France. This ancestral alliance had diverted to Paris almost the whole of the meagre stream of the Scotsmen who kept contact with the affairs of the Continent and the great Powers were content to remember that Scotland swung in the wide path of France as the least of her satellites. The only serious rival was England and the conflicts between that country and Scotland were regarded as questions of purely domestic and insular policy, which left the Continent unconcerned. Even when the religious struggles developed, the Calvinist interest was provided for by English support and the Catholic by that French policy which was inspired by the House of Lorraine.

Nevertheless, that attraction which Spain, as the champion of ordered Catholicism, exercised upon the mind of the Celts had also,a repercussion in Scotland. For compared to Spain the French Court, even when the Guise faction held power, represented the political side of the Church, while King Philip stood in open defence of the old Catholic order. Thus, while the political friends of Queen Mary never ceased to look towards France, those Catholic elements, who for one reason or another had kept aloof from her rule, saw the only fulfilment of their hopes in the Spaniards. This will account for the comparatively slight interest in Spain, while the ' French ' Queen was still on the throne, and it was only when she was imprisoned, and the French Court for the time being compromised by the desire for alliance with England, that any serious plan was put forward for the granting of military aid. The circumstances of the moment made it quite out of the question for the French to give any definite support to the idea of the Northern Revolt, so that when the rising had failed and the Catholic fugitives had fled to Scotland for safety, it was clear that it was only from Spain that even a purely private expedition could come forth to their help. The distance to the coasts of Spain made assistance from that quarter difficult, so that the only plan, which could have a chance of success, was relief from the Low Countries, which were still loyal to that Crown. Yet even so it was not so much a hope of real succour as the last plan of the Catholic leaders to avert the effects of the victory, which the Lords of the Congregation had gained.

The hopes set upon Spain came therefore from the remote Catholic lords, who had for the most part never been treated with friendship and sometimes even with enmity by Queen Mary. Moreover, it was the combination of the English political exiles with their Catholic hosts in the Highlands that brought this movement about. It was in fact an abortive attempt of the great Highland families to gain something of a counterpoise both to the English alliance of the Protestant lords and to those ancient bonds which united the Queen's close friends to France. The ultimate aim was, of course, the achievement of a greater measure of their own political power, as well as the continued practice of their age-long religion. There is perhaps something in the wide spaces and in the less complex thought of clan rulers which drew the O'Neills and the Gordons, and at moments even the Campbells, to the idea of alliance with Spain. For the devotion of their clansmen introduced always a certain regal quality into their outlook, which was thus best satisfied by a free union of monarchs under the leadership of the symbolic Empire of the Western seas and the Catholic Majesty of Spain. Besides there was always the glamour which surrounds the unknown, and it was a true calculation that the accurate French knowledge of Scotland could soon appraise the value of Gordon support, just as London could estimate almost exactly the power of O'Neill. But, until the beginnings of this conflict with England, Spanish policy had been hardly concerned either with Scotland or Ireland, so that at Madrid or at Brussels an importance was given to the ' princes,' both in Tyrone and the Highlands, which at the Courts of Paris or London they could never hope to receive.

Yet, before considering the negotiations between Alva and the Gordons, it is essential to examine briefly the working of the official Queen's party, for it is not possible to appreciate the gulf which divided these leaders in their attitude towards Spain without a clear understanding of the Queen of Scotland's approach. All the original Marian party were to a great extent left untouched by a plan of succour from Spain, for, as far as the Queen was concerned, France as represented by her uncles of Guise was the first line of defence, and the aid from Spain would depend directly on the point to which Spanish policy would come into line with the Guisards. It is surprising also how imposing was the diplomatic representation that the Queen of Scots could still keep at the Courts, for, even though she had fled from Scotland nearly two years before, nothing could take from her the rank of the Widow of France, and this very real status, backed by the control of the royal lands in Touraine, on which her revenue was originally charged, came to reinforce the almost sacrosanct claims of her royalty. Besides at this time Edinburgh Castle still held for her, as did Lord Fleming in the West at Dumbarton, and the Queen maintained her ambassadors at the Courts of England and France and even accredited a new envoy to Rome from her prison at Chatsworth. And just as the Queen's incontrovertible rank as a Dowager of France gave her a status, which her actual position in Scotland could not provide, so also her envoys abroad were supported as much by their episcopal character as by her letters of credence. Thus the Bishops of Dunblane, Glasgow and Ross in their embassies were received as members of the Catholic episcopate and this rank also gave them the power to receive ecclesiastical benefices, which would provide an income abroad. In this way Bishop Chisholm of Dunblane received by Papal appointment the small see of Vaison near Avignon and Bishop Beaton of Glasgow was Commendatory Abbot of Sié and held the Treasurership and Priory of Saint Hilaire in Poitou.

There were also the pensions still paid to Maitland of Lethington and Kirkcaldy of Grange and all the façade of Secretaryships of State, which masked what had by now become the remains of a monarchy. Besides such official representatives as Lord Seton still retained their regular money gifts and their Orders, so that there remained a real semblance of political weight in the slow movement of the machine which still swung on with decreasing momentum during the twenty years which separated the Queen's defeat at Langside from her death. It was the revenues of the Crown matrimonial of France that enabled it to maintain a slow motion, since the official power lay with the Ambassador to that Court, who as the Queen's Treasurer also held control of the purse strings. Thus from 1568 until 1587 there was a headquarters for the Scottish party in the Bishop of Glasgow's lodgings in the precincts of St. Jean de Lateran at Paris and to this centre all the policies of the Queen of Scots sluggishly flowed. A certain aristocratic leisure pervaded them, for their leaders had come to rest, long before the arrival of the Tridentine spirit, in the unreformed and upper reaches of the Church, and it was obvious that their natural sympathy was for the great lay lords of their acquaintance rather than for the bustling clergy of this newer age. The Queen of Scotland's party attracted therefore to itself all the English gentlemen of position like the Pagets, who paid their accustomed devotions at the Cordeliers and considered that a steadfast adherence to religion did not necessarily imply a desire for the close companionship of priests. Besides, in the Paris of those days, the episcopal *mensa* could always provide a very welcome entertainment, distinguished by a most careful *menu*, enlivened by sufficient, but not too acute, a wit and all conducted with as much decorum as a man of breeding would find to his taste. If at times the continuance of the Scottish party seems remarkable it should always be remembered that it reposed for its everyday existence on a very assured and solid basis, the French revenues settled on the Queen of Scotland and even if the mill ground cumbrously it would never stop as long as these were paid.

This was the official Queen's party irretrievably linked with the Catholic movement in France and unable to separate itself from the interests of that country, which in financial matters gave it its life. This placed an inevitable restriction on every movement towards Spain and left open to them only those courses of action which had gained a certain approval from the Lorraine faction in France. In such a sense Lord Seton could be spoken of as a ' Castilian ' and receive the flatteries of a pension and the knighthood of Santiago for his third son, Sir John, who was being brought up at Alcala in Spain. But such measures did not in any way advance matters, for they only served to establish the Scottish Queen's party at a point in the then interlocking diplomacy considerably past the broad-minded Left of the Spaniards and a little beyond the Catholic Right of the French. There was, nevertheless, a moment when direct Spanish action was possible after the rebellion in England had broken and there was for once the conjunction of the disappointed, fierce English with the only elements in the Highlands, which were at the same time Catholic and vocal. Yet through it all in the background there remained the official French party, and it was also necessary to contend with the weight of the Hamiltons.

On 20th December, 1569, the ruined leaders of the Northern Rising, disappointed in their last effort at Naworth Castle, made their way at night across the border into Liddesdale and were received by Black Ormiston and his men.[1] They were fiercely angry at the

[1] On 22nd December Lord Sussex wrote that ' they remain under the conduct of Black Ormiston, one of the murderers of Lord Darnley, and John of the Side and the Lord's Jock, two notable thieves of Liddesdale.' Cal. S.P. Dom. Add., 1566–79, p. 160.

treachery of Leonard Dacres and already quarrelling among themselves, the older, simpler mind of Northumberland and the young,
unstable Westmoreland, destined always to be as weak as water and
now a penniless exile at twenty-six. Surrounding them and remaining
close to the Northumberlands in the general dispersion, there was a
group of the chief squires of the North Country, whose power had
for so long depended on their near alliance with the Percy name,
men like Thomas Markenfield and the Nortons and the Tempests.
The short rebellion was over and the effort to re-establish the Catholic
religion by a march southwards and to secure the freedom of the
Queen of Scots had failed. Waiting in the Lowlands with his own
soldiers, and anxious to secure some means which would enable him
to attack Queen Mary's supporters in his country, the Regent Moray
calculated where he should strike with the only weapon at his command. There was no doubt that Northumberland would be the most
profitable and for no other rebel would the English pay so high a
price ; but it was necessary to strike quickly, while the leaders were
still enjoying the hospitality of the petty Border lairds and before
they could reach the greater houses, for there the proposal to surrender a guest for money might fall like seed upon a stony ground.
As it was, Harlaw held out for a good figure, but before Christmastide
was over the Regent was at Jedburgh, and Northumberland was in
his hands. But there was no further opportunity for bargaining, for,
by the time this matter was completed, the other leaders had left the
holds of Liddesdale and come down to the houses of Queen Mary's
friends. There at Ferniehurst with Sir Thomas Ker or with his
brother-in-law, Sir Walter Scott, at Branksome they were safe for the
time from all pursuit. Three thousand men from their own lands
were ready to muster for these chiefs, and although the Regent came
' within a quarter of a mile of Farn Hyrst, he had none left save his
own men, so that he returned to Gedworth (Jedford) and said he
rode but to view the woods.' [1] From this moment until they sailed
from Scotland the English rebels lit everywhere the flame of rebellion
in their passing and aroused the hopes of assistance out of Spain.
Lord Westmoreland and Lady Northumberland were by now the
surviving leaders, and for a time they remained together. There was
no concealment and Sir Robert Constable, who was sent over by the

[1] Cal. S.P. Scotland, 1569–71, p. 47.

English Government as a spy,[1] found Westmoreland at Ferniehurst, ' not secretly kept, but walking before the gates openly with seven servants standing by.' Lady Northumberland and some of her husband's gentlemen were also staying there,[2] while old Mr. Norton and his sons and servants were at the Sheriff of Teviotdale's house at Cavers, five miles to the west, and a rather noisier party of the younger men, including Mr. Egremont Radcliffe and Sir John Neville, were among the guests at Branksome with the Scotts.[3]

Nevertheless it was a calm less real than apparent, for it was clear that the Border chiefs could not maintain for an indefinite period the expense of these guests, and there was always the positive, but unmentionable danger that one day one of these hosts might receive an offer of money large enough to be tempting. This was the idea of Constable whose effort to induce Westmoreland to return to England and throw himself on the Queen's mercy had not unnaturally failed. The description of Sir Thomas Ker as ' covetous and poor '[4] was made with regard to this principle, and it was certainly clear to Elizabeth that she could get back her rebels at a much cheaper cost, if she managed the business direct without giving the Regent a chance to appear as the middle man. For all these reasons there was early in January a general drift of the fugitives away from the Border. The first to move was Lady Northumberland, who made her way towards the sea coast to the greater security of the Humes. But as the journey lay through the open and cultivated country, where the lower reaches of the Teviot meet the Tweed, it was necessary to start before midnight with a strong bodyguard of horse as a protection against the wandering free troopers, who might be returning like the Eliots to the security of Minto or to the strongholds about Mospatrickhope. Even so, such dangers of the night time were greatly preferable to meeting the Regent Moray's army in the day, and it was not yet light when,

---

[1] He was a cousin of Westmoreland and corresponded with Secretary Cecil under the assumed name of Francis Haigh, apparently accepting this service to gain a pardon for his doubtful past. When in the service of Lord Leicester he had been ' one of them that helped to steal his plate.' Cal. S.P. Dom. Add., 1566–79, p. 193.

[2] A letter of Sir John Forster to Lord Sussex, dated 7th January, 1570, states that ' the Earl of Westmoreland lies in the overmost chamber in Ferniehurst Tower and Lady Northumberland in the lowest chamber,' and although they must have been somewhat cramped it was a happy contrast to those first days of misery in ' John of the Side's house, a cottage not to be compared to a dog kennel in England.' Cal. S.P. Dom. Add., 1566–79, pp. 185 and 162.

[3] Their movements are recorded in a series of dispatches in Cal. S.P. Scotland, 1569–71, pp. 47–60 and Cal. S.P. Dom. Add., 1566–79, pp. 160–93, *passim.*

[4] Letter of Constable in Cal. S.P. Scotland, 1569–71, p. 52.

to the westward of Hume Castle, Sir Thomas Ker handed over to Lord Hume's retainers the dangerous custody of his guests. Stiffening the support for the fugitives there was the new leader, Kirkcaldy of Grange, the father of Ferniehurst's first wife, who demanded that he and Lord Hume should take the offensive for Northumberland's rescue. At the same time the hopes of those who favoured a Spanish trend and that desire for Alva's support, which the English fugitives had brought into Scotland, received a confirmation in rumour. As Governor of the Low Countries all the Spanish forces in Northern Europe were under Alva's command, and it was said that he intended to send troops for the relief of Queen Mary's fortress, Dumbarton, and also that ' the Duke of Alva and his power are ready and some of his horsemen are shipped, but no one knows of their landing when or where.' [1]

Then suddenly everything was changed by the assassination of the Regent Moray by the Hamilton faction. The murder took place on the morning of 24th January, 1570, as the Regent was riding through the streets of Linlithgow, and when James Hamilton of Bothwellhaugh, who had fired the shots from behind a curtain in the lodgings of My Lord of St. Andrew's, escaped past the sheltering high houses and rode away across the fields to Hamilton Castle, he had laid the first hopes of the English exiles in ruins. There was an immediate reaction, which favoured the Government, and all parties, including the Hamiltons, were loud in denouncing the crime, while general reconciliation took place by the corpse of the Regent. The new Presbyterianism which had affected so many, even of Queen Mary's supporters, was a powerful solvent of any alliance with Rome and, for instance, the slow political evolution of Grange's standpoint was checked and he bore the late Regent's standard at the triumphantly Protestant service with which he was laid in the grave. Those whose political ties were too close with the Hamiltons were the loudest in denouncing the murder and among them Lord Hume, while the temperature of the political side of his hospitality to the exiles fell several degrees. Under these circumstances there appeared the first

---

[1] Letter of Allen King to Sir Henry Percy, dated 6th January, Cal. S.P. Scottish, 1569–71, p. 45. Two days earlier Sir Thomas Gargrave had forwarded a letter to Cecil. ' We hear from Antwerp that the Duke (of Alva) is making great provision of shipping and is taking up soldiers ; some say for Spain, to assist the King against the Moors, who win country daily ; but most say it is to assist our Moors in England.' Cal. S.P. Dom. Add., 1566–79, pp. 179–80.

signs of that *rapprochement*, which grew close as the summer proceeded, between the English fugitives and the Catholic Earls in the North, Huntly and Atholl. In both cases they were innocent of the murder and had Catholic interests at stake, but neither party seriously pretended regret for the death of the Regent, who had been more instrumental than any man in pulling down throughout Scotland those altars at which their forefathers had worshipped. But before describing the meeting of Westmoreland and Lady Northumberland with the Huntlys, it is necessary to consider the position in Scotland of the Hamiltons, whose ill-advised murder of Moray had caused the crumbling of the first house of cards, which the exiles constructed.

The Hamiltons were in appearance the leaders of the Scottish Queen's party, but they represented a force in Scotland on which no one could ever depend. The Duke of Châtelhèrault, the head of the family, was, after the Queen and her son, the lawful heir to the Crown and it was the danger and pride of the Hamiltons that they stood too close to the throne, while this combined with the caution native to their stock to prevent them from ever coming to a compromising decision. They did not know which of the many opposing movements might deliver Scotland into their hands, and therefore at each crisis they are found not in the centre of the political stage, but in the wings waiting. There were many of them, even among the main branch of the stock, and in dependence a whole host of house friends and kinsmen, all awaiting such leadership as might be forthcoming from the cautious, aged and weary-eyed Duke of Châtelhèrault. The essence of their position lay in a certain outward adherence to the traditional alliance with France, double-crossed by sound pledges to the Court of Elizabeth. In religion they were not divided, for they would never allow that to happen, but they were at different periods disposed on opposite sides. Unlike England, where the lords had to depend in the general scramble on what they could obtain from the Crown, there was a system in Scotland by which bishoprics and abbacies were gradually accumulated into the great noble families and then, when they had become Churchmen to the core and were loaded with benefices, they would ' untrammel their conscience from Popery ' and in freedom swallow the lot. There was needed in this case a *finesse* which the Hamiltons well understood, for it was necessary to show themselves profoundly and devotedly Catholic to obtain those ecclesiastical riches with which to turn against Rome. Even so, a doubt hung over all their religion and at any particular moment they would always keep one of their leaders, who was content to be considered a Catholic, more often than not the Duke's brother, the Archbishop of St. Andrew's ' that godless and bloody man.' [1]

As an immediate result of the murder of the Regent Moray the Hamiltons, who had hoped to gain, were checkmated. Like all the numerous political assassinations with which this period of Scottish history is starred, this killing also suffered from a very evident lack of concealment of the traces of the conspirators, which the clamour and noise inseparable from such actions in Scotland inevitably brought to the light. Thus the murder of Moray was as little concealed as the slaying of Rizzio, and it was only a timorous affectation of ignorance which could persuade the burgesses of Linlithgow that they could not discover the murderer when they saw the Gudeman of Bothwell-haugh streaking foam-flecked over the fields.

Yet even so and although James Hamilton of Bothwellhaugh had fired the shots which proved fatal from the window of Archbishop Hamilton's house, this was not sufficient, on account of the feudal power which the great houses possessed, to deliver the chiefs of his blood to their enemies. The Duke of Châtelhèrault and the Archbishop were for this reason believed when they both denied any complicity, for in the delicate balance of power in that monarchy in which kingship had foundered it was not possible for the accuracy of their words to be tested. Yet although their excuses met with acceptance, the whole situation was changed by the murder, for the searchings of heart that resulted were not so much among their open opponents as in the ranks of their nominal friends.

It was extremely desirable for the great lords in Scotland, who were seldom without their weapons and with their servants similarly armed, that the practice of murder should not settle into a habit, as in those feuds to extermination in the Cinquecento in Italy, tales which the travellers from Rome with the old Catholic bishops had carried, so that in the hard northern life of their country they remained as part of the literary background, incoherent and rich. Besides it was the doubtful condition of the Hamiltons that left opinion uncertain and now madness had settled down upon the Duke's eldest son, Arran,

[1] Proclamation of the Secret Council. Cal. S.P. Scotland, 1569–71, p. 65.

who wandered in charge of retainers across the rough farms of his lordship, dreaming of yellow ganders by the sea at Blackwaterfoot.[1] For a cloud of insanity hung over this family, settling also on Lord Claud's later days, a form of melancholia which for many of the Hamiltons seemed inescapable despite, or perhaps on account of, that ceaseless web of their plotting from which they could never break free. Meanwhile the Hamilton heirship to the throne was a motive always close to the surface, and now that Moray was dead it could only be vaguely predicted who would prove the next victim. At the same time there could not fail to be a certain gratitude in the mind of the Queen's supporters towards those who, for whatever motive, had pulled their chestnuts out of the fire.

This will perhaps serve to explain the changing attitude of the Marian leaders in the months that now followed. At the first news of the murder the manner in which Kirkcaldy had rallied to the other Protestant leaders seemed to foreshadow a complete abandonment by the Marians of all foreign projects, but at the end of February the last flicker of the English rebellion, the unsuccessful attempt of Leonard Dacres to capture Lord Hunsdon, encouraged the exiles and, although he had failed, the ride of his men into Liddesdale proved that there were still Englishmen ready to take arms for religion. In consequence Lord Hume became interested again,[2] and in March a meeting was held between the Northern Earls, Huntly and Atholl, and the Hamiltons to formulate a joint basis for action, but this proved abortive, and as a result of their failure there was no longer any hope of success in the Lowlands of Scotland. Without the Hamilton power, the Queen's scattered adherents in the South could never summon a rising, and the English exiles therefore made their way to the North, menaced by the English army, retained on the borders, which on 29th April had taken Hume Castle. Two days earlier Lord Seton, one of Queen Mary's most devoted adherents, had arrived at Holyrood House [3] with Lady Northumberland on their journey to the more secure Catholic power of the Highlands. Before June Lady Northumberland was established in Aberdeen, while Westmoreland and Tempest had

---

[1] Details of Arran's sickness are provided in the letters of Argyle and Randolph. Cal. S.P. Scotland, 1509–89, pp. 178 and 202.
[2] Letter of Randolph dated 2nd March states that Hume ' has forsaken Religion and now hears two or three Masses daily with Lady Northumberland.' Cal. S.P. Dom. Add., 1566–79, p. 429.
[3] Richard Bannatyne's *Journal of the Transactions in Scotland*, p. 412.

also arrived, and a meeting was summoned at Huntly's castle, Strath-bogie, where the northern Catholics were to wait for the messengers whom Alva was sending.

Here at once the atmosphere was quite different for at last the exiles were freed from all the complicated and clogging circles of interest by which the slow movement of the machinery of the Queen's party was hindered. It was no question of an idealization of the Highland lords with their direct and sanguinary policies, but it must have been a relief to see more clearly the permanent and tangible objects towards which their self-interest was turning, instead of the obscure tangled aims which moved the great southern leaders who maintained the outward tradition of a subtle and mannered royal Court. For it was a noteworthy fact that the lords like Morton and Bothwell, who had achieved the brutality and the guile of Renaissance Court life, could never attain either to the subtlety or the clearness of vision which had brought to success the careers of the Italian despots they admired. Besides, as long as they remained opposed to the Queen, all the rivals in these uneasy politics had no alternative but to rely on Elizabeth, while if they should turn to Queen Mary there was the Court of France as her shadow, but in foreign affairs, as in Scottish, the Highland lords remained free.

For in the North the English exiles had reached the area of that self-contained, independent existence of the far Celtic fringes, which in Scotland, as in Ireland, implied an ultimate desire for true sovereignty which is found expressed in every manœuvre, whether of the Gordons or the O'Neills. Thus the Hamiltons sought to obtain control of that Governmental machine, which the northern clans simply wished to evade. It had been one of Queen Mary's difficulties in Scotland that her rivals and would-be supplanters were always so close to her, for if possessed of a measure of favour they were forever beside her, like Douglas of Morton whose narrow and crafty eyes followed her from chamber to chamber, and, if some hurried royal anger had driven them out of the precincts, they only retreated for a moment over the brow of the hill to re-form and to gather. It was this factor that made the disasters of the reign so Byzantine, heavy with all the close, scent-laden air of a palace intrigue ; for the death plots of Darnley and Rizzio were both hatched at Holyrood in the gloomy and small rooms of the courtiers. By contrast with the tapestried curtains behind which David Rizzio's body lay with its sixty-five wounds, while the elaborate dishes which the French cook had prepared for the Queen grew cold on the table, the episode of the Gordons suggests a wide freedom. They wished to escape from the Queen, not to come too close to her policies, and there could be few deeper contrasts to this supper table at Holyrood than their own disaster, Corrichie, where the old Huntly had died with his pipers and his clansmen about him under the clear northern night sky of his country.

It was this independence which provided the key note, for the Gordons would act as the Scottish Crown's viceroys, but never as servants and the campaign of 1562, which had led to the death of the old Earl at the hands of the Southerners, shortly after the return of the Queen from abroad, had arisen from that impracticable, yet haunting desire to mate his son, Sir John, with the Sovereign. At this time, in the early part of 1570, the spring after Moray was killed, the head of the clan was George, fifth Earl of Huntly. He was a leader after the old Highland fashion, a man now entering upon middle age, who, in spite of his part in the life of the Court, was not really at ease when away from his clansmen. Among them he was almost a king with his power over West Aberdeen and at his back the impregnable hold of the mountains, and beyond these he had friendship, almost of the nature of an independent alliance, with his kinsman, the Stewart of Atholl. It was the good fruit of this steadfast alliance that when Huntly should ride through the hills either up Deeside from his southern lands at Aboyne or from the Bogie through the long valley to Badenoch, he would come down through the Forest of Atholl to the house of his friends. On the east there was a long harrying of the weak power of Findlater and further south a state of intermittent war with the Forbes', while this was as he would wish it, the life that he knew, for no one had right to command him to set his claymores at rest. A clear light is thrown upon his activities by the detailed account that Bannatyne has preserved [1] for us of the way that he met with his death. He had risen early at Strathbogie on this morning of late October and he had gone alone into Winton's Wood and had killed three hares and ' ane tod ' before he had returned home at twelve for his dinner. ' At the dinner he cryed for ane futeball that he

<hr>
[1] Richard Bannatyne *Journal of the Transactions in Scotland*, pp. 484-5.

micht play after none and reprovit Jhone Hamiltoun verie bitterlie because the ball was not reddie.' Then he settled a case that was brought to him and he went out again to his sport, but at the second ' stryke ' of the ball he fell down and was laid with his back to a peat stack until he was carried unconscious ' within the grit chalmer of the new work of Strabogie ' to the round chamber where he died.

In sharp contrast to this ancestral simplicity there was his brother, James Gordon, the Jesuit, whose life foreshadowed the future, for he had been brought up in France and was a professor in the college at Paris, accomplished and fervent. Standing between these two types there was the third brother, Sir Adam, a Catholic swordsman familiar with the ways of the Court, who was carrying on a perpetual struggle with his brother-in-law, the Master of Forbes. Yet, if he was favourably considered at Holyrood, he had lost nothing of fierceness, as the flames bore witness as they arose in the wake of his riding, like the House of Towie, that notable burning, where he had left the lady and her children and the twenty-three servants all dead in the fall of the Tower. It is not surprising with such holocausts of swift violence that religion in that northern country should be sometimes shadowed by magic, whose practices could alone give expression to the hate that ' fire raising ' engendered. Nor is it out of keeping that, although the Gordons had acquired the office of bailie of the church lands of Aberdeen from their aged uncle the Bishop, their own prelates at this period should have served the episcopate only in name. And throughout this there sat in the inner rooms at Strathbogie the mother of the Gordons, the old Dowager Countess, who had brought with her the witch women and the strange blood of the Keiths.

Joined for the moment with Huntly and Atholl and forming the third power in the central part of the Highlands was the chief of the Campbells, Argyll. In the greater questions of policy these lords had a checking and controlling influence, even where their direct rule had ended, over the whole breadth of the country at the latitude of the Grampians. To the West of the comparatively weak power of the Atholls, who nevertheless had command of the one road from Perth to the North, there lay those broad and high tracks through the heather which led up through the trough of the mountains to the peat bogs of Rannoch. And from the southern end of Rannoch Moor there began the levels of Glenorchy, Campbell country, which led down through the lower slopes of Macallum Mor's kingdom to the hills of Lorne and the little harbours with the beached Irish galleys and the guardian Isles of the Sea. Here were bards from Ireland and a traffic borne by the galleys and the Gaelic songs and the speech, all those last signs of the Celtic twilight that lingered. Yet if it was this essential unity of outlook that linked the Irish and the Highland Scots, it was also the strong extension of the Government, working equally from Edinburgh and Dublin, that came in time to force the legal day.

Beyond the compact dependence of Huntly and Argyll there lay the changing and widening sphere of their influence, that gradual extension of the Campbell power westward and southward and the vaguer and less defined Gordon ambitions. Northward of Rannoch and among those shifting lines of Macdonald there was to be found the slow westward move of the Gordons and the power of ' good friend-ship.' Even in 1546 the old Earl of Huntly had been stirring these waters until his nominee had gone down before the Macdonalds in the fight at Blar-nan-leine on the shores of Loch Lochy. Now again they were playing on the rivalry of the factions, the great powers of Argyll and Huntly overshadowing the independent Balkans of Scot-land. At the moment Alastair nan Cleas of Keppoch, Alexander of the Shifts, seemed the most suitable client to assist the building again of that league of Glengarry, Keppoch and Lochiel, which in return for assistance against the Campbell encroachment would accept the distant protection of the chief of the Gordons. Yet, even so, to achieve any measure of success in the North, both Argyll and Huntly had to deploy all their power, not only as leaders of clansmen, but as chiefs who alone could treat with the Crown in the Lowlands, just as in Ulster where also the relations of O'Neill with Dublin governed his own control over his subjects.

In the Highlands, as in Ireland, it was the need for the constant reinforcement of their power among their own people that led the great Celtic lords to value their political life in the capitals and the contacts, distant and often hostile, that they continued to keep with the Court. Thus Argyll had been a Lord of the Congregation and Huntly had temporized in religion and opposed the Queen in her early policy, so long as the Stuart rule remained strong. Again Atholl, although always a Catholic, was opposed to the Queen at one stage in the last Bothwell period, for it was essential for the Highland lords to preserve their independence of Government. Yet no sooner was the Queen's cause defeated than all these three chieftains became her supporters, since it was vital for them to maintain themselves free from the encroachments of Edinburgh, and it was now the old Lords of the Congregation and the Regency leaders who stood to them for that southern, strong centralized power, which in every varying phase they detested.

It seemed clear that Spanish aid would ease the whole situation and would in any case serve as a valuable piece in all the various moves that the leaders adopted to keep themselves and their clansmen free from the Southrons. Besides, lately, the detail of Highland policies had been greatly refined since they had gained Lethington's [1] friendship, so that when the English leaders came into the North they found that the most cultivated of the Scottish officials had already gone into the mountains before them. But it was the misfortune of the English exiles that, while Maitland of Lethington was an admirable intermediary between their own southern manners and the less elaborate northern approach, he failed to possess any interest in that one subject, religion, for which all their sacrifices were made. It was in the nature of William Maitland to drift with the tide of affairs, convinced that the old religion was doomed and that the new preachers and Knox had contrived no alternative palatable to one who had known the wide scepticism of the last years of Francis the First, when Marot had drawn back from Geneva and the Plèiade was rising. There was nothing easier for one whom the Renaissance influence had led to disbelieve in the possibility of attaining to ultimate Truth than to protest against the positive doctrines of the Catholic religion, but, when this was done, the successor, that gaunt Predestinarian frame, which was the sincerity beneath the self-interest, appeared much more repellent. His whole career was in fact overshadowed by the tragedy of the expatriate, for his foreign upbringing, under the Renaissance influence of the formative years, had produced a habit of mind unique in his country.

Nothing could make Knox so angry as the still waters of Lething-

---

[1] The impression made by his broad, almost international, outlook, is preserved in a contemporary note. 'And the said Lard of Ledingtowne, whose hoill study was to have a suer friendship betwixt the two realms; at leist a particular faction in Scotland inclyning nether to England nor France.' Cal. Buccleugh MSS., i, p. 23.

ton's thought, and it was a hatred which caused much of the rancour at this stage in the quarrel. Added to this the power that Lethington possessed of influencing the feminine mind was viewed with contempt in his country by the Calvinist lords, slow witted, but masculine, with their hands on the money. There was something of dalliance, too, in the motives that led him on this hazardous journey, for he had married Mary Fleming, one of the Queen's four Maries, and now gave a tempered philosophic support to the cause she so hotly espoused. Then again by this marriage he had been brought into the family circle of the great Catholic lords and he had gained all their confidence. Here there was an union of the ancestral Scottish tradition with his own wide-minded France in his wife's aunt, the Countess of Atholl, that masterful lady and her sister-in-law, Lady Fleming. With Lady Atholl in particular he had a great influence in this time of her fortunate marriage after her previous husbands, Lord Grahame and the Master of Erskine, had been laid precipitately in the grave. And here the Highland strain came again, for she had read with a great magician and had the power of casting the spells.[1] Lady Argyll, too, was a friend, the Queen's elder sister, and all the while Knox's anger mounted as Lethington made his way northward thoughtfully and with care. ' About the same tyme,' wrote Knox's secretary, Bannatyne, ' the Counsell of Athole held . . . where heid of witt Mitchell Wylie with his sore feit was.' [2] It is possible to possess an intuition too keen for success, and it was Lethington's misfortune that the conceptions of his rivals were so early mediæval that no Macchiavellian weapon was sufficiently blunt to succeed.

By June the leaders in the North were gathered together at Blair Atholl and at Strathbogie, the strongholds of the clans. In the Gordon fastness there were Huntly and his brothers and the English guests, Westmoreland and Lady Northumberland, living in an atmosphere still ancestral and Catholic, where the services of the Old Kirk were unbroken. Here was a countryside which, even through the next century, followed its unchanging traditions with Mass said in public by my Lord Huntly's chaplain in the Raws of Strathbogie and in the Brunt Kirk by Deveron, while the altar lamps were kept burning in

---

[1] An instance of this reputed power was the casting of the pains of Queen Mary's childbirth upon Lady Rires mentioned by Bannatyne, p. 238.
[2] Bannatyne, *Journals of the Transactions in Scotland*, p. 37.

the Gordon's house, Place of Gight.[1] Among all Queen Mary's supporters there was no other house quite so Catholic. Far away in the West at Dunoon there was the shrine destroyer, Argyll, with old Châtelhèrault, an incalculable portent, and at Blair Atholl besides the lord and his wife there was the tireless, but invalid, Maitland of Lethington. Behind these again there were the Queen's Lords, like Seton and Livingstone, who rode to the Blair either from Dunoon or Dumbarton, which was lately re-victualled, and to Blair Atholl also came Huntly. All these men came riding in, each with a fresh plan of action based on policies deeply divergent, but it was no accident that led Lethington to choose this vantage ground in the struggle, so that all their efforts were countered by the Secretary's delicate webs.

Spain, as a Sovereign Power, remained the last Catholic hope of the exiles, and for the Celtic minds it contained the deep fascination which arose from that recognition of prestige and status which the greatest monarch of Christendom was always free to bestow. Thus Strathbogie and even Dunoon were affected by the hope of armed forces from Flanders and of those victories in the Highlands which they would then have power to achieve. For to them Queen Mary was far away and her cause but a pretext, a cover for those elemental desires which controlled them, and it is typical of the remoteness of these lords that even the once godly Argyll was shadowed by a wide reputation for a ferocity barely concealed, so that the Countess of Argyll should dread that she might meet with her husband, foreseeing that at Inveraray she would surely find a ' dark end.' Yet it was just these desires, however disordered, for freedom that provided an ample material for a fast alliance with Spain and had there been no others in question except the exiles from England and the chiefs in the North, a Spanish invasion might have developed, like the later expeditions which King Philip sent over to Ireland to sustain the hopes of his friends.

This was the spirit at Strathbogie during the period of waiting for the messengers to come over from Alva, but there was a Lowland wind at Blair Atholl. They had called over Lethington and had brought him into the North and to his clear sight the only remedy for the

---

[1] The papers from the Archives of Propaganda printed in Appendix viii of the *Blairs Papers*, 1603–60 by M. V. Hay throw light on the continuing Catholicism of this region as does the statement of Fr. Christie in 1654 that ' the Marquis of Huntly dyed in the Bog (of Gight) Catholik, F. Grant, Mr. Lumsden and ane Irish preest present.'

political situation, with which alone he was concerned, was a balance of factions.[1] Beyond Huntly there was the more moderate Atholl and then still further removed from all these northern ambitions the Lowland Marian lords like Seton and Fleming and in the wings Châtelhèrault and the Hamiltons waiting. These were all on his side, and he was concerned with distribution and balance, so that among the contending Regency factions some might be won for the Queen, with the result that imperceptibly the balance would slide until at last the victory was gained. No one was more free from illusion than Lethington, who had an unparalleled knowledge both of Queen Mary [2] and her opponents, and he worked, clearsighted and cautious, while this principle stood forth most evident that, so long as his supporters were numerically weak, conciliation was needed. He could not allow an invasion to antagonize possible friends, so that he was forced to keep fast to diplomacy in foreign relations, for thus only could he hope for success, by a balanced adjustment, a compromise. It was in this way that he had spent the last ten years of his service, sacrificing inessentials for peace. The two elements which had made the recent situation more complex were the insistent claims of the Catholics and the hospitality which had been granted to the clamorous exiles.

To the English exiles, the messengers which Alva was sending provided a fine opportunity for a landing of troops and for a Catholic rising aided by Spain, but to Maitland their use was quite different. They were valuable not for what they could bring, but for the chance which their coming provided of removing embarrassing guests, those English Catholics whose departure would facilitate a more smooth political course.

It was perhaps this intention which led to the decision to transfer the northern meeting from Strathbogie to the calmer atmosphere of Blair Atholl, where the Queen's friends [3] could more easily gather.

---

[1] The following sentence proves his desire for accommodation and balance. 'The greatest poynt,' wrote Lethington to an unknown English Councillor, 'will stand in taking ordour with the Quene of Scotland quhilk being weill handellit may content the tane and put the tother out of fear.' Warrender Papers, i, p. 79.

[2] The fact that the Queen, although she had officially pardoned Lethington, had never really forgiven him for his actions during her reign only made his judgment more clear. This attitude of Queen Mary's would seem to have been unknown to Lethington's son when he wrote his uncompleted *Apologie for Williame Maitland against the lies and calumnies of Jhone Leslie, Bishop of Ross, George Buchanan and Williame Camden as Authors Inventors and Surmisers,* printed in Scottish History Society's *Miscellany,* ii, pp. 153–228.

[3] A statement of Francis Bertie gives an impression of the life of this circle. 'Francis,' said the Bishop of Ross, 'Kan you read Itallian. I canne not well understand, praie you inglisshe yt me.' Cal. S.P. Scottish, 1571–74, p. 13.

For in his cabinet in this house Atholl kept the cypher that he used to communicate with the Queen's envoy in England, that loquacious and indolent gourmet the Bishop of Ross,[1] and here there was gathered a company which lived on the happy memories of the Court of Queen Mary, where the minor lords like the Flemings had seemed quite close to the throne. Another advantage of Blair Atholl lay in its central position, so that the envoys from Spain could not penetrate so far without danger, while the French aid for Dumbarton could be used as a counterpoise. Everything was to be done to make the situation more calm and to remove the centre of political gravity away from the Gordon country from Strathbogie, which commanded the claymores, to Blair Atholl which looked down on the plain.

It was on 14th August that the long expected messengers, a Scotsman, John Hamilton and two of King Philip's subjects, arrived at Aberdeen in a Flemish ' pynk.' There they were met by Huntly's brothers, Robert and Sir Adam Gordon, and were brought to the Kirk of Tullycht in Cromar and then to Strathbogie,[2] but they went no farther for Huntly was away at Blair, and they were forced to await his return. It is a matter of doubt as to whether, as Randolph reported, the envoys later went on to Dunkeld, but in any case a full plan was prepared for them. They were to return to Flanders with the chief English exiles, Lady Northumberland, Westmoreland and Tempest, and also with an accredited Ambassador, Seton. Nothing could have been more flattering than to send to Alva a man of Lord Seton's position to represent the Queen's interests, and the Commission was drawn out most honourably in the name of James, Duke of Châtelhèrault, George, Earl of Huntly, and Archibald, Earl of Argyll, who were represented as sending George, Lord Seton to the most excellent Prince Ferdinand, Duke of Albany, Viceroy of the people and provinces of Lower Germany, with full power to treat

[1] The character of this prelate shows the unbridgeable gulf between the outlook of the wild Highland Gordons and a Marian Court Bishop. The Bishop of Ross notes in his diary that on 13th June he had a bath for two sundry days prepared with hot water and sundry herbs as ' reid roses, vialet laiffis, camavyne and malvie.' On 23rd he refers to Chisholm's passage with money and munitions and on 29th August to two pairs of perfumed gloves he had lately received. Cal. S.P. Scottish, 1569–71, pp. 529–42.

[2] Report of 23rd August confirmed by Lord Saltoun's letter in which the foreigners are described as ' a Florentine called Cæsar Ruspoty and a Pikart called Philip Hensier. Randolph, the English envoy, added that they were gentlemen to the Duke of Alva. Ibid., pp. 323–5. Bannatyne describes the messengers as ' two gentlemen with Mr. John Hamiltoune called the skirmisher fra duck d'Alva.' Op. cit., p. 35.

with the King.[1] With whatever intentions King Philip had embarked upon this adventure, he could not be dissatisfied with the response he received, and there was that concession to Huntly of the second place in the patent and for the exiles the distinguished position they were accorded as envoys and the protection that Seton was to provide for themselves and their train. Nevertheless, this was a victory for Lethington, and in his eyes a danger averted, for the old movement of the pendulum had begun swinging again. Brussels was not to be the end of the journey for Lord Seton received instructions to go later to France and to visit as early as possible the Cardinal Charles of Lorraine.[2] This was in the regular motion of the Scottish Queen's party, the inevitable counterpart to the dependence of the Regent on English support. Thus the re-victualling of Dumbarton by Vèrac [3] was as legitimate as the introduction of Sussex's army, which the new Regent Lennox effected, and was a well-recognized counter in the political struggle. Spain was an unknown force, and Lethington had prevented a blazing torch being cast on the always inflammable Highlands, for, although Huntly cherished other ambitions, it was the future united Scotland that Lethington gave his last years to serve. There had been no open struggle before the strife of religion and Lethington, impatient with this side of the question, was anxious for peace. Now he could go forward slowly with all his pieces assembled,[4] the Hamiltons and Huntly and the Marian lords, while already his plans had borne fruit in the reconciliation of Argyll. The weakness of the body and the paralysed state of his legs only rendered more acute the clarity of his mental outlook as he gradually surmounted the obstacles before peace. If he never did achieve this it was in great measure due to the hatred, which he always vainly hoped to assuage, between the strong Presbyterian lords in the Lowlands and the Catholic clans in the North, and then the Gordons escaped his control and there

[1] Cal. S.P. Scottish, 1569–71, p. 305.
[2] *Ibid.*, p. 304.
[3] 'About the end of August came from France . . . ane schip with famous embasadour Mosr. Virak (of whom we hard before) a notable pyrate. With him he broght some oringes, some reasinges, sum bisqueat bread, some powder, some bullet and so of omni gaddarin he broghte a maledictione to furneis Dumbartoun.' Bannatyne, p. 38.
[4] There is a sharp contrast between the calm outlook of Lethington and Bannatyne's bitter account of this episode, with its slander on Lady Northumberland, who has never elsewhere been attacked. 'To bring better tydinges was direct ane embassadour of the femening gener the Ladie Northumberland. . . . With hir were joyned to give hir comfort in the schip the vyse Lord Seatoun ; a meitt match, a Scottis cucold and ane Englis mesmonger who knoweth hir better judge what I spare to speik. About the same tyme the counsell of Athole held two or threi dayes, whare heid of witt Mitchell Wylie with his sore feit was.' *Op. cit.*, p. 37.

followed the murder of Lennox and the hanging of Archbishop Hamilton. Yet in spite of these ultimate failures he achieved much for the peace of the country, and it was the beginning of a long calm in Scotland when Sussex was persuaded to withdraw his troops across the Border and the exiles at last put out to sea.

CHAPTER VII
THE VACANT SEE OF ARMAGH

This brief episode deals with the life of Archbishop Creagh, a prelate, disinterested and devoted, who came from the quiet work of the provincial priesthood to a troubled year in Ulster and a long imprisonment in the Tower. He saw Catholic Europe in the first period of the Conciliar Reform, passing with devotion along those highways which so many adventurers were soon to tread. As far as Ireland was concerned he was the first and most apostolic of the exiles. In his country the conflicts with O'Neill indicate the first state of that high family which was to change so rapidly, as well as the tangled relations between Tyrone and Argyll and the Scotsmen to the North. His career thus provides a prelude to the consideration of all those political and social problems, which were to dominate the immediate future of that country, while his own single-minded desires serve in some measure to explain the attitude which the Papacy adopted towards the Queen's dominions. In contrast to all the men whom very varied motives were to lead, as in the case of Stukeley, to ask the aid of Rome, his aims were simple. The political confusion which was so soon to cloud each situation is illuminated by this figure.

THERE are few groups whose policies seem more involved and tangled than those which gained a fluctuating control in the Ireland of Elizabeth, whether among the Irish, or the old Anglo-Irish or the settlers. The struggles between the rival leaders within a clan, which was itself in a state of intermittent conflict with its neighbours, were echoed not only in the greater political dissensions, but also in the government of the Church. The continued rule of the Catholic bishops, who had survived from the reign of Mary, side by side with the new prelates who had been established under the Elizabethan Act, reflected this disorder, while the hesitant state of certain bishops and the existence of an increasing number of episcopal appointments, straight from Rome, only added to the confusion. At the same time the fidelity to the Old Religion shown by the many Religious, who were able in the more distant parts of the country to continue their community life unhindered, was counterbalanced by the lax example of the *soi-disant* Catholicism of the Earls. And in the welter of this confusion, which even the general antipathy to England could not make clear, there was placed the primatial rule of Richard Creagh.

THE VACANT SEE OF ARMAGH

Archbishop Creagh was not only raised by his position above this labyrinth of dispute, but he was also by temperament outside it. In another sense he was also outside and apart, for it is not dogmatic quarrels that have ever disturbed the Irish Church, and, although Richard Creagh was twenty before the work of the Council first began, his life and rule had no need for the new spirit of reform. Hearing in Rome, on his way to consecration, of the completed results of all these labours, he accepted with gratitude the decisions of the See of Peter and those safeguards of which in his own life he had no need. There was in him the spirit which is at the root of all Catholicism, whether of the Middle Ages or of Trent. He was entirely unaffected by the political quarrels of the time, for these matters held no interest for him, while the detachment of his dedicated life increased as he grew older, in contrast with the comfort of his secular beginnings. At Limerick in his father's merchant house and in the voyages which he made in his father's ships he was far removed in spirit from the cabins and the huts beyond the gates. The Latin and the Spanish, the ornament and the necessity of the leisured trade with Spain, carried him still farther from the Irish life beyond the city and the deep-rooted Christian spirit of this ordered round, the prayers before the altar lights in the harbour churches in Ireland, Portugal and Spain gave to his mind that sense of the indivisibility of the Universal Church which he was never afterwards to lose. It was in one of the quayside churches of a Spanish port that he decided to spend his life in the service of religion, while it was at the University of Louvain that he received the priesthood and in Limerick that he spent his years of work. Circumstances thus aided in the slow formation of a character singularly impervious to external change. The sheltered life of a wealthy merchant's son gave place to five years' work among the poor, teaching the children of the city. It was a form of work in which he could concentrate as he desired upon the spiritual welfare of his people, without concern either for the local politics or for the great affairs of State. There were few centres where the Catholic life could continue with so little disturbance in that epoch of revolt as in what were in many ways almost the City States of Ireland, and, if Waterford can alone claim the title 'Urbs Intacta,' Limerick in the sixteenth century followed close to her in the walled protection of her calm.

At the age of thirty-seven, when he was engaged on what had

119

become by 1562 his still more obscure and hidden labours, Richard Creagh was discovered by the Papal Legate, David Wolfe, who saw in him a priest of considerable attainments, naturally retiring disposition and rather delicate health, made remarkable by his utter lack of interest in the shifting politics of the outside world. It is this last quality of complete detachment, which provides the guiding mark to his career. The Legate's letter resulted in a summons for Creagh to go to Rome and there he received consecration on Low Sunday, 1564, as Archbishop Primate of Armagh. There was on his road a whole group of prelates interested in the affairs of the Church in England and in Ireland, the Nuncio to the Most Christian King, Monsignor Prospero Publicola Santa Croce, Bishop of Chissamos, the Archbishop of Rossano, Nuncio to the Catholic [1] King, who was in Rome during a portion of his visit, and all the advocates of a forward policy who had influence in the Curia or with the Pope. But this left him quite unaffected, for, as he afterwards declared in England, ' I intended if God would, for to enter into such religion as I should there in Rome see best or most agreeable to my weak complexion, but as I was commanded by obedience to take my way to Rome, so being there ready for to enter the religion of the Theatines, otherwise called Paulines, dwelling at Montecavallo, I was commanded by the Cardinal (of Gonzaga), under pain of obedience, to change nothing about myself till I should know further of the Pope his will.' [2] It is easy to picture too that ' poor table and house ' of his Roman sojourn, the gradual abandonment by the greater prelates of the companionship of one who had so little interest in affairs and that occasional hospitality at the English College, which the Bishop of St. Asaph would provide.

A circumstance enables us to fill in again this Roman life, for on his return to Ireland the Archbishop was taken and examined by Cecil in the Tower. He had never denied the right of Queen Elizabeth and he had nothing to conceal, while his absorption in an unique object precipitated a humble-minded accuracy of reply. He had stayed where possible in the new houses which had been lately founded by the Society of Jesus to which his supporter Fr. David Wolfe belonged, and all his living had been provided by the Pope ; for it was but right that the Living Peter should give succour to his children, six crowns

[1] Cal. S.P. Roman, 1558–71, pp. 60, 91 and 255–77, *passim*, for the circle of Continental prelates who corresponded about the English and the Irish Church.
[2] State Papers, Ireland, Eliz. xii, 33.

a month for house rent in the year that he was kept in waiting and then, when he was consecrated, 'a robe of blue unwatered chamlet and wearing apparel of three sorts.' He seems to have accepted with complete assurance and repeated, even to his examiners, the casual and inaccurate statement of Cardinal Morone that ' the Queen would shortly turn to the Catholic Faith,' and he set out from Rome with only one servant a poor Ulster scholar. Keeping to the track of the Jesuit houses and aided by the letters of Fr. Wolfe the new Archbishop stayed a week with the great protector of the Society the Cardinal Truchsess von Waldburg at Augsburg, where he obtained relief from the pains of the ague he had caught on his journey. Then passing northwards from one religious house to another, he came to Franciscans at Antwerp and at last to Louvain, where he gave a banquet to the doctors in his robes. Passing through England, he had accepted as a servant an Irish boy whom he had found at Rochester begging in the streets and on reaching Ireland he was immediately arrested.

How strange in this period and country is such simplicity ? Other prelates were involved in every form of diplomacy and disturbance, but his own words as to his intentions are most clear. ' Being asked what he would have done if he had been received Archbishop of Armagh, saith, he would have lived there quietly. Being asked what he would have done if he had been refused, he answereth, that he would have gone to Louvain to his track again.' [1] Coming from a man whose movements and speech were marked by such an absence of the tortuous sixteenth-century precaution, it can hardly be doubted that this phrase rings true. Almost immediately after his last examination he escaped from the Tower [2] on Low Sunday, 1565, and made his way to Louvain and in the following year at last reached Ulster by the familiar route from Spain.

He had come at length to the appointed place of his labours, for *in vinea Domini* it was Ulster, which had been entrusted to his care. There was a population with a profound reverence for the name of Catholic, a strong body of Franciscan Friars, a disorganized and

---

[1] The details of these examinations which took place on 22nd February and 17th and 23rd March, 1565, are preserved in State Papers, Ireland, Eliz., xii, 33, 59 and 60, while considerable extracts have been published in *The Reformation in Ireland under Elizabeth*, pp. 119–32, a work in which the Rev. M. V. Ronan has provided a scholarly study of the intricate changes in the Irish Church.

[2] An account of this escape, which the Archbishop considered miraculous, has been published in *Spicilegium Ossoriense*, i, p. 41, from the Vatican archives.

scattered clergy and one predominant lord, the Great O'Neill. The political details were beyond the pale of his experience, Louvain with the long calm years of study and Limerick with its quiet well-ordered work, and he did not possess any more desire to mingle in these, to him, barbaric policies, than in the suaver movements of the Roman Court. It was obvious, however, that, as the spiritual head of a people in a time of trouble and danger, he must keep close to the springs of their temporal government, which were in this case centred solely in the Prince.

In that spiritual order, with which his interests were alone concerned, he could see most clearly the condition of the Irish without a shepherd, while his lack of political zest had freed him from illusion where the personal character of the leaders was concerned. Shane O'Neill, Earl of Tyrone, was at this time thirty-six years of age and at the height of that success which had gained for him from his followers the title of *an dio mais*, the proud, and from the English the respectful sobriquet of the Grand O'Neill. He had recently defeated the McDonnells and the Scots at Ballycastle and James and Sorley were his prisoners of state, taking the place of Calvagh O'Donnell, whom he had for three years exhibited in chains as an indisputable evidence of his power. Behind this there was a tangled history of alternate friendship and enmity with his cousin Sir Turlough and perpetual blood feud with his nephew, Dungannon, whose father, Fedoragh O'Neill, he had murdered. While below these the 'urraghs' moved in intricate and changing dependence and among them his chief supporters, the O'Donnellys with whom he had fostered. In addition he kept 600 men 'as it were his janyzery about him' and 'agentys contynualy in the coor of Scotland and with the dyvers potentates of the Irish Scottes.'

On the ecclesiastical side, his chief friend was his foster-brother, the Dean of Armagh, who had Englished his name as Terence Daniel and still found it convenient to support the Pope; nor was Shane free from the suggestions of a sacrilege. He had dissolved his first marriage with a MacDonnell of Cantyre and was now living with the Dowager Countess of Argyll, who was the wife of his former captive, O'Donnell,[1] but during the years of this adultery he had received the

---

[1] Bagwell complicates the matter unnecessarily by supposing that Lady Argyll was the wife of Archibald the fifth Earl and that O'Donnell paid him a pension for her use. She was in fact

Communion secretly from Bishop Quadra,[1] as a mere means to establish his *bona fides* with Spain. Whatever his ignorance of the intricacies of northern policy, the theological implications of this action, the apparent and callous neglect of that purity of Christian life with which the reception of this Sacrament must be approached, could not have been lost upon Archbishop Creagh.

There was in Shane O'Neill nothing of that ' civility,' which marked the later generations of his house, and there can have been few greater burdens than the constant company of such a man. In the morning when he woke from his stupor, refreshed by the clean air of his country, was the best time to approach him, for his mind was then clear, as is shown by the description of his day, which Lord Deputy Sidney sent home to the Government. ' In the morning he is subtle,' wrote Sir Henry, ' and then will he cause letters to be written either directly otherwise than he will do, or else so doubtfully as he may make what construction he likes and ofttimes his secretary penneth his letters in more dulled form than he giveth instruction, but in the afternoon, when the wine is in, then unfoldeth he himself, *in vino veritas*, then showeth he himself what he is and what he is likely to attempt.' [2] And then, when the Archbishop had taken his departure and Shane O'Neill was far gone in wine, he would order Lady Argyll to be brought to him out of that dungeon where it was his pride to keep her in fetters. It was a satisfaction to O'Neill, who boasted that he spoke no tongue save the Gaelic, to wound the O'Donnell so deep in his pride by keeping for his pleasures the Lady of Tyrconnell and Argyll, reputed ' very sober, wyse and no less sotell, beyng not unlearned in the Latyn tong (speakyng) good French and, as is said, some lytell Italyon.' [3] Even so, there was no point of contact between the Archbishop and a woman, who was said to have surrendered her husband to his enemy to become O'Neill's mistress.[4] Besides her

Catherine McLean, the third wife of Archibald fourth Earl of Argyll, whom O'Donnell had married after her husband's death in 1558. Although Tyrone may have gone through a ceremony with her in 1565 any lawful marriage was impossible and he certainly regarded himself as free to propose himself as a husband for Queen Mary when Lady Argyll was still with him.

[1] Letter of Bishop Quadra to Cardinal Granvelle, dated 3rd April, 1562. Cal. S.P. Spanish, 1558–67, p. 235.
[2] Sidney Papers, *passim*. As regards the quotation *in vino veritas*, it is perhaps only fair to mention the bottle sent in the time of Sidney's predecessor, Lord Sussex, to effect O'Neill's removal, ' per potionem vini in quo clam venenum,' as Shane's secretary wrote.
[3] State Papers, Ireland, Eliz., iii, 84.
[4] Cal. S.P. Irel., 1509–73, p. 172. A letter of Lord Justice Fitzwilliam to Cecil contains a reference to the capture of O'Donnell and the Countess of Argyll by Shane, which he fears will prove to be the act of the wife.

knowledge consisted of the phrases of Latin and French learned in the days when, as the young wife of Argyll, she had attended on the Queen Regent Mary of Guise at the Scottish Court of her exile and this had nothing in common with the Archbishop's scholarship. While beyond this there was something of the tigress strain in the Countess of Argyll, the wild blood that she had inherited from the Dowart McLeans, and she was at the heart of all the feuds of O'Neill and O'Donnell, those sudden betrayals which made the shifting changes of fortune so startling. Every week of this year there were changes, some alteration of loyalty between O'Neill and O'Donnell on the part of the remote ' urraghs ' on their borders and then as the gallow-glasses came riding in, with their rough frieze cloaks flying, O'Neill would rouse himself for a moment and then sink heavily at his wine.

In contrast to this there was the peaceful life at Louvain, the eight years of devotion and scholarship which Richard Creagh had passed in the colleges, with no more disturbance than the clatter of the country people coming in to the market or a detachment of Spanish infantry marching, and all the streets filled with a host of students and friars and monks, a veritable City of God. Then, when the lectures were over, there had been those disputations with his companions against that quiet background, the peace of Brabant in summer, the stiff poplars along the road to Aerschot and the still, slow water beneath the trees, and in the afternoon the choice of Vespers, either with the Canons at St. Gertrude or in that spiritual calm that was never broken, the Charterhouse of St. Mary Magdalen beneath the Cross.

As it was he was compelled to go with Shane to Inish Darell and back to Dunavally, with this man for whom moral sanctions had no force. In the summer the Cathedral at Armagh was burned down by the clansmen, for matters were becoming more difficult and in August O'Neill was made Traitor and began a feverish plotting with Argyll and Queen Mary and then doubled back on his tracks to attempt to make peace with the once conquered MacDonnells. At the end of October on the Vigil of Ss. Simon and Jude, messengers rode in with the news that Calvagh O'Donnell was dead, that he had fallen from his horse in a fit as he went against Derry. Then, gathering all his forces, Shane O'Neill set out on a forced march on Tyrconnell, which led to disaster.

THE VACANT SEE OF ARMAGH

At the beginning of this campaign the Archbishop left him and after journeying through the North, was captured again and handed over to the Government by the O'Shaughnessys in the first weeks of May. Less than a month later, on 2nd June, Shane O'Neill, who had reached the end of his tether, was murdered by the MacDonnells at Cushendun as he came to seek peace. The Archbishop was taken to Dublin, where he escaped again, but was re-captured before the end of the year and sent on to London, and although he was never actually tried for high treason, he was never released.[1] The Irish regarded him as a priest who had selflessly tried to serve God and opinion made him a saint, for to them it seemed that he had no other idea save to foster the spirit of Christ in his country. This was a standpoint that in part the Government shared, as is shown by a lucid phrase of the official dispatch, that the Archbishop was 'a dangerous man to be among the Irish, for the reverence that is by that nation borne unto him and therefore fit to be continued in prison.' In prison therefore he remained for eighteen years until he died on 14th October, 1585, the morrow of the Feast of St. Edward the Confessor. The purely political effects of his rule were slight.

[1] One construction put on these years in prison has interest. Among the innumerable charges made against Sir John Perrot, there appears 'item. Favour to Dr. Creagh,' an accusation certainly false. It is to be found in a collection of points written out in Burghley's hand on 15th November, 1591. Cal. S.P. Irel., 1588–92, p. 439.

CHAPTER VIII

SIR THOMAS STUKELEY'S DESIGN

In this study a very marked contrast appears between the disinterested endeavours of Archbishop Creagh and the episodes of Sir Thomas Stukeley's career. The latter would seem to have been a pure adventurer whose life on the Continent from 1570 till 1578 consisted of a series of attempts to stimulate the Catholic Courts against England. It is this characteristic which gives to his intrigues a significance which neither his personal influence, nor his prestige would merit. He was of reasonably distinguished descent (although his claim as a son of Henry VIII, which forms an interesting parallel with the similar assertion of Lord Deputy Perrot, need not be regarded too seriously), had maintained contacts at Court and had held a military command of some importance in Ireland. These assets secured him a hearing and, during his eight years abroad, he was able to get into touch with all the political forces opposed to the Elizabethan *régime*. The attitudes taken up by King Philip and by the Papal Nuncio towards an aggressive policy against England is seen reflected in these dealings; while the support which Stukeley obtained from the English Duchess of Feria provides an instance of the value which the Catholic exiles set on good breeding. The pre-occupation of the Roman Curia with the question of his heretical status is also shown clearly.

A contrast is provided by the opposing parties in Spain, the Ferias with their English connections, aristocratic in tone, who supported Sir Thomas, and the official and ecclesiastical group who favoured the Irish churchmen abroad, who were seeking for aid. The opposition between Sir Thomas Stukeley and the Archbishop of Cashel is clear cut, while in a later development the Irish supporters concentrated on Fitzmaurice's claims. In this matter Fitzmaurice appears as the spiritual heir of Archbishop Creagh, completely disinterested and rather improvident. After Stukeley's failure to obtain any serious aid from Philip II, his negotiations with Don John of Austria and Pope Gregory XIII in turn illuminate the politics of this time. As in Spain, so also in Rome, his claims gave rise to two attitudes, sharply opposed, the Pope's generous support and the profound distrust felt by the 'Cardinal Secretary. The influence of Paolo Giordano Orsini as a chieftain of bandits and the unsatisfactory condition of public order in the Papal States are discussed as preliminaries to the eventual grant of a Papal commission. The evidence as to Stukeley's intentions in setting sail are examined, and his position is compared with that of Hawkins and Drake who had never left Queen Elizabeth's service. Finally those relations with King Sebastian of Portugal which led to his death are described. Thus in the light of the career of this man all the varying attitudes of Western Catholics towards England and their different plans of aggression can be clearly discerned.

It is a mark of the Catholic Church that she has always retained in her allegiance the most diverse racial types, while among her adherents are those who possess all the shades of experience and temperament, however conflicting. For this reason a greater unanimity was to be found in the sixteenth century among her opponents ; for the matters on which they were united were nearer at hand, the secular state and the national idea that they fostered or perhaps such a general concept as liberty. But even such an ideal as freedom, in its political and temporal sense, must possess a continuous contact with the life of the world and the measure of possession is tested by the material gains it achieves. Thus the fulfilment of those ideals for which the reforming parties were striving would be reached in this world, peace under an ordered calm reason, an efficient state of prosperity and, for religion, preachers to lead the peoples to the great open bibles, which should radiate that Divine and pure clear light of the Gospel. This was the standpoint of Melanchthon, and it was evident to his supporters that, once this reign of pure truth was established and the mediæval fogs blown away, the world would go forward in happiness, still in terrestrial existence, but free in the daylight of God. The greatness of these events went to justify such a contention and, if there was ever a moment in which the towers of the ' City of the Sun ' could almost be made out on the skyline, it was at this time of the overthrow ; for those who believed in the changes. It was natural, therefore, for all, who were elated at the thought of the good that must come from so much evil cast down, to believe in Utopia. Yet there is a great contrast in outlook between the men who construct such fantasies and those others dissecting with patience the detail and stuff of their dreams, and it is only a normal development that the more careful Utopian students seldom accept the religion of Campanella and More. For it was at once the interior strength and the external weakness of the Catholic Church that the aims which she set before her children were essentially spiritual and directed in the first place at the liberation of the soul, so that they looked forward to the stainless rising of the Bride of Christ, resplendent with the glory of the Saviour at the gateway of the tomb. ' I am the Alpha and the Omega, the beginning and the end,' and in the peace of God they would reach at last to union. But it was the very strength of this exalted hope that made their perceptions of earthly values keener, for until their journey was completed they would never expect an end to strife.

This recognition that, even among the most zealous defenders of their Faith, they could not hope to find accord, so long as racial differences continued, was a commonplace to all those Catholics who sought to restore the ancient Church. Thus, however bewildering the disputes and quarrels that eddied round King Philip's Court in Spain may seem to us, they did not dim the ardour or reduce the religious zeal of the rival factions and the Pope knew that he could count upon them all. It is always in reaction to some outside force that the condition of affairs is most clearly revealed and, for the understanding of the attitude of the different parties in Spain, we need just such a touchstone and, as far as the Catholic exiles were concerned, this is provided in Thomas Stukeley's meteoric career. For Stukeley was outside, if not aloof from, these sharp religious disputes, a carefree adventurer clogged always by enemies, and in the midst of these Catholic exiles he appeared as a portent, a shooting star falling in the austere Spanish heavens and revealing as it dissolved.

It was in the spring that had succeeded the publication of the Bull *Regnans in Excelsis* that the *Trinity* of Bridgewater, owned by Captain Stukeley, commanded by Robert Kean and manned by a mutinous Irish crew, carried its owner into the port of Vivero de Galicia and so into Spanish life. It was the morrow of the feast of St. Mark, 24th April, 1570, and the Court of Seville had entered upon that routine of business, untempered by any very severe religious exercise, which marked, for King Philip, the spirit in which the household of the Catholic King should welcome the joyous calm of the weeks of Paschaltide. There were various matters of importance before the King, the completion of the final arrangements for the creation of the Spanish Cardinals in the May conclave and the details of his fourth marriage, the dispensation and the proxies and the bride's journey; for the King was about to marry his eldest niece, the Emperor's daughter, the Archduchess Anne, a pale tall girl, with that long and sad face and the heavy jaw that had marked the house of Austria and its thin exalted blood. Her painting in the stiff German manner had provided the measure of happiness and an approach to intelligent emotion on the part of Don Carlos, King Philip's crazy son, whose affianced bride she had been in his last years. Yet the King at forty-three, with that high conception of his royal duty that sustained him, seemed hardly to consider the personal element in such a case, for the

SIR THOMAS STUKELEY'S DESIGN

Catholic King, who was always the greatest of suitors, need therefore never be the first. Besides it was an essential characteristic of His Catholic Majesty, whose profoundly Christian character is sometimes overshadowed by that austerity which is to our minds so unfamiliar, always willingly to accept a sacrifice as a pledge that obligations were fulfilled. Especially when contrasted with the *insouciance* of the French Monarchy it is a very impressive quality that unending and increasing sacrifice which from the days of *Los Reyes Cattolicos* has at times been offered by the Crown of Spain.

It was a moment too in King Philip's life when, the affections of his youth behind him, he had not yet gained that support of the love of his eldest daughter, who was to encourage his later years, and he was left alone, in that isolation which he knew so well how to increase. In his family there was no companionship save for his sister the Princess of Portugal who lived in her widowhood in that devoutly regal atmosphere of the Descalzas Reales, with the Poor Clares of Our Lady of Consolation spread out fan-like at her back. This was an application of his principles, to be thus surrounded by a house of prayer, and the monastery of the Escorial also was finished, while King Philip lived in one wing of his palace in that newly quarried wilderness of stone.

And in these circumstances the King considered Stukeley. He had his dossier, careful and now complete. In the first place he was a gentleman and had held a high position of trust in Ireland, from which country he now came. He had the support also of Sir Henry Sidney, who was a serious nobleman and of an excellent manner, and he was strongly recommended by the Ambassador Guerau d'Espes. In addition he had brought with him, as a pledge of respectability, a young and legitimate son. To set against these assets there was the doubt as to d'Espes' judgement, which was not unnaturally already troubling the King, the fact that Stukeley was without substantial funds, that he had lived for some years as a pirate and that he had played a rather shady part as a Spanish mercenary in the late Emperor Charles' time. Meanwhile Stukeley was at Vivero and let him remain there, for the affair of the Moriscos was nearly over and the seizure of the treasure fleet by the Queen of England caused Philip's mind to turn towards the North, and now it was always possible that he might there come in useful. As for the fellow's protestations of religion, they were clearly worth nothing, but, after the shameful trickery of that other pirate John Hawkins, it was a relief at any rate to deal with a gentleman. Besides as he was going North to Madrid he would send him 200 ducats to keep the matter in trim, but there were other affairs so much more important, the Duke's dispatches from Brussels and all the marriage arrangements, the new frescoes at the Escorial and details of a fresh pattern of dark, rich chased armour, and the Governorships in Peru. And in that May all these things were passing before the restless and cold eyes of the King.

It was not in the nature of Thomas Stukeley to move unprepared, for he had been for five years in tentative negotiation with Spain [1] and he knew that, for a gentleman who lived by his wits, it was necessary to possess a powerful backing of friendship for fear that he might fall below that standard in servants and dress which was necessary to avert the danger of being thought to be a predatory rogue. It was essential therefore to rely on a patron and he had decided that his position should hinge on the Duchess of Feria. This was in any case the most fortunate channel through which the English Catholics could make their approach.[2] The highest rank was essential to secure a constant use of appeal to the Sovereign, and the Duke of Feria, a conscientious, silent and deeply extravagant man, had the rights of the first-class grandeeship and the privilege that the command of the royal bodyguard carried, even for those who no longer had active charge of the post. 'Her Ladyship's Grace of Feria' had therefore a right of entry into the Presence and of appeal to the King of Spain to which none of the exiles could aspire.

In this spring of 1570, when Stukeley was descending upon Vivero, Jane, Duchess of Feria, was holding what was in reality the shadow of a Court in the palace of Zafra, her husband's great fief in Southern Spain. She was now thirty-two years of age and had held a great position in the Europe of her day, ever since Queen Mary had singled her out as the favourite of her Maids of Honour and had raised Mistress Dormer to a distinction far beyond her father's rank. That journey which she had taken from England on Queen Mary's death, as the

---

[1] Letter from the Ambassador Guzman de Silva to the King of Spain, dated 8th October, 1565, 'Stukeley says that Sidney is very anxious to take him to Ireland by means of which he hopes, in case Your Majesty were so pleased, to be able to effect something in that Island.' Cal. S.P. Spanish, 1558–67, p. 488. Another letter protesting his Catholicism was sent on 25th May, 1566. *Ibid.*, p. 550.
[2] A list of the English Catholic pensioners in Spain which is preserved in the Record Office, S.P. Dom. Eliz. CV, 9, is printed at the end of this volume. It is significant that it should be directed 'To the Duchesse of Ferya her good grace.'

bride of the Spanish Ambassador de Feria, was a symbol of the calm progress of her life, with six English gentlewomen in attendance, and Mrs. Clarencia, the Queen's nurse with her, and a household of twenty in her train. England and Spain were at peace, and she corresponded with the English lords and the ministers and her own family and was everywhere honoured, and as a greater tension appeared in the strain of the policies, so also did the increasing circles of her protection ripple more wide. The matter of the exiles of the Northern Revolt had been troubling her lately, and the dispute between Lord Prior Shelley and her own old friend Englefield and the troubles in Flanders. At Zafra it seemed so strange, all this danger to Holy Religion, while the vines ripened in May in Estramadura in the long, unbroken Christian field of that country, which ran to the mountains eastward at La Granja de Torrehermosa and far again to the South, where all the Christian blood had been spilled in defence of the Cross. The gallery with its great range of long windows, which the English Duchess had built, in the massive castle at Zafra looked down on the Feria villages, which, compared to the rest of Europe, were so recently conquered for Christ, and along their roads to the further bastions of true religion, to the Guardian Towers of Villa Garcia and to Jerez of the Knights. And in Madrid and still more at Feria the whole of the background was filled by her life of devotion with Padre de Figueroa, her husband's Jesuit brother and the devout, ageing and widowed Duchess of Arcos. Then, at the time of Vespers, the English Duchess would go down through the private passage, with the link boys leading the way, to her own chapel in Zafra, where the nuns of Santa Marina were maintained for chanting the hours, and kneeling at her prie-dieu of honour, with the worked armorial silk and the pages beside her and the servants grouping behind, it was difficult not to believe that the whole of Europe would echo the Christian calm of this land, where over every detail of life the ancestral peace of the Old Faith rested. And then the letters began to come in about Stukeley's arrival.

Like many devoutly Catholic great ladies, the Duchess of Feria, while possessing a decided *penchant* for converts, greatly preferred that they should be well bred. For her own position resembled in some degree that of the great Victorian converts of established social prestige, who also stood enveloped in the shadow of persecution,

THE CELTIC PEOPLES & RENAISSANCE EUROPE

although in their life it receded, while in hers it always advanced. Yet her Elizabethan contemporaries could not deny that she possessed, what was for them, the soundest of all reasons for being a Catholic, the fact of her marriage to a man, whose political and social duties involved the practice of that particular faith. As for Mr. Stukeley, she remembered him from the days of Queen Mary, when he had been assiduous at the Court and had had considerable dealings with her friend, good Sir Francis, who controlled the office of Wards.[1] He came of a sufficient family, but she had not met his wife, for that was since she left England and she gathered that he had married for money someone of whom she had not heard. There had been one little boy whom he had brought with him. But the deciding factor was Sir Henry Sidney, her uncle, with whom she had always continued to remain on excellent terms.[2] With her own extravagant husband the Duchess could now understand Uncle Henry so well, the debts and the curious moods,[3] and with it all that courtly fine manner as she had seen him last in the late Queen's Court at St. James' with his square Tudor-like features and the golden beard that depended from his smooth, pink, heavy cheek.[4] And Uncle Henry had recommended Mr. Stukeley most strongly ; they had been intimate friends and he was reputed a gallant captain in Ireland, where together they ruled the ' savages ' for so many years. But Mr. Stukeley, like a brave soldier, had sacrificed all for religion, and it was clearly her duty to help him and so she would write to the Nuncio for whom she had the highest regard.[5] Besides she realized that he would have difficulties with the Irish ecclastiastics already in exile, whom her husband had always advised the King not to assist.[6] For herself, in spite of the respect due to the purple and on account of all they had suffered in defending Holy Church in their country, she could not deny that these

[1] In a letter of 15th September, 1558, Queen Mary informed Sir Francis Englefield, Master of the Court of Wards, that she had granted the wardship and marriage of Sergeant Prideaux's son to Thomas Stukeley. Cal. S.P. Dom., 1547–80, p. 156.
[2] As witness a letter of the Duchess of Feria to Sir Henry Sidney, dated 13th June, 1576. Cal. Sidney Papers, p. 114.
[3] Sir Henry Sidney, writing to Lord Leicester on 19th May, 1577, described a false report from Ireland as ' but one of the crabs that the cankered trees of this cursed country, for want of better sap, bring forth.' Cal. Carew MSS., ii, p. 81.
[4] An excellent impression of Sir Henry in his heyday is provided by the painting in the National Portrait Gallery.
[5] A letter from the Nuncio, Archbishop Castagna, dated 5th February, 1571, and addressed to the Cardinal of Alessandria, refers to the Duchess as ' a most Catholic and Christian lady,' and shows that the good opinion was returned. Cal. S.P. Rome, 1558–71, p. 377.
[6] Report in Cal. S.P. Foreign, 1569–71, p. 315.

THE DUCHESS OF FERIA
Antonio Moro.   From the Portrait of a Lady supposed to be
the Duchess of Feria in the Prado.

Photo · Anderson.

prelates were difficult, but with Mr. Stukeley it would be so different. All the English ladies at Zafra were most anxious for news of their country and especially Margaret Harrington, now in permanent exile from Exton, and it was now so long since the Duchess had seen her young brother and sisters, Robert, who was now growing tall, and Catherine who was soon to marry a son of Lord St. John. It was a piece of unexpected good fortune that, while it was an obvious duty and charity to help Mr. Stukeley, it was such a pleasure as well.

For six weeks the *Trinity* had lain at anchor in Vivero River without any news from the Court and matters were now getting difficult with the mutinous Irish crew who would never have agreed to embark had they not believed that it was an ordinary voyage back to England. The *alcalde* of the small port was cold and all Europe knew of the crossing, for Stukeley had burned his boats and ahead lay starvation. There was no posting road, no diversion, as he remained in the afterguard of his ship at Vivero in that lonely river, nothing save an occasional rider from the horse fair at Ortigueira and the solitary mountains. Then in June the first instalment of money, 200 ducats, arrived from the Court, but with it there were orders that Stukeley was not to remove from the harbour. Still, so long as he could hold out, this was merely a time of waiting to learn the result of a hazard, one of those casts of the loaded dice on which his life rested. Finally, on 17th August, the long-delayed messengers came with that summons to the King of Spain's Court, for which he had passed through such risks. This letter of summons with the moneys that the King now provided and the appointment of suitable quarters, with Don Francisco de Marles the King's Taster at His Majesty's charge, was the most needed gift of good fortune in Stukeley's stirring and venturesome life. For all was now smooth and the influence of the Ferias and of Don Guerau d'Espes could not fail to provide a wide series of chances for the display of that *camaraderie* in arms which had formed his chief social asset. Yet it would have proved so much simpler if the issue of religion had not been forced to the front by the needs of the time, for he was made for the comradeship of free-spoken soldiers, not priests, and now he had to learn all their words and their jargon. It has surely a claim on our sympathy, this spectacle of the honourable bandit enmeshed in religious dispute.

His Excellency Monsignor Giambattista Castagna, Archbishop of

Rossano and Apostolic Nuncio at the Court of the Catholic King, was a calm and experienced, and above all judicial, prelate. His training had been in the law schools of Bologna and as Refendary in the *Segnatura ;* he was himself the nephew of the late Cardinal of Santa Anastasia, the lawyer Jacovazzi, and behind him stretched all the weave of that tradition, administrative and legal, that ruled the Papal Court. He was forty-nine and already the future was fore-shadowed, the Cardinal's hat and the Curia and then at last the Tiara, for through his work lay implicit the marble repose of that effigy at the Minerva under the keys, and this figure of Urban VII makes it easy for us to picture Archbishop Castagna, with the great nose and the grave, bearded countenance and the calm serene manner.

For the Nuncio, this Spanish appointment had proved a most difficult post, the constant disputes over the Milanese question and Sicily and the old theories revived of the *Monarchia Sicula* and then the *exsequatur* in Naples. Besides he had been confirmed and not chosen by Pius V and at times the Pope drove his own policy, the intensive reform of the Orders and, on the other hand, the cold-ness towards the Court, when the Carranza affair was in question ; and all the time there was difficulty with Cardinal Espinosa, the Minister and the cold, polite sovereign. And then there came the Duchess of Feria's letter in favour of Stukeley. The Nuncio, although personally quite uninterested in these adventures of the sword, was favourably disposed to any advice from that quarter, and it came as a relief, too, after the inopportune and vexatious persistence of the Irish Archbishop. For there had been in Madrid during three years the exiled Archbishop of Cashel, Maurice Reagh McGibbon, a fiery and patriotic prelate with torrents of uncontrolled energy and no sources of income. It was known that he had the confidence of the Irish and of the Desmond leader, Fitzmaurice, and it was reported that in Ireland, even when an Archbishop, he had attacked his foes with a skeyne ;[1] but on the other hand, he had sent in his ardour a list of Irish supporters, which was palpably false,[2] and he had seriously irritated the Cardinal Secretary and was out of favour at Rome. Now the Archbishop was a marked opponent of Stukeley, and this was an

[1] Loftus MSS., Annals A.D., 1567.
[2] The list included, as among those prepared to support the Pope and the King of Spain, the names of the Earls of Desmond, Kildare, Ormonde, Clanrickard, Thomand and Tyrone, together with all the barons, nobles, knights, cities, towns and the whole community of Ireland.

added reason to grant him protection, and he might in fact prove a means of procuring that prelate's removal and at this stage an interesting canon law case developed.

It was the matter of Stukeley's request for an absolution from heresy and apparently also from the result of the actions of *communicatio in sacris* in which it seemed he was involved. The circumstances of the English petitioner were set forth most lucidly and he was certainly free from the status of *excommunicatus vitandus* which was regulated by the constitution *Ad evitanda*, which Pope Martin V had laid down. There were the Leonine constitutions, *Supernæ Maiestatis* and *Exsurge Domine* to be considered, but the ruling, which seemed to govern the particular case, had been formulated by Paul IV in *Cum ex Apostolatus*, ' qui quoquo modo hæresis propagationem sponte et scienter iuvat . . . suspectus de hæresi est.'[1] However, to be argued against this there were the affidavits, sworn by the petitioner, which maintained that in matters of heretical worship he had been outwardly consistent only and that the oath, which he took to the Queen, concerned his temporal allegiance alone. He admitted eating meat on the forbidden days, and that he had held the lands of an abbey, but this he was prepared to restore, and his penitent state was most clear, for all the Christian precepts and duties were very faithfully observed. After referring to the written permission, which he had received from the Holy See through the Cardinal Secretary, to absolve even cases of heresy, the Nuncio wrote that he was anxious to submit this matter to His Holiness' judgment, while pointing out that the petitioner might save considerable delay by asking for absolution from the Cardinal Inquisitor. It was an unusual and very novel question, the exact point at which *de facto* the penalties of heresy were incurred and the decision of Rome would be awaited with considerable interest. The Nuncio ' had told the poor gentleman not to despair '[2] and this was much needed advice, for, although Stukeley had told many a fantastic tale in his time, it was terrible for an upstanding freebooter that it was upon these small pitiful lies that there depended his dinner.

Except for this difficulty, Stukeley's affair at the Spanish Court went smoothly enough with the usual quota of open and avowed

[1] A doctrine embodied in this form in Canon 2316 of the Codex of Canon Law.
[2] Letter of Archbishop Castagna to Cardinal Rusticucci, dated 24th September, 1571. Cal. S.P. Foreign, 1558–71, pp. 353–4.

enemies denouncing that 'rakehell Stukeley'[1] as a desperate pirate together with the secret opponents, both belonging to categories which dogged his footsteps through life. The point of view of the Irish he could understand clearly enough, especially after two of his own mutinous crew had joined the Archbishop's supporters, for they wished for freedom, while he was a Devonshire adventurer merely using the name of their country. At the same time, even in this, his want of prudence and management in this world of *finesse* is apparent, for he decided that his conscience compelled him reluctantly to discover the Archbishop's dissolute life. This was unwise enough on the part of an excommunicate heretic, an attack on a prelate whom scandal had left quite untouched, but he followed it up by calling him a 'mere Dominican friar,'[2] which was a serious error, when both the Pope and the Cardinal Secretary belonged to that Order. But it was all so difficult, this ecclesiastical detail, and, when his mind went back to his careless boyhood at Aston, Stukeley must surely have wondered whether he had chosen aright or whether his desire for the company of men of distinction and rank had not in this instance betrayed him. For after all, his friendship with soldierly leaders like Sir Henry Sidney and the late Shane O'Neill had set him on unfamiliar courses and had brought him at length to Madrid and these perils. All the assertions that he had made that he was a son of Henry VIII and the titles that he assumed in Madrid, Earl of Wexford and Marquis of Leinster,[3] had not the value of cash[4] and he might have been wiser to have stayed in his old profession of piracy and developed the schemes he had made out in 1563 for the conquest of Florida. It had been a mistake in his judgment to return to the Queen's military service and how differently his life would have turned if he had only joined forces with Hawkins? Even that terrible disaster at San Juan de Ulloa had been of use to its victims and then there were the successes; for it was truly a matter for envy, on this hazardous inadequate pension, the thought of those cargoes as the English ships slipped through the Carib waters with fifty odd negroes *optimi generis* under their hatches. Even if he had only one little cargo, provided the physical

---

[1] Letter of Lord Morley to Lord Burghley. Cal. Salisbury MSS., ii, p. 97.
[2] Relation in Cal. S.P. Irel., 1509–73, p. 446.
[3] Letter of Lord Morley to Lord Burghley in Cal. Salisbury MSS., ii, p. 97.
[4] According to a letter from the Queen to Sir Francis Walsingham, dated 11th February, 1571, she marvelled that the King and Council should give credit to such as Stukeley, for he had not the value of a 'marmaduc' in land or livelihood. Cal. S.P. Foreign, 1569–71, p. 404.

specimens his men took were well chosen, they were worth £160 apiece, and this would have soon set him up, far away from the draughts of the ante-chambers of the Nuncio's palace and the tall Castilian footmen with their insolent eyes. It was true, of course, that he was now past his first vigour and that at forty-five one had less desire for adventure, but then there were the rewards at home in his country, and Humphrey Gilbert, who had served with Stukeley in Ireland, was to use these to advantage and so also did his young brother from Withycombe Raleigh. And instead of this honour in England he was dancing attendance in Spain, supported by money from priests and talking of a barefoot pilgrimage, while the Pope delayed reply. The great forces of politics were here so detached and remote, while on that inland shore, which Hispaniola guarded, there lay that Indian fortune, which would now elude his grasp.

An equilibrium reasonably stable was at this time maintained between the opposing forces in Spain, for Ruy Gomes with the King's favour had an unassailable power, while Alva although his influence was weakening was still very far from defeat. Vaguely the military party with Feria tended to support the great Duke, while the Gomes faction reached out, through that labyrinth of the secretaries, which the bureaucracy had called forth, towards the ecclesiastics and a general line of policy more suave and considered. All the same, there was hardly conflict between them, for however much they might deceive King Philip in detail, the ultimate decisions of State always came from the unapproachable and remote mind of the sovereign. Stukeley was accustomed in his previous career to have the accounts that he gave of himself either refused or accepted and, in these more direct eventualities, he always knew how to act, but now he was caught in a web of shifting responsibilities and written memorials and about his case the leaves of the State papers drifted. Apart from the Ferias he was alone, with the vague support of the soldiers and of the advocates of a militant policy, but on the other hand Ruy Gomes had decided with reason that the Archbishop of Cashel represented more nearly the true Irish opinion and on that account was inclined to be hostile, while ' Cardinal Siguenza and Secretary Cayas began to mislike Stukeley's evil behaviour towards the Archbishop.' [1] And then all the great churchmen, sweeping by in their courses, began to oppose

---

[1] Relation dated 2nd May, 1571. Cal. S.P. Irel., 1509–73, p. 446.

him, not because they were prepared to admit the Irish prelate even to an inferior seat at their tables, but because they sensed that with all this parade of piety the English adventurer was attacking their order. The Cardinal of Tarragona and the Archbishop of Seville, Cardinal de Zuniga Avellaneda, were united and guiding them there was the Cardinal Espinosa, Bishop of Siguenza and President of the Council of State. They were unfavourable, unhurried and calm, for there were other matters, so much more important for these statesmen than such casual adventure. Instances are provided by that negotiation through which Cardinal Espinosa was enabled to act as a strainer to sift the harassing news from the Netherlands, which was undermining the fortunes of Alva, and the financial arrangements of Ruy Gomes with their Excellencies of Medina Celi for the purchase of the aggregate of the fiefs about Pastrana to establish his Grandeeship in Castile.

At Rome all these affairs received attention, the representations of the Nuncio in Stukeley's favour, but also the complaints of his conduct from the Archbishop of Cashel, the testimony of their Eminences of Seville and Tarragona and the Lord Cardinal of Siguenza's detailed State paper. Even making allowance a serious doubt remained as to the accuracy of the submissions and the Pope Pius V, preparing for his crusade against Islam and weighed down by the burdensome charge of the safeguard of Christendom, decided on 31st October [1] that the absolution ought not to be granted. It is a strange commentary on the cross-currents of the period that it was just this adverse Papal judgment against Stukeley which tipped the balance at the Court of Spain in his favour. The question of the leadership of the relief expeditions was difficult, and Philip II saw himself as Stukeley's only protector and then the King had been angered by the trickery of Hawkins and still more by the increased help from England for the rebel ' sea beggars.' To toy with the idea of an expedition to Ireland might frighten Elizabeth and then its abandonment could be used as a lever to induce her to refrain from aiding the Low Country rebels. The Royal Council of State considered the choices before them and if an expedition was threatened Stukeley would have a value which the Archbishop lacked, and then the Pope's refusal gave him a complete

[1] Cardinal Rusticucci wrote to the Nuncio that the absolution craved by that Irish gentlemen (Stukeley) has been considered by the Pope and definitively it is decided that it ought not to be granted. Cal. S.P. Rome, 1558–71, p. 366.

dependence on Spain, while the prelates always possessed a second line of defence. It was not an important question, while Cardinal Espinosa pursued his gradual accretion and the slow intake of power, but at least it was a good thing to have it provisionally settled. The Archbishop of Cashel left for Paris and, as a gesture against England, on 22nd January, 1571, the third Sunday after Epiphany and the Eve of St. Raymond of Peñafort, His Catholic Majesty conferred the knighthood of Calatrava upon Thomas Stukeley.[1]

Now at last his hopes were revived of setting to sea and gaining plunder once more and his plans were encouraged. Santander was to be the embarkation port for this journey, and four well-equipped warships and two armed barques were demanded to transport the 3,000 foot soldiers and the 500 horsemen. With his true sanguine hopefulness Stukeley was prepared to raise these on his credit without any sums on account, and he offered to capture and burn the fleet of Aquines, his old associate Hawkins, and then to make himself master of Cork and of Waterford. Alternatively he was ready, now that Philip II was suffering from Treslong and his *Gueux de Mer*, to burn and sink all the galleons that the Queen of England kept in the Thames. Yet it must have been with foreboding that he made these courageous proposals, for he had gained experience already of the dilatory Spanish affairs. As for King Philip, he had reached the opinion that his gesture of defiance to England had been rather too definite and that it was wise to draw back, so that only a fortnight after the grant of his knighthood, Sir Thomas Stukeley, as he was always now called, received his dismissal. ' You must be satisfied,' wrote the King through Secretary Cayas,[2] ' with His Majesty's good will, for that you certainly have, and you depart much in his favour, which is the chief matter to be considered by a person of your quality ; and, as this is His Majesty's final decision and admits no reply, I have seen fit to apprise you thereof, that, having learned it, you may depart as soon as ever you please. God be gracious to you.'

Stukeley went therefore to Rome and in the feverish rush of that summer he joined the army that Don John of Austria was gathering

[1] It is, however, a mark of the inaccuracies spread about Stukeley, even in his good fortune, that the Venetian Ambassador, referring to this ceremony in his letter from Madrid of 19th February, 1571, describes him as ' an Irishman, a person of quality and exiled by the Queen.' Leonardo Donado to the Seignory, Cal. S.P. Venetian, 1558–80, p. 464.
[2] Letter of Secretary Gabriel Cayas to Sir Thomas Stukeley, dated 8th February, 1571. Cal. S.P. Rome, 1558–71, p. 385.

at Naples to attack the power of the Turks, and at the battle of Lepanto he commanded three galleys. Yet even so that was in the nature of a crusade, not well thought out and profitable warfare, and beyond the absolution from heresy it gained him nothing. The stones of Rome were now familiar and the future was empty, for 1572 held for him only a period of waiting, as he watched the wealth of the Indies percolate through that great administrative machine of the Council. If he had never left orthodox piracy, 1572 would have meant something so different, that great attack on Nombre de Dios and the Treasure of the World, the false calm in the quivering August heats in the Caribbean and from the East past Maracaibo the hurricanes approaching over the empty and treacherous waters. All those forces from which he now suffered, he could gird at in freedom, for it was on the mule trains of the Isthmus that there came the Indian gold, but Stukeley had chosen the wrong banner, and he whose sword might have conquered the World's Treasure was crushed by the golden chariot of Spain. It is the last humiliation for one who has always played the favoured prodigal to find himself with Lazarus at the gate.

The privateers sailing from England were able to retain their own freedom, unhampered by obligations ; for there was a tacit understanding as to the sources from which they would hope to gain profit. It was a system which gave every scope for initiative, severely practical and yet free. But in the Catholic South it was different and, once the hope of an immediate expedition to Ireland had vanished, it was necessary to find a protector and then to raise capital and, finally, which was a difficult matter, to fabricate a plausible plan of campaign. The hopes of Don John of Austria would seem to provide a solution and during the next four years such chances, as Stukeley might gather, depended entirely on the fortune which attended his protector's ambitions. It was no question either of any equality or of a personal friendship and Stukeley was growing old for the gaining of chances, which depended on the art of the courtier. Yet, beyond this, there was no hope, save an existence of continually decreasing prosperity as the payment of the King of Spain's pension fell more and more into arrears. Besides, for adventurers of Stukeley's position it is all important to make a good first impression to carry off the tales, which are not always quickly accepted, concerning the posts of honour sacrificed and the heavy despoiling of wealth. But, as the years went by, the impressiveness of Stukeley's position in England was inevitably bound to decrease, and then he had a misfortune, through the death of the Duke of Feria in the year of Lepanto. And even as the result of much painful effort it was not until 1575 that he succeeded in attracting the attention [1] of Don John of Austria.

It was in the autumn of that year that they met and Don John was wintering at Naples as Lieutenant-General in Italy for his brother, King Philip, with his affairs in the unquiet guidance of Juan Escobedo. He was then just thirty years old and wayward, with something of the charm of the old Hapsburgs, Maximilian I and Philip, but with the lighter frame, an inheritance from that fair stock of Bavarians whose daughter had for a moment obtained the fleeting and remorseful fancy of the middle-aged Emperor. It was this difference of bastardy which created an uneasiness in his ambition and caused those doubts of his loyalty which were natural to the cold nature of his half-brother the King. Before his mind, profoundly disheartened by the failure of his African venture and all the useless blood that was spilled at Goletta, there rose the thoughts of a marriage with the beautiful and imprisoned Queen of the Scots, and then the gaining of the throne of England and the assured royal status. And in this plan Sir Thomas Stukeley might help, an excellent soldier, who had served under him at Lepanto and had relations, almost of friendship, with the leading Orsini. Escobedo would easily manage to arrange for the meeting. It was not that the young General was at all cold in this matter, for on the contrary it was deeply bound up with his hopes, but there was all the difference of a generation between them, and he had had no experience to gain him that tolerance which life in Spain could not bring. It was a difficult matter for Stukeley, nor was he successful. For Don John was formidable in his arrogant youth as he stood, the halberdiers from Valencia around him, with his long and carefully curled hair and the short Spanish beard and the pale and lengthy moustaches he had gained from the Blombergs. The steel cuirass suggested that affectation of action, which the warm stream of the Court life in Naples was sapping, while the flung crimson scarf belied the armour, as did the embroidered gold silk and the pearls. It was difficult too for such a leader to understand poverty in a man of fashion and taste, for his credit so far had

[1] An attempt to construct an itinerary for Stukeley at this time would suggest that he left Spain for Rome before 12th February, 1575, and visited Don John at Naples shortly after 17th October.

141

no limit, and in his soundings from extravagance to extravagance he had never yet reached the rock bottom of refusal, although he had so often cast the lead. But Stukeley was fifty and careworn and almost shabby from his four years' endeavour [1] and, although it occurred to the Prince that he might be useful as a guide, he did not strike him in the light of a leader and still less as a potential friend and companion. To Stukeley it was perfectly clear that in the Prince's scheme he was worthless, and he went back to Rome, while Don John, fingering the badge of the Golden Fleece that he invariably carried, turned again to his city, to his *inamorata* and to the cavaliers riding along the new way, the Toledo, and to the diverting tricks of the lion he had tamed when in Tunis.

Nevertheless it was Sir Thomas Stukeley's persistence which at length received a reward; for the plans of Don John shifted, and then he received the Governor-Generalship of the Low Countries from Philip II and he was gradually brought to abandon all hopes of invasion. He was at that time at Marche-en-Famine, where Stukeley had followed him after many useless journeys between Rome and Madrid, and, on this breaking up of his hopes by the pressing need of the Spanish party in Belgium, Don John wrote a warm letter of recommendation [2] to Rome, which just came at the turn of the tide in his follower's favour. Now that Don John was removed, the situation was clearer and the evident unwillingness of the King of Spain to involve himself further left the field open. Since formerly there had always been some chance of a Spanish attack or at least of a semi-official 'armada' under Don John; but once these possibilities were removed it remained purely a question as to whether any pressure could be brought to bear on the Pontiff.

With the departure of Don John from the scene the plan had shifted back again to an invasion, not of England, but of Ireland, for which the various Irish prelates, whom the last two Popes had created, were clamouring. Besides, James Fitzmaurice Fitzgerald, the leader of the Irish in Munster, had been in the ports of Brittany for nearly

[1] According to a letter from Cardinal Galli to the Bishop of Padua, Nuncio in Spain, dated 24th May, 1577, 'Stukeley . . . is as full of ardour as he is destitute of funds.' Cal. S.P. Rome, 1572–8, p. 311.

[2] Letter from Don John of Austria to Pope Gregory XIII dated 17th February, 1577, five days after the signature of the Perpetual Edict, 'I entreat your Holiness ever to make especial account of Thomas Stucley, for I warrant you his good qualities merit it and will daily merit it more and more.' *Ibid.*, p. 291.

two years attempting to get together a force for a Catholic invasion and, although it might seem at first glance that these diverse forces stood in the way of Stukeley's success, they really conspired to assist him. For the English knight was a necessary link in the chain between the Italian churchmen and the less sophisticated zeal of the Irish. Even James Fitzmaurice with his devotion and courage and his almost mystical faith had not the art to convince the Roman officials that his proposition would pay. No one could equal Fitzmaurice's faith and his ardent desire for the victory of the ancestral Christian religion under its natural leaders, the great feudal lords of the Irish ; but he was, in a sense, too zealous for prudence, nor would he stir far from those ports which faced the Atlantic across which he longed to return to his country. He would not make the journey to Rome and all his energies were devoted to rallying his countrymen in the valleys of Munster, to fortifying his cousins, Sir John and Sir James of Desmond and that careful hunchback, the Earl, and to praying that God should grant the victory to his servants, so that once more the bells of the monks should ring out from their tranquil belfries at Askeaton and Monasternenagh over the length and the breadth of the Forest of Desmond. ' *In pace et tranquilitate spes nostra Jesu et Maria* ' was the heading he used for his letters and in all that he did his quiet courage is apparent, as in his words to his old friend, David Wolf, ' and I besyche youe lovinge gosope so to speak to the Pope and tell him that I am ready to perform his Holiness his will and pleasure.' [1] There was no doubt at all of his zeal, but it was suggested in Rome that Stukeley, as a leader, would have a more practical mind, and this was correct, for nothing could be more cogently and severely practical than Sir Thomas' outlook.

The situation that Stukeley discovered in Rome and which at last brought him to fortune was that created by a Pope, very aged and laborious and consumed with great zeal, well served by a careful diplomacy, but lacking in executive power. As a result of this combination the Pope was in a position where recognition and status could be more easily granted than money, but these gifts had their value, for Gregory XIII at seventy-six had a dislike for changing his ministers which ensured a stable *régime*. The Counter-Reformation was well

[1] From a letter in the Vatican Archives quoted in the Rev. M. V. Ronan's study of *The Reformation in Ireland under Elizabeth*, p. 517, a work which contains a most lucid study of Fitzmaurice's movements.

under way and was yearly gaining momentum, and the spirit was wholly progressive, but there was a weak point in the administration, and Stukeley, who during his years of waiting had become attuned to such things, grasped the chance it provided. For while James Fitzmaurice used ' his ancient gosope ' David Wolf as his agent, an old priest long past activity, who was not even greatly valued by the Jesuit General, Father Mercurian, Sir Thomas Stukeley more prudently chose the noble prince, Don Paolo Giordano Orsini, Duke of Bracciano and chief of the bandits. In order to understand this element in the situation completely it is necessary to consider the changing relations between the Pope and Orsini and also between Orsini and Stukeley.

Paolo Giordano Orsini was a puissant and magnificent lord whose expenses bore no relation to his sources of income. He was close on forty and in the last few years a change had come over his life since the early days of his gallant deeds at Lepanto and his following of St. Philip Neri, when with Colonna and the other nobles of Rome he had knelt in the public hostels to wash the feet of the poor. The sedate Marcantonio Colonna might regard this as a salutary penance, but for Orsini it was altogether too much, for he had grown up in the wide freedom of that dying Renaissance splendour in the household of his happily childless uncle, the Cardinal Sforza di Santa Fiora. The need of the sums that his brigands paid him in tribute, the failure of his marriage, stately and Medicean and barren, and the weak hold of the Papal Government had all combined to loosen his framework of values and then he was caught up in that passion for Vittoria Accoramboni, which led to disaster. Already his prestige had suffered severely, and he was unfortunate in the profound impression which was caused by the death of his wife, after supper at Cerreto Guidi, on one of the Duke's rare visits to his Tuscan villa, as a result of ' an apoplexy caused by the bathing of the head.' His reputation therefore was damaged and sinking, but to what degree this increasingly sinister fortune had forced itself on the mind of the Pontiff is exceedingly doubtful, for the Duke was placed in that moment of transition when he was no longer burdened by the Pope's affection, but was still in full enjoyment of his power. Yet every step which took him away from the company of the new holy Cardinals brought him close to his old companion in arms, the experienced Stukeley. It was at this point that the Duke made his offer to provide some of his servants for the projected journey to Ireland, to undertake the raising of 600 men in the States of the Church and to find volunteers for a galleon from among his own vassals. It is difficult not to believe that this offer was made with some knowledge of the use that the troops would be put to, but it solved a difficult problem, while the continued support, which Stukeley received both from the English faction and from Dr. Lewis, the Papal Refendary, decided the question. He had had to wait five years for his ship, while the English gained theirs at once, but at last he was a general at sea, but this was hardly the view which the Pope took of the matter.

The beginning of that auspicious journey was the climax of Stukeley's good fortune, as he rode down to Civita Vecchia with the standard that the Holy Father had blessed and the new patent which created him Marquis of Leinster. To the venerable Pope, whose expectations were apt in these years to overbear his more prudent opinions, it was a matter for happiness that all the Irishmen, who strove for the Faith, were united at last and that a praiseworthy zeal had been shown by Don Paolo Giordano of whom his officers were sometimes inclined to be unduly complaining. It was surely a reasonable hope that Providence might come to the aid of Fitzmaurice and the English knight and the bishops, once they had planted again the standard of Christ in that holy soil of Yrlanda. For a wonderfully sanguine belief in the Faith's strong and quick victory coloured the mind of the Pope, filled with the thought of the urgent need of his vigilance, *speculatorem dedi te domui Israel*. Besides, it was a good augury also, those long Advent lections with the straining words of Isaias, ' glorify ye . . . the Lord God of Israel in the isles of the sea.' He would himself go down to the port to give the benediction to these soldiers, and on 23rd January he rode out from the City on his great white charger with his long mantle white against the caparisoned red of the horse cloth [1] and the falling snow-coloured beard, serene, a Melchisedec in the valley of blessing.

The attitude of the Papal Secretary, Cardinal Galli of Como was a very different affair, for, with that shrewd and hard outlook of the Comacene peasant, he disliked these out-of-work soldiers, a dangerous element in the City, with their useless and arrogant sword play ;

[1] Michel de Montaigne, *Journal de voyage d'Italie*, i, pp. 224–30.

besides he knew the opposition,[1] and he had the reports about Stukeley and how he relaxed from piety, that essential and terrible strain. It was so different from his own life work, that hard-working zeal as the confidential servant of Antonio, Cardinal Trivulzi, then after his death the secretary's post and old Cardinal Gaddi and, when he had lost his new patron, all the start over again and the slow gaining of confidence with Gian Angelo Medici. Yet he had always striven and provided a loyal and calm service, so that even Charles Borromeo had attested his probity, and, if the chance of a conclave had made his master Pope Pius IV and he had been carried to greatness, it was clear that no man could have been more devoted, nor deserved more good fortune. As to how far Sir Thomas Stukeley deserved any good fortune he was in his own mind perfectly clear, and it was such a relief now that he had departed. The Cardinal did not feel called upon to accompany the Pope to the ceremony of granting the blessing.

In fact by what was perhaps, in consideration of the general intentions of Stukeley, a fortunate chance the Papal Blessing was never imparted, for life on a pirate ship can always be carried on fairly smoothly in the ocean, even if it is necessary to resort to *force majeure*, the difficulty lies in setting out to sea. In this case ' an uproar and mutiny had broken out among (the sailors) as they insisted on having two instalments of their pay before embarking,' [2] a very natural precaution, for those who had the courage to take service on the well-found ' galleon of the English Duke.' Besides, there was difficulty about the Bishop of Killala and the eight Irish priests and students, who had received orders to embark. This was the opportunity for them to show that apostolic spirit for which their English *confrères* were so marked, and, as far as the Cardinal Secretary was concerned, it would remove the whole group nearer to their own native country and away from all the cross-currents of the life of the City. However it is easy to understand the Irish standpoint, for these men had struggled for three years to obtain the command of their forces for the

---

[1] On 11th May, 1577, Bishop Sega, Nuncio in Spain, had written to Cardinal Galli that ' it will be well to walk warily in dealing with Stucley,' while the English Ambassador Wilson, who it must be admitted was too interested to be a witness, referred to him as ' a broken braggart and impostor.' In his reply of 1st July the Cardinal, after mentioning the King of Spain's commendation of Stukeley, refers to his own opinion. ' If he is poor and broken', he wrote, ' the reason is that he is an exile from home ; if he is a braggart the reason is that he desires to return home ; but that he has been dismissed by the Catholic King is not true.' Cal. S.P. Rome, 1571–8, pp. 305–6 and 319. It is easy to read here the Cardinal's opinion about a man whom he could not refer to more frankly because of the Papal support.

[2] Cal. S.P. Rome, 1572–8, p. 375.

THE BURIAL OF THE COUNT OF ORGAZ
El Greco. From the Church of San Tomé at Toledo.

devoted and Catholic Fitzmaurice and now they were to be handed over to the ' Marquis of Leinster,' while only an Irishman could fully grasp all that was implied in that ironical title.

And Stukeley was horribly ready to take in these passengers, for he had a fine ship, the *St. John*, and 600 armed men in his service, and he was only too anxious to accept the care of a guest who might prove a good hostage. However, he was successful in applying the pressure, and the ship set sail with the Most Illustrious Lord Marquis, as Sir Thomas now styled himself, secure at last after his efforts and the guests of honour in the stern cabin divided between anger and fear. The orders were to sail direct for Ireland with secrecy and despatch, but instead Stukeley put in first at Port 'Ercole, and then at a whole string of harbours, Palamos, Salou outside Tarragona, Alicante, Cadiz,[1] and everywhere he announced that here was a force against England. At this date we cannot decide what plans he considered as the galleon sailed through the warm spring Mediterranean weather, putting in for a week or so at the harbours and on all sides spreading the news of a voyage whose discovery could only end in his death. But it is possible that, until the more attractive Portuguese plan had fully matured, Stukeley welcomed his episcopal guest as a means to procure his own pardon. For, if he could arrange to hand over to the Queen these unarmed, but valuable, priests and one or two Papal officials, he could have set up as a privateer on his own with the fine ship that the Pope had provided. It is quite clear that this possibility was present to the agitated minds of the Irish,[2] and meanwhile Stukeley was living in the various harbours of Spain on the Pope's money and in a style befitting a gentleman. It was obvious that, if the heads of the Papal Envoys were impaled on the town gates of Waterford, Sir Thomas would reap a considerable benefit. He must, however, go ashore for another procession, for this was the holy season of Lent.

It would seem, from the reports sent in later, that it was only during his stay in these Spanish ports that he decided to embark on

---

[1] A copy of one of Stukeley's passports given at Cadiz in the ship called *Saint John Baptist* on 8th April, 1578, gives his titles as Baron of Rosse and Idrone, Viscount Murrowes and Rinshelagh, Earl of Gerfort, and Catherlonsi, Marquis of Leinster and General of Our Most Holy Father, Gregory XIII. Sidney Papers, i, p. 263.

[2] At Lisbon the Irish priests asserted ' That hated as he is in Ireland they hold it for certain that he (Stukeley) will lead them all to death.' Report of Roberto Fontana, Cal. S.P. Rome, 1572-8, Appendix, p. 567.

the Portuguese venture, but meanwhile the Papal officials were not unnaturally disturbed by so much delay and, when the rumour reached Lisbon that the Marquis was decided to call at that port, the Apostolic Collector, Monsignor Fontana put out in a frigate to remind him of the dangers of landing. But this was a subject on which the views of Stukeley and the prelate were directly opposed and, after all these arid years haunting the Chanceries, it must have been a pleasure at last to have the power to act with decision. For a situation had developed at Lisbon which seemed to open before him a lifetime of profit, since the young King had decided to go to war with the Moors, and there was all the difference between the Lord Marquis' situation with 600 men and a galleon and the misery, when surrounded by plenty, which Thomas Stukeley endured.

Dom Sebastian, the young King of Portugal, was at Belem, when Stukeley arrived, preparing the magnificent obsequies for his grandmother, Queen Catherine, who had been Regent for so many years, 'a lady of old world prudence and holiness of life (and) of venerable majesty.'[1] The political situation was curious, for there was no Nuncio to the Court, and the King's uncle of Spain was remote, while the Castilian Ambassador held aloof in his palace. For the King was ridden by dreams of an African conquest and driven onwards by a feverish energy in which perhaps the result of so many generations of inter-marriage shows forth ; since it was the energy not of strength, but of weakness, that last fever in which he was anxious to stifle the doubts of his manhood. Behind the throne, in the confined policies of the kingdom, there was the influence of his old teacher, Father Luiz Gonçalves, who supported the King in his refusal to marry and in his visions of a new Christian Africa. The late Nuncio had quarrelled with this excellent priest, and it is certainly possible that the latter made an imprudent estimate of his pupil's motives and powers ; for, as the history of St. Francis Xavier can show us, the house of Coimbra was not the most securely established in the nascent Society. On account of the views which the Nuncio had expressed, the King was not in very high favour in Rome, and the King of Spain, whose advice was neglected, disapproved of these unbalanced military schemes and of the director of revenue, Alcaçova. And to the

[1] Report sent in 1575 by Monsignor Gian Andrea Caligari then Nuncio. Cal. S.P. Rome 1572–8, p. 198.

young King isolated and full of adventure, pacing the royal cloister at Belem in his enforced mourning seclusion and waiting for the hunting to which he was so soon to return in the forests of Cintra, there came the Lord Marquis Stukeley.

To Stukeley the prospect of joining the fight with the Moors was entirely agreeable, for in the past Hawkins had run the slave trade from the Gold Coast, but here there would be whole trains of slaves to be had for the asking, and for a man of his almost crude tastes there would be few pleasures beyond the reach of a vizier in Africa. In the meantime there had of course been reverberations when the use to which he had put the money of Holy Church was apparent, and only the Bishop of Killala and his priests were contented; for by this means they were free. Amid all this excitement the Cardinal of Como was admirably judicial and in no way surprised. ' His Holiness wonders,' he wrote [1] drily to the Marquis, ' how it was that though you could go ahead without passing by Lisbon, you set yourself to lengthen 300 miles of journey in order to strike on this rock. . . . I would have you be mindful of your promise and give his Holiness no further cause for such disgust as he has now felt.' And by the same post a letter went also to the Nuncio in Madrid. ' This is God's affair,' [2] declared the Cardinal, ' and therefore we must believe that it is guided by His infallible providence and assume that all is for the best. You on your part will take care that the 20,000 crowns be not by chance recalled.' A postscript to this is provided by a letter of Stukeley's shipmaster, which was given to the Nuncio Monsignor Sega and sent on to the Cardinal. ' Captain William Cleyborne,' [3] so ran this document, ' being apprehensive of death has bidden me in his name to let you know that which, if he had been able to arrive in safety at the City, he would have let his Holiness know; to wit, that Stucley is quite unfit to be entrusted with the conduct of this or any other business; especially because, on seeing that James Geraldine was granted an equal share with himself, in the division of the 20,000 crowns, he said that he would make those by

---

[1] Letter from Cardinal Galli to the Marquis of Leinster, dated 30th May, 1578. Cal. S.P. Rome, 1572–8, p. 446.
[2] Letter from Cardinal Galli to Philip Sega, Bishop of Ripa and Nuncio at Madrid, dated the same day. *Ibid.*, p. 445.
[3] Letter from Bishop Sega to Cardinal Galli, enclosing the statement of Captain William Cleiborne, formerly master of the *St. John* in the service of the Marquis Stukeley and then on his deathbed, 8th August, 1578. *Ibid.*, p. 484.

whose authority it was done repent them of it ; that he would sell the Pontiff's arms, and with the Pontiff's soldiers betake him where he might make spoils ; that in fine he would give the Pontiff's chair, or the Pontiff thereon, a rude shaking. Nor could Cleyborne ever discover that Stucley had a mind to contemplate going to Ireland.' Perhaps the detail is prejudiced and inaccurate, for Cleiborne was not without his enemies, but the conclusion is unmistakably sound.

On 26th June Stukeley sailed with the King for Africa and after weeks in the camps outside Arzila the forces were engaged at Alcacer-quibir. It was in the morning of 4th August, the feast of St. Dominic, and by mid-day, after the fierce fighting, Dom Sebastian and his ally, Mahomed XI, as well as his enemy, Abd-el-melek, were all slain in this battle of the kings, the Bishop of Coimbra also and the Lord Marquis Stukeley. The last weeks of the adventurer's life were assuredly the most pleasant, after all the years of his suffering, for he was immersed until the moment of the battle in the dreams of these very concrete favours, the dancing boys and the Circassians, the train of ivory and the gold. And considering this, it is remarkable how much of the religious life of the time is revealed in the stormy change of a career, which could hardly have proved more remote from religion. The Cardinal accepted the intimation of this fresh disaster with the same unaltered calm. ' As to Marquis Stucley's effects,' he wrote[1] to Monsignor Fontana, ' you, in concert with the Commissary San Joseffi, will be at pains to make the best possible profit of them, and thereby pay, in the first place, the debts incurred by him to the Reverend Chamber ; and, if there should be aught to spare, it may be given to the other creditors, or the heirs. You will also keep an eye on the said Joseffi, so as to safeguard for the benefit of the Reverend Chamber all that is in hand, whether money, or arms, or munitions, or victuals.' Few statements can better express, so serenely and completely, how little an adventurer can achieve.

[1] Letter from Cardinal Galli to Monsignor Fontana, Apostolic Collector at Lisbon, dated 27th October, 1578. Cal. S.P. Rome, 1572–8, p. 520.

CHAPTER IX

THE CHARACTER OF DESMOND

The following chapter links up the policies of the Celtic exiles abroad with the actual situation in Ireland. Before 1588 the relations of Spanish agents were chiefly concerned with the great lords in Munster, while the affairs of the Pale were considered as matters of secondary interest. The key to the situation lay in the position and character of Gerald, Earl of Desmond, who ruled as the chief of the Geraldines from 1558 until 1583. During this period the power of the Fitzgeralds was completely destroyed, the balance of power in the South was disturbed and the Butlers of Ormonde were left without an equal or a rival in Munster. At the same time the direct military rule from Dublin was enforced, there was a great re-distribution of land and the foundations of the Ascendancy system were laid down securely. It was the rebellion and the consequent destruction of Desmond which alone made these social changes possible. The position of the chief had also a greater importance from the custom of primogeniture, which in Ireland was but half-understood and which the possession of an ancient earldom involved. The combination of two diverse elements in the Geraldine organization, a chief in some degree Anglicized depending on a body of supporters wholly Gaelic in feeling and tone, tended both to the essential weakness and the apparent prestige of the head of the family ; while the curious personal character of the last free Earl of Desmond notably enhanced this remoteness. The physical weakness from which he suffered, for he was almost a cripple, the absence of religious feeling, since partly through his education he could never take this matter seriously, and the deep-seated and intricate family feuds raised barriers between the Earl and his natural supporters. On the other hand his lack of a systematic education, in contrast to his stepson, Ormonde, and the consequently transparent character of his guile, made him an unacceptable companion to the English lords. Under these circumstances the distrust of the Government and the Queen towards him became habitual, while a certain fear of his own wild swordsmen, his gallowglasses, was never absent. Besides, he had to contend with that bitter enmity which any Desmond would provoke in the hereditary rivals, the Ormonde connection and the McCarthys, and in the new menace of the settlers. A jealousy, easily aroused, is perceptible in all his dealings with Fitzmaurice.

For these reasons it is not difficult to disentangle his line of policy which in the last free Earl of Desmond has such importance. The details of the little Spanish and Papal forces, the Smerwick expedition for instance, have beside this a trivial significance. Two men alone seem to have influenced him, his cousin Fitzmaurice by repulsion, and Dr. Nicholas Sanders, whose persuasions in an unfortunate hour sealed his fate. The power which the Earl lost was never recovered and neither the Sugane Earl, nor the Kinsale expedition produced a serious effect. Both on account of its intrinsic importance and viewed as an introduction to the political situation in Ireland, from a remote and unusual standpoint, the destruction of the Desmonds and the irremediable loss of their power will illustrate the first direct collapse of a complex Celtic organism when faced with the new national State.

THE CELTIC PEOPLES & RENAISSANCE EUROPE

In regard to sources, the State Papers and similar documentary collections can be assessed by the same standards used in dealing with similar evidence relating to England and Wales. When the Annals of Loch Cé, Ulster and the Four Masters are in question, the passages are cited for the purpose of testing the reaction of different sections of Irish opinion to public events. In order to avoid the suggestions of anachronism, which linguistic purity would convey, the Elizabethan spelling of Gaelic names is in most cases retained in the form in which it appears in the State Papers and Annals.

THERE are so many ways of approach along which the situation in Ireland under Elizabeth can be envisaged. Considering only the ancient forces in that country, the native septs and those families which had adopted a Gaelic fashion of life, there were three main lines of external reaction and contact. These were the attitude of the Papacy, and in this matter the life of Archbishop Creagh throws into relief each degree of ecclesiastical contact, the opinion in Spain, which can best be viewed in the light of the effect which James Fitzmaurice produced when he emerged as a political factor, and lastly the judgement of England, which the disturbed career of the last Earl of Desmond reflects. The three angles of vision imply sharply contrasted variations of outlook and desire, the theological aspect at Rome, the wide Spanish policies and the political aim of the English, economic and firm.

The whole of Munster beyond the Butler lands was influenced either mediately or directly by the Geraldine rule. It was therefore a matter of the gravest importance, in a country where the high lords ruled so strongly, that the English governors should understand Desmond. On the other hand, if the Earl were to succeed in preserving his power it was essential that his appreciations of current events should prove just. In this case it was exactly the failure of this personal element which led to disaster; but some understanding of that confused Geraldine background, with its shifting and vehement forms, is needed to grasp the idea of the pressure against which Desmond lived and of those flaws which led to his ruin.

The decline of the Geraldine influence may be considered to date from the death of the fourteenth Earl of Desmond. The summer of 1558 had found this Earl already ailing,[1] wearied by his early years of

---

[1] Letter of Lord Deputy Sussex to Secretary Boxall, dated from Leighton 4th August, 1558, ' the Earl of Desmond not dead, but past recovery.' Cal. S.P. Irel., 1509–73, p. 148.

struggle and by the maintenance of a strict and ordered law. The Lord Treasurership, which he had held with one break for sixteen years, and the carrying out of the administrative tasks of Southern Ireland had taxed his strength, already worn by that unremitting vigilance which was needed to maintain, for such a period, the burden of this uneasy peace. The murder of his predecessor at Leucansgail, on the Friday of Passion Week in 1540, had closed for the time the vendetta which had divided the Geraldines throughout his childhood. Private war and a vivid personal religion, murder and long ascetic expiation, had been a part of his close familiar life. Earl Maurice of the Chariot, warlike and lame, had held the reins of the administration lightly and deep private feuds had flourished; while the young James had often been taken as a boy to Tralee, to the house of the Friars Preachers, so that he might reverence his grandfather the Knight of Desmond, that holy firebrand, who now gave himself to prayer. A deep connection, which ran through all the Irish history of the time, united the two aspects in the life story of this powerful and venerable man; the Dominican John of Desmond, ancient and hardy, with his stumblings at Latin in choir and his quick, rude singing, and the young Knight who had sown the seeds of all the turmoil by his fratricide, that angry murder of Earl James FitzThomas in the winter of fifty years before. So much of Geraldine history is contained in these two episodes of Sir John, the heavy rosary swinging lustily as the old Friar tramped with vigour through his serfs, and that earlier scene at Courtmatrix, when the attendants had fled and the Earl's body lay bleeding on the fresh-strewn reeds on the flooring, alone in the great hall with the Earl's brother.

For sixteen years the strained quietude had lasted; but nothing could be more certain than that the Desmond volcano would soon heave again. Nor had this Earl been prudent in his marriages, that careless system of partly complete and undissolved alliance which was to bring to Ireland so many ills. His present Countess, by birth a McCarthy of Clancare, was his fourth wife, while each predecessor had been a lady of indisputable, nay distinguished, rank. At the same time a canonical flaw, consanguinity, had been found in his first marriage,[1] with a daughter of Viscount Fermoy, and the children of that

---

[1] By a curious error Joan Roche, this wife of his youth, is described as Desmond's great-niece both by the *D.N.B.* and *Complete Peerage*, where she is stated to have been a daughter of Maurice, sixth Lord Fermoy, whose own marriage with Eleanor Fitzgerald only took place

bed declared incapable of succeeding. A fruitful occasion of discord was thus provided within his own family between the three opposing series of children, Thomas the Red, his eldest, disinherited son, Gerald, the child that his second wife had borne to him and the small boys of his latest marriage, all of whom would grow up into conflict. To complete this intimate group, there remained in the background the Earl's brother, Sir Maurice of the Burnings, a capable and most resolute man, who had successfully arranged the destruction of his cousin, the previous head of the family. As the Earl's illness progressed, it is not surprising that the whole fabric of Desmond power became weakened. The last years had brought him honour, the confidence of Queen Mary, the professed friendship of Lord Sussex. The long minority into which the neighbouring earldom of Ormonde had fallen helped him, and when his strength at last gave out, as he lay with the Franciscans around him in his castle at Askeaton, he left his country peaceful. It was the autumn that Queen Mary died and the Earl's burial took place with great magnificence on the Feast of All Saints in his own monastic church, where on the next day, the Commemoration of All Souls, the Friars sang High Mass of Requiem for their founders as the law, which was still in force, prescribed. It was the last year that they could offer to God this public and official intercession, nor were any of the succeeding Earls of Desmond to have the fortune to die thus in peace. ' The Earl of Desmond . . . died,' [1] begins the Annalist's entry for 1558. ' The loss of this good man was woful to his country, for there was no need to watch cattle or close doors from Duncaoin (Dunquin) in Kerry to the green bordered meeting of the three waters.[2] And his son Garrett was installed in his place.'

Gerald Fitzgerald, who now became fifteenth Earl of Desmond, was to manage his power in Munster for a precarious twenty-five years. It was a difficult and troubled inheritance, and he lived to destroy it completely. In this complicated series of changes and shifts,

after 1590. She appears, in fact, to have been a daughter of Maurice, fourth Lord Fermoy and consequently a cousin of Desmond. A letter from Robert Remon, Augustinian Prior of St. Katherine's without the Walls at Waterford, to the fourteenth Earl of Desmond, written in London on 24th March, 1558, illustrates the care which the latter took over some matrimonial affairs. The Prior wrote that he was about to go to Cardinal Caraffa, Legate in Flanders or Brabant, for a dispensation for Desmond's daughter, Onoria, and McCarthy Mor. Cardinal Pole, he asserted, did not possess the necessary powers. Cal. S.P. Irel., 1509–73, p. 143.
[1] Annals of the Four Masters, 1558, p. 1561.
[2] The meeting of the Suir and Nore below Waterford.

which ended in an utter disaster, the key may be sought in the character of the young Desmond chief. As the brief description of the background has suggested, the characteristics of the Fitzgeralds of Desmond, which remain most fixed in the memory, were a fierceness in action, almost barbaric, and a strongly marked vein of religious devotion, both qualities in which the young Earl was lacking. A physical weakness and a certain state of ill health, whose nature is not clearly defined, made him almost a cripple,[1] and this gave a very real insecurity in the midst of his clan and bred in him a jealousy and fear of his neighbours. Had he been the mere petty chief of some little sept up in the North, it is probable that he would not have ruled long; but the great Desmond Earldom, securely established since the first days of Edward III, bound his clansmen uneasily to a system of half-understood primogeniture. This was sufficient to retain him the headship, but it was no guarantee that an invalid could exercise it in peace. Yet, if Desmond was crippled, he could still be devoted and saintly and would on that title receive an allegiance as the holy lord of the South; yet here again the jealousy and distrust, to which he gave way so easily, had eaten into his nature and these alone would have turned those springs bitter from which his life of devotion must flow. He was thus completely remote from all those living around him and he took that remedy which lay nearest at hand, a refuge in craft and in guile. Isolated and utterly friendless, deception, that too soft pleasure, entranced him. But here again, he had lost his great opportunity, for, although this political craft was the talisman of the age, he lacked the education to use it. Twice he had been offered, and his father had been pressed to accept for him, an education in England, first under Henry VIII and then by Protector Somerset, who wished [2] to make him a companion for the young King Edward VI. However, his father refused, hardly on account of his Faith, for the occulting light of the old Earl's religion was in shadow at these particular times, but from his fear that his power would be broken,

---

[1] His thigh had been broken by a pistol shot fired by his stepson, Sir Edmund Butler, at the battle of Affane in 1565, but the consequent injuries do not account for the innumerable references to his physical weakness. Lord Deputy Sidney declared ten years later that the Earl could hardly ride and 'had to be holpen to his horse,' while it was reported in 1579 that 'Desmond hath a great palsy and is very sore benumbed, but his tongue is not out.' Cf. Cal. S.P. Irel., Cal. Carew MSS. and Sidney Papers, passim.

[2] Letter written in the King's name to the Earl of Desmond on 24th October, 1547, with the offer 'to have your eldest son to attend here upon us and to be brought up in our company.' Cal. S.P. Irel., 1509–73, p. 78.

if he gave up his heir to the King. Could he have foreseen the manhood of that son it is not likely that he would still have thwarted his solitary chance to reach fortune.

All through his life there is apparent that lack of experience of the contemporary and alien culture of England, which the Franciscans, whom his father maintained had no power to impart, as they taught him in the summer at Askeaton in the shade beneath the trees. If he had been taken to Court, he would also have developed more gracefully that sense of religious 'indifference' after which he ineffectually yearned; yet it was his strange destiny that one who so wished for the shallows of a mere religious observance should have been forced out into the deeps of a vehement Christian endeavour, those strong tideways of the spirit in which James Fitzmaurice moved. And perhaps the limits of his unhappiness were reached when, at last fully caught in the toils, he rode drenched and sad through his mountains with the cry of ' Papa Abu.' But, instead of the English Court, there had come his marriage, when he was not yet out of boyhood, with his cousin the Countess of Ormonde, that mature and strong-minded wife. The settlement of various claims on the Fitzgerald inheritance of Lady Ormonde's branch of the family had dictated such an alliance; but it was singularly imprudent if the so necessary increase of Desmond's personal prestige is considered. The seven turbulent stepsons, the wife older than his own mother,[1] the inevitably barren marriage, were all factors tending to concentrate the public mind on his weakness. It is true that he survived his wife, for this he could hardly avoid, and that he married again and had children; yet the blight had lain on his prospects during fifteen formative years. These were the years when he should have been mastering the manners and ways of the Court, as his stepson, Ormonde, was doing;[2] for, when he came to London at last as a kind of semi-state prisoner, his chance lay behind him. During his years in England, from 1570 till 1573, living for the most part at Southwark with Sir Warham St. Leger, Desmond made no impression. He was incurably monogamous, his manner was supple and obedient, he could write a fair, round hand. He had,

---

[1] According to a letter from Walter Cowley to Thomas Cromwell, dated 21st December, 1531, 'Lord Butler married to the heiress of Desmond.' Cal. S.P. Irel., 1509–73, p. 8. Her future husband was not yet born.

[2] His stepson's precedence as Treasurer of Ireland as early as 2nd August, 1559, was especially galling. Cal. Patent Rolls, Ireland, p. 433.

in fact, politically speaking, all the virtues ; but the graces were lacking and it was with these alone that he could win the Queen. It was a desperate misfortune to lack that bluster and presence by which Shane O'Neill was able to carry off a brief visit. Compared to the truculence of the North, Desmond cut a sad figure, guileful and weak and fairly illiterate and, as far as the Queen was concerned, he did not make a conquest.[1]

He failed in London and Kerry and also in Dublin, while the situation became still more bitter through the favour that the soldiers from England would show to his brother. The Lords President would like a great huntsman, whatever his political views, and Desmond saw Perrott, for instance, favouring his brother, Sir John, but no despatch came from England to suggest that the Earl should be won.[2] As the chief of Desmond his power was elaborate and there was always much administrative work to be gone through ; but in circumstances so primitive that only rude physical health could sustain it with pleasure. The taking and granting [3] of refections, the duties owed by the Knight of the Valley, the customs paid by him in meat and drink, the ' bloodsheds ' reserved to the Earl's uses, the dues of a half-marshal by inheritance, the profits from the courts of liberties and the payments from the baron royal's courts, these matters grated harshly on his ear, as the stewards and captains made return to him while their soiled fingers drummed on the rough scabbards.

The provision by the rhymers' lands of candlelight seemed a custom so remote from the ordered calm that he desired ; for how could a Prince rule with prudence when the necessities of his household depended upon the veiledly insolent loyalty of the moody and wavering bards. Yet this was one example from many ; for all his life he was forced to preserve the reign of this undisturbed custom, as his rents came in to him slowly, cumbrous and primitive. A strong light is thus thrown on the amenities of life in Desmond by an account of the duties that the clansmen owed to their chief. At Kilmallock,

[1] A letter from the Queen to Ormonde, dated 22nd April, 1575, contains a phrase typical of her mistrust. ' We pray you still to have an eye to the behaviour of the Earl of Desmond, who cannot be thought altogether ignorant of . . . councils and designs.' Cal. Carew MSS., 1575–88, p. 13.
[2] Instead the Queen declared in a letter written to Lord Deputy Sidney on July, 1574, that she misliked the slender dealing with Desmond and also Desmond's rude and barbarous answers. Cal. S.P. Irel., 1574–85, p. 35.
[3] These and the subsequent details appear in a schedule of Desmond's lands under the date 1572. Cal. Carew MSS., 1558–74, pp. 414–8.

for instance, he would have the right of hospitality from the chief magistrate, known by the old-fashioned title of sovereign of the town, and would receive the stores prepared against his coming, the bread, ale and *aqua vitæ* and the candles, the household utensils and the bedding, the fixed and unchanging dues which they owed him. These symbols had done service for years, the objects, ancient and musty, and the bedding of honour brought down from the loft, where it was preserved from the damp for an honourable visitor. Around the Earl, in contrast to the rough frieze of the portreeve, there would stand the military officers, seneschal, constable, vice-constable and marshal, with behind them the captain of the gallowglasses, contemptuous, impatient, made for war.

Yet, if Desmond had not the leadership that his nobles desired, he was still more remote from the other classes in Ireland. He had no ties of blood with the North, nor with the lords of the Pale, and his marriages only brought him in contact with the, now hostile, Butlers. His second wife, Eleanor Butler, a daughter of the careful old Lord Dunboyne by Desmond's cousin, Cecilia McCarthy, was still a mere child and brought no powerful assistance;[1] while his own sisters were married to the local chiefs in the South, McCarthy More and Fitzmaurice of Kerry. Besides, the feuds with the Butlers of Ormonde, which began in 1565, made any journey to Dublin most dangerous and, however much he might desire it, Desmond had not the address to convince the Deputies that he was loyal. Still, if he could hardly leave Munster, at home he was beset by his rivals; not only his elder half-brother, Sir Thomas, whom he displaced[2] with comparative ease, but also by the Knights of Desmond, Sir John and Sir James, with their mutterings, and by the Captain of Desmond, his cousin Fitzmaurice.

It was only to be expected that Sir Maurice (a totane) of the Burnings should transmit to his son the position of the thorn of the Desmonds. There was no question of the latter intriguing[3] for a

---

[1] Certain 'English' sympathies were discernible in this second wife, and a desire to keep on good terms with the Deputies. In the Sidney Household Inventory there appears 'a casting bottle which my Lady Desmond gave your Lordship (Sir H. Sidney) for a New Year's gift.' Cal. de Lisle and Dudley MSS., i, p. 276.

[2] Letter of Henry Ackworth to Burghley, dated from Waterford on 20th May, 1574, 'Desmond has imprisoned Sir Thomas of Desmond's lady and banished him.' Cal. S.P. Irel., 1509–73, p. 24.

[3] The testimony that Fitzmaurice never claimed the Earldom of Desmond is clear. In the Papal documents he is referred to as James Fitzgerald or James Geraldine. Cal. S.P. Rome, 1572–8, *passim*. He occasionally used the style James Geraldine Desmond. On the other hand abroad this was much misunderstood.

place of supremacy; but he carried away the clansmen on a wave of increasing enthusiasm for his martial spirit and glory; for James Fitzmaurice Fitzgerald possessed all those qualities in which the head of the family was lacking. However this disinterested endeavour and the pure flame of religion in time induced Fitzmaurice to go to seek aid from abroad, an action which came to Desmond as an unexpected relief. For long he had attempted to counter his cousin's hot-headed zeal[1] by circuitous movements of caution,[2] but now he could show himself, for once, sincere and consistent : even the Queen of England herself was not more anxious than he, that Fitzmaurice, once safely removed out of Ireland, should remain overseas.

The mere elimination of a possible rival was hardly sufficient to secure Desmond's peace; but the nearest approach to contentment he was destined to know, in a life both isolated and troubled, came to him in those years, from 1575 till 1579, during which his cousin Fitzmaurice was absent. Even then he had to contend with his turbulent brothers and a comparative absence of strong opposition was no substitute for support. It is essential at this point to envisage the Earl's position in regard to the rest of the Geraldines, for this alone gives the key to so much of the subsequent action.

The first in official rank among these embarrassing kinsmen, the next heir after the Earl's child, Lord Garret,[3] and the obvious guardian of the Earldom, was Desmond's brother of the full blood, Sir John Fitzgerald; a man whose position as the senior male agnate would, in the event of the Earl's death or imprisonment, entitle him to a rank, which the old Scottish title of that period so well expresses, like the Tutor of Rothes or the Tutor of Mar. The Earl's upbringing as the eldest son had done something to separate him from this vehement and irresponsible brother, a separation which his half-crippled condition made wider. To Desmond it was clear that in his brother there was concentrated all that hot-blooded inheritance of their

[1] This is instanced in a letter sent by Fitzmaurice on 12th July, 1569, from Martynstown to the Mayor and Corporation of Cork requiring them 'to aboolissh oute of that cittie that old heresy newely raised and invented, and namely Barnaby Daaly and therin that be Hugnettes, boothe men and women.' Cal. S.P. Irel., 1509–73, p. 413.

[2] In contrast to Fitzmaurice's action is Desmond's prudence as shown in his declaration of 28th June, 1562. 'I do firmly vow and promise,' he wrote to the Queen, 'that I will, to the uttermost of my power aid and assist the Bishop . . . to cause the honour and divine service of Almighty God to be maintained . . . in all churches in the realm of Ireland . . . as is and shall be ordered by the laws, statutes, and orders of the realm of Ireland.' State Papers, Eliz. Irel., vi, 30. Yet. he was not trusted.

[3] He was at this time (1579) a child of eight and inclined to be sickly.

mother, an O'Carroll of Ely, that pure Gaelic strain which had some-how passed the Earl by; and their attitude to this O'Carroll grand-father is typical: to Sir John he was the Lord 'Maelruanaidh the noblest, the most illustrious of the Gaels of Leth Modho and the most destructive to the Foreigner,'[1] but to the Earl, regarding only his inferior possessions, he remained simply old Sir Maolrony. And then there were his brother's fierce ridings, while he had to be helped to the saddle, and it was clear that the younger man was the hero of the Geraldine gallowglasses, as he rode out a-coshering; for he was surely ' the best Earl's son for bounty, nobility and dignity that ever came out of the Geraldines, though he had no inheritance but his own energy.'[2] To a mind like the Earl's this atmosphere roused suspicion, and it would seem that he was not only uneasy, but also always a little afraid and that it was chiefly the driving force of his jealousy which contrived to conquer his fear. Nevertheless, in spite of their constant 'jars,'[3] these misgivings would appear to have been quite unfounded: besides, when he acted apart from his brother, Sir John as a younger son could obtain very little support.[4] On the whole, Desmond's calculations could in this matter bring him relief.

The question of the next brother, Sir James of the Musters, was rather more complex, for, while on the one hand he had a potential hostility to the head of the family, his whole manner and outlook was less Gaelic, as his examinations when a prisoner show. He had been the youngest son of Earl James by his late fourth marriage and was separated by twenty years from the Earl, his half-brother. Lord Sussex had been his godfather[5] and he had been brought up in Eliza-bethan Ireland; hence the difference between his religion and that of

---

[1] Annals of Loch Cé, 1532, p. 278.
[2] Ibid., 1581, p. 446.
[3] Letter of Sir William Drury to Lord Burghley, dated 6th January, 1579, from the Fort of Philipstown, ' Jar between Sir John and the Earl.' Cal. S.P. Irel., 1574–85, p. 154.
[4] A letter from Lord Deputy Fitzwilliam to the Privy Council, dated 23rd November, 1574, refers to the Queen's warrant for an estate to Sir John of Desmond of £100 yearly, Ibid., p. 44. This is the more significant in view of his small inheritance. The Queen might show favour to any Geraldine except Desmond.
[5] The report of Sussex's journey, dated 25th July, 1558, gives an impression of the last period of official Catholicism. ' Sunday the 26th June in the afternoone at the Bishop's house in Limerick was bishoped James, the son of the Earl of Desmond. The Lord Deputy being Godfather called the child James Sussex of Desmond. On Sunday the 10th July, after the High Mass in the great church of Limerick, the Earl of Thomond and all the freeholders of the county were sworn upon the Holy Sacrament with all the relics of the Church, as bell, book and candle light.' Carew MSS., vol. 621, f. 20.

his brother, Sir John of Desmond, the elder being fervently, but the younger more intermittently, Catholic. In general he followed Sir John, so that Desmond was forced to negotiate through his elder brother when the loyalty of both was in question. Moreover, there had been one serious quarrel lasting two years between Desmond and Sir James; for the Earl had been unable to resist the temptation to deprive him by chicanery of the inheritance, which his father had left him. At this juncture Sir James of Desmond had successfully relied on the English [1] and the matter was patched up at last, [2] and he received his disputed castle, the Fort of the Three Enemies, significant name. Another element of some importance remained. Sir James' mother had been Eveleen McCarthy, and he was thus a nephew of Desmond's inveterate rival, the Earl of Clancare. A change of the tide might have made him a candidate for the headship, especially as Sir John was still childless, and the uncertain McCarthy powers to the southward, always prone to hostility, might rally to make him the head of the Geraldines for the sake of their kinship. Yet in this case also Desmond had the satisfaction of remembering that the appanage, which Sir James had at last wrung from him, was a quite insufficient base for attack.

Still there was one direction in which success was complete and the Earl could pride himself on the skill with which he had managed the affairs of his elder half-brother, and he was right to regard him now as a negligible political factor. For Desmond could well understand that there was a degree of friendship with Government which would be bound to destroy all influence over his own most difficult men. Sir Thomas of Desmond had over-passed this limit in his subservience as a Queen's man, while the impossibility of ever regaining his vanished local prestige made the Government unwilling to use such a valueless tool. This was not the only occasion in Irish history when the Government, seeking to buy patriots, refused to make offers to those whose fallen credit with their countrymen made them hardly worth the trouble of purchase.

Beyond the Earl's brothers the wide Desmond kinship stood ranged, headed by the Seneschal of Imokilly, John FitzEdmund

---

[1] Letter of the Queen to the Lord Deputy, dated June, 1575, from the manor of Hatfield, instructing him to put Sir James Fitzgerald in possession of the land given him by his father and now withheld by the Earl of Desmond. Cal. S.P. Irel., 1574–85, p. 71.

[2] Letter of Sir William Drury to the Privy Council, dated 24th April, 1577, 'Sir James of Desmond reconciled with the Earl and takes meat in Dowalla with a large force.' *Ibid.*, p. 113.

FitzGerald.[1] Here again Desmond could consider with reason that he had managed to counter an enmity. It was true that the recent quarrel, caused by complaints of the Earl's excessive coshering,[2] still rankled in the childlike and proud mind of the Seneschal, and that he had become sworn man to his brother-in-law, James Fitzmaurice; but mercifully this defender was absent. The same confidence could apply to the White Knight's position, a man more conciliatory perhaps, with a considerable stake in the country and recently seized of his mother's lands [3] through her death. He also had followed Fitzmaurice and indeed had once been to France with him, rather in the capacity of young companion and page, than as friend, and he, too, remained quiet now that Fitzmaurice stayed out of the country. As a convenient foil in the background there appeared the ageing figure of Sir John FitzEdmund of Cloyne, astute and always ready to trim his sails for the light airs from Dublin.[4] During the ordered peace of four years, Desmond for once knew good fortune.[5]

The only permanent trouble arose from James Fitzmaurice, a man whom it was not in the Earl's nature to understand more than partially. That consuming desire for the victory of Religion and for his free nation was most unsympathetic to Desmond, in so far as he could apprehend it at all. He could, however, benefit from this unworldliness and from the peace-bringing conviction that Fitzmaurice would never equip an expedition from Spain with success. Meanwhile his inborn subtlety, acting through a temperament inexperienced and supple, induced him to send encouraging letters, if only to keep control of Fitzmaurice's friends in his country; but his suspicions were always increasing. Granted that Fitzmaurice professed to be loyal, might Desmond's power not go down in a national rising? This would not be permanently successful, for Desmond knew enough of

[1] A triple tie bound the Seneschal to the parties to this internal Geraldine conflict. (I) He was a cousin in the male line to the Earl. (II) Through his mother Shiela O'Carroll he was a first cousin to the Earl and Sir John of Desmond and a nephew by marriage of Earl James. (III) He had married James Fitzmaurice's sister. The last tie was the strongest.
[2] The cognate rights of quartering men and obtaining supplies which the notion of ' coshering ' upon the lands of dependants implied were obviously a fruitful source of dispute between a chief and his followers.
[3] Cal. Fiants, Elizabeth, No. 3583.
[4] Letter of Sir George Bourchier to the Lord Deputy, dated Kilmallock 23rd December, 1573. ' The Earl of Desmond would do great mischief, but for the Countess and John Fitz-Edmond's continual crying to him.' Cal. S.P. Irel., 1509–73, p. 534.
[5] The document relating to the Countess of Desmond printed in the Appendix to this volume contains an eloquent tribute to the concord of the Earl's domestic life. It also throws a new light on his physical state.

the resources of England and Ireland to understand that point clearly, but the rising might last long enough to destroy him. On any English basis of law Fitzmaurice could never inherit; yet he had an undeniable claim in a Gaelic uprising. The very absence of primogeniture would be a revival of the old custom, as against the rigid English procedure, and then he had been recognized in 1567 as Captain of Desmond, almost as 'Tanist' perhaps; no man could claim that he had not his share of high blood, with his father, Sir Maurice of the Burnings himself 'Mac an Iarlas.'[1] Meanwhile, he was still overseas and Munster was peaceful, while the death of Stukeley would seem a good omen and Fitzmaurice's first attempt at an expedition had failed, and he had, in fact, suffered repeated disaster. It seemed really improbable that he would ever return to disturb the Earl in his country.[2]

At this point it is necessary to consider more closely James Fitzmaurice's purpose, the motives which led to his action and the separation between his ideas and those within which the Earl could range freely. As a constructive statesman Fitzmaurice was entirely lacking in the power to visualize the new conditions in Ireland, and, as far as government was concerned, he followed the old traditional ideas of his country. In this Desmond could clearly perceive the weakness which he shared with the rest of his kindred. It was in the sphere of religion that miscalculation arose; for, if Fitzmaurice retained mediæval political theories, he also possessed a religious faith, deep and unclouded. And here Desmond's essential weakness betrayed him; for he was no more naturally religious than Ormonde, and this lack led them both into errors of judgement. Still, while Ormonde with the equipment of sixteenth-century England had thus gained the power to ride the whirlwind, Desmond hesitated between the cen-

---

[1] The title 'Mac an Iarlas' gives an instance of how deeply the Gaelic mind had been impressed by the Saxon dignity of the Earl.

[2] On account of the confusing custom of using the father's name as well as, and sometimes in place of, the Fitzgerald, it would be well to resume the list of the leading Geraldine characters. James, Earl of Desmond left four sons; by his first doubtful union with Joan Roche, Sir Thomas of Desmond, by his second wife, More O'Carroll, Gerald, Earl of Desmond from 1558–83, and Sir John of Desmond, and by his fourth wife, Eveleen McCarthy, Sir James of Desmond. He also left two nephews, James Fitzmaurice Fitzgerald and John FitzEdmund Fitzgerald, who were known as James Fitzmaurice and the Seneschal of Imokilly respectively. There were also two cousins, Edmund FitzJohn FitzGibbon, known as the White Knight and Sir John FitzEdmund Fitzgerald, who usually appears as Sir John FitzEdmund of Cloyne. To be distinguished from these are the three Fitzmaurices of Kerry, who descended eventually from the same male line, Thomas Fitzmaurice, Lord Kerry and Lixnaw, generally referred to as the MacMaurice or the Baron of Lixnaw, and his two sons, Patrickeen and Edmund FitzThomas.

M 2

turies, deprived of intuitive sympathy, lacking acquired knowledge and hesitating thus his cause was lost.

A contrast between Desmond and Fitzmaurice can alone explain the barrier between them. The latter had been waiting four years in the Continental ports towards Ireland to fit out his expedition, and time and again he had suffered misfortune, while his sense of chivalry, almost mediæval, had proved a hindrance in practical matters. To a lord of his rank those details of seamanship, in which Stukeley had proved himself adept, seemed hardly his province, as was seen in that first disaster when he came out from Mass on the Feast of Epiphany to find that his crew had mutinied and that the ship, his only possession, was even now moving down the fairway and standing out, with his loyal men turned pirate, for some more prosperous and less empty sea. And in 1579 he was still in Galicia. Below him in the harbour at Corunna, beyond the red tiles of the fishing quarter, Pescaderia, he could make out the mastheads of a new vessel of whose eventual purchase he felt sure. Meanwhile he must not forget his prayer; since without the aid of God's mercy how could he hope to bring back the Faith to his people ? He had knelt for so long before these Tabernacles by the waterside, which the drawn-out delays had made familiar; Nuestra Señora de la Angustia at Ferrol, and the weathered parish church at Ribadeo with the ship models hanging in the chapels, a mark of the gratitude of sailors protected by Our Lady of the Sea. And as he came from his Mass at Corunna in the old churches of the Ciudad Alta, from Santa Maria del Campo or Santa Barbara, it seemed so short a journey to his country. The ruined Tower of Hercules on the promontory beyond the City was the last link with that Ireland, which it faced; for it had surely been built by the good King Breoghan[1] and he had heard many tales concerning it, as he had sat on the ground before the peat fires, while the bards would discourse on noble themes, such as befitted Sir Maurice ' a Totane,' in Desmond in the long wet winters. Then, again and again, the messengers came from the Court with letters to show that his negotiations ran crooked and that another long delay was essential. Yet these pains but intensified his ardour, for he was privileged to bear the Cross. Upon these Galician fields the shadow of the reign of Christ lay tranquil, as he

---

[1] The following phrase suggests its use in common parlance. ' O'Donnell and his saffron-clad heroes sail swift ships from Cuan an Chaislein to the tower of Breogan on the Groyne.' Cf. Annals of the Four Masters, 1602, p. 2293.

made his way along those narrow sunken paths, the *corredoiras*, riding deep between the maize and orchards to the city of St. James his patron, Compostela. Faith he had always possessed most strongly ; charity had urged him on this four years' journey, and as he knelt on the stone flags of the Cathedral, with the floor space crowded for the *fiesta*, the Portico de la Gloria behind him and the great silver censer swinging slowly from the roof, he did not fail to receive the strength of hope. These central mysteries which the long ceremonial of the Christian Church enshrined, the adoration of God which arose from the people of Christ in their untrammelled freedom, gave unity and peace to all his thought. He would give his life to preserve and maintain them. But such was not the Earl of Desmond's opinion ; for Fitzmaurice's hope, however spiritual, was the chief cause of Cousin Desmond's fear.

The Earl, balancing factors, at enmity with his kinsmen, but content with that tortuous pleasure which intrigue could still bring, had stifled opposition with prudence. Without the carefree innocence of his rieving kindred, unfortified by the confidence of England, he could yet precariously maintain his lands in quiet. And in Spain there was James Fitzmaurice with the ties of his loyal hot friendship and his visionary zeal. The peace which both men desired belonged to differing and conflicting orders, nor would Fitzmaurice have denied that, as far as Desmond's uneasy quietude was considered, he brought not peace, but the sword.

Then, in the summer of 1579, James Fitzmaurice returned. The future of the Irish in Munster depended to a great extent on Desmond's course and his character and outlook can alone provide the key to his subsequent action. A consideration of Desmond's conduct in detail will help to explain the disaster which followed ; for this destruction seems almost inevitable, once his personal ideas are weighed, those conflicting elements of pride and of jealousy and, throughout, that profound inexperience of the minds from which he was isolated. At this perilous moment, when a false step meant ruin, Desmond was still unable to fathom the reactions set up [1] on those forces which now hemmed him in, English Deputy, new settler, lord of the Pale, or Scot.

[1] Letter from Edward Waterhouse to Walsingham, dated at Waterford 22nd August, 1579, ' John of Desmond was in all things pleasured by the Lord Justice (Drury) who meant to have been a suitor for a pension for him.' Cal. S.P. Irel., 1574–85, p. 182. In this question the animus of Waterhouse against Drury must not be forgotten.

The spring of 1579 found Desmond in his own country moving with that dry weather, which had succeeded to the winter rains, through the various hunting lodges of his lands. The ships with fish and general cargo, as they came into Dingle or the Kenmare River, would bring the latest news of the Spanish preparations; but the expedition had been so long delayed, and these plans so often failed completely, as in the case of Stukeley about whom there had been such bruit, that there seemed no reason for undue disturbance. Besides, at the moment, his brothers seemed satisfied, for a real friendship had sprung up between Sir John and the English agent, old Mr. Davells, and he also seems to have received marked favour [1] from Lord Justice Drury. Any idea of jealousy must have been submerged in relief that, if his younger brothers had such good standing in the eyes of the Government, they would be likely to support him against an invader. At the same time it was flattering that James Fitzmaurice, so far as reports could be gathered, never failed to recognize him as his chief. Under these circumstances it certainly seemed that there was no great need to fear for the future, while Desmond's relations with his wife went on smoothly, and it was clearly an advantage that the Government had formed the impression that they could rely on her aid.[2] Meanwhile, the Earl had acted lately with great circumspection. He had not failed to ask pardon during the winter for a recalcitrant cousin and had sent the welcome news home that ' the Seneschal of Imokilly stands in point of agreement.' [3] The advices which he received from the shipping, as to Fitzmaurice's movements, were duly despatched,[4] and he had lately written [5] to the Privy Council about a freight of gold on his palatinate of Kerry, which he desired to preserve for the Queen. It was a question of treasure trove, not merely wreck right, and this would surely produce an impression.

---

[1] A letter from the Queen to Sidney makes her attitude quite clear. ' Suffer not,' she wrote, ' that Desmonds deminge deedes, far wide from promised workes, make you trust to other pleage than either him selfe or John for gaige : he hathe so well performed his Inglesche Vowes that I warne you to trust them no longer than you see one of them. Prometheus let me be, and Prometheus hath bine myne to long. I pray God youre olde strainge shepe late (as you say) retorned into fold, wore not her wolly garment upon her wolvy back.' Sidney Papers, i, p. 7.

[2] John Verdon had written on 28th November, 1578, that ' The Countess of Desmond (is) ever looking to settle all things according to the English manner '; while on 6th January following, Sir William Drury had written to Burghley that the Earl and Countess of Desmond were in good tune. Cal. S.P. Irel., 1574–85, pp. 154–5.

[3] Letter of Desmond to Drury, dated 28th November, 1578, at Adare. *Ibid.*

[4] Letter of Desmond to Drury, dated 20th April, 1579, at Dingle and enclosing the deposition of Pierre Gance of St. Malo. *Ibid.*, p. 167.

[5] Letter of Desmond to the Privy Council, dated 9th January, 1579, at New Castle. *Ibid.*, p. 156.

His letters show that it was with a light heart that he heard that James Fitzmaurice had really arrived. On 17th July the ships from Spain anchored in the afternoon outside Dingle, while the Earl was at his hunting lodge near Cullen in the Wood, rather over forty miles to the eastward. The Portreeve sent [1] the news to his chief by a runner, and a day later Desmond composed [2] a most dutiful letter for England : he was ready to venture his life in Her Majesty's service, but he naturally required advice how to act. The next day he wrote [3] more strongly and with a facile piety, which he wrongly judged would come opportune, to declare that he had all his force and that he hoped with the hand of God to expel this traitor ; and after this settled down quietly.

If only he could persuade his brothers to follow his prudent tactics, the Fitzmaurice affair would collapse. Already he had gathered that the actual military aid that had been brought over was small, and that the invaders would be entirely dependent on the support that they could obtain. He had so often heard his men mutter of what they would do when Fitzmaurice returned and, after all the trouble, it seemed to him that the matter was planning out smoothly. Fitzmaurice could not succeed as long as the Earl's men held aloof, and after a serious military check his power would be broken and there would no longer be need to fear him as a rival. Over against Fitzmaurice's single-minded devotion, there stood his cousin, pain-racked and weak, with his mind unwaveringly and consistently tortuous. If Fitzmaurice should succeed, he would be in effect the ruler of Desmond ; but it was essential if he was to fail that his cousin must not possess an overt share in the tragedy. Meanwhile, on the edges of his country there remained the armed threat from Ormonde and the more remote English ; and in consequence the situation was now become complex, so that, although the Earl had the craft, he had not the experience, nor the wide education to make his casts with success. Moreover, this fortnight's inaction cost him the remainder of his reputation in England, and he never regained it. Then on the 2nd August his own brothers broke away from him and went out into revolt.

Old Mr. Davells, the Sheriff of Cork, and the Provost Marshal of

[1] Letter of the Portreeve of the Dingle to Desmond, dated 17th July, 1579. Cal. S.P. Irel., 1574–85, p. 173.
[2] Letter of Desmond to Drury, dated 19th July, 1579, at Cullen. *Ibid.*, p. 172.
[3] Letter of Desmond to Drury, dated 20th July, at Whitestown. *Ibid.*, p. 174.

Munster, had been away on a tour of inspection and on their return journey had arrived as far as Tralee. That night, as they lay in bed at Rice's wine tavern, the Geraldine brothers came down from the hills and filled the streets of the little town with their clansmen. Then, alone, they broke into the inn and Sir John and Sir James of Desmond, who would never leave a great honourable killing to others, strode into the bedroom and despatched the ancient, dazed men with their swords.[1] They were now committed irrevocably, and the situation became still harder for Desmond. The hope of Fitzmaurice's rapid departure decreased and he could no longer count on his own gallowglasses. Yet he was even less inclined now to join the invaders. John of Desmond, with whom he kept up an irritable and half-subdued quarrel, had received a warm welcome and a grant of the second rank in the force; so that, should he decide to support them, Desmond would have to reckon with both his cousin and brother in every council of war. Besides, the form and substance of Fitzmaurice's new proclamation were alike most uncongenial. There was, for instance, that sentence in the Gaelic letter sent out, which had filtered down through their leaders to each Hebridean gallowglass that Desmond maintained in his pay. 'Advise every one of your friends,' [2] wrote Fitamaurice, 'who likes fighting for his religion and his country better than for gold or silver, or who wishes to obtain them all, to come to me . . . and find each of these things.' Religion and His Holiness' banner, whatever appeal such ideas may have once had for Desmond, his policy of cautious submission had long since charmed them away. The proclamation, too, had contained a most distinct threat. 'They surely that come first . . . must of necessity occupy the chief place in His Holiness his army.' There could be no doubt that Desmond had forfeited his place to his brother and then

---

[1] The account of Davells' murder given by Thomas Russell in his *Relation of the fitz Geralds of Ireland*, written in 1638, ed. Hayman and Graves, p. 29, is amplified in Bishop Carleton's description; which gives the version, accurate or not, destined to be received as traditional. In regard to the conversations reported it is difficult to see on what evidence they could have been based.

[2] Letters of Fitzmaurice. Two statements typical of the political and astrological traditions among the victors should be here recorded. 'But see what mischiefe,' wrote Russell, ' sprung from ye malice of a woman. For Dame Elleynor Butler, Countess of Desmond, and then the mother of one only son, opposed herself against this James Fitzmaurice and with reasons, perswasions, teares and imploringes persuaded the Earl her husband not to dismember his patrimony.' The second entry is very curious. ' Let this be remembered,' he continued, ' that few years before Sebastianus his overthrow in Affrica and that long and miserable warre begun by James Fitz Maurice and continued by the Earl of Desmond ; a strange starre commonly called a comett, or rather that you will call it soe Apinoment in the Chayre of Cassiopia's Constellation, appeared in November 1573.' Russell, *Relation of the fitz Geralds of Ireland*, pp. 25 and 28.

there came those phrases of exalted religious enthusiasm, which grated upon him so much. The fight for ' the Cross of Christ and His Holiness his banner, for both which I,' Fitzmaurice continued, ' as well as all other Christians, ought to spend our blood and, for my part, intend at least by God's grace, Whom I beseech to give you all, my lords, in this world courage and stoutness for the defence of His Faith and in the world to come life ever lasting.' Desmond had a knowledge of London and as a prisoner he had seen English power. For twenty years he had managed to keep the control of his country, and now there came this cousin with his monastic ideals and his preaching. If by any chance the invaders should conquer, all the glory would go to Fitzmaurice, and it was clear that he would be deposed. If, as would seem almost certain, Fitzmaurice's force was destroyed, Desmond would lose everything at the hands of the English, once he had compromised himself in the least. These were the two alternatives should he favour the newcomers. On the other hand, if he marched against them, a proceeding altogether insane, his bonnaughts would revolt and refuse to fight against this popular leader. The religious element came in here again. His early training, his father's casual shifts and the mature wish to satisfy England, in order to keep his lands free, had driven the Earl into devious courses, where the seeds of his personal religion had perished. But, if Desmond had forgotten Holy Ireland, his men would respond to that call, so that to attack was clearly impossible, while there was always the danger that he might carelessly be murdered by some over-zealous dependent, if he moved to the sacrilege of opposing the Vicar of Christ and his banner. He was therefore forced to the course of an inactive support of the Government; a position more and more difficult, as each subordinate leader went out to the rebels, while in England Desmond's stock sank low and touched bottom.

After these years of waiting Fitzmaurice remained alive a month in Ireland. For the first fortnight he had sent out messages and had gradually gathered support,[1] and then came the killing of Davells and the crucial accession of Sir John and Sir James of Desmond.[2] Follow-

[1] Letter of Edward Waterhouse to Walsingham, dated from Dublin 23rd July, 1579, ' Friars practise with O'Rourke, O'Donnell, Turlough Lynagh and the Scots.' Cal. S.P. Irel., 1574–85, p. 175.
[2] Letter of Edward Waterhouse to Walsingham, dated from Dublin 3rd August, 1579, 'Sir John Desmond more dangerous than the rebel both for his credit and his bloody mind.' Cal. S.P. Irel., 1574–85, p. 178.

ing upon this emergency, the measures in Dublin grew sterner,[1] especially against those wandering bards [2] by whom communications were fostered. And then quite unexpectedly the news came that Fitzmaurice had been cut off and killed by the Burkes at Castletown in Limerick on 17th August in a casual skirmish. If he had died three weeks earlier it seems almost certain that Desmond would have been saved. Freed from this rebellion the Earl would have left a quiet inheritance and the Dukes of Desmond would have more than filled, during the long years of the Ascendancy, the place of Ormonde and Kildare. As it was, the murder which Sir John of Desmond had committed made pardon upon submission impossible. The authority of the Catholic forces devolved upon him and the situation changed for the worse for both brothers.[3] In the case of Sir John of Desmond there was a lack of that power of inspiring loyal friendship, which Fitzmaurice possessed, nor could he act freely apart from his brother. The hopes of gaining O'Rourke or young John Burke [4] of Leitrim were vague and, without a real leader in the South, the movement of rebellion was crippled.

The chief immediate effect of Fitzmaurice's death, as far as Desmond was concerned, would seem to have been a deepening of the already heavy suspicion with which the English in Ireland watched his every movement.[5] Since Sir John of Desmond was his brother, it seemed an obvious duty that the Earl should bring him to heel. But it might reasonably have been asked whether under such circumstances the Queen would have been prepared to grant him a pardon after her two leading officers in the South had been slain. And, if this pardon was not forthcoming, how could Desmond survive in his country after he had delivered over his brother to the Englishmen's halter ? Besides, this was always presupposing that he possessed the power to

---

[1] Order by the Council of Ireland, dated 9th August, 1579. Leaders of blind folks, harpers, bards, rhymers, and all loose and idle people having no master to be executed by martial law. *Ibid.*. p. 179.

[2] This was an old weakness of Desmond's. On 22nd February, 1563 the Earl had promised that he would ' henceforth . . . not give any manner of reward for any such lewd rhymes under pain of forfeiting double the sum. As those rhymers, by their ditties and rhymes, made for divers lords and gentlemen in Ireland . . . (make) commendation and high praise of extortion, rebellion, rape, rapine and other injustice.' Cal. Patent Rolls, Irel., pp. 481–2.

[3] Letter from Lord Chancellor Gerrard to Burghley, dated 16th September, 1579, ' John of Desmond sleepeth not and hath a perilous head.' Cal. S.P. Irel., 1574–85, p. 187.

[4] Malby's Remembrance, dated 22nd August, 1579, ' John Burke has waded so far in ill actions that he will trust his life to no man's courtesy.' *Ibid.*, p. 182.

[5] As evidence of the immediate re-percussion, two letters were written to Walsingham on 22nd and 23rd August, the first from Malby stating that Desmond was protecting the rebels and the second from Drury referring to suspicions of his disloyalty. *Ibid.*

put down the rebellion; but, as he gathered his force at Askeaton during this difficult month, the Earl was the nominal leader of a rapidly vanishing host, while as they moved from one camp to the other his followers would never consider that they really transferred their allegiance. It was the most difficult point in the matter that Fitzmaurice had always remained so embarrassingly loyal to his titular chief. But, supposing he had brought these Geraldine forces to action, he could hardly imagine that either side would be prepared to engage in a conflict. This was no raiding foray, but the semblance of a war of religion, and in this case, as far as Desmond's men were concerned, the religious ideas were identical; in the whole country, apart from Fitzgerald of Cloyne, only the Earl himself did not share them. If Desmond's men would not fight against the Pope's banner, which was the symbol of all their religious belief, and if Fitzmaurice's followers refused to take action against their lord, the great Earl, it would have proved almost impossible to have arranged for a battle. In such a case, all the marchings and counter-marchings and the insincere parleys of Desmond fall into their place; for he could do little else save to strive desperately hard to pacify the officials.

This was the cause of his strange action in offering up Bishop O'Hely by which he endeavoured to provide for the English an acceptable sacrifice. The Bishop, a Franciscan from Connaught who had spent some years in Spain and had been appointed to the See of Mayo by the Pope when he was in Rome three summers before, had come in the ship with Fitzmaurice. Now that the band was dispersing, he made his way to Askeaton accompanied by two of his scholars, one of them a son of O'Rourke, expecting to find a most cordial welcome,[1] for Fitzmaurice had always spoken so highly of the Earl's respect for the Church. To Desmond, however, it seemed that, after his changes and troubles, he had at last received an undoubted piece of good fortune; still further enhanced by his own lucky, or perhaps intentional, absence. The prelate was received with distinction by the Countess of Desmond, and the party were sent on their way towards Limerick, after their hostess had passed word to the English and

---

[1] They were at any rate sufficiently valued in their country. 'The Bishop O'hElidhe, i.e. the paragon of learning and piety of the whole world and the son of O'Ruairc, Connbrathar the son of Brian come from the east after their education and tour.' Annals of Loch Cé, 1579, p. 427.

arranged for their capture. It would seem that the Irish never grasped the Desmonds' share in this action; but the whole episode goes to prove that at this time in mid-August the Earl had no intention of throwing in his lot with the rebels, but was only bent upon keeping the control of his country in peace. This event throws distinct light on Desmond's religious position and the equanimity with which he could view the Catholic Episcopate. It cannot be forgotten in the later period in the shoutings of ' Papa Abo '[1] and in that reverence with which the Earl was forced to receive the Pope's ' ewer and bason.' At any rate the Irish opinion of the hanging of Bishop O'Hely was sufficiently definite. ' That was a pitiful deed,'[2] runs the entry of the Annalist, ' to put an honourable most pious bishop and a friar minor of noble blood to death in an unbecoming manner.' Ormonde would have held Desmond's opinion that this hanging was by no means an unbecoming manner of death for a bishop; but this only stresses still more their isolation in Ireland.

Towards the end of September Desmond made yet another effort to satisfy the officials, who were by this time prepared to admit his powerless[3] state. He delivered over his son, Lord Garret, who was at Askeaton with his wife, to the Lord Justice Drury as a pledge of his loyalty. Again it seems clear that, even at the end of September, he did not foresee that he would be involved in desperate and irremediable quarrel. Yet as each week passed the English became increasingly hostile. On 16th September an official had written[4] to England that ' Desmond is preparing his forces to very ill purpose,' and two days earlier there had come in the first hint of an alien influence, ' Sanders persuades Desmond.'[5] In these words the disaster which overtook the Geraldine power is foreshadowed.

Yet before dealing with Sanders, it would be well to consider the attempts to pacify Dublin which Desmond continued to make. The next development in the situation was the serious illness of Lord

---

[1] The surrender of Bishop O'Hely should be contrasted with the scene described by Pelham eighteen months later (28th December, 1580). ' The Earl of Desmond guardeth the Pope's ensign with all his own household servants and in all his skirmishes and outrages crieth " Papa abo." ' Cal. Carew MSS., 1558–74, p. 191.
[2] Annals of Loch Cé, 1579, p. 428.
[3] Letter of Malby to Walsingham, dated from Kilmallock 10th September, 1579, ' Desmond has not three men in his service that will follow him on Her Majesty's service.' Cal. S.P. Irel., 1574–85, p. 185.
[4] Letter of Waterhouse to Secretary Wilson, dated 16th September, 1579, at the camp of Aherlow. Ibid., p. 187.
[5] Letter of Drury to Walsingham, dated 14th September, 1579. Ibid., p. 186.

Justice Drury, which, beginning in mid-September, resulted in his death at Waterford on the thirteenth of the following month. This brought the military situation into the control of his subordinate, Nicholas Malby, who was given his mandate. A certain urgency in the handling of the situation is notable because Malby's new power depended upon the life of his chief. The illness was, from the first, known to be grave, and Malby's commission terminated, temporarily at least, with the Lord Justice's death. Undoubtedly this time factor hastened the crisis.

The beginning of the correspondence was friendly. On 28th September Malby, as Governor of Munster, wrote [1] to the Earl, desiring his assistance and advice in council. It was this letter which occasioned the first sign of hostility into which Desmond was betrayed. Three days later he wrote [2] from Askeaton that ' his plot ought to have been followed and that the army should not spoil his tenants.' A certain injury to his military pride is suggested in the rejection of his plan of campaign ; but he had marched in the previous month with Drury on the border of the Great Wood to search for his brother, and he knew how weak were his own forces. On the next day the Governor replied [3] that Desmond's presence would avail more than his absence could do. It was a manifest threat, and only fourteen miles of open country lay between the Earl's house and the English forces. Desmond at once became careful, and, with that somewhat obvious prudence in which he took his naive pride, a despatch was returned [4] the same day giving news of his brother John's doings in the depths of the woods. The following day, Saturday, 3rd October, after a feint had been made, he bravely sent [5] a description of a victory won over the rebels stating that he hoped ' to light on the residue that are fled.' Taking him at his word, Malby retreated,[6] promising that he would give Desmond much honour and favour if he would ' get that papistical and arrogant traitor Sanders, who deceived with false lies, to be arrested.' It was impossible for the Earl, helpless against the Geraldine forces, to continue upon such a line, and he returned to his

---

[1] Letter of Malby to Desmond, dated 28th September, 1579, at Limerick. Cal. S.P. Irel., 1574–85, p. 190.
[2] Letter of Desmond to Malby, dated 1st October, 1579, at Askeaton. *Ibid.*, p. 190.
[3] Letter of Malby to Desmond, dated 2nd October, 1579 at Limerick. *Ibid.*
[4] Letter of Desmond to Malby, dated 2nd October, 1579, at Askeaton. *Ibid.*, p. 190.
[5] Letter of Desmond to Malby, dated 3rd October, 1579, at Askeaton. *Ibid.*
[6] Letter of Malby to Desmond, dated 3rd October, 1579, at Limerick. *Ibid.*

original method, marvelling[1] that Malby should destroy his poor tenants. Here there was a suggestion of appealing to Cæsar, but by now it was already too late. The same day, a fact which indicates the rapidity with which the riders passed on these level roads, the Governor replied[2] with a peremptory command that the Earl's presence at Limerick was necessary to show his obedience. This was the turning point, and yet it is hardly possible to maintain that Desmond's fear for his safety was groundless. At the same time his retreat to the southward settled his fate. Malby marched to Askeaton summoning[3] the Earl or the Countess of Desmond, or, failing their presence, Maurice McSheehy to a conference; but the Earl had fled and his castle was empty. There was no doubt as to the Governor's intentions, for a letter written to the English Government on the Sunday had made these very clear. 'To have instructions . . . ,' Malby had begun,[4] 'how I shall deal with this mad brained Earl, the only Archtraitor in all Ireland.'

Desmond had now only one hope left, the possible mediation of Ormonde. This stepson from whom he had been so long estranged, now changed almost out of recognition by the favour of England and the Court, had the one advantage of a determined enmity against Malby. It was a slender hope on which to rest his fortune. The older man began[5] appropriately enough by a reference to his dead wife, Ormonde's mother, and to the injury which Malby had done to her grave at Askeaton and then, settling down to his task, harried and desperate, his secretary took down once again the well-worn and familiar phrases of loyalty. He referred to his successful opposition to the Traitor and to the O'Flahertys, to John of Desmond's most cruel murder of Davells and to his own fear that his brothers would imbrue their cruel hands in the blood of his wife and his son. As to the truth of all these facts he desired Ormonde to certify Her Majesty. The effort failed[6]; Ormonde forwarded the letters from the 'lewd

---

[1] Letter of Desmond to Malby, dated 6th October, 1579, at Askeaton. *Ibid.*
[2] Letter of Malby to Desmond, dated 6th October, 1579, at Limerick. *Ibid.*
[3] Letter of Malby to Desmond, dated 8th October, 1579, at Askeaton Abbey. *Ibid.*, p. 190.
[4] Letter of Malby to Walsingham, dated 4th October, 1579, at Monasternenagh. Cal. S.P. Irel., 1574–85, p. 189.
[5] Letter of Desmond to Ormonde, dated 10th October, 1579. *Ibid.*
[6] The last half-hearted effort concerned the new Lord Justice Pelham. 'I have been made acquainted by the Earl of Ormonde,' wrote Pelham on 24th October, from Cashel, 'with such letters as you (Desmond) wrote to him, finding yourself grieved with the dealings of Sir Nicholas Malby. . . . I wish you to come hither. Use no delay for I will not lie idle.' To this letter Desmond replied on 28th October from Askeaton: 'As I cannot presently repair to your

Earl and his traitorous brethren' to England and Desmond joined his brothers in revolt. He could hold out no longer between John of Desmond and the English forces; still it is doubtful if even then he would have succumbed had it not been for the presence of Sanders.

In the Earl's complete isolation one figure continually increased in significance, that of Dr. Nicholas Sanders, the Legate. As in the case of Fitzmaurice, here was a character quite beyond the Earl's comprehension; but in this case the absence of understanding went hand in hand with attraction. Still it would serve no purpose to describe the various motives which led the bewildered[1] Desmond to fall under this spell, until the outlook of Dr. Sanders is considered, and the circumstances which had induced him, a middle-class Englishman from Surrey, to strand himself among these barefoot kernes. The matter is the more important because the character of this man, Fitzmaurice's companion and effectual legacy, was a determining factor in the course of rebellion.

No other figure, among those concerned with the period of the religious changes in England, conveys quite the same impression of whole-hearted absorption in a cause, a devotion which was at once so hard and unyielding, self-consuming and pitiless. English on both sides, with an upbringing, cultivated and peaceful, backed by an assurance of an easy future, such as the life of a scholar at Winchester did not always then imply, the young Nicholas had grown up with his inevitably accommodating parents in the quietude at Charlwood Place. Even then those first low slopes of Surrey echoed all the London change; the bustle of the Court, with which in its lower and less fashionable aspects the Sanders were in some degree connected, came up to these unexciting meadows. It was a world where prudent caution reigned, with no exaggeration in the *tempo ;* the whole careful movement symbolized both by ease and by restricted freedom, the horsemen trotting on the Godstone road.

Nicholas Sanders had no more connection than any other meteor with these surroundings; but characters as uncompromising and as

Honour I have sent my wife to declare the causes of my present stay and how my country has been burned and spoiled.' A further letter arrived on 30th October, offering ' to serve against my unnatural brethren ; the traitor Dr. Sanders and their adherents.' This also in Desmond's continued absence proved unsuccessful. Cal. Carew MSS., 1575–88, pp. 158–61.

[1] In regard to Desmond's character, Lord Deputy Sidney, not on this point an unfriendly witness, had written to the Queen twelve years before : ' The Earl of Desmounde a man both voide of judgement and will to be ruled.' Sidney Papers, i, p. 29.

stern were to come from the same circumscribed background, those Puritan leaders who would rise like hawks from the elms in Huntingdon. They and their successors, the early firm-driving Empire builders, were men whose native strength was quite untempered by those influences which have given their more accustomed moulding to the race. For Sanders was seized by and lived for an idea; a strong driving force which would have seemed, as in the case of Puritans, to have withered his humour. The delightful wit, the carefree gaiety, which played about the lives of the English Martyrs was absent in him. There are also indications that he was an uncomfortable and in a sense a lonely man. His late ordination at thirty-six perhaps accounted for the fact that something of the ecclesiastical layman clung to him always; for he had been a man past thirty, a Lecturer at New College in Canon Law, when he had been fired by a passion for the Tridentine Reform in its austerity. Considering the supple characteristics of his generation, it is interesting to observe in this Roman Legate those traits which are often thought so English, a character quite unresilient, straight, unbending, tough.

With all his strength he served this purpose, the new life of a reviving Church; conflict of the mind, not only in the study, but on the Christian forum became a necessity which his nature craved. The terms of the Canon Law lay down the matter clearly, and he gave himself to the capture of the citadels of the spirit,[1] to the subjugation of rebellious minds. There was no vagueness in his sense of values, nor in that firmness with which his soul abhorred all heresy as treason against God. National preferences quite vanished in this fire; his own ties with England now hung loose, the father dead, the mother through his influence an exile. He was not Italian, but de-national, spending his life in frontier garrisons on the contested Marches of the Faith. The Jesuits of the Canisian school were perhaps the closest to him in affinity; but there was in Sanders a solitariness and a custom of unheeding fervent judgment which could not have been permitted to survive in that calm balance the Ignatian mould. The position as a *littérateur*, which he had gained early, made him both outwardly

---

[1] A letter from Bishop Sega, Nuncio at Madrid, to the Cardinal of Como written on 22nd November, 1578, expresses this characteristic clearly. 'Sanders is determined to go with him (Fitzmaurice) and His Majesty at my insistence is content that he should let him go, since I have more hope in the prudence, judgement and much religion of this man than, I might almost say, of an entire army.' Cal. S.P. Rome, 1572–78.

receptive of social customs and *persona grata* [1] in the Catholic world. The Cardinals had used him : Morone, Hosius, then Commendone had requisitioned his ardour in their turn. Poland, Lithuania and the closing sessions of the Great Council were followed, however, by a contrast, seven years as Professor of Theology at Louvain, unwelcome calm. This, the period of his writings and of the *De Visibili Monarchia Ecclesiæ*, gave him the experience of an intellectual conflict ; but the peaceful life, the opiate quality of this dreaming town, urged him to break out towards the battle, the physical combat for the Catholic rule. Besides, in this environment he can never have been altogether at his ease, while the letters in which he adopts the trivial politenesses of the day ring falsely from one of his unyielding temper. The uncertain fires of such a temperament, that scorn of weakness which he did not share, cannot have been pleasant for his fellow-exiles in the trials of their personal defeat. The bitterness, too, is never absent from his polemic, as in the too-famous passages [2] in the *De Schismate Anglicano*. But through this, as in his earlier work, there can be discerned his urgency for a life of action.

A letter from this period reveals the contrast. In the document in question, which by a casual chance has been preserved, the Professor of Theology writes [3] to Lady Northumberland on a point as technical as would prove suitable to her sex the recommendations for the drafting of official Latin letters. Questions of French and Italian scholars are discussed. The writer suggests that she will have about her the flower of Louvain and finally, to close with the gifts of courtesy which that age demanded, he mentions a ' picture on a table ' which he has entrusted to Sir John Neville for her Ladyship's acceptance. How different from this was his self-chosen destiny ? Back in Poland with the Prince Bishop of Ermeland and the Bishop of Zante [4] his life had been strenuous. There he had done real work and not trifling, com-

---

[1] *Cf.* Letter of the Countess of Northumberland, Sir Francis Englefield, Leonard Dacre, etc., to Cardinal Hosius, written at Brussels 29th June, 1573, in favour of ' the Cardinal's quondam pupil Nicholas Sander.' *Ibid.*, p. 119.

[2] Such phrases in reference to His late Majesty as that ' the royal household consisted of men utterly abandoned, gamblers, adulterers, panders, swindlers, false swearers, blasphemers, extortioners and even heretics ' must have caused deep offence to the many Catholic squires of the Court circle. Sanders, *De Schismate Anglicano*, trans. Lewis, p. 24.

[3] Letter from Dr. Nicholas Sanders to the Countess of Northumberland, dated 17th January, 1572, at Louvain. Cal. Salisbury MSS., ii, p. 4.

[4] Better known by his later title as Cardinal Commendone. Stanislaus Hosius was generally styled the Cardinal of Ermeland, after his elevation to the Sacred College. Cal. S.P. Rome, 1572–8, *passim*.

posing those elaborate despatches which the traditions of the Nuncia-
ture had prescribed. Those rooms at Piotrkow in the winter that the
Diet sat were firm in his memory ; the ramshackle, doubtful walls of
that notable's house which had been placed at the Nuncio's disposal ;
the damp stains but half concealed by those damask hangings, the
travelling furniture [1] of rank, which the servants of His Most Serene
Lordship had set up ; and on the coarse rough table the candlesticks
from Italy. Beyond the heavy table, the fire of pine cones blazed, with
burning rosemary to give forth in the room much needed sweetness,
as the rats scampered in the barns below. And, as he wrote, the lords
would stride in for their audience with their Latin speech, weird and
self-conscious, the crude rich chasing of the heavy scabbards, the
tarnished opulence of fur. Outside in the deep snow of that northern
winter the gentlemen of the *szlachta* passed and re-passed in their grey
Masovian cloaks ; in all the fury of their new conventicles, threatening
and Calvinist.

Sanders determined that once more he would come to grips with
the Church's opponents.

The call to Rome in the weeks before Pope Pius V died and the
Curial offices which he then received brought Sanders into contact
with James Fitzmaurice in whom he found that Christian paladin for
whom he had so long been seeking. It was in Rome, too, that Sanders
and Fitzmaurice had gathered from the Franciscan convent at Ara
Coeli, Fr. O'Hely and his charge, O'Rourke. All those elements of
hardship and of danger, which this Irish expedition inevitably involved,
appealed to Sanders. His years at Louvain had brought him into a
clear knowledge of the unsuccessful conspirators, and there was no
one among the exiled Catholic laymen to compare with Fitzmaurice
if simple piety and berserk courage alone were in question. But the
expedition was to prove a most severe test of Sanders' devotion. It is
not difficult to understand, given this accumulation of data, the basis
from which he approached the problem of Desmond. Fitzmaurice,
whom he admired so greatly, was killed ; he would make the best,
therefore, of the surviving material. John of Desmond with all his
strangeness had valour, and then there came Desmond's own case.
Dr. Sanders knew nothing of him at first hand ; for he had retired
overseas before the period of the Earl's somewhat squalid visit to

---

[1] *Cf.* the inventory of Cardinal Pole's furniture. State Papers Dom. Elizabeth, i, 10.

London.[1] The reports he had heard before his landing had not been encouraging; but, on the other hand, Fitzmaurice always maintained a deep loyalty to him. One recent episode had affected their future relations. There was a great gulf fixed between Dr. Sanders and Bishop O'Hely,[2] and that innocent, rather arrogant boy on whose rank as the son of O'Rourke, the whole party insisted; but still they had gone to Desmond and then had been taken and hanged. Close as had been his relations with Fitzmaurice, one fact emerges clearly that natural personal affection did not enter into Dr. Sanders' relations with Desmond.

By the time of this last effort after Fitzmaurice's death, it had become very clear that the situation had arrived at a deadlock. John of Desmond could hardly hope for a pardon, and yet his brother's hesitation prevented wide action. Whatever he might manage in Kerry there was no chance that the rebellion would spread throughout Ireland unless the Earl of Desmond supported it strongly. No chief in the West or the North would engage in revolt, unless it was certain that those struggling in Munster had the whole Geraldine force to support them. This becomes especially clear in those dealings with Ulster and the Scots in which the Earl later engaged; for it was the name of Desmond alone which could move them to action; although even here his physical weakness and the absence of personal friendship with the northern leaders considerably diminished his power of appeal. Yet, the adhesion of Desmond remained the solitary although insecure hope of rebellion. All Sanders' past experience and his strong, detached courage is displayed in the way that he dealt with this new manœuvre.

To Desmond in those first sanguine moments when he fell under Sanders' sway, it must have seemed that here at last he had found a servant worthy of his high and princely [3] endeavours. As to the

---

[1] Two extracts give a vivid impression of this visit.
   (a) On 21st December, 1567, Thomas Scott wrote to Cecil to notify that Sir John Desmond fell sick between Stone and Lichfield, so that they had much ado to get him to Lichfield. Their greatest lack is money for the conveyance of the said Earl (of Desmond). Cal. Salisbury, MSS., i, p. 349.
   (b) On 6th June, 1571, Sir Warham St. Leger wrote to Burghley that 'the Earl and Sir John have but lately recovered. Their health cannot be long being pent up in so little a room as they be.' Cal. S.P. Irel., 1509–73, p. 450.
   [2] A reference in a news letter written to Walsingham by Denis Molan on 7th June, 1578, gives an impression of the prelate, 'this Episcopus Maionen preaching in Spain and " craving every other where for him " (Fitzmaurice).' Cal. S.P. Foreign, 1578–9, p. 7.
   [3] As a proof of Sanders' reputation. 'At Betanzos (within 3 leagues of The Groyne) it was reported that the Pope had made Dr. Candares, Lord Chancellor of Ireland.' Occurrents, 1580. Cal. S.P. Rome, 1572–80, p. 500.

Doctor's birth, he had full information. He came, it seemed, from that middle state from which the Queen of England, and the great kings of Europe as well were accustomed to select their advisers. The physical handicap under which Desmond laboured, the ' palsy,' which already afflicted him and the troublesome effects of that old wound at Affane combined to make him appreciate the unbending strength of this new friend. And, as he realized the gulf in rank between them with pleasure, it was a balm for the Earl to consider those other high princes who had once held the service of this great minister whom he had gained. Then Sanders, rising to the occasion, with that disregard for his own preferences which the fires of his nature brought forth, would re-assure him. It was a fact, he had firmly declared, that the hand of God had removed [1] Fitzmaurice that the Earl might come into his own. All Desmond's desires seemed satisfied by this new and almost obsequious courtesy from a man whom the outside world would regard with attention. The bitter memories of forty years, the harsh treatment of the English Governors, the disdainful neglect in England, the sense of isolation from his own people, were to his final misfortune charmed away. Even in the matter of religion this last phrase touched a chord. His separation from the Catholic outlook would have made the task difficult for many envoys; but here Desmond could be moved by this man, so strong and so learned. With religion absent, superstition in the sixteenth century was never far away, and perhaps Providence had intended to use him. It was a suitable thought for a leader whom failure at the English Court had made doubly conscious of his great feudal position, exalted and princely.

As a result of the submission of Desmond's will to the Legate's strong purpose, all the disasters of the Geraldines followed. The chance of united action, never hopeful, soon vanished and the whole long train of misfortune, the massacre at Smerwick, the capture of Sir James of Desmond and the death of his brother, Sir John, dragged them down slowly. The aid from Spain was from the start insufficient and the ultimate reduction of Kerry was merely a question of time. Lady Desmond made a fruitless effort to secure mediation; [2] but,

---

[1] Sanders used this argument from the action of Providence rather freely. ' God permitting your father to be taken prisoner,' he wrote to Ulick Burke on 27th October, 1579, ' meant to warn you, his sons, to provide as well for his liberty as for your own.' Cal. Carew MSS., 1575–88, p. 159.

[2] See the document relating to the Countess of Desmond printed in the Appendix to this volume, p. 476.

once the Earl had gone into rebellion and had been proclaimed traitor, the enemies of his house would make sure that this charter of their liberty was never rescinded. Ormonde and the new English settlers had far too much to gain by the absolute permanent destruction of Desmond. In the length of the three years' struggle other forces, and notably Baltinglas and the Nugents, came to the aid of the Geraldine faction ; but from the going out to rebellion the fate of Desmond was sealed.

To Nicholas Sanders, as he passed with the Earl through the woods, it was obvious that good had been done, for as a priest he could see the firm hold which the Catholic Faith had regained [1] in South Ireland. He was past fifty now and the fever had weakened his limbs. News had been brought to him lately of the death of his leader and chief, Cardinal Hosius, Bishop of Ermeland, the *Cardinalis meus* of the days of his youth. The end had come at the villa at Capranica where the Cardinal was resting from the heats. For Sanders this closed an epoch, that intimate life of the Papal City with the Cardinal discussing in that measured fashion which Peter Canisius so commended, the despatches which the couriers had brought from Poland or some complex plan for Irish aid. It was from just this life that Sanders turned, the too great calm and order for one who was by nature a strong fighter, the slow rising from *siesta*, the heavy atmosphere beneath Janiculum, the burden of the hot unmoving air. He was not made for this existence, guarded by the drowsy majorduomos, gazing somnolent upon the hot flagstones while he worked and wrote with His Eminence, silent, untiring, as the Piazza di Santa Maria below him lay under the changing Trastevere sunshine. He had chosen the hardships of his Irish journey freely and, considering the effect which the Fitzmaurice venture and the Desmond Rising had produced in bringing before the Irish the vivid remembrance of their Catholic Faith, he could rest contented. The words with which he closed his life,[2] as he lay at night pain-racked and destitute in the Wood of Clonlish, are not those of an unhappy man. ' Unge me Illustris

---

[1] The evidence of a hostile seventeenth-century witness would have satisfied Sanders ' But the truth is his (the Tower Earl of Desmond's) religion was the only cause that bred this coynesse in them all ; for, if he had been Romish Catholick, the hearts and knees of all degrees in the Province (of Munster) would have bowed unto him.' *Pacata Hibernia*, Lib. 1, cap. 14, p. 890.
[2] The date of his death is unknown and even the vague April, 1581, is a conjecture. There is reason to believe that the Government considered that he was still alive on 18th February, 1581. Cal. S.P. Irel., 1574–85, p. 287.

Domine,' he began,[1] turning with courtesy to his companion, Bishop Cornelius O'Ryan, ' extrema unctione olei morientium, nam hac nocte sum e vita discessurus, a creatore meo vocatus.' The entry in the Annals of the Four Masters inscribes [2] his epitaph. ' Dr. Saunders died in the wood of Claenglaise. He was the supporting pillar of the Catholic Faith.' Nevertheless, this was not of very much comfort to Desmond.

The Earl survived Sanders two years, dying at last at the hands of a kerne in the deep tracks of the wood of Glanageenty on 11th November, 1583. Thus closed his brief St. Martin's summer. There was a truth in the saying of his captor, when he asked for mercy : ' Thou has killed thyself long ago.' He had, indeed, on the day that he accepted Sanders and the open rebellion that this implied. The fighting of his men through these uneasy years had caused a legend to arise about his name. He became Earl Garret of the Raids and every Geraldine action was an aid to his glory. ' And there was no one in Erinn,' the entry runs,[3] ' whose equal he was not in nobility, honour and in power, and by whom more Saxons died and who put the Queen to greater cost.' And he was to die among portents. ' The cuckoo called at night at Ard-mic-Grainne . . . and that was a great wonder ' ; a bitter recompense for all his loss and the Wasting of Desmond.

[1] This account of the Anointing obtained by Philip O'Sullevan Beare from his father, who was one of the knights at Sanders' funeral, suggests the polite and quick Latin speech which was the medium of his communication with the priests of the Gaeldom. For this death scene see *Historiæ Catholicæ Iberniæ Compendium*, t, ii, lib., iv, c. xvi.
[2] Annals of the Four Masters, 1581, p. 1762.
[3] Annals of Loch Cé, 1582, p. 456.

CHAPTER X

THE RISINGS IN THE PALE

In this chapter the reaction of the Anglo-Irish to the new power of the English settlers is considered, the scene chosen is the Pale, where the struggle between the old-established families and the Elizabethan officials was fought out, and the time, those spring months of 1580 when the rising discontent was soon to issue in the Baltinglas Revolt. But, before discussing the Anglo-Irish of the Pale, the Gaelic background of the great lords must be considered, for in the Tudor scheme their position as earls gave them a place at the summit of the newly wrought system. In addition they had this value, that as a counterpoise to the new officials they were the only element in Ireland on whom the Anglo-Irish of the Pale might rely should they choose to revolt. The Burkes of Clanricarde are chosen as a typical instance of those lords, vague in religion, by turns Henrican and Papal, moody and fierce, surrounded by a court with bards and secretaries for Irish and Latin letters, yet perpetually insecure from a fear of the ' tanistry ' which they had disowned, and a network of rivals. Their privileges, like the right of giving the judicial rod, were vague and their signs of honour, primitive ; even their wealth, which lay in the great herds of cattle, was mobile.

In contrast there was the Anglo-Irish element, distinguished usually by the use of English as a first language, combined with a more settled conception of life, and a desire for peace and good trade. They were loyalist in the sense that they controlled the judicial bench and the administration and were linked with the merchant classes in the rich seaport towns. But their position was menaced by the arrival of a stream of officials from England, whose power became increasingly greater as the Government became more ' direct.' These men, English by birth, coming usually from the landed class and possessing therefore influence, but no wealth, were marked by a cool judgment, an inheritance of adventure and an attachment for the name of Protestant, which they considered to be synonymous with their race. There was also a further division between the officials in Dublin and the military men ; while, above them and detached, there ruled the Lords Deputy. A consideration of Ormonde's attitude completes the list of the forces which converged upon Dublin.

All these five elements were involved in the Baltinglas Rising which ultimately failed because its leader was unable to persuade the other Anglo-Irish lords of the Pale to join with the clansmen. In the background the old Ormonde and Kildare feud played into the hands of the Government through Kildare's weakness and Ormonde's strength. In this light, the connection between the Baltinglas Rising and the so-called revolt of the Nugents of Delvin is clear. The first rebellion led to the meeting at Tara between Baltinglas and Kildare and the Anglo-Irish Lord Delvin, when the latter promised a friendly neutrality. This doubtful attitude then caused their arrest, which led to a hurried attempt on the part of their friends to release them, the Nugent Revolt. As a result of these risings, the new settlers who had suppressed them were left strongly entrenched. It was in fact a victory of the settlers, aided by a benevolent Viceroy, over the Anglo-Irish lords. In the next chapter the settlers are again seen victorious over a Lord Deputy, Sir John Perrot, who dared to oppose them.

THE CELTIC PEOPLES & RENAISSANCE EUROPE

As in all the disturbed movements of the Irish the Desmond Rising was reflected in the lands within the English Pale. That area of the more settled country inland from Drogheda and Dublin had been for long the stronghold of the Anglo-Irish, but the lines of demarcation were not clear, and the increased ' civility,' which the Henrican changes had brought about, tended to obliterate by degrees the old distinctions. Thus the Earldoms which the great chieftains had received from Henry VIII had brought them to the Dublin Parliament to sit beside the Anglo-Irish peers. And under such influence the habits of speech and dress, the whole of the mental outlook, was slowly changing. Much had been loosened by the nominal acceptance of the Henrican version in religion, a recognition which was in part the price of the new hereditary lordships. Yet on the other hand the friaries often survived their nominal suppression, retaining in many cases their corporate existence [1] and still providing the tutors for the young generation whose fathers had agreed to renounce the Papal Supremacy. This religious confusion, often made much more complex by the quasi-matrimonial arrangements in which the great lords had indulged, was reflected in secular matters. The loosening of the ties with their clansmen and their religion, the insecurity of the new links which were not yet forged securely, both contributed to that instability to which they were naturally prone. These are the lines along which the tentative and only half-meant revolts can best be explained, that uncertainty of the great chieftains which kept the Pale in disquiet.

A concrete instance of this changing is the policy of the McWilliam Burkes of Clanricarde.[2] They had received an earldom from Henry VIII and this advantage over the rest of the clan made them loyal, and they accepted the English religion in name, and the second Earl of Clanricarde quarrelled with the Church as his last three marriages

---

[1] Instances of the fashion in which the religious lives still continued are provided by the struggle of two bands of friars for the honour of burying Lord Inchiquin in 1597, and the protection afforded to the friary at Multifarnham by the Nugents of Delvin. The Franciscan Bishop Brady of Kilmore, who survived until 1607, invariably wore the habit and, together with his retinue of confessor, chaplain and acolytes, made this latter house his headquarters. The houses of Ros Irial and Moyn, both Clanricarde foundations, also survived. *Franciscan MSS.*, printed by C. P. Meehan, pp. 24–74, *passim.*

[2] A quotation indicates the deep internal feuds of the Burkes. ' If Redmond (Burke),' wrote the Annalist, ' would be satisfied with one mantle's breadth of his inheritance or patrimony from Sruthair to Abhainn-da-Loilgheach, he (Clanricarde) would not give him so much as a reward for war or peace.' Annals of the Four Masters, 1598, pp. 2056–7.

were made while his first wife was living. She was a stormy O'Brien, and survived him and he drove her out of his house as a witch and forced her back to her kindred in Thomond. But, even when he was an old men, his troubles increased, for, while his third [1] wife also was living, a Butler from Meath in the plains, he went through a form of marriage with a daughter of one of the Burkes and again with the child of McBrien I Ara, for he could not so far insult them as to take a mistress from that honourable house.

Then the sons of his marriages quarrelled and he claimed to the English Government that he had executed one of his children and a nephew and fifty of his principal followers, who went into rebellion. There followed a feud with his sons, but he relieved them secretly, sending caskets of money and jewels by a foster-brother and meeting them by the ford of the river to persuade their return to obedience. They agreed to give half their goods, ' both corn and horn ' [2] and he sent their offer to Dublin and this marks their preoccupation with the herds that made their great fortune. Then the old Earl with his bards and his secretary for Irish letters, Fyneen McMoeltroly, [3] would move uneasily from Ballinasloe to Dunkellin and back to Loughrea, sending his herds west to Claregalway when troops moved over the Shannon and intercepting the messages which came north from the Desmonds ; for he kept a semblance of loyalty. He was astute, but failing in body, worn out by his women and their quarrelling sons ; but most of all, he feared a punitive raid with the memory of the smoke of the burning farms of the Lower Burkes drifting south from Iar Connaught and the flickering of that year's fortune as the ricks burned against the sky.

Clanricarde died [4] in 1582 and his children came into their freedom, while John, Lord Leitrim, the second son, had a child by his sister, Lady Mary Burke, a wayward fierce woman, who already had a son

---

[1] Only his second wife retained her honours ; ' the Countess of Clann Rickard, Margaret, the daughter of Donnchadh son of Conchobar O'Briain, the best woman that was in Erinn in her own time died this year.' Annals of Loch Cé, 1568, p. 405.
[2] An offer made in 1577, ' half their goods, moveable and immovable, corn and horn.'
[3] This Secretary derived a special importance because Clanricarde could speak only a little English. Cal. S.P. Irel., 1575–86, p. 163.
[4] For the history of the Clanricardes see Cal. S.P. Irel., 1509–73 and 1575–86, passim, but for the details of the second Earl and his sons particularly the Elizabethan State Papers MSS., Vol. lvii, 39 and Vol. lxiv, 24–42.
A reference by the Lord Deputy throws a light on the vicissitudes of these leaders. ' The Erle of Clanricarde,' he wrote, ' is yet so over ruled by a putative wife whom he now kepeth as ofte tyme, when he best intended, she forceth hym to doe worst.' Sidney Papers, i, p. 29.

by O'Rourke; but the weight of the grave sin of incest now moved them to penance. After this the Burkes abruptly returned to the Church and became for 200 years the support of all the priests and friars in Connaught. But, in spite of such plunging and turmoil, it was only the Geraldines who went down in the reign of Elizabeth after the inexorable victory of the wasting of Desmond, nor did all these changes of the outer septs prevent a certain prosperity when the clans were allied; so that, after the agreement of 1571 between O'Neill and McDonnel, a report was sent to the Deputy that 'there are more ploughs in Clandeboy than there has been this hundred years.' Yet this was only a moment's respite, for the personal adventures of leaders had in each case significance, and Thomond was under control, since the Earl had pledged his estate to a merchant in Limerick. Such lords knew little of money and thought in terms of heads of cattle and payments in kind, rents paid in fodder and privileges like the giving of the judicial rod, and even their signs of honour were primitive, as McCarthy's present to the Spaniards of *aqua vitæ* and a sodden hog dressed with bread. Besides this, many outbreaks were due to restlessness as their imagination soared on the wings of their bards, while they sat over the peat fires in the winter and every meeting was sealed by great bouts and feats of endurance; so that, after one such gathering of honour and rank in the spring of 1583, the messengers rode south, declaring that Turlough O'Neill's trances had overcome him at last[1]; but the magnificent physique of the old man triumphed and, after twenty-four hours, the clouds passed and he rode away raising the North in his name.

In contrast to these perennial revolts of the outer septs, which were the immediate reaction of the Irish to any rule which was more than a shadow, there was the steady slow ferment of the lords in the Pale. For Dublin and the country around it and the fortified towns were dominated by the Anglo-Irish, a name which later obtained a wider significance, but which conveyed at that time a community as widely separate from the native Irish as Lowland from Highland Scots. There was this difference, however, that intermarriage was frequent, and some families of French or English descent had 'gone Irish,' while others had formed ties through the practice of fostering in the

[1] Cal. S.P. Irel., 1509–73, p. 443 for the ploughs in Clandeboy and 1574–85, p. 222, for McCarthy's gift and pp. 446–7 for Turlough's surfeit.

forest lodges with the wilder clans to the West. The test of the Anglo-Irish was perhaps the use of English as a first language, combined with a more settled conception of life and an English standard of luxury. They were loyalist towards England in the sense that they controlled the administration and the judicial posts, and because, possessing the trade, they desired settled conditions, while the rest desired war. Besides, the wealthy merchants in Galway and Waterford were inseparable from the gentry and intimately bound up with the great settled estates, since their profits came from the carrying trade and the sale of agricultural produce. Now straddling these sections there had been the great house of Kildare, but their leadership had been ruined in the rebellion of 1535, which had cost Silken Thomas his life. As long as the Kildare rule survived, the Anglo-Irish had governed the country and filled the great posts, relying also in a measure on the Geraldine support from the hills; but once the English rule was direct there came a whole class of officials from England and, between the new-comers and the clans, the Anglo-Irish struggled for breath.

They were long accustomed to the harrying raids, the ride of the spears from beyond the Brenny, galloping in the long dark of a moon-less night to the Red Moor in Meath and the drive of the cattle back before them away to the North from the settled land; but the ' under-takers ' threat was unceasing, conflict at the Council, charges to the Deputy, the slow unyielding process of the Court.

It was this new element of ' undertakers,' too, who introduced a fresh bitterness into the struggle, and it was to the credit of these clear-sighted officials that they saw that there would have to be conflict every inch of the way. They were English by birth, coming usually from the landed class, having therefore influence, but no wealth, and an inheritance of adventure. In religion they followed the Queen, but with a tenacity for the name of Protestant,[1] which they held to as a sign of their race. They were possessed of a cool judgement, nor did they underrate for a moment the sacrifice that they made in consenting to live at all in, what was to them, a barbarous land. But they could not retire, for their success depended on residence, just as in the case of the earlier nabobs in India, whose great fortunes were the direct result of a very personal contact such as Warren Hastings maintained

---

[1] As a mark of commendation, the phrases of the Reforming Party came early into use, and thus in 1572 Lord Deputy Fitzwilliam is found writing to Burghley that ' the Lord Chancellor is godly and cannot be corrupted by gifts.' Cal. S.P. Irel., 1509–73, p. 464.

with the Begums of Oudh. These riches were the result of shaking the pagoda tree with judgement and care, and in Ireland the case was the same, for whether the career was military or administrative, although the means used were different, the end was identical. Thus in a military career the first effort was to secure through influence an Irish command and then promotion came quickly, if determination was shown.

Closely allied with these military governors were the English officials in Dublin, astute men who were perhaps hardly qualified for similar office in England, but who had obtained this employment because they were willing to go into exile. There was, however, a certain divergence of view as the Queen was parsimonious and, if, for instance, the Master of the Ordnance wished to succeed in his office, peace was essential, as his margin of profit could not become good unless he preserved his scanty material. This also applied to the Master of the Horse and the Marshal and others in charge of equipment, and the revenue officials were similarly in a difficult place, as the Queen demanded a good showing and it needed skill to provide a sufficient profit to reconcile them to their arduous life. But, in the last resort, they all stood or fell together, and for this reason it was essential that the permanent officials should be maintained without changing. As they grew old and their ill-health developed, they were driven back on one another, especially as the body of hatred both in Dublin and the country increased, and a lifetime of service seemed too short to win a reward from a soil so harsh and ungrateful; but to the clans and the Anglo-Irish their achievement seemed solid enough.

Above all these parties stood the Lords Deputy appointed by the Queen and with direct access to her, but still to some extent at the mercy of the governing cliques at the Court. They associated chiefly with the English officials, but their whole outlook was different, and they were also in close touch with the Anglo-Irish, who had seats at the Council Board as they still retained the judiciary, and with the lords of the Pale, while again, independently of the provincial governors, they would sometimes keep their own agents with the clans in the North. They were men of a wide experience, and their horizons were not bounded by Ireland, for this office was only an episode in a successful career and would perhaps be rewarded by some great post on the Council or, as in Sidney's case, by the Presidency of Wales and the quiet honours of Ludlow.

An intimate acquaintance with the Court gave them links, which the officials did not possess, with the English wives of the great lords, like Lady Kildare, and they commonly possessed some almost unbreakable support to maintain them, as in the case of Perrot's supposed royal paternity or Fitzwilliam, who had the Cecil connection, or Sidney with his brother-in-law Leicester. They were very remote from the shifts which their subordinates often employed, and this gave them sympathy with the Anglo-Irish lords, quiet men like Dunsany and Gormanston, whose small castles rose stiffly from the fields about Dublin or by those little ports which faced towards England. It was pleasant for Lord Deputy Sidney to ride out to Gormanston, where his host would have an understanding of wine and an interest in the new styles of building and in racing greyhounds for coursing,[1] all lit by a calm judgement, the happy fruit of a security that both landlords possessed. But the Lord Deputy's card-playing at night with his Master of the Ordnance, Mr. Wingfield, was a different affair. It was true that Mr. Wingfield was a most courteous old gentleman and, on the mother's side, well connected, and that Lord Sussex's charge of treason had been dropped and his dismissal by Fitzwilliam rescinded, but still he had had his vicissitudes. Even when out of office, Lord Gormanston had his house by the sea and Sir Henry Sidney had Penshurst, with its great trees and its deer, but Mr. Wingfield had nothing. It is no wonder that he took trouble with his table of Ordnance, well balanced and very impressive and fortified by imaginary cannon in his ruinous keeps.[2] In this case the driving power is manifest which led the English officials to their final success. It was a crucial matter for them to retain their position, for the viceroys from England could retire to their sheltered estates, but if they

---

[1] Lord Deputy Perrot was particularly interested in the breeding of Irish wolfhounds both black and white, while at a later date Sir S. Bagenal refers to 'a great white dog, the most furiousest beast that ever I saw.' Cal. Salisbury MSS., 1st November, 1602, and Fynes Morison also pays a tribute, 'the cattle being in general very small and only the men and greyhounds of great stature.' *Itinerary*, pt. iii, bk. iii.

[2] The Elizabethan State Papers MSS. provide the stages of Mr. Jaques Wingfield's career. He began his service in 1534, but in 1562 he was deprived of all his offices by Lord Sussex on account of untoward conduct in the field against Shane, vi, 196, and in 1573 Fitzwilliam wrote 'Jaques Wingfield treads the same cross paths,' xli, 511, while in 1581 Sir G. Fenton refers to his negligence and plain corruption, lxxxvii, 336. In 1583 he countered by laying 'sinister informations' against Sir H. Wallop, but Perrot opposed him also and he died in 1587 deeply in debt to the Crown.

once lost their foothold they perished. Thus this division of opinion explains why the Irish would sometimes appeal, away from the provincial governors, to the deputies, whose very broadmindedness was the ultimate cause of their fall. The attitude of the Protestant Deputies to religion was typical; most of them were indifferent, Erastian and uninterested, with that sceptical Renaissance outlook, which the frame of mind of the Queen had provoked. On every question they lacked a vital interest in Ireland, and therefore they had to give way to their subordinates' vehement zeal.

In addition to these four groups, the Irish clans, the Anglo-Irish, the English officials and the Lords Deputy, with the continuity and force of the Crown, there was one man who, throughout the reign of Elizabeth, controlled so marked an influence and so great a force that he stood for a fifth element in the conflict, the power of the Butlers of Ormonde at the gate of the South.

Thomas, tenth Earl of Ormonde, was a man of great strength of character, loyal and tenacious, a mirror of all the honourable but unimaginative Butlers. The accident of his education at the Court of Edward VI had made him a Protestant or rather had imbued him with the lasting belief that the Catholic religion could not be true. In his manner and speech he was English with a short black beard of the Court fashion and an elegance in dress, wearing the restrained jewellery which the custom allowed. As a child he had been fostered with Rory O'More, but his subsequent training had separated him from his six Butler brothers. They were rebellious and Catholic and had been brought up by their mother the heiress of the elder branch of the Geraldines, who had married in her strong middle age the young Earl Gerald of Desmond, so that they were involved in all the tangle of hatred that had sprung from the murder at Leucansgail and the earlier death of Earl James at Courtmartix at the hands of Sir John. In addition there was constant dispute as to their mother's land and her dowry and the inheritance which her grandfather the fighting Bishop McBrien had left. But Ormonde had no sympathy with the Desmonds and their great feastings, bards coming from every house in the South and beeves driven as tribute through the forest of Desmond and the Franciscan friars maintained at Askeaton and the riding in of the young men, pretentious, grandiloquent as the bards in the Castle. Still less had he any contact with his father's cousins the Cavanaghs, with their outworn saffron, the masses of hair and the swords. His own duty was to maintain order and to safeguard his lands which stretched across the roads to the South, as they ran through the two Ormondes from his earldom of Ossory. It was a rich and fertile district, stretching right down the Suir Valley, but there was constant need of policing to ward off attack from the Graces, who lived as brigands in the high woods of Aherlow, or even in the interior of his country from the disturbances of O'Maolryan in the fastness of Solloghade or from Lord Upper Ossory[1] in the boundary dispute.

Into all these matters Ormonde entered with zeal, for he had that soldierly, rather stern love of duty in which the Butlers excelled. His was an isolated position,[2] for, while he was so far apart from the Irish, he was cool towards England, since he could not fail to perceive the intentions of the English officials, who were settling down on the country like locusts, and he could not forget the poisoned death of his father, the banquet of that autumn evening in Holborn, when he was fourteen and the old Earl and his steward and sixteen servants dead at the table. Allowing for certain exceptions, his relations with the Lords Deputy were good, but again these were distant, for he had such great power that they were not at their ease, since an adverse report to the Queen might cause their recall. With the Anglo-Irish his relations were closer and the three Butler peers, his Uncle Mountgarret and his cousins from Cahir and Dunboyne in the Pale belonged to this party; but with these men, even with those who had been brought up in England, there was the barrier of religion, for they all held to a Catholicism which he harshly despised. He was perhaps more fortunate in his relations with his subordinates than with his equals, yet another sign of his military temper, and especially with those men among the Anglo-Irish, who had lived in dependence on his family for years, like the Master of the Rolls, Sir Nicholas Whyte, who pleased him by a standard of worldly knowledge to which only the judges in his country attained, coupled with a clear-sighted judge-

---

[1] Ormonde put much vigour into his action against 'that most wicked and detestable old traitor Piers Grace' and his ally, Barnaby, Lord Upper Ossory than whom 'there was not a naughtier nor more dangerous man' in all Ireland. Cal S.P. Irel., 1574–85, pp. 224 and 237.

[2] On 7th June, 1581, Lord Upper Ossory wrote to Lord Leicester, 'I have been in prison six months through the malice and hate of my great enemy the Earl of Ormonde.' In the following March Sir N. Malby was drawing up a list of charges against Ormonde, his consistent enemy; while in March, 1583, Sir Henry Sidney declared that 'the Earl of Ormonde (my professed foe) sometime with clamour, but oftener with whispering did bitterly backbite me.' Cal. Carew MSS., ii, pp. 320–50 passim.

ment and perhaps most of all by an indifference in religious affairs. Catholic piety and especially the pilgrimages such as his brother Sir Edmund Butler arranged to Holy Cross Abbey, caused vexation to Ormonde, whose mind was concentrated on the safeguarding of highways and the strengthening of fords and the arrangements for the sale of the crops. His lands were almost a principality, and he had the isolation and influence, if not the material force, of such power and a certain slow pleasure in the administrative machinery and in his gift of protection. The prosaic quality of his mind aided his fame in contrast to the soaring imaginations of Desmond and the mounting fantastic glories of O'Neill's wine-clouded dream, for it was a relief to turn to Ormonde's calm judgement with its heavy if monotonous movement, the ground swell of thought.

This was the situation in the summer of 1580 when, after the hay harvest, Lord Baltinglas [1] joined the rebellion which was always flickering in the recesses of Wicklow, in the thick woods which guarded Glendalough of the Churches and the Glenmalure Water, which had proved for the O'Byrnes an impregnable hold. This Baltinglas Conspiracy is one of the most obscure of the period, both in its causes and hopes and in the connection with the Nugent plots that succeeded it. The confusion arises from the fact that every one of these five sections of opinion were prepared to be loyal at a price, and similarly were ready to put down rebellion, provided that their own terms were received, and in the case of this conspiracy it would seem to be the long strangling pressure of the settlers, which brought the Anglo-Irish to action at last. It is here that the significance of this rebellion is seen, for it was the first time in the reign that the English-speaking gentry had thrown in their lot with the clans, and it is only by a gradual reconstruction that we can discover, in a case where there are so few documents, how the Anglo-Irish would have used their success and what really they wished to achieve.

James, third Viscount Baltinglas, controlled all the land for over twenty miles along the slopes west of Wicklow, living at Kilcullen, a small town in the north of his property, near the Fitzgerald lands in

---

[1] The exact geographical distribution of the Baltinglas influence is fixed by a document, compiled when all was over and entitled, the lands of Viscount Baltinglas attainted. 'The lordship and late monastery of Baltinglas, the lordships and manors of Kilcullin and Harryston; the manors of Tobber, Rathernan near Dublin and Cahill; villages, town and woods in the Counties of Dublin, Kildare and Catherlogh and the barony of Fort O'Nolan.' Cal. Carew MSS., ii, p. 370.

Kildare. He was a devout Catholic, maintaining the Franciscans in Kilcullen and as an Anglo-Irish leader he had joined with Trimlestown and Lord Delvin to protest against the levying of cess, but, apart from this, he had been peaceful, though his brothers were troublesome.[1] His house was close to the stream of traffic, so that the gentlemen who fitted into the great semi-feudal structure of Ormonde would dine with him as they came riding home with their armed retainers from Dublin. Kilcullen was a centre of order where English was spoken, and it could be a strong refuge from the dangerous clans ; for although it faced towards the calm plains of Leinster and the travellers went down in safety to Seven Stars westward, behind lay the mountains. From the edge of the Eustace land, the tracks led up to the thickets where the O'Byrnes lay with their swords, and this is the most clear explanation of the Baltinglas Rising, for the Viscount was allied with the clans and two of his aunts had been sent into the mountain fastness as brides for Brian McCahir Cavanagh and O'Toole of Magnelle. A long period of discontent, due to loss of power and the coming of settlers, prepared this rebellion ; but Baltinglas miscalculated in his hope of raising the Pale. At the moment of the rising, the Desmond Rebellion was alight in the South, supported by Dr. Sanders the Nuncio, and there were stirs in the North and in Connaught, so that it seemed a fortunate time, but the very activity of the clans made the Anglo-Irish suspicious. Baltinglas, whose land ran up to the hills, understood the wilder clans and their leader Fiagh McHugh O'Byrne of Malure, who had ravaged with his brother-in-law, Rory O'More in the spring raid of nine years earlier and had now called out his followers again to avenge his murdered kinsman, the Kavanagh ; but, although the leader might understand the O'Byrnes, they were feared by the lords in the Pale, and it was these allies that prevented him from gaining supporters. Seen in this light, the Baltinglas Conspiracy has a slighter importance, for it was not so much a rebellious movement of the Anglo-Irish as the case of a solitary chief from their leaders, whose Highland blood and sympathies conquered as the result of the long suppressed feud with the English.

The early events of the rising after the fight at Glenmalure con-

---

[1] A report of Lord Justice Drury to the Privy Council dated 20th November, 1578, states that at Kilkenny thirty-four persons were executed including a blackmoor and two witches by natural law, and that it had been thought fit to keep the two sons of the (old) Viscount Baltinglas safe in Dublin Castle for some hurts lately done by them. Cal. Carew MSS., ii, p. 144–5.

firmed this ; for Baltinglas was joined by a natural son of his brother-in-law Butler of Roscrea and, in August, Garret Jones came to him bringing 'calivers and furniture from her Majesty's store,' for 'he had been entertained to serve against the rebels with fifty men for the defence of the Pale.'[1] In the same month Edward Butler, another of Ormonde's turbulent brothers,[2] came into Clanricarde with a hundred swords and kept to the mountains, and meanwhile there were communications with Desmond. 'A messenger with a green hat whose name was Robert Morris came from James Eustace. He brought no letters, but only signs, which were known to the Earl, and John of Desmond prepared himself for a journey.'[3] The same messenger stated that McWilliam Eighter had four hundred Scots with long swords, who would come to help Desmond, and the North was stirring ; for, according to the Knight Marshal's spy, Baltinglas had sent his chaplain, Sir Manus, to Turlough O'Neill to persuade him to join with the Munster rebels and O'Rourke from Connaught and appointing a meeting in Meath.

In May it was reported that O'Donnell and O'Neill had sent their wives into Scotland for soldiers, and in July that four thousand men were to be hired and the galleys of the O'Malleys and the O'Flaherties were sent to transport them, and in August two thousand were said to have landed in Ulster. They came across with the favouring tide on the calm moonless summer nights from Cantyre and went ashore on those beaches where the tangled woods of the Glens of Antrim came down to the sea, so that before sunrise they were lost in the trees. Every moonlight Turlough O'Neill made 'his continual gatherings' and the revolt of Clanricarde's sons 'disquieted Connaught . . . but like wild wolves they kept the woods and the mountains.' In the South, Desmond sent his own household servants to guard the Pope's standard and his men adopted the war cry of Papa Abu and, finally in August, Sir John of Desmond and Dr. Sanders himself, after taking refuge in Aherlow were passed in safety by the

---

[1] According to the notes made on 31st August, 1580, by Sir Nicholas Malbie. Cal. Carew MSS., ii, p. 311.

[2] Described by Malbie as 'Edward Butler, brother of my Lord of Ormonde, whom he hath banished for his dissolute life.' *Ibid.*, p. 311.

[3] From the tenth item of the examination of the captured friar James O'Haie before Sir Lucas Dillon on 17th August, 1580. Cal. Carew MSS., ii, pp. 308–10. This is confirmed from other sources and by information from Ormonde. The movements in Ulster were reported by Sir Nicholas Malbie and Lord Justice Pelham and are confirmed from the Scottish side by reports among the Scottish State Papers.

Graces of Leix, whence the O'Mores led them to the strongholds of Baltinglas and O'Byrne. When these were the wild fruits of the rising, it is not strange that the Anglo-Irish of the Pale stood aloof.[1] This fear of the kernes riding down on the farms was one of the two elements that Baltinglas had to contend with in his appeal to the Pale and the other was the strange character of the Earl of Kildare, who still led as the first among equals where his father was master.

Gerald, eleventh Earl of Kildare, was at this time fifty-five years of age, delicate and, although well proportioned, so small as to be almost deformed, perhaps the result of a weakened strain from his mother, who had had dwarfs in her family, the Dorset Greys. He was the child of a second marriage, and, when he was ten, the power of his family was ruined in the rebellion of his half-brother Thomas. Lord Gerald, as he was called, was sickening with small-pox and he was still so little that he could be packed into a hamper by his tutor and sent away for safety to the fastness of Offaly. Then he lived with his aunt, Lady Eleanor, in the wilds of Tyrconnell and was sent, an abrupt contrast, to Rome to the charge of Cardinal Pole, his relation. There he lived in the house beside St. Mary in Cosmedin, and in the summers in the Governor's house at Viterbo, for the Cardinal was Legate of the Patrimonium and he travelled with all the magnificence of Farnese Rome. A slight and undeveloped boy of fifteen, quite without letters, such an upbringing could only serve to increase his native indecision of character. He had personal courage, which he showed when fighting with the Knights of Rhodes against Turkey, and he had moments of the traditional Fitzgerald anger; but in all major matters he was submissive. Perhaps his reserve, due to his weakness, made him remote,[2] but he never acquired either reputation or friendship, passing through his service at the Medicean Court and his long years in Ireland without making any impression, seeking only for peace.

[1] The Irish account of Baltinglas' first victory at Glenmalure helps to explain this. 'The defeat of Glen-Malura was inflicted on the Saxons by the sons of Roland Eustace and by Fiacha son of Aedh son of John.' Annals of Loch Cé, 1579, p. 431. An interesting contrast is provided between this entry in Loch Cé and the later Munster classicism of O'Sullevan Beare, ' memorabilem pugnam ad muluriam sylvam committunt ubi Greium Anglum Iberniæ proregem acie superarunt : octingentos milites occiderunt, et inter illos crudelem Catholicorum carnificem Franciscum Cosbium Lissiæ præfectum.' Historiæ Catholicæ Iberniæ Compendium, t, ii, lib., iv, c. xv.

[2] Nevertheless to the Irish he was a protective and portentous figure, as the following entry among the chief obituaries will show. ' The Earl of Cill-dara's steward, Meiler Husè died this year.' Annals of Loch Cé, 1582, p. 455.

o 2

Although his education had been so profoundly Catholic, he was indifferent in these matters also, becoming Protestant to please Edward VI and Catholic again and then Anglican and then finally returning to Catholicism through the strength of his wife. He had made a Catholic marriage, wealthy but of no great rank, with the eldest daughter of Sir Anthony Browne, who involved him in later trouble through the doings of her brother, Charles Browne at Santander, an exile in the service of Spain.[1] The Earldom had been restored to him and this gave him a rank in the Pale above and apart from the others ; but he never acquired great wealth, while a perhaps nervous attachment to gambling sapped his resources. Unlike Ormonde his relations were strained with the Government, due to his hesitating policy in the case of the Fitzgeralds of Desmond. Finally he was appointed as General of the forces against the rebels, rather because the Deputy thought that in his weakness this would bind him than on account of any personal trust. It was this man that Baltinglas rode out to meet at the Hill of Tara on the morning of Wednesday, the 4th of July, 1580, to persuade him to become the leader of the rebellion in the Pale.

This was not the first time that Kildare had been approached with such plans, although the earlier schemes had turned on his son, Lord Gerald, who, had he survived, might have become the leader that the Irish desired ; but he had died in England[2] in the early 'twenties and had been buried in St. Alban's Abbey a fortnight before. The great and ramshackle household, which Kildare maintained at Rahangan, was a breeding ground of petty intrigue, and seven years earlier Richard Stanyhurst, who had himself been trained overseas, formed a plan to carry over Lord Gerald to Spain and so the idea developed, mounting from one fantasy to another to marry him to King Philip's daughter and bring him back to Ireland as King. Stanyhurst, who was at the time tutor, told Lalor the Seneschal and then Parson Canton was made privy to the enterprise and told Hussey, who in his turn brought the story to the Earl, who was greatly offended. No one knew better than Kildare how dangerous the rambling talk of

---

[1] Charles Browne's name with the note ' like to be serviceable when occasion shall be offred ' appears in a list of English exiles in Spain. S.P. Dom. Eliz., cv, p. 10, printed at the end of this volume.

[2] The Kildares maintained constant contact with England and earlier in the same year their Seneschal had been sent to London with £100 in rents for Lord Gerald and had lain three weeks in Holborn at the sign of the *Crown*. Cal. Carew MSS., ii, App. p. 486.

some disappointed scholar over his fire in the evenings could become in the hands of his enemies and in this case the Government professed to believe that, if not Kildare himself, his Countess paid considerable heed to these schemes.

It was partly the greater freedom, which the Irish Lords possessed in religious affairs, that caused this suspicion, for in Ireland, while the priests and friars were hunted, the households of the peers were immune. They could all maintain Catholic chaplains and keep in their service men like the Seneschal Lalor, who had been abroad to Louvain, and at Rahangan, for instance, there were rooms kept for the priest Rochford, while Sir Nicholas Eustace, one of the Baltinglas clan, was Lady Kildare's personal chaplain.[1] Then of course there were the Irish, McGeoghegan and his son Brian who had murdered his other son Rosse, 'the one assured servant the Queen had in Offaly,' and old McGilpatrick and the swarm of Geraldine bastards. With so many friends in that household, Baltinglas might be justified in his hopes of the Earl, who was surrounded by all these men who had suffered in the destruction of the chieftains of Leix, which Captain Cosby had arranged, the blood of the Rath of Mullaghmast calling for action. But in reality Kildare had no thought of rebellion, for although Turlough O'Neill riding through Ulster in the high steeple-crowned hat that was the mark of his civilized pride, might dream of himself as a new King of Ireland with Emain Macha re-arisen and the North ruling again, and Desmond in Munster might have similar hopes, Kildare had travelled and knew well that the rebels had nothing to offer him. Baltinglas played with the Papal title of Viceroy, and so it seems did Lord Gerald, but Kildare only wished to keep a security, for he knew that if he went too far on the side of the English he might die at the hands of his disappointed supporters. In this difficulty he called in his son-in-law, Lord Delvin, on whose advice he then much relied,[2] to come to the meeting at Tara and with the assistance of this

[1] According to a letter from Lord Chancellor Gerard to Walsingham, dated 18th February, 1581, the Countess of Kildare is to hear that Her Majesty is not ignorant of her harbouring known Papists combined with Sanders in her house and the open passage Rochford had at Rahangan where his books were kept. Sir Nicholas Eustace, priest, who for the most part kept at Rahangan would depart thence to gentlemen's houses and there at Mass swear men to join the rebels or at least not to be against them. Cal. S.P. Irel., 1574–85, p. 287.

[2] On 22nd December, 1580, Lord Deputy Grey wrote to the Queen that Delvin had an obstinate devotion to Popery and was a wicked creature, who had ruined the poor Earl. Cal. S.P. Irel., 1574–85, p. 275. His Catholic zeal is shown by a hostile reference to a venerated shrine he maintained, 'a gay master god with glass eyes in the Baron Delvin's island near Athlone.' S.P. Irel. Eliz., MS. 131, f. 64. *The first number gives the volume, the second gives the first page of the document.*

197

man, who though of much greater decision of mind was confronted by similar problems, he prepared his reply.[1]

Christopher, fourteenth Lord Delvin, was thirty-six years of age and had, like Ormonde, been brought up in England, for his father had died young, leaving him to the guardianship of Lord Deputy Sussex, who had sent him to Cambridge and this put something of a barrier between him and his kindred. Thus his next brother, William Nugent, spoke Gaelic and his English was so strange that it could not be understood by the gentlemen of the Pale and hardly by his uncle Judge Nugent. The importance of the Nugents lay in their sympathy with the Irish and they were more likely to favour rebellions, for like the Eustaces their forces were always hanging on the edge of the Pale, since their strength lay above Meath in the bog and the heather. Strategically they depended on the alliance of the O'Reillys of Breffny and on this by the favour of the Great O'Reilly, ' a very honest man, but old very impotent and bedrid,' [2] they could rely. A strong Catholicism and a mutual loyalty united them, although within the family there were very marked contrasts, particularly between the restrained Lord Delvin, with his interest in books and his great architectural plans, and his brother, William Nugent, the firebrand, who had carried off his wife, Janet Marward, from her guardian at the point of the sword and who knew his way blindfold through all the mazed intrigues of the Irish.[3] Then again Nicholas Nugent, their youngest uncle, was Chief Justice of the Common Pleas, cultivated and sober and the popular leader of the pro-Irish party in Dublin, while the other uncles were Gaelic on the edge of the wilds, Oliver at Ballina, Gerald at Lissaghnedan and James at Coolamber, men of great authority on the border, who could rouse and pacify clans. These men exercised on their nephew, Lord Delvin, the same pressure [4] to join in rebellion that the Geraldines and their Irish followers had used with Kildare. In fact, all three Delvin, Baltinglas and Kildare were being urged forward by their supporters, but only Baltinglas

---

[1] Sydney Papers, i, p. 102.

[2] Unpublished documents, preserved in the Public Record Office, dealing with the relations between Baltinglas, Kildare and the Nugents are summarized in the Appendix to this volume.

[3] This aspect of the family is represented by the address in Gaelic to Janet Nugent, *Sined inghen Uateir*, a lament for the death of her son the heir of Skreen, now preserved as Egerton MSS., iii, f. 80.

[4] The pressure of the outer Nugents is clearly seen in the imposition of fines for refusal of cess payments, recorded under February, 1578, in the Entry Book of Orders and Decrees of the Court of Castle Chamber, Dublin. Cal. Egmont MSS., i, p. 7.

had yielded, for he had none of the experience of European conditions, which the others had gained.

Failing an agreement to take the field together, an arrangement for mutual protection was made. Kildare, who had the supreme command of the Government forces, agreed to take care that none of his zealous subordinates should be allowed to capture the rebels, and on his part obtained a pledge from O'Byrne that he would spare the Fitzgerald lands and carry his raids towards Dublin more to the eastward. Before separating, they arranged for messengers to keep one another in touch, one of the Geraldine bastards representing Kildare, while William Nugent acted for Delvin and Baltinglas sent messages through his English wife and his sister, Lady Upper Ossory. The place of meeting was to be Monkstown, four miles outside Dublin, which had belonged to Lady Baltinglas' family, the Travers. Plans were made for communicating with Richard Eustace, Lord Baltinglas' youngest brother, who was studying in Paris, and became a priest later in Rome ; for the usual channel through the Waterford merchants, who looked after the Eustace affairs, was stopped since the rebellion. The other four brothers, Edmund, William, Thomas and Walter, were with Baltinglas in the hills, for they had only a younger son's portion, land worth £40 a year each, and depended upon him. Arrangements were completed for the purchase of powder and calivers, a most necessary weapon, from Walter Sedgrave and William Fitzsimmons,[1] merchants in Dublin. This was made easier by the relationship of their agents, for, while all this side of Baltinglas' affairs were in the hands of Christopher Barnewell, much of the loose organization of the Kildare estates was controlled by Robert Barnewall, who also belonged to that clan. At the same time the lands which the rebels had held, including the estate of Mr. Eustace of Castlemartin and that of young David Sutton of Castleton, were to be protected by Kildare, who could give a certain proof of his loyalty by the zeal with which he demanded the custody of the Baltinglas property.[2] Finally Sir

---

[1] These merchants would seem to have belonged to the same firm as Alderman Christopher Sedgrave, who possessed a small demi-round tower with two vaults, one equal with the wall with three ' lowps,' the other with a pair of stairs going up unto it from the city wall. Mr. Nicholas Fitzsimmons had a similar tower 32 feet high, with four stories and three lofts, in another part of the wall. Cal. S.P. Irel., 1574–85, pp. 454 and 591. Alderman Sedgrave was the third husband of Lady Trimlestown, who was connected with the Nugents, and the Fitzsimmons had relations abroad including Laurence Fitzsimmons in Rome, so that these towers were perhaps store-houses for the rebels easily accessible on the outer edge of the wall.

[2] The total value of all the lands of Lords Baltinglas, Delvin and Kildare and Mr. Sutton is given as £6,000 a year in Elizabethan money, equivalent perhaps to the purchasing power of

Nicholas Eustace was to be sent round to all the houses of the Pale to persuade the gentry to swear that they would not bear arms against rebels. Then they separated, Baltinglas and his kinsmen riding back to the mountains again, Lord Delvin returning to his house at Westmeath and Kildare to Rahangan, whence he refused to come for consultations in Dublin, and wrote to Walsingham saying that ' he was like to die ' [1] and pleading his sickness. The result of this meeting had therefore been disappointing to Baltinglas and even more so to the enthusiastic supporters of Kildare and Delvin, since time was in any case on the side of the English. To the Government also it was unsatisfactory, as there was always a possibility that these Lords might be forced to rebel, and it was difficult to decide the right moment for action, which was complicated by the zeal of the settlers, who were afraid that a heaven-sent opportunity of degrading their enemies might escape. Of course, as in all the cumbrous conspiracies of the period, the moves were perfectly known to the Government ; but in this case a special clamour was caused by the intervention of the Archbishop of Dublin.

As Kildare rode away from this dialectical victory, he fell in with another company, that of the Protestant Archbishop and Keeper of the Great Seal, Dr. Adam Loftus, a grave noble-looking divine with a bald crown and a great white beard, who led the more moderate or, so to speak, the right wing of the settlers. He was the first of a house, which was to be bound up with many of the fatalities of Ireland ; for he ruined Kildare and then with all his class achieved the ruin of Perrot and one of his family was the instrument of Strafford's disaster ; while the Marquessate of Ely was one of the most costly of the winding sheets with which the Irish Parliament was laid in its grave. The immunities, which the Catholic Lords enjoyed, provided a certain guarded and prescribed intercourse with the bishops, and as a result Sir Nicholas Whyte, who was a Catholic, at least in name,[2] could be

£48,000 a year and on a similar basis the property of Mr. Sutton would be worth £2,400 a year, that of Mr. Eustace of Castlemartin £1,600, and Mr. Eustace of Cardiston £480, the portion of the younger Baltinglas sons would be equivalent to an income of £320, while Eustace of Cardiston had goods and cattle worth £3,200 and David Sutton's brother John who was landless had the equivalent of £7,200 in money and £2,400 in cattle. But of course the Suttons were among the richer landowners of the Pale. Elizabethan State Papers MS. 98, f. 85.,

[1] Letter of Kildare to Walsingham, dated 19th September, 1580. His cause was not assisted in London by the dispatch sent by Sir W. St. Leger to Burghley five days later, asserting that Charles Brown, the Countess's base brother, had come with the Italians. Cal. S.P. Irel., 1574–85, pp. 253–4.

[2] All his family remained Catholic, nor does his acceptance of office under the Crown in Ireland prove much, but a letter to Walsingham, in which he sends him ' a sanctus bell and

called upon to write to England that the Archbishop was a good father to his many children. In this connection, it was in fact these twenty Loftus children who determined the resolute financial policy which marked this man of peace.

Dr. Adam Loftus' career had begun in Ireland, where he had come as chaplain to Lord Deputy Sussex, which led to promotion to the see of Armagh when he was twenty-eight and then six years later to Dublin and to legal office as Keeper of the Seal and as Chancellor. It was a hard struggle, as he could not obtain possession of Armagh at all, since it belonged to O'Neill, but he was a Yorkshireman with a strong sense of reality, and it was a great contrast to a younger son's place on the lands of Swineside, the big yeoman's house in Wensleydale where he was born. So he pushed on slowly from Termonfeckin outside Drogheda, with £20 a year, to the town of Tallaght, which was part of the temporalities of the see of Dublin, under the Wicklow Hills and finally to the building of Rathfarnham. Fortunately he had opportunities in later life; for he was not only Lord Chancellor, but, on the Ecclesiastical side, ' Chief Commissioner in the High Commission and Principal for the Faculties and Archbishop of Dublin, so he is all in all.' In his position, too, where so much depended on the prudent disposal of parsonages and glebes, in places to which it was hardly possible to send a minister, a level head was essential. This he possessed, and such charges as were produced against him were abandoned; for he had a solid support and the firm influence of the settlers.[1] He was a heavy man, suffering from an infirmity of the leg and from the quartan agues, grave, ' reverend ' after the fashion of the times, and with a weight of determination, which made

another toy ' taken from Fitzmaurice, shows that he at any rate knew how to dissemble his fervour. In 1590 his son Andrew Whyte figured in a report as ' a most dangerous Papist.' Cal. S.P. Irel., 1588–92, p. 365.

[1] Accusations against the Archbishop made in 1590 by the Deputy Remembrancer, Robert Legge, included the concealment of fines, the granting of ante-dated bonds and the retention of many churches and livings to maintain his children; also specifically the acceptance of a bribe from the Dean of St. Patrick's and a present of hogsheads of salmon to procure the release of Sir John O'Doherty from the Castle. His friends on the Bench, especially Sir Robert Dillon, had incurred justified suspicion and the Serjeant is described as ' very timorous, heavy and sleepy in Court, but doth nothing.' Another accusation of Andrew Trollope in 1581 stated ' it is very likely to be true that the Lord Bishop of Dublin is a partner in the profits of the Commission of Faculties and anything almost will be suffered in Ireland for gain or friendship.' He had borrowed £400 from Sir William Drury ' and to defray all charges and get more money for his sons and daughters many think maketh him to have a cheverell conscience.' Elizabethan State Papers, Irish MSS. 85, f. 39 and 150, f. 52. These accusations were made by his own followers, but it must be said that the Government did not proceed with the charges.

him the most dangerous of the enemies which the hesitant and doubtful Earl could chance to meet.

The conversations between Kildare and the Archbishop ran along the lines which could be foreseen from a knowledge of character. The Archbishop first inquired who had led the troop of horse, which he had seen at Killeen. Kildare, having at first concealed their identity, was obliged to admit that Baltinglas has been there and following up his advantage the Archbishop suggested that the Earl ' should take Sir John Harryngton's horsemen for the present apprehension of the Viscount,' to which Kildare replied that he was his kinsman and that his country would hate him and that it would be a perpetual reproach to his house, if he should apprehend him. The Archbishop countered this firmly, and Kildare, who as the Queen's General, had no adequate reply, offered to ride to Maynooth the same evening and to send to Baltinglas to come to a meeting next day at which the Archbishop could arrange for his capture. He indeed rode off at once to Baltinglas, but only to warn him, and when the Archbishop came on the following morning he proposed another plan by which Baltinglas could be arrested at a meeting at his house at Monkstown late in the week. Having thus gained time for a safe retreat to the mountains, there was a final meeting [1] at Kildare's house in Dublin, from which the Archbishop came away determined to ruin him. Nor did Kildare's action assist his cause, for he refused to come to Dublin and fell into passionate speeches, ' sometimes braying out with oaths and saying this were enough to make a man break out,' and then would come fear and a sudden calm and an altered mind.

These occasional Fitzgerald angers only showed the more clearly that nervous solitude in which he suffered the increased tension of a situation already dangerous, acting on a temperament which deformity and a foreign training had combined to render doubtful, solitary, apart. But in England, where all these reverberations sounded fainter, there was hesitation as to the course, for, while there was a certain danger in leaving Kildare at liberty, it would be a great asset in case of a more general rebellion if he could be retained in freedom even as a nominal supporter of England. Although the usual time for the rebellions had not yet come, there was always the fear that the com-

[1] Elizabethan State Papers, Irish MS. 84, ff. 36, 38, contain a series of thirty-seven interrogatories administered to Lord Kildare and twenty-two to Lord Delvin, after their capture : while Kildare's conduct in the summer is described in Carew MS. 607, f. 76.

THE RISINGS IN THE PALE

bined pressure of Desmond and O'Neill and the Pale rebels might cause the clans to revolt. The Scots had already crossed in the later summer, creeping down the coast of Ulster to the western ports, but the Irish in Connaught would wait first to gather in their harvest[1] especially in those great fields in the West in Mayo to which the English rule had never come. Then, after the autumn sowing and before the worst of the rain, they would ride down into the settled land to plunder, plunging eastward through the long winter night and raising the Nugents and their friends in the Pale and the old clans in Leix and Offaly and all that host of enemies around the edges of Ormonde, who hung about the fringes of the hard Butler rule. But November came with no sign of trouble, and O'Neill was peaceful, and it seemed that, although winter had brought security to the recesses of Desmond, it was already known to the clans that the revolt in the South was failing and that all the rebellion moved brokenly on a faltering wing. Besides, Sir James of Desmond was captured and already the Nuncio Sanders was dying, so that this lessening hope, which spread so fast through the clans, kept them back from an action.

Yet this made the settlers more clamorous for the arrest of Kildare and Delvin, now that winter was safe and they hoped that a premature revolt of their followers would give them the chance they desired, to prove, as they would have put it, which of the Anglo-Irish lords were loyal to their mistress. The Government yielded and, on the 23rd of November, Kildare and Delvin were arrested, and this action was immediately followed by that confused series of events which are known as the Nugent Revolt, of which only the results remain clear, the death of the leaders and the transfer of the Anglo-Irish land to the settlers. It was a clear succession of cause and effect, for the Baltinglas Conspiracy led to the meeting at Tara and the friendly neutrality of Kildare and Delvin, while this doubtful attitude caused their arrest, which was followed by a hurried attempt to release them the Nugent Revolt. After this, there was quiet and a calm season and the plains of Meath an English field and the Irish tenants reaping.

The arrest of these chiefs at once placed those anxious to rebel in

---

[1] A letter of Sir Nicholas Malbie, dated 15th September, 1583, contains an instance of this practice, ' O'Wrourcke wrote to me that he would keep the peace usque ad festum Omnium Sanctorum (1st November). His meaning thereby was to get in his harvest and then break out. O'Connor Dun's son who married O'Wrourcke's daughter refused to come to me and set on fire his fathers castle, who is blind and 100 years old.' Cal. Carew MSS., ii, p. 363.

the weaker position, but William Nugent rode off to the west to the moors where Sir Thomas Nugent's lands reached up to the O'Reilly's Country in Cavan. His uncle Nicholas, who was the more cautious, followed to persuade him to come back to Dublin, but without any success, and William Nugent rode on, arriving on Christmas Eve at Cloneen, the most northerly and isolated of Lord Delvin's houses, near the head waters of the Erne beyond Gowna, and then, in the New Year, he crossed over the border to the O'Rourkes and O'Reillies to raise them in rebellion. There was a certain agreement and some sharp raiding and then he came back to the Pale in secret to make an effort to persuade the Anglo-Irish to free themselves from the settlers by a joint attack with the clans.[1] From one point of view, the moment was favourable, as opinion had been influenced by the arrest of the leaders and by the eager quarrelling among the settlers for the Baltinglas land; but on the other hand it was clear that the Government was expecting and almost provoking a rising, and it was knowledge of this factor which kept the rich men immovable. Lord Gormanston protested his loyalty, as did the old blind Lord Howth and even Lord Dunsany,[2] who was stepson of the Great O'Reilly, refused to come forward; so, driven down to the prosperous squires, Nugent attempted to gain the Plunkets and Barnewalls, but this also failed, and he was compelled to recruit his forces from the young and the landless.

Then gradually, by playing off all the submerged feuds and smothered rivalries of the country, William Nugent collected support, chiefly from the Cusackes, who were dependent on the Nugents and had a feud with the 'English' Dillons and then from the Scurlocks of Scurlockstown, a minor family whose situation was complicated by enmity with the Lismullen Cusackes from which their relations with the other branches of that family at Ellistonreed and at Cassington seemed to be free. John Cusacke of Ellistonreed was the chief agent employed, going to Lady Delvin, with a plan for the surprise

[1] In every such united effort the Anglo-Irish were obliged to face English ridicule. The attitude of derision is clearly expressed in a speech by Sir Robert Cecil. 'Harrington . . . hided and was put to a shamefull flighte by the sonne of a Mountayne Kerne Teffmakewe.' Star Chamber Speeches, Farmer Chetham MSS., i, pp. 1–24, printed by the Surtees Society.
[2] Lord Howth may have been deterred by his recent imprisonment for cruelty to his fourteen children and for beating his butler, who had given bread and drink of a better sort to Lady Howth who was kept as a prisoner, perhaps on account of a feud with her family the strong stock of the Plunkets of Beaulieu. Cal. Egmont MSS., i, pp. 11–2. Lord Dunsany, on the other hand, was quiet and scholarly, a devout Catholic and the head of the Guild of Our Lady at Killeen with a poor and embarrassed estate.

Map of the Irish Pale and Wicklow.

The places marked are referred to in the text in connection with the Baltinglas and Nugent Risings.

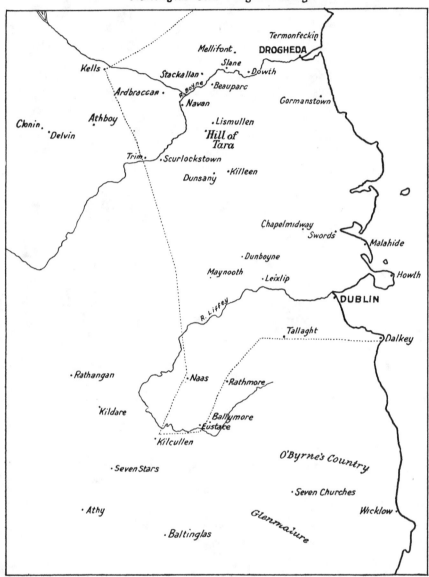

The dotted line marks the boundary of the Pale.

of Dublin Castle and the release of her father, and then to all the houses in the safe fields near the city, to Chapelmidway and the Cusacke cousins at Kilbride, where it would be dangerous for William Nugent to venture. Then again Cusacke would ride through the rich and well-policed lands of the Boyne, moving up through the river valley from Drogheda, gathering young George Netterville from his father at Dowth, failing to gain Mr. Fleming from Slane, but obtaining one of the Plunket sons from Beauparc, only to fail with their cousins at Stackallan over the river. As he moved up-stream to the upper river by Lismullen and Scurlockstown he had greater success till he came to the wild country where Nugent was hiding, concealed in the barns on the farms of his servants. And then, gathering supporters from the edge of the Pale towards Ulster, from Drakestown and Dromisalot, John Cusacke held a meeting at Ellistonreed in the summer, ' standing by his harvest folk in his fields,' when they agreed to ride to the safety of Castletown Delvin, where William Nugent with thirty kerne of his clansmen and O'Reillys met them in the thickets of the Grove of Dyrrys to devise the details of a new campaign.

Yet, with so small a force, they could do little, a constant raiding of the guarded cattle, the more ambitious burning of Mullingar, Athboy and Trim, where the settlers had now gathered, an act of personal vengeance against Mr. Moore at Mellifont, the driving of Bishop Jones' kine, an ineffective, undistinguished list. Then, for a local feud, they rode into the Plunket's country with behind them the flame and smoke of Sir Lucas Dillon's manor and the cattle showing faintly in the byres, a noble effort as they swept into Rathrannan, ' the bright of the moon to spoil and burn.'[1] By this time it was a desperate effort, though perhaps William Nugent hoped that such a display of force would bring the wavering lords into action at last, but in reality it was the chief means by which the Government achieved his destruction.

It had been a fortunate summer for the English with the Nuncio Sanders dead and a successful raid into the O'Byrnes' Country and the burning of their chief house, Ballinacor and Desmond ineffectually suing for mercy. The Government in Dublin, perfectly aware of the

[1] Examinations of prisoners in Elizabethan State Papers, Irish MS. 86, f. 19 i–iv, ff. 67, 72, 80, 87 i–ii, and MS. 87, ff. 22 i and 44 i. There are personal details of the Nugents in MS. 88, f. 44, i, the confession of John Cusacke of Ellistonreed is contained in MS. 88, f. 47, i, while MS. 86, f .30 includes Wallop's letter about Baltinglas.

general movements, had only to decide on the particular methods for obtaining their evidence. The decision was taken that the first attempt should be made with John Cusacke of Cassington, who as a first cousin of Delvin's was in some sense the leader. Although, as they regretted, the officials in Dublin possessed no ' engine,' [1] such as that which it was customary to use in the Tower, they were completely successful and procured the necessary evidence through a promise of mercy which they did not fulfil. In the following February, they obtained the condemnation of Justice Nicholas Nugent for treason on the evidence of John Cusacke of Ellistonreed, whom they had arrested not only for rebellion, but for attempting the murder of Sir Lucas Dillon and who earned a pardon for this notable service. In the same winter of 1581 William Nugent escaped to Turlough O'Neill and thence to Scotland, while the rebels in Wicklow were already hard pressed in the autumn, and Sir Henry Wallop wrote to Walsingham as to their plight : [2] ' The O'Connors have kept very quiet, but by reason of their wood and bog we cannot light on them. They dare not stay ii nights together in any place, nor lie within five miles of where they sup. And even in like sort is it with Baltynglas and Phelim O'Toole. We are informed that Baltynglas mindeth to go into Spayne hoping to get shipping about Wexford, which to prevent we shall use our best endeavours.' But Baltinglas was successful, and he took that road to Spain from Ferrol to the Court, which has always been strewn, as thickly as camel bones on a desert track, with the end of Irish hope.

When all this struggle was over, Kildare and Delvin, who had been taken to England, were allowed to return home under *surveillance* to a country where the spirit of the Anglo-Irish was broken. Henceforward there was no need to reckon with them as a party which might foster rebellion and, with the wasting of Desmond, the South, too, fell to the settlers. It took a quarter of a century before the power of Ulster was broken at the Flight of the Earls, but before that the settlers had already conquered the Viceroy. During the Baltinglas and Nugent Revolts, the Deputy Lord Grey of Wilton was in every way in sympathy with the dominant English, but, under his successor,

---

[1] A letter of The Lords Justices in Dublin to Walsingham in 1583 complains that they have neither rack nor engine of torture in Dublin Castle to terrify Dr. Hurley. They suggest that the Tower of London would be a better place for one so inward with the Pope and Cardinals to be examined. Elizabethan State Papers, Irish MS. 106, f. 7.

[2] *Cf.* Letter of Geoffrey Fenton to Leicester, dated 1st September, 1581, ' the Viscount Baltinglas wandereth in great astonishment.' Cal. S.P. Irel., 1574–85, p. 317.

Perrot, there was a struggle against the Viceroy from London on the part of the settlers, which ended with their complete and permanent victory. As a political force apart from them, Ormonde alone survived, but his power could not outlive him, for the Anglo-Irish were in very much the same dilemma in which sometimes the Indian Princes were placed and their failure was inevitable when they first lost the support of the Crown. If the settlers won they would lose their land by lawsuit and their power would depart, but they must have known what would have been their fate in a great uprising of the outer Gaelic Ireland, the Pale alight and the clans riding, the death of the sword.

CHAPTER XI

THE FALL OF LORD DEPUTY PERROT

The following study of Sir John Perrot's rule in Ireland concerns the conflict between the new English official settlers and the alien and superior, but transitory, power of the Governors from England. Already, after the victory over the old Anglo-Irish families of the Pale which has just been considered, the new English settlers were asserting a right to the sole government of the country in which they had planted their stock. Providing that the Deputies sent out from England would support their position, the settlers were ready to serve with these passing and casual rulers. It was Perrot's decision to rule with independence that forced the settlers to show their strength and give battle. The four years of his government, from 1584 till 1588, the period immediately succeeding the Nugent and Baltinglas risings, thus passed in continual conflict, which led in the end to a victory for the new settlers. The foundations of that system were laid by which the Crown was to agree to leave Ireland to the Ascendancy Party. At the same time, a consideration of Sir John Perrot's rule throws light on the Wales of his time, for he had been a great figure in Pembroke and, among his supporters in Ireland, the Castle Welshmen form a curious group. In the correspondence of the time, the diverse characters of his opponents, the Lords Justices Wallop and Loftus, the Knight Marshal, Sir Nicholas Bagenal, and Auditor Jenison, stand contrasted and every reaction to his strong rule is clear. In the background Perrot's friends, like the Judges, Sir Nicholas Whyte and the Dillons, represent the survival of the old Anglo-Irish opinion, which had gone down with the Nugents; while behind them there is the constant Butler power and O'Neill. Farther west, almost indistinguishable in this struggle, there are the Gaelic Irish, whom the next chapter describes. Just as in the case of the North Welsh families, so also in these Irish studies, the same factions appear with their changing *rôles* at each stage of the quarrel. In this instance the Bagenals will form an example, for, while they were powerful in their influence on Perrot, they were destined in the decade to follow to provide the sharpest of the irritants which acted on the mind of Tyrone. It is typical of all the political families which Ireland received, that their influence was alternately bent on the official framework at Dublin and on the forces of Gaeldom. This chapter deals with Ireland as seen from the Castle, the next study, on the Armada, with Ireland seen from the sea.

IT would be a difficult thesis to prove that Ireland was ever during any prolonged period ruled from without, for, until the changes under Henry VIII, it was not the English Crown, but the clans and the Anglo-Irish who in reality controlled Irish affairs and as soon as these were destroyed their places were taken by the English settlers who came to succeed them. During the seventeenth and eighteenth centuries it can be maintained that it was not the Crown, but the English in Ireland who controlled the chief power, and in the stream of Elizabethan Deputies the rule of Perrot has this significance that it saw a challenge to the Crown control by the settlers, which ended in victory. And this was because of Perrot's strength, not his weakness, and because he recognized the menace to the direct power of the Crown, which came from the settlers encouraged by their recent victory over the Nugents. The foundations had been laid in the political defeat of the Anglo-Irish, but it was from these Council Board quarrels that the Ascendancy Party arose and their success was assured in that moment when the English officials obtained the support of the Queen and when the defeated Viceroy sailed home for England leaving the country in the hands of his enemies. This was a curious episode too, a struggle between winter and autumn, for while Perrot was ageing, his adversaries were chiefly the ancient officers, who had already given a lifetime of service, steeped in the especial traditions, both in practice and theory, which rule in that country required.

There are few prominent men whose careers appear so widely different in their public and in their private aspect as the less prosperous Elizabethan courtiers and in the instance of Sir John Perrot, who was chosen Lord Deputy of Ireland in 1584, this is in particular the case. His general reputation was that of an outspoken administrator of proved courage, who had had a certain experience of the country as President of Munster and who was reputed to enjoy the complete confidence of the Queen. It was known that he claimed to be a son of King Henry and his Court favour was regarded as a tacit recognition, while his loyalty was as undoubted as his sound Protestantism, for he had been accused of sheltering heretics in Queen Mary's time, and beyond all this he was understood to possess an ample fortune. It was a matter of favourable comment, too, that he had never received any gifts in land or money and he was indeed regarded as an honourable free-spoken gentleman, adequately wealthy and somewhat impaired in health, which was held to account for the rural leisure, which for the last ten years he had enjoyed.

In reality the situation was much more complex, for he possessed a certain directness both in speech and action, which had hindered the even development of his fortune, although like many others of

THE CELTIC PEOPLES & RENAISSANCE EUROPE

presumed royal descent he had reaped all the advantages of a double paternity, being as much a Tudor as the Queen would let him at Court and in the West always a Perrot. His estate at Haroldstone in Pembroke with extensive sheep runs in the hills was the second largest in the County, and he had some house property in Haverford, but his total legitimate income never exceeded £1,500 [1] a year. At the time of his Deputyship he was rather poorer, and considering the great state that he maintained, such resources were quite insufficient. His secret outgoings were tremendous, and this was the result of his temper of mind, for his life was starred with quarrels, but there was never a peacemaking and death alone ended his feuds. Thus he quarrelled with Lord Pembroke at the Council Board, so he had the Herberts against him ; then there was a dispute with Lord Essex over Lamphey and a constant feud with the Bishops out at St. David's, while his relations with the greater gentry were bad and the poorer squires were banded against him and all this cost money. To recoup himself he bought the Borough Council of Haverford, which appointed the revenue officers and the customers, and he proceeded to derive an income by encroachment and the seizure of houses and from illegal tolls at Haverford Market, the best in the County. He was for a time Vice-Admiral of South Wales, and, as the competent authority for the suppression of piracy, had the option of purchase and could condemn any vessel and he was accustomed to hold selected foreign merchants to ransom. At the same time the Pembrokeshire people put themselves completely into his power, since neither gentry nor merchants could resist the temptation to buy stolen goods, while Perrot received everything through his servants the customers.[2] But his expenses far outran his receipts, and he gladly accepted the office in Ireland to escape from a harvest of trouble. There was, however, another difficulty, as his ill-health was worse than was thought, since he suffered from stone and his digestion was ruined, and he was in fact breaking up, for he had never denied himself

[1] The income of Haroldstone was normally £1,000 and the house property brought Perrot £100 a year, and at the time of his death his sheep and cattle were valued at £1,000 and the plate and household effects at £900, while there was £200 in ready money in the chest. Cal. S.P. Irel., 1590, *passim*, and Inquisitions Post Mortem. A complete survey exists in Lansdowne MS. 172.

[2] Eliz. State Papers, Dom. MS. 124, 16 and 28, and Haverford West Borough Accounts. List of abettors of pirates MS. 120, 75–78 and Cal. S.P. Scottish, ii, p. 82, while a charge of ' Lxix very slanderous articles ' is given in the Acts of the Privy Council under the date of 4th July, 1581.

pleasure. In addition to the local hatreds there was hardened enmity at Court from the Cecils[1] and from 'his frisking adversary,' Lord Chancellor Hatton. Nothing was more calculated to disturb the settlers in Ireland than the irruption into their close corporation of this man with his curious pride of birth, courage and magnanimity, his wrecked vigour and pressing imperious need.[2]

The appointment was made in January, 1584, and the Lord Deputy arrived in June to find the waters, which had been disturbed by the disappearance of Sir Nicholas Malby, still rippling into eddies, for the whole stream of official life had been affected by the going down of such a great career. It had been a life not rare among these high officials, a man of powerful office as President of Connaught, who had lived strongly ever since his pardon from the death penalty for coining,[3] which was one of the unstable enterprises of his youth, before he received the control of the Crown forces and could plan and act upon a national scale. He had weathered many storms, the normal stress of a civil service as yet incompletely organized. There had been, for instance, a charge in 1582 of thirty-four articles from his Clerk of the Council, which he countered by an accusation of 'evil and corrupt carriage in his office,' and this from a man of Sir Nicholas' rank was accepted.[4] A long-standing quarrel was kept up with Lord Justice Wallop, and there was bitterness against 'his consistent enemy,' Ormonde,[5] and all this was maintained under the pressure of a financial strain, which was ever increasing. And so the approaching death of Sir Nicholas Malby, dying at Athlone in the midst of his enemies, worn out after fifty-four years of hard life, caused a commotion. The Lord Justice wrote for the reversion after his death 'for he is past recovery,' although he had still a month to live, and Sir William

[1] It would seem from the State Papers and Salisbury Correspondence that Walsingham was a friend and Hatton an opponent of Perrot, while Burghley was the friend of his enemies. In regard to the many details of corruption the ethics of the official life of this period should always be borne in mind.

[2] As regards Perrot's personal appearance, Gaspar Thunder, one of his spies, describes him as ' a tall proportionate, square man,' but this may have been flattery, while Sir Robert Naunton commenting on his resemblance to Henry VIII, states ' his picture, his qualities, gesture and voyce . . . will plead strongly that he was a subrepticious child of the bloud Royall.' Fragmenta Regalia, p. 42.

[3] Diary of Henry Machyn, p. 290.

[4] Cal. S.P. Irel., 1574–85, p. 360.

[5] Sir N. Malby complained in March, 1582, that ' when two choice persons were entertained for the killing of the traitor Seneschal (of Imokelly) and had undertaken the same, the matter not being revealed to any . . . save only to the Earl of Ormonde, these executioners were no sooner arrived at the camp, but they were apprehended by the Seneschal and charged with the practice and for the same executed, to the great grief of the persons that entertained them.' Cal. Carew Papers, ii, p. 327.

P 2

Stanley put in a counter-petition and the royal agents made ready to settle down on his widespread interests on various charges of fraud. These were transgressions permitted to his strong-handed justice, but which in his weakness the Crown would remember. Finally there was the most successful stroke in this matter, Lord Justice Wallop's decision to pass a grant of Athlone to himself before the new Deputy should appear. In addition to this great affair there was the rivalry in the departments, one of the feuds between the revenue and administrative officials, which had resulted in the discomfiture of Mr. Jacques Wingfield. As was customary, and indeed but decent, pawns were used and John Shereff, a Clerk of the Ordnance, brought forward the charges of extortion against Mr. Masterson and laid ' sinister informations ' against the Lord Justice.[1] Mr. Wingfield reluctantly upheld his subordinate, but there was a miscalculation, for Auditor Jenyson, although an enemy of Wallop, could not be induced to attack him ; so the attempt was a failure.[2] The few months before Perrot arrived were passed in clearing up Shereff's affairs and dividing his fortune.

These were the actual matters, which agitated public opinion, but they were merely the result of the friction between the strong men of the party ; for on Perrot's arrival there were two wings of the settlers, the heavy methodical, mercantile influence of the Lords Justices and the auditors and the more variable moods of the soldiers. Beyond them stood Ormonde outside and apart. The fall of Perrot and the diminution of direct royal power was caused by all three ; for he had a quarrel, temperamental and deep with the Justices, then a heavy combat with the revenue officers and, when the settlers closed ranks, the soldiers, too, were affected. Even so, how much might Perrot have retained had he won Ormonde and this failure destroyed the last of his chances. But it is the character of the two predecessors, who as Lords Justices had shared all power, that provides the background for this complicated struggle ; for they were divided between their distrust of Perrot and a not unnatural anxiety that London should always be provided with a favourable interpretation of their zeal.

---

[1] Cal. S.P. Irel., 1574–85, pp. 480–1.
[2] Mr. Wingfield retired to England without resigning his post. Details of the long career of this official, ' his untoward conduct in the field ' in 1562, ' cross paths ' in 1573 and ' plain corruption ' in 1581 are recorded in Cal. S.P. Irel., *passim*, while obligations of honour appear in Sir H. Sidney's Accounts, Cal. De Lisle and Dudley MSS., i, p. 415.

THE FALL OF LORD DEPUTY PERROT

And in this connection it is difficult to disentangle the different *rôles* of Walsingham and Burghley, the two channels of approach to London, with whom these officials correspond. It is, however, worth noting that both the protagonists, Sir Henry Wallop, and Lord Deputy Perrot, were distrusted by Burghley and had Walsingham's 'friendship', and it is perhaps this fact that even avowed enemies must use the same channels which preserved for so uneasy a period the *status quo*.

The character of Loftus, Archbishop of Dublin, is perhaps seen to best advantage in the Baltinglas affair, that cautious tenacity, which marked his actions and the sense of personal dignity sustaining him in what was at moments a somewhat isolated course. Sir Henry Wallop had many points of sympathy with his colleague, but the most marked feature of his character was a certain rather modern trend and outlook, which was a notable assistance in dealing with Perrot, who entirely lacked his financial acumen. He was a sober gentleman of a most respectable character, going everywhere with Lady Wallop and her 'sweet babes,' with a Puritan bent in religious matters, a regular churchgoer sitting under Archbishop Loftus and approving his sermons. Coming from an established family in the County of Southampton, he had already a certain prosperity, when he decided to leave his seat in Parliament and go to Ireland to build up his fortunes.[1] With a desire for the protection of the letter of the law he felt at once a distaste for the soldiers and the lesser officials, nor could he forget that it was a condescension for him to come at all to such a country, to leave Farleigh Wallop and all that settled home life, the great stone gates and the quiet wind in the beeches as he rode back from one of My Lord's dinners at Basing. But now he was surrounded by men whose future was very doubtful and who had had some painful 'experiences' in their past, and it is sufficient to mention in this connection the contrast between Wallop and Malby. The Vice-Treasurership of Munster had been the occasion of his coming, and to this the Lord Justiceship was added, both offices giving him the change that he needed. His concentration on business had brought its rewards, but he was without friends, a rather humourless man 'in nature and condition somewhat sour,' as Malby described [2] him, and not one who

---

[1] Letter on his commercial views. Molyneux MSS., vii, p. 629.
[2] Letter of 14th September, 1582. Cal. S.P. Irel., 1574–85, p. 398. For detailed references to these quarrels, see the note on personal feuds at Dublin printed at the end of this volume.

could royster through his extortions. But, in addition, the enterprises which his influence had floated involved him in difficulties all over the country; for not only were there the wide lands of the House of Bagetragh near Dublin, but also the lease of 12,000 acres of abbey land at Enniscorthy, which he had obtained on most favourable terms and the abbey lands of Adare. He had, besides, interests as an exporter through the trade in ship planks and wine staves to Spain, which he had set going. There were also his alum mines in Kerry and in England the veins of metal on his Somerset manor of Worle, calamine stone and the lease to dig it, and he had offered half shares to Walsingham in return for his help.[1] His chief anxiety was that his friend the Archbishop should not again share his power; for he had early seen that Perrot 'carried an unfaithful heart,' and he had a determined prescience of the ruin that might lead to his fortune. To complete the picture of this party among the settlers it is necessary to recall the figure of Ormonde's enemy, Sir Warham St. Leger, the Provost Marshal of Munster, who exercised much influence, although he did not actually appear during these years in Ireland. He was not a man of great energy, but rich and, according to Ormonde, ' one who does no good, but drinks and writes false advertisements.'[2] At the time of Perrot's appointment he was living at Leeds Castle in Kent and had been injured by a post-horse falling upon him, but his significance lies in this that he represented to some extent the settlers at Court. He had many influential connections as a brother-in-law of Lord Abergavenny, and he was always able to add force to the accounts of the troubles in which Perrot was so soon involved.

In quite another sphere from the Lords Justices, but connected with them because their occupations were not military but civil, were the Crown Auditors under the leadership of Mr. Thomas Jenison, who was steadfastly accumulating a fortune to buy a landed estate for his family in England. For all these revenue officials it must have been a pleasure to associate with men of such influence had it not been for the difficulties which their official position entailed. Thus Mr. Jenison was always ready to produce his own accounts, which would give adequate satisfaction to any Government; for he had learnt

[1] Letter of 13th July, 1583. Cal. S.P. Irel., 1574–85, p. 457.
[2] Letter of Ormonde to Burghley dated 5th July, 1585. Cal. S.P. Irel., 1574–85, p. 456.

THE FALL OF LORD DEPUTY PERROT

wisdom since his first dismissal for the too courageous defalcations of thirty years earlier; but the auditing of Sir Henry Wallop's balance-sheet was a nightmare. Yet it was this duty which gave him among the settlers a position of power, for he had the right to withhold the royal approval from these expenses; but Mr. Jenison behaved with great prudence, choosing always rather to give his benediction to their efforts, a slow but certain road to fortune, instead of giving way to the tempting efforts of those who must rely upon his official assistance as the only way to blast a friend's career. He was in all things a sensible unimaginative man, and although he received some relief from the remedy of an old blind Irish priest, his outlook was somewhat coloured by the gout. Sir Henry Wallop refers to his ' great cunning and little conscience '[1] and also accused him, without ground, of Popery, for his son was Catholic; but it would seem that he himself was indifferent in contrast to Sir Henry's sober hatred of Rome. The root of the jealousy was the knowledge so galling to Wallop, that, because he was Auditor-General, a man like Jenison, who was certainly not his equal in rank, married to the Groom Porter's daughter and haunting the back purlieus at Court, a man, too, who had received sentence, whether or not he had actually been long in gaol, should have power over him from the Crown. But how much more painful was it to the other party, the soldiers, to feel this civilian control, especially to a man, whose sword had served his country for years, like the Knight Marshal, Sir Nicholas Bagenal, who drove a heavy fortune in Ulster.

At the age of seventy-four Sir Nicholas was the leader of the military settlers, an unusual character with the isolation which their conflicting interests made common among his equals in Ireland, and with an unsolved and difficult past. Brought up in Newcastle, the son of a tailor, there had been an undefined connection with the Earl of Tyrone, and then there was a murder trial and a pardon [2] and later a very dubious transaction with Stukeley as to the sale of his offices under the Crown,[3] but now for nearly forty years he had been Marshal. All the intricacies of that border were known to him, but his methods were a great contrast to Malby's, for he would sit cold with age in his northern castle, playing off one leader for the price of

[1] Letter to Walsingham dated 17th March, 1583. Cal. S.P. Irel., 1574–85, p. 434.
[2] Letters and Papers, Henry VIII, 1542, No. 1182.
[3] Correspondence in Cal. S.P. Irel., 1509–73, pp. 292–7.

another, selling always the peace. The North was full of his sons, Sir Henry with whom he had quarrelled, but to whom he secured his great posts, Samuel an adventurer, Ralph, a well-known swordsman in Dublin, and the unfortunate Dudley, who had married the Archbishop's daughter and paid a great sum for the Kavanagh's country and who was killed in an ambush when riding to recover four cows in Idrone.[1] All the Bagenals in some sense stood aloof, and there were repeated attacks on their courage, not it would seem the result of any lack of personal bravery, but because they always honoured the arrangements they had made with the enemy. With all these reserved areas and this interlacing web of affairs conflict was certain, nor was Sir John Perrot the man to avoid it.

It was not until 21st June, 1584, that the new Lord Deputy received the sword of state from the Archbishop in Dublin, but he brought with him a direct freshness in contrast with the honeycombed affairs of the settlers, for he was a man of large mind, anxious to make the most of his power, and with a zeal for the Queen's cause, a *magnifico* as the Renaissance lords would have put it. Even his ideas about money were in contrast with the slow care of the English officials, for he had no desire to make a great fortune, but merely to pay for the splendid state he maintained, an effort which his extravagance made always impossible. The difficulties began at once with a first skirmish with Wallop, who was characteristically engaged in removing from above the Attorney-General of Munster, an indiscreet man, who had been charged with nine several treasons and was being slowly driven out of his post. He was also involved in some way with Francis Lovell,[2] the Sheriff of Kilkenny, which was perhaps a side move against Ormonde his enemy, but the first meeting was a victory for Perrot, since Wallop was forced to surrender Athlone,[3] which the Deputy declared might be used as a capital. Meanwhile there was also difficulty with Auditor Jenison and in August Perrot set out for the North to aid O'Donnell against a Scottish invasion, and this was carried into an attack on the McDonnell's and Sorley Boy's country, which it was hoped would increase the royal prestige

[1] Report in Cal. S.P. Irel., 1586–8, p. 289. Archbishop Loftus referred to Sir Henry Bagenal as 'this decrepit and innocent old gentleman.' *Ibid.*, p. 359; but in this point of view he was singular.
[2] Just before Perrot's arrival Ormonde wrote to Burghley of Lovell's malice, 'he is as bad a man and vainglorious a fool as may be.' Cal. S.P. Irel., 1574–1585, p. 515.
[3] Cal. S.P. Irel., 1574–85, p. 506.

and set up the Deputy.[1] It was a question of cows, and these it was thought might prove a solution like Sir Francis Drake's prosperous voyages, which cost the Queen and her countrymen nothing. In October Perrot was jubilant and wrote ' Sorley who was lord over 50,000 cows has but 1,500 to give him milk,'[2] seeing a delightful vision of 48,500 giving milk for himself, but unfortunately matters were not really so simple, for by these direct raids he had stirred up a hornet's nest. The Bagenals, with their balanced and profitable peace, were disturbed by such an intrusion and joined the ranks of his enemies, while Auditor Jenison, whose system was thrown out of gear was loud in complaint.[3] As a result there was trouble behind Perrot in Dublin, and then the hopes of the cows vanished and he came back south to find Loftus an enemy. This was the inevitable result of the educational scheme, which Perrot had brought in from England, although it was not a question that interested him ; for his own training, though soundly Protestant, had been very scanty, the ' new learning ' at St. David's in the time of the troubles, when the Canons played cards for candles in that desolate spot and one kept a tavern [4] in the Close, while the wind howled through the Palace, whose roof had been prudently stripped by the Bishop to portion his daughters. However, it was a well-thought-out plan to deprive the Archbishop of more than half his see's revenue, besides incidentally turning his Cathedral into a court house, for there would be judges in the Canons' houses and two new colleges with the endowment of £1,000 [5] a year and then came the Deputy's contribution, the idea that Perrot College would be a most suitable name.

In all the turmoil of these difficulties one man stood the Deputy's friend the Principal Secretary Fenton. He was an observer of very

---

[1] As a mark of the preservation of external unity there is no reference to his quarrels in the account of Perrot in the Annals of Loch Cé, ii, p. 461.

[2] The great herds of Sorley McDonnell's country were famous, and kine had also been the occasion of O'Donnell's appeal against the annual invasion of Scots, since he wrote to Perrot, ' two thousand well appointed men have landed in the country and have not left a cow in M'Sweeny's country, which was the best man of his name under me.' Cal. S.P. Irel., 1574–85, pp. 520 and 532.

[3] Protest to Walsingham that he was not ' a corrupt man.' Ibid., p. 529.

[4] Register of the Chapter Acts, St. David's MSS., ff. 52, 57 and 241.

[5] Outlined in a letter of 21st August, 1584, and contrasting in its sobriety with Perrot's military plan of seven towns, seven castles and seven bridges to hold Ireland. Cal. S.P. Irel., 1574–5, pp. 524 and 532–3. This has the appeal of symbolical numbers to the Celtic mind seen in Harleian MS. 4181 and especially in the contemporary prophecy in Mostyn MS. 133, ' Ffower beastes shall bind thayre tayles."

acute perceptions, a fine scholar and a *littérateur* who had translated Belleforest's Tales, a friend of the late Deputy's wife, Mary Sidney, persuasive, not without charm. At this time, unfortunately, his financial state was precarious, nor was the effort that he made to stabilize it by marrying Bishop Brady's widow successful. It was obviously to his interest to support a superior who had gained the Queen's confidence.

Meanwhile the Lord Deputy's troubles were increasing, for a determined effort to rid himself of Auditor Jenison failed, as the Government refused to accept his account of ' his sickness and slackness,' and then all the rumours from the Northern Camp filtered back to London against him. There was first Christopher Carliell's complaint to his uncle Walsingham that ' Perrot's insolent speeches to all men will not be slightly digested,' and the still harsher words of an unknown captain [1] and then in the midst of the trouble he fell out with Ormonde. It was over the interminable quarrels between the royal official Lovell, with the settlers behind him, and Ormonde's deputy, Shee, and, as Wallop disliked them both, it might have been easy to reach an agreement ; but Perrot arrested Shee and so lost the support of his only powerful friendship. And then with Dublin and the North against him Perrot alienated the South by quarrelling with the President of Munster, John Norreys, under the cover of whose official position Wallop was attempting to manœuvre a patent in woad.[2] Yet at the same time the submission of the Irish [3] assisted Perrot with the Government in England, and his position was made much easier by the deaths of Baltinglas and Kildare, so that in the quarrel between the Deputy and the settlers a kind of stalemate was reached. Nevertheless he sent Fenton to England to give his version of the University question, and this stirred up the episcopal anger against him, so that the Archbishop wrote of his daily threatenings and his harsh and bitter letter, while Loftus' brother-in-law the Bishop of Meath complained of his fury.[4] During the summer a certain boycott of the Lord Deputy

[1] This letter of 2nd February, 1585, after stating that Captain Dudley Bagenal had borrowed a round blow on the ear from Sir W. Stanley and referring to Sir Henry Bagenal's precipitate flight from Glenarm to Knockfergus, continues, ' I was amongst the rest as a common town dog at every hunter's call, appointed to attend his Lordship (Perrot), but now turned off to get my food where I may.' Eliz. State Papers Irel. MS. 114, f. 62.
[2] Cal. S.P. Irel., 1574–85, p. 556 and Alnwick MSS., vol. vii, 24.
[3] *Cf.* the solitary entry in Thadeus Dowling's *Annales Hiberniæ* for 1583–8. ' Johannes Perrot . . . Hiberniæ pacificavit regnum.'
[4] Letter to Walsingham, dated 15th August, 1585. Cal. S.P. Irel., 1574–85, p. 576.

was developing, and he was made to feel the insecurity of his English support all the more as he had sponsored another project for an expensive attack on the North. In September he was writing[1] to Burghley, bewailing his misfortune in receiving no answers, stating that he was not to be blamed for the design of converting St. Patrick's into an University and claiming that he gave good suppers for all who would come, although, as Dr. Hector would testify, it was twenty-three years since he had been able to eat in the evening. During the autumn, too, he had succeeded in arousing the fierce enmity of Sir Richard Bingham, a most strong-minded man, over a deal in house property, which he had cancelled,[2] and at the same time Sir William Stanley left Ireland. In an unlucky hour Stanley and the Deputy had come close together, the result perhaps of a certain resemblance in outlook, that military temper and breadth of vision and that spirit of the true adventurer, the contempt for mere money, which both heartily shared. This was the more unfortunate because, even before he left Ireland, Mr. Arnwood, a well-to-do pirate, had warned the Government against Stanley, and the surrender of Deventer to the Spaniards was not the least among the many misfortunes, which made Perrot's ruin complete.

As the autumn rains came down on the capital, the Lord Deputy was almost isolated, surrounded by the steadfast and strong enmity of the settlers and in his determination not to surrender his power he roused yet further anger by his reliance on the only elements in the Council opposed to them, the judges,[3] Sir Nicholas Whyte and the Dillons. Sir Nicholas was a wise and generous man, whose position was strong in spite of the constant attempts to assail it, for while he had the full support of his countrymen, whom he always befriended and the friendship of Ormonde, standing godfather to Lord Butler at Carrick, he could also count upon Burghley. It had been necessary for the Treasurer to maintain a correspondent of rank, intimate with, but apart from, the Deputy and the settlers, to inform the Queen of affairs and since this was Whyte's position he was perfectly safe. The connection with England was a policy that the Anglo-Irish had always

---

[1] Elizabethan State Papers, Irish MS. 118, f. 13.
[2] Cal. S.P. Irel., 1586–88, p. 23 and for Mr. Arnwood's letter in which he refers to his refusal of £100 from the Spaniards, Cal. S.P. Irel., 1574–85, p. 529.
[3] This opposition appears in Wallop's letter to Walsingham of February, 1583, 'there is not a malytyerser man in this land . . . nor a greater ypocrite and dissembler' than Sir N. Whyte. Cal. S.P. Irel., 1574–85, p. 428.

maintained, and in Sir Nicholas' restrained approval of Perrot,[1] and in all his comments on affairs there is a philosophic and calm, yet determined attempt to support a strong Government, as against the depredations of those who had realized at last all that Ireland could be made to provide. The character of the Dillons was more doubtful, and they were pursued with an inveterate hatred on account of their share in securing the conviction of Nugent; for it was believed that they put pressure on the jury, 'compelling them by malice to alter the verdict,'[2] and besides, while on the one hand they were the great supporters of the English exaction of cess, yet in their private lives they were Catholic. They had a special importance, for the cousins and especially Sir Lucas were the richest commoners in the country, and were so profoundly loyal that they were never suspected, yet they had a brother in Rome with the priests, but they kept their private preferences in subjection. The simplest explanation that these contradictions will bear is that they were manœuvring for position to obtain that peerage which they felt was their due and which came in the next generation, when Sir Lucas' son was made Earl of Roscommon. Now in addition to these lords of the Council there was also another body on which Perrot relied, the Castle Welshmen whom he had planted, Richard Meredith, his chaplain and Dean of St. Patrick's, Philip Williams, his secretary,[3] Charles Trevor and another Thomas Williams, his cousin, whose appointment gave particular offence to the settlers.

In the summer Perrot had begun to develop suspicions of Fenton, which were further enhanced by Bingham's inopportune victory, throwing up into relief the re-capture of Dunluce by McDonnell and overshadowing the early northern victories on which the Deputy had based his prestige. In his plan for a new northern campaign he had the support of Dillon and Whyte,[4] whose interests were confined to

---

[1] In regard to Sir Nicholas Whyte's connections with the Baltinglas party it is worth noting that in his testament dated 3rd May, 1592, Sir John Perrot states: ' I deny that I was in any confederacy with the Viscount Baltinglas . . . or ever heard from the Viscount Baltinglas in all my life.' Cal. Salisbury MSS., iv, p. 193.

[2] Sloane MS. 4993, f. 130.

[3] It is clear that Williams had been ingratiating himself with Perrot while still in service at Tintern in 1572. Alnwick MSS., vol. vii, 7 and 8.

[4] A letter of Wallop dated 23rd August, 1586, states, ' All that are here (Dublin) of the English Council dissuade the Deputy what we may, Sir Lucas Dillon and Sir Nicholas White, his only favourites, sooth him in that and all other things. The reasons that move his Lordship to go, as I conceive are two : the first to pull from Sir Richard Byngham, whom assuredly he hateth, the credit of the service, the second his greedy desire to gain cows and to spare at home.' Elizabeth State Papers, Ireland MS. 125, f. 62.

the Pale, but as usual a determined attack from the settlers. In this case his enemies found a friend in the Queen, so that in the autumn of 1586 his position was weaker, for he had received a severe rebuke from Elizabeth. ' Let me,' wrote the Queen, ' have no more such rash unadvised journeys without good ground as your last fond journey in the North. We marvel that you hanged not such saucy an advertiser as he that made you believe so great a company was coming. I know you do nothing but with a good intent for my service, but yet take better heed ere you use Us so again.' [1]

After this the separation between the Deputy and the settlers was almost complete, so much so in fact that the officials decided to tamper with the Castle Welshmen in order to remove or confirm the suspicions, which the determined isolation of Perrot had caused them. Among the Welshmen Dean Meredith was the most loyal, being very anxious to please his protector by demolishing the fabric of the Cathedral, which the Deputy had placed in his hands. The others, however, were not a source of strength, but of weakness, for it was not in their nature to refuse a good offer. It was essential for the settlers to discover the Deputy's moves and in October some letters were missing and Philip Williams was cast into gaol. The method of approach had been delicate, and this is the Archbishop's explanation of how the documents found their way to his hands. ' The accident fell at first of my Lord's (Perrot's) own open dealing in his chamber, which some other that is towards him, that he least suspecteth, gave ear unto at his chamber door, and undesired of my part and at that time utterly unknown unto me, was moved, when by hearing the letter read he perceived I was so maliciously shot at, and so watched an opportunity while Williams was sent away to write other letters in his own chamber, to convey that letter from My Lord's own board to a friend of mine that brought it to me when I was sitting in the Chancery, and returned it again to the place whence he took it, before Williams could come back again with the business he had in hand. In as strange a manner, though after another sort, was the copy of the letters against Sir Henry Bagenall gotten and brought unto me without his knowledge or fault.' [2] It is hardly surprising after this

---

[1] Elizabethan State Papers, Ireland MS. 123, f. 34, supported by a statement of Wallop asserting that there are not 600 weaponed Scots in the North of Ireland and these but baretailed beggars. Cal. S.P. Irel., 1586–88, p. 144.
[2] Elizabethan State Papers, Ireland MS. 130, f. 38.

that not only Williams, but also his servant, Zacharie, who was accused of 'discovering' the letters were cast into 'a woeful chamber' in Dublin. This unfortunate incident brought affairs to a head, for it was clear that either Loftus must lie under suspicion or else he must free Williams and ruin the Deputy.

Quarrels and high words at the Council Board followed, and then, with the evidence before them, the settlers decided they had the strength to launch an attack, which took the form of reports written to Burghley, who was known to be an opponent of Perrot. The Deputy had given free rein to his tongue, so that on the 1st of December Marshal Bagenal wrote from Newry a general account of the charges. 'The Lord Deputy countenanceth the baddest and wickedest sort of people, against the Governors of the several provinces, greatly to the impeachment of Her Majesty's service, and vilipending of their authority, and withal the terms are so vile and opprobrious as beggars, squibs, puppies, wherewith ordinarily he doth use all of Her Majesty's Council, as were it not in regard of the place he doth possess, no man is able to endure at the hands of any subject.' This was followed up, four days later, by a letter from Loftus with the more substantial complaint that the Deputy removed suits from Chancery for his favourites to decide and also from the Chief Justice Gardiner, who represented the settlers, the Court of Castle Chamber being referred to in these terms : ' For in case any gentleman makes petition to have his cause considered of before the Council Board his Lordship's common answer is this with great fury. What tellest thou me of the Council ? What care I for the Council ? They are all of them but a sort of beggars and squibbs, puppies dogs, dunghill churles, yea even the proudest of them come here with their hose patched on the heels. And also terming the Queen's Chief Justices at the Law, ten shilling knaves, using such other reproachful and despiteful terms against us, that we find ourselves both greatly discontented, discouraged and disabled from doing of any good.' The next day Sir Richard Bingham wrote to support this, complaining of the Lord Deputy's uncourteous terms and bad speeches, 'such as for modesty's sake I omit to write here.'[1] Then a week later the Archbishop took up the same tale,

---

[1] Elizabethan State Papers, Ireland MS. 127, f. 1. Bagenal's letter, f. 4 Loftus' first letter, f. 8 Bingham's letter and f. 25 Loftus' second letter. On 24th July, 1587, Bagenal reinforced these by a letter to the Queen imploring her to save him from ' the Lord Deputy's hands, which it appears he would gladly imbrue in guiltless blood.' Cal. Salisbury MSS., iii, p. 269.

adding the serious charges that the Deputy had attempted to make a *concordatum* with him, whereby two hundred of Her Majesty's beeves should have been converted to his private commodity, and, after expressing fears for his life from his outspoken loyalty, he sat down quietly in Dublin to await a successful reply.

Perrot isolated in Dublin Castle determined on a drastic remedy and, since he was convinced that Secretary Fenton had betrayed him, he cast him into prison for debt. This was in connection with a sum of £50 which he had borrowed from the Deputy's servant, Mr. Russell, who dealt in such matters, and for £20 10s., which Mrs. Fenton had imprudently borrowed from Perrot himself, who was in these questions Henrican and quite free from that chivalrous convention, which a later fashion brought in. At the same time he managed to throw into prison one of the Archbishop's daughters, for it was not to be supposed that all that numerous family could keep so rigidly to the right side of the law ; but the principal Councillors, conscious of their letters to England, were most careful to provide the Deputy with no excuse for arrest. In February the Deputy received orders from England for Fenton's release, and at once his enemies gained two fresh charges against him, but while Fenton could only produce a tale of some dubious financial transaction,[1] Philip Williams had a more encouraging story with vague menaces to the Deputy. This the Archbishop with a perfunctory show of regret smuggled out of the prison and away to the Council. Meanwhile Perrot realized that his side could be best assisted by a serious charge pressed home on his enemies, and in May with good fortune one of O'Neill's messengers, Cullan, fell into his hands with letters from Turlough, and, what was more important, some compromising Bagenal material in which Sir Henry's honour was touched. This was an opportunity for humbling his rivals, but it led to the climax of these Council Board quarrels, as the old Marshal at seventy-six hurried south to the rescue. On arriving at St. Mary's Abbey he demanded immediate audience and challenged Perrot's right to examine the prisoners, ' for I mistrust there will be false measure used,' cried the Marshal. After a heated exchange, for it was an Henrican scene and Perrot was at his most Tudor, the Marshal declared ' If you were not Deputy I

---

[1] It was said that Bickerstaffe, the Lord Deputy's servant, had been minister under one Spark, a scrivener of London, at the time of his bankrowting and was not thought to be free from suspicion of that falseness. Cal. S.P. Irel., 1586–88, p. 269.

would say you lie. Because you are Deputy I will not say you lie, for I care not for Sir John Perrot.' 'If I were but Sir John Perrot,' replied the Deputy, 'I would teach him that came from a tailor's stall to use me thus.' 'Well because you dote I will bear with you, otherwise I would commit you to prison.' At this point, according to Sir Nicholas, the Deputy beat him to the ground. Still the versions diverge, and it is not impossible, as Perrot suggested, that the old man had fortified himself with liquor, so as to be able to exchange his senile timidity for a truculent defence of his son.[1] The accounts of this episode made a painful impression in England and the release of Williams was ordered at last, while Perrot could not redress his position, since the Queen's rebuke had prevented a military venture. The fact that Perrot sufficiently appreciated Bingham's soldierly qualities to challenge him to a combat added a final fantastic touch to the doom of his rule.

There was a lull for the last few months of his term, when the settlers had conquered and while the Government was slowly choosing a Deputy. Yet during this time he only intensified his disputes, quarrelling again with Ormonde about a levy of cess and watching the death-bed of Jenison, cold and unfriendly.[2] In December Sir William Fitzwilliam was appointed and the settlers had won, but the quarrels around Perrot were not appeased by his fall, and after he had sailed for England in June, 1588, their determination pursued him. And in this connection it is necessary to consider the baser instruments, which the Castle employed, men who at that period were inseparable from any *régime*, spiteful yet powerless, except when it should suit the great lords to employ them. One of the marked results of the quarrel with the English officials was the fact that even the lesser agents became Irish or Welsh. The system of retaining fees, by which the great men could know through their household servants the intimate thought of their friends, had bound all the English together against him and so the Castle Apothecary [3] was retired on a pension.

---

[1] The accounts of this encounter are to be found in Cal. S.P. Irel., 1586–88, pp. 351–377, *passim*.

[2] In a letter of 16th February, 1588, Perrot stated that Auditor Jenison ' lived like a hog and died like a dog.' Elizabethan State Papers, Ireland MS 133, f. 51. His increasing sickness also made Perrot more bitter, for he wrote to the Queen on 23rd September, 1587, ' my disease doth so trouble me as I cannot ride.' Cal. Salisbury MSS., iii, p. 285.

[3] Mr. Thomas Smythe, a valued and permanent official, had been Chief ' Potygarie ' since 1556, and had been prominent under Lord Sussex when the solutions that were provided for Shane O'Neill's removal failed of their effect. He had the confidence of Mr. Fenton and was Sir Henry Wallop's ' only physician,' but with the general public, who knew him as Bottle Smith, his reputation was sinister. Cal. S.P. Irel., *passim*, and Cal. Carew MSS., 1515–74, p. 349.

THE FALL OF LORD DEPUTY PERROT

This particular post was filled by Mr. Thaddeus Nolan, who was neither discreet, nor experienced and the other appointments were also unhappy; while among the very lowest ranks of this service there was a wild man, who was in the fulness of time to prove fatal to Perrot, Denis O'Roughan with his beard red as blood. He had of course no power of himself, but he had the good fortune to be chosen as the instrument of destruction. In consequence his last years were peaceful, but it is impossible to know what his first years had been, for his history opens in gaol, in the dungeons in Dublin. It seems that he had once lived abroad for his country and he is always described as a priest, but this may merely have meant that he had been a resident for the Government in some college in Spain. Certainly he was now a stout Protestant with apparently two English wives in Chester and Dublin, the second of whom promoted his fortunes; but it seems likely that he disguised himself as a hedge priest, when travelling on the Deputy's service. Like all such men, he had two sources of income, the greater sum being derived from the manufacture and sale of documents particularly warrants, in which he would seem to have managed a partnership with some of the Welshmen in the Castle and especially Charles Trevor. A quiet blackmail among his fellow-servants and also against Mr. Registrar Byrde, a man of quite a different social position, completed his more obvious activities, and, although of course not faithful, he was certainly zealous and in the course of his official business had severely injured his nose. In another age he might not have been raised from obscurity, but when the opinions and expressions of individual leaders were of so great importance it belonged to Statecraft to possess a sure knowledge of every part of the field; but these developments were still in the future and Perrot returned sullen in safety to England.

The alarms of that summer, the destruction of the Spanish Fleet and the subsequent fear as to the influence of the Spaniards cast upon Connaught combined to keep Perrot's affairs in the background, and he remained in Pembrokeshire,[1] at Haroldstone and Carew, zealously active in forwarding to Court [2] such news of the Armada as was

---

[1] As late as 14th May, 1589, Perrot signed Privy Council letters from Whitehall, Cal. Saville Foljambe MSS., p. 63, while on 10th May Sir T. Heneage could write to Sir G. Carew, 'Sir John Perrot is especially trusted by Her Majesty.' Cal. Carew MSS., 1589–1600, p. 5.

[2] The letters in the Stradling Correspondence xl and xli with their reference to the purchase of ' 20 milche kyne ' contain almost the only allusion to his ordinary rural pursuits.

brought in by the fishing vessels at Milford. But, when this excitement had died down, the Councils at Dublin, now closely united, encouraged the accusations against their old chief. Fitzwilliam was unobnoxious to Ormonde and extremely acceptable to all the settlers, elderly and an invalid, said to have been ruled in his first Deputyship by his wife and now to divide the power with her daughter. The settlers controlled him with a rule that became strong with the years, for his qualities and failings were theirs. There still remained the Anglo-Irish judges in Dublin, and it was evident that, if the accusers were given their head, this last opposition to the settlers might vanish and the permanent fall of their friend would settle for ever the menace of a Perrot revival. So in the spring of 1590 news came through to England that Denis O'Roughan, whom the English always called Rowghane, was writing[1] a book of his charges and the Deputy discovered a close inquiry essential and finally Sir John Perrot and Sir Nicholas Whyte were placed under restraint, while Dean Meredith, now Bishop of Leighlin, was soon sent to join them.

The first of these charges was O'Roughan's assertion that Perrot had written a letter to King Philip, five years before, offering to obtain for him England and Ireland, if he could have Wales as his portion. To this and to all the charges Perrot made a characteristic too rapid reply. He referred to the ' ill character of the hellish, false, suborned priest,' nor did he spare the Lord Deputy, ' for the father of this last forgery hath had no worse nurse to pamper him than Lady Dier, appointed by the Deputy her father, and free access at all times to the Deputy's Secretary Philip Williams a most wicked man.'[2] Then finally the matter of bribing Lady Dyer[3] by cows was brought up, and all this stirring of the muddied waters only injured his case, for the affair was well planned. First there was the evidence of O'Roughan and the rest of the Deputy's blades, who were prepared to risk an adventure, then there was the sober testimony of Mr. Williams, now

---

[1] ' Sir Denis is now writing a book of informations. One of the constable's men bit off a piece of his nose and he can now only write in short fits.' Cal. S.P. Irel., 1588–92, p. 305.

[2] Cal. S.P. Dom., 1581–90, pp. 659–678, *passim*.

[3] On 30th April, 1590, Lord Deputy Fitzwilliam wrote to Burghley in this connection. ' The report made of cows that my daughter Lady Dyer was to have for preferring a partner to McMahon's country is untrue. It may be some one has given out that speech, who knows better how to cast about for a cow than I or any of mine : but if ever there were such a motion or meaning for her, for me or for any of mine . . . let God wipe us all out of his book and so your Lordship may see how slanderously and injuriously I and mine are dealt with.' Elizabethan State Papers, Ireland MS. 151, f. 93.

THE FALL OF LORD DEPUTY PERROT

Permanent Secretary, and the valued evidence of Mr., now Sir, Geoffrey Fenton, and lastly the admissions from the friends and supporters of Perrot, once they were securely in gaol. The settlers were in no hurry, and the charges took more than two years to complete, but the chief point was gained already when Perrot was under restraint, which later became more strict, when he was closely confined in the Tower. The first capital point was the letter, but here arose some difficulties, for several men O'Roughan, Roger Bullock, Charles Trevor and Byrde were charged in turn with its forging, nor was O'Roughan's own story consistent, as there were confessions and counter-confessions and an understanding of the Lord Deputy's hand was to these men professional knowledge. The same difficulties applied to the charge of Perrot's Confession to O'Roughan, the Mass stipend he offered[1] and the Mass which was alleged to have been said in his presence. After the many months employed in sifting this evidence, which became more complex because one of the chief witnesses Trevor was an open rebel with O'Rourke, they came to the charges by the persons of greater repute. These were divided into two sections, the charges of leniency to Papists, which the Archbishops of Dublin and Cashel preferred, and the accusations of contemptuous words of the Queen, which were in the first place vouched for by Williams. In this matter they had better fortune, for the freedom of Perrot's speech was well known and, apart from the coarser words, which stood under Williams' name, Sir Nicholas Whyte was brought to admit that he had said the Queen's timidity hindered his service and had referred to 'the paltry sword' of his mistress.

Gradually the other charges vanished to make way for this one, for O'Roughan's suggestions that he had had Michael Wheeler killed by his servant, John Morgan, to prevent the seizure of his letter to Spain and that he had employed Walter Reagh to remove Dudley Bagenall were dropped, as was the accusation in connection with Perrot's attack on O'Byrne, which he skilfully defeated.[2] Simi-

---

[1] Perrot's Protestant Faith appears perfectly clear in his Testament and he firmly adhered to the doctrine of Justification by Faith, concluding his Will with the sentiment, ' farewell world with all thy vanity and soon may I come to Heaven, where is all unspeakable glory.' Cal. Salisbury MSS., iv, p. 196.

[2] Perrot wrote of ' the ill course of living of Feagh McHugh and his followers. His people lived like wolves, foxes and bears that prey upon all things.' He referred to Thady Nolan's mixture which was intended to poison Feagh McHugh, but which was not successful. Cal. S.P. Dom., 1581–90, p. 691.

larly the evidence of his apothecary, Thady Nolan, was not considered worth purchase and the charge that Perrot had said that he hoped ' to send the proudest of the Council of Ireland riding on cowlstaves (cabbage stalks) out of Castle Street ' [1] was regarded as frivolous, while a circumstantial account of his support of a rising by O'Rourke in order to embarrass Lord President Bingham was likewise watered down to a charge of connivance at the dragging of the Queen's image at the tail of a horse and a sufferance of rhymers.[2] All the more serious charges and especially the rigmarole of the Spanish letter were quite palpably false and Perrot might yet have been saved had he not affected the Queen in her vanity and especially in his coarse taunts at her fear. Although he had Sir Christopher Hatton [3] against him, it was from Ireland that the moving power for his ruin came [4] and this was complete, for it was only his death in prison in the summer of 1592, which saved him from the scaffold. Nevertheless, from the very first moment of his blundering opposition to the officials in Ireland his ruin was sure, for he had stumbled across a group already too powerful and organized to accept such a setback. The enmity of the settlers, both civilian and military, was a constant factor, and growing with each fresh attempt that Perrot had made to increase the power of the viceroy. There was no possibility of a balance with the aid of the Anglo-Irish, even had they possessed the requisite strength, since their enmity towards England still smouldered since the Nugent arrests and finally Ormonde, with all the great power he controlled stood aloof. The most widely gathered support, used with a serene and wise judgment, could alone have staved off a disaster, but to all this closing circle of enemies Perrot could only oppose

---

[1] Statement of O'Roughan on 6th January, 1592. Cal. S.P. Irel., 1591–4, p. 167.

[2] In this matter Perrot answered concerning the Rhymers of the North, who went to dwell under the Earl of Thomond in his waste country, that he never saw any of the rhymes that they made against the Queen. The rhyme on the O'Conor Don that ' the swift hungry greyhound would drive all Englishmen over the salt sea ' was typical. Cal. S.P. Irel., 1588–92, pp. 386, 724. The absence of any reference to Perrot in the considerable collection of Gaelic poems in praise of O'Rourke (now known as Egerton MSS. 111) would also support his assertion that there had been no alliance.

[3] A misconception has arisen owing to a statement in Dwnn's Visitations, i, 90, giving the parentage of one of Perrot's natural daughters as ' Mam hono Elsbeth Hatton v. Syr Kristor Haton,' which has led the author of the article on Perrot in the D.N.B. to found Hatton's hostility on the seducing of his child. But since Sir Christopher was never married, the daughter in question must have been illegitimate and in that case it is improbable, according to the standards of the time, that he would have been displeased that a child, to whom he had given no endowment, should form a connection with a courtier of rank.

[4] Perrot clearly believed this when he wrote to the Council in December, 1590, saying that he knew he would see but few of his writings, ' if Sir Jeffry Fenton came to the fingering of them.' Cal. S.P. Irel., 1588–92, p. 702.

the tempest of his vehement mind. It was the case of a struggle between an individual, representing the power of the Crown, and a great corporation and his relentless and slow destruction was merely the inevitable self-protection, which such powerful bodies employ.

CHAPTER XII

SIR WILLIAM STANLEY AND WALES

In this section the surrender of Deventer is the central episode. This garrison town in the Eastern Netherlands was given up to the Spaniards by Sir William Stanley who held it under the Earl of Leicester, the leader of the expeditionary force which Queen Elizabeth had sent to aid the Dutch in their revolt. This action had many diverse effects, one of which, its contributory influence towards the fall of Perrot's rule in Ireland, has already been discussed. Stanley had been an English leader in Ireland for fifteen years, and his garrison was composed of Irish troops. His connection in the public mind with the Babington Plot and the circumstances of his treason widened the gulf between the Catholic and conforming elements among the squires, carrying one stage further the development of public feeling. Among the Catholic exiles the influence of this accession to the Spanish party was very great. Hitherto, if the northern rebels be excepted, the exiles had left England freely and regarded themselves during the thirty years of peace as merely temporarily resident abroad. This was the position of the Welsh exiles, not only of the priests like Clynog and Lewis, but also of laymen like Sir Edward Carne. The solitary exception among the earlier group was the young Hugh Owen, who joined the Spanish military service, that cosmopolitan but still exclusive freemasonry of the sword. It was Owen who prepared the way for Stanley and became in time his chief assistant. At this point the difficult episode of Dr. William Parry, the Welsh Member of Parliament who was executed for treason, is considered.

The situation in the Netherlands which preceded the surrender of Deventer is then described in detail; the conflict between Leicester and the States, the jealousies of Norreys and Stanley, the unusual position of the envoy Wilkes. The lack of intervention on the part of the Secretaries of State, the continued management of affairs by Leicester, who was himself an absentee, mark out the difficulties by which the Government was faced when opposed by a favourite of rank. The maintenance of Stanley at his post, in spite of so many urgent warnings from the Dutch, is seen as the action of a great noble, uninterested and ill-informed, but determined to guard his *protégé*. The factors which led to Stanley's treason are in turn accumulated, his discontent and jealousy and the indiscretions in England into which his sense of injustice had betrayed him, the fear of disgrace for these imprudent actions, the isolation. The influence of his new-born Catholicism, the effect of an innate conservatism which led him to prefer the Spaniards to the Dutch and the independent semi-feudal outlook, that impression of the Fronde, which his position as a Stanley had induced, complete the picture. It is this last factor which has importance in regard to his relations with North Wales; for, after the die had been cast by his surrender, he was constantly occupied by the problem of a Derby succession to the throne. The possibilities of the situation centred round the figure of Ferdinando, fifth Earl of Derby, who represented his grandmother, a niece of King Henry. The characters of Ferdinando and William Stanley are then contrasted, and the plots with which their names are both connected are examined. In regard to these latter details, a number of unsolved doubts at once arise, which only become more complex when the death of the Earl eight months from his accession had caused such schemes to be first shelved and then abandoned. But in all the conversations on the Continent there seems to be stress laid upon North Wales. The influence of William Stanley, extending through Chester and the Marches, brings in again the squires of the Irish road.

In the mid-sixteenth century when the national and cultural barriers were still so strong, and when the mere personal contact, such as that which the Welsh prelates could make, was to prove of so little avail, there was one manner of life which brought intimate understanding, that polite and still exclusive freemasonry of the sword. It was necessary, however, that those who gained admittance to this favoured company should forego the ancient spirit of their own country and adopt the speech and train the processes of thought and use the phrasing of the *lingua franca* of the camp. It was among the Spanish soldiery and the French *Ligueur* captains, their allies, that this basis of social intercourse grew firm, welding into its own strong amalgam, the stray Flemings, Burgundians and Walloons, the nobles from the Rhineland and the Hapsburg territories in Alsace and even the light Italian cavaliers. All had been physically able, armigerous and poor, and the honour of their service had now brought them a loyalty as its seal, even for those whom mercenary prudence had first induced to serve the Crowns of Spain. Polite, covetous, unimaginative, at once coarse-fibred and sincere, the collective opinion of these officers accepted religion in its stride. There was no question of a refusal, nor possible reason to hesitate in accepting the official religion under whose banners they waged their campaign, and it seems probable that it was seldom devout enthusiasm which stirred in these soldiers, but rather an utter contempt for the way of life of their rivals, so religious and so *outré*. What the captains of the Spanish camp hated was all this parade of religion and righteousness and a God-fearing life, Coligny reading the Bible with his son-in-law, Téligny, stiff-jointed, demure, and the shadow of Theodore Bèza. They could understand better the fighters like Poltrot de Méré, the murderer of Guise, though even then it was hardly in accordance with honour to shoot the Duke in the back. It was not the only occasion in history when revolutionary thought proved abhorrent to the military mind, and in this particular instance the Low Country duties were full. The scene was complete, the life of the garrison, free within its conventions, the hunting parties at Aerschot with *Monseigneur le Duc*, the influence of the General, Alva, a frigid but now remote star, and then the evenings and wine accepted up to that limit which a man of spirit could bear, and in the background realities, taken so much for granted as to be at times almost forgotten, the Catholic Throne and its framework the unchanged Christian Church. The Spanish captains, profoundly unimaginative, moved in a social country, where the light came down from the Catholic heavens ; such secure immensity caused them to cease to trouble, no sensible man would think about the sky.

It was into such a close military circle that some of the exiles from Britain penetrated with time ; but it was only the most adaptable who could pay the price of absorption. The exiled Welsh priests and the English squires, like the Pagets, were prevented by their strongly marked character and their more national outlook from contemplating this change, while Stukeley was always too much the adventurer to be approved by a conventional group. Yet this was a well-defined type the Anglo-Spanish soldier and in the career of Hugh Owen such a fortune is traced, from the first days when the military men had been put ashore upon Flanders until the time when those well-seasoned veterans, whom Mr. Fawkes had supported, could plan out their adventures in the camp before Ostend.

It is almost inevitable that following out such a course the character of Captain Owen should seem blurred and indeed somewhat unimportant ; but it is just this lack of clear outline which is notable in all those who receive so readily the stamp of an alien culture and the absence of very defined characteristics only makes the general outline of the military opinion stand clear. It had been the landing of the dispersed survivors of the Northern Rising upon the Flanders coast, which had produced the first contact between the soldierly group of the exiles and the organized military mind of the Spaniards. Foremost among such exiles, implicated in the Ridolfi conspiracy and reaching the Low Countries not long after Northumberland's followers had been shipped abroad from the North, Hugh Owen was destined as the interpreter of the military exiles to the official circles in Spain. He had been one of the gentlemen attending upon old Lord Arundel and had held something of the rank of a secretary, deep in his confidence, engaging on behalf of that numerous Fitzalan alliance in the dangerous plots of the time. It is certain that he came from North Wales and was closely connected with Lleyn ; but the careful identification with Hugh Owen of Plas Du is a matter not yet clearly proved. At any rate it is perfectly evident that his birth carried some degree of prestige and the circumstances of his service, the business relations with the Ambassador, Ross and with the younger Stanleys of Derby gave him that power to rely on the repute of such an acquaintance, which still possessed a considerable value for the graded hierarchy in Spain.

And at this point we must consider the various Welshmen who were now to be found on the Continent to appreciate their effect upon Captain Owen, their failure and his success. Dr. Owen Lewis and the clergy held a position already made clear and, when they are left out of the question, it is seen that the few survivors belonged to the old urbane school of the voluntary exiles. It was this group which Sir Edward Carne had so eminently adorned when, as the last English Ambassador to the Pope, he had chosen to remain abroad till his death in the City where his friends were to raise that reposeful epitaph for him in the forecourt of the church of St. Gregory on the Coelian Hill. Just such a disposition of mind, eirenic and calm, was shared by Sir Thomas Stradling, Carne's cousin, and the contact which the latter maintained with the Continent was inspired by this spirit. It is a peace of the older world that still breathes in his letters to Spain, where his daughter Damasyn was Maid of Honour to the English Duchess of Feria, and again in the contacts with Mistress Stradling, his sister, who lived as a *Béguine* at Bruges. In all these scenes, in the old age of Stradling and Carne, but perhaps most of all in this *Béguinage*, we can see the ancient customs slowly coming to their death. Yet this was an ending, not of religion in Wales with its strong Celtic lines, but only of that calm rather Anglicized standpoint of the squires in Glamorgan ; the great manors beside the Bristol Channel, the quiet, protected cornfields of the Vale. Among the *Béguines*, every detail showed a delicate charity, the little houses and the books of prayer, a life of peace retaining all the spiritual contentment of the old monastic state. And then with the ringing of the evening *Angelus*, when the sisters had reassembled from their missions of charity in the town, there would come the cumbrous closing of the great outer gates, as the lights behind the lattices were kindled, while

233

the leaves of the plane trees still showed up darkly against that stone wall coping which enclosed the empty court. This is the note of the voluntary exiles, a lingering affection, a passing away.

Here there are two types sharply contrasted, the new Spanish soldiers, capable and concerned with the perfecting of their unrivalled military power, and the survivors of a religious disaster, bent on preserving their spiritual freedom and treasuring memories, and those delicacies of personal conduct which they had received as a gift from the past. Then in the summer of 1570 the exiles reached Flanders from Scotland. The career of Owen has this significance that it reveals the successful association of a military exile with the matter-of-fact Spanish captains at a time when the bulk of the fugitives concerned themselves with the past. These were the ' hot Louvainists,' Lady Northumberland in her piety and her gentleman Lygons and the ladies who had crossed with her and Lady Hungerford, the Duchess of Feria's sister, women devoted and brave, but lost in their mourning. Around them grouped the survivors of the men who had supported the Percy, Edward Dacres and Frank, and John Norton and old Sir John Neville.

Owen had sympathy with them and especially for Lady Northumberland, dignified in her convent in her long widow's weeds ; but his interests lay in the practical future. They, on the contrary, would forever gaze back to the good Catholic days, as they sat with Sir Francis Englefield, their oracle, an elderly and devout cavalier, who would speak of his rents, now held up in England, and of the plans he had formed for assisting the English Carthusians. It was pleasant indeed to sit in the temporary guest-house in the Rue Sainte Claire at Bruges and to discuss with old Dom Maurice Chauncy the fall of the Charterhouse and the glorious deaths of the martyrs, with those delightful personal touches about Dom Sebastian Newdigate, Anne Hungerford's uncle, of whom they were all now so proud. And then, in other surroundings, when the conversation turned worldly Sir Francis would deliver his *dicta* on the need that William Dormer should make a good Catholic marriage and on young Lord Cumberland's future, for it was said that he had been taken away from the charge of Lord Montague. Then he would share with the company his news letter from England which Lady Waldegrave or Lady Petre had sent him and, as the ladies sympathized with his ailments, he would

hobble down the stone stairs with his man and so home to the Widow
Haghelu who looked after them both in the house opposite the *logis*
of St. André facing the square. The times had been different when as
a boy he had ridden in Berkshire ; but he did not forget that an excellent priest, who had given him the benefit of his mature judgment,
had reminded him that there was much that was apposite in the writings
of Father Ignatius to a state of adversity. But Hugh Owen, whose
cast of mind was so different, had no great zeal for these things, but
looked to the future, to the surrender of Sir William Stanley and the
soldiers trapped in Deventer.

England and Spain were at peace, and this state was still to endure
for sixteen years more. The soldiers therefore had no very vivid
interest in the doings of exiles, however dissatisfied, who had come
from a country with which the Majesty of Spain was still friendly.
In the eyes of the Civil Governors due account was paid to position,
with Sir Francis Englefield first, as a Privy Councillor of that Kingdom
during the years when it received the benefit of His Catholic Majesty's
rule. Then came the Countess of Northumberland, a lady of very
high rank, belonging to the Blood Royal of England through one of
those left-handed descents with which the Low Country mind was
familiar. Below her, marred by his attainder in England, there ranked
the young Earl of Westmoreland and then the whole list of political
exiles, whom the failure of the Rising had cast on these shores, and
mingling with them were the gentlemen, like Sir Richard Shelley,
Lord Prior of St. John, and the elegant Mr. T. Copley, who had left
their country for pleasure without any compulsion. The Duke of
Alva, His Majesty's Governor, fully discerned implications which the
situation involved, the freedom of intercourse possible with Sir
Francis and the Lord Prior and the greater caution invariably needed
in dealing with the English Queen's foes. Nevertheless, it was to be
remembered that King Philip had graciously granted pensions to a
considerable number of exiles, and that they had, in the Duchess of
Feria, a spokesman at Court. Yet it had to be admitted that they did
not constitute a grave problem, nor were their dealings of interest.
With His Majesty's temper of mind, there was no likelihood of a war
between England and Spain, and it was clear that those who had been
in rebellion would not be allowed to return, while as to their plannings
and schemes the Duke was little concerned, and he placed no reliance

at all on Don Guerau, his colleague in London. While the rebellion had been in progress there had been a definite political problem and the subsequent events in Scotland had provided an opportunity for a slight military gesture or more correctly a diplomatic *démarche*. But, now that the exiles had reached Flanders, the episode never of any very great interest was in his eyes concluded.

The Duke of Alva, who was now advanced in the sixties, had had occasion to visit the North when attending his royal master at the celebration of his second marriage with the late Queen of England. His memory of the ceremonies in Winchester and of the slow progress to town, as the Court spread itself out between those strange hedgerows, sufficed to dispel the illusion that any serious importance could be attached to these exiles. Besides, as the reverse side to that severity for which his rule has been known, Alva had a distaste for the small coin of devout conversation and for the intimate family concerns of a well-defined social strata, which was all that ever resulted from their windy, extravagant hope. Those ' in religion,' the monastic communities like the Carthusians and Bridgettines and the more loosely ordered *Béguines*, were different ; but then they did not presume to possess a political value. This was a time at which the religious campaign of the seminary priests and the later military adventure were both still undeveloped, and it was not under persecution, but in the oblivion of those files, which already marked the first bureaucratic government in Europe, that the hopes of the exiles were buried. Thus the North Country and Welsh interest among the exiles began slowly to vanish, while the Irish and the ' Scottish ' party had hardly yet appeared on the scene. Alva was almost surrounded by all the surging troubles of the Netherlands in revolt and he could well afford to neglect these failures from England. It is the importance of Hugh Owen that he survived to become a leader in a later and fiercer time.

The fourteen years between the establishment of the northern exiles and that first military accession which the surrender at Deventer was to provide passed in a condition of peace, growing from year to year more strained and uneasy. Yet the developments among the exiles at this period, episodes which are now suggested by the names Fitzmaurice and Stukeley and the Baltinglas-Desmond revolts, belong almost exclusively to the history of Ireland and caused, therefore, no great concern among the English living abroad whose insular character was already deep-rooted and strong. Opposed both to the English and Irish, there were a few resolute exiles, led by Hugh Owen, who in this decade found themselves assimilated increasingly to the Spanish military spirit, passing from that somewhat confined atmosphere of the English refugee gentry to the wider life of the camp. It was, as has been suggested, a manner of life on which racial origins counted for little, but the English element in the Spanish service, though small, paved the way for Sir William Stanley and Yorke, the only military accession of value which the exiles were to receive.

But in these intervening years Owen was also involved in a strange case that of Dr. William Parry, his intentions and his designs, the *data* for whose solution would still seem insufficient. Even the origins [1] of Dr. Parry were obscure in his time, a contemporary pamphlet describing him as ' one of the younger sons of a poor man named Harry ap David who lived in North Wales at the village of Northoppe in Flint,' and his mother as ' the reputed daughter of a priest named Conway from Halkin,' while the poems of his period describe him as ' a man of goodly lineage whom his countrymen would willingly place at the head of affairs.' And this seems but natural in one who abroad was the underpaid secret agent of Burghley, but who at home was considered as the ' Pearl of Gwynedd ' and the ' Peacock of Cheshire.'

As far as the exiles were concerned, his brief connection with them must have served rather as a warning than an encouragement. He had been a familiar figure for some time, one of those gentlemen who were employed to keep Lord Burghley informed, and he acted in various capacities, as a tutor and a bear leader, a series of ill-defined duties which in no way served to conceal the source of his income. It was understood that he was of good birth, a fact for which Owen could vouch, and a violent and pragmatical fellow with a certain moneyed connection with the legal circles in England and accustomed to use with effect the designation of a Doctor of Laws. The style of

---

[1] The generally accepted version makes Parry a younger son of Harry ap David of Northope by his second wife. It is to be noted, however, that in the pedigree of this family of North Welsh squires, given in Lewys Dwnn, *Visitation of Wales*, ii, p. 326, his name does not appear. It is, however, asserted by Sir Samuel Meyrick in a note that he was one of the thirty children of this gentleman, who according to Parry's own account died in 1566 at the age of 108. His exact parentage is a question still surrounded by considerable doubt.

In regard to Hugh Owen it is his place in the family tree which is doubtful. Sir John Wynn describes him as ' Hugh Owen . . . a younger brother of an ancient gent : house called Plas Du.' *History of Gwydir*, p. 72.

LL.D. was of considerable value in providing a veil, even if rather transparent, for his somewhat doubtful pursuit. And then Parry ' had begun to mistrust his advancement in England,' and had been reconciled to the Church. It was at this point that Owen gave him assistance and, after a brief and embarrassing intimacy with those he had shadowed so long, he set out for England. It was now January, 1584, and Burghley's reception of his former agent was curious. He had his *dossier* in detail very complete, the two marriages and the law-suit with his stepson about ' embecilling,' the flights from his creditors in 1571, 1579 and 1582, the death sentence for burglary which had arisen from one of these episodes and then the reprieve. The dis-quieting character and insufficient detail of his later reports had been noted and the very strange circumstances of his last visit abroad. Here was a man without a shred of reputation remaining. It is interesting to note the course of action which was pursued. A careful consideration of these facts led Burghley to offer him a seat in Parlia-ment and he became Member for Queenborough.

As soon as he had entered the House, Parry protested against the Bill for dealing with Jesuits and Seminary priests, was arrested and again released. Then a second arrest followed and a confession that he had intended to murder the Queen, later a retractation, much play with an entirely non-committal letter which the Cardinal of Como had written, and finally his execution for treason with every barbarous rite. The dates are noteworthy, since the whole affair was so rapid. In January the Doctor landed at Rye, in November he was elected for Queenborough and on 17th December he made his protest in the House. His second arrest took place at the beginning of February, 1585, and his execution on 2nd March. In the absence of sufficient evidence it is a baffling minor affair ; but one fact alone remains certain, the assured sagacity with which Lord Burghley had acted. He did indeed deserve the reputation of having again saved Her Majesty's life. For the exiles it was a painful matter and will serve as an indication of the measure in which the affair of Sir William Stanley came as a relief.

An appreciation of the career of Sir William Stanley is of crucial importance for an understanding of the point of view of the exiles and as a stage in the gradual hardening of the opinion of the ruling classes in England against that Catholic religion to which they had all so lately belonged. It also provides an instance of that intercourse between the squires of the Welsh Marches and Ireland, which the new system of rule in Dublin and the service there called forth. For, although he came of purely English stock as a cadet of the Earls of Derby, Sir William Stanley had his home and all his landed interests in Hooton in the Wirral. In an age when mere physical distance counted for so much, this closeness to the Marcher area has its own value, and it was not without importance in his life that as Stanley would ride across his western farms on that low swell of ground where the heavy fields rose slightly above the levels he could see beyond the waters fringing Deeside that permanent guardian line, the hills of Wales. Thus his youth connected him with the circuit courts of Chester and that squirearchy of his County, with which the greater families in North Wales, like the Bulkeleys, were allied ; while a long service in Ireland gave him contact with the leading officials of his time. The Babington Plot, so closely bound up in its ramifications with his country, had an influence on his own disaster, while his actions also contributed their damage to the final downfall of Perrot's rule. By repulsion he affected the loyalty of the English Catholics at the Armada period, while his treason served to introduce a different tenor into the movement of the exiles still abroad. Yet all these effects were produced by a single action, the only notable work of his career, the surrender of Deventer. It is necessary to consider in some detail the circumstances of this event.

The policy of opposition to Spain which the English Government had so long pursued, had led at length to an act of almost overt hostility the expedition which the Earl of Leicester had taken, after the assassination of Orange, to the aid of the States. Thus an English army was established in Holland to aid the revolted provinces to continue their struggle with Spain. In that period, however, the influential leaders were few, and, in studying the list of the captains, the familiar names come again, Norreys, Killigrew, Pelham, the seasoned warriors from Ireland and then the young lords of the Court, Philip Sidney and Essex. The first year of the expedition was now over, Zutphen fought and Philip Sidney killed, when William Stanley received the charge of Deventer.

He was close on forty years of age, worn by fifteen winters on the Irish service, which he considered ill requited, with a discontent fast turning into rancour, blocked in his prospects, poor. His father's vigorous age and the chances of rule at Hooton, which were thus denied him, emphasized the impression of his poverty, and it was clear that officially he was a fading star, for in the Netherlands, as in Ireland, his rival Norreys was preferred before him. It would seem clear that Sir William had at first accepted this military charge without foreseeing the outcome of his service. The sharpness of his discontent had been responsible for certain indiscretions on his visits to England and he became increasingly conscious that his reputation had in some way been clouded by the Babington Plot. Walsingham had always proved friendly and Stanley decided to write to him to remove the danger from these suspicions. 'I protest,' wrote [1] Sir William 'that Jacques my Lieutenant whom I have loved very well in respect that the Vice Chamberlain put him in his place is thought to be one of the odious (Babington) conspiracy against Her Majesty.' This was the first sign of alarm, and it is significant that no message was ever to be received to reassure him. His soldiers raised in Ireland now also caused suspicion,[2] as did the subordinate Catholic officers whom he maintained. The correspondence, which follows, will indicate the sequence of the changes as Sir William Stanley garrisoned Deventer while the northern winter settled on that town.

The Earl of Leicester, the chief of the expedition, was in England and the diplomatic agency was held by the Secretary of the Council, Thomas Wilkes, who had been sent out to manage his recall.[3] The Hague was headquarters for the senior military officer, Sir John Norreys, from whose jurisdiction Stanley had recently been able to cast free, and on the Dutch side there was the authority of the difficult Councils of the States. The first signs of trouble appeared late in November in a letter addressed by the Magistrates of Deventer to the Council of State, complaining that Stanley had brought the Irish from the forts beyond the Yssel into the town. 'Against our will,' wrote [4] the Magistrates, 'we have abandoned to him the Noremberger

---

[1] Letter of Sir William Stanley to Sir Francis Walsingham, dated 10th October, 1586, from the camp before Deventer. Cal. S.P. Foreign, 1586–7, p. 188.
[2] Leicester had written to Sir Francis Walsingham on 15th December, 1585, to send him 'a 1000 of your Irish idell men, such as be not only in her majestyes pay but very mete to be out of their countrey.' Leycester Correspondence, Camden Society, p. 26.
[3] This opposition was at first not manifest, and Leicester, writing of Wilkes on 10th August, 1586, calls him 'a marvellous sufficient man.' Cal. S.P. Foreign, 1586–7, p. 122.
[4] Letter of the Magistrates to the Council of State, dated 21st November, 1586. Ibid., pp. 241–2

Gate. He is going on to dispose of all merchandise and other traffic leaving the town, tears up the passports which we give and seems to direct all things to the end of forcing all good burghers to fly from the place when it will fall into the hands of the enemy (which God forbid). Truly in our extreme misery and desolation, worse even than that of Bergen op Zoom we had not expected that we would have secret enemies who would plot for us such calamity.' On 9th December, the complaints having reached him by the proper channels, Wilkes wrote two letters to Leicester and to Stanley to make his view of the situation clear. In these letters there appears clearly his complete distrust of all such rumours, for it was so manifest to him that there were many ways in which these foreign burghers would be likely to resent the English rule. Among the leaders of an expeditionary force, so infrequent and uncertain in its pay,[1] it was necessary to forage for a living; such repercussions would almost seem inevitable when Stanley and his soldiers wintered in Guelderland. 'The magistrates of Deventer,' wrote [2] Wilkes, 'sent great complaint against Sir William Standley . . . that he seeketh to take from them the keys of their gates, seized and holdeth their strengths within that by force . . . and albeit for my own part I do hold Sir William Standley to be a wise and discreet gentleman . . . yet when I see how heavily the matter is conceived here by the States and the Council I do fear that all is not well.' This same suspicion that undue exactions from the burghers had caused this stir is reflected in Wilkes' letter to Sir William. 'They have complained,' he wrote [3] the same day to Deventer, 'that you have done many things to the wonderful discontentment of the whole inhabitants. For mine own part I have always known you to be a gentleman of value, wisdom and judgment and therefore should hardly believe any such thing to happen where you command.' Five days later, refreshing the memory of an ancient feud, Sir John Norreys sent by post to Burghley. 'As I did presume,' he wrote,[4] 'so I find Sir William Stanley and Mr. Yorke here to oppose themselves against me.'

---

[1] A letter of Anthony Gawdy to his nephew Philip Gawdy, dated at Bergen-op-Zoom, 30th May, 1588, states that 'Bergen is full of captains and good soldiers in want of money and apparel.' Cal. Gawdy, MSS., p. 30.
[2] Letter of Thomas Wilkes to the Earl of Leicester, dated 9th December, 1586. Cal. S.P. Foreign, 1586–7, p. 261.
[3] Letter of Thomas Wilkes to Sir William Stanley, same date. *Ibid.*, p. 263.
[4] Letter of Sir John Norreys to Lord Burghley, dated 12th December, 1586, at the Hague. Cal. S.P. Foreign, 1586–7, p. 266.

THE CELTIC PEOPLES & RENAISSANCE EUROPE

The question of Sir William Stanley was not a matter upon which the authorities in England were destined to the enjoyment of much peace. Only two days later despatches contained the rumour that he had asked for a special church to have Mass said and Stanley himself was stimulated to reply. 'I have given none any commission of either aye or no,' he wrote [1] to his enemy, Norreys, ' so trust I that Sir John Norris my good friend hath given no authority to any of his to report that we here have demanded a Church to say Mass in. And for my own person it is ready for Her Majesty's service to discharge all honourable actions amongst which I prefer the charge which it has pleased his Excellency to lay upon me.' It was, however, his misfortune that nothing could settle calm on these reports. The method of approach was more circuitous, complaints from the States to their own Dutch Generals with an eventual hope that the removal of Stanley, which seemed to them so essential, might at last be obtained by direct negotiation between the States General and the English Queen. To the clear-sighted citizens of Guelderland it was very evident that they must leave no stone unturned to save themselves from the power of such a friend. The first move was a letter sent from the Councillors of the Duchy of Gueldres and the County of Zutphen to the military commander, Count Neuenaar. 'We are advertised by two persons coming from Zutphen,' so the Councillors declared,[2] ' that a lieutenant of the garrison of Deventer has been two days in Zutphen where he had much intercourse and good cheer. The Irish are great Papists and in close friendship with the burghers of the Roman religion.' Already, however, a fierce denial of any treachery had been sent by Stanley's subordinate, Rowland Yorke, who commanded the capture of Zutphen sconce. 'As to what you have been told,' wrote [3] Yorke to the Council, ' of my lieutenant an honourable gentleman and only adopted son of the Baron Zouch: their author I declare (be he whom he may) to be a poltroon and a false liar. These evil spirits have slandered me also.' Here again Wilkes found it necessary to write to Stanley of the disturbing character of

<hr>

[1] Letter of Sir William Stanley to Sir John Norreys, dated 14th December, 1586, at Deventer. Cal. S.P. Foreign, 1586–7, pp. 272–3.

[2] Letter from the Council of Gueldres to Count Neuenaar, dated 14th December, 1586, at Arnhem. Cal. S.P. Foreign, 1586–7, p. 273.

[3] Letter from Rowland Yorke, dated 10th December, from the fort of the Velue before Zutphen. The signatures of subordinate officers are appended for confirmation. Cal. S.P. Foreign, 1586–7, p. 273.

these reports. ' The Council of Gueldres advertize,' he wrote [4] on 17th December, ' that a lieut. of some English company at Deventer hath had access to the enemy at Zutphen and that the Irish of your regiment (being for the most part Papists as it is supposed) do enter into a very straight league with the Papists of Deventer whereby there are grown some conceits that there is intelligence with the enemy to betray the town of Deventer. Albeit I trust that be no such matter. Yet I pray you to have a careful eye to the Irish people.' The signs were accumulating and this defence of the military leader whose reputation was so closely threatened seems almost a refusal to read warnings in the sky.

With the Christmas snow falling upon Deventer, in the enforced military inaction which the slow freezing of the waterways had brought about, an opportunity is provided for considering the position from the standpoint of Leicester and Stanley, the choices which lay before them and the reason which would seem to govern the indifference, in the face of so much warning, which the high command in England had displayed. The Earl of Leicester was now approaching his sixtieth year and had been accustomed all through his mature life to a constant and undeviating power. It was the form of power which could only be exercised by a great noble, personal in its incidence and its scope, very remunerative. The detail of administration, the tireless middle-class activities of the new bureaucracy, all the careful achievement of the Cecils was foreign to him. In regard to Stanley the whole question turned upon this outlook. The political interests of a great lord of Leicester's distinction were eclectic from choice, since his prestige would enable him to put forward and sometimes to carry his personal opinion upon any measure of policy on which he might choose to reflect. Thus, while Burghley and Walsingham were concerned with every aspect of the realm's business, Leicester confined himself to the greater questions, the matter of the Queen of Scots, the support of the high Protestants upon the Continent, and a firmly aggressive attitude to Spain. This was the contrast in the region of the advice that they tendered, an opposition which also appears very clearly in the different methods by which Leicester and Burghley obtained their greater rewards. In the case of the bureaucratic

[1] Letter from Thomas Wilkes to Sir William Stanley, dated 17th December. *Ibid.*, pp. 278-9.

ministers the rewards came to them slowly on the long skein of their weaving, the toil, unceasing and constant, the myriad details with which their work was connected, the gradual changeless accretion as the threads of each fresh transaction were gathered into their hands. They were as fortunate as they were wise, and it is pleasant to reflect amidst those apostrophes of praise which rose sweet to Burghley's godly ear that, as far as the carcase of the State was concerned, this Sampson had indeed taken the honey.

The methods of Leicester were more direct, and he had a favourite's licence, so that he was accustomed to ask openly for grants which the lesser statesmen could only with slow prudence acquire. Now in their relationship with the rest of the world this contrast arises again, for Burghley and Walsingham neither intrigued nor complained against the Queen's other servants, but corresponded with all and only withdrew their support when it seemed that Her Majesty's interests would be hindered by further encouragement. Thus Stanley corresponded to the very last with Burghley and Walsingham. But the more open autocratic methods which Leicester employed resulted in a definite attitude towards all his subordinates. In the case of Sir William Stanley the situation was clear. Leicester regarded him as very definitely a *protégé* and was perfectly aware of his discontent with the Government which only seemed to bind Stanley the more closely to him. His interests in Denbigh had given Leicester an understanding of the influences in North Wales and Cheshire and he fully appreciated the sway which Stanley exercised in those parts. As to his chief ground of complaint, the neglect of his claims in the great partition of Desmond, Leicester knew himself clear, for the Irish situation was not a department of policy in which he had ever been tempted towards intervention. Besides, for Stanley's successful rivals Leicester had no great liking, for so many of the new settlers in Ireland were dependents of his enemies, Sussex and Essex. In this matter he had even assisted Stanley in his feud with Sir John Norreys, although the latter was a very capable officer who had destroyed a record number of ' savages ' and a horde of their barbarous women in a highly successful affair he had carried through at Rathlin. The second ground of complaint against Stanley was the dislike felt for him by the Dutch, another point upon which Leicester could sympathize. Lastly there was the charge of treachery among

THE EARL OF LEICESTER

From an engraving by Robert Vaughan in the National Museum of Wales.

the Irish, but it was perfectly clear that no danger arose from that quarter so long as Stanley was firm. It was probable that he had been somewhat imprudent in the fines that he had levied from the close-fisted Dutch, but beyond that there was hardly likely to be any real excuse for complaint. It was said that Stanley was a Catholic, but how common it was in these days to hear such a charge ; Leicester was a man of the world and could well conceive that there were sympathies for the Old Religion at Hooton, but Stanley had always been reasonable, and it seemed incredible that now, after twenty years of sensible conduct, he would allow a mere private opinion to influence an important affair. And then in Holland the distances were so small, for Leicester remembered so well the confined spaces of Zeeland and the bells of the Lange Jan Toren, which could be heard with a favouring wind through the length and the breadth of the Province, ringing for assemblies in the high air of Middelburg. These were his own Dutch memories, the open windows of a Zeeland summer, the bells ringing above him as he sat in his house in Lange Delft, the soldiers clanking across the Singel of the ramparts, the look-outs in the tower above the Abbey and on the seas beyond Vlissingen the crowding English sail. It seemed that there could be no danger in giving Sir William Stanley the charge of Deventer. Exact knowledge was not considered necessary by the Earl of Leicester, and this episode of Stanley and Deventer was not the only time his vagueness played him false. It was in a very different light that the situation presented itself to Sir William Stanley.

He was, it is true, hardly a very serious Catholic at this period, and the custom of long acquiescence was most strong. It is to be noted also that the only evidence adduced for his long-formed intention to betray his charge was a despatch [1] of the former Ambassador, Don Bernardino de Mendoza, written in Paris ; its author had been expelled from England two years previously and was known for his political prophecies, vivid, inaccurate, wholly misleading. The very doubtful character of this evidence does not in any case carry the matter further than the suggestion that Stanley had turned over these possibilities in his mind. But the dominant influence in his conduct

---

[1] The letter sent by Don Bernardino de Mendoza to Philip II on 13th August, 1586, refers in a list of those ready to rise to ' Sir William Stanley a soldier of great experience, who has come over from Ireland by the Queen's order with 1000 troops mostly Catholics to pass over to Flanders. When he is obliged to go to Zeeland he promises to pass over on the first opportunity to the Prince of Parma.' Cal. S.P. Spanish, 1580-6, p. 604.

arose from isolation and from fear. The effect of such a fear, irritant though groundless, was to bring to execution a project which ran counter to the whole previous current of his life. For Stanley was alone, surrounded by subordinate officers of quite unequal rank and with the constant murmured plots of Rowland Yorke. He had certainly been imprudent, there had been communications of some kind with the Babington conspirators and the Government suspicions were aroused. How easy it became for him to give way before the fears of that lonely winter as the suspicion fed by Rowland Yorke became more strong that he could not go back in safety and that in England lay arrest. For Yorke it was a very different matter, for he had never been beyond suspicion, a strong adventurer of the sword, suspected and imprisoned, then a captive of Parma, an equivocal and doubtful prisoner, a Catholic who owed his preservation to the prudent clemency of that prince. And here he was Stanley's solitary guide.

Communications could at this time barely be maintained, for the firm hold of the Spanish troops in Zutphen increased the isolation as Stanley settled down within Deventer. He was far from the coast with a road difficult and sometimes dangerous to reach the Hague. The Province of Overyssel on the eastern march already felt the slow return of the Spanish rulers and there was a party favourable to their former sovereign within the town. None of the protection of the canal and dyke land surrounded him ; but only the sandy heath and the pine forests, defenceless and desolate. The full monotony of this distant guard, the absence of any serious Dutch authority, the constant murmurings of the burghers combined to keep Stanley insecure. How clear it seemed that all aid was out of reach as he moved from the house of the Three Herrings through that pretence of a market, which the Spanish hold on the surrounding lands had strangled, to the few offices of the provincial city, the Weigh House with its cupolas and the red tower above the Mint. Upon the tower of the Groote Kerk appeared the words, weathered now but omnious, ' Consule '— ' Fortis Age '—' Fide Deo '—' Vigila.' Only five miles south along the Yssel the bells from the Wynhuis Tower at Zutphen marked the headquarters of the Spanish troops and westward there ran the only but dangerous way to safety the road to Apeldoorn. There was a negligible stream of traffic and no messengers upon the road, except on the days when Yorke came riding a roundabout way enough from

SIR WILLIAM STANLEY AND WALES

his outpost before Zutphen the Veluwe. This was a disturbing messenger for Stanley's mind at such a time, suggesting to him that no safety remained in the English service, and that it was only the distance from the capital which had so long preserved him from arrest. Two letters reflect this state of mind, an appeal which Stanley sent to Walsingham on St. Stephen's Day and a Christmas note to Norreys. ' I know you are inclined to judge well of us,' he wrote [1] with hesitancy to the Secretary of State, ' I am at this turn driven to lodge all my apparell to pawn in the Lombarde for money to pay for meat and drink ' ; while in the letter to his military rival the sense of isolation stands forth clear. ' For I rest here,' he wrote,[2] ' on the confines of the world, neither expecting nor accepting any good, but hardly bestead. Money we have none, nor any other joy save this, that I must merit heaven with patience.'

Yet, if the prospect towards England was so gloomy, there were a number of unusual circumstances in the situation as far as the Spaniards were concerned. In the first place England was not at war with Spain and the Queen had herself declared in accents of courageous insincerity that she wished that the Seven Provinces should return, subject to certain safeguards, to the Spanish Crown. At the same time the sentiment in favour of legitimacy was already strong, and, like all conservatives with a Catholic trend, Stanley could hardly avoid an inherent prejudice in favour of the lawful sovereignty of Philip. In addition, any sympathy that might at one time have existed between the English and the Dutch had now worn thin and even Wilkes, who represented the cautious opinion at that time, referred [3] to the enmity of the Dutch generals ' Counts Hohenlohe and Moers who have done almost nothing but drink and banquet for ten or twelve days together.' In Stanley's case this feeling was heightened by the peculiar dislike shown him in Holland and, as he thought of the constant intrigues against him and of the envoy van Schagen Bersingerhoren with his long persistent complaint, he could hardly feel much compunction [4]

---

[1] Letter of Sir William Stanley to Sir Francis Walsingham, dated 26th December, 1586. Cal. S.P. Foreign, 1586-7, p. 287.
[2] Letter of Sir William Stanley to Sir John Norreys, dated 25th December. *Ibid.*
[3] Letter of Thomas Wilkes to the Earl of Leicester, dated 4th January, 1587. Cal. S.P. Foreign, 1586-7, p. 308.
[4] Complaints from another angle are contained in a letter dated 16th February, 1587, from Colonel Fremin to Lord Willoughby, Governor of Bergen-op-Zoom. ' Your Lordship knows the humour of these (Dutch) nations who need a good schoolmaster with the thunderbolt of Jupiter in his hand.' Cal. Ancaster MSS., p. 44.

as far as the Dutch were concerned. What exactly was his position ? He had undertaken to hold Deventer for Leicester. It was therefore not really the Queen's business at all. But then Leicester was in England and it was doubtful if he would return. Altogether it could hardly savour of treason how he acted in this private affair. He had a chance of weighing both sides, for he had served under Alva in his first days of soldiering and now he had experienced the Dutch and their methods. Such specious reasoning[1] was of course not wholly sincere, but in an age of formalism such technical points had their value. Besides, his discontent and his fear of disgrace in England would magnify and distort all these aspects in the wintry camp of Deventer alone with the burghers. Every indication would show that he did not regard his action as an irreparable breach with his country ; but rather as the act of a member of the opposition in the complicated moves of the Court. The seventeenth century example of the Fronde provides a clue to the outlook of many of the politically minded Catholics abroad in the years between the Queen's accession and the final outbreak of war. And this is particularly true of Stanley whose high military service and claims to office combined with the influence of his great feudal family to suggest those later French leaders. The case of Yorke was very different. He could indeed use most of Stanley's arguments, but he had never reached the high commands. As a mere private Captain, long distrusted, his actions had none of the significance of his chief's decision ; for the whole importance of the Stanley episode turned upon the distinguished career that Sir William was completing, the great office for which he was marked out, the claims which the Queen considered she possessed on his good service. It is remarkable that till the very end Leicester and Wilkes still kept to their position.

The States General, finding their former efforts unsuccessful, now endeavoured to approach Leicester directly. A strong letter was sent from the Council of the States, enclosing a memorandum of the further reports of Stanley and showing the dangerous condition of Deventer.

---

[1] The distinction between the service of Leicester, regarded as a private individual, and that of the Queen is perhaps valid ; while it seems that Stanley could also plead the permission given him previously by Leicester to leave the service of the States. The excommunication of 1570 which had not previously disturbed him, does not seem to have been a moving factor in Stanley's action. In Allen's argument it was only given a third place after the duty of rendering up towns ' unlawfully holden' and the position of the Flemish rebels had been discussed. *Cf.* Allen's *Defence of Stanley*, Chetham Society, pp. 1–31.

SIR WILLIAM STANLEY AND WALES

' He (Stanley) speaks,' so they declared,[1] ' very disrespectfully of the Council, of Norris and Wilkes, and told the agent (of the Council) "Io recibo cartas como cartas pero hare come soldando," treating him with contempt and extorting money from him. If good order is not taken some great disaster is to be feared.' Such a warning could hardly be more plain, but Wilkes thoroughly irritated [2] against the Dutchmen still maintained that there was only a financial difficulty at stake. In a letter sent to England the next day, after referring to his correspondence with Leicester whom he terms Themistocles, he again presses his view of this affair. ' Stanley,' he wrote,[3] ' is not contented with the entertainment of £40 sterling a month, but has seized £10 a month over from the Commissaries. He is charged with taking from the poor villages near abouts, weekly for the provision of his table, one whole ox, three sheep and a hog or in lieu of the hog 20s. sterling.' On the same day that Wilkes was engaged with his judicial picture, while he was balancing Stanley's latest crime, ' the taking of a hog or in lieu of the hog 20 shillings,' the Governor of Deventer delivered up the keys of the city with all that it contained, the garrison and the discontented burghers to the representative of the King of Spain. The following morning a messenger came riding to the Hague bearing a letter from John Norreys. ' Here is come even now,' wrote [4] the fortunate rival, ' news from Amersford in the report of certain soldiers that Sir William Stanley hath delivered Deventer to the enemy. If it be so I must account that all Overyssel is lost and the country in great danger and our journey quite defeated.' Stanley was immediately declared a traitor and entered the Spanish service, many of his subordinate officers [5] and all the Irish troops whom he commanded following him in this course.[6]

---

[1] Letter of the Council of State to the Earl of Leicester, dated 18th January, 1587. Cal. S.P. Foreign, 1586–7, p. 319.
[2] An example of this imitation among the soldiery appears in Colonel Fremin's letter, dated 28th January, ' You knew how our States have treated me one month's pay in seven months.' Cal. Ancaster MSS., p. 44.
[3] Letter of Thomas Wilkes to Sir Francis Walsingham, dated 19th January. Cal. S.P. Foreign, 1586–7, p. 322.
[4] Letter of Sir John Norreys to Thomas Wilkes, dated 20th January, 1587. Cal. S.P. Foreign, 1586–7, p. 326.
[5] The surrender of the Veluwe Fort by Yorke, which took place the same day, was almost lost sight of in the general excitement. In the final arrangements Captain Thomas Salisbury, one of Stanley's staff, was the go-between who kept Yorke in touch with Deventer. Cal. S.P. Foreign, 1586–7, p. 488.
[6] According to a letter of Colonel Fremin to Lord Willoughby dated 28th January, 1587, ' the traitor Marchant has sold the castle of Wauw for 48,000 florins and has retired with his company towards the frontiers of France.' Cal. Ancaster MSS., p. 43.

In England the news produced an effect profoundly damaging for the Catholic cause. The long favour shown Stanley by his patron only heightened the general anger, the crop of suspicions pushed up anew and the half Conforming Elizabethan gentry moved another stage away from Rome. This episode continued the process that the Bull *Regnans in Excelsis* and the Babington Plot had begun. To those squires who were anxious to find good reasons for not opposing the Crown it began to be clear that there was no way in which they could fulfill their duty to the Queen and to England more fully than by partaking of the new Sacrament which Her Majesty had set up. Already the beginning of the Cavalier mind is seen forming. Yet in contrast to all such expressions there survives an interesting report of the Venetian Ambassador in Paris, a paper objective and calm. ' Colonel Stanley,' declared [1] the Ambassador, ' an Englishman of high nobility belonging to the house of Derby has surrendered Deventer spontaneously. Stanley says he came to this resolve upon conscientious grounds as he knew how just were his Catholic Majesty's claims upon that place. . . . Near Zutphen an Englishman surrendered to the Duke a fort of great importance ; this he did out of gratitude to the Duke, who, a year before, had spared his life.' As far as motives for the action are concerned there is little more to be said on the matter.

If the surrender of Deventer caused such a profound impression in England, it was inevitable that the accession of Sir William Stanley should have a lasting effect on the English exiles abroad. From the first there was no doubt as to how he would range himself coming at once into the heart of Spain's military system. His young brother, who had served with him at Deventer, and Captain Yorke and the subordinate Catholic officers, Salisbury and the Eatons, formed a quite definite group bound together by the view that the Government took of their action. This was what Hugh Owen had always desired a forthright and soldierly company with whom he was also in sympathy through their North Welsh connections, and at last events happened quickly. For the exiles of the Northern Rising the long waiting, now fifteen years, without hope of return had proved galling, but the definite declaration of war at last fixed the issue. In the month

---

[1] Letter of Giovanni Dolfin to the Doge and Senate dated 27th February, 1587. Cal. S.P. Venetian, 1581–91, p. 249.

which followed Stanley's surrender, February, 1587, the Queen of Scots was beheaded and in April Drake's fleet sailed into Cadiz, thus destroying the last pretence of neutrality. Eighteen months later all immediate chance of an invasion of England was over with the Armada destroyed. The exiles settled once more into their old rival factions, and it is interesting to see the part that the Welsh group now played.

Sir William Stanley left an impression, recorded by Parma, of disinterested reserve. The Governorship of Mechlin provided him with new duties, and he was now an acknowledged leader, but, even so and in spite of the pronounced ' Spanish ' views he adopted, it would seem that he regarded the affair as a Fronde, a dislocation of Government which forced him to action. It is along such lines that the ideas of the leadership and perhaps the succession to the English Crown of Ferdinando, Earl of Derby, his cousin, would seem to have made their appeal. His own lack of intimacy with this younger man and the secret Catholic practice of Ferdinando's mother both provided a scope for his planning. The old Queen must soon die and his cousin had definite claims as the grandson of King Henry VIII's sister Mary.[1] It was a simple plan, in fact altogether too simple, but one which his companions could easily grasp. The remembrance of the Isle of Man as the stronghold of his family floated before him and then the thought of support he might raise in North Wales. It is clear at this period how anxious the English abroad were to avoid the proposal of giving their Crown to a foreigner and this reservation was one which had an important effect on their outlook. To Stanley, whose family had given the Crown to Henry VII at Bosworth, it would prove just such another adventure over again with Derby cast, all unconscious, for the part of a Richmond. In these hopes the Spanish party received the support of that section known as the Jesuit group on the Continent. It was a case of mutual attraction. The military system, the practical methods, the clear-sighted outlook and vigorous action which marked St. Ignatius' Company appealed to the soldier in Stanley, a point of view which he shared with the

[1] If the descendants of King Henry's elder sister Margaret were excluded as foreigners, and if Lady Arabella Stewart should be regarded as Scottish, the Crown would vest in the younger sister's descendants. But a doubt could be raised as to the legitimacy of Mary's elder daughter, the Duchess of Suffolk, on account of the doubtful status of Charles Brandon's earlier marriage. If the Suffolk line were excluded as illegitimate, the succession would pass to Mary's younger daughter the Countess of Cumberland, whose only child, Margaret, Countess of Derby, was the mother of Earl Ferdinando. It was a just possible line, but much less reasonable than those of Lady Arabella or the Suffolk representative, Beauchamp.

great Spanish captains. Stanley was an Englishman with an understanding of North Welsh conditions and some slight admixture of
blood, since his grandmother had come over the border, Grace Griffiths
from Penrhyn ; but in a house of that high distinction the male line
pruned in accepting the qualities of each fortunate bride. Stanley was
therefore utterly remote from the ancient Celtic outlook of Clynog
and Cassano, poetic and vague, while the definite standpoint of such
Englishmen as Parsons and Holt appealed to him strongly. He could
see the need of radical changes and they would help him to arrange
them on an ordered conservative basis. This was a view in which
Owen also concurred, for his English upbringing and his position in
Arundel's household had given a slightly sophisticated trend to his
mind ; while no one agreed more completely with Stanley than
Parsons. Above all, Father Parsons desired an utter casting away of
the new religious system in England and for this task he found strongest
sympathy among those whose actions prevented a return to their
country. He wished for a complete purification of the whole public
system in England ; but there would be a purification indeed before
Stanley was allowed to return. Then he had a quite just appreciation
of Stanley's worldly position, an accomplishment which the Welsh
priests sadly lacked. Again he had a very clear knowledge of this
leader's military value, compared to the out-of-date details which good
Sir Francis produced, and he knew the temptations of those who had
left England freely. He could, in fact, within his perspective apportion
means to their end.

A pleasant contrast is provided by a letter of Thomas Morgan of
this date in which the vague hopes of the old Welsh party are compared with this precision. Bishop Lewis of Cassano and his chaplain,
Lewis Hughes, had cast their minds back to the conditions of Wales,
and Morgan whose relationship with the Queen of Scots and the Pagets
marks him as the interpreter of so many moods expresses this also.
' If any of their cousins' or friends' children be apt for learning,' he
wrote [1] to his brother Rowland, ' he would have him bring some of
them over. He thinks there should be some toward youths in
Tredegar, the Vanne, Llantarnam and Bedwelty, the lords of which
places he honours and remembers them all to God. He desires Powel
the priest to try and send Mr. Lewis of St. Por of that side the seas

---

[1] An intercepted letter. Cal. Salisbury MSS., iv, p. 8.

well appointed. If Mr. Lewis would come to him he would be glad so he would conform himself to the Catholic Faith.' In this connection it should be noted that England was in a state of war and that Mr. Lewis of St. Pierre on whom the plan depended was not a Catholic, yet it was a happy and pleasant reverie, instinct with that sense of old Welsh kinship and with the desire that the spirit should once more be free. Fr. Parsons' precise ideas were very different, totally lacking in that Utopian folly of the Welsh suggestion, but weapons of precision sometimes fail.

It would seem to have been during 1591 that the Government first corresponded[1] about Sir William Stanley's scheme. Several barren years had passed since Father Parsons had adopted the proposal that the Infanta should succeed to the Throne. This was a fantastic plan, sufficient in itself to show how remote that priest had become from the thought in his country. The idea that Philip II possessed any possible claim, through a far distant Lancastrian inheritance, was not even plausible, and such rights as he inherited would obviously pass to his son, the Prince of Asturias, later King Philip III, a boy of thirteen; but the successor designate was the King's elder daughter. The only vague chance of success would have lain in the accession of James VI of Scotland under the tutelage of Philip II and married to the Infanta; but Fr. Parsons never perceived how impossible it was that the English in the present state of the national temper should accept the Daughter of Spain. This was the rock on which every plan foundered, the fact that, if the Queen were to be killed, the party of the strong anti-Catholics would surely be swept into power. All that could really be hoped for was that a friendly Prince should succeed to the Queen's peaceful deathbed and that date seemed remote. The Scottish party of course favoured King James; but any hope of united intention with the high Spanish party had vanished when in 1589 he was married to the Lutheran Princess of Denmark. For these latter the case now presented itself as a question of finding a suitable Catholic. Two lines were excluded at once, those of Lords Beauchamp and Huntingdon, the one representing the Suffolks and son to the Erastian Lord Hertford and the other possessing the

---

[1] One of the earliest references is contained in a letter written by Fr. Parsons to John Cecil, a priest at Lisbon and dated 13th April, 1591. Opposite the phrase, ' Again I request you that my cousin's matter be dealt in secrecy,' the words ' by his cousin is meant my lord Straunge ' are written in the margin. Cal. Salisbury MSS., iv, p. 104.

Clarence inheritance as the strangely Puritan son of that Katherine Pole who had been the favourite niece of the Cardinal. Among the English possibilities this only left remaining Lady Arabella Stuart,[1] a woman unfitted for leadership and closely bound to the Court and Derby's son, Ferdinando, Lord Strange. It was not altogether a fortunate choice on which the Catholics were forced to rely, the personality of Henry, Lord Derby being the first obstacle to success.

At a period when the character of each leader counted so strongly, the whole trend of the Stanley power was determined by the religious indifference of Henry, Lord Strange. Just as the very different Elizabethan career of Philip Howard has had so strong an effect upon the Catholicism of the Norfolks, so Derby marked out his family's action, an attachment to the Crown, and in consequence to the State Church, so profound that it permitted from the calm of its security an assured yet casual tolerance of Rome. The dominant figure at this moment[2] was the fourth Earl, who had been known before his succession as Lord Strange and had ruled his house for nearly twenty years, a man somewhat pompous, as the episode of his golden breeches clearly shows, a strong supporter of the Government, rather heavy, a magnate of affairs. Religion had never been of interest to him, in spite of the Catholicism of his brothers, and he had been unfortunate in his domestic life,[3] reputed also too careful over money.[4] As Lord Lieutenant of Lancashire and Cheshire, he was very zealous against ' secret or church papists '[5] and in the overshadowing power of the Father at that time he was able to neutralize effectively any attempted manœuvre of his son. Thus there was no hope in any case for the Catholics, so long as the old Earl of Derby lived; for the *Patria Potestas* still had strength to secure the whole of the Stanley interest in an almost effortless control.

---

[1] Lady Huntingdon had been the great-granddaughter and heiress-general of George, Duke of Clarence, younger brother of Edward IV, and Lady Arabella was the first cousin of James VI, King of Scotland over whom she possessed the advantage of being English by birth.
[2] As late as 20th May, 1593, there was no question of the Earl's ill-health. *Cf.* a letter of the Privy Council which he signed on that date. Cal. Burford Corporation MSS. Var. Coll., i, p. 60.
[3] A letter from Margaret, Lady Strange to Sir William Cecil, dated July, 1567, shows that a long series of quarrels had led up to the separation which took place about that time. Cal. S.P. Dom. Add., 1566–79, p. 33.
[4] According to the statement of Lady Strange's woman, Mrs. Calfhill, her husband had kept her short of money from 1559 until 1567, when a definite arrangement was prepared. *Ibid.*, p. 43.
[5] Letter from the Earl of Derby to the Council, dated November, 1592, in which he refers also to his apprehending of priests. Cal. S.P. Dom., 1591–4, p. 288.

SIR WILLIAM STANLEY AND WALES

It could not be said either that Ferdinando, Lord Strange would seem a hopeful candidate. He was at this time a man in the early thirties, a patron of the stage and in some slight measure himself also a writer. In his favour there stood only the fact that he had never obtained the Queen's graces. Those sandy moustaches and the little peaked beard and the roving, mild blue eye were of a quality to leave the Queen untouched. Against him was a complete absence of any interest in religion and the fact of his marriage. The daughter of Sir John Spencer, a garrulous, litigious [1] woman, whom he had married before his majority, was hardly a fit consort for the Throne. But, worst of all, a certain intimacy had sprung up, dating from the time when Robert Cecil served the Earl [2] at Dover, between the mild Lord Strange and Burghley's gifted son. A certain mutual lack of aptitude for outdoor sports may well have formed the link in what was, in the Catholic eyes, this inconvenient bond. [3]

Nevertheless, gloomy as the prospect might appear, there was no other candidate, and Sir William Stanley pressed for his adoption. The events which now followed are obscure and admit of several explanations. It would seem probable that a messenger was chosen as soon as the old Earl's health began to fail to test the opinions of Lord Strange. Richard Hesketh, a cadet of an excellent family in the North, first appears in this episode in September, 1593, a traveller from the Low Countries into Kent. By fairly direct stages [4] he made his way to Lancashire, arriving at New Park on the day that the old Earl of Derby died. [5] A few days later he met Ferdinando, the new Earl, by appointment at Bruerton and was handed over to the authorities, by whom he was executed for treason on 29th November. Hesketh was introduced to the Earl by Sir Thomas Langton, known

[1] There were, for instance, prolonged lawsuits with her brother-in-law, and after her husband's death she declared herself dissatisfied with an offer of £20,000 for her three daughters and £5,000 in dowry for herself. Cal. S.P. Dom., 1595–7, p. 155.
[2] Letter of Rob. Cecil to Lord Burghley, dated 16th February, 1588. 'I will obey your fatherly counsel about my duty to God and to the Earl (of Derby) whose follower I am. My health is good, especially when I take in the mornings in the top of the castle the hungry air of the seaside.' Cal. S.P. Dom. Add., 1580–1625, p. 241.
[3] A letter from Earl Ferdinando to Sir Robert Cecil, dated 16th September, 1593, conveys this well. ' How near you are to my wife,' he wrote, ' I need not tell you ; how dear to me time may show with my good fortunes make show of.' Cal. Salisbury MSS., iv, p. 3.
[4] He stayed at the *Bell* Inn at Canterbury, where Richard Baylye entered his service, and then passed by Gravesend to London, staying at Mr. More's house at Paul's Wharf. Cal. Salisbury MSS., iv, pp. 408–9.
[5] On this occasion he did not see Lord Strange, but delivered his letters to Sir Edward Stanley, one of the old Earl's Catholic nephews. Hesketh asserted that the letters had been given to him at the *White Lion* at Islington by Mr. Hickman, the Stanleys' factor, and only contained London news. *Ibid.*, p. 409.

255

alternatively [1] as the Baron of Walton and the Baron of Newton, a gentleman in Lord Derby's service and a distant relative through the Monteagle Stanleys. It is significant that, although Sir Thomas had been a Recusant for six years and was asserted to possess the confidence of Sir William Stanley and the Cardinal, he was not molested. The situation is complicated by the very remarkable paper that now fortunately appeared [2] containing references to the 'hallowed crown' that was to be sent to Lord Derby and the Spanish military aid he could count on. The talent which the Government possessed for producing the necessary documents had caused suspicion to be cast even on the existence of this impracticable scheme and it is possible that the authorities, after capturing Hesketh, considered that the moment had come to make use of this happy event. Nevertheless, if proof is needed that Hesketh came upon some mission [3] to sound Derby's intentions in however tentative a fashion, it would be supplied by the great agitation into which the Stanleys were thrown. Two of Sir William Stanley's sons were being brought up as pages at Lathom and Derby set himself elaborately to explain. 'In respect of this late action of their father's,' he wrote [4] to Cecil, 'I have forbid them for a time. . . . They are very good comers to Church, grieved at their father's courses, young when he left his country like a traitor and now able to judge of such an action.' In a letter sent a day later he was still dwelling upon the same subject. He begins by referring to Hesketh the lawyer, 'brother to him I brought up,' who seeks only to cross him. 'Though it be but a trifle,' Derby declared,[5] 'yet would I be loth to be thwarted by so mean a man. I think he is angry that I used myself so honestly touching his brother.' Nor was Lady Derby free from alarm. 'I doubt not,' she began [6] to Cecil, 'but he (my Lord) shall be crossed in Court and crossed in his county, but I imagine his uprightness and honourable carriage, will, by the

[1] He was correctly Sir Thomas Langton of Walton Hall, lord of Newton-in-Makerfield. He had been a fugitive since the slaying of Thomas Hoghton in a fray. *Cf.* Lord Burghley's Map of Lancashire, Catholic Record Society, Misc., iv, p. 180.

[2] A detailed report was preserved by Lord Burghley. Cal. Salisbury, MSS., v, pp. 38–9.

[3] In a letter to William Waad, written by Hesketh on 5th November, 1593, he states that 'the Cardinal . . . hath made me the *enffant perdue* as I wrote to the Cardinal I thought I should prove.' Cal. Salisbury MSS., xiii, p. 493.

[4] Letter from the Earl of Derby to Sir Robert Cecil, dated at New Park, 8th November, 1593. Cal. Salisbury MSS., iv, p. 412.

[5] Letter from the Earl of Derby to Sir Robert Cecil, dated 9th November, 1593. Cal. Salisbury MSS., iv, p. 412.

[6] Letter from the Countess of Derby to Sir Robert Cecil, dated November, 1593. *Ibid.*, p.428.

means of so good friends as your father and yourself, be able to support him against any malice.' These are not the letters of a man who feels that he has never been in danger.

As far as Sir William Stanley was concerned, he was credited with the intention of wishing to establish contact with Derby through Father John Gerard.[1] There was much to be said for such a plan, since the elder brother, Thomas Gerard, was a personal friend of Lord Derby and in attendance upon his wife. Yet it would hardly seem that Father Gerard was quite the right choice; for excellent as he proved with the rough country squires, the arrival of so elaborate a layman was calculated to terrify the already much shaken Earl.[2] The description of this famous Jesuit makes the point very clear. ' Mr. Gerard,' so runs the admirable account,[3] ' was of stature tall, high shouldered, black haired and of complexion swarth, hawk-nosed, high templed and for the most part attired costly and defencibly in buff leather, garnished with gold or silver lace, sattin doublet and velvet hose of all colours with cloaks correspondent, and rapiers and daggers, gilt or silvered.' The arrival of this determined hawk-nosed man with his spade-cut beard and moustachios, his rapiers and daggers, was not likely to leave Lord Derby reassured. Only at the price of a courageous capture could he have reached at last to peace and this perhaps John Gerard understood, for he wisely never came.

At Valladolid, enjoying that hospitality which the English College now provided and always chafing [4] at this half-pay life, Sir William cast his mind on further schemes; but this was to prove Lord Derby's

---

[1] According to a letter of John Fixer, dated 22nd May, 1591, Sir W. Stanley ' hopes in Lord Strange who might be influenced through John Gerard, a priest, brother to one of his familiars.' ' The drift of his letter, in the opinion of J. C., dated 3rd July, 1592, ' is charging us by means of John Garrat, a priest, to make trial of my L(ord) S(trange).' ' Was asked by Sir William,' so runs the confession of Henry Walpole, ' to deal with some priest that might get access to Lord Strange, now Earl of Derby, Gerard he thought a fit man.' Cal. S.P. Dom., 1591–4, pp. 40 and 519 and Cal. S.P. Dom. Add., 1580–1625, p. 336.
[2] A letter of the Earl of Derby to Sir Robert Cecil, dated 13th October, makes it clear that he was in no state to meet Gerard. ' I am glad,' wrote the Earl, ' to hear that the lewd fellow (Hesketh) hath shown himself as base in mind as he is bad in manners. I wish that such vile men may never more have strength . . . and pray that all men ever carry like faith as myself.' Cal. Salisbury MSS., xiii, p. 491.
[3] Description. Cal. Salisbury MSS., xi, p. 365.
[4] An interesting note of a memorial of what Colonel Stanley had lost throws light on this dissatisfaction. He has lost (i) his patrimony of the Stanleys of Derby, (ii) his charge of the artillery in Ireland four thousand ' ducados,' (iii) his charge of Master-General of the infantry camp three thousand and sixty ' ducados,' (iv) his wages as Colonel of the companies three hundred and thirty ' ducados,' (v) the wages and perquisites of the Governor of Deventer, and (vi) for a company of two hundred men which he governed with a lieutenan in Ireland one thousand and three hundred ' ducados ' in the year. Valladolid MSS., legajo 6, preserved in the English College there.

only Christmas, for in the new year he was taken ill and on the sixteenth he was dead. The episode was brief and inconclusive, and it is probable that it will never really clear.

Connected in some way with this matter, evidently in the same region of ideas, was the plot of Yorke and Williams. Again the bare facts stand out distinct enough. During the following July Henry Young, Richard and Robert Williams and Edmund Young were arrested in England on a charge of treason. It appeared that Young and Yorke, who was a nephew of Rowland Yorke of Zutphen, had been reconciled by Father Holt[1] and they admitted serving in the Low Countries. Edmund Yorke, a young and rather fashionable[2] but extremely empty-headed man, had been serving in the Queen's forces as lately as the previous March.[3] Richard Williams, who took delight in hawks, had however been attached for some time to Sir William Stanley's regiment. He was said to be a nephew of Mr. Sheldon[4] at Beoley and to have influential connections; but it was clear that at the moment he was down at heel and unable to pay the rent of the house in the market-place at Brussels which he shared with his friend. Robert Williams was from Dublin, had been one of Sir William Stanley's Irishmen and was now in the service of Edmund Yorke. These details and the fact of the executions for treason are alone certain.

There remain, however, the somewhat lurid purposes that were attributed to them, either in their own forced statements or in the confessions of their friends. It is the difficulty which surrounds such information that the only possibility of pardon was on occasion to pitch the story high. They were speaking, too, of a foreign country and of events which inevitably were unknown in England. On the other hand it could be objected by those who prefer to accept these

---

[1] During his examination in the Tower on 12th August, 1594, Edmund Yorke declared that he had been reconciled by Fr. Holt, who gave him 12 crowns at parting and told him to remain a Catholic. Cal. S.P. Dom., 1591–5, p. 539.
[2] A letter from Edmund Yorke at Abbeville to Wm. Munning at Monsr. Ercknells at Dieppe, dated 21st March, states that his baizes of cloth of gold will do him much credit, and he is not to lay them in pawn. *Ibid.*, p. 470.
[3] A letter from Otwell Smith to Lord Burghley, dated at Dieppe 2nd March, 1594, described Captain Yorke's speeches as suspicious and declared that he is thought to have left the town and gone over to the enemy. *Ibid.*, p. 451. Captain Mosten had gone with him, and they had joined with Franklin and Captain Rourke, ' no well wishers to the State.' *Ibid.*, p. 485.
[4] It appears that Mr. Ralph Sheldon had nine married sisters, but none of them married to Williams. If he was a nephew therefore this must have been *à la mode de Bretagne*. The cousin-ship claimed with Sir Griffin Markham may have arisen through Mrs. Edward Sheldon who belonged to that family. *Cf. Visitation of Warwickshire*, pp. 2–3.

travellers' tales that it is often the details, rather than the main line, of their reports which ring fantastic.

The story pieced together runs as follows. Sir William Stanley was reported to have said [1] that ' if the Queen were dead he would go to Scotland with his regiment, make it strong and go to the Earl of Derby as would all England.' Alternatively ' they were to move some rebellion in the Earl of Derby's name though he was not privy to it.' [2] At the same time collateral evidence was put in [3] that ' Lord Strange, though he was of no religion, should find friends to decide a nearer state than these titles (Lord Treasurer, etc.).' As to more precise details, Young declared [4] that Williams had decided that ' it was better to raise a rebellion in North Wales, where his father and friends all Catholic live, his uncle, Mr. Sheldon, would help with money, also Mr. Pew who keeps a pinnace and dwells on a fortified rock and so draws the people to him that in two parishes near him, scarce three or four go to church.' The same deponent was also responsible for the statements that Captain Middleton was to keep the Irish Seas and prevent any ship annoying Pew's pinnace and that Conway Castle could be taken in one night. There is little known of Young's reliability of a witness beyond the fact that he appears to have been very skilled in making poisons. He was also employed by Richard Williams to write his letters and was in depressed circumstances at Brussels, selling his cloak through Wright, ' a man of many words.' Yorke in his confessions blamed Williams, describing his readiness to kill the Queen at the instigation of Stanley,[5] while Williams in his turn posed as an honest robber, giving that crime as an excuse for his foreign service and insisting on his loyalty to the Queen. It was stated that he had used an ' engine ' for breaking open the Church treasure at Winchester and that this was taken to Whitehall for an attempt to force the Queen's Jewel House. Williams was

---

[1] Examination of Edmund Yorke, dated 12th August, 1594. Cal. S.P. Dom., 1591–4, p. 539.
[2] The same continued on 20th August. *Ibid.*, p. 547.
[3] According to a speech of Philip Woodward reported by William Goldsmyth to Sir Robert Cecil on 11th July, 1593. The second half of Woodward's alleged statement that ' Sir Thomas Cornwallis and his sons were happy in that they suck honey from spiders ' does nothing to give an impression either of the genuine or serious character of the whole. *Ibid.*, pp. 335–6.
[4] Declaration of Henry Young, dated 16th August, 1594. *Ibid.*, p. 545.
[5] It must be admitted that Stanley seems to have been unfortunate in his servants at this time, for neither his steward, Mr. Greene, ' a tall black man, slender faced and very fine (who) hath a grace in casting his hands,' nor his page secretary Tony Jones, ' a little young man fully faced with auburn hair and curly locks at his ears ' can be considered very reliable. Cal. Salisbury MSS., iv, p. 500.

said to use coining irons in his cousin Sir Griffin Markham's chamber at Grays Inn and Sheldon was supposed to give money for a rebellion in Wales.[1] It is hardly possible to disentangle this farrago. Yet there is one phrase which keeps a suggestion of accuracy, such as these wild details lack. ' Stanley,' declared Yorke, ' was waiting for the Queen's death when all England would go to the Earl of Derby.' Perhaps this may suggest the real clue.

After the death of Ferdinando, Earl of Derby there was no possible hope from that side for the Catholics, since his claims [2] went to his daughters, whose mother was under the influence of Secretary Cecil, while the Earldom passed to his brother, who was married to Burghley's ward and granddaughter, Elizabeth Vere. It is a tentative suggestion that all these allied ' plots ' were the wreckage of some unthought-out plan, based on a desire for Derby's succession with Catholic aid from the North and from Wales. This would not by any means imply the Queen's killing, but an organization and readiness to take action when the signs of a serious illness should appear in her now ageing frame. Such talk would have come to an end in the February of 1594, when the news of the Earl's death would reach the Low Countries. It may even have been the abandonment of this purpose which led these stray swordsmen and Yorke, who had come to them later, to return on some private and non-political venture. Nevertheless, it does not seem fanciful to imagine that in the end they were captured because of the talk in the Low Country inns in the winter, while they gazed, thinking of what plan might turn to profit, at those disastrous pictures in the fire.

Surviving these troubles, Sir William Stanley and Owen, whom he used for his fine Castilian speech,[3] gradually settled and weathered ; while the Spanish military system, its arteries hardened already,

---

[1] These further details come from repeated re-examinations. Cal. S.P. Dom., 1591-4, pp. 539-48.

[2] Two independent details show the value which contemporary opinion set on this claim. In a report of the Council of State to Philip III, dated 11th July, 1600, after various alternatives it is suggested that ' the son of the Earl of Worcester, an English Catholic of good parts, although he has no claim to the throne might marry the daughter of the Earl of Derby. Cal. S.P. Spanish, 1587-1603, p. 664.

In a letter from Francesco Contarini, Ambassador at Paris, to the Doge and Senate of Venice, dated 25th April, 1599, it is stated that the Hugenots also suggest a wife for His Majesty (Henry IV) ; among others a Princess of the House of Saxony and an English lady, a daughter of the Earl of Derby, a relation of the Queen of England, through whom the King would acquire a certain claim to the English throne. Cal. S.P. Venetian, 1592-1603, pp. 566-7.

[3] A letter to Thomas Barnes, dated 7th September, 1589, states that ' Owen is gone to be his (Stanley's) prolocutor, being very perfect in the Spanish tongue and of better audacity to speak. Sir William has always used Owen thus.' Cal. S.P. Dom, Add., 1580-1625, p. 280.

passed over its prime. Plans were still being considered for the surrender of fortresses[1] and Stanley had already developed into that
'bogey' in England, which he was destined throughout life[2] to
remain. He belonged to the failing generation, and in his letters it is
perfectly clear that the causes which prevented his return into England
passed quite unperceived. The French party returned, but not the
Spanish.[3] Charles Paget took up again his interrupted rural life,
while William Stanley still remained an exile. Hugh Owen, Don
Ugo, that lesser man, would seem to have been absorbed into the
Spanish system; but for Stanley there was no such easy course.
With that quasi-royal status of his family and the faint suggestion of
the Fronde, there must have been in those fierce Castilian winters
amazement mingled with regret that he could not, even at the Peace,
return to Hooton. The Queen was dead, and still it was forbidden.
That long old manor house in the black and white of Cheshire, the
slender turret which rose above the roof line, the lighted windows
when his friends came in from hunting and sat with their tankards
resting on the bare oak of the banquet table, these things were forfeits
to a new-found national sense. The etiquette had now become much
stricter. The technical reasons which satisfied his action held good no
longer; for he was in a sense a late feudal survivor, keeping that line
of approach from which a Percy or a Stanley could take an independent action towards the holder of the Crown.[4] Yet the last feudalism
of the Northern Rising had not long survived the downfall of the
Old Religion and the new spirit would reject this standpoint for that
nationalism which the Universal Church could check no longer.
There had come a new dominion of the soil and the literary symbols
in their changing, the Divine Right of Kings, the Patriot King, were
received and buried by the Hooton oaks.

[1] According to the Confessions of Henry Walpole, July, 1594, ' Owen said that Sedgrave
an Irishman had dealt with Mr. Sidney the Governor concerning selling Flushing and that one
Creakes was sent to Lord Boroughs.'   Cal. S.P. Dom., 1591–4, p. 534.
[2] As witness a draft of a letter from the Duke of Buckingham to the Spanish Ambassador,
' some . . . had confessed that the said Sir William (Stanley) was not only privy to the plot of
the gunpowder treason, but that it was he who chose and sent over Faux.'   Cal. Drummond
Moray MSS., p. 116.
[3] It is noticeable that Sir John Wynn's account of ' Hugh Owen who was ye privat Counsell
to ye Prince of Parma ' is favourable.   History of Gwydir, p. 72.
[4] For this doctrine also the high royalism of James I could not forgive him. ' Sir William
Stanley now laments,' wrote James Wadsworth, ' his misfortunes and, if His Majesty of Great
Britain would grant him pardon and leave to live the rest of his days in Lancashire with beef
and bag pudding, he should count himself one of the happiest in the world.'   The English
Spanish Pilgrim, 1629, p. 69.

THE IRISH SCENE

At this point the forces of Gaelic Ireland are for the first time directly considered. The Anglo-Irish lords of the Pale bound by a long tradition of judicial and administrative service to the idea of the English Kingship were always influenced in a measure by England. It was in fact a settled custom of adherence to the Central Government on the part of Lord Delvin which lent an emphasis to the Celtic sympathies of the younger Nugents. In a still more marked degree the great political importance of the Desmonds had served to strengthen their links across the Channel. The custom of an ancient earldom, the primogeniture which this implied and the frequent high office which was granted to the Fitzgeralds of Munster all served to bind chiefs of this great family in, at any rate, intermittent contact with the English Crown. Hitherto the greater part of the connections between Ireland and Western Europe during this century had been confined to these groups and to their supporters or to the town merchants of Galway and Limerick. The Irish clergy, who were found abroad, had nearly always been to some degree mellowed by similar meetings. It was only when the ships of the Spanish Armada were wrecked on the north and west coasts of Ireland that the Spaniards first came into contact with the old Gaelic civilization.

A contrast is at once evident between the cultures of Ireland and Wales. The mediæval Welsh culture had always possessed a certain Latinity, which is emphasized by the claim made by many great houses to a continuity of lineal descent from the ' purple clad,' the constant boast of the blood of Tacit or Macsen. The Roman Emperors in Britain were never far in the background of Welsh consciousness. On the other hand the mediæval Welsh culture had been profoundly and integrally affected by the Anglo-Norman culture. Its Celtic elements served, however, to keep it distinct, since in so far as they were Celtic, pre-mediæval and pre-Roman, they were utterly alien to the men of the East or the South. In addition to the persistence of the tribe, a feature which was by this period of much less significance, the development from a society of the ' La Tène ' age was most apparent. This society, essentially aristocratic, based upon a multitude of kernes and kinsmen, implied by the lords ' dun ' as its centre. In Wales this system was vanishing with the great native lords like the house of Dynevor, and in the Elizabethan period only survived as an echo lingering in the hills. In the Hebrides it had been fading with the destruction of the Lordship of the Isles, but in Ireland a form continued : there its death agony ended with the Flight of the Earls.

The coming change in Ireland was already clear, hastened by Henry VIII's Act of 1542. Thus until that period Thomond had been controlled by the O'Briens, the chiefs of the Dal Cais, ruling by the Brehon Law. But in 1542 Murrough of Thomond ' came in ' and in the next year received the lands as an earldom, while in 1558 his nephew was inaugurated in the English fashion. A poem written about 1550 describes the situation completely. [1]

It was just the aristocratic quality of such a society, which gave significance to

[1] ' The race of the O'Briens of Banba under Murrough
Their covenant is with the King of England
They have turned and sad is the deed
Their back to the inheritance of their fathers.'

263

these changes. Such a surrender to the new system had an effect upon the clans of the West of Ireland, almost as disintegrating as that of the collapse of the High-land Macdonalds on the fate of the Islesmen. In the case of the O'Neill power there was a great change between the outlook of Shane O'Neill and his nephew, Earl Hugh. The old civilization remained less affected in ' Fermanagh of the bend-ing woods ' or in Tirconnell.

Celtic Ireland had remained almost unaffected by the recurrent waves of influence which had gone to the making of mediæval Europe and were now destroying it. It had no share in those common memories which still united the other nations of the West, memories of Roman order and of Roman law, of a hierarchy of officials and the sovereignty of the State. Besides, even feudalism had suffered a sea-change as it crossed the Irish Sea. It was this barrier which led the English to regard as ' savages ' the magnates who ruled West of English Law, an inevitable consequence of the profoundly alien character of the Celtic civiliza-tion. The society dominated by Shane O'Neill was a legitimate development of that of the Cuchulain cycle. Few customs could be more remote from sixteenth-century Europe than those which still survived in the elaborate ritual of the chief's ' dun,' the right to ' the shouldier place ' and ' the hero's portion,' the precedence of the well-descended kinsmen, the presence of the bought women and the wolf-hounds.

Such a life had been an anachronism in the mediæval system, and there was no place for it in Renaissance Europe. The mutual incomprehension of the Irish chieftains and the officials of the New Monarchy in Spain suggest that the Irish wars would have been inevitable, even if Catholicism had remained the State religion in England. Doctrinal differences only served to embitter the struggle and to emphasize its cause, the fundamental divergence between the Celtic con-ception of a ruler and the new conception of the State.

CHAPTER XIII

THE SPANISH SHORE

This episode deals with the wreck of the Spanish galleons cast upon the west coast of Ireland when the Armada had failed. It is intended to indicate the contrast between the extremes, the western Irish, like Brian O'Rourke, and the courtly grave Spaniards of whom de Leyva stands as a type. In the earlier chapters and especially in those on Stukeley and Stanley, some impression has been given of the outlook in Spain, while the O'Byrnes who stood behind the Baltinglas Rising and the Irish troops in Deventer have suggested that permanent background of Gaeldom against which the English settlers in Ireland and the Castle politics moved. The actual meeting proved how impracticable was the idea of alliance with which the Gaelic Irish and the Spaniards had toyed. All the details of Irish life which are mentioned are intended to stress the unbridgeable difference of outlook. The life of O'Rourke at Muinter Eolais, the bards and their legends, the picture of his cousin of Spain as the head of the house of Miledh was not further from the Spanish opinion of that day than the reality of the ten hundred cows before his rath on which his wealth depended and the constant internal feuds of the clans. It is in this sense also that the usquebaugh, the smoke vents and the drawn matting all indicate a civilization several centuries remote from the Spaniards. The rivalries of the Burkes and Graine O'Malley support the impression which the details of O'Rourke have built up. In contrast stands de Leyva, an accomplished cavalier, reserved and deliberate, whose mind ran on the *finesse* of diplomacy necessary in dealing on behalf of His Catholic Majesty with the little Courts of South Europe. The central incident is supplied by the wreck of his galleon on the Donegal coast and the camp he set up there until he was rescued again and then drowned by the rocks of Dunluce. The details which surround this episode make the irreconcilable divergence very clear.

THE idea of an alliance does not of itself imply contact and when two different stages of civilized life are in question, the chief danger to guard against is a meeting of principals. In nearly all cases suitable agents are employed, who can give to the people in the more simple country such impression as it is desired they shall form, and it is only some uncommon disaster that can bring together a representative body of such nominal allies. There is no parity here with the welcome given to strangers, whose lives are unknown, as in that innocent wonder at the Sailing Gods in Samoa, nor is there the usual development of hatred and admiration and barter, when the periods meet. This case is the rare event of the strain placed on a lifelong apparent friendship by the unforeseen meeting of allies, whose habits of thought are divided by centuries, and it is seen nowhere more clearly than in that meeting in Connaught, in the summer that the Armada scattered, between the Gaelic chiefs and the Spaniards.

In the case of the Spanish Armada the Irish for the last thirty years had gazed towards Spain, but on account of the difference of outlook it was the most desperate evil for the Spaniards to be cast on the shore of their allies, when the galleons were caught off the Isles in the first Atlantic gales of September. There was no hope of contact between minds, whose ideas had developed along planes so divergent. The Spaniards, who so unexpectedly found themselves in these cold seas, were typical of their countrymen embarked for a more urbane conflict conducted on that chess-board pattern to which their severe and unimaginative leaders were fettered. In the packed galleons with every kind of soldier and priest there was all the atmosphere of their country, where the Renaissance had been touched and stiffened by austerity and where the Nationalism was devout, with an attachment to *El Rey*, as representing their earthly sovereignty and to *El Emperador*, that term of which St. Teresa was so fond and on which they dwelt, ever conscious of that Divine Omnipotence under their monotonous and wide horizon. On the material plane they were always mindful of the unconquered Spanish Infantry and aware of, though half despising, the gold of the Indies behind them. But the Gaelic Irish were of the freshness of the Celtic Ages before the reign of law and no understanding could be established between the ship-wrecked Spaniards and their hosts in the Gaeltacht. Until they were captured or died, the Spaniards would never seem to have fathomed that dreamlike political innocence of the Irish and the meaning and ideas of these soldiers were never grasped by the clans, neither when they gave free reign to that wild hospitality, which the Spaniards barely survived, nor when in the wake of a more primitive instinct they gloried in the sight of the bodies of such strongly armoured lords on their beaches.

The contrast was accentuated still further because the poor lands on the coast were held by the fishing clans, dependent on the great families, whose strongholds lay inland. Tyrconnell and Connaught still kept a life of their own, unless the machinery was set in motion for some terrible raid, and the first news would be swept across this land by the runners; so that when the Spanish galleons were sighted the pivot of action would be not the sea villages, but Brian na Murtha O'Rourke's rath in Muinter, twenty miles from the coast. The strange interplay that ensued was the result of that drifting mist through which the clans looked upon Spain, where that Great King ruled, who was their equal and friend, proud to assist them. The case of Brian O'Rourke, who held the chief power in Leitrim, will show how remote were their sympathies and their methods from the lords of the Pale. To such a man it would always seem a balanced alliance, for, as he thought on the ten hundred cows by his rath,[1] the bards before the great fires in the evening would picture, for his massed followers, his cousin of Spain, the head of the house of Miledh, who lived with the Pope in a palace of gold beyond the Tower of Breoghan, a Prester John of the South. Then the High Kingship of the Gael would flicker in the firelight at Muinter Eolais before him, as the bard O'Maelchonaire described the Southern King and his master and their parallel glory; for to the Gael an alliance with the foreigner was not the foundation of independence, but the last ascent and the climax. It was only when the embers were cold that O'Rourke might consider Cousin Spain as a rescuing friend; for the rest they were equal. And then all these negotiations had the quality of a dream, since the chronicler knew of King Sebastian's death at Alcacerquibir, but was sure that his friend the Persian King would march across to avenge him, and Guise was ' Duic Guiber,[2] a good duke of the King's house of France.' Again and again we find this long clinging haze, ' the excellence of the hand of O'Dalbaighe,' [3] Alva disgraced and now dead, and even in regard to the lords of the Pale, a kind of ritual chant, Baltinglas and ' all the good heirs of the Foreigner, the eighteen heirs of the nobles of the foreigners of Midhe.' [4] But even in regard to O'Rourke this is only part of the picture, for with his neighbours he was courageous and practical and it was a constant unceasing fight to remain the chief of Hy Briuin. He had lived dangerously, but, although it was twenty-six years since his brother, Hugh Galldha, had died at his hands, there had always been rivals to encumber his

---

[1] The lesser McSweeney rath was described as ' the white rath, lime white with the red hung hall.' Egerton MSS., 111, f. 87.
[2] Annals of Loch Cé, 1588, p. 488.
[3] Ibid., 1581, p. 446.
[4] Ibid., 1581, pp. 445–6.

path, and this had required a constant clearing away of the luxuriant undergrowth of his kindred, his other brother, Hugh Boy, and his nephews, the last of whom Teige Oge had only recently succumbed in his dungeon. Every year he had brought the Scots in the summer, five hundred 'red legged' Albanachts, useful but expensive, and then there were other contracts with O'Flaherty of the Axes and Cuconnaught Maguire. At the same time there was the alliance with the Burkes, for Lady Mary had given him an heir, and a severely practical arrangement with Mr. O'Crean,[1] a Sligo merchant, whose wife had become his most permanent mistress. Now it was on this plane that he became conscious of the Spaniards, men who were dejected and strangers, expensive to feed, but with arms of great value. There they stood, dispirited and dripping from the waters, men who had appeared to him always as great shadows in the smoke from the fire.

In all these embarrassments there were two possible courses of action, for he might play for safety and despatch them on the shore, thus establishing a claim with the Queen and obtaining the undisputed possession of the arms they had landed, and in this connection the little brass cannons from the wrecks, the 'loud mouthed roarers' of the annalist, tempted him sorely. The alternative was to spare them for use as his mercenaries, driving a bargain with the starving men, which would save him from hiring the Albanachts, whom he would have had to pay from the price of his harvest. The first plan was the more prudent course, and with Perrot as Governor he might have pursued it, but the exalted mood rode him again and he could see, through the fumes of the usquebaugh, the grave Spanish captains with their gold chains, serving before him, so he sent letters of welcome and aroused his supporters.

Owing to the north-easterly gale the galleons were cast ashore on the rocks of Mayo and Donegal, and the success of O'Rourke's support would depend on his influence over the lesser Burkes and McSweeneys, who held the pathways up from the beaches, while a more difficult problem arose along the hard coasts of O'Dogherty's Country. Over the long shore of Mayo the havens were held by the Burkes, who generally assisted O'Rourke, although weakened by the

---

[1] As a reward the bard refers to O'Crean with charity as 'the least wicked merchant that was in Erinn,' while the bastard 'Brian na Samhthach was the tower of the battle for prowess.' Annals of Loch Cé, 1590, p. 512 and Annals of the Four Masters, 1604, p. 2349.

hidden internal feuds, which consumed them. Their enmity towards the Governor was incessant,[1] and they were more Gaelic than the Irish themselves, for all trace of their foreign kinsmen had vanished, and, while Brian na Murtha had the Latin tongue and could sign his name to his deeds, the Burkes made their marks, leaving to the scribes of their household the making of letters, from which through their princely blood they were free. Any progress to united rebellion was hindered by their half-smothered rivalries, although since the death of Sir Shane McOliverus, the McWilliam Iochtar, there had been a most uneasy peace for the English. The difficulty had been caused by the forceful policy of the succeeding McWilliam, Sir Richard the Iron, Risdeart an Iarrain, who had married the heiress of the Sea O'Malley and had hoped with her help for an overlordship. Then Sir Richard died and the clan united in putting forward Burke of Castlebar for the headship, but they were hardly prepared to sacrifice their lives for a cousin. Before the rebellion was properly started in the summer of 1586 the Burkes all submitted and accepted the death of their leader, and this led to a breach with the Castlebar line.[2] The Tyrawley branch were also divided, Walter Kittagh the left-handed supporting the Government, while his brother, Shane of the Mountain, led the surviving Scots from fastness to fastness. A fresh leader was proposed in the Blind Abbot, William from the house of Rossreala, who had the Lower Burkes at his call and a claim to the chiefship, which his family supported, while in the background there was the figure of the Devil's Reaping Hook, determined and sinister. This was Ricaird Demhan in Chorain McRicaird McEamonn, the chief of the Burkes of the Crooked Shield, astute after an earlier manner, who fostered rebellions, which broke when his friends had declared, and then submitted to await the reward of his labours. He had indeed survived through well cal-

---

[1] It is only fair to state that this sentiment was returned as witness the Governor's appreciation of the leading members of the family. 'Walter Kittough is wise enough, but too weak to attain the M'Williamship. The Blind Abbot was never wise, steady or honest. He doats for age, is very beggarly, overborne by his children. Edmund Burke of Cong called M'Thomas Yvanghny is a very handsome man; always out for fear of the law for killing Ulick Burke of the Neale.' Letter of Sir R. Bingham to Walsingham. Cal. S.P. Irel., 1588–92, p. 241. In fairness the Burke's Book of Complaints should also be studied. 'Edmund Burke of Castlebar the chiefest of all the Burkes, was hanged at Toghu without any trial of the country. He was an old man of more than 80 years impotent by reason of the loss of his leg two years before.' Ibid., p. 263. 'Clanricarde has many enemies in his own country and many carry wounded hearts at the Earl of Thomand's greatness.' Ibid., p. 263.

[2] A very detailed note on the septs of the Burkes in Mayo was prepared in 1587. Cal. S.P. Irel., 1586–8, pp. 214–5. In 1586 Bingham considered William the Blind Abbot, as the capital traitor of them. Ibid., p. 132.

culated submissions, but there was bitter feeling with the sons of the men, whom the Government had decided must die to preserve him. Sobriquets like his were considered an honour and the name of the Fiend of the Sickle, though given in anger, was accepted in pride. Here in the proud formula ' I the Blind Abbot declare,' which the McWilliam gave to his scribes at the sacring ceremonies at Rahessekyre, lay the epitome of the period, religious instinct, hierarchic power and the guile of simple men.

The clans immediately allied to O'Rourke were bound to support him and in this way he could rely upon Thadeus O'Clancy [1] of Dartry, the head of the house of Macnahoidchi, the Son of the Night. Similarly McSweeney ne Doe and McSweeney ne Bannagh would follow him and this gave the control of the south coast of Tyrconnell. But even in these cases, where a personal friendship was certain, the rivalry within each sept was so keen [2] that there were always leaders ready to take advantage of any open decision. Thus once Brian na Murtha had declared for the Spaniards there were two Queen's O'Rourkes on the wait to dethrone him, since the custom of tanistry prevented the evolution of a sacrosanct line. In this way the position of Thadeus O'Clancy was typical, for he had attained the power on his brother's murder in 1581,[3] while there was not only an ' English ' rival, his cousin, Boethius Clancy from the Fields of Liscannor, but more serious the steady increasing power of Maelsechlainn, which grew till the open struggle in '90, when he killed Thadeus and became the Queen's Clancy.

Beyond the immediate range of O'Rourke's alliance there lay the O'Flaherty's Country, which was also reached by the federation of the West Connaught havens under Graine O'Malley of Carraic an Chobhlaigh. She was the valiant Grace of the Tonsure, who led her own vessels to piracy and hoped for a complete control of the West by the Sea O'Malleys of the Six Islands, aided by the O'Connors of Sligo and the O'Malleys of Murrish and the little tribes by the Sea. At the moment this western alliance was loyal to England, although Graine

---

[1] The unequivocal character of the spasmodic relations of the Government with these septs is notable. Thus, after a visit to O'Clancy, Bingham wrote on 16th August, 1586, to Perrot, ' I will go to M'Gawran lying between O'Rourke and Maguire and cause him to submit himself and yield composition for his land or else I will give him a wipe of a thousand cows, wherein Your Lordship shall not, I hope, mislike my doings.'   Cal. S.P. Irel., 1586–8, p. 140.

[2] McSweeney ne Bannagh had killed his predecessor on the uplands of Doirinis on St. Bridget's Day of this year (1588).   Annals of the Four Masters, iv, p. 1867.

[3] For the murder of the Queen's Clancy.   Annals of Loch Cé, 1581, p. 446.

O'Malley was described as ' a notable traitress and nurse of all rebellions these forty years,' but her enmity with the Burkes would lead her to welcome any effort against them, for her son, Theobald of the Ships, as a son of Sir Richard the Iron, had a claim as McWilliam, which his kinsmen denied. It was this Burke and O'Malley quarrel of four years before, which made it certain that there would be no mercy for the Spanish crews, who were cast on the Islands.

When this crisis arose the O'Flaherty, Sir Murrough of the Battle Axe, threw in his lot with O'Rourke, for he was seventy-five, a man grown ancient in pardons and he had been at the Dun-an-oir with Fitzmaurice; but his clan was divided and after a struggle the Sea O'Flaherty followed O'Malley. There was hesitation, for the Sea O'Flaherties were sons of Donnal an Chogaidh, who had been assured cousin in nine degrees to Sir Murrough, and they hated the Governors for the death of their brother Eoghan *per dolum* in 1586. Yet they could not stand out against the ships from the Islands, and their father had once been husband to Grace of the Tonsure, and they had followed her galleys in their constant untiring assault on the not very valuable traffic to Galway. It is strange that had Theobald Burke been elected chief of Clanwilliam the invaders would have found men their friends and every pinnace and skiff a help to the ships in their sinking. As it was, the fleet beating down from the outer ocean could not know that there was friendship on the northern coasts of Mayo, but from Erris Head southward only death, whether in the storm wrack still breaking over the galleys beached on Achill or in the summer weather of that sheltered water, where McGeoghegan of the Sails had placed his beacons to light his ships upon the western sea.

In this brief contact between the Spaniards and the Irish neither party had any accurate notion [1] of the life of the other and if, when the runners came through the storm with the news that the Spanish vessels were sighted, O'Rourke had allowed himself the wildest dreams of good fortune, still less did Don Alonso de Leyva realize his perilous state among Christians. The driving rain and the miles of turf and the white thorn hedges were what had been expected in Spain, nor was the poverty of the cabins surprising, but in the temperate South one could not imagine the effect of the storms on the

[1] This is seen in the only commodities that they were able to exchange; for, according to a report of 26th October, 1588, ' the Spaniards would give the country people a caliver for a mutton.' Cal. S.P. Irel., 1588–92, p. 65.

usquebaugh, the smoke hanging under the great hall rafters with the vent closed and the matting drawn tight and the clansmen shouting.

Don Alonso de Leyva, Lieutenant-General of the Armada and second in command of the troops under His Excellency the Duke of Medina Sidonia, Captain General of the Ocean was a man of middle age, reserved and deliberate in his movements, an accomplished cavalier and the chief personal friend of King Philip. He was tall and slender with the careful beard of the period and smooth fair hair, a man rather attentive to his dress and appearance, devoted to the King, but for the rest somewhat detached.[1] His last service had been a term of military command in Milan just completed and he had an aloof and discerning acquaintance with the policy of the little Southern Courts. Loyalty to the dynasty had been bred in him, for he was a son of Charles V's great general, the Prince of Ascoli, and he had had difficulties and setbacks to contend with, the very delicate negotiations over patronage with the Archiepiscopal Curia in Milan and the some-what disheartening correspondence with the Serene Courts of Mantua and Savoy over the frontier fortresses in Montferrat. Italian was his first language and his ship's company had come from Italy with him, sailing in one of the large galleons only recently withdrawn from the trade to the Levant, *La Rata Santa Maria Encoronada*, with a very adequate supply of chaplains, some of them carried for secretarial duty, and a name given in honour of the last mystery of that Rosary, which in Spain served both as the devotion of the simple and for the most cultivated, meditative prayer. Every day past the Hebrides brought *La Rata* into warmer waters and Don Alonso towards the life that he had known, intimacy with the military advisers, a certain distrust from the Grandees of the Council of Castile and the King's devoted personal friendship. Against the familiar background of the Escorial there remained a troublesome question, the refusal through the Grandees of a request for the privilege for the Ascolis to remain covered in the royal presence, a matter of quarterings, which the Marshal of Court Ceremonial disputed. But Dowdaire O'Malley was waiting for corpses from the galleons cast ashore by the sea.

[1] Two interesting descriptions of de Leyva were given later by prisoners. James Machary ' saith that Don Alonso for his stature was tall and slender, of a whitely complexion, of a flaxen and smooth hair, of behaviour mild and temperate, of speech good and deliberate, greatly reverenced not only of his own men, but generally of all the whole company.' Also ' George de Venerey of Candie in Greece sayeth that Don Alonso was a whitely man with an Abram beard.' Cal. S.P. Irel., 1588–92, pp. 98–9.

DON JULIAN ROMERO
El Greco.   From the Prado.

Photo : Vernacci.

It was only fortunate that, since they were cast on the outer rocks of Erris, they could not make their way to the shore, where the ' Supporter of the Destitute and Keeper of a house of Hospitality ' awaited their landing.

The fleet had kept together and, although *La Rata* was fast upon the rocks, one of the Andalusian galleons, the *Duquesa Santa Ana*, took off the ship's company and set sail once more for Spain. But in the westerly gale that arose they were driven back upon Ireland, making the harbour of Loughros near the west point of Donegal, which lay in the McSweeney's Country, and it was from this anchorage that messengers went south to O'Rourke with the news that the Spaniards had landed.[1]

In all this strange episode it is most curious that de Leyva would seem never to have fully understood the dangers about him, for injuries in the landing, when his leg had been crushed by the capstan, kept him to his tent. He had come ashore on uninhabited beaches, for there were not even the huts of a fishing village and on all sides the heather came down to the shingle ; but since he could not walk, nor even ride, the state of the country was hidden. Then there came news of the *Girona*, a galleass from Naples, and two other vessels, which had put into Killybegs, and he was carried by four of his Spaniards through the woods and up into the high bogs on the slopes of Mulmosog and then down again to the sea. Here he was surrounded by more than a thousand Spaniards, the crews of four vessels, and established his camp between the thick tangled oakwoods and the shore and all the time O'Rourke was sending his messages. The early and harsh autumn kept him under canvas, but it was a real Spanish camp and organized, with passwords and the standard with the castles on the gold of Castile flying in the keen wind coming over the trees from the empty heather, and this made him judge affairs in the light of civilized warfare, for he had no means to check information as he looked out on a desolate sea.

---

[1] The reports which reached Dublin show the form in which the news first came. On 8th September Sir R. Bingham reported that ' the Devil's Hook, a notable malefactor of the Burkes in Mayo hath of late taken a dozen skiffs . . . into the islands there,' while on 10th September agents declared that ' it is said Sir John O'Dogherty himself hath been in speeches with them (the Spaniards), for that he hath a fair target, a murrion and a halberd of theirs which argueth to be received rather as a gift.' Three days later a report from Galway was sent in of ' one of their ships ventred at a place called Burris, whereof 16 of the company landed with chains of gold about their necks,' and on 18th September Mr. Comerford wrote of the galleon at Torrane, ' James Blake, Moilmory M'Ranyll, Thomas Burke, M'Inabbe, took out of the wreck a boat full of treasure, cloth of gold, velvet, etc.' Cal. S.P. Irel., 1588–92, pp. 29–42.

THE CELTIC PEOPLES & RENAISSANCE EUROPE

Had he known of the death of Don Pedro de Mendoza and the massacre at Torrane and the fate of *La Trinidad Valencera*[1] on the coasts of O'Dogherty's Country, he would have gained a new light in which to read his despatches. As it was, while the preparations for repairing his ship were completing,[2] he heard of the *Princeps Tironiæ*, a most convincing address, for O'Rourke invariably used Latin when he wrote by his clerics, and of the *Dominus Carolus Flavus*, as he always signed himself, whom a great marriage had brought to Strabane.[3] And then even in the somewhat bizarre Latinity he could make out the figures, so like that Renaissance court scene on which his memory alone could rely, the princes of Tyrone and their Scottish allies and the whole garnished with the signatures of ecclesiastics of rank, the Dominican Prior and the Primate of Armagh, and every assurance of friendship. This must have seemed just an episode in the return journey to Spain, in which he alone had success in all that disastrous adventure, for he could hardly regard the kernes seriously and he had confidence in his officers and his soldiers, so that he sailed North to the islands to meet the young Prince of Tyrone.

O'Rourke must have regarded this as the completion of his planning, for de Leyva had left many apparently noble captains behind him and he had taken Irish and Scots pilots, so he would surely return. Besides the Spaniards at Killybegs were still heavily armed and ' the fiery red shot vomiting guns ' were ' loud in their roaring,' while all this delight in such uproar was merely another facet of the pleasure in physical strength that the chieftains displayed. Sorley Boy McDonnell, as *Carolus Flavus* was more commonly known, rode, although long past eighty, to carry his bride to the Rowte, that tangled fortress which he had ruled since the death of his brother, Black Coll of the Horses, and the landless men shouted as those illusory princes, Shane McShane and Hugh of the Fetters, rowed in their surf boat from island to island.

In place of the wavering hope from the Spaniards, the real result

---

[1] Lists of the wrecked galleons are preserved in Cal. S.P. Spanish, iv, pp. 337 and 463, Cal. Carew MSS., ii, p. 472 and Cal. S.P. Irel., 1588–92, pp. 26–97, *passim.*

[2] According to the information of a spy, ' the third (Spanish ship) being a galley and sore bruised with the seas was repaired in the said harbour with some of the planks of the second ship and the planks of a pinnace which they had of M'Sweeney. The Spaniards gave M'Sweeney at their departure 12 butts of sack wine and to one Murrough Oge McMurrough I Vayell four butts.' Cal. S.P. Irel., 1588–92, p. 65.

[3] Report of 27th October, 1588, ' Sorley Boy McDonnell was lately at Strabane to consummate his marriage with O'Neill's daughter.' Cal. S.P. Irel., 1588–92, p. 63.

of the landing was the awakened wrath of the English and the Burkes were crushed,[1] when Bingham and the settlers forced the pass of the Gap of the Wind, and then the O'Rourkes went down in their last stand at Dartry and ' the Breifne was burned in that hosting' and they made ' a polished garment of the province of Connacht.' [2] But the wild life of the Irish could never penetrate to de Leyva. It was a delicate problem as to who should go in the galleass, beyond the complement of the rowers, as there were not only the Italians from *La Rata* and the rather middle-class afterguard of the store ships, but from the *Santa Ana* some most distinguished ' hidalgos,' friends of the Duchess of Medina Sidonia, who had embarked in the Andalusian galleon she had named from her saint. Finally all the most influential officers were received in the galleass and set sail for the friendly ports of the princes, since de Leyva lying injured in camp had never heard of the massacres and Muinter was out of his reach and he could not imagine Shane and Hugh of the Fetters, his ' princes ' gazing to sea through their matted hair with their one battered long ship drawn up on the beach out of reach of the breakers. An alliance between such extremes could end only in massacre, and when soon after sailing the *Girona* and her company were lost at midnight below Dunluce on the rocks at the foot of the castle, Don Alonso de Leyva and the Spaniards were received by a merciful sea. In a case where there is so wide a gulf in outlook between allies no peaceful ending is possible, for either the more modern and powerful equipment will reduce their simpler companions to slavery or if, as in Ireland, the power lies with the more mediæval nation the outcome is assuredly fatal, for with that clear determination, which no law had yet trammelled, they could not hunger for long for the ornament and arms of their neighbours without exerting upon them their ruthless strength in its pride.

[1] Yet even as late as January, 1592, there were still six Spaniards with the Burkes in Mayo. Cal. S.P. Irel., 1588–92, p. 452.
[2] This reference and that to the burning of Breifne come from the Irish records, Annals of Loch Cé, 1589, p. 494 and 1590, p. 512.

CHAPTER XIV
THE SCOTS OF THE OUT ISLES

Two distinct problems are presented by the presence of the marauding Islesmen in the reign of Elizabeth. Their descents upon Ireland to aid in rebellion had a definite effect in prolonging the resistance of O'Neill and the clansmen in Connaught, while in the wider political sphere the English Government made some attempt to control them by bribery. The key to the position of the Islesmen lay in the destruction in the fifteenth century of the great centralized power of the Macdonalds, Lords of the Isles. The haphazard and disorganized nature of all their later political action is the result of the consequent absence of leadership. Had the Lords of the Isles still survived the Islesmen would have developed a political power similar to that of the Ulster O'Neills and would have acted as a recognized force in the changes of policy. Thus Philip of Spain could negotiate with O'Neill, but the Islesmen no longer possessed a paramount leader. All the confusion that followed derived from that fact.

The relationship between the Irish chiefs and the Islesmen was based upon contract entered into for a fixed and brief period during which the leaders of the sub-clans of Macdonald and the local headmen in the Islands, like McLeod and McDougall, bound themselves to supply a number of swordsmen and galleys. There were a series of hereditary feuds dividing the Islesmen in the absence of a chief lord, and these are referred to in passing. The effect of these further dissensions is shown by the fact that, although in the open market it was nominally possible to hire a very large number of swordsmen, the actual figure available at any one time was severely reduced by the difficulty of persuading hereditary enemies to fight on the same side in a struggle.

The strongest united power was that of the southern Macdonalds and the most lasting effect of these movements was their gradual transplantation from Cantyre into Ulster and the results which this change produced on the fortunes of O'Neill and Campbell. The short sea passage, a matter of two or three hours with a favouring tide, between Cantyre and Ulster also gave to this branch of Macdonald an importance in sudden emergencies, which the galleys from Skye and the Hebrides could never possess. This new Irish settlement of the Macdonalds, which is commonly held to date from the defeat of the McQuillins at Rowte at the battle of Slieve an aura in 1558, is associated with the name of Sorley Macdonald (or McDonnell), otherwise called Carolus Flavus, whose Latin name suggests the influence which the Court of Tyrone possessed upon Scotland. One result of this transference and the consequent hostility of O'Neill and O'Donnell was the development of a certain alliance between the English Government and Sorley McDonnell. A similar conflict in Scotland between the Macdonalds in Cantyre and the encroaching power of the Campbells led to temporary alliances, even less well-assorted, between Tyrone and Argyle.

The degree to which the policy of the Islesmen was affected by the designs of Huntly and Argyle on the Nordreys and Surdreys, as the two groups of islands were usually known, is considered and their general plans are examined with particular reference to that earlier contact with Foreign Affairs described in the chapter on the Spanish Project in Scotland. The Gordon centre of power was too remote to act as a serious menace, and the Campbells failed to dominate the Islands chiefly because they were a land and not a sea-power. At this point the importance of the McLeans of Mul is considered, as they were the outposts of the Argyle ' friendship.' The second connection between the English Government and the Isles now becomes clear, for just as the McDonnells were influenced from London through Dublin, so the McLeans were reached by Cecil through their agent in Edinburgh. The object of the somewhat hesitant bribery in the last ten years of the reign was to prevent the Islesmen from sending galleys to assist the rebels in Ireland by stirring up those ancient feuds to which reference has already been made.

Finally the differences between the Islesmen and the Irish are mentioned, together with the remarkable, but sometimes superficial, points of resemblance. The contacts between the O'Neills and the outer world had raised a barrier which would always divide them from the Islesmen with their unchanging simplicity, while the picture of the life of the Islesmen forms a counterpart to that drawn of the Irish in the previous chapter. Their remoteness of spirit was the cause of the irresolute and uncertain character of the intervention of the Islesmen in the political life of this time. They could only have acted as a deliberate force if they had possessed one supreme leader.

IT is a curiosity of sixteenth-century politics that, while the great nations were already organized and on the outer fringes the old feudal system survived, there should have seemed to have been in West Scotland so many men masterless. There was no parallel at that time in Europe to these Western tribes, warlike and restless, hanging like a cloud on the horizon of the old feudal Ireland. In the extreme North, in the Orkneys and Caithness, life was still organized on the lines of a firm social pyramid where each line would lead to the apex, that chief of the Sinclairs, the key to whose almost inscrutable policies now seems to be lost to us. Again in Northern Ireland there was the ultimate, although indirect, power of the O'Neills or O'Donnells through the system of ' urraghs.' Even in those parts of Ireland where the control of the main power would seem less direct, there was always, among the great chiefs or their rivals, some high Gaelic leader who was known as the final authority for the acts of the clansmen. But in the Western Highlands and the Isles, we do not hear of any power which can be compared with that of the princes of Ulster and the most common reference is to the hiring of ' red Shanks ' or Albanachts, not an alliance of equals, but a bargain of commerce. It was nothing in the structure of life that had produced such a difference, for the basis of clanship and service continued unbroken through all the sea divided land of the Gaeltacht from the northern creeks under

Cape Wrath, where the galley crews in the winter could feel the approach of the ice, to the calm of Valentia River and the warm Kerry waters.

Everywhere the sea clans followed the same way of life, the fishing, the casual piracy and occasional conflict, with the galleys acting as transports for the swordsmen of their country who, in the intervals of their service, would eke out a hard living from those stony and gale swept lands, which rose out of the seaweed. Among these local chiefs there was also a kinship and all the waterside movements were known from McGeoghegan of the Sails in the south to the McNeill ships in Barra. Yet, it was when they were considered on a national scale that the contrast was striking, for the McGeoghegans were affected by Fitzmaurice and the Clancare McCarthys, and these were influenced by the Geraldine movements, so that throughout Desmond, the ideas of the Gaelic lords found an echo. But in the Isles it was different, for there the fighting men each followed their immediate chieftain and even the shadow of a high leader was absent.

During the fifteenth century the Lords of the Isles had played in the West Highlands the part which in Ulster was the lot of Hy Niall and, even in 1588, the islands seemed masterless; for they had not yet recovered from that sudden disaster when the political fortunes of that great house had foundered. All the West and the galleys of every sea clan had acknowledged the Macdonalds as Lords of the Isles and now they had gone down like the sun and the outer seas were all strewn with their wreckage. There only remained the sub-clans of Macdonald, like the house of Alastair of Oronsay and over on the mainland the Clan Ian Abrach and the Clan Carrach and the weak lords of Clan Ranald and in the Route, Carolus Flavus. These were the broken remnants, leaderless but still linked together, which the storm had cast shorewards. In the background there arose the traditions of an immemorial lordship and of the sconced torches flaring in the long hall of Ardtornish and of their high burial stones, which still stood in the wind of Icolmkill. One hundred and eighty galleys had followed their call to Knockfergus and the old men had heard from their fathers of that sea fight off Mull, when John, Lord of the Isles, had been stabbed by his bastard; while they had all known the Lord Domhaill McAengus, the last of the claimants. His had been a chequered and violent career, while the lordship slid down into darkness under the blows that Ian of Sleat and Alastair Macdonald of Islay had dealt to their rival. And this in turn arose from the killing which had brought him to power, when his ship had found at Oronsay the Lord Alastair of Lochalsh. There had been white clouds upon the Paps of Jura and gulls had come inland to the cornfields and the Macdonald power did not survive these portents of stormy weather and a gale of wind.

There were still remaining the local chiefs on the islands, like the McNeills and McLeods at Barra and Harris, and the other McLeods at Dunvegan, stable, unconquering and unconquered, and all the parasite chieftains, like McDougall of Lorne and McNaughten, Gaelic Princes of Hesse, eager to hire out their swordsmen to help in a conquest. But such men had only small power, since their leader had vanished, and they could not formulate policy, but could merely contract out their swords. And, now that they had no strong defenders, they could no longer hold their religion ; for on this wild coast they were strongly possessed by a reverence for the graves of their fathers laid in that holy sod of Icolmkill. Yet it was nearly thirty years now, in 1561, since the heretics had cast down the three hundred high crosses and laid bare ' the fair bodies of the Kings of Fingall at the Teampull Odhran of Iona.' By the past and the present they had been left deserted.

In addition, their defenceless condition had attracted the greed of the great mainland chieftains, Argyll and Huntly. For over sixty years they had been gradually consolidating their paramount power and working towards a control of the islands, the Gordons with their eyes on the Nordreys, the Hebrides and their satellites, stretching away from Ardnamurchan Point to the north, and the Campbells eager to cover with their own network of alliance the Surdreys, those islands which lay in a ring on the outer shores of Argyll. But these were mere shadows of danger, the threat of subjection and not its achievement and the distance of the real Gordon power kept the Northern Isles safe. For they had no ships and not even a foothold on the coast, and it was only a question of the trouble that their emissaries caused among those eastern sub-clans of Macdonald whose aspirations to headship they cherished. Much more immediate was the danger which came from the Campbells, although these had so far been hampered by their weakness in galleys. Yet the islanders trusted too much to their straits to protect them, so that even this danger from the South could not make them unite, and there was something too in their standpoint of the old hardy contempt and a belief that contact with the Southrons had made the Campbell turn soft. For they could not imagine that the power of their swords could go down before a Macallum, apostate from the ways of his fathers, Saxon speaking, ' a son of the cowhide '; while in this last phrase was summed up all that angry dislike for a parchment legality, on which the Earl of Argyll now relied, and for the time this was justified, since the islands seemed safe. Yet it was an uneasy freedom that the western galleys enjoyed in an age when, throughout Europe, the lawless centres of anarchy were submitting at last, and Argyll was only a danger because of his support in the South in the calm, settled Lowlands. The islanders were to go down fighting with their wild Highland indiscipline and their primitive arms against a power which they could not understand, for the force by which they were broken was the same that fifty years later caused the fall of Montrose, that reign, increasing, dominant and centralized, the power of gold.

There was also the interaction of the Irish quarrels and the consequent hiring of galleys and the precarious maintenance of that independence, which they contrived so long to preserve. For, if Ireland was the market for the sale of their swords, its existence in continuous warfare provided the demand [1] for swordsmen of that roving and carefree temper which the Scots Isles could supply. Besides, at times the galleys would even bring powder [2] to Ireland to continue the struggle, and it was therefore the unrest in Ireland which served to keep all the galleys of the Out Isles in movement and free.[3] So far as any continuous development can be traced in the fitful and irresponsible ties of alliance, based on a purely mercenary system, it is the gradual building up of the Macdonald power on the coast which was to become McDonnell of Antrim and the consequent movement and extension of the Campbell rule in Argyll. Beyond that there is

[1] Evidence of this is supplied by the letter, dated 17th July, 1570, from Walsingham to Sir Henry Sidney stating that ' we hear that one Angwys and McConnell of the Scottish Isles hath in readiness nine score galleys for the transporting of men, as we take it, for Ireland.' Cal. Sydney Papers, i, p. 123.
[2] Report of Sir H. Docwra. Lambeth MSS 632, printed in *Miscell. Celtica*, p. 287.
[3] It is significant that, even in time of peace, it was agreed between the first Earl of Essex and Turlough Lynagh in 1575 that ' for the better security of his person O'Neill may have 300 Scots in wages provided they be of the nation of McAllins and Campbells.' Cal. Carew Papers, 1575-88, p. 235.

the satellite McLean rule in Mull at enmity with Macdonald and in half-friendship with Campbell and the effect which the turn of the Queen of Scotland's affairs and Queen Elizabeth's hesitant bribery had on their action. Even in these greater changes, like the McDonnell successes in Ulster, there is something of the movement of waves that constant repetition of the Scottish swords cast on those beaches and then their retirement and their return. But beyond the immediate following, the 'household men' of the Cantyre Macdonalds, there were all the galleys and swords from the Hebrides and the sub-clans, men unknown to Dublin and Edinburgh and beyond the reach of all offers, save those which would come from Hy Niall and the high lords of Connacht.

For that reason, the only vantage point from which to make out this confused and dark sea is where the waves break upon Ulster in the fitful light of that day and it is only when the Government looked northward that their continuing ranks are for the moment illumined. Even back in 1538 Alastair Macdonald had been leading his men into Ireland and three years earlier an English agent had written of the endeavour of O'Neill to draw the Scots from the Out Isles of Scotland for a rapid summer campaign.[1] All through this century the movement continued,[2] and, even when the northern galleys were absent, the men of Cantyre could cross to Ulster in two or three hours with a favouring tide from Machrinhanish, where the galleys lay drawn up on the firm white sand of the bay out of reach of the breakers. Only a westerly gale could make this harbour unsafe and once the sea crossing was over they could put ashore at Port Brittas or the little creeks of the Glinns. It was a question for Dublin to note, but not to prevent, such invasions, since for that they were powerless, and underlying the false hopefulness, such as is shown in Sir Thomas Cusack's report, we can see how complete was the islanders' freedom. 'And hard it is to stay the coming of them,' wrote Sir Thomas, 'for there be so many landing places between the highland of the Rathlyns and Knockfergus, and above the Rathlins standeth so far from defence as it is very hard to have men there continually being so far from help.'[3] And all this

[1] Letter of Sir W. Skeffington dated 17th June, 1535. Cal. Carew MSS., i, p. 67.
[2] According to a description of O'Doghertie's country in Ulster in 1586, 'His country lying upon the sea and open to the isles of Ila and Jura in Scotland is almost yearly invaded by the Scots who take the spoil of it at their pleasure, whereby O'Doghertie is forced always to be at their devotions.' Ibid., ii, p. 435.
[3] Report made in 1553. Ibid., i, p. 243.

while it was only the Scots, who landed when Ulster was troubled, who came into view, for nothing was known of the galleys which gave support to the rivals in the distant struggles in Connacht, and it is difficult to date with accuracy such events as the defeat at the Pit of Destruction, that creek in the rocks under Coll, where the McNeills of Barra on their way to their galleys were set upon by McLean.

In the South matters are plainer, for Sorley McDonnell held for forty years a certain control of the southern ships of the Isles, which was backed by his own fleet of twenty-four galleys. He had made the swordsmen from the Rhinns of Isla and Cantyre familiar in all the long Ulster conflict and his Macdonald inheritance gave him a certain claim on the friendship of the sea clans to northward. But it was not until 1559 that the battle of Slieve an aura, an almost casual encounter with the McQuillins of Rowte, gave a permanent shift to the balance of power in the North. Until this time there had been the Macdonald outposts in Antrim, but the real centre of power of the house of Ian Mor, son of Ian of the Gifts, Lord of the Isles, lay in Scotland, in that square stone castle in Isla, where the tracks shelved down to the sea and their galleys lay beached or at anchor in the calm of Loch Indail. Southwards there could be seen in clear weather the cliffs of the Rathlins and to the east the high moors in Cantyre, but the policy of the Lord Alastair, Sorley's father, looked northward to where the galleys from the Firth of Lorne would come down through the tideways and so out westward to the open waters between Iona and the Ross of Mull. Besides Alastair's wife was one of the northern Macdonalds from Ardnamurchan in Mull and he had lived in the time when it was still within hope that the Lordship of the Isles might revive,[1] since, in these regions of ancient tradition, a system of tanistry had prevented that almost sacred attachment to the senior line of descent. Thus there was always a chance for a leader, who possessed the right blood of Somerled, to come to supremacy and in this claim they were equal, for, now that the line of Ardtornish had vanished except for the bastards of Sleat, all the surviving sub-clans were equal.

So although the Macdonalds made their living in Ireland, fighting and hiring out men, they always returned to the Isles, where the idea of hegemony wavered dreamlike before them. But by the late 'fifties

---

[1] In fact the unknown author of the ' Taladh an Leinibh Ilich ' claims all Western Albyn for a croft of the crown-descended lords of Islay with the bird land and the stag land and the islands and all the seas from Mannin to the Moyle.

it was clear that they could never unite and Sorley began the slow transference from Cantyre into Antrim,[1] a gradual and increasing displacement, the pressure of whose new settlement provided a lever. Thus in Ulster it was circumstances and not their desire, which determined their standpoint, and the heavy pressure of O'Neill and O'Donnell caused the McDonnells to rely on the South and to place their moves with a view to reactions in Dublin. As a result they came ultimately to the strange position which left them as survivors in Ulster, when the old chiefs had gone, still Catholic but loyalist perforce, until in his dealings with Lord Antrim Charles I, who sundered so many loyalties, broke theirs also at last. But this was two generations away in the future from Sorley McDonnell, whose manner had put on a new grandeur as he sat at Bonamargy in the Prior's cell by the harbour, where his galleys had come up on the tide, and listened to the man of God, so prudent and holy.

The new name that he chose was characteristic of the old magnificent Ireland and the high lords of Gaeldom, Carolus Flavus, a name for which even his next brother James, who had been taught by the Dean of Holyrood to make his own letters, was hardly an equal. With this change the old connection which Sorley McAlastair had maintained with the Outer Seas broke and, while his men come out into the light, the northern ships still elude us. But just at the moment of the transition we can see the detail quite plain, as in the spring attack of 1565, when the Macdonalds were gradually strengthening their foothold against the strong pressure of O'Neill of Tyrone. It was after the Easter festivities that O'Neill made his gathering and, when the news came of approaching attack, the Scots in Ireland with Sorley lit the warning fires above Murloch to summon their kinsmen. James Macdonald with the three hundred 'household men' of his permanent service had been keeping the feast at Saddell, where his race was accustomed to pass the seasons of penance in the house they had founded, and there from the monastery beneath the elms by the shore he could see the answering light on Sareadan till the coast beacons burned again over the harbour and the quiet creek and the long, beached galleys. This was a warning for which his men were

[1] According to a contemporary description, the landing-place in the Glins ' is backed with a very steep and boggy mountain and on the other part with the sea, on which side there are very small creeks between rocks and thickets, where the Scottish galleys do commonly land.' Cal. Carew MSS., ii, p. 437.

prepared, and they crossed on the calm tides of May Eve to Cushendun, and yet even so when all these movements are known they can only show the proportion of action that a searchlight reveals and beyond are dark waters.

This gradual displacement of the Macdonalds [1] and the division thus made in the sphere of influence of the clan inevitably led to a slowly developed attack by the Campbells on the point of weakness, Cantyre. There was a certain quality of watchfulness which was for long associated with the Macallum, a capacity in the Campbells for biding their time in contrast to the Highlanders, whose minds were chained as far as politics were concerned to an immediate future, to the harvest and the next season's fighting. But to Argyll it was clear that the southern Macdonalds lacked the power to preserve both Antrim and Cantyre, and it was as the ultimate reward of this fore-sight that the Scottish inheritance of the Ulster Macdonalds dropped like heavy fruit into his hands. It was a contrast which the seventeenth century repeated, and in the case of the dealings of Macdonald of Glencoe and the first Earl of Breadalbane, we can see again that cal-culated Campbell success, which the just appreciation of the time factors had brought them. To a great extent it depended on a know-ledge of political detail available to Argyll with his stewards and his agent at Edinburgh, but inaccessible to those Highland chiefs in the Isles who did not know letters. Thus at first Argyll supported a Macdonald and O'Donnell alliance, for, as far as Scotland was con-cerned, the success of the Antrim settlement could not fail to weaken his rivals; but, once the Macdonalds were committed to this Ulster adventure and were settled in permanence, the Campbell policy veered to a support of O'Neill of Tyrone who could keep Sorley in check. The career of Argyll's sister Agnes, who possessed as her own inheri-tance the island of Gigha, clearly marks this change in the wind, for the first compact was sealed by her marriage with James Macdonald of Cantyre, while the shifting balance was shown when she was again a peace offering at the wild ceremony on the cliffs above Rathlyn, which made her the wife of O'Neill. It was a slow policy of balance which two generations pursued, for friendship and yet independence towards the King of Scotland was needed and a working alliance with O'Neill

[1] According to a report of 1570, ' James McDonnell has many carpenters come out of Scot-land to build him a house in the Red Bay.' Cal. S.P. Irel., 1509–73, p. 170.

to keep Macdonald in check, and there was a subsidy from England to manage and the closing of the lines of access along which help for his rivals might now come. Yet this was essentially a policy of encroachment on the mainland, the marking and the seizure of fields, which left Cantyre to become in 1594 a Campbell possession. But how little affected by such conflicts were the lives of the reiving clansmen on the sea ? For even the influence of Argyll was too southern and too compromised to penetrate northward beyond their neighbours on the coast of Mull.

It was thus the position as the northern member of the Argyll ' friendship '[1] that gave significance to the harbours of McLean. For on the outer flank of the Campbells there stretched the power of McLean, who held Morven and controlled the rocky creeks for the galleys on Mull, where the Captain of Aros and the Captain of Lochbuy and their leader, the Baron of Dowart, would call in their men from the high bare fields of their countries to come down for a launching. Here was the last outpost of the southern influence from the capitals where McLean could still appear as a lord ' bred in civility ' and as such capable of understanding the offers that might be made him for a serious service. An old clan, now resurgent, they kept close to Macdonald and Campbell to partake of their fortune, and, although riven by internal feuds between the head house at Dowart and the lesser chieftain on Coll, they could drive a hard bargain. It was a matter of dealing with O'Donnell, after a subservient circumvention of Argyll, and then defying Macdonald, with a hope always in the background that an avowed hatred for Elizabeth's enemies would draw forth some aid from the Queen.[2] It was in this mood that the chiefs of the clan, as they sat in the narrow-roofed Council hall at Lochbuy under the low strong arches, where the stone flags and the rushes seemed never dry from the sea, considered the offers that their agent, Achinros, had extorted. For Islay was exposed to the men of

[1] Hector McLean had been married in 1558 to Lady Janet Campbell with an exchange of land in Knapdale, while the appearance of Lachlan McLean in a list of the Catholics makes it probable that his mother, Lady Janet, was one of the fiercely Catholic women, whom by contrast the calculation of Macallum had produced, like Lady Agnes O'Neill and her sister-in-law, the Queen's friend, Lady Argyll. Cal. Registrum Magni Sigilli Regnum Scotorum, 1546–80, p. 300. A letter from the laird of Carmichael dated 1st June, 1582, states that ' at the pleasure of the Duke (of Lennox) there are Huntly, Seton, Ogilvy, the Prior (of Pluscarden), McLane, Balfour . . . these are Papists.' Cal. S.P. Scottish, 1581–3, p. 121.

[2] An account of the negotiations between McLean and the English envoys, Wotton and Bowes, carried on through John Achinros, Steward of Dowart, is contained in Cal. S.P. Scottish, 1585–98, *passim*.

Argyll and neither party could be sure to return in safety with hostile galleys off the Ross of Mull. But farther North such policies vanished, for the march and counter-march of the Campbells left the free lords without any concern, and in Ireland we have the Macdonalds and beyond them the Campbells and then the McLeans, but the islands are nameless.[1]

Yet beyond Mull there was still one more link between the islands and the wider policies in the lives of those Macdonalds who were affected by the Gordon ambitions in the North. This was merely a shadow of force playing on the eastern Macdonalds in Glengarry and Keppoch, and even so it did little more than give them a glimpse of the stiff and primitive organization of the Gordon affairs and the slow jolting and creaking of the great wain of Huntly. It was down through Glen Mor, where the Caledonian Canal now passes, that the Gordons drove their power, with their outposts at Lochy and their strength at Loch Ness and then pushing westward against the mountains by the sea with the transplanted and satellite Grant of Glenmoriston. And it was here that they met with the inland Macdonalds of Glengarry and Keppoch.

Theirs was an influence remote and at best at second remove, the passing shadow of Huntly, a chief who was never destined to appear in the picture. These were his ambassadors, the Inverness Grants, a sideline dependent and recognizing the chiefship of Freuchie, where the strong stock of the eastern Grants was gathered, increasingly rich and relying on Huntly. Comparatively newly arrived among the great families, their coffers were swollen with the spoils of Clan Chattan and from the wide church lands in Strathspey, while their firm link with the Gordons was one which the bond of the man rent made stronger. Besides it was just in these doubtful years in the 'seventies that the Grants were making new headway, and that through the aid of other clans also the Huntly power was advancing. Slowly they were pressing forward their influence to the western sea coast and not in Glenmoriston only, but to the lands beyond Loch Ness, to Castle Urquhart and its barony and to the hill lands above Loch nan

---

[1] In addition to a reference under 1557, the only mention of the McLean in the 'Annals of the Four Masters' is to Shane O'Neill's capture of Calvagh O'Donnell and his wife, the daughter of MacGilleain in 1560, pp. 1555 and 1577. The only reference in the 'Annals of Ulster (or Senat)' is under 1523. 'Mac Gilla Eain, namely Lachlaun son of Echaun, one who was of great fame and of vigorous hand, was slain in treachery by the Knight son of Mac Cailin in the town of the King,' iii, p. 551.

Eun, while the bastions of this power towards the seaboard were in the west Sgurr nan Conbhairean and Carn a Choire Buidhe and Mhic an Toisich farther to the north. The emissaries from these outposts brought a reflection of the Huntly policy, which even succeeded to the point that Lauchlan McLean himself was to join their standard at Glenlivet; but this high talk with the chieftains never reached to the islands, nor even as far as Applecross and the Highland clans on Skye. The tracks beneath Sgurr nan Conbhairean and the mountains of the remotest Gordon hold led down from the head of Glenmoriston through the pass of Clunie to the upper waters of Lochalsh; but it was only there that they made contact with the Macdonalds of the Sea.

Still farther north there was another contact when the chiefs from the Northern Hebrides met the influence of Sinclair. Yet this was a quite different matter, for Huntly represented a reaction to the great central policies in England and Scotland, feeling these changes as much as Argyll or as O'Neill in Ireland, but the Sinclairs were so far away as to respond only to the stimulus of the feud against Huntly and in spirit they were as remote as the islands. With the Norse colouring of their background such Sinclair episodes, as we can now discover, suggest rather the Mediæval Norway and the feuds of Jarl Birger. On the other hand, the death by poison of the Earl and Countess of Sutherland, the details of which Sir Robert Gordon of Gordonstoun has preserved, suggests an age still more primitive, the Earl, already in agony in the Forest of Helmsdale, warning his young son as he came in from hunting that on his life he must not touch the meat. And then came the forced buying by the Sinclairs of the wardship of young Sutherland and the changed colour of a feud within their ranks and the Master of Caithness dying of thirst at Girnigo in his father's prison. It seems almost Biblical, little scenes with the same clear-cut simplicity and behind each the northern sorcerers and the white beard of Caithness.

Yet this influence, only dimly discerned, was also a great landward and not a sea power facing, as did the northern Gordons also, towards Norway and with its back to the forests of the seafarers' country, to Mackay at Eddrachillis and to the McLeod lands on Assynt. There was therefore no means of continuous political approach to the islands and through the telescopes of London and Dublin, and even of Edinburgh, all these men were the same, for in each case the identical terms could be offered. On their side the clan leaders were wise in the choice of their agents who were able to speak in the current language of politics and to persuade the English Queen's envoys of their masters' alliance and power. A clear instance of this is the recommendation from Sir Edward Wotton regarding McLean, which in 1585 he sent home to Walsingham. ' I am (for mine own part) of opinion,' wrote Sir Edward,[1] ' that, if Her Majesty would bestow a yearly pension of one hundred or two hundred Pounds upon Makclan, it would save her four thousand or five thousand pounds every year in her Irish expenses, for the Makclan (being a greatly lord in the Highlands) and having a deadly feud against Angus, upon whom he bordereth, were he Her Majesty's pensioner would be ready at all times whensoever either Angus or Sorleboy should start into Ireland to spoil and burn their countries.' It all seemed so simple and the only thing left of importance was to settle the price, and, although this proved an obstacle, ten years later McLean himself proposed, through his agent John Achinros, that he should be employed in this service. In the spring of 1595 McLean had reported that three thousand men were going from the Isles to the rebels and, in return for a thousand crowns for himself and a *douceur* of fifty crowns for his steward, it was asserted that he had prevented nine hundred Islesmen from sailing. As a result in the next year there came offers of an annual pension, which was succeeded by a recurrent period of English economy,[2] and then in August, 1598, McLean was reported dead in Ireland, murdered at a tryst by his enemy, Angus Macdonald. This negotiation provided the basis for the only impression that the great powers had decided to form of the North, parallelled by the reference of Spottiswood to McLean's ' civility and good manners.' [3] Yet there was always the danger that this civility and good manners might not stand too

---

[1] Letter dated 22nd August, 1585, the quarrel with Angus Macdonald had been raging in 1562.   Cal. Hamilton Papers, ii, p. 682.
[2] Lauchlan McLean wrote to Mr. Bowes from Dowart on 20th December, 1595, that he marvelled at the story of the token, that it was so long in coming and wished to know whether the promise would be kept or not.   On 8th June, 1596, McLean at the devotion of Her Majesty gave thanks for £150 sterling and the promise of a pension, but on 11th May following, his agent wrote of McLean's intention to send his men to Tyrone, if his services were not better esteemed in England.   On 26th July, 1598, McLean informed the Queen through his agent that if he did not receive any more recompense than mere words he would not be subject to her any longer and eleven days later he was dead.   Cal. S.P. Scotland, 1589–1603, pp. 702–712, 736 and 753 *sqq.*
[3] Spottiswood, *History*, pp. 348–9.

stringent a test and when McLean succumbed to temptation, while the *Whyte Hart* was anchored off Mull, he had cried out over the body of the murdered mate, Walker, that ' Englishe men's fleshe would make Scottishe dogges runne well,' [1] as he ordered the remains to be cast to his staghounds. There is only a very little help to be obtained from the observers in solving the problem of the Western Isles.

For it is most remarkable how little effect was produced by the presence of all these fighting men in the islands, a threat which exercised the mind of the Government, but never issued in dangerous action, and since the political and administrative sources of information are so meagre, it is through the cultural aspect of the question that such a failure can be best explained. Time and again the Scots galleys came down upon Ulster, but in the great crises they are lacking and the chief cause of this apparent inaction would seem to be the disaster which had overtaken the Lords of the Isles. It was not in the antiquity of their power that the surviving chiefs were inferior, but only that, once the Macdonald was gone, none of them possessed that great influence which would inevitably have lifted them into contact with England and Scotland. The power that was wielded by Huntly and Argyll in Scotland and in Ulster by the O'Neill would have come also to the Lords of the Isles and with this power, knowledge, a contact with a wider experience that the Islesmen could not now attain. Then while there was a rift of temperament and experience between the island chiefs and the high lords of Ulster, there was also a deeper divergence between their retainers. It is again a case where effective contact was prevented by a difference of outlook, for the islanders were purely of the Middle Ages and struggling out of a darkness still more primitive, while in Ulster, however strong the old enchantments, they had suffered the customs of the time.

At first it is the points of resemblance between the leaders of the Islesmen and the great lords in Ireland which are the more striking, for the highly inflected Irish Gaelic was the courtly tongue from Dunvegan up north to Ardtornish. Thus a lord from the Isles would use the present tense or change his first consonants like any noble in Ulster, while the fact that the untutored Islanders could never rise to such nicety only emphasized the strong ties which bound leaders

[1] Cal. S.P. Scottish, 1574–81, p. 669. A most interesting study of the structure of Highland life at this period is contained in *The Loyal Clans*, by A. Cunningham, published by the Cambridge University Press in 1932.

together. Besides, unlike his followers, no chief of the Macdonalds and especially Sorley could ever look upon Ireland as ' the place oi his strangerhood.' He knew that he shared the same background and the height of the glories, for he came of the house of Eremon, the King's son of Miledh of Spain, through Conn of the hundred battles and Coll the noble [1] and he was thus of the ' fuil is feith nan righ,' the crown descended, to whom pertained a great house and the half of Albyn, whose likeness was Cuchulain and he the sun arising [2] and to whom was the headship of the Gael.

Yet the O'Neill and O'Donnell, whom the Elizabethan wind had changed in its passing, could hardly have so considered the strangers. They must have been appalled by that unrelieved and unchanging simplicity, for the newcomers had none of that subtlety which befitted a noble in sixteenth-century Gaeldom. To them guile was an expedient rather than an accomplishment, and even their magnates, Macdonalds, Macdougalls, Macnaghtens, were almost equally difficult as hosts or as allies, powerless to appreciate the delicate balanced conventions on which Irish diplomacy swayed or to attune themselves to the slow classical metre and the consonants chiming. In this case the occasional jarring effect of Sorley's false stresses and faulty mutations only marked the contrast more strongly between the prosody, careful and fine webbed, in which the last Earl of Tyrone had delighted, and the camp-fire songs of the Scots. True the language was a link between them, but for the Irish it was their own past calling, and from this they turned away ; for the Ulster lords had their minds bent to the southward on the Great King and the Pope, while the Islanders still brooded on their legends which echoed back across the endless sea. Thus O'Neill, absorbed in that detailed policy which the century had taught him, would be constrained, when a guest at Dunluce or in the high rath of Macdougall, to stay with his host over the usque-baugh between the feast and the peat smooring, while the ' filé,' the island poet, chanted in long monotony and in the shadow stood the ' red shanks ' with their long and flowing hair. What strange play for a great lord, these continued unending recitals of the same monstrous adventures of some Macmhicalasdair or Macmhicailein or of the deeds of the speckled water horse or the trout singing, and all

[1] A descent described at length in the ' Taladh an Leinibh Ilich.'
[2] As in the invocation to the Lords of the Isles, ' Buachaille nan Eilean.'

the men with a rock-like faith in these sagas. And this instead of discussing such matters as are of concern to the well born, chess or the details of prosody or the pedigree of the new hunting dogs. There was in fact a gulf too wide to be bridged, an entire difference of period between the Scots and O'Neill, for it was the mind of every Scottish leader that ' his likeness was Cuchulain and he the sun arising,' and he was an anachronism in the Elizabethan Cycle, since with his ' red shanks ' he had strayed from the cycle of the ' Tain.'

Since this was the case with the leaders, the ' red shanks ' were yet more strange again, for in Connaught they had fought at their ease, but this was Ulster where the O'Neill had wide contacts and their old spell was broken. For the background of the Albanachts of the Islands was a simplicity, whose secret was lost to the over subtle leaders of the King's sons of Eireann, deeply based on the legends of their people, the stag tryst, and the prowess of their chieftain and the white gleaming of the spear heads and him putting out the stars. In religion, too, they could remember the glory of the seven priested Mass and the gold-covered hand[1] of Columcille and ' S'Orasa nan ceall's na dideann,' Oronsay of the Sanctuary and the Cells. It was so simple, in spite of the ornate phrasing, to think of themselves as mere swordsmen, the ' Gruagach,'[2] so flame-keen bladed, with a skin like the snow and it falling, elk-backed and eagle-eyed, launching the ' birlinn.'[3] Before them were the horned sea creatures, the white-shouldered galleys in a night of stars, sweeping south to harry the Eilean Uaine or moving to rescue the land of Ulster, where the fawn-eyed heroes dwelt. Behind them were all the ' Siol Mhorgan ' and the younger branch of the Mackay and the galleys of McNeill, most famous for their reiving, and the ' long ships of the blood of Norman,' the McLeod. They were like the mists from which they came, nothing practical, nor solid, for they had none of the gains of the prosperous pirates of less empty channels and, unlike their Irish neighbours, the music of the lowing of the conquered cattle was a sound that could not fall upon their ears. To them any such tangible evidence of prosperity seemed infinitely far off and remote, as they drove their

---

[1] Such phrases from the ' Buachaille ' are repeated in the Red and the Black Book of Clanranald.

[2] There are references to the ' Gruagach ' in the *Laoidh an Amadain Mhoir.*

[3] The *Iubrach nan Guala Geala* deals with ' the white shouldered birlinn cresting the sea foam,' the galleys embarked on their quest.

galleys in solitude to conflict under the guardian spirits of the sea.

In Ireland, and especially in the West, this primeval spirit also still lingered, but in that country there were always chiefs, who could in a measure interpret their life in the outer world's language. It was true that this was deceptive and that the gulf between the Celtic life and the new customs of Europe was by now unbridgeably wide, but with the Islanders there was simply no contact. As a mark of this isolation even the Spanish Armada could hardly disturb them, except for such slight stir as the Tobermory galleon made, and once the Macdonalds were settled in Ireland they lost all touch with the Isles, which was marked by that moment of time when Sorley Boy Macdonald became Carolus Flavus. In addition, to the islanders, the Macallum was always remote, for their minds went back to their chiefs, who, during the rise and fall of the 'filédecht,' were invested at Cille Dhonan on the stone of girding with the lordship of the Isles. If these lords had survived, they, too, would have led their clansmen away from this dim primeval custom into the troubled half-light of O'Neill and of Huntly ; but, as it was, the islanders were destined to remain, just over the edge of all policies, unreal and phantom, in the state of Hy Brasil, timeless and protected by their solitary waters.

CHAPTER XV

THE CORNISH AND WELSH PIRATES

A consideration of the piracy practiced, for the most part in their home waters, by Cornish and Welsh sea captains in the reign of Elizabeth shows how very remote this work kept from any questions of national policy. A loyalty to the English Government is very marked and is explained by the nature of the traffic. This was controlled for the most part by a group of landowners, who not only financed the ventures but acted as receivers, a position which their possession of foreshore and coves and even in some cases of private harbours made very secure. The local officials of the Admiralty most frequently connived at this practice and the immunity of the pirate ships when they put in to these harbours of refuge is clearly shown. As regards the subsequent transfer of these stolen cargoes, a certain risk was involved, but this was countered by the success with which the wealthy organizers of the traffic succeeded in influencing the juries in the localities where they held their lands. The landowners who embarked upon this work were nearly all connected by friendship and often by blood, so that an exchange of port of arrival could be arranged and the contacts between the Rogers at Lulworth, the Killigrews in Cornwall and Sir John Perrot and his supporters in Pembrokeshire increased the assurances of safety. The political careers which each of these families pursued at the English Court led them to avoid even the distant appearances of treason, while during the later part of the period it was perhaps the knowledge of the Government that these traffickers were very patriotic which led to some laxity in their suppression. Details are given of the profits which could be gained, figures kept at a low level by the character of the coastal trade, and also of the difficulties which captains experienced in attempting to embark upon this business without the partnership of the influential receivers. A sharp contrast is shown between these men and the pirates of Munster. The fact that this English piracy was organized by men who gave general support to the Government is sufficient explanation of the fact that Catholic pirates were few. There was also little contact with that freer life of the Indian Seas into which some of the more adventurous captains would graduate. The absence of contact between this work and the landing of priests is very significant. In Wales likewise it was not the old Celtic and Catholic elements, but the Anglicized townsmen who were involved in the traffic. As far as the corruption of officials is concerned an interesting parallel is suggested with the state of affairs in the Ordnance Office, which forms the subject of a later chapter. If the question of relations with Spain on the part of the officials in these two offices is considered, it should be remembered that the apparently clearer record which the Admiralty servants seem to possess, when compared with the Ordnance officials, is in part explained by the lesser temptation. London and not the smaller ports of the Bristol Channel where the customers dwelt was the centre of Spanish intrigue. The semi-feudal element in the continuance of this piracy, especially in Cornwall, is interesting. Financial stringency was the cause of the payment of the necessary bribes, while the removal of the menace of Spanish invasion allowed the Admiralty to take measures which had been neglected during that danger. The necessity for providing authorities for the numerous charges of official corruption accounts for the close annotation of this chapter.

THE CELTIC PEOPLES & RENAISSANCE EUROPE

THE Elizabethan age witnessed a curious phase in the history of piracy. The undertakings off the western coast became purely commercial and the sea voyages of the pirates were brief, but they produced a safe profit. There was neither excitement nor cruelty, and the characteristic of the English pirates was a caution occasionally tempered by avarice. Their success would have been much more prolonged had the capitalist landowners, who financed them, not proved themselves such imprudent investors ; for an elaborate system of piracy was carried on intermittently during the whole of the reign. Arrangements between the gentry, the local officials and the pirates ensured the safety in normal times of this organized traffic, while different companies often sailed together and divided the spoil of the trade routes ; for the landowners who supported them were allied from Kerry to Dorset. A few of their havens, one in Dorset, one in Cornwall, three or four in Ireland, and one or two in Wales, were immune from sudden attack. These were nearly always privately owned, some of them were never used for legitimate traffic, and they were all more or less secret ; moreover, no search was ever successful. In Cornwall and Wales it was impossible to muster such forces as the Crown controlled without arousing suspicion, so that none of the captains were ever taken while unlading their cargoes in secrecy, for while the night riding and all the cumbrous machinery of private search was set into motion, they stood out for the moonless sea and were gone by the day ; but it was essential that this security should continue if the traffic was to succeed.

There were many reasons likely to induce the gentry to take a share in this piracy—the safe profits, the slight risks and the opportunity for obtaining a valuable return from the possession of foreshore and coves which were otherwise useless. The cargoes alone were often worth £1,000,[1] and the receiver of course made the bulk of the profit. It seems that in Cornwall the pirate obtained one-fifth of the value, the receiver taking the risks of disposal, but the absence of any very great reward was compensated for by the regularity of the captures, since the normal limits of action were the Isle of Man and

---

[1] The more normal figures for coasting traffic varied between £150 and £400, while the value of ship and cargo might rise to £4,000 or £5,000. In 1592 four barques on a voyage from Bristol to Carmarthen were despoiled of silks, velvets and wines to the value of £10,000. Acts of the Privy Council, xix, 367, xxiii, 112, and xxvi, 204, and Cal. S.P. Dom., Addenda, 1580 1625, p. 230.

Belle Isle. Sometimes ships were boarded at night, but this occurred chiefly in Falmouth Harbour, where the ships often lay near the mouth of the river some miles from Penrhyn. The most lucrative form of piracy seems to have been the attack on the coastal traffic, as household goods, especially plate, were easily realizable, and in Ireland these were nearly always sent by sea. The regular trade most frequently interrupted was that in Spanish and Gascon wines for Ireland and Bristol, and cargoes of wheat and salt were often taken, while sometimes British ships returning with fish from Newfoundland or Portuguese barques sailing for France with spices were captured and occasionally a Santander coasting vessel with Spanish iron.[1] If the cargoes could not be disposed of in England or Wales, they were taken to Ireland, and in the last resort were sent away to the coasts of Galicia or to obscure Portuguese towns like Avero.

This traffic was fairly safe for there were no warships in the Irish Sea, except on rare voyages to interrupt communications with Spain and half-private expeditions like Sir Peter Carew's. There was no regular patrol along the Welsh coast, and the official guardship of the Vice-Admiral, the *Flying Hart*, seems to have made Newport her headquarters until in 1578 she was plundered by pirates. During the whole of this period no pirate in the Bristol Channel was ever taken at sea, and in southern Ireland, except in Youghal, Cork and Waterford, they were equally safe, while no really prominent pirate was ever arrested in Cornwall and Pembroke. The receivers were in a still better position and victualling was easy, for the royal officials in the West were corrupt and had direct intercourse with the pirates on a friendly basis of commerce. The deputy Vice-Admiral of Bristol was accused of releasing pirates for bribes, and the customer inward of the port was convicted of sinister dealings. He deceived the revenue and, together with the comptrollers and tide waiters, shared £20 or £30 from the customs on ships coming in from the Straits, and at Cardiff also there were constant complaints.[2] The comptroller of the port was ordered to be set in the pillory, and when the chief local

---

[1] The goods were distributed at the most favourable markets. One hundred and twenty thousand fish were landed at Studland in Dorset and pearls were brought to Cork and Youghal for sale to the Irish.

[2] For the instances of corruption at Bristol and Cardiff, *vide* Acts of the Privy Council, ix, p. 366 and Cal. S.P. Dom., 1598–1601, pp. 56–7.

pirate arrived in Penarth Roads with his prizes it was with the serjeant of the Admiralty that he stayed.[1]

The conditions of the traffic made the rovers completely dependent upon the owners of the coast. In former times isolated pirates had used some of the private harbours, but the improvement of the roads and the increased importance of the landowners, who still kept their armed retainers, made this impossible. There was also no longer any safe refuge between Lincolnshire and the Isle of Wight, and the Channel pirates could not beat up all the way north to Ingoldmells. The most suitable harbours were Lulworth, Helford, and Laugharne, but the pirates could only succeed with the help of the lords of those countrysides. Lulworth Cove was of minor importance, for there was no roadstead for ships, and no vessel of more than eighty tons could lie inside the harbour ; besides the local authorities were suspicious, and most of the landing of stolen cargoes had to be carried through during the night. Laugharne was safer, and the lordship belonged to Sir John Perrot, who had recently built the castle, so there was little danger of interference, but the harbour was unprotected, and there was no market town within reach. Helford Haven was a much better refuge than either for there was a good anchorage for ships of two hundred tons, quite sufficient for the piracy along the coast, and there were only two small fishing villages on the shore. The harbour was fed by no river and was quite deserted, yet it was a good centre for dispersal, and Truro was within reach ; while if the cargoes could not be sold in Cornwall they could be sent across to Brittany from Penrhyn. This countryside was controlled by the Killigrews of Arwennecke, and it was their support of the pirates that led to the elaborate system of harbours of sale and harbours of refuge that were organized for piracy under Elizabeth.

The Killigrews were a great Cornish family, and were hereditary royal governors of Pendennis Castle, while Sir John Killigrew was Vice-Admiral of Cornwall. They were attached to the Cecils and had considerable influence at Court, and their income from land was £1,000 a year. In virtue of their position they had also a certain unofficial control over the movements of warships in their harbours, and from the early days of the reign until 1598 they were the mainstays of piracy.

[1] State Papers. Dom. Eliz., xxiv, p. 16.

THE CORNISH AND WELSH PIRATES

John Killigrew was a recognized leader,[1] while his uncle Peter had sailed the Irish seas as a rover and his mother, Lady Killigrew, was accused of leading a boarding party at Falmouth and murdering a factor in a Hanseatic ship for the sake of two barrels of Spanish pieces of eight.[2] In normal times prizes were sent into Falmouth, but when there was any risk Helford was used, while their dependants, the Michells, acted as receivers at Truro for the sale of the goods. The great house of Arwennecke, built in 1571, was near a solitary part of Falmouth Harbour and close to the open sea, and Killigrew's influence in the West Country was great, so that he acted with much independence, selling the royal provisions in Pendennis Castle, which had a hundred pieces of cannon when he came to command it. In 1597 a pirate came into Falmouth and found some royal ships riding at anchor; but Captain Killigrew went aboard them and agreed with the senior naval officer, Captain Jonas, 'for £100 not to take them but to go into the country till they should get out.'[3]

Other Cornish gentlemen followed the Killigrews, but they were less daring and far less successful. Mr. Prideaux encouraged piracy round Padstow, where a secret hiding was arranged below the cliffs,[4] and Mr. Roscarrock of Roscarrock hired two pirates to attack the galleon *Lombardo of Venice* as she was passing along the coast. In Wales also there was a similar system, and the pirates brought their prizes to Milford Haven or to Tenby, which was quieter and where the deputy Vice-Admiral was a friend.[5] In reserve there was Laugharne and the landing-places of Cardigan; and Cornwall was always the centre of the organization. Killigrew's kinsman, Sir John Wogan, when Vice-Admiral of South Wales, was prosecuted for piracy during these years and kept two great guns with four chambers at Boulston to command the river approaches to his house. John Godolphin, a Cornishman and another cousin, was Sir John Perrot's steward and

---

[1] Among Killigrew's relatives engaged in this traffic, besides his father, mother and uncle, were his first cousins, John Michell and John Penrose of Kethicke and his more distant cousins, Thomas Roscarrock of Roscarrock and John Maderne. His maternal grandfather, Philip Wolverston was a pirate in Suffolk. See the Visitations of Cornwall, and, for the individual charges, Acts of the Privy Council, vols. iv, ix–xii and xvi and Cal. S.P. Dom., 1547–80.

[2] Cal. Salisbury MSS., v, p. 519 and an account of 'that Jezebel' by Hals in *Parochial History of Cornwall*, i, 388–9.

[3] Cal. S.P. Dom., 1598–1601, p. 40.

[4] Acts of the Privy Council, viii, 23. There were other hiding places near the coast at this period, a refuge for stolen goods used by pirates in the Dale of Emyland in Cardigan and a cave by the sea-shore about three fathoms deep in Caernarvon used as a meeting place for priests . State Papers, Dom. Eliz., cxxviii, No. 35, and Robert Owen, *Cymry*, p. 116.

[5] Acts of the Privy Council, vii, p. 148.

managed much of this side of his affairs. And in Ireland there was much the same situation, for a western base was established near Tralee by the Vice-President of Munster, who was a neighbour of the Killigrews and sat in Parliament for Liskeard. The Dorset receivers were related, also, and a constant communication was kept up by means of the pirate companies passing along the coast so that John Killigrew had relations with all the pirates from ' the Terrible John Piers,' who worked with his mother, a well-known witch in Cornwall, to the Lord Conchobar O'Driscoll and ' Sir Finian of the Ships.' [1]

The methods of communication between the pirates and their supporters varied from place to place along the coast. At Lulworth some fishermen acted as lodgers of pirates and in Wales the rovers could lodge with the agents of Sir John Perrot, but it was only in Cornwall and Ireland that hospitality was openly practised. The more respectable pirates stayed with Lady Killigrew at Arwennecke, and Captains Heidon, Lusingham, and Corbet went with their crews into Beerhaven Castle as guests of the O'Sullivan Beare,[2] but in Dorset it was dangerous for these seamen to stay long ashore. Arwennecke had a private landing-place, and at Beerhaven they were received publicly, but Bryanston was several miles from the sea. The pirates were accustomed to lie off Melcombe Regis and their captains seldom ventured on the coast, although there were eight lodgers of pirates at West Lulworth and four more in the neighbourhood. The cargoes were landed chiefly after dark and taken ashore in the fishing boats of Lulworth and stored at Mr. Francis Rogers' house, while later they were taken in carts at night across the wheat fields to a manor belonging to Sir Richard Rogers, a considerable landowner of those parts. The tenants acted as carriers and brought supplies for the pirates down to the coast, and the fishermen carried out the provisions in their boats, for most of the stolen goods were bought by Sir Richard Rogers of Bryanston and his four brothers, while nearly the whole of the traffic was carried on by their men.[3] The whole system was very compact. Nevertheless, caution was necessary, for the Vice-Admiral of

---

[1] See odes of Tadg MacDiarmaid Oge and Donnchadh O'Fuaithail in *Miscellanea Celtica*, pp. 340 and 370, and *Historiæ Catholicæ Iberniæ Compendium*, iii, lib. vi, c. 8; lib. vii, c. 1; lib. viii., c. 3.
[2] Cal. S.P. Dom., 1597–80, p. 251.
[3] State Papers, Dom. Eliz., cxiii, No. 29 and cxxiv, No. 16 contain detailed accounts.

Dorset, Lord Howard of Bindon, was hostile and was building the castle of East Lulworth at this time. It was in fact only the necessity for a landing-place some distance up Channel that induced the pirates to use so dangerous a harbour. Later, with the capture of various pirates in 1581, owing to the guard kept by the Howards, it seems to have been abandoned by the various companies. Dartmouth was used as a temporary centre during the mayorality of the Plomleighs, but it soon proved a failure, although until the end of the reign Helford, Milford, and the Irish ports remained places of refuge. But, in addition to these embarrassments it would be a serious error to neglect the deep social distinctions among those who followed this trade.

The pirates of the outer Channel could be divided into three classes, two of these being professional; some were recognized leaders of companies and often worked together, dealing directly with their most important supporters, while others were also professional but of less standing. These hired themselves to the smaller gentry often for the speculation of a single voyage or adventure, and in addition there were various seamen who indulged in casual and rather timid piracy from time to time. Captain John Callys was an excellent example of the first type, Captain Maris of the second, and Captain Arystotle Tottle of the third.

Captain Callys was a cousin of William Herbert of the Earl of Pembroke's family. He had served as captain under Sir John Berkeley, a distinguished naval officer, and his chief associations were with Glamorgan, where he had many friends among the local landowners, to whom he sold calivers. The comptroller and the serjeant of the Admiralty at Cardiff were among his intimates, and his company was well known in all the ports. He had stayed often with his cousin, had been entertained by Francis Rogers, and he had relations with the O'Sullivan Beare. Though working sometimes alone, he was frequently in company with either Court Higgenberte or Robert Hickes,[1] a Saltash captain, and he had haunted the Irish seas with James Heidon, the sole survivor of the earlier and more aristocratic band of 1564. Besides these men, there were other confederates and, although the

---

[1] Hickes was one of the few English leaders of western companies to be hanged at Wapping. William Appleton alias Captain Smith also suffered. Edward Herberde cut his throat and Piers was killed in a fight at sea, but many of the chief pirates died peacefully in different seaport towns, like Captain Grainger at Portsmouth and Captain Clarke at Gravelines.

field of action was usually limited to the mouth of the Channel, he had landed goods in Denbigh and captured a prize off La Rochelle. In May, 1577, he was arrested in the Isle of Wight and £22 7s. was found upon his person; but as he consented to furnish a complete list of all his receivers, among whom was the deputy Vice-Admiral of South Wales,[1] any further career in western waters was closed to him.[2] The leaders of companies were sometimes foreigners, like Court Higgenberte or Count Hekenberch as he was often called and Symon Ferdinando Portingale, but the English were mostly from the yeoman families of the West, although Edward Herberde was a servant of Sir John Perrot and Griffith was a wealthy squire.[3] The prospects were excellent for those who were able to retire in time.

Captain Maris had a certain official status as lieutenant of an Irish castle, and was one of the undertakers of Munster and a tenant of Sir Edward Denny. He seems to have sailed always in the service of others, for he made a voyage for Sir Thomas Norris, the deputy President of Munster, and was probably at one time in the service of the Killigrews. Finally, he attached himself to Sir Edward Denny at Tralee and Tawlaght Castle was given to him as a permanent centre for trade, and in this he was more fortunate than his companions. Other hired captains appear in the records from time to time, but they were usually Irish and their work was ill paid and perilous, since at the best they could be employed by a syndicate, like Andrew Battyn, who was commissioned by a group of Somersetshire squires and Bristol merchants to command the *Pleasure* for an extensive voyage. The prospects of these hired bravos were always very poor, although the casual pirates had better fortune, and Captain Tottle made £100 by his adventure, but then they usually had some other occupation. It was not always easy for a professional pirate to obtain a ship for any normal voyage.

The pirates were on the whole loyal to their comrades, but their dealings with the receivers were rather more dubious, since most of

---

[1] State Papers Dom. Eliz., cxiii, No. 24. The details of Callys' career are contained in State Papers, Dom. Eliz., cxii, No. 5, cxxiv, No. 16, addenda xxv, No. 60, Acts of the Privy Council, viii, p. 230 and ix, pp. 73, 89 and 337.
[2] Captain Callys' later life was unfortunate. Friends offered £500 to save him and he was pardoned at the request of the Earl of Morton, who had a personal interest; but in 1580 he was ambushed in the Orkneys and fell upon evil days, losing his independence. Two years later he commanded the pirate ship *Minikin* for Mr. Bellingham off the East coast. He was eventually killed in Barbary. Cal. of State Papers, Scottish, v. 308 and 449; vi, 513–14.
[3] Cal. S.P. Dom., 1598–1601, p. 293. He is said to have had £500 a year in land.

the Government information came from confessions and Callys, for instance, gave a complete list of all his supporters. This was perhaps an act of vengeance, for Thomas Lewis of the Van in Bedwas had been guilty of treachery. He was a magistrate and had long had dealings with the principal pirates, supplying his town house in Cardiff and his country manors from the spoils brought ashore at the Roads of Penarth. These matters had always been arranged by personal interview, so that when he was accused in later years, when the search was more stringent, he was able to clear himself from suspicion by arresting Court Higgenberte and Portingale,[1] when they came to his house. The wider question of loyalty to the Sovereign was more difficult to determine, but the possibilities of treason lay chiefly with Spain and Barbary, and as regards the Spanish offers the pirates were usually loyal. At their trials they referred to the great bribes that they had refused as a reason for mercy, and only one pirate is recorded to have delivered his ship to the Spaniards. The numerous Englishmen concerned in the preparations of the second Armada do not seem to have engaged in this traffic, but the dealings of the pirates with Spain opens up the question of their relations with Ireland, for the lords in Munster were valuable customers, and when the English markets failed cargoes could nearly always be sold in that country. All the harbours were open, especially during the first twenty years of the reign, and there was no need for elaborate precautions, since the inner harbour at Killybegs, protected by Rudraighe O'Donnell's[2] fortress, was no safer than the O'Driscoll's open roadstead in Roaringwater Bay.

There was much generous hospitality and little rivalry, and this was always maintained, for Sir Finian O'Driscoll was a dependent and agent of the O'Sullivan Beare,[3] who with his cousins, the McCarthys, controlled a long coast line. Yet the whole objects of the English and Irish pirates were different, for all these Irish leaders looked with a favourable eye on the service of Spain and regarded their occupation in the light of adventure, but the English were organized. This was their livelihood, commercial and passionless, and they never regarded their work as a glorious warfare like the impoverished heroes of Ireland,

---

[1] Acts of the Privy Council, ix, 268. While foreign leaders of companies were often captured, the English who were hanged were usually the meaner pirates, like Hogges, Thomas Halfpenny and Robert Trosher. *Ibid.*, ix, 240, and x, 351.
[2] Annals of the Four Masters, vi, 2221.
[3] Appendix on the O'Driscolls by John O'Donovan in *Miscellanea Celtica*, referring to Philip O'Sullivan Beare, *Historiæ Catholicæ Iberniæ Compendium*, 1621.

who, when they had beached their galleys with the valueless, pitiful spoil, which was all that the empty waters of the seas below Connaught would yield, would be met by the bards of their race, singing the praise of Lord Tibott na Longe or of Graine O'Malley at Carraic an Chobhlaigh.[1] But there is little evidence of communication between the native lords and the Killigrews and the connection gradually ended as profitable markets were opened up by the settlers.

The increase of the professional element in the pirate bands is very marked during the reign, for the younger sons of the Cornish gentry soon tired of this traffic. Two were killed before Havre and many, lured on by the very attractive price ' per head ' of the negroes, drifted off to the Indian waters, while others, and these were the more experienced investors, retired ashore like Peter Killigrew and financed the piratical ventures instead of sailing themselves. The few who held on were, like Justinian Talcarne, seldom successful,[2] and with their departure the bands adopted more orderly methods. There was no accusation of cruelty in the western seas after the case of Captain Anthony Courtenay in 1564, for the regular wage-earning commanders, like the Hickes and Battes combination, could hardly afford to indulge themselves in these passions, and the rather monotonous routine developed much caution, while this is particularly notable in the dealing of the pirate captains with Barbary. Edward Glemham, a Suffolk squire who was quite independent, sold English captives as slaves in Algiers,[3] but the western leaders were normally on a regular service and preferred a safe profit. A curious unpublished document among the confessions in the Domestic State Papers at the Record Office [4] throws some light on this aspect. William Thickyns confessed his dealings at Milford Haven. ' Batts had a ship of cxl tonnes,' the confession begins, ' and lay there with nothinge in her but men and ordinance. He this deponent (as he sayethe) fell to practize with Captain Batts, fyrst whether he would goe withe this deponent into Barbary uppon certen goode which this deponent did disclose unto him, and he said yea witheall his heart . . . and he said he would goe

---

[1] Annals of the Four Masters, vi, 2091. The only instance of similar popular fame in Wales was the case of Nicholas Hwk, Hwkes, or Hookes, ' the great pyrate,' who left twenty-seven children in Aberconway and was himself the twenty-fifth child and fifteenth son of a merchant of that town. Lewis Dwnn, *Visitations of Wales*, ii, p. 162.
[2] For an account of his misfortunes see State Papers, Dom. Eliz., cxxiv, 16.
[3] Acts of the Privy Council, xxviii, p. 247.
[4] State Papers, Dom. Eliz., cxxiv, No. 66.

withe this examinant, but for his former contracte withe Sir William
Morgan Knt, who was so worshipfull a gentleman that he could not
finde in his heart to break his wordes to him.' It is to be noticed
that Mr. Thickyns was a gentleman who claimed to be the agent in
England for the King of Barbary, Captain Batts was a western pirate
who had recently captured six hundred and thirty-four elephants'
teeth in the outer Channel, while Sir William Morgan was Governor
of Dungarvan, Marshal in Ireland and one of the Vice-Admirals of
South Wales.

This reference to Sir William is typical, for, while the pirates were
tolerably loyal to one another and rather treacherous towards their
supporters, the organizers of piracy were always most generous.[1]
Their relations with one another were excellent, and although a large
proportion of Cornish landowners were concerned with the pirates,
there was no encroachment and it was only in Pembroke that there
was bad feeling as a result of Perrot's inveterate feuds.[2] There was
much mutual assistance, and, while Lady Denny received stolen goods
at Tralee,[3] she was aided by her mother, Mrs. Edgecumbe, who was
charged with wrecking at Marazion,[4] and by her uncle, Sir Richard
Rogers, who sent stores to the pirate ships at Lulworth when they
were slipping down the coast. They were loyal to the Government,
and only Killigrew was in his later necessities betrayed into communication with Spain, and this led to his ruin, but his overtures were
probably not serious and only a last attempt to gain money to escape
his embarrassments.[5] The whole atmosphere was far too respectable
and the perquisites of enlightened sportsmanship received such
recognition that it was hardly to be considered that any gentleman
would put himself out of the pale by such underhand dealing. With
the exception of Mr. Lewis' case the relations of the squires with the
pirates were condescending, yet friendly, nor was it their fault when
in the end their abettors were taken. They were in no danger of
execution themselves and they were bound in loyalty to do what they
could for their less fortunate friends. Such minor pirates as were

[1] This of course only applied to the regular captains. Interlopers were severely discouraged,
and Sir John Perrot imprisoned for two years without trial a young Scottish pirate, Alexander,
son of Monane Hog.   Cal. S.P. Scottish, ii, p. 74.
[2] State Papers Dom. Eliz., cxxiv, No. 28.
[3] Cal. S.P. Irel., 1588–92, p. 192.
[4] Acts of the Privy Council, ix, 28.
[5] Cal. Salisbury MSS. ix, p. 376.

foolish enough to be captured, often by some drunken imprudence, were usually acquitted by the respectful and feudally minded juries in Cornwall and there were repeated escapes from Dorchester prison; while the Killigrews used their influence in Devon and, when Clinton Atkinson was in Exeter gaol, he was given the most favourable testimonials by the mayor of the town. Nevertheless there was a considerable activity on the part of the Cornish officials, and, although they were not so indiscreet as to take any men of importance, a negro and various Frenchmen were sent up to London. Even on the way to the capital, pirates, who were neither black men, nor foreigners, had no need to surrender their hopes, and a whole company of freebooters, on the road to the Tower, were able to escape in the woods about Cobham.[1]

It was of course only the condition of the Admiralty officials in outlying parts, who had never recovered from the demoralizing influence of Lord Seymour, which made all this possible, for, if the last of his captains who became regular pirates seem to have disappeared in the reign of Queen Mary, the minor port officials of his period survived very much longer. In this matter the Channel ports were alone efficient, for the Vice-Admiral of Essex had victualled a very barbarous Scottish pirate on the Colne, while the Vice-Admiral of Norfolk demanded £80 for intervening to save two Danish ships and the servants of the Lord Admiral in Lincolnshire had established a ' rovers ' base at Ingoldmells.[2]

Yet if the Admiralty had much to do with the continuance of this traffic of piracy, they seem to have little responsibility for its collapse; for apart from measures such as the local guards of 1581, which closed the eastern Dorset refuges to the pirates, the first serious decline in their prosperity was caused by the outbreak of the war with Spain. The loss of the Spanish trade reduced the profits considerably, while the temporary naval concentration on Plymouth made work much more dangerous, and besides there was always the French competition, not only the official privateer like Espinay de Saint Luc, but also the less scrupulous rivalry of Captain Gargantuan.[3] The custom or

---

[1] For the instances of jury corruption and arranged escapes see Acts of the Privy Council, v, p. 362, vii, p. 207, xvi, p. 13 and xiii, p. 188, and Cal. S.P. Dom., 1547–80, p. 687.
[2] For these cases of Admiralty connivance see Acts of the Privy Council, ix, p. 30, xi, p. 12, and xii, p. 351.
[3] Acts of the Privy Council, vii, p. 392.

keeping armed retainers was dying out even in the remoter parts, so that the activities of Killigrew's men were thrown into prominence, and at the same time the balance of wealth in the counties was changing, for the Killigrews had conducted the piracy in too lavish a manner, and it was the smaller men who made profits. Thus Sir John Killigrew had died in debt for £10,000 and during fifteen years his son had still greater misfortune, for he tried too many experiments. His marriage paid off most of the debt ; but later he became feverish, and besides rack-renting his tenants and robbing strangers both by land and by sea and indulging in casual wrecking, he seems to have been imprudent in accepting money from Spain, and he certainly sold the provisions of Pendennis Castle. But the expense of maintaining armed guards and the bribery at Court exceeded the profits, for there were so many men, who had the power to betray him, while his spectacular failure,[1] on his £20,000 debt, frightened the others. Sir Richard Rogers was dead and his sons had grown old, while Perrot had died in prison and Sir Edward Denny had retired to his Hertfordshire property, and it was just the personal character of the control of the trade which caused it to fail, when it was deprived of the backing and aid of these gentlemen. With the decay of retainers the maintenance of private harbours became an impossible task, and the pirate ships returned to legitimate traffic.[2] Besides, the background had been a series of rather intimate friendships, but most of the second generation were elderly at the end of the century and their successors did not renew the former relations.

In 1559 all these families had been wealthy and on the side of the Government, and of course their leaders were loyal and in any case foreign ships suffered rather more than the English. Moreover they had relations at Court, and Sir John Perrot himself was a favourite, while the Dennys and Rogers had influence and Sir Henry Killigrew, from motives of mere self-interest, would have done all in his power to preserve the house of Arwennecke. But at the end of the century many of these families were ruined, for Perrot and the Killigrews were suspected of treason and most had been extravagant gamblers ; while the

---

[1] There are details of Killigrew's extortion and of his final embarrassments in Cal. Salisbury MSS., v, p. 378 and xi, p. 376.
[2] The names of pirate ships in western waters were peaceful. The *Tiger, Dragon* and *Sea Dragon* worked in the Mediterranean. Among the chief ships in the Channel were *Mary Fortune* and *Mary Grace*. Others were *Fortunatus, Neptune,* three *Dolphins, Prosperitie.* Acts of the Privy Council, ix, xviii, xxiii and xxvii and Cal. S.P. Venetian, ix, p. 547.

commemorative feasts at Arwennecke and the great banquets [1] for the Admiralty servants were ruinous and had their sons wished to continue the piracy it would not have been possible. This traffic had grown up under the shadow of the powerful protectors and it could flourish only with aid, so that once these wild squires were fallen, and the corrupt officials exposed, the piracy ceased. The growth and success had been in part due to the abnormal stress of a period, when any crime unconnected with treason seemed hardly worthy of punishment and the absence of violence and the purely commercial nature of the whole transaction had at first helped to prosperity. So long as the leaders could safeguard their harbours, the working expenses were small, but, as soon as order was established in Cornwall, it was necessary to bribe a whole countryside and there could be no profit.

[1] Cal. S.P. Dom. Add., 1566–79, p. 536, *passim.*

CHAPTER XVI

THE LANDING OF THE PRIESTS

It is intended in this brief study to make the connection between the general political activities of the Catholic exiles and the means by which the priests were introduced into England in defiance of the newly passed law. In this case the way of life described in the chapters on the Welsh exiles abroad and Sir Thomas Stukeley's design forms the background from which the priests abroad had set forth, while the studies of the Cornish and Welsh pirates and the Elizabethan Ordnance officers deal with the men among whom they were thrown in their attempt to return into England. The question of bribery is also prominent in these later chapters, and the detail of the traffic established for the landing of priests shows the reactions of the English seamen to a temptingly diverse choice of lucrative offers. It is noticeable that many captains preferred the prospects of a straightforward piracy to an action which might involve them in the toils of religious dispute. The distinction between politically minded Catholics abroad and the missionary priests appears clearly, and an impression is given of the very complex system of secret service which had developed under the Cecils, and is here seen at the most efficient phase of its work.

THE problem of the means of entry into England was one which could not fail to exercise the proscribed English priests, for it was a matter always difficult, involving dangers which, with the passing of the penal laws of 1586 and the outbreak of the war with Spain, became acute. An intricate organization was essential and the success both of the secular clergy and of the Jesuits in landing their members on English soil and conveying them to places of comparative safety was only achieved by frequent alterations of their long-considered plans. The remarkable character of the achievement is further indicated by the fact that in a work demanding so complete a secrecy no less than nine groups of men were involved in the different preliminaries to each affair.

In the first place there were the priests in the colleges and the Jesuits and the agents, on the whole faithful, whom they employed, then the English Ambassadors at foreign Courts and the numerous private representatives of the Queen's Government, and, besides, a very varied band of agents, some of a less reputable character, engaged by the Cecil family or by the other prominent advisers of the Crown.

Direct contact existed only between this last group and the second, for it was inevitable that some few of the men, into whose hands the priests were forced to trust themselves, should be not only in a desperate need of money, but also subject to pressure on account of the too adventurous actions of their past. In vague connection with these men was a body of English gentlemen living abroad, some of whom possessed a quite meticulous sense of personal honour. In England there were the agents of the Spanish Government, usually soldiers of unblemished and distinguished character who were accustomed to invite themselves to the houses of embarrassed country squires on the score of some ancient friendship formed when King Philip was in England or a comradeship in the camp at Gravelines. These men of course vanished with the outbreak of the war, but there was also watching these proceedings a body of alien merchants living in London and enjoying the favour of the English Government as the agents of the Portuguese Pretender and of a wealthy merchant house at Amsterdam. After being for ten years the chief enemies of the Spaniards, they had transferred their services at a most favourable moment; their race, for they were Jewish, lent them a calm detachment in the religious aspect of this dispute.

Except for the priests, who were of course apart, all these men passing along the high roads to the ports of Europe were in some sense equal, for they were all moneyed and had merchandize and wives. In particular it was a considerable advantage for an English private agent to be married, since this would give that appearance of stable respectability so necessary in this profession which was always hazardous and often vagabond. But below these mingling groups who were in contact, however dubious with the Great, there was always the numerous company of the broken men. These were a constant difficulty, men who were prepared for the most dangerous enterrises and against whom there was a death warrant in their own country; the death warrant and the danger of starvation made any risk seem light. To reach England therefore the priests had to pass the observation of the Queen's Ambassadors, the Queen's private agents and Mr. Secretary's private agents, and then there was the danger of the broken men along the quays. In England there were all these over again as well as King Philip's agents. Dr. Lopez and Mr. Anes sat detached in London with each department of their business kept perfectly distinct. They might explain the whereabouts of the English Fleet to the Spaniards and this was valuable, but uncertain, or they might indicate the hiding place of priests to the English Government and this was yet more valuable again.

Yet in this question, with the detailed reports [1] that the members of these different parties sent, the chief difficulty is to establish a control of the sources; for it is natural that the priests should not willingly have committed to writing the details of their evasion of the law and in this matter the narrative of Father Gerard, S.J., forms one of the very few outstanding exceptions. On the other hand, the reports sent in to the English Government are most copious, but they suffer from the disadvantage that their writers depended for their livelihood on the continued production of a mass of exact and detailed information. The English agents were men of proved capacity, and it is an added difficulty that their descriptions, though sometimes inaccurate, are invariably precise. In this connection the constant use of the word ' Jesuit ' causes some trouble, for it was often employed when speaking of the secular clergy and the agents had sometimes a very highly coloured notion as to what sort of character could be fittingly covered by this term. These details can, however, be checked to some extent by the confessions of the captured men and by the reports sent in to the foreign Governments and in this way the line of the actual voyages to England can be recovered as well as the framework of that complicated system, which the rigorous persecution forced the Catholics to set up.

At first the priests landed at the ordinary ports in disguise, and in fact Fathers Parsons and Campion, who were the first Jesuits to reach England in June, 1580, landed at Dover. Rather earlier the harbour at Rye had been used, for the Customer there was a Catholic and it was easy to slip away across the solitudes of Romney Marsh to the Recusant houses in East Kent. Besides, in those days of peace it was a simple matter to sail from any Channel port, while the priests in Spain were accustomed to embark at San Lucar de Barrameda,[2] a

---

[1] It is to be noted that the insularity of the official envoys often deprived their despatches of much value. Dr. Henry Man who, when Ambassador to Spain, mentioned in a letter to Leicester of 21st April, 1568, that ' I have declared to Wry Gomes ' was evidently no reliable guide to the affairs of that country. Cal. Pepys MSS., p. 113.

[2] Letter from Emmanuel d'Andrada to the Queen, dated 13th August, 1591. ' All vessels from San Lucar to Newcastle should be searched as Father Parsons sends his spies that way.' Cal. S.P. Dom., 1591–4, p. 86.

private harbour owned by the Duke of Medina Sidonia on the Andalusian Coast. The Duke was a considerable benefactor of the exiled
priests, a warm admirer of the new Society, and Father Parsons was
honoured by his friendship, so that everything was arranged with
great simplicity in a town where all the merchant captains were his
tenants and the customs officials in his employ. On the English side
Arundel harbour was used, for the whole countryside was controlled
by the Fitzalans, and the Catholicism of their stewards was a guarantee
of support in the earlier days. Altogether until 1586 the actual crossing
was simple, provided that the traveller was prudent and had a sufficiently convincing disguise, for it was a mere question of a landing in
secret and a ride before chance of discovery to the safe shelter of
friends. In this way Fathers Southwell and Garnet were put ashore in
East Anglia and Father Leighton was to have been landed from the
fishing smack *Hopewell* at Poole ; [1] but the outbreak of the war with
Spain put an end to this casual adventure, and it was replaced by an
elaborate method, which was used during the sixteen years from 1587
till 1603, when the persecution was fierce.

The system worked in this fashion. On leaving his college each
priest was directed to one of the chief managers of the traffic and was
given his journey money *pro viatico*, a sum which varied very considerably, but which was sometimes, in the case of the Spanish Colleges,
fifty crowns or perhaps, as an alternative, ten crowns, two hundred
and fifty *reales* and a horse.[2] The men from Seville often went to the
house of a friend of the priests at San Lucar, while those from Valladolid sometimes stayed with Nicholas Baldwin at Palencia, a day's
ride along the high road to the sea. Mr. Baldwin, a Cornishman from
St. Mawes and now a prosperous merchant, married to a Spanish
lady, was a benefactor of the English College and accustomed to
entertain the English priests. The priests going from St. Omer would
lodge at the inn kept by William Randall [3] at Dunkirk. He was from
Weymouth, a skilful mariner and pilot, a man very resolved in his
religion, prudent and growing old, who kept the best table in Dunkirk
and was married to a Flemish widow of that town. Should they come
from Brussels or Louvain, the travellers would meet together at the
house of Adrian de Langhe, the postmaster of Antwerp, who had

---

[1] Examination of the mariners of the *Hopewell*. Cal. S.P. Dom., 1581–90.
[2] Confessions of William Jessop in 1600. Cal. Salisbury MSS., x, p. 341.
[3] Cal. Salisbury MSS., iv, p. 588.

THE LANDING OF THE PRIESTS

managed the correspondence of the priests with England since 1582.[1] He was expert at secret writing both in lemon water and in milk and was accustomed to make the passports, usually in Sir Thomas Baskerville's[2] hand, so essential to adventurers in disguise. It was probably in these houses that the final costumes were adopted and not in the colleges, whose entrances were watched by the representatives of the English Government and whose kitchens were haunted by Cecil's men.[3]

For the sake of ease and rapidity of movement it was usual to adopt the costume and manner of gentlemen of rank and thus Father Ancott wore a tawny satin doublet with a pair of black velvet hose, while Father Barnwell, a tall man with a flaxen beard and fingers lame from racking, wore a similar dress, and Father Oswell,[4] a tall black-haired man who passed for a soldier, had a plain doublet of fustian with a pair of round fustian hose of the same, laid with gold lace and a white high hat very flat in the crown. This dress was in keeping with the customs of the period, adequate and discreet; but the exiles did not always follow such discretion. A young man disguised with a pair of red breeches and yellow stockings, who was quite unacquainted with the Society, was arrested as a Jesuit at Rhynbercke, being captured by a most experienced investigator, Captain Loon, who had a wide knowledge of European languages and had lived familiarly among the Jesuits at Rome. In the same way a wandering Englishman of fifty-five was declared without any reason to be a Jesuit. This man, who had dyed his beard and hair black and gave his occupation as a farmer, huntsman and innkeeper, was a discharged servant of the Arundells of Wardour, who, after maintaining a precarious livelihood in Paris apparently as a receiver, had been reduced to experimenting[5] in poisonous compounds at the sign of the *Angel* in the market-place at St. Omer. An exile with a damaged reputation was invariably described as an agent of the Society. In connection

---

[1] Letter of W. Williams to Walsingham dated 18th September, 1582, ‘Lange the post was a bad man and carried many evil letters.’ Cal. S.P. Dom., 1581–90, p. 70.

[2] Cal. S.P. Dom., 1591–4, p. 497.

[3] *Cf.* the case of James Lomas an English agent, who lived at Seville in the house of the Archbishop's cook. Cal. S.P. Spanish, 1587–1603, p. 219.

[4] The descriptions of the three men were obtained from the confessions of William Astell, made on 22nd February, 1598, while the reference to Oswall is confirmed by a letter from Thomas Bruges to Essex from Vivero on 6th March, ‘this Oswall, a priest . . . is a man something tall of stature, his hair black.’ Cal. Salisbury MSS., viii, pp. 59 and 63.

[5] Examination of William Thomson alias Carre on 18th March, 1592. Cal. S.P. Dom., 1591–4, p. 203.

with this question a charge brought against Mr. Randall should be mentioned. According to a report contributed by Richard Topcliffe in 1593, he had been engaged in devising poisoned fireballs in collaboration with an old lame devil at Dunkirk and the ' poisoned conclucyon,' as it is described, was said to be in his desk there ; but it seems unlikely that an elderly innkeeper, who according to his adversaries was very prudent, should involve himself in this affair. It is therefore clear that the reports of the English agents as to the activities of the Jesuits in France should be treated with considerable reserve.

On leaving the houses where they obtained directions and disguise, the priests went carefully on towards the sea ; for it was one of the effects of the state of war that a long land journey now became essential, since direct passage from Spanish soil became impossible and the southern route had fallen to disuse. As late as 1591 there was some traffic from San Lucar to Newcastle, but only neutral ships could be made use of and any vessel from Spain aroused suspicion. But it was more usual for the priests in Spain to go northward overland to San Sebastian and thence by sea to Bordeaux, trusting to find a ship for England in that crowded port. Sometimes the journey was made direct to Saint Jean de Luz or Bayonne, but this had the disadvantage that there were English agents watching at all the gateways into Spain. Occasionally the more adventurous would sail from Bayonne to Fowey or St. Germans, but it was safer to land among the crowds of the Port of London than for a stranger to go ashore on the remote Cornish coast, so that most of the priests reached England by the short seaway from France. It was on Calais therefore that the travellers converged, riding along the roads from Dunkirk to St. Omer, or the road from Italy and Paris or coming into the harbour on board a merchantman from Spain. The journey from Bilbao took nine days and the passage money was six golden crowns, and Father Oswald Tesimond, S.J., for instance, was one of the well-known clergy to arrive this way.

There were many reasons why Calais should have been chosen. It was a Catholic town with a Governor well disposed to the higher clergy and attached to the interests of the League, the secular priests, as well as the religious, were most friendly and the Dean of Calais himself arranged these English journeys. The *Mermaid* Inn was in the hands of excellent Catholics, as were several other houses in the

Map of the Western Approaches.
The position of the North Spanish ports in relation to the Celtic countries is indicated.

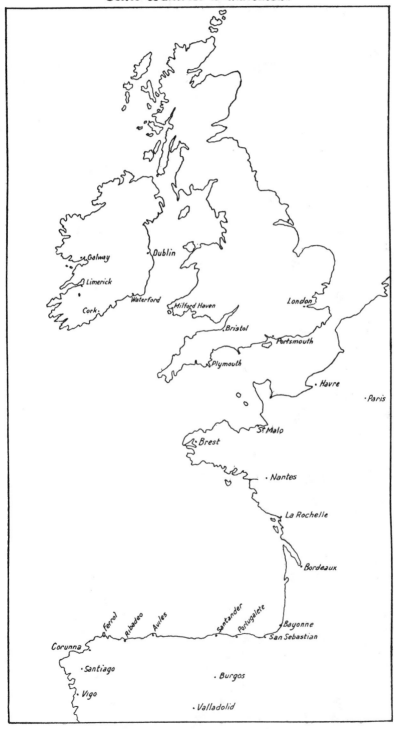

town, and the exiled priests could count upon a following, numerous and loyal, among the captains of the port. Captain Jacobson,[1] an experienced pilot, was the chief of this party and carried disguised travellers across the Channel, rounding the North Foreland and landing them on the beach at Reculver in the dawn of the long winter nights; while Captain Cornelius Nabs and Monsieur Gibels [2] sailed betweeı London and Calais Sands, charging a fare of forty shillings for each passenger, so that it was a profitable as well as an adventurous pursuit. In the last years of the reign this way by Calais seems to have been the only route, for in 1592 the English Government managed to stop the sending across of ' Jesuits ' from Middelburg, which had been arranged by Mr. Cook [3] for seven years and the success of the Navarre party at Boulogne, where the Mayor used to send dispatches [4] to Sir Robert Cecil, made that port difficult. Thus, with every detail concentrated upon Calais and with Dunkirk and Antwerp as the mainland bases, it is easier to see the effort that the English Government put forth to shadow the priests and stop them on their way.

Difficulties would be met with at the very outset of the journey. One of the Queen's agents was stationed at the sign of the *God of Love* in the Rue Saint Jacques at Paris and another at the *Launce Couronne* at Liège, while Thomas Barnes, a most trustworthy man, lodged at the *Golden Ape* at Tournai to report on travellers coming from Brussels and Louvain or from Bar-le-Duc and Pont-à-Mousson by the road from the Ardennes. At Calais it was necessary to avoid the *White Swan*, where the English agent, Monsieur Hans Poulson, was living and Lord Burghley maintained a correspondent there as well, while there was always danger from the stray English sailors about the port, men like Mat Howson who bargained for passages on the wharfside and were ready to take smugglers or gunrunners or priests. There was no security in trusting to men who were always balancing reward against profit. Besides this, there were civil servants

---

[1] Cal. S.P. Dom., 1601–1603, p. 41.
[2] Cal. Salisbury MSS., xii, p. 231.
[3] Cal. S.P. Dom., 1591–4, p. 298. The references for this section are confined for the most part to the names of individuals ; details of landing places and halts which are too numerous to receive individual mention will be found under date in the Calendars of State Papers, the Acts of the Privy Council and the Calendars of the Salisbury MSS.
[4] Letters of warning were sent on 5th June, 1598, and again in October. Cal. Salisbury MSS., viii, pp. 195, 396. And this letter, written later in the year, is most revealing. ' Cest ce a quoy,' wrote the Mayor, ' l'on doibt bien prende garde, car je vous asseure que les Jesuites des Pays Bas ont une intelligence grande avec les cordeliers de cette ville, tant pour faire tenir leurs lettres et passa leurs gens vers vous, et a Calais ils ont la doien ou curé.' *Ibid.*, p. 556.

employed to investigate the manufacture of passports in co-operation with London decipherers, and this affair seems to have been managed by a confidential agent who lived at Antwerp under the names of Sterrell, Robinson and Saint Main. Even the crossing had its own peculiar dangers, for it was impossible to keep so organized a traffic secret. The English public money had been laid out to great advantage and one of the trusted captains, who took the priests across, had been induced to enter the Government's employ, so that it was an irretrievable misfortune for a weary traveller, who had avoided so many dangers, to be landed on the English shore by Captain Gelpe.[1]

For the arrival at London changes of plan were constantly needed, and at first it was often the custom for priests to land on the Essex shore and make their way across country to Braddocks and then ride in with Mr. Wiseman to London. For seven most perilous years, from 1585 until 1592, they were accustomed to go on landing to the house of an Italian [2] who kept a bowling green at the Moorfields end of Bishopsgate Street; but this in turn was discovered and then Mr. Middleton, a merchant in Holborn, received them, until Father John Gerard was captured in 1594. This only indicates some of the methods of passage, and after the landing there was a constant alteration of choice. In this way certain of the messengers chose to lodge in Billingsgate at the *Swan with Two Necks*, but for others and in especial the Jesuits, it was necessary to lodge, in accordance with the disguise they assumed, in the respectable parts of the City. Mr. Lawrence Povey, for instance, who lived at the *Mermaid's Head* in Fleet Street was particularly concerned with those coming from the sea, and then when their costume was completed they could go to private houses in Drury Lane, or, as Father Parsons did, to one of those rather expensive inns in Holborn where the Catholic gentry used to lodge. But here there was grave danger, for Mr. Henry Knowles was constantly in this neighbourhood, a man very active in all the Recusant concerns, who was employed by the Government to move in the more expensive Catholic circles about the town. Meanwhile there were always the great Catholic households as unchanging centres of refuge, and at Southampton House, still a stronghold even after the death of Swithin

[1] Cal. S.P. Dom., 1598–1601, p. 377.
[2] Cal. S.P. Dom., 1591–4, p. 298.

Wells, Lady Cornwallis would shelter Father Gerard,[1] while at Arundel House Father Southwell lay concealed during the years of the imprisonment of the Earl. In these establishments with their many courtyards and outbuildings and their gardens stretching from the river to the Strand, with their troops of servants and loosely attached dependents, it was easy to lie secret, for no entry could be made without a definite search warrant, and there was always the influence that could be brought to bear to check this by Lady Southampton or Lord Henry Howard in political circles or at the Court. This can be regarded as the end of the immediate journey; for these great houses, safer, except in moments of unusual danger, than the remote but less protected country manors, provided the nearest approach to security that the priests in England could ever hope to reach. Yet how few were fortunate enough to find a shelter there.

In addition to the actual journeys of the English priests there was all the system of the correspondence that they maintained both with their immediate superiors and with Rome, and in this matter also there is considerable detail still extant. In 1592 Mr. Thomas Payne, a haberdasher living against the Counter in the Poultry, and Mr. James Tayler,[2] whose house was by the conduit in Fleet Street, were receivers of letters, but it seems likely that the messengers they sent over to Middelburg [3] were not in the secret. Most of the actual arrangements seem to have been made by Monsieur Dierick Hendricks, a substantial merchant in Blackfriars, whose brother Peter lived at the sign of the *Golden Horn* in the Rue Perpot at Antwerp and managed the Continental side of this traffic. A perhaps less trustworthy agent was Monsieur Gaspar,[4] a Dutchman, who received the letters from Father Parsons in Spain at his house near St. Katherine by the Tower. The fact that he had formerly been in the service of the Cardinal of Portugal, whom he had left for reasons undisclosed, might seem a qualification with a double edge.

In order to stop this correspondence the English Government appear wisely to have concentrated their efforts on Antwerp; for it

[1] Cal. Salisbury MSS., xi, p. 387.
[2] Letter of Fr. Robert Parsons, S.J., to Fr. Simon Swinborne, S.J., dated 10th February, 1592. Cal. S.P. Dom., 1591–4, p. 181.
[3] Middelburg was also the centre from which students for the seminaries re-embarked. On 30th December, 1597, Tobias Parry confessed that he had gone as pilot in a small Middelburg fly boat to San Lucar on All Saints Day last, landing twelve English scholars between 18 and 25 years of age. Cal. S.P. Dom., 1595–7, p. 554.
[4] Examination of Henry Sise, 8th August, 1594. Cal. S P. Dom., 1591–4, p. 538.

seems that once they reached Flanders these missionary letters, protected by their cypher, were sent through the ordinary posts, and,
although this presumably only applied to a portion of the correspondence, to the Government every letter was valuable. By a fortunate
chance all letters in charge of the royal posts were kept a day for
weighing at Madrid and Antwerp, so that on payment of a retaining
fee of twenty-eight ducats a month to one of the postmaster's clerks, the
English agent had the opportunity of a hasty perusal,[1] while at a more
expensive rate any really necessary document could be lost on the way.

At Antwerp, which was one of the great centres of the exiles, the
Government had made the most lavish arrangements, taking fully
into account the different shades of conduct which so delicate a situation then required. In the first place and somewhat remote from
practical affairs there was Mr. Thomas Morgan, an impoverished
Welsh gentleman, a Catholic with an implacable dislike for the Society,
who lodged in the postmaster's house with the carriers from England [2]
and moved in the polite circles of the City. His pronounced views
upon the conduct and aims of the Fathers of the Society and his
financial embarrassments were levers upon which the English worked
and his presence in such a place had its own value, since, although he
was a loyal servant of the Queen of Scots, his antipathies could be
used to prevent the smooth running of the machine. Then for
definite information there was Mr. John Lee, a merchant living at the
Golden Stag, who went about among the solid mercantile community,
maintaining contact with Monsieur Jasper Himselroy, who dealt in
English passports at the sign of the *Gilded Head*, and with Mr. Ver-
stegan [3] the Catholic printer, who lived by the Bridge of the Tapestry
Makers and helped the missionaries in this the most essential point of
their disguise. Lastly there was the confidential agent, living at that
time as Mr. Sterrell,[4] a man versatile and astute, who kept in touch
with the house in Black Sisters Street, whence letters were written
to England in faint orange juice and milk [5] and with a very dubious

---

[1] Accurate details of the transactions of Mr. Borrell and Senor Martinez, one of Don Juan
de Tassis' clerks, are preserved in Cal. Salisbury MSS., viii, pp. 180 and 184, and Cal. S.P. Dom.,
1598–1601, p. 47.
[2] Papers relating to the charges against Thomas Morgan, filed at Brussels on 12th February,
1590. Cal. S.P. Spanish, 1587–1603, pp. 565–9.
[3] Cal. S.P. Dom., 1591–4, pp. 478 and 520, and Cal. Salisbury MSS., iv, p. 499.
[4] He stated that he had laid out £26 in coming and in procuring passports and that he could
not live in Antwerp under £140 a year. Cal. S.P. Dom., 1591–4, p. 217.
[5] Cal. S.P. Dom., 1591–4, p. 207.

establishment under Italian management in the Rue des Juifs, where reliable and soldierly men could be hired for an adventure. In the poorest quarters of the town there was a common lodging-house for seamen called the *Pied Ox*, where the sailors of the ships for England met together. Here there was no question of finding swordsmen, but ground unicorns' horns [1] and compounds of a very potent nature could be obtained. This also was under observation. It was a system beautifully balanced and complete.

In all these affairs the English Government paid their agents on a dual basis, partly on a fixed retaining fee and partly on a sliding scale, according to results. This provided a very adequate livelihood and, as an instance, Monsieur Chasteau Martin, who was Lord Burghley's representative at Bayonne, had an allowance of twelve hundred crowns a year, which was maintained until he died at his post in the cold winter of 1596.[2] All risks were covered by a complete form of insurance as is shown by an interesting memorial for a claim, which was written in 1599, and describes the qualifications of Mr. Thomas Harrison. ' I have sundry times,' wrote [3] this faithful servant of the State, ' very dangerously adventured to have my throat cut as may appear. In the house of the Lord Seaton I lay in policy to discover Holt the Jesuit fourteen days and caused him together with myself to be apprehended at Leith with all his packets for France and Spain. In Colchester, by Mr. Secretary's devise I was consorted with one Deane and Shelley a seminary and lodged fourteen days in the outward prison to intercept all their letters, which was also done to the discovery of a number of traitors.' By profession Mr. Harrison was a writer, an agent of the second rank living in Isleworth, who was familiar with the Yeomen of the Guard and had done good service for Lord Rich. As in this case, previous service was always the best claim to further reward, while the reliability of these agents was increased by a definite salary and by the impossibility of obtaining other employment should they incur their master's displeasure. Besides, the reports which all the agents sent home regarding the activities of their colleagues ensured the competence and relative loyalty of the whole secret service.

---

[1] Examination of Simon Knowles on 30th March, 1594. Cal. Salisbury MSS., iv, p. 499.
[2] Letter of Fr. Robert Parsons to Don Juan de Idiaquez. Cal. S.P. Spanish, 1587–1603, p. 633.
[3] Cal. Salisbury MSS., ix, p. 87.

Under these circumstances it was a considerable triumph that so large a number of priests were successfully landed in England, but they had this great advantage, an endless opportunity for alterations of plan. They had friends in all the French ports and could make rapid changes of hiding place among the Catholic houses in England. It must have been difficult for an agent even with the most roving commission to trace the movements of men who could rely on so many supporters.

CHAPTER XVII

THE ORDNANCE OFFICE AND GUNRUNNING

A consideration of the question of gunrunning naturally follows the sections which deal with piracy and the illegal entry of priests. In this case a parallel with the Elizabethan coastal pirates is suggested by the connivance of the officers of the Ordnance in the traffic. The distinction between ordinary corruption and that which was tinged with an unpatriotic character, as a result of the outbreak of the war with Spain, is clearly shown. At the same time the workings of the Ordnance administration throw light upon the relations between the subordinate officers and those Court officials who enjoyed the supreme responsibility and the titular honour. The feuds which these class distinctions engendered were not without a certain political importance and a side of the official careers of public men, which often caused them much embarrassment, is explained by these intermittent quarrels. The manner in which the great officers of the Crown had imprudently delivered themselves into the power of their subordinates is also apparent. In this matter the details of the corrupt practices in the Ordnance Office are connected up with the hindrances which the incipient bureaucracy could often place, as in Ireland under Sir John Perrot, upon the activities of their chiefs. It should be remembered, however, that, even before the Spanish War, the Ordnance officers lay under the temptation of offers of purchase from abroad.

In the later years of the reign the Ordnance Office provided a field for the Earl of Essex's casual activity. The constant influence of the Cecils in all departments of Government coincided and sometimes conflicted with Essex's exercise of his power. The earlier portion of this chapter is thus chiefly concerned with gunrunning to Spain; while later the effect of this corruption upon the political chiefs is considered. In this way an introduction is provided to an examination of Essex's influence which was so strongly bound up both by opposition and friendship with the surviving Celtic movements in Ireland and Wales.

THE official organization of the spending departments, which were in time to develop into the Civil Service, has always suffered in the earlier stages of their life from the disease of malnutrition. Pay for the soldiers was essential and opportunity was needed by the sailors, but for the patient and obscure beginnings of the Civil Service there was no such haste, and yet it was necessary for these officials with their acute minds to obtain some living for themselves and their dependents, although they could not receive that prompt payment which was reserved for soldiers and spies, nor could they turn to the easy plunder which the Spanish Main could provide. At the same time the ease with which the courtiers could obtain their large grants

319

THE CELTIC PEOPLES & RENAISSANCE EUROPE

only emphasized the poverty of the needy officials, who were tied through life to their cumbrous and rickety tables and could not even reach Ireland, that country where the eastern sky towards England was dark with the vultures. For the emblems of Elizabethan adventure were double-headed and fierce and those figures of the English eagles sailing by Valparaiso, magnificent and golden, were changed in the light of the cold north weather to vultures hovering merciless in the wintry Munster sky. It was typical of the public finances of the period and of the manner in which every form of income was dried up at the source that only a very small proportion of the moneys could come in safety through that *barrage*, which the men around the Queen's throne brought to bear.

In addition the calculated parsimony of the Queen emphasized the unequal character of this division, for it was essential that the public expenses should be kept down below a certain figure and part of the lavish income of the courtiers could only be secured by the exercise of a rigid economy towards subordinates, whose meagre pay had frequently to be kept well in arrears while on some occasions it was suspended altogether. These considerations are in part responsible for the curious disorders in various branches of the public service and in particular in the Ordnance Office, for, since officials were so badly paid, the royal policy was strangled. In this connection the phrase of Lord Mountjoy, writing to Sir Robert Cecil in 1600, about the Ordnance officials in Ireland and their master can be seen to have a much wider application. ' He (the master),' wrote Mountjoy, ' hath such a mean entertainment for his under officers that they cannot be of any sufficiency or of any great sincerity.' [1] Again and again we find in the complaints of the Ordnance Office in England the phrase of the impossibility of discovering officials of ' any sufficiency or ability.' But it is not ' ability ' in the modern sense of that word that was lacking and the officials could never be accused of any useless concealment of their talent. On the contrary, they used every talent to the utmost, but it was just this successful use of their position which prevented them from giving any real obedience to the Queen.

They were men of the office desk lacking that incentive to the more respectable adventures, like the strong sword hilt of the Spanish Main. Instead they were quiet officials and often given to religion, so

[1] State Papers, Eliz. Irel., xcvii, 21.

320

THE ORDNANCE OFFICE AND GUNRUNNING

that in one case the note, 'a very religious man and very well acquainted with the ordnance,'[1] is found appended, and they seldom ventured far from the Tower of London and from the ancient tallies and the heavy desks. Far beyond them and with a merely nominal connection with this office work, there moved the great courtiers, men, suave and easy in their manners, but financially not porous, and, if there was one factor which had taught these subordinates self-reliance, it was the knowledge that the masters in the spheres above them had effectually dammed the flow of gold.

Fortunately starvation was never a pressing danger for the officials of this time, but it was a fruit of that sense of joint responsibility, which even a very simple organization now implied, that the lords who had diverted the public moneys could not, for that reason, feign an ignorance of the source from which their inferiors were kept supplied. This was in contrast to the case of the Secret Service, where a system of balances and checks maintained a state of relative efficiency, while the independence of the ministers who maintained these private agents allowed a very wide freedom for their acts. It was on the other hand the misfortune of the spending departments, even in their rudimentary forms, that the acting head of the office and his subordinates were equally responsible to the Queen, so that, while the ministers could always get rid of a private agent without serious lack of prestige, there came a moment in the Ordnance Office, when the scandals were so serious that the only safe course for the Master of the Ordnance was to ignore them and to pretend that Her Majesty had not been 'deceived.'

A particular interest attaches to the history of this department on account of the illicit export of ordnance to Spain and because of the misfortune that led Essex to assume responsibility for its affairs with that peculiar fatality that led him to accept and even to covet any position that was hazardous and ill starred. In this way this Government office became at first a vulnerable point in the Spanish attack, while later the storms of Essex's political life broke over these bureaux.

Until the outbreak of the war with Spain the administration creaked forward slowly aided by that doubtful equilibrium which a balance between the lack of money and the absence of an urgent need of spending could provide. The supply of funds trickled forward

[1] Cal. Salisbury MSS., ix, p. 340.

very slowly and yet in a time of peace there was no need to be much prepared, for the atmosphere was slumber-laden, and if matters were brought very nearly to a standstill this was made easier by a general agreement that there was no pressing necessity to move. At the same time, even if the stock of ordnance and munitions could be left in security unreplenished, it was necessary for the Ordnance officers to make a living and a complete immunity from imprisonment or censure was not an adequate substitute for bread. In such circumstances it was the obvious course for the officials to derive a secure income from their position without any further drain upon the funds and in this case the inordinate determination of the Crown to obtain a revenue without adequate expenditure only placed the situation in their hands. It was in some sense a repetition of the connivance of the Admiralty officials in the case of piracy, for in both instances the root cause was a lack of sufficient payment for the under officers, and the result a loss to the Exchequer in the end.

As in other cases, so also in the Ordnance Office, it was from the misuse of an intended Government remedy that the illegal income was derived. By an effect of that inter-departmental jealousy, which is found even in the most undeveloped organizations, a certain tightening had already taken place in the Ordnance Office regulations in 1574, as a result of the work of Mr. Baker, a zealous Admiralty official. The spoiling of the oak woods in the Sussex Weald was held to involve an injury to the easy supply of masts for English vessels, while it was alleged that the iron from the Wealden furnaces was sent abroad. An order from the Privy Council was issued with a view to counter-acting the effects of this abuse and a central control was soon established which was to cause the Crown revenue to increase. It was the same underpaid officials who controlled the profits of this yield, but in this case they were unanimously certain as to whom such benefits were due. ' All ordnance,' so ran the order from the Council,[1] ' shall be shipped . . . or brought by lande to the Tower Wharf and there be solde to Englishe merchauntes or to such straungers as dwell in this realm and are owners of any shippe or parte owners which merchauntes shall enter into bonde to the Queen Majestie's use in the office of the ordnance that they only buye them for the furniture of Englishe shippes and not to make a sale of them unto any straungers

[1] Acts of the Privy Council, 1571-5, pp. 254-5.

out of the realm. The casters of the said iron pieces shall yearly deliver up true certificat unto the Master of the Ordinance as well what number of peeces they cast as also the names of the parties to whom they sell them.' It was clear that 'bonds' and 'true certificats' were thus destined to supply the income for which the ordnance officers had looked in vain.

It was at first a purely commercial question and happily unconfused by those issues of patriotism which were so soon to disturb it. Ordnance was shipped abroad, sometimes for the Sultan of Morocco's new armaments and occasionally for the Spaniards or for the benefit of some other Power, which, when all were at peace with the English, was an entirely private affair. Meanwhile, behind them to drive forward this commerce, there was the influence of the rich South country gentry, men of the new governing class like the Sidneys,[1] whose son, Sir Philip, was joint Master of Ordnance, or the Sackvilles, who had great interest in the forges throughout the Weald and in Kent. Besides all the gentlemen who had forges in their possession had sunk capital in these efforts and now demanded return. It was the chief effect of the Queen's economy that, if they could not find a market in England, they must send their products abroad and this involved them in a dual payment or tax to the Ordnance officials. For in the first place there was the price that was given for the unbroken quiet of the Tower, where the officials concealed their surprise that there was so little traffic, and then there were the definite payments in return for valuable service, when the Ordnance officers would sign and vouch for the furnace accounts.

Far above them was the Master of the Ordnance now approaching the thirtieth year of his tenure, which was the most substantial reward that the Queen had bestowed on Lord Ambrose Dudley, who had the merit to be the Lord Robert's brother. Lord Ambrose, now Earl of Warwick, was ageing in heaviness, spending his time far from the Court at Bath taking the waters, and in any case there would not seem to be any good reason to disturb affairs in the Office. The representatives of the iron trade were among his dependents and friends, and their political influence in the country had value; besides every

---

[1] For an account of the Sidney ironworks at Robertsbridge, cf. Cal. de Lisle and Dudley MSS., pp. 305–18. In regard to the gunrunning to Morocco a document from the Record Office with explanatory notes is printed in the appendix, p. 487. The State Papers contain many references to this Moroccan traffic, particularly between 1580 and 1582, and these are described briefly in the introduction to this unprinted paper, p. 486.

indication would show that Lord Warwick was perfectly willing that all his dependent officials should obtain an adequate income, so long as there was no suggestion that he should be obliged to provide it himself. In the moral sphere especially it seemed there was hardly a problem, for the whole question was a simple matter of passing the customs, until suddenly the war came with Spain and this changed the whole issue.

The character of an act is modified by circumstances, but it was the difficulty of the Ordnance officials that no further solution was put forward through which the question of their means of livelihood could be broached; but a light was thrown on the unpreparedness of the office and the controversy added bitterness to its tone. A letter from the Council to the Lord Admiral and Lord Buckhurst shows how this rapid change had come about. 'Whereas (as their Lordships knows),'[1] wrote the Council, 'there were bondes taken of soche as made iron ordynaunce within the County of Sussex that they should sell none to anie that should transporte the same, nor themselves cause anie to be transported beyond the seas, and lykewise certyfie monthlie to the Lord Admyrall and to th'Office of the Ordinaunce what quantitie was made by anie of them, and to whom the same should be sould and uttered; which having not been performed because their Lordships sawe the lyttle regard the oweners of furnysses and the makers of those peeces had of theire bondes, and how yt impaired the estate that the enemies of Her Majestie and the Realme should not be furnished out of the land with ordynaunce to annoye us, therefore their Lordships thought goode to praie theire Lordships to cause the justices of the Peace were the forges were to take a true inventory.'

It was at this stage that a new source of income was discovered for the Ordnance officials and there began those revelations of the 'searchers out of corruptions and deceits,' which were to embitter the life in the Ordnance Office through the reign. An accidental circumstance contributed to the difficulty of the position, due to the fact that the Masters of the Ordnance through their long acceptance of the situation, and in consequence of the small pay which their subordinates received, were compelled to take a roseate view of the smooth running of the office, which no crisis from below had power

---

[1] Acts of the Privy Council, 1589–90, p. 8. *Cf.* Document printed by David and Gervase Mathew in the *English Historical Review*, January, 1933.

to shake. There was no possibility therefore that any ' difficult ' official would ever vanish from the Ordnance desks above Tower Wharf, for on the one hand, the so-called ' deceivers of Her Majesty ' were always supported by authority and, on the other, the zealous ' searchers out ' naturally remained within the office, where alone their talents could find full employ.

The first rumours of war in the autumn of 1587 had quickened this activity and the Surveyor of the Ordnance, Mr. Powell, had written to the Queen offering to expose frauds in the Ordnance Office and accusing the old Earl of Warwick of great oppressions and Mr. Painter of false recording in the office books.[1] But this was only a sequel to charges of corruption which had already been levelled against Mr. Powell,[2] and in the result there was stalemate, and they all went on working together, but with a rather strained stiffness and a con- siderable increase of caution in the management of their private affairs. The negotiations, too, became changed, for what had been the almost open arrangements with the light-fingered and hearty gentlemen of the good days of peace had now become a serious business secret with the Low Country merchants. Back in the late 'seventies there had been an easy traffic, with Mr. Woollcombe selling bronze guns to the Mayor of Laredo and Mr. Gulston of Plymouth with his little twenty-eight-ton ' bark ' at San Sebastian alongside the quay and a brisk sale of cast pieces, sakers, falcons and minion falcons to the Spanish firms and the French.[3] Even in 1580 Mr. Fermer, a Sussex gentleman, who had had the ill fortune to be arrested, was released, since ' he humbly confesseth his fault of sending over iron cast ordinance into Spayne ' ;[4] but the war had changed everything and without it there would probably have continued that reign of old custom without scandal or bitterness.

After all, Drake had been an unlicensed pirate, and, as long as there was peace, certainly no one could complain if ordnance was sent over also to the Spanish Royal Navy ; yet the effect of these careless sales might well seem disastrous and a document among the ' adver- tisements ' sent from Spain in 1586 bears this out. ' The ships at Passage,' wrote the English agent,[5] ' have as yet but little ordnance

[1] Cal. Salisbury MSS., iii, p. 280.
[2] Acts of the Privy Council, 1587–8, p. 137.
[3] Cal. S.P. Foreign, 1577–8, p. 10.
[4] Acts of the Privy Council, 1580, p. 378.
[5] Cal. S.P. Foreign, 1585–6, p. 641.

and all they have is cast iron. What a blessing God hath bestowed upon our native country and how it has been abused ; all Christendom durst not look the navy of England in the face were they not replenished with English ordnance. God grant it may be treason the transporting any out of the realm that is for service either by sea or land.' There is already marked here the turning tide and then once the war had broken out the illegal export from the furnaces of the Sussex gentry ceased, but nevertheless, as the need became still more acute, foreign merchants came in to take their place in this traffic, a secret careful affair of false lading papers. But now it was a matter of treason at second remove, for, while it would seem that the patriotic squires were quite free from suspicion, the pressure on the middle man was increasing. An assertion in regard to this point, which is apparently well founded, was made by the investigator, John Borrell, who, writing in 1598,[1] demanded that the licence for Lord Buckhurst to export one thousand tons of ordnance to Flanders, France and Scotland should be withdrawn, because the pieces were transferred into ships bound for Portugal or for Spain and were used against England. He supported this contention with the statement that ships sailing from Spain for the Indies or for Brazil mostly carried ' cast pieces of iron,' and that men ' never see no cast ordnance of iron, but such as is made in England,' as all seafarers are agreed.

It was this new form of traffic which was in the background of all those troubles which were destined in time to threaten the Ordnance, for there were all the dubious merchants like Monsieur Michel Antrambly[2] of St. Malo, who had succeeded in obtaining £1,000 worth of guns, and behind them the chief Spanish agents, like Arteaga and Palafox,[3] with their much larger offers. The rate of purchase was high, twenty-two shillings the hundredweight for pieces of over fifteen hundredweight and nineteen shillings for all ordnance under that weight, while promises of a heavy deposit and suggestions of a life pension were mooted. It was a matter of neutral harbours, Hamburg and Rotterdam and perhaps this suggests remoteness and the Spanish letter which Juan de Ambias received[4] in the safety of

---

[1] Cal. Salisbury MSS., viii, p. 182.
[2] Acts of the Privy Council, 1596, p. 399.
[3] It should be noted that in this case the lateness of the information, a letter from Richard Tomson, dated April, 1593, throws some doubt upon the seriousness of the offer.
[4] Letter dated 10th April, 1591, from Richard Horton at Madrid to Juan de Ambias, attached to the suite of the Duke of Feria at Milan, ' Aqui recibimos cada dia in quantidad artileria de

THE ORDNANCE OFFICE AND GUNRUNNING

Milan seems more far away still and equally incapable of disturbing so solid and essentially English an office. Yet it was just this secret traffic, however remote and distant it sounds, which caused the uneasiness in the Ordnance Office, for it brought treason uncomfortably close and that was the ominous word which was to prove the downfall of Essex, who among his innumerable facets controlled the Ordnance at the end. Again, with their pressing need for an income, the Ordnance officials did not distinguish sufficiently between peace time and war, and this involved a system, not so much of definite and thought-out intrigue, as of a constant casting about in every direction which would seem to promise result. And then, when the old Earl of Warwick was dead, they received as their master the young Earl of Essex, while for some years the affairs of the office still ground onward slowly.

It is the appointment of a new Lieutenant-General in the person of Sir George Carew which has served to reveal to us the true state of affairs. Warwick had been old and aloof and Essex's wavering interests were still far away from these details of the basis of military life, but Carew was still a young man and methodical and one who could realize that there were alternative methods of bringing success to his office besides that blind acceptance which his seniors had always preferred. Sir George was one of the first of the courtiers to go down among the officials, entering as a stranger, as one whose round of life constantly led him away from his official house in the Minories and out west of the City to the pomp of the Court and to the library, where that antiquarian collection was forming, which of itself gave him the rank of a liberal patron of art. It was indeed a contrast from which there developed a struggle between the new Elizabethan Court manner and the honeycombed stronghold of a life, unpretentious and rooted, nor could it be doubted as to which was the stronger. For, although strange and sometimes devious men and far from the main stream of their time, the under officers of the Ordnance were yet the forerunners of the Civil Service and, beneath the ebb and flow of this tangled conflict, there arose the slow victory of the middle class.

The headquarters of the Ordnance were far from the Court, and it is only this new intrusion which can show us how strong the

Inglaterra por via de Lubeca, Embden, Bremen y Hamburgo, y lleban los mercadores de lla sin suspecho con navios cargatos de carbon. Todo haze il dinero.' Cal. Salisbury MSS., iv, p. 103.

bureaucracy in chrysalis had become. The appointment of Sir George Carew was made in the summer of 1592 and even ten months later he had not yet forced an entry. ' That which grieveth me,' he is found writing [1] in May, 1593, ' is the contemptible dealing of the keeper of the store, who (if he be an officer) is but to keep and deliver and not to comptroll or equal his authority with mine who (until Her Majesty make a Master) am the first in the office. Heretofore in the like unrespective manner he hath often used me, which I have swallowed.' But a year later a fuller understanding had come to him and we obtain a more complete picture of their strength. ' By the favour of your father,' wrote Carew to Sir Robert Cecil,[2] ' with your help unto Her Majesty, I was removed from my place in Ireland to the office which now I hold. To discourse unto you all my griefs were exceeding tedious, for I do not pass a day without new occasions and with infinite repentance for leaving my office there, which was of good profit . . . to wear my days in this troublesome place where I have at no time found either profit or ease ; and thereof you cannot marvel, the allowances being so small as they are and, which is worse, my fellows in office so corrupt and of such malicious spirits as but in hell I think their matches can hardly be found. That I have been a careful servant to Her Majesty your father doth partly understand, who doth know that before my time the Queen did pay far greater rates for her munitions than now. In other things I have corrected their accustomed abuses, so as to myself they have often complained that like the dog in the manger I did purpose both to starve myself and them, which has won me such hatred amongst them as I know when I shall offend in the least it shall not be forgotten in information to do me disgrace. Hope did persuade me that as their falsehoods were discovered and proved they would be displaced, but that hope is almost lost, for I understand Powell, under a pretence to do Her Majesty some service, doth assure himself to hold his place ; if he do the rest will be less afraid to commit falsehoods and the office will ever more remain in trouble. His hopes are builded upon your father's favour. . . . But if the office be so accursed that he must return, then shall I rest out of all hope to purge it from corruption and

---

[1] Letter from Sir George Carew dated at the Minories 16th May, 1593, and apparently addressed to Lord Burghley. Cal. Salisbury MSS., iv, p. 315.
[2] Letter from Sir George Carew dated at the Minories 30th June, 1594. Cal. Salisbury MSS., iv, p. 555.

infamy or to lead any quiet life in it.' The introduction of another courtier, Sir Edward Hoby, into these surroundings made Carew's position still more difficult as his letter of the following June makes clear. ' If possible I do beseech you,' he wrote again to Sir Robert Cecil,[1] ' to rid me of the late charge you imposed upon me. I hold it to be less cumbersome to rule the apes and bears in Paris Garden than to govern this one untamed Hoby (Sir Edward), who never yet could be brought to know his keeper longer than he pleased, nor be reclaimed from his haggardly wildness, by nature incident unto him ever since he was hatched.'

And then there comes a great change in the last letter of this strange correspondence. For by September it was clear that the permanent officials had conquered and it was Carew now who was forced to defend himself from their charges. He began by reminding Sir Robert that he had been ' long weary of this unquiet office, wherein is small profit and infinite vexations,' [2] and after asserting that ' the monstrous abuses he knows of in the office are reformed,' there appeared the first signs of alarm. He continued that he is told that the Queen is daily troubled with information and new devices, as if corruptions in the office were yet in their infancy and daily increasing, and this only wearies him in the service. This is no argument that he fears complaints out of guiltiness, but he would be glad in his soul if the Queen should command him to some other service and, if in arrears, he would repay the uttermost farthing. After the lofty style of his entry, this marks a contrast, the result of the strong bond of union which the Ordnance Office maintained, in spite of its internal seething feuds and its jealousies, in the face of the courtier. How aloof and remote had Sir George Carew ridden down to the Minories, determined to bring to calm order these shifty quill-driving clerks in the Tower, condescending and concealing politely those too cultured tastes which they could not be expected to share, and with his mind free from the desks to return to the pleasant thoughts of the ranks of his folios. But in five years they had worn him and now he was timidly offering to repay the last farthing.

---

[1] Letter of Sir George Carew to Sir Robert Cecil, dated 7th June, 1595. Cal. Salisbury MSS., v, p. 235.
[2] Letter of the same to the same, dated 14th September, 1595. *Ibid.*, v, p. 377. Details of Sir George Carew's service in Ireland and the state of the Ordnance Office there are provided in a note printed at the end of this volume, pp. 497–500.

And this was not the only disturbance which the Ordnance Office had strength to repel, since the intervention of Essex had no better fortune. It was in 1595 that he had accepted the Mastership [1] and gradually every influence among his great following bore its share in the development of the affairs of the Ordnance. In the first place, one of Essex's followers was appointed Surveyor, Sir John Davis, a soldier of fortune, who had ' served in France and the Portingal journey, in the Low Countries, almost four years, at Cales and the Islands.' [2] This was sufficient to prove him a valorous fighter, and it seemed hardly likely that the barricades of the Ordnance chamber would hold against one who had broken Cadiz. Then again Davis was a man of studious invention, which was itself an asset of value, when the apprenticeship to the study of cannon balls was the search for the philosopher's stone, and, if, behind the life of the zealous official, there was the entire region of his private affairs and his profitable marriage and bargains, across the whole of the background lay the dreamland of alchemy. He had also the reputation of a practical man of affairs and was in addition possessed of self-confidence as his application for office makes clear. ' I enclose,' wrote Sir John Davis [3] to Essex on this occasion, ' the short collections of my former studies in artillery, wherein, if I had but that practice, as this place doth of necessity draw a man unto, I would not doubt but in short time to discover the true effect of artillery more sufficiently than hitherto hath been by any of our nation.'

It would seem surely improbable that such a paragon should not succeed and at the outset Essex and Davis also found men ready to make revelations, a matter which was considered worthy of the casual thought of the patron, as an exchange of correspondence between his secretaries confirms. ' You know the multiplicity of his (Essex's) business at his being in England,' wrote [4] Mr. Temple to Mr. Reynolds, ' would not permit his honourable apprehension to descend unto the ordering of those meaner services. The lieutenant there is he unto whom my Lord hath committed the direction and carriage of the office during his absence : so as I marvel he refuseth to give order in

[1] He was already referred to as Master on 6th September, 1595. Cal. S.P. Dom., 1595-7, p. 99.
[2] Letter from Sir John Davis to the Earl Marshal Essex, dated 16th November, 1598. Cal. Salisbury MSS., viii, p. 440.
[3] Cal. Salisbury MSS., viii, p. 440.
[4] Letter dated August, 1599. *Ibid.*, ix, p. 340.

that behalf. There is a servant of my Lord's called Christopher Bird, a gunmaker and a man both very religious and very well acquainted with ordnance matters, having been a long time trained up in the Tower. I have recommended him for one who is able to do . . . special service in that place. Take knowledge of him he can discover many abuses.' And then the note of the Essex encroachment ' Sir John Davis and I have conferred.'

Nevertheless, in their own way his efforts were just as little availing as those of Carew had been and before long he had conflict with the Ordnance officials, while a letter from Sir George Carew's uncle, Mr. George Harvey, who had for many years served in the office, makes the whole position most clear. ' On the second of February last,' wrote Mr. Harvey [1] to Sir Robert Cecil, ' I was deputed to the lieutenancy of the Ordnance in the absence of Sir George Carew. I am and always have been very loth, so that her Majesty be truly served, to give distaste to any man, but now I must beseech your aid for suppressing such violent humours as are come amongst us. On Thursday the thirteenth of March, myself and the officers being in the office, Mr. Paulfreyman, this bearer, being sub-treasurer and speaking for her Majesty's benefit and Sir George Carew's security in paying of an allowance of £20 per annum to the keeper of the Store, given and set down . . . by the officers only, without any further warrant, it pleased Sir John Davis to call him a " saucy companion " and to say it was an indignity not to be endured by the officers. . . . Hereupon Sir John Davis growing in choler threatened to thrust him out and so rising from his stool took him by the shoulders and not being able of himself to do it, he called his servants William Scott and another ruffianly fellow whose name I know not into the office.' Then after a long recital he continued, ' I doubt not but Mr. Lieutenant (of the Tower) will avouch the same, also the indignity which before him Sir John Davis did offer me in saying that I was insolent and but a deputy. If these savage courses may have passage I shall not be able to do her Majesty the service which I willingly would.'

In the following autumn the dispute was carried yet further over the insufficiency of the principal wheeler and the respective duties of the lieutenant and yeomen. The officer had declared that he was ' a

---

[1] Letter dated 4th April, 1600. Cal. Salisbury MSS., x, pp. 100–1.

leader of men, not a leader of carts,'[1] and Mr. Harvey again wrote to Sir Robert that Sir John Davis, 'a shepstar's son hatched in Gutter Lane,'[2] plotted that no man should serve her Majesty in the office save himself and his followers. This dispute took place in the winter, while the troubles in London were growing and Essex was waiting, before the storm of his rising broke over the City and swept away in its passage his *protégé* Davis. But the real significance of these Ordnance quarrels does not lie in the leaders of struggle, like Carew and Davis, but in the influence of the permanent officers, whose power remained hidden, for, if it was the prevalence of corrupt practices which had caused the downfall of the courtiers, it was this very obscurity which allowed the officials to proceed with success. They did not desire to quarrel with the Court or the courtiers, for the nominees of the Queen had their sources of income with which they had no wish to tamper, as long as they were permitted to continue in peace their own search for a livelihood. But the interference of Carew or Davis meant conflict; for the Ordnance Office was organized in those ancient quarters, ' neighbouring the safest prisons in the Tower,' to carry on Her Majesty's business of the Ordnance and to keep the munitions well supplied, while providing an adequate living for the officers without any embarrassing tax upon the Queen. They were an interesting body of men, these Ordnance officers, each one so strongly entrenched that no scandal could move them, so that even the most stringent official inquiry would leave them untouched in their place and their ranking. During a lifetime together there was not one who had not at some time or other placed his reputation within the control of his neighbour and it is a result of a situation where all stand and fall together that the interlocked suspicions must produce a tranquil peace.

First of all there was Mr. John Lynewray who had served sixteen years in the office and had specialized in ' the discovery of abuses, forgeries and deceits.'[3] For the last six years he had been ' called forth on all great foreign services,' which is not surprising considering his previous interference with his senior colleague, Mr. Painter, ' when for four years he had been employed in searching out the strange

---

[1] Account of the conduct of the munition in 1600. Cal. Salisbury MSS., x, p. 457.
[2] Letter of Mr. Harvey to Sir Robert Cecil, dated 28th November, 1600. *Ibid.*, x, p. 399.
[3] Docquet of services in the Ordnance of John Linwray, 1601. Cal. Salisbury MSS., xi, .551.

forgeries and deceits used by Paynter and the rest whereby H.M. was defrauded in that office of £60,000.' It is easy to understand why, after this adventure, he preferred the prospect of service in foreign countries to the occasional asperities of office life. It was this same Anthony Painter who had contrived to make the position of Sir George Carew so difficult, and now aimed at the Surveyorship of the Ordnance, a post from which he could exercise control. He insisted on his qualifications and in particular on the very doubtful merit of ' having been brought up in that office ' [1] since a boy, and, like all his colleagues, he was not slow to rebut an accusation, charging Mr. Lynewray, his accuser, of defaulting with £7,000,[2] and in turn blaming all the deceits upon Mr. Powell. It is a matter for some surprise that this ancient man should still have been assisting at the Ordnance and all the more when under charges, like those which Mr. Painter preferred against him, so very sweeping and concise. It was now fourteen years since the conviction in the Court of Exchequer which Mr. Painter had had the good fortune to secure against Mr. Powell had ruffled their daily life in the office together, but at last the compiling of the docquet was completed and ' Mr. Powell's manifold embezzlements, deceits, selling her Majesties wages and much other abuse ' [3] was written clear.

And, behind these principal figures, there were the other officers, whose method of livelihood was not so spectacular, like the clerk of deliveries, Mr. George Hogg, who declared that many offences had been committed in the office of the Ordnance, as the record of the Exchequer could testify, but that he had always been free from attaint. Then in the background there was the venerable figure of Bagnoll, the clerk of the Ordnance, ' who had served most honestly in the office these thirty years,' but even he had taken his place with the others as ' a principal discoverer of many deceits.' [4] The figures of money, too, in the cross-accusations went mounting until the summit was reached in a letter from Harvey. In framing this further indictment

[1] Letter of Anthony Paynter to Sir Robert Cecil, dated 30th March, 1600. Cal. Salisbury MSS., x, p. 86.
[2] Letter of George Harvey to Sir Robert Cecil, dated 13th October, 1601, ' I may not neglect anything concerning the reputation of my nephew (Sir G. Carew) and therefore make bold to acquaint you with the lewd proceedings of one Anthony Painter, who, out of malice because he could not be surveyor hath preferred an information into the Exchequer against Mr. Lynewraye for an account of provisions amounting to £7,000.' *Ibid.*, xi, p. 426.
[3] Letter of Anthony Paynter to Sir Robert Cecil, 1601. Cal. Salisbury MSS., xi, p. 560.
[4] Letter of Sir Thomas Heneage to Sir Robert Cecil, dated 25th August, 1595. Cal. Salisbury MSS., v, p. 347.

he referred to ' Rowland and Painter's services wherein Her Majesty lost and was deceived almost £100,000,'[1] and then he went on to ask that ' the premises should be reformed,' but under the circumstances it is not unnatural that those who wished seriously for a reformation should have had to cherish such a hope in vain.

Here the methods and even the objectives were altered, but the *personnel* of the Ordnance outlasted all changes. In the first period the export was hardly concealed, and then, when war was declared, there had been a short interval when the traffic in guns was controlled by the factors, men like Novy of Shoreditch,[2] and finally, once this stage was over, it became a question of false bills of lading. The maintenance of a convenient official ignorance, which this last method must involve, was a simple affair for the officers and resulted for the Spaniards in great and immediate gain as the report of the purchase of vessels in 1601 has made clear. ' No ship ought to depart out of this realm,' so ran the paper,[3] ' before they have put in sufficient bonds for the bringing back of their ships and ordnance. Divers evil persons have most unnaturally, by colour of feigned voyages some for the Straits, some for Leghorn, Venice and other places, conveyed to the King of Spain divers tall and serviceable ships of England with all their ordnance. One was called the *Margaret* of London which was sold at Lisbon by Lucas Felix ; another called the *Pretence* alias the *Saint Andrew*, carried away by James Upgrave ; a ship called the *Refuge*, one Salesburie captain and John Links master ; another ship called the *Guift* of London ; another called the *John an Baptist* which was one of the best merchants' ships in England, she bore three tier of ordnance on a side, which ship with all her ordnance and furniture was sold to Philip Barnardo, an Italian merchant dwelling at Crutched Friars in London, who sent her on a voyage as it were for Italy, but she is now in Spain in the King's service. Another ship called the *Fox* of Horne, the master Simple Sunderark, took in 31 pieces of English ordnance in the Port of London and the rest of her lading at Dartmouth, who went from thence to St. Lucas in Spain and there

---

[1] *Ibid.*, x, p. 399.
[2] The Privy Council report on 8th September, 1591, that ' one Novy dwelling in Shore-dishe has been and is a daily conveyer and transporter of ordinance as well to her Majesty's enemies as to other places. He is himself of small ability and a dealer or factor in these matters.' Acts of the Privy Council, 1591–2, p. 430.
[3] Letter from William Hunt to Sir Robert Cecil, dated 1st August, 1601. Cal. Salisbury MSS., xi p. 314.

delivered all the said ordnance and other lading. Another ship of Hull, the owner Thomas Brian, laded in the Port of London great store of ordnance and other munition as it were for Melven, but it was all conveyed into Spain. A number of ships more as yet unknown are in the same predicament.' It is an important fact, when considering the illicit income of the Ordnance officers, that these ships nearly all sailed out from London Pool to the Spaniards.[1]

No economic disaster is so serious as that starvation of resources which an inadequate circulation brings about. The Ordnance Office with its thick parchment rolls and the big tables, where the water came dripping through the heavy and damp walls of the Tower, was the home of one of the first beginnings of the official middle class of the country. The England of Piers Plowman had vanished, ' to dig I am not able,' and the early history of the Ordnance Office mirrors the effect of the spectre of starvation upon the habits of a middle class.

---

[1] The case of Edmund Mathew of Radyr provides an instance of apparent gunrunning from Wales. On 5th April, 1602, orders were sent from the Privy Council ' to put down Edmond Mathewes esquier for casting any Ordnaunce at his ffurnace neere Cardiff in Wales because from that place very easilie they may be caried into Spayne. And if a due accompte be taken for v or vj yeares laste past, all ot the moste parte of Thordnaunce wch he hath made . . . shall be fownde to haue ben stolne beyonde Seaes, and the officers of that Porte are very poore men and such as dare not displease him.' State Papers, Dom. Eliz., cclxxxiii, 73.

CHAPTER XVIII

THE WELSH ASPECTS OF THE ESSEX RISING

The series of studies which form the last three chapters of this volume is centred around the Earl of Essex's public career. This favourite did not possess any capacity for continuous political action, but he has gained his importance from the fact that his talents made him a lodestar for the young men of his time. The first of the three chapters deals with the influence in Wales that he exercised, the second with his contact with the Celtic influence which the O'Neill represented, and the last with that new outlook in England in which the Spanish political influence is seen to have vanished at last. His sudden fall has revealed in very great detail the workings of his ' interest.'

In Wales Essex had the hereditary influence of the Devereux in Carmarthen and Pembroke which made him the spokesman of the Welshmen among the great lords. In addition his immediate household was filled with Welshmen, and he provided the prestige which was translated into active influence by Sir Gelli Meyrick his steward. The power of Essex in Wales is seen in the development of Sir Gelli Meyrick's career, while in the documents concerning his fall the influence and aspirations of the other Welsh groups are revealed. The Welsh military adventurers, whom Sir Roger Williams had led, the group of squires in the Southern Marches and the representatives of the older stocks in Central Wales thus stand contrasted. Behind them there are the younger sons of the North Welsh gentry, who already had a military connection with the Court. The legal standpoint of the members of the Court of the Marches is also seen opposed to that tenacious adherence to old custom which characterized the more remote Welshmen. A picture is thus provided of the shifting outlook and ambition of these conflicting Welsh groups who were never again to have the chance to come so close to the throne. Above them and rendering all their efforts vain was the Queen's favourite, Essex, whom they could use, but could not control. In the end it was his permanent careless *insouciance* which was to destroy him.

It is the natural result of the suffusion of a small and privileged group by certain well-defined and concrete ideas that in the course of time an Admirable Crichton should appear possessing all that the elect could strive for and desire. Thus Cecil and Walsingham were in a sense the creators of the Elizabethan system, but Philip Sidney and Essex were the fruits. Sidney was indeed the Bayard of the Elizabethans, but this very trait implied in him a certain quality of simplicity, in his case a cultivated and over decorative, but still chivalrous simplicity, which prevented a full absorption in the Renaissance mood.

336

THE WELSH ASPECTS OF THE ESSEX RISING

Robert Devereux, second Earl of Essex, was free from this handicap, for he would never have failed upon any occasion to wish to be wiser than the children of light. He was in fact the embodiment of all that the close Court circle might desire, adventurous with a great magnanimity, independent in mind and free, with a high and generous temper that needed magnificence. His gallantry gave satisfaction to those, who, having garnered the wisdom of the Egyptians, could pour out their treasures unhindered by the inhibitions of the mediæval Christian masque. Essex was thus the darling prodigy of the Elizabethan Age, which applauded and caressed and flattered and then Moloch-like consumed him.

His whole life was an adventure in freedom aided by his Italian-instilled ideas of an independent *magnifico* and although his father had been an Erastian on the Genevan model, this influence faded when Essex had left the stiff tutors at Chartley. He took his freedom, too, from the obligations in marriage and he went his way heedless of the power of the Ministers and he passed free of the Queen. And at the end, when he was pinioned and his followers were taken, he was the only one of the peers to be sacrificed and escaping at length from his friends as well as his enemies, he went forward to a future in whose existence he did not believe.

It was a development of the Italianate theories of the Court that Essex had few friends, but many supporters, and it was the detachment of his remote spirit that enabled these to be saved at the end. The Celtic imagination exercised a certain fascination upon him and he constantly used the Welsh squires in his service, while his English officials were in comparison kept at a distance and he was never fully understood by his equals. He was entirely aloof, relying on an unchanging wind of royal favour with the sails of his future full set for the Fortunate Isles ; but his supporters could not be expected to share his detachment.

To obtain an impression of the network of interests, with all the web of officials and agents that the career of the great lords implied, is usually exceedingly difficult, for it was in each case the result of a slow process of building and the shifting interests and the gradual dissolving of these local hierarchies can hardly be checked. Thus it is most difficult to visualize the ramifications of Leicester, who with Essex had the only great household whose administration impinged upon

THE CELTIC PEOPLES & RENAISSANCE EUROPE

Wales.[1] We can see something of Leicester's actions in his lordship of Denbigh, his harsh rule and oppressions and the form of his chief supporter Doctor Ellis Price of Plas Iolin with his white jacket and the broad turnover of his clerical calling, the lank yellow hair, the thin beard and the pious cast of the countenance of that long acquisitive face.[2] But everything else is in darkness, for Leicester died at peace and his system gradually faded, while with Essex the system was complete at the time of the Rising and in the light of that final catastrophe all the details stand clear.

An impression of Essex's surroundings and the degree to which his plans for revolt were connected with a refuge in Wales can be seen by studying his agents in the summer of 1600, the last year of his freedom. The Earl of Essex was at this time thirty-three years of age, although he looked younger, for he was tall and slight and fair skinned, with the trimmed close beard then in fashion.[3] He had in his manner a carefree arrogance that issued in quarrels, so that Cecil and Raleigh and many at the English Court were his enemies, while at the same time he inspired in his young contemporaries and even in his wife a constant affection, which he had not the power to return. His marital freedom brought him his most lasting opponents and the cases of Lady Mary Howard, Lady Southwell and Mrs. Russell united whole groups of Court families against him, but as long as the Queen's favour held he could regard them with a careless defiance as he followed his fortunate star.

It was partly this unheeding indifference which gave to his Welsh supporters such a power in his business, for someone must watch over his interests, and it chanced that, since Chartley was damp and there was no adequate house on his manors in Essex,[4] he had passed a considerable part of his boyhood at Lamphey. He had thus a neg-

---

[1] From 1595 until his death in January, 1601, the second Earl of Pembroke was often an invalid, and, although Lord President of Wales, was unable to exert a great influence. Besides all the interests of the Herberts were now centred in Wiltshire at Wilton. S.P. Dom. and Hatfield Papers, *passim*. Similarly the influence of the Earls of Worcester at Raglan did not become powerful till the seventeenth century, and Lady Russell, writing to Sir Robert Cecil in 1597, asserts that ' an inheritance of £10,000 . . . should be a sufficient portion for an Earl of so small revenue and so many children as the Earl of Worcester.' Cal. Salisbury MSS., vii, p. 267.

[2] From a portrait at Bodscallan described by Pennant in 1784 in his *Tour of Wales*, ii, p. 330.

[3] Description sent by the Ambassador Francesco Gradenigo in 1596. Cal. S.P. Venetian, p. 237.

[4] Nevertheless, Essex's influence in East Anglia was considerable. He held, for instance, the office of High Steward of Dunwich and in September, 1596, nominated a Parliamentary Burgess for that town. Cal. Dunwich Corporation MSS., pp. 82–5 ; while the details of the Essex Manors of his ancestor, Lord Ferrers, are preserved in a land survey of 1420–8. Cal. Essex MSS., p. 332.

THE WELSH ASPECTS OF THE ESSEX RISING

ligent familiarity with the heavy squires about Pembroke, as he rode out hawking among them, tall with his slim figure and the slight stoop of the shoulders and the jewel-sewn gloves from Paris in his slender and delicate hand.[1] At least he had more acquaintance with them than with the country gentry round Chartley, where honest Richard Bagot had a free rein in his local affairs,[2] but this Welsh connection brought profit and there was a most tedious increase of business and the acquaintances of his boyhood were ready to manage his interests, so with relief in his gesture he surrendered them into their grasp.

Three generations of Devereux had built up this connection, a constant record of labour thrown away at last by a prodigal. They were a family of Herefordshire squires, who had hoisted themselves by two strategical marriages [3] to the last rank of the poorer barons and then to the Earldom. Administrative offices carefully nursed were the foundation of their prosperity,[4] for the isolated, haphazard lands, agricultural holdings round Chartley, a couple of manors in Hereford and the Bourchier farms scattered in Essex could not of themselves provide for the pomp of magnificent state.[5] But the Chief Justiceship of South Wales had helped them to an influence in Carmarthen, mayoral appointments and the parliamentary election, and they had obtained from Bishop Barlow the episcopal palace at Lamphey, and this had gradually led on to borough influence throughout Wales. It was a solid basis of interest, and then at twenty the young Essex became the Queen's favourite and it acquired an added significance ; but the same cause, which increased his influence, led him

---

[1] According to Sir Henry Wotton's description.

[2] Bagot MSS., printed in Hist. MSS., Comm. Reports, iv, pp. 128–38. The only other Staffordshire gentleman of whose services he seems to have made use was Sir Walter Aston, who acted for him in 1590.   Cal. Bagot MSS., p. 138.

[3] Sir Walter Devereux became first Lord Ferrers of Chartley by marriage in 1461, while his son married Lady Cecilia Bourchier, sister to the last Earl of Essex.

[4] For the Devereux influence as High Steward of Builth see *Dialogue of the Government of Wales* by George Owen of Henllys and *The Description of Pembrokeshire*, where the eight Devereux livings in St. David's are mentioned, both printed in the *Cymmrodorion Records*, iii, pp. 185, and 1892, ii, p. 219. The mayoralty of Pembroke was in their control, see ' Letters and Papers of Henry VIII,' 1537, *passim*, and in 1537 Bishop Barlow was writing ' Griffith ap Owen and John Lewis the Treasurer . . . are loose livers and sworn chaplains and lovers of Lord Ferrers.' The first Earl of Essex in particular had much influence in his birth place, Carmarthen, being referred to as ' Gwallter a'r Devrasaid Iarl Caermyddin ' in an ode quoted in *Carmarthen Antiquarian Society's Transactions*, i, p. 135. Evidence for the Devereux influence in the nomination of burgesses for Parliament in Hereford is to be found in the Corporation MSS. of that city.

[5] Besides the property was always deeply encumbered, for in 1576 Essex's father owed £10,000 to the Queen and other debts of £25,473 and was forced to raise £10,000 by the sale of the lands he had been granted in Cornwall and Yorkshire and by 1590 Essex's own debts had reached £22,000.

339   z 2

THE CELTIC PEOPLES & RENAISSANCE EUROPE

to despise it. As a boy Essex, with his sister Dorothy and her raw, provincial lover, Tom Perrot, had been prudently kept by his mother at Lamphey,[1] a great house partly in ruins, which stood solitary and stranded upon those level windswept fields, which lie open to the Atlantic beyond Carmarthen Bay. There was no wide estate and not even a park around Lamphey Palace, which was destined to remain the unripened fruit of a sacrilege, so that it is not surprising that, when he came to his power and to that splendour which he had always desired, Essex seldom returned for long to this home of his childhood. But his Welsh acquaintance remained, clinging to his new-found prosperity, and in an inconsequent mood he left his patronage, and the fresh value it had gained, in their power. It was the direct result of this policy that when he had lost the royal favour and was standing at bay it was upon the support and advice of these Welshmen that he was forced to rely; but in studying this influence there appears at once the great divergence of character between them and their master which makes it more difficult to assess the trend of that personal power which Essex first exercised in indifference, but at last in desperation when there was no hope eastward of Wales.

Sir Roger Williams, who was dead at this time, had been the first of his Welshmen and had taken the young Essex at nineteen to the Portugal Fleet. He came of the Penrhos family, which he considered highly distinguished, and after a dubious youth, about which nothing quite certain is known, he had settled down as a fairly respectable soldier, exceedingly and recklessly brave, but with a judgement clouded by drink. In time he had even gained a position at Court, as a butt for the Queen's coarse humour,[2] a privilege to which the rest of his countrymen could never hope to attain. For ten years he had acted for Essex as agent and confidential adviser, until he died one night of a surfeit, leaving to his patron all he possessed,[3] the Spanish spoils which included £1,000 worth of jewels and his penniless cousins,

---

[1] Lady Essex, who had planned this delicate transition in her first husband's lifetime, was engaged in becoming Lord Leicester's third wife, while his second was living. In this the younger children would have been no assistance, but she kept her eldest daughter at Court, the beautiful and wanton Penelope.

[2] As in the anecdote, ' Fah, Williams pr'y-the begone thy bootes stinke,' reported in *The Merry Passages* of Sir Nicholas Lestrange. Harleian MSS. 6395, printed in part by the Camden Society, 1839, p. 47.

[3] Sydney Papers, i, p. 377. It is interesting to note Wotton's theory of Essex's rise. ' Always certain it is,' he wrote, ' that he (Leicester) drew him (Essex) into the fatal circle from a kind of resolved privateness at his house at Lampsis in South Wales.' Sir Henry Wotton, *A Parallell between the Earl of Essex and the Duke of Buckingham*, pp. 57-8.

the Meyricks, Gelli, Francis, Simon and John. Among these brothers Gelli Meyrick had been Steward since 1587, but it was only on Sir Roger's death that he came into real power, which was marked by the knighthood which Essex conferred on him after his able division of the spoils of Cadiz. Sir Gelli was fortunately the very last man to dream of burying his talents, and it was a curious situation into which Essex had incautiously drifted, for all the Welsh patronage went through the Steward and Sir Gelli, who in London was merely a factotum, in Wales was almost a viceroy.

Sir Gelli Meyrick was a man of parts, possessed of determination and leadership, some ten years older than his patron, brought up on his mother's manor at Hascard near Lamphey, quickwitted and penniless. His position as the son of a Bishop did not then carry the prestige that the rank later acquired, and he was only one of the six children of his father's stormy old age, when Chancellor Meyrick of St. David's had prudently married a gentleman's daughter. But it was a marriage without money behind it, for the sums were vanished [1] long since that he and his fellow canons had extorted by the robbery and sale of Church plate, and he only lived for three years as Queen Elizabeth's Bishop of Bangor. It was a fortunate hour in which the young Gelli was received into the household of the Devereux as attendant to Sir George, a weak and garrulous knight who lived on the bounty [2] of a nephew, Lord Essex. Besides, this position as youthful attendant and steward increased a pride in his rank and in the descent from the princes and Gelli never forgot that his father was an Esquire's son in the North, while the three allied clans of his kinsmen, Bodeon, Bodwrgan and Bodychan, arose in the background. It was fine, too, the House of Bodwrgan, with its two chimneys and the painted shield over the hearth and the lean-to byres and the sties, and the serving men coming from Malldraeth across the drained heather and through all, and above the Anglesea accent, the voice of the ' Esgwier.' [3]

This was the whole root of his unusual position which gave him

[1] They were spent on ' shameless whoredoms ' according to a letter of Meyrick's co-religionist Bishop Ferrar, printed curiously enough in Foxe's *Acts and Monuments*, vii, p. 17.
[2] A letter from Sir George Devereux to his nephew dated January, 1599, is typical. ' I might go beg, I know no friend that will give me a mile's meal. My host where I lie hath pawned all he hath to relieve me. These are the debts I owe £151. Friend me this once.' Cal. Salisbury MSS., ix, p. 52.
[3] Lewys Dwnn, *Visitation of Wales*, i, p. 137. Niceties were added to the Meyrick arms at this period including ' two porcupines passant argent incensed and unguled gules.'

a special value in the eyes of his master, for he was regarded as a mere soldier of fortune [1] in England, while in Wales he was admired and respected, but it was his misfortune that in this matter Essex followed the English. In the extreme divergence between the Welsh view and the English there are constant references to his poverty, like the comment that his brother Francis was ' horsekeeper to the Devereux ' [2] and the savage attack on Sir Gelli by Sir Anthony Ashley. The division of the spoils of Cadiz was the occasion on which the following diatribe was called forth. ' But I doubts these matters will be procrastinated unless you strike the stroke. I have sent you (Sir Robert Cecil) some two or three leaves in haste written of the discovery of Sir Gilly's late practice against me, vouchsafe the perusal. Excusing the errors escaped in writing and I dare warrant that before I have done with the gentleman I will make him fit to return whence he came, when his worship was first taken up by Sir George Devorax from playing at whippergundy (a Welsh play) in a poor red pair of hose, his father the priest Sir Richard not being of ability to maintain him otherwise.' [3]

We have here as later in the Arnold Depositions, with their scornful reference to ' the son of the priest,' a real factor in the English attitude towards Meyrick, due to a lingering recollection, not so much of a celibate sanctity as of a priest's bastard as socially the last rung of the ladder. But how far this was from the conceptions of Gelli and the Welshmen ; for he was not the son of one of the New Preachers (Yr Newydd) who had the long gloom of the Puritans with their trim burgess-like air, but his father's priesthood was ancestral. Rowland Meyrick was indeed fortuitously an Erastian Bishop, but before that he was a priest of the order of Ednowain of Llanbadarn, who was sketched by Giraldus, patriarchal and living on benefices, which had remained age-long in his stock. Such a man controlled the farmers of his country, superior in his knowledge of cattle and pleasuring himself in their households, for he came of great lords of the House of Llywelyn ap Heylin and own cousin to Tudor. Who could fail to respect him ?

It is these differences in outlook which only serve to reveal the

---

[1] Those who wished for a favour called him Sir Guyllyam, while his enemies contented themselves with Sir Gilly, but beyond his own borders the true pronunciation Sir Gaili Myerick was unknown.
[2] Cal. Salisbury MSS., x, p. 93.
[3] *Ibid.*, xxii, p. 584.

widening gulf that existed between the thoughts of Welsh soldiers, that insistence on their race's prowess and the value they placed on the lordship of their few bare acres of soil, as compared with the sophisticated minds of the courtiers. To the Welshman a cave would suggest the rock defended soil of Eryri, but to the courtiers the thought of a cave would mean only Boccaccio. This is borne out by the account of the House of Gwydir, in a rather earlier time, from Sir John Wynn's 'Memorials.' Meredith ap Jevan ap Robert came to Nantconway 'so that he should find elbow room in that vast country among the bondmen, for he had rather fight with outlaws and thieves than with his own blood and kindred, for if "I live in myne own house in Evioneth,[1] I must either kill mine own kinsmen or be killed by them." And this he said truly for John Owen ap John ap Meredith, in his father's time, had killed Howell ap Madoc Vaughan of Berkin, for no other quarrel, but for the mastery of the country and the first good morrow.' This was still the attitude of the Meyricks, Trevors and Salusburys, at least in the younger branches, where the servants in the manor farms struggled together, urged on by their masters. But to such a condition of life the minds of Essex and the cool sedate courtiers were quite unresponsive, for in place of these Celtic angers and wounds and the brave high lights of speech, they lived with a well-guarded intercourse smooth and deceptive and calm. Thus when united in opposition the English supporters of Essex favoured conspiracy, while the Welsh hoped for rebellion, and both these plans, separate and mingled, passed through that secret and aloof, but impetuous mind, on which all their hopes rested.

In considering their influence on Essex it is necessary to stress the simple and direct ideas of Sir Gelli, for here was neither diplomacy, nor a delicate balance of factors, since he was his lord's loyal supporter and surely ' the mastery of the country and the first good morrow ' was a sufficient reason for strife. This simplicity is seen in Sir Gelli's handling of the situation at Cadiz and in his later action on the Marches, while in Wales it was the source of his strength. In the attack on Cadiz he had of course a good share in the profits, but he also succeeded in concealing six hundred Barbary hides, an important line in silk stockings, a chest of plate with a hatful of pearl and some amber and

---

[1] This Anglicized form of Eifionydd, which Sir John Wynn uses, has an interesting counterpart in the transitional Iuionith, which appears in Leland's *Itinerary*, part vi, f. 47.

the contents of a mercer's shop in velvet and silks. When charged by Sir Anthony Ashley with this, he put in a most straightforward defence, explaining that it was a case of misguided family affection, for his brother ' being at the bridge, when the spoil of the quarter was made, received nothing,' so that he ' had sought to advantage himself ' by speculating in India hide, and both he and his brother had combined to obtain three hundred pairs of silk stockings to flood the market in London and had gained control of a mercer's shop, ' which was of small value . . . as I shall prove.'¹ And after this, when his patron's influence had saved him, he had made a reputation for prompt and determined action among the Essex House group. From that time, until his last fall, Essex would seem to have consulted him always, and there is much evidence of his power in Welsh matters. In a letter to Cecil, Sir Gelli declared that he was ' a bad writer,' and there is no reason to suppose that this was mere modesty, but what he lacked in accomplishments he made up for by shrewdness, and he possessed what were then the old-fashioned virtues, for, by nature a cattle raider, he spared his master's kine.²

It must have seemed so appropriate to him that in Wales he should be almost a Palatine and restore his clan's fortune, but in all that curious distorted mirror of the old Queen's romantic affection there are few things more strange. The favours which Sir Gelli Meyrick ground out heavily across the country, riding with his boots splashed to the thigh, would never have come near him but for the vanity of his aged sovereign and the effect now wrought upon her by the sight of the young Essex, slender and slightly stooping, with his back against the light. There was nothing less certain than Sir Gelli's power, which was like the unreal light of an eruption reflected in the sea ; but, although the royal passions might waver, the complaints sent in to London show that, while it lasted, it was felt.

According to a letter to Essex,³ ' most of those that wear your

¹ The charges of embezzlement and the defence are to be found in Cal. Salisbury MSS., vi, p. 568 and xiii, p. 582, while the counter-charges against Ashley appear in Cal. S.P. Dom., 1595–97, p. 283 *seq.*
² A letter from the Lord Admiral Howard to Essex is a real proof of this zeal. ' If you will have me to do for you anything Sir Gylyam Merrike shall not be more readier nor with more love to do it.' Cal. Salisbury MSS., vii, p. 444.
³ Cal. Salisbury MSS., viii, pp. 422–3. Two instances, a century apart, will show the persistence of the Welsh attachment to the ' Devrasiaid ' ; the fifteenth-century ode by Lewis Glyn Cothi, ' awdl i dri meib syr Thomas ab Rhosser,' Y Dosparth I, xiii, in honour of the Vaughans of Bredwardine and the Elizabethan poem by Davydd Benwyn, ' I syr William Herbert o St. Gilian,' Baglan MSS. 8, Cardiff Library.

honour's cloth in this country (of Wales) it is to have your honour's countenance and to be made sheriffs, lieutenants, stewards, subsidy men, searchers, sergeants on the sea, mustermen—everything is fish that comes to their net. When the last sheriffs were made, your Lordship should (have) come to your chamber and have said. " Lord Meryke, I have made all the sheriffs thou wouldst have me make in Wales save one." So with the officers and brags, they oppress all her Highness' poor subjects. When they are together about any bad matter they will say it is a shame for them all if they cannot make a jury, being the Earl of Essex's men, to serve their turns in Herefordshire, Brecknockshire, Carmarthenshire or Pembrokeshire.'

There are no sufficient grounds in this letter for any real accusation of tyranny, but the suggestion that Sir Gelly Meyrick exercised a determining power does not only rest on such private letters of grievance, but is reinforced by the statement of the high officials at Ludlow.[1] It was an influence exercised through the power of Essex with the Queen and depended in certain cases, as in the pricking of sheriffs, on the personal choice of the sovereign, while in others, where the posts were themselves unimportant, it was due to the refusal of the immediate patrons to risk making Essex an enemy. The Welshmen came to Meyrick for their advancement and he, using Essex's name as a lever, obtained for them offices, which men were unwilling to refuse to the favourite. All this would tend to increase the prestige of the master, and it was part of Essex's power, which he used with so much unconcern, that he was solely concerned through Sir Gelli with advancing his *protégés* and he would never stoop to consider, when promoting his followers, the enmities he would heedlessly rouse.

In the course of this process Sir Gelli Meyrick had come to fortune by reasonable stages and the first step had been the marriage in 1584 with a young and childless widow, Mrs. Gwynn of Llanelwedd, and in time he inherited also her father's house at Gladestry. Then Essex had procured for him Wigmore Castle, which became his chief home,[2]

---

[1] Sir Richard Lewkenor wrote to Secretary Cecil in 1601, ' I assure you that the fall of the Earl (of Essex) in those places where he was greatest is not grieved at, because I do generally hear that he was, and the rather by Sir Gelly Merrick's means, often very chargeable and burdensome unto them and Sir Gelly Merrick himself lived by such oppression and overruling over them that they do not only rejoice at his fall but curse him bitterly.' Cal. Salisbury MSS., xi, p. 44. But this was written when the men who had not received favours had come back to power.

[2] Richard Symons' *Diary*, p. 262.

and the parsonage of Knighton and a London house in St. Clement's. It was a leisured progress and Sir Gelli must have felt that Essex owed it to his own rank to advance him, and it caused no particular friction, except a sharp protest from Pembroke, which was later withdrawn, against his inclusion as lieutenant in his wife's county of Radnor.

The complaint of Lord Pembroke to Cecil throws light on the whole situation, showing Sir Gelli Meyrick as the subordinate, forceful and loyal. ' I understand,' wrote Pembroke,[1] ' that the letters I wrote to the lords were received by my Lord of Essex with scoffing laughter and my judgement disallowed as having omitted Sir Gilly Meyrick, a man by his lordship reputed most sufficient. . . . I know that Sir Gilly Meyrick is a knight ; I hear that he is rich ; I mislike not his credit and envy not his wealth ; but I know also that he is the Earl of Essex's household servant, not residing in Radnorshire and born and bred elsewhere, nor of kin to any there, only brought thither by marriage with his wife and she no inheritrix neither as I am informed.' As this letter shows, there was never any question of Sir Gelli acting as anything more than an agent, nor any suggestion of any independence in Wales. Thus had Essex died earlier the plans for a military rising would never have come to a head ; but it was part of Sir Gelli's character that he took a pleasure in struggles with a loyalty quite mediæval, which was in no way affected by the current ideas of his age, and if Essex should fail, through his diplomatic supporters in England, the Welshmen would save him. Thus in 1600 when Essex was again at liberty Sir Gelli Meyrick was more ready than ever to ride out in the quarrels and he made his own preparations. Those unobtrusive years, while he was becoming through his master a power in the country, had given a real opportunity, for while Essex's courtly advisers could predict a triumph of statecraft, he could take the field with his men. He saw the whole situation so simple and clear-cut, the old Queen and her high-born favourite and the new men plotting against him. His patron's enemies were his own, Raleigh and Secretary Cecil ; for who were they to compare with the blood of the Devereux and Llywelyn ap Heylin ?

To the careful diplomats who surrounded Essex any course was preferable to an open, armed struggle ; for men like Francis and

[1] Letter dated 26th June, 1598.   Cal. Salisbury MSS., viii, pp. 232–3.

THE WELSH ASPECTS OF THE ESSEX RISING

Anthony Bacon could well gauge the military power of the Cecils and to these experienced courtiers the whole future of Essex depended on the susceptibility of the old Queen to his influence. It was a situation delicately balanced, for there was always the possibility that the Queen's affection for the favourite would survive all his angers and sulks and those mad, rash actions, such as his sudden return from the Irish command, which had already given to his enemies such a powerful lever. But it was true that in a sense it was this same rash and feckless indifference that gave him his power with his sovereign, for this flickering of his youthful spirit was a salve to Elizabeth's vanity, until he defied her. There was always an appeal for the Queen in what was, at its best, Essex's very personal loyalty, and it was a pleasure for her to defend her friend from her servants. Failing the Queen, there was always the chance of Essex obtaining the ear of King James, and here the unknown factor was the influence of Secretary Cecil in Scotland. Yet it was not unwise to imagine that, with Elizabeth dead, the Cecil reign would be over, for no man could be Pope twice and the tastes of the King of Scotland were at the opposite pole from the Queen's. Even if this should imply some months of retirement surely they would ride into calm fortune with the turn of the tide. But, for all these plans to mature, one thing was essential, no armed force should be used, for they had an accurate gauge of the strength of support they could count on and they knew that if Essex rode armed, it would be on but a short journey to the water gate and the Tower.

It is notable also that these diplomatic supporters were the only members of his *entourage* who had a real knowledge of the thoughts of the Court, for the peers, like Southampton and Rutland, were young men blinded by an over romantic affection, who lived in a world with no place for reality. For the rest the Essex House circle, whether on the side of the secretarial staff or on that of Sir Gelli and his Welshmen, was quite out of touch with the Court, since they had no right of entry and only a distorted and second-hand knowledge of the life of the sovereign.

Sir Gelli Meyrick was thus quite unaware of these subtleties and all that he could see was the great Earl, his master, attacked and the Welsh with a power to defend him. He had in addition two qualities then most valuable for enrolling recruits, administrative experience as

Marshal of the army in Ulster, when Essex was Viceroy, and a wide tolerance not only of religious practice, but of theory. As a child of the Queen's Bishop, Sir Gelli had no actual leanings to Rome,[1] but he had seen certain aspects of the New Religion too close for enthusiasm. It was a great thing at that time, when so many of the squires were still Catholic, that a young soldier could find a commanding officer so free from all prejudice, a man who could enjoy as well as anyone the heavy coarse talk of the camp without blaspheming against the Faith of his fathers.

Even so, Sir Gelli Meyrick's purpose in forming these connections with the younger squires in Wales and the Marches and their motives for joining him were of course radically different. At every point in his life we find this great personal devotion to Essex and the determination to use force to support him, but the extent of the assistance that he could derive from the squires was never put to the test. In the case of the Catholics there had been a half permanent connection through the protection which he had afforded them from the ill-managed recusant fines, but even here it was hardly a question of an armed revolt being proposed to them. The Herefordshire squires, for instance, lived in a world infinitely remote from affairs, since they were accustomed to stay on their lands, and the prosperity of their orchards and fields gave them employment, unlike that bare hill manor soil which drove the Welsh to the capital. Nevertheless, the reports taken when the conspiracy broke show that there was strong support for Essex amongst them. According to the notary public, John Bird,[2] ' Roger Vaughan, John Seaborne of Sutton Esq of £600 in lands of Herefordshire and Roger Bodnam of Rodrasse (Rotherwas) in the same county, like many other justices and gentlemen, namely, Owen James alias Morgan, being matched with Sir Gelly and most inward of his secrets, have been and are held for most obstinate papists and all their wives ; and albeit some of them (by dispensation from the Pope for saving their fines according to the statute) may sometime be seen at church, yet never received they the Communion ; and by letters procured from the Earl (of Essex) stopped the course of

---

[1] Nevertheless, such converts to Catholicism as George Barlow, Sylvanus Scory and Sir Tobie Mathew had been reared in the new episcopal nurseries of St. David's, Hereford and Durham.
[2] Cal. Salisbury MSS., xi, pp. 106–8. The fact that John Bird had had twenty-eight years of State service does not of itself prove him veracious, but his evidence is in great part confirmed by the Bishop of Hereford's report.

law for indicting them by Sir Gelly's means; such was his power as no judges at the assizes could bring them under the laws and so live incorrigibly and are most dangerous to the state. Sir Gelly could not be ignorant that their houses were ever places of refuge of traitorous priests which labour the disturbance of the state and of mass mongers; by bearing out of whom and their adherents he made his corrupt gain of £400 or £500 yearly.' Still, in spite of these brave phrases as to the disturbance of the State, there was no group among whom Meyrick laboured who would have proved less hopeful for his master's cause, for in Herefordshire they had prosperity and not even the Civil Wars disturbed their quiet acres. The chances of realizing his plans increased as Sir Gelli moved westward.

It is a little further into the Welsh hills that there is found established the next group of dependents that the fall of Essex has revealed. But in this case there was a closer connection with the Earl's great household, the men concerned were neighbours and in one way agents, acting for Meyrick on his journeys, and there was over all a brooding sense of financial insecurity, which these remote hill manors so frequently suggest. At Llanthony, lying in those narrow high fields, which the mountains shadowed, it was very clear to the squires that, beyond their ungrateful and rockbound farmlands, they had nothing else to rely on save their noble friends and their swords. This was more profitable for Sir Gelli's endeavours than the English side of the March, where, whatever the Recusancy fines might come to, men lived in generous seasons, in the windless calm of the apple-heavy orchards, amid a soil which would never fail to yield its fruit.

Before studying the Llanthony group in the papers of the Arnold Deposition, it is necessary to give some impression of the informant from whom Cecil's information was derived. Paul de la Hay was an adventurer who had married one of the eight daughters of William Cecil, the owner of what they rather needlessly described as the mansion house of Alt-yr-Ynis, a manor farm in Monmouthshire within the hills. As far back as 1596 de la Hay had preyed upon old Lord Burghley's love of pedigree and the pretended relationship with the father had led to a precarious correspondence with the son. But Lord Burghley's character was singularly well balanced, for while he was devoted to the pursuit of genealogy he had a just appreciation of money values and would not pay even for the most courageous [1] flattery, except in kind. A feud with the Arnolds, who sought for fortune by a different road, was of long standing,[2] but nevertheless, de la Hay's report, backed up by local corroboration, is not without its value for Sir Gelli's ways. The unprejudiced preamble [3] explains that it is a cross-examination on points already verified by witnesses of Dame Margaret Arnold of Llanthony, of Mary Whore her daughter and of John Arnold her son, who was reputed to be her husband's child. After this the questionnaire begins and comes rapidly to the point. 'Did you Dame Margaret in rejoicing sort say " Mary, I always thought that God would hear my prayer in the behalf of that good Earl of Essex." And did you Dame Margaret or you John Arnold say, " I warrant that corrupt fellow the Secretary will rue the time that he ever opposed himself against the Earl of Essex." William Herbert of Walterston, gentleman, saith that he heard them use these words.

'Did you Dame Margaret at your table at Llanthony in Monmouthshire at dinner the 11 of December last say " Now the Court of Wards is ruled all by Coucks, cooks and none but coocks," naming Sir Robert Cecil to be a cook by his mother, Mr. Bacon the like, Mr. Coocke her Majesty's attorney and Mr. William Coocke. And did you say to Harry Prosser (gentleman, servant in livery to the Earl of Essex), he being at dinner with you, " Fellow," striking him on the shoulder, " be of good cheer, for shortly shalt thou see the lord and master to flourish, and also shalt thou never see a Cooke to bear office in that Court or elsewhere, and that shall we see shortly, if we live, for, I tell thee Harry, my son John knoweth more than a few men in Wales." Herbert was then at the table with the said Harry Prosser, Dame Margaret and her daughter Mary and Alice daughter of James Baskerville, Esquire. Two Welshmen and Philip the butler attended the table.'

After various other queries we come to the specific questions for

---

[1] In 1600 when writing to Cecil of a quarrel as to the wardship of the infant daughter of Mr. Barole of Bunshill, he states that while attending Divine Service he was ' violently pulled out of the seat in church belonging unto this house and where men now living did see Richard Cecil your " tresayle " use.' This is an audacity which even the French affectation of ' trisaieul ' cannot conceal. Cal. Salisbury MSS., xi, p. 413.

[2] ' Sir N. Arnold had brought a blind man as evidence of copyhold lands by the running water of Monnowe, as likely to be true as that within 60 years Themes did run where St. Gilles Church now standeth.' According to a letter of de la Hay in Cal. Salisbury MSS., xiv, p. 125.

[3] Depositions of 14th March, 1601. Cal. Salisbury MSS., xi, pp. 125–127.

John Arnold. 'How often were you in London before the 8 of February last ? How often during your abode repaired you to Essex's house and there had you any conference with him or with Sir Gilly Meyrick ? Herbert confesseth that William Watkyns of Longtown, steward of the said Arnold's courts, told him that Arnold lay in Southwark and by water commonly came every day to Essex's house to Sir Gilly Meyrick. It is well known that of late Arnold chiefly depended upon Gelly Meyrick, who as reported with Captain Lee or Captain Salisbury christened Arnold's son in London.' Finally there came this question, ' did you say " Before the corrupt Secretary so should have his will (as to ruin Essex) it would cost 1000 mens lives." and that the " Tower of London would be broken " ? ' After these assertions, which witnesses supported, there was added the following note, unassisted by any evidence, but provided to give a flavouring to the whole. ' Harry Prosser of Walterston is said to be one of those that killed one Mr. Powell of Radnorshire to pleasure Sir Gelly Meyrick and since killed one Stumppe of Walterston aforesaid. For the doing of these murders he was supported by Meyrick and he has never been tried for them.'

It is to be observed in connection with this inconclusive affair that the absence of Arnold in Wales at the time of the Rising saved him from penalty and the accusation from test. But if we abandon the last charges against Meyrick, as unsupported by evidence, there is still enough in the whole story to suggest a household where Sir Gelli was powerful and his patron's word law, for Prosser was certainly gentleman in livery to Essex and the Baskerville guests had a distant blood descent from the Devereux, before they were famous. However much we may distrust certain detail, this is a picture, blurred but perhaps not unlifelike, of those country manors where Meyrick would ride, the great man fresh from the Court and bearing good tidings. But it is to be noticed that these alliances never bore fruit, since Wales was not roused up for Essex and although Meyrick went sowing across the breadth of the country, no armed men sprang up from these dragon-born seeds.

Before considering Sir Gelli's more successful endeavours, a note of the talk of the serving men will give the sense of the changes when the speech of the manors found its way to the ale-house. The conversation in question, reported by Mr. Garnons of Crickadarn, one of those diligent inquirers whom Cecil's success had produced, shows accurately enough the mind of the Welsh serving men, dependents of the Radnorshire Vaughans, in the weeks when their master stabled in London, while the crisis was brewing. According to this letter a gentlewoman, who had been sitting in a low chamber by the ground within the court of the inn at the Sign of the Checker near Charing Cross, deposed [1] that ' she being alone sitting upon a chest near the window overheard a serving man under the window say to another, " Is great Robin out ? " " No," said the other, " I would he were and if he were he would make little Robin Rydeck and all his friends flee to the hedge." " Well," said the other, " a day will come that will pay for all. I can tell the man (Essex) hath many friends in many places of England and especially in the Welsh shires of Carmarthen, Pembroke and others adjoining as far as the sea coast, and I warrant he hath enow in Herefordshire, Radnorshire and other places as far as great Roger Vaughan goeth." " Yea," said the other, " all the Vaughans wholly and all Sir Gelly Meyricks friends." ' After this the informant adds a little less reliable evidence to tighten up and give a balance to the whole. ' Another time Mr. Powell of Carmarthenshire having said to this reporter that Sir Gelly Meyrick was now so stout that he would know nobody, she repeated the speech to Mrs. Powell. " Yea," said the latter, " the priests son hopeth for the day that I trust he shall never see." '

Here we see the links between Welshmen, the last remnant of that feudal outlook which bound together the lords and their vassals ; for Sir Gelli also would think of Great Vaughan and his kinsmen, phrases which to Essex's English supporters would seem merely barbaric. There was this same sense of the racial stocks of their chieftains, the blood of Bleddyn ap Cynvyn or Elystan Glodrydd, dim, ancestral princes, whose simple emblems still held together the clan in its branches. The boars' heads and the lions in the halls of these families were the symbols, weakening but not without power, of that unity which bound the nobles of Powys, each separated by the mountains, living with their flocks around them in the wooded folds of the hills. When Sir Gelli had ridden well past the border and had reached Radnorshire and the heart of his country, he had greater success and the measure of his good fortune was the sound of the grooms' voices,

[1] Cal. Salisbury MSS., xi, pp. 133–5.

Map of Radnorshire and the Central Marches.
The strongholds of Essex's Welsh supporters are marked as well as the chief Catholic houses on the English side of the Border.

Chirbury

MONTGOMERY
Lymore

Church Stretton

Newtown
·Kerry

Bishop's Castle
·Plowden

Wenlock Edge

Kerry Hill

Clun Forest

·Clun

Stokesay

R. Teme

Llanfair
·Waterdine

Leintwardine

LUDLOW

·Llanbister

Knighton

Brampton
Bryan

Abbey
Cwmhir

R. Lugg

Wigmore

Lingen

Orleton

R. Eithon

Radnor Forest

Presteigne

Llanvihangel nant Moylyn ·

.RADNOR

Kington

Leominster

Gladestry

·Hergest

.BUILTH

Bodenham

·Aberedw

·Rhos Goch

·Painscastle

·Sarnesfield

Crickadarn·

·Clyro
·Hay

·Bredwardine

The Black
Mountains

HEREFORD

R. Wye

The country within and to the west of the dotted line lies at an elevation of over 500 ft.

talking of Great Vaughan and his Welshmen in the court of a rich London Inn.

With the Herefordshire squires there had been only the ties of service rendered and received to bind them together, while with families, like the Arnolds at Llanthony, there was a common dependance on the work of the Essex estates, but in Radnorshire all was quite different. Here Sir Gelli could also rely, besides his power with his master, on the feeling of kinship of the older Welsh stocks, jealous of the Englishry and of the ever encroaching Courts of the Marches. The few English settlers were regarded with suspicion and became naturally Government agents, men like Mr. Fowler from Abbey Cwmhir, where Bishop Lee had established his Staffordshire kinsmen, and Mr. Bradshaw of Presteigne, the lieutenant, whose father had been steward[1] to the Sidneys and who had gained his power through the English service at Ludlow. All that was bizarre to English eyes in Sir Gelli appealed to these lost ' barons ' in Radnor, for he belonged to the high tribes of the North, and he was the heart friend of the Devrasaid, those powerful nobles. It was not a question of finding many supporters, for in that bare country the families were scattered and the old stock of Ferleix, those who carried the boars' heads of Cadwgan ap Elystan were inevitable leaders of that moorland and forest between the upper waters of the Severn and Wye, where the Teme and the Lugg and the Eithon pressed eastwards out of the hills. In the south there was the outpost of the Devereux in the Baskerville[2] house at Aber Edw and then further down the valley, where the Wye turns east to England, the open lands of Clyro, where Sir Gelli's cousin, the great Vaughan, guarded the entrance into Wales. And then, each controlling his own valley, there came Mynachdy and Pylaley of the Pryses, who shared the blood of Elystan with the Lloyds of Borthy Crwys, beyond the Brecknock border, and with the Broughtons in the north at Bishops' Castle on the skyline against the English March.[3]

Every phase was represented in this last union of the stock, for both the Anglicized Richard Broughton, that legal-minded, rather fastidious antiquarian, who had been a trustee for young Essex,[4]

---

[1] Cal. Salisbury MSS., viii, p. 232.
[2] Lewys Dwnn, *Visitation of Wales*, i, p. 257.
[3] For the sixteenth century Elystan kindred see Dwnn, i, pp. 140, 242, 252.
[4] Montgomery Collections, xiv, pp. 121–3 and State Papers Dom., 1591–7, *passim*, give details of his ventures in slate mines in Corndon Forest, the crown leases in Kery in which he dealt and his slow judicial and administrative career.

and the old Lloyd of Borth y Crwys, whom Lord Ferrers had employed
for the rougher kind of Welsh-speaking business, the bartering down
of the hill farmers' sheep, only represented two different facets of their
clan. Besides, the management of the county and of the rather
rudimentary official life of the district was controlled by the families
of Cadwgan ap Elystan; for not only were the Devereux affairs in
their hands, but the members for the borough and the county, James
Pryse and his cousin Stephen, belonged to this race, which also
numbered a clear majority of those few recurrent names in the rota
for Sheriff. Thus their common duties and their blood descent kept
them together and differences of outlook and fortune seemed trivial
when they remembered that they were of the high blood of the almost
Arthurian princes. And their memories went back beyond the legendary
mediæval glories of Ferllys to the earlier hold of their race, which
the great red marsh, the Rhos Goch, guarded, the standing stones of
Llys Ifor, last relic of the ' Imperial purple clad ' Ifor ap Severws.
This was an atmosphere with which Sir Gelli was familiar, the long
bardic chants of his childhood, and he knew it also from the stories
of his mother's grandfather's race. For himself of course he remembered that in Wales Gwynedd was always the leader and he preferred
more recent distinction like his illustrious cousinage with the roses of
Tudor. In the same way Sir Gelli was always acceptable to these
Radnorshire lords, for he had two characteristics, which marked him
apart from the meanly descended officials; there was no doubt that he
was of high noble blood, but happily much less noble than they, and
he was an aid against the encroaching power of the English, for it
was partly the cause of their deep-seated resentment the ribaldry with
which their tales would be heard in Ludlow or London. And in the
centre of this clanship there stood the house, which Sir Gelli's marriage
had brought him, the Court of Gladestry, so that Radnor was now all
linked together by the failing memories of a common ancestry and
by new ties of Devereux service.[1]

For all this riding about on Essex's service only strengthened the
old racial instinct of the Radnorshire squires, as they came passing

---

[1] Of course the English families like the Fowlers and Bradshaws and the Cornewalls of
Stanage stood altogether apart, remote from the Celtic life of the county. They more often
lived in the towns, as the Bradshaws did at Presteigne, and were supported by the small English
element, which the ecclesiastical jurisdiction of Hereford had brought to the townships. In
addition they had the assistance of one Welsh family, the Lewis', but these were bound up with
New Radnor, for their house at Harpston was close to its gates.

from Bishop's Castle, thirty miles away, to Gladestry, past Knighton where the bridge was built of stone, then by the mountain track which fell down to Llanelwedd or by the drying stones of the river bed, beneath the hanging woods, to the houses at Llanfair Waterdine. As in these ridings, so also in the pilgrimage of Sir Gelli's career, the Court of Gladestry was in a sense always the end of the journey, where he would plan for his tomb, the effigy recumbent and generous and the smooth marble pillars.[1] Sir Gelli would think, too, with that English veneer, which experience had brought to his nature, of how he would be carried out magnificent with the bier and the torches, along the four miles of his avenue, past the young oaks he had planted across the rise and fall of the sheep runs. No one in Radnor could equal what he was building for the tomb of Gladestry, and, when he had his supporting pillars and canopy and his new hatchment displayed, his own herds from Llanvihangel nant Moylyn would not be more amazed at his splendour than the lords of the county.

Here in Radnor Sir Gelli was fully at ease and could taste his good fortune. His wife's line were more powerful men than the Meyricks, but by how much he had surpassed them, as he sat at the high table in his hall at Gladestry, sipping his wine in the English fashion, with his men-at-arms crowding the gate, a lord among the chiefs of the country, but how much greater than they, for who in Radnorshire possessed a great starched ruff and a jewelled sword and who could equal his wealth ?

In this centre of Wales there was a support for the Devrasaid and dislike for the Cecils and a readiness to assist Meyrick's patron. But it was the difficulty of Sir Gelli's position that he had gone too far west, he had crossed the border, and it was very hard to make use of the Welshmen or to explain their cumbrous utility to the Essex House group, where the fine gentlemen lit with a touch of mockery their calm and sceptical talk. There they sat listening to Southampton and Essex, the guests of their patrons in the cave of Boccaccio, but this only made it impossible to bring in those who really almost lived in the caverns. It was the contrast between those Middle Ages, from which the Welsh had not yet departed, and the quick mind of the Italian Renaissance, for it was one of the minor tragedies of Essex

---

[1] Lord Lincoln applied for the pillars after Sir Gelli's fall as too fine for a traitor's tomb. Cal. Salisbury MSS., x, p. 38.

that those who are reared on Tasso and Ariosto can no longer sound the blast on Roland's horn.

But, before considering the other aspects of this inability to unite the Welsh supporters of Essex with the English, a digression dealing with the religious aspect of the case is essential. Essex we can see in his calm and indifference uniting all parties and, therefore, the chosen patron of Catholics, but the difference of outlook even in religion between the English and Welsh was too deep for one policy. The variation of attitude between the old English recusant squires and the Catholic members of the Essex House circle was sufficiently striking, but it was as nothing when compared with the gulf which divided Charles Danvers or Francis Tresham from the Radnorshire Vaughans, although these were both Catholic.

Essex's friends were in the main converts, familiar with the religion of the Imperial armies and with the Catholicism, hard riding, loose tongued, yet devoted, of the French *ligueur* captains. The pleasures of keen argument, the sharp logical conclusion of the Fathers of the Society and all the antique Roman splendour drew them; for it is sometimes forgotten that, before the time of Gibbon and the Encyclopædists, a taste for the classical antiquities was best satisfied within the Roman fold. But most attractive of all to them was the fact that, among the innumerable facets of that universal creed, Catholicism was in the sixteenth and seventeenth centuries the religion of the swordsmen of Europe and as such it set its seal upon their faith.

All the forces of the Catholic reaction played upon those cultivated circles in London and abroad, where the friends of Essex moved, and Wales was neglected. It was not a purposeful, but rather an almost necessary, neglect, for there was so much work and so few priests, and even when they had penetrated to the West the missionaries were absorbed by their ministry to the strong Catholic manors of the English March. Radnorshire had been far from an episcopal centre, remote from St. David's, to which its scattered parishes belonged, with no monastery of importance save Cwmhir, a house which had never entirely recovered since the times of Glendower and the flames of his rising. There were monastic granges dependent on Cwmhir, scattered across the breadth of the country, such as those at Mynachdy and Clyro and the Cistercians on their journeys supplied that duty of giving the sacraments, which the impoverished parish clergy, whose tithes had been granted away in England, could only barely fulfil. It was a religion deep-rooted and slow, and it lasted when the abbeys fell, so long as the monks and the old priests were living. But by 1600 they had all vanished and for their ministrations the people depended on such occasional visits as the priests from beyond the border could manage, riding into the mountains from the centres at Sarnesfield, Orleton or Lingen or from the Catholic houses beyond Leintwardine. Besides these men were English and foreigners and they could hardly make themselves clear. So we have the attitude of the Radnorshire squires, attached to the saints of their ancestors and to the solemn Communion and Shriving and to the protection of the Lord Michael the Angel, to whom they had put up so many shrines. They had all been baptized fairly with the Blessed Water, and they would have no dealings with ' Yr Newydd.' When the law commanded under pain of fine, they might go rarely to the local preaching, but more they would not do, nor was there insistence in this remote country. Men like the Great Vaughan were well determined that they would not drink, nor let their children drink, of the sacrament of the New Preachers' wine.

It was this remote standpoint and the foreign Welsh speech of their preference which governed and restricted the political usefulness of Sir Gelli's supporters. They were profoundly attached to the Tudors in their hazy and sanguine conception of the Welsh character of that race, but they could have no love for the Cecils and for that tight bureaucratic Government, handed on by Burghley and Walsingham. The appointments from the Court of the Marches, the lawyers and time-serving officials, mark a complete contrast to their rooted ancestral custom, and the keen search for the royal prerogatives, which the judges maintained, was a cold comfort for those who were bred on the thoughts of their illustrious lineage, with the bards praising their race. Under the Devereux, with the Welsh Queen relying once more on her nobles from Wales, there would be good times and a freer rule once the lords of high blood had returned. Thus it was a static and not a dynamic support that Sir Gelli obtained, for he could not bring such men into contact with Essex, nor could he move them. It would seem that this was the motive which induced him to support the plan of a refuge in Wales. He was quite out of touch with the inner Court circle and he knew his power with the

Welshry, and, if Essex would come down to Wales, his countrymen would support him. It was a strange plan and one which for Meyrick and Essex ended in tragedy, the case of an agent, loyal and courageous, striving to furnish a military force for the support of his master. Yet Sir Gelli could never fully grasp the significance of Essex House, the labyrinthine activities of that centre of all disaffection, for in time everyone came there who had any grievance, whether political, literary or religious against the ruling power.

The Cecil rule had been long and the young men had grown up beneath it and England has always needed a two-party system. There had been no rule of favourites or of ministers in the past which had proved quite so lengthy ; but of all these diverse currents Meyrick was unconscious as he sat with his Welsh friends, dependents of Essex, Captains Owen and John Salusbury, those excellent swordsmen, in Peter Wynn's lodgings [1] at the back of St. Clements. There they could speak and plan as if they were back in their country and their master's future was dependent upon their own prowess. If Essex would come down amongst them it would seem so easy a matter to raise the Welsh counties, for the Radnorshire squires were only a single instance and they had friends scattered through Wales from Caernarvon to Pembroke. This was their plan then, an open rebellion, a *coup d'état*, not against the Queen, but the Government. In Essex House and Drury House and in the dependencies of these great lords, round Charing Cross, there were other cabals and scheming, but above and untouched by them all Essex passed remote and indifferent. It seemed natural to him that a great man should have clients and enemies, yet both of these groups were the cause of his downfall. A contemporary pamphlet on Essex's death suggests something of this aloofness, the difference in quality of his spirit, for its very title, the ' Finding of the Rayned Deer ' portrays him. It is the fate of such creatures to perish and the ' Rayned Deer ' foundered at last.

[1] Cal. Salisbury MSS., x, pp. 42–3.

CHAPTER XIX

ESSEX IN IRELAND

The rule of Essex in Ireland has been worked out in some detail, since it is particularly notable in showing the now established power of the Settlers and because of the change in Essex's policy when he actually met with Tyrone. As far as the O'Neills were concerned, this was the last great success of the reign and the attitude of the Earl of Tyrone shows the farthest stage that they advanced in 'civility.' Already there is a great contrast between Tyrone's standpoint and the attitude of Shane O'Neill, which was discussed in the seventh chapter on Archbishop Creagh. Turlough O'Neill, who had been the power in the northern background to Sir John Perrot's rule, was in a midway position between them. It is of note that it was at this moment when Tyrone succeeded in exercising his influence on Essex that he himself was subject most completely to the influence, or rather the fascination, of Spain.

In the case of the official classes at Dublin the power of the Settlers, which was on the increase during the Baltinglas and Nugent rebellions and which proved triumphant against Lord Deputy Perrot, had now reached its apex. The attitude of Ormonde, which was considered during the Grey de Wilton and Perrot *régimes,* had still further hardened with age in its opposition to the Gaelic life of his country.

At the same time the more irresponsible elements, among Essex's following, whose rise to power has just been described, coalesced in this adventure and it was in Dublin that the alliance became firm between the Welshmen and Essex's English military friends. In the background, while the Viceroy was marching, there were two forces in waiting, the Government patient in London and the new English Settlers. In contrast to those Celtic influences, which now helped to sway Essex, these two powers in essentials agreed. This six months' journey in Ireland was in fact an attempt by Essex, aided by the forces from the Celtic fringes whose power would so soon disappear, to recoup by a military victory his political fortunes.

IT is a strange contrast that arises between the staid and careful Government of the settlers in Ireland and the sudden, adventurous irruption of Essex; between that slowly moving and laboriously constructed machine, through which the settlers obtained a sufficient wealth from the country, and the chance following of this inconsequent viceroy, the soldierly vagabonds and the amazed, but still polite, courtiers. The decision to come to Ireland had been the unconsidered result of a Council Board quarrel, one of the fruits of an unreflecting and careless bravado, which caused Essex to desire the Viceroyalty to recoup his political fortunes. Among all the rulers of

Ireland the Earl of Essex alone set out for that country with the sole intention of achieving a military glory, and yet there were few other governors who have proved so ineffective.

For this brief episode contains at the same time the last successes of that mounting, free Celtic spirit, which dominated one facet of the mind of Tyrone, and also the beginnings of an organized conspiracy in Essex's favour. At the moment when the Irish were weaving counter-plots against Dublin, the Viceroy's followers were thinking of London and the overthrow of the Government, but the actions of both were dominated by that prudent and now permanent group of the Dublin officials and settlers, who attended to their immediate interests amid all this chimera. Essex was to die on the scaffold and Tyrone was to vanish from Ireland with the Flight of the Earls, but the settlers continued unmoving for they had factors on their side which their adversaries did not possess, time and the power of slow thought, and these gave them the country. If the deputyship of Perrot shows that opposition to the settlers could lead only to ruin, that of Essex has proved that no solid achievement was possible without their assistance, and if the success of Mountjoy's rule was contrasted this was in part because he was always known as their friend.

For Essex, time was the factor on which everything now depended, since a speedy victory was essential to enable him to come home to the Court as a conqueror, so that for him an immediate defeat of Tyrone was imperative; while what the settlers required was the destruction of the power of the Irish, which if necessary could delay for a period, as long as it should in the end be permanent and complete. Thus the settlers had come to Dublin to make their fortunes in Ireland, but the friends of Essex had crossed to Ireland to make their fortune in London, which was a much more difficult thing. As long as military affairs should go well, Essex's entourage would bear their temporary exile in the hope of a rapid return to England with the power to form Government; but when the victory was delayed they began to drift into dangerous courses. Essex intended to return swiftly to London and, as Cecil's enemy and a victorious leader, he would replace him in the Queen's confidence: now two things were essential, he must return home very soon and he must obtain the Queen's confidence, but his ignorance as to how this was to happen is merely another evidence of the loose threads of his thought. It was at this juncture, while their leader was carefree, that the Earl's supporters formed plans, while Tyrone and the Irish temporized and in the background the settlers waited.

It was raining, and already the ' dead of the night ' of 10th April, 1599, the Thursday in Easter Week, that Essex reached Beaumaris, after he had pressed the new post horses from Aberconway over the last stages of his road. The journey had been tempestuous ' over Penmaenmawr in the worst way and the extremest wet I have endured,' [1] with intervals of a calm April, as when he had found a light breeze at sunset that same evening, which had carried the *Popinjay* and the other naval pinnace across Beaumaris Bay. Ever since leaving Chester he had been in doubt as to whether he should follow the land route [2] with his soldiers or sail in the pinnaces, which were then stormbound in the Dee. There had already been difficulties with the Queen, which made his conquest harder and he was suffering from ague, and from every point, whether in the main cabin of the *Popinjay* in Hilbrey Harbour, or at the different houses along the road, he would pour out letters, despatching courier after courier to London, and writing with equal openness, both to his enemies and to his friends, heedless of consequence. After his brief angers and hopes, he would return again to the tale of his sickness, for ' neither can rheumatick body promise itself that health in a rotten moist country.' [3] This was a great part of the difficulty, for although he was only in his thirty-fourth year, and retained all his carefree indifference, his health was already doubtful, [4] and he was leading a whole body of gentlemen, who had followed him so readily when he was sailing through that warm clear weather in the ' Indian Seas.' But then they were all volunteers eager to have the honour to serve under his Lordship, and every engagement meant plunder, while now they had to wait in quarters at Dublin and deal with the settlers, before they could even get at the ' savages ' and this in ' a rotten moist country.'

At Beaumaris, Sir Richard Bulkeley entertained Essex with splendour, while all day the rain came driving down against the new

---

[1] Cal. S.P. Irel., 1599–1600, pp. 2–12 for an account of this journey, supported by Essex's letters in Cal. Salisbury MSS., ix.

[2] ' There be four score horses laid at every post, twixt this (London) and Chester and so to Holyhead, for him and his followers and as many by the way of Bristow.' Chamberlain's Letters, p. 49.

[3] Cal. S.P. Irel., 1599–1600, p. 1.

[4] On 29th November, 1599, it had been reported that the Earl of Essex was extreme ill of the stone, which takes from him all rest. Sydney Papers, ii, p. 145.

leaded panes and the winds prevented his sailing. As it was, in the end the passage was stormy, and Essex was forced ashore with his gentlemen near Lord Howth's house, eight miles from Dublin;[1] and on the fourteenth he made his state entry, with all his staff and the latest fashions from Court, so that the Irish were amazed at the great sixteen-pleated ruffs and the new short cloaks, the mandillians fringed with glass bugles and the fantastic, opulent swords. Here were no petty soldiers of fortune, but the favoured of Nonsuch and Greenwich,[2] courtiers who were proud to call cousin with such ' a prime man of nobility ' as the new Lord Lieutenant. Two Earls, Southampton and Rutland, each with his following, were attached to this party and there was such movement and bustle that it might have been Cadiz that they had come to despoil, instead of the friendly city of Dublin. The Irish were impressed by display which left the settlers unmoved, and the rhymers set to work to record the effect of this richness. It is curious that from this adventure there remains but one memorial, for, in a slight engagement in the hills with the rebels, the plumed hats of some of these courtiers were lost in retreat and these remote high fields in Wicklow became known as the Pass of the Feathers.

At the same time as Essex was making his state entry, Sir Henry Wallop, the Treasurer, lay in his agony at his house in Dublin, and at eight o'clock that evening he died ; while a few days later the Earl of Kildare, following the Lord Lieutenant, was drowned in the Irish Channel in the wreck of the packet, a barque of thirteen tons, on the Thursday, ' the night whereof was so tempestuous.'[3] But these changes, so significant for the settlers and for the Anglo-Irish, meant nothing to Essex, who was merely using the country as a battlefield, which would lead him to favour. In his correspondence he hardly referred to them, but was still occupied solely with his supporters, so that his view of the situation was not that of a governor, but of a general, whose outlook was bounded by the immediate needs of his staff.

[1] Cal. Salisbury MSS., ix, p. 134.
[2] Chamberlain had written that Essex ' shall carry a great troop of gallants with him, if all go that are spoken of, as the Earls of Derby, Rutland and Southampton, the Lords Windsor, Grey, Audley and Cromwell, who stands to be Marshall of the Army, besides knights sans nomber, Sir Ferdinando Gorge, Sir Henry Davers, Sir Charles Davers, Sir Charles Percy, Sir Charles Blunt, Sir Thomas Egerton, Sir Thomas Germin, Sir Alexander Ratcliffe and I know not how many more.' Letters, Camden Society, 1861, p. 38.
[3] Letter of Sir Anthony Standen to Sir Robert Cecil. Cal. Salisbury MSS., ix, p. 144.

ESSEX IN IRELAND

It was in connection with his great train of followers that Essex's first clash with the Queen had occurred. By his unusually wide patent he was enabled to make many appointments, but not those to the Council in Ireland, yet when he reached Dublin it was just these higher appointments that he was anxious to fill, to remove his friends from the interference and control of the local officials. The first contest was over a place in the Council for Essex's stepfather, the Marshal, Sir Christopher Blount, which the Queen refused to concede. Then, before he could forget this setback, there came a second refusal to accept the Earl of Southampton as General of the Horse, and then an order to send home Lord Rutland, who had come 'without Her Majesty's leave.' And these jars came before he could set his army in motion, with a suggestion from the Council that the sands were fast running out and a note of bitterness, too, in their letter, when they spoke of his support of his friends, 'in receiving them you have done amiss.'[1] These quarrels also had a lasting effect, for the friends, whom the Government had insulted, remained about Essex to provoke that anger, which came so easily[2] to him, and to make plans for close self-protection, to make themselves safe from the Crown. Yet amid all these quarrels and the arrogance and the heat they engendered, the experienced Castle officials were patient. They did not conspire, they did not even complain against the Queen's Governor, but they waited with that patience, which Irish life had taught them, for the coming of the clearly seen end.

It would of course be false to suggest that Cecil received no advices, and he had naturally taken the precaution to place about Essex's table a few exceptionally trusted personal agents, but there was no movement against him; yet there was what was in the end to prove even more damning, the calm recital and the dispassionate collation of all that was transitory and vehement in his mood. On coming to Ireland Essex had found Tyrone in the North, seven miles beyond Newry, hidden in the bog-circled forest of his intricate fortress, protected by this wettest of Aprils and by the still slowly rising rivers and the not yet ended rain. In the South there was Tyrone's vassal, the Sugan Earl, who held that great name of Desmond, which for the Eliza-

[1] Letter of the Privy Council to Essex, dated 13th May.   Cal. S.P. Irel., 1599–1600, p. 34.
[2] Twelve years earlier in a letter to Lord Willoughby dated 30th July, 1587, Martin Frobisher had declared that 'my lord of Essekes was gone in a feume from the Courte as fare as Margate.'   Cal. Ancaster MSS., p. 49.

bethans had filled all their childhood, and southwards also there was Ormonde. The lesser victory would prepare for the greater, for that harrying of the North when the ground had hardened and then Tyrone's life would be spared and Essex would only need to gather the fruits of his conquest. Meanwhile Ormonde would supply the local knowledge and his own troops the courage and skill, for Essex always maintained the firmest and proudest belief in the military quality of his friends. There was much to recommend Ormonde to him, a man of experience, not in Essex's eyes very clever, and, although of most ancient lineage, his inferior in rank. All the difficulties that he had had with Lord Nottingham were over, for no one could dispute in precedence with the Viceroy and this was an essential to the full development of magnificence, as the Italians would have conceived. So he took his way southwards, writing to London of his coming campaign against that 'unwieldy coward'[1] Mountgarret, and the citizens breathed more freely as his great train moved out of Dublin, with its still unresolved jealousies.

The Earl of Ormonde was now entering the last phase of his rule, and, as he approached seventy, any hope or misgiving or indeed any serious interest in these successive governors from England was over. It had long been clear that, however much the Queen might value his services, she would never entrust him with the government of the country, and his own life was now centred on his still active rule in the Ormondes and over the manipulation of the Butlers in the face of conspiracy. The sense of order and the prudence of his old age and, perhaps more than all else, his innate distaste for Catholicism had always kept him from the acceptance of any rebel proposal. Yet the rest of his clan were constantly shifting from loyalty into rebellion ; for in the more important revolts it was necessary that the Butlers should have representatives of standing in the ranks of the rebels, and it is noteworthy the great importance that the native Irish attached to those peerages, which the King had conferred. When they went out into revolt, they might abandon their earldoms, but all these titles were the price that they had been able to extort from the English and as such a guarantee of their worth. In this latest revolt, after the defeat of the Blackwater, Ormonde's cousin, Edmund, second

---

[1] Letter of Essex to the Privy Council, dated 28th April. Cal. S.P. Irel., 1599–1600, p. 20. *Cf.* Sir Warham St. Leger's reference to Lords Roche and Mountgarret, 'both are old and unwieldy and have good store of land.' *Ibid.*, p. 27.

Viscount Mountgarret had gone to represent the Butlers in the plans of O'Neill. Now that the new governor proposed to march down through Leinster, it was prudent that Mountgarret should be recalled and his penitence vouched for by the ever loyal chief of his family. As far as Essex personally was concerned, Ormonde was perfectly informed of everything that had led to this journey. They were of different generations and without any sympathy ; but Essex in Ireland could not survive unless he was supported and Ormonde stood by, detached and observant, but he did not feel called on to give any special assistance.

The march southward began, and Ormonde brought nine hundred men to the meeting, and there was also the fortunate submission of his cousin Mountgarret. It was six months since this old peer had sided heavily with the rebellion, entertaining at his house at Bally-ragget those who favoured the most desperate courses and marrying his eldest son to the ' Northern Traitor's ' daughter, Lady Margaret O'Neill. A system of alliance had arisen and all his daughters [1] were bespoken in the chief houses of Ireland and he thought himself of the Earldom of Ormonde, for he had ' a great sting [2] of mind ' against his cousin the Earl. It is true of course that, had O'Neill been entirely successful, there might have been this change in the Butlers, but Ormonde knew that a complete victory was out of the question and short of that he was safe. As a matter of fact the first movements from England had brought Mountgarret to reason and these great plans and alliances vanished and the Butlers once more provided a united support for the Crown. Only the younger men were still out and this involved Essex in a minor action, the reduction of Cahir Castle, which was made all the easier because Lord Cahir, who was a brother-in-law of Mountgarret and one of the new Butler peers, had already submitted. There would seem to have been a good deal of play-acting [3] in both these submissions and in any case to bring the

---

[1] His daughters described as Margaret, Marie, Marget, Elish and Joan had been suggested as brides, the first for Desmond, the second for Kavanagh, the fourth for O'Donnell and the fifth for O'Moore. His sons, Richard, James, Edward, Thomas, Theobald, John and Gilbert followed their father ; but it was said that long before Mountgarret came out ' he had long covered the sparkles of rebellion in the hid ashes of dissimulation,' and that ' all this time he went about the bush and pretended the Queen's service.' He asserted that when the Lord Lieutenant had sent him prisoner to Dublin he commanded the horsemen to cut his head off by the way. MS. History in State Papers, Eliz. Irel., vol. ccv, 74.

[2] Cal. S.P. Irel., 1598–9, p. 338.

[3] A letter from Mountgarret to St. Leger, dated 24th May, runs as follows. ' For so it is that by the prosecution of my Lord of Ormond in doing me hurt, I am driven to run for my life

Butlers into line with Ormonde was not an important achievement, since the allegiance of the head of the family was never in doubt ; but such as it was it would prove Essex's only success.

As he rode south, through this unfamiliar country, Essex became more and more dependent upon his personal friends, whose military quality he rated so highly, and he was still sanguine ; for he was away from Dublin and correspondence diminished and he always hoped that Ormonde would show him the Sugan Earl, so that there could be a spectacular capture. ' The advantage that we have,' as he wrote from Kilkenny, ' is in our horse, which will command all champaigns, in our order, which the savages have not ; and in the extraordinary courage and spirit of our men of quality.' [1] This represented perhaps his last moment of calm, as he sat in the tapestried room at Kilkenny with the great trees and the plain and that peaceful river. It seemed, as they sat together in their high chairs of state, carved and elaborate, with the worked leather panels, that with Ormonde's aid he might carry success, for outside was a scene as quiet almost as England, ' champaign country,' and beside him was his now aged host with the white beard and the old-fashioned courtesy, who would certainly prove a sure guide to the ' savages.' Whether it was that such a description as ' savages,' when applied to his kinsmen and friends, did not seem amusing, or whether he saw too clearly how little these English swords could achieve, Ormonde said nothing ; he did not guide the campaign and Essex passed on his way.

From the first his expedition seemed hopeless, for the rebels never stirred from the edge of their woods ' further than an old hunted hare doth from her covert for relief.' [2] All the same, they were ready to harry the stragglers and to cut off an independent party riding alone, and it was in this way that Sir Thomas Norris, the President of Munster, was attacked and wounded on 30th May, as he rode home from Buttevant. From Clonmell and Cahir, Essex's army pushed on to Askeaton and then he turned back and marched to the coast at Dungarvan. On his flank there hung the White Knight, who was royal sheriff of Cork, but whose loyalty was justly suspected, and

among those whose company I least desire. I was assuredly advertised that he procured the Council's commandment for the apprehension of my children and myself, only to rid us of our lives.' Cal. Salisbury MSS., ix, p. 140.

[1] Letter of Essex to the Privy Council, dated 20th May. Cal. S.P. Irel., 1599–1600, p. 36.

[2] Harington, *Nugæ Antiquæ*, i, pp. 278–80.

in a horse litter beside him was the President Norris suffering from a wound at the base of the jaw bone. The Sugan Earl had abandoned his stronghold at Connaghe and retired to the woods and all the greater men in the South kept an uneasy and sterile semblance of loyalty. Then Sir Thomas Norris' wound began festering and he was carried to Mallow to die, while his brother, Henry Norris, the Colonel-General, was hit in a chance encounter which likewise proved fatal. And there was nothing to set off against the deaths and these losses, no victory in the open and not even an independent rebel submission. Kilkenny seemed far away, as Essex marched up and down on the edge of the impenetrable Forest of Desmond, and every day his army grew smaller, partly by the garrisons, which he detailed to hold all the fortified towns, and also to some extent through desertion. At last, when June was already advanced, the army marched into Water-ford and found once more a prosperous city, with wine and good bedding; but there were also letters waiting for Essex and certain news from the Queen. In the first place Sir Henry Harrington's force had been defeated in Wicklow by the kernes of Phelim McFeagh O'Byrne, although they had especially sent forward 'a rhymer to feed (this chief) with fair words.'[1] There was also the first sign of doubt as to Essex's policy on the part of his Irish officials, as Sir George Carew's letter to Cecil makes clear,[2] and finally there was a harsh note from the Privy Council and another rebuke in the long list of complaints against his use of Southampton.

His recollection of all these past quarrels was hazy, as he marched through the South, and he thought them forgotten; but his farewell to the Queen had been angry and every month they were drifting apart. Essex had written, before leaving Dublin, to ask for more swords, and the tone of the Councillors' letter well reflected the hardening mind of their Sovereign. 'For the swords desired by your Lordship (which you know well is a new demand and must pass by a new warrant under Her Majesty's hand) we must say this unto your Lordship,' wrote the Council from London, 'that in respect you had a provision in surplusage of arms, when you first went over, we did not expect to have been driven to deal with the Queen so soon

---

[1] Letter of Harrington to Lord Chancellor Loftus. Cal. S.P. Irel., 1599–1600, pp. 58–60.
[2] He asked for two months' more pay for the soldiers, for 'either the soldiers must be cessed on the country or else feed on the Queen's victuals, which ought to be preserved until Essex's journey into the North.' Ibid., p. 32.

for any extraordinary demands of that kind.'[1] The second letter concerning Southampton was in a still harsher vein, and ran, ' Her Majesty is much displeased . . . and taketh it offensively that you would appoint his Lordship to that place and advice, considering that Her Majesty did not only deny it . . . but gave you an express prohibition to the contrary that he should not be appointed thereunto.'[2]

The immediate reaction to these letters was an outburst of affection for his personal friends, who were ready to sacrifice so much in his service. The high Renaissance mood rode Essex again in the face of these pricking, clogging officials and his reply rings like a challenge as he set out for Dublin to punish, with a Roman severity, the loss of discipline in his triumphant war. ' I am now hastening back to Dublin,' wrote Essex, ' but will pass through the county of Wexford and the Ranelagh, both to give order for those parts and to seek some revenge on those rogues, who, in my absence, had the killing of our base, cowardly and ill guided clowns.' ' I am advertised that they have drawn to them besides the forces of Donnell Spainagh and the Kavanaghs and Feagh McHugh's sons, and the mountain gallowglasses, all the force of the Moores and Connors, and of Tyrrell with his bonnaughts. But surely this blow cannot so much appal our base new men, as it doth inflame the hearts of our commanders and gentlemen of quality, whose forwardness I shall have no less labour to restrain than to encourage and bring on the meaner sort.'[3]

This mood was further intensified by the effect of these Court attacks on his friends, who were drawn still closer to him as every post made it more certain that their whole future service depended upon the favour which their victorious chief could procure. All Essex's friends had now gathered round him, the inner circle of his relations and equals, Southampton, Rutland, and Sir Christopher Blount, and then his intimate household companions, Sir Henry Danvers, and Cuffe and Sir Gelli Meyrick, and beyond them the host of his supporters, dependent and military. Here Meyrick's touch was

---

[1] Both this and the succeeding letter were dated 10th June. Cal. S.P. Irel., 1599–1600, pp. 60–1.

[2] As an instance of the degree to which this royal displeasure with the results of the Essex Expedition was public property, John Chamberlain wrote to Dudley Carleton on 28th June that ' the Queen is nothing satisfied with the Earl of Essex's manner of proceeding, nor likes anything that is done ; but says she allows him £1000 a day to go in progress.' Printed in Chamberlain's Letters, p. 51, published by the Camden Society, 1861.

[3] Letters of the Privy Council to Essex, both dated 10th June. State Papers, Ireland, Eliz., Vol. ccv, 79 and 84.

in evidence, for, as the backbone of this company, there was a strong Welsh contingent, men like Sir John Vaughan of Golden Grove, who had married Sir Gelli's daughter, and all the younger sons from the north, Captains Ellis Floyd, Peter Wynn, Foulk Conway and Trevor. In Essex's immediate entourage there were such old campaigners as Sir Mathew Morgan and Captain Ellis Jones, who had served in the Netherlands, and in Munster were the South Welsh squires, like Kemeys and Progers and Philipps, while in Connaught there was Sir Henry Davies and the already doubtfully loyal Hugh Mostyn. The less influential soldiers were stationed in all the fortified garrisons, as Captain John Salusbury in Leinster, with Richard Croft from the Marches, and in Offaly Captain Owen Salusbury and, at Newry, the energetic Captain Blayney from Powis, and in charge of the discipline of the army the Provost Marshal, Owen ap Hugh.[1] When we consider how long Sir Gelli Meyrick had been recruiting his friends, it is not surprising to find the Welshmen so predominant.

Now, when Essex reached Dublin, these influences came to surround him and the support of the Welsh squires at this juncture assured them that power in his councils that they never afterwards lost. Alone among the followers of Essex, the long Munster campaign had not left them discouraged; for they were men, serviceable and used to hardship and fighting, while the young poets from Essex House wilted, with none of the movement of the Spanish Seas to sustain them and no hope of a fortune. When this first campaign was over, the Welsh soldiers settled down in the wet weather to enjoy the gambling and the fairly good wine and the cards; but the friends of the Essex House circle, anxious for London again, missed the life of the Court and the witty talk and the plays, as they sat over the fire in their lodgings in Dublin, with their finery drenched as the rain fell without ceasing. They were men of fashion and property, and nothing would have induced them to come out of Egypt into this desert, except the belief that they would reach the Promised Land quickly, and for this reason they had entrusted the patron with the care of their future; while in contrast the Welshmen were soldiers, made for endurance, and they had given Essex their swords. It was at this period in Ireland that there were changes among the Viceroy's sup-

---

[1] List of officers with the army in Ireland appointed to take the field with the Lord Lieutenant on 28th April. Cal. Salisbury MSS., ix, pp. 145–8.

porters, so that the soldiers from the Court group, like Sir Christopher Blount and the Danvers, took part with Sir Gelli Meyrick and his hired captains. It is true of course that the two opposing groups of supporters, the military and the courtier, had very unequal opportunities to discover the actual state of affairs, so that any comparison would be unfair which contrasted Sir Gelli Meyrick's long devotion with the determination of Sir John Harington that he ' would not be wrecked upon the Essex Coast.' [1] It might be said indeed that the outcome of the situation, which these gatherings in Ireland was to foreshadow, was rather the shipwreck of Essex on the Welsh coast, cast up there by the storms of the Irish Sea.

Now that Essex had returned to Dublin again, the question of the attack on Tyrone loomed up in the foreground. To the Viceroy and his following Tyrone was merely a name, the chief of those ' savages,' whose conquest would so soon establish their reputation for ever; so that all were agreed on the imperative necessity of immediate action, now that at length the dry weather was coming. The reports which Sir Ralph Lane had prepared at the time of the Munster campaign were just ready and it was in the light that these papers provided that Essex and his friends approached the problem of the organization of victory, which was complicated by the aid and encouragement that Tyrone received from the Scots. When considering the various stages of Essex's rule, it is his ignorance that is perhaps most surprising, and this was the inevitable result of his own temperament, aloof and uninterested, and of the attitude of the officials towards him, courteous, but without hope in his victory and therefore unhelpful. He had their official reports, but not their private opinion and it was this poverty of his knowledge which always gave the enemy the power to surprise him. Not that Essex and his counsellors considered for a moment that their information was in any way lacking, for on the contrary they were convinced that they had at their disposal all the facts necessary to arrange for a conquest. It is the importance of this report on the North that it really contained all the points of view and the facts, on which Essex had to base his decision.

' Tyrone,' so the report began, ' holds one resolution firmly, viz. to make strong fights upon every pass from Ballenemoyrie forwards.' The rebel chief is then described as protected by ' the invincible fastnesses of Tyrone, together with the desert, craggy and boggy mountains at Sleoughe Gallaine (Slieve Gallion), containing forty miles in compass, with the great woods of Killaltagh, Kilwardin, Killaleyrto and Clancankie (which he means to make a bawn for his cows, whilst the soldiers must hunt after them and take their bane in them). These fastnesses were inevitable stops to the journeys of all former Deputies into Ulster, in times of far easier wars than this is like to prove. Scots come to Dundrum Bay and Strangford River . . . and as for Shane O'Neill his sons, these great pledges are kept in an Island in Tyrone within a certain lough, called Lough Insellin, within the great fastness of the country called Killelewtre.' It is suggested as a remedy that ' the three great lords should be entertained, which his Lordship may yet assuredly do, viz. Donnell Gorme,[1] Lord of Jura, the sons of Angus McConnell and the sons of McLane. The use of which must be resolutely this ; . . . his Lordship then (when he, Tyrone, least thinketh) to enter upon him with 4000 Scots, in the heart of all his great fastnesses of Tyrone, by the Ford of Tewme in Killewtre amongst 4000 cows ; which fastnesses also they may sit down in and ensconce themselves there, having taken his cows, before he and all his can turn themselves to stop any part of that breach, which that furious and unlooked for battery shall have made upon his strongest rampier ; having such a kennel of hungry, starved hounds at his heels to break their main herd, and to enter his park and royal chase of Dungannon ; being therewithal to have them so nigh neighbours unto him, as once in fourteen hours at their pleasure to attend his stirrup at his own gates, which will course him and his followers more ways than one.' [2] Confused as was the impression that such a report must have made on Essex's mind, which was now constantly turning to the thought of London again and that life he had sacrificed for the moment, one thing at least remained clear, that Tyrone was followed by ' a kennel of hungry, starved hounds.' Now this was just the impression that Essex had always possessed, when he had stopped to consider the matter at all, on those occasions when the conversation had turned for a moment on that wet country, where his

---

[1] It is an instance of the continuity of this policy that Lord Deputy Sidney, writing to Burghley in 1568 had urged the Queen to procure the devotion of Donnell Gorme McDonald, Lord of the Out Isles. Cal. S.P. Irel., 1509–73, p. 393.

[2] Reports printed in Cal. S.P. Irel., 1599–1600, pp. 69–76. Scots galleys had come to Strangford on 15th June of the same year. The writer had obtained many of the topographical details from a redshank.

father had lost so much money. Beyond that, Ireland had merely remained a political abstraction, whose governorship possessed the reality of a Council Board pawn and which he had so long considered as a place for the removal of rivals and a grave in which their reputations would quickly be buried.

Just in the same way might some Grandee on the Council at Lisbon have treated the Indies and the governorship of Goa d'Orada, although it is hardly conceivable that he would ever have consented to go there himself; but with Essex there was always a lack of balance, an equilibrium that was never quite stable, as is shown by the fact that it was not the reality of military conquest, but the fetish of military glory, a phantom, that he pursued.

When the question of a campaign in the North was considered, Essex was faced with the wastage of his forces, which had now sunk from the sixteen thousand [1] foot soldiers and the cavalry arm of one thousand six hundred, which he had at first been granted, to an effective force of between three thousand five hundred and four thousand ' strong and serviceable troops.' This was the result in great part of the garrisons that he had stationed through the towns of the South and was also caused to a certain extent by desertion, while it is probable that the number of sixteen thousand men, which the Queen had accorded him, was far in excess of the total effectives. Certainly reinforcements were needed, and Essex wrote to the Queen, asking for the permission ' to entertain ' two thousand additional men, until the end of the harvest.[2] Even so he did not reveal his full plans and he had filled a letter, written on his journey to Dublin, with an ill-timed and heavy metaphor,[3] which was intended as a complaint of his enemies on the Council. Only five days before Essex reached Dublin, Sir John Shelton had been killed in the North, in a sortie from Ards, of which town he was governor, and in another encounter Sir Henry Danvers was wounded. There was unfortunately no one

---

[1] On this point Chamberlain had written to Carleton on 15th March that ' his whole forces are said to be 16,000 foot and 1400 horse, but when they shall come to the polle I fear they will fall short.' Chamberlain Letters, p. 49.

[2] Letter of Essex to the Privy Council, dated 15th July. Cal. S.P. Irel., 1599–1600, p. 94. The phrase ' for the army was everywhere very miserable, especially those poor men that had been eight weeks in the field ' is an instance of his tactless re-iteration of circumstances which could only redound to his discredit.

[3] ' But as I ever said, I ever must say, I provided for this service plastron and not curate; that is I am armed on the breast, but not on the back.' Ibid., p. 77. These complaints against his enemies, disguised under the metaphor of breast and shoulder armour, seriously offended the Council.

less fitted than Essex to realize the cumulative effect of these episodes,[1] as successive couriers brought the news to the capital.

He was now happy again and imagined that others should be, but instead his rule was disturbed by a sharp reprimand from the Queen. 'We have perceived,' she wrote, 'by your letter that you have arrived in Dublin. Yet have you in this dispatch given us small light either when, or in what order, you intend particularly to proceed to the Northern Action. Wherein, if you compare the time that is run on and the excessive charges that is spent . . . yet you must needs think that we . . . can little please Ourself hitherto with anything that hath been effected. For what can be more true (if things be rightly examined) than that your two months' journey hath brought in never a capital rebel, against whom it had been worthy to have adventured one thousand men. For of their comings in that were brought unto you by Ormonde (namely, Mountgarret and Cahir) whereupon ensued the taking of Cahir Castle, full well do we know that you would long since have scorned to have allowed it for any great matter in others to have taken an Irish hold from a rabble of rogues, with such force as you had and with the help of the cannon, which was always able on Ireland to make his passage where it pleased. . . . Whereunto we will add this one thing that doth more displease us than any charge or expense that happens, which is, that it must be the Queen of England's fortune (who hath held down the greatest enemy she had), to make a base bush kern to be accounted so famous a rebel, as to be a person against whom so many thousands of foot and horse, besides the force of all the nobility of that kingdom must be thought too little to be employed.'[2]

Now in all these cases Essex's imagination was clouded by the memory of the Queen, who had yielded so often to the spell of his presence; but for the friends, who were in his widespread, unconsidering confidence, it was more and more evident that an immediate victory was essential. Yet although Essex agreed with this in the main, he still imagined that all would be well, if only he was back once more at the Court. Every rebuke from the Queen made his friends increas-

---

[1] He did not see that his complaint, contained in a letter of 13th July to the Council, regarding the conduct of his troops who 'have laid still like drones without doing service and now have been beaten hard under the fort' was in itself an indictment of his rule. Cal. Salisbury MSS., ix, p. 231.
[2] State Papers, Ireland, Eliz., Vol. ccv, No. 113.

ingly desperate ; but on Essex it had the reverse effect and convinced him that Tyrone was of comparatively little importance, beside the necessity to return to England to bring this woman back to her reason. However, he ordered an attack on Ulster from Connaught by the forces of Sir Conyers Clifford, the President.

Ten days later another letter came from the Court, and to everyone except Essex it was now unmistakably clear that the Queen's mind was settling and that the lines along which it had hardened were not to be changed by a mere conversation. The same phrases appeared again, only put much more strongly. 'If then you consider what month we are in and what a charge we have ever been at, since the first hour of your arrival . . . you may easily judge that it is far beyond our expectation to find you make new doubts.' 'You have broken the heart of our best troops and weakened your strength upon inferior rebels and run out the glass of time, which can hardly be recovered.' And then at the thought of her defiant subject, Tyrone, the Queen's imagery mounted, as she wrote of the encouragement of her enemies, ' especially when these base rebels see their golden calf preserve himself without taint or loss, safe as in his sanctuary.' [1] Nothing could be more clear to Essex and his friends than that, as far as they were concerned, a safe sanctuary was the very last thing that this disturbing journey to Ireland could give them. And then there came the news of the defeat of Sir Conyers Clifford in the mountain bogs of the Curlews.

This was the result of a sudden attack from the O'Rourkes, and Sir Conyers had been slain and also Sir Alexander Ratcliffe, his Colonel. Not only this, but the troops had broken and fled, and there were rumours as to the conduct of the acting Governor, Sir Arthur Savage, who was said to have run away and caused the loss of the treasure.[2] This produced an impression in Ireland very different from the unsurprised and despondent calm with which the Court took such a disaster ; for Essex and his friends were confirmed in their desperate distrust of their troops and of all those who, like Sir Arthur Savage, stood outside their own circle. But Sir Alexander and Sir Conyers had often dined at Essex House with the gentlemen in those good days

---

[1] Letter of the Queen to Essex, dated 30th July. Cal. S.P. Irel., 1599–1600, p. 106. The preceding letter was dated 19th July and the defeat at the Curlews took place on 5th August.
[2] In addition to this charge there are references to the alleged ' miserable and sleepy disposition of the Governor of Connaught, Sir Arthur Savage.' Ibid., p. 502.

in London and now every hope of advancement at Court would end if Tyrone could repeat his friends' victory. This was the climax of that unhappiness and discomfort, which had only deepened during the five months that they had been in the country and which had led the Viceroy's followers to include the ' savages ' and the settlers and their own underpaid troops [1] in a general atmosphere of distrust, which was increased by their knowledge of how hostile the Government and the Court were becoming. They would have cheerfully accepted the daylight hazards and the obvious risks of the fighting in Spain and the Netherlands, but this was so different and in face of Sir Conyers' disaster they felt that, at the end of the attack on the North, they too would be lying dead in the heather.

However much they may have desired a quick victory, this defeat pulled them up short and they counselled delay. With this new plan the volatile mind of their leader concurred and, only a week after their last letter for reinforcements was sent, they despatched fresh proposals. But the Government in England worked steadily and surely without changing their standpoint and although, to Essex and his followers, Tyrone was a pawn to be used for their fortunes, to the Queen he was a rebel against her authority, and his chastisement was the sole justification upon which these burdensome expenses were based. On 9th August therefore an immediate reply from the Queen, addressed to both Essex and the Council was sent over. ' The letter,' she wrote with decision, ' which we have read this day from you of that Council concerning your opinions for the northern action, doth rather deserve reproof than much answer. . . . But we do see bitter effects of our long sufferings. . . . Yet may not our kingdoms, our honour and the lives of our subjects, both at home and abroad be still dallied withall. Do you forget that within these seven days you made a hot demand for 2000 men for this action and now, before you have answer, send us tidings that this huge charge must leave Tyrone untouched ? Lastly for Lough Foyle, which still you ring in our ears, to be the place that would most annoy the rebel, we doubt not but to hear by the next that it is begun and not in question.' [2]

[1] The letter of Essex to the Privy Council, dated 14th August, brings out this last point, ' Her Majesty in the list payeth many, but hath her service followed by few, for every town and place of garrison is an hospital, where our degenrate countrymen are glad to entertain some sickness as a *supersedeas* for their going into the field. Believed it cannot be what baseness and cowardice most of these troops are grown unto.' Cal. S.P. Irel., 1599–1600, pp. 123–4.
[2] Letter of the Queen to Essex and his Council. Cal. S.P. Irel., 1599–1600, p. 115.

This insistence from London on an immediate march into Ulster drew for the moment all the followers of Essex together. The unreliability of the troops, which the disaster in the Curlews had made clear, produced a lasting effect on those soldiers who had hitherto favoured every policy of aggression. The courtiers, already depressed, realized that there were dangers compared to which even the melancholy and tedious waiting at Dublin was preferable, and even those military men who were not dependent on Essex and were inclined to deride each new plan, could not but agree as to the necessity of postponing this attack on the North after the lesson that Sir Conyers Clifford's defeat had now taught them. As a result of the present policy their lives were directly in peril, and they decided to make another attempt to explain their views to the Queen. In fact, among those groups that were to be found supporting the English *régime*, one alone, the strong class of the Castle officials and settlers, remained indifferent with regard to the Ulster campaign. There was no danger that they would be involved in this immediate fighting themselves, and on one point they were certain, Essex and all his untrained new gentlemen could never succeed and it was a matter of indifference as to whether his defeat and recall came sooner or later, or what form it should take. In this turmoil they waited in silence.

All the same it was necessary for preparations to be made for a journey and for Essex to move off to the North, even though he might hope that the Court would soon countermand such a hopeless offensive. On 21st August the letter of the Lords and Colonels of the army [1] supporting the Deputy's standpoint was sent off to the Queen, and a week later Essex set out for the North, establishing himself at first at the Bishop of Meath's house at Ardbraccan. Among gloomy supporters Essex alone remained hopeful, for there was always in his mind the belief that an interview with the Queen would end every difficulty, and he was anxious for London. Besides he felt perfectly sure that if there was insistence from the Court he could, when he wished, always make them see reason. If he had been allowed to follow his feckless instinct in this, his career might not have come to disaster ; but it

---

[1] Among the eighteen signatories to this memorandum, Lords Southampton and Monteagle, Sir Mathew Morgan, Sir Henry Danvers, Sir Charles Wilmot, Sir Thomas Jermyn and Arthur Champernowne belonged to Essex's personal following, Sir Edward Wingfield, Sir Oliver Lambart and Sir Henry Docwra were soldiers who had served under him abroad and had received their posts through his influence, while Sir Samuel Bagenall, Sir Francis Darcy and Sir Edward Herbert were experienced officers, who supported him on military grounds.

was his misfortune that the military supporters, who were aware of the small chance of success if he should rely solely on his personal gift of persuasion, were insistent on a course of action which could have only one end. The Queen might be devoted to Essex and ready to yield to his wishes, when he came suppliant and alone and she could grant all his requests, as he knelt before her, impulsive, with that quick charm still manifest under the new seriousness of his state. But Elizabeth possessed a great measure of that royal dignity, which it satisfied her so much to assume, and once her Deputy should bring his swordsmen along with him and his horde of slow-witted admirers and especially his odious secretaries with their too nimble wit, then she would prove adamant. Among the episodes of her cousin's history that she remembered were the details of Rizzio's death, that March evening at Holyrood with the nobles, brutal and clumsy, with the candlelight on their swords, the spilled wine and the hard flushed faces, and in the inner room and defenceless the Queen standing alone. Elizabeth was determined that into this trap she would never fall, and Essex, who might have won her, solitary and unprotected, was ruined once he made display of his supporters and called to his aid the sword.

But meanwhile the preparations at Ardbraccan were going forward for the Northern March and after all these months the Viceroy's mind was coming at last to consider the problem of Tyrone. It was prudently a long time since the latter had appeared at the Court and so far as he considered the matter it would seem probable that Essex had no idea what to expect beyond the general note of barbarity, which all his letters show, that he always linked with his rudimentary ideas of the Irish. This meeting with Tyrone shows, more clearly than any other detail in his changing and purposeless life, the readiness to receive impressions, which Essex always retained, and the disastrous powers he possessed of translating such fleeting impressions into permanent political act. His soldiers following him loyally and his courtiers, trying to anticipate each unrelated and varying mood, were alike powerless to restrain him and yet this was most important for them, since all the future depended on the way he was managed. As for the settlers they could remain passive, for even a mere consideration of the financial side could now show them that this marching and counter-marching must surely end very soon.

Neither the settlers, nor the Viceroy's followers had any very clear notion about Tyrone's position and aims; yet this was the less important since a meeting with him could never greatly affect them, but it was quite different for Essex with that undecided, poised mind, which the Renaissance had made so open to influence. Although Tyrone probably never understood this, and it was Essex's fortune, not his, that was changed in the end, he had to deal now with the only man in the Elizabethan official life of the English, who would really give him a hearing.

It is necessary to take some account of Tyrone's position with regard not to the Irish chiefs, but to the Government. In this brief Irish journey Essex never really came into contact with the other chiefs like O'Rourke and O'Donnell and the Irish in Desmond, so that their movements meant nothing to him and he never troubled himself on this matter; but in the case of Tyrone a personal meeting was the means of deflecting his policy. The impression made by Tyrone caused Essex to change his opinion and to agree to a truce, but this truce brought him back to the Court to justify himself to the Queen, and the ride to Nonsuch contained in seed all the elements that produced the catastrophe. Tyrone had grown old in presenting to a long line of deputies the picture of the Queen's loyal subject, and each one had at first looked on him with favour, but it was Essex's misfortune that he at first thought him a 'savage' and then suddenly almost a friend.

Hugh O'Neill, Earl of Tyrone, was now in his sixtieth year, an ancient among chiefs, whose position and career had made him an isolated figure in Ireland, for, while he controlled all the undoubted power of the chief of Hy Niall, he also possessed, in his own eyes, the accomplishments of the great lords of the Court. This was an aspect of which he was never unconscious, and it was just because he was so learned and accomplished that he felt that he could meet the Viceroys as an equal and he regarded the letters from Spain and from the Pope as a tribute not only to his power, but to his Latinity. Those six years which he had passed as a hostage in England when, as the young Lord Dungannon, he had developed his talents at Court, had taught him all the ways of the nobles in London, as ' with sufficient equipage and orderly respect ' he had ' trooped in the streets.' This was an impression, which he was confident that the last thirty years could not efface and it governed his actions. The great Queen was his friend and how often he had protested his loyalty, but it was the settlers who were his enemies, the ravenous low-born English, deceitful and cunning. Leicester had been his chief friend, and how many times they had pledged wine together, and even now the sight of the Queen and Lord Robert and all the pleasurable scandal of '62–64 was still fresh to him, but these raw settlers knew nothing of Leicester, except perhaps as his servants.

The thought of the Bagenals was particularly unpleasant, with the long forty years of their enmity and the bitter memory of his foolish third marriage. His first wife had been one of his own blood of the high-born O'Neill, though he had defied Holy Church in his wildness, and then he had taken the daughter of illustrious O'Donnell, and when he was a personable, grown man in his fifties he had fallen for Mabel Bagenal, that slender, weak, English child. The horrible untrue lies that her brothers had then spread about him still rankled, as if he was not a great lord who had danced with the Queen. And then there had been the prudery of that low-born, heretic chit, who had refused to associate with the ladies of distinguished blood from his ' urraghs ' whom he had taken into his household when he yielded to nature. Yet he had been so patient and kind with the child and had explained again and again that she was Countess of Tyrone, a place which no one could take from her. Fortunately that was all over at last, and it was one of his happiest memories that at the strife of the Yellow Ford it had been his own men who had slaughtered her base brother, Sir Henry. Now that Mabel was dead, he had learned prudence and his new wife was a daughter of Magennis of Iveagh, a staunch and fine woman.

It was in these tangled private affairs and in his ancestral outlook on religion that Tyrone had retained most strongly the old spirit of the Hy Niall. To his Cousins of England and Spain there was added the Holiness of the Lord Pope as the corner stone of this Trinity, and this was only natural to Tyrone, for he protected all the holy men in his country and although he had that weakness, which afflicted many great lords, he was determined to make a good end and in this he succeeded. Meanwhile none of his ancestors had received such letters as he had from the Lord Pope, and he was to receive the great gift of the Phœnix's Feather.

Nevertheless, there was a great contrast between Tyrone and his predecessor, Sir Turlough, for the former considered these great marks of esteem, the ' Penna Phœnicis ' and the high-sounding titles, as a tribute not only to his power, but also to his ' civility ' and his wisdom. He was well aware that there was no one like him in Ireland, as he sat, with his black velvet jagged with gold edging and his many-pleated stiff ruff in his private chamber with the tapestries hanging on the rough, heavy walls, talking with Henry Ovenden, his new soft-spoken adviser, while the Spanish wine stood before them in the thin foreign glasses. However wild may have been the background of his life it was these things, the courtesy and the careful fashion and the hesitant words of Italian, that separated Tyrone from his friends among the old Irish. As he sat through the evenings, in his costly and ceremonial velvet, discussing with Ovenden the letters from Spain, it was not possible for him to think without serious disquiet of the ' urraghs,' for he had so little in common with the strongest of his supporters, like the ' high born haughty O'Hagans ' or even the Maguires of the Spears. What he desired was that power and equality, which would keep him in state as the friend of either England or Spain. It was only his more fantastic supporters who dreamed of him as the High King of Ireland and who seriously thought that the position of the Sugan Earl as his ' urragh ' meant tribute. Yet he had indeed done wonders and had turned Munster ' to a trembling sod ' [1] at his feet ; but he was inclined now to live on the glories of the past, Beal an Athe Buidhe and the slaughter of Bagenal. Since he admitted the great power of Elizabeth of England and Philip of Spain, his own desires were concentrated on Ulster and he would never seriously march south, if he could keep Ulster secure. After all he was ageing and he wished for honour and the respect due to his name. It would seem to be this that explains his repeated submissions and at the end at the Flight of the Earls, when he saw that England would never be friendly, he sailed away to the south to find protection and friendship from his Cousin of Spain and from the holy Lord Pope.

This explains too his attitude towards Essex who was the son of his friend and from whom he would surely receive more honourable dealing than from his forerunners, that succession of Boroughs, Fitzwilliams and Perrots, whose *milieu* had been so different. The

[1] This phrase has a melancholy interest as one of the last instances of the unrestrained magniloquence of the Annalists, a final metaphor.

POPE PIUS V.

Sebastiano Ricci.   From the Church of the Gesuati at Venice.

Photo : Alinari.

truce of the ford of Anagh Clint depended on the fact that Tyrone came South to treat Essex as an equal, and although the Viceroy had always thought him almost a ' savage,' yet neither was anxious for war.

On 28th August Essex had written home to the Council saying, ' I am even now putting foot into my stirrup to go to the rendezvous at the Navan,' but the Queen had given no further sign.[1] At the first sight of his army the thoughts of victory had risen again, and two days later he wrote in the most hopeful strain to the Court. ' I hear even now,' Essex began, ' that Tyrone is coming into the Brenny and hath sent for all that he can make in the world ; bragging that he will do wonders. But if he have as much courage as he pretendeth we will on one side or the other end the war.' [2] This was sent by Henry Cuffe, a most unfortunate choice, and reached the Queen, sheltering at Hampton from the last of the heat. The new mood of her changeable deputy naturally hardly affected the Queen, but there was no way in which Essex could have played more directly into the hands of his rivals ; for on this document there remains a marginal note placed there by Sir Robert Cecil, ' here was no sign of a parley toward.'

Yet, before this despatch had reached London, Essex's outlook was changing again and he remembered that he had only 2,500 men, while all the time the forces of Tyrone became stronger. And then on 5th September Henry Hagan came under safe conduct[3] to ask whether Essex would consent to meet Tyrone in a parley. Remembering the wild men of the O'Moores and Kavanaghs,[4] Essex agreed and, with that chivalrous unwisdom to which he so frequently fell agreed that they should be alone at this sign of submission. The obvious danger of treachery was one that he was perhaps justified in incurring, but it was the suggestions of his opponents in England that he had most reason to fear. But on the next day he went forward to Anagh Clint, the ford of the river, to hear what Tyrone had to say, and at this moment Essex's open mind betrayed him again into an action which proved the turning point of his life. With that receptive mind, which the Italian thought of his period had brought him, he saw Tyrone first with surprise and then with a pleasure which gave

[1] Cal. S.P. Irel., 1599–1600, p. 136.
[2] Ibid., p. 137.
[3] Cal. S.P. Irel., 1599–1600, p. 145.
[4] For an account of the submission of these leaders. Ibid., p. 140.

way in turn to a calm sense of relief. Well mounted and with the armour that the courtiers of the period then used, Tyrone rode forward to meet him to the northern bank and then onward into the river, so that the slow stream of the August waters came close to the polished stirrups and to the new elaborate spurs. There bareheaded and with an old-fashioned courtesy Tyrone set forth his proposals, dignified in his obeisance and submissive in all things to the Queen. It was on these ceremonial occasions, in fact in set conversational pieces, that Tyrone could be most impressive and this was the man whom Essex had thought a barbarian. The next day[1] the meeting was repeated with six companions a side and the Viceroy was conquered; for without loss of dignity Tyrone could not have shown greater respect,[2] and now that Essex could see the true situation, his terms seemed most reasonable, merely a truce for the winter, peace on both sides until May, and through it all he had showed the profoundest submission, not only to the Queen, but also to Essex. It was such a great satisfaction that everything could be settled so simply and it merely proved to Essex how simple it was to rule Ireland, so long as he was the man on the spot.

But when he turned and marched back to the Pale he found how strange was the attitude that the settlers took up to this meeting, for what seemed to him a master stroke of his rule was to them a surrender. The wildest rumours were current, since there had been no witnesses of the first meeting and he found that he had raised a whirlwind which his own indiscreet and bellicose followers would be quite unable to lay. After this there were to be exalted moods and periods of feverish activity, but in Essex's life the tranquil hours were past. The officials in Dublin were now clearly hostile,[3] and he saw that it was essential

---

[1] It is clear that no reliance need be placed on the statements of Udall, a spy, who made capital out of ' one, whose name he doth not remember, that lay in a bush near the place of the conference between Essex and Tyrone.' Such charges were the inevitable result of the solitary meeting. Later Udall fell into disfavour for borrowing money from Lord Bath and Sir Griffith Markham by ' a cosening trick and a coney catching device of his to serve his turn upon us.' Cal. S.P. Irel., 1599–1600, pp. 319–21.

[2] The phrases of Tyrone's speech at Anagh Clint, as given in the report in the Trevelyan Papers, ii, pp. 101–3, do not suggest that this particular account is reliable.

[3] This hostility was first clearly expressed in the letter sent to Cecil by Sir Geoffrey Fenton on 30th August. ' I know not, nor shall know nothing,' he wrote, ' other than by the market for that I am still left at home, as I have been in all journeys since His Lordship entered into charge . . . it is my part . . . to carry my comfort in silence, till my twenty years service be thought worthy of better measure.' This was a midway stage in their correspondence between the tempered complaints of 7th May, when Fenton wrote that he was ' hardly thought of ' for his inwardness with Sir John Norreys, and the open hatred to which on 3rd December he felt he was now strong enough to give vent, ' His Lordship (Essex) you know was hardly conceited

that he should return and visit the Queen, for she would understand and would yield in affection and with her experience she could not fail to acknowledge the wise plans he had made. Besides he would be back once more in London in his element and his old power would return, while in the background there were the military men, his supporters and the figures of Gelli Meyrick and Sir Christopher Blount, his stepfather, with the power, if not of controlling, at least of riding the storm. It was a question as to whether he should take over his army or come, as Christopher Blount would prefer, with a chosen body of swordsmen or perhaps keep both in reserve. In the end he took only six friends when he set out from Dublin and held the rest of his followers in waiting, for he was so sure that once he returned he would be able to scatter the advisers, who were coming between him and the Queen, since she could not fail to recognize that his rule in Ireland was wise.

At Nonsuch, where the Court had now moved the Queen received the last disquieting despatches. Tyrone was a rebel in arms, still in the field, and there was no reason in these phrases of his submission, bare-headed, riding into the water, most courteous. Yet Essex, who could do nothing and who had concluded a shameful truce without any authority, had collected enough swordsmen in Dublin to make any prudent sovereign uneasy. There was only one thing that would be worse, if he should desert his post without leave and come back to the Court, keeping his swordsmen ready, a threat in the background. On the morning of 28th September Essex and his companions rode under the great gate at Nonsuch and he penetrated alone to the chamber, where the maids of honour were busy preparing the Queen for the day.

Essex was careless, and once more confident that he could exert his accustomed authority, but his horse's hoofs on the gate stone at Nonsuch had aroused the Queen's memory [1] of the long succession of nobles who had come too close to the throne. There was that changing group of Scots Lords, who had surrounded her cousin, and no one knew so well their fierce strength and their greed as the English

of me before ; but now since he hath discovered that I am an open professed party on your side . . . my portion will be far more sour and full of peril. . . .' Cal. S.P. Irel., 1599–1600, pp. 27, 139 and 297.
 [1] 'She (the Queen) entertained him courteously, but not with the countenance she was wont.' Sir H. Wotton, *Memoirs of the Earl of Essex*, p. 15.

Queen who financed them ; for she had thus all the knowledge of the woof of the under side of the carpet. In England there was the line of great lords, in her father's reign and her own, who had aroused that too keen sense of danger, which the Tudors always possessed. To the calm and detached Essex, so remote from reality, it seemed that his every decision had been lucid and clear,[1] but to the Queen he now stood before her, a noble, disobedient and armed, who had toyed with rebellion. No one save Essex could be surprised at such a development, and to all observers it was clear that during his rule in Ireland he had covered the first and longest of the stages on the road from great royal influence to the Tower.

[1] In this one solitary observer supports him. ' And wee,' wrote John Trevelyan, ' all hope of pease and that the Earl Terron wilbe a true subiecte and sende in his pledges.' Trevelyan Papers, ii, p. 103.

CHAPTER XX

THE CLOSE OF THE CENTURY

The general situation at the close of the century and in particular the last effects of the Celtic influences in politics at the end of the reign, can best be viewed in connection with the closing stages of Essex's life and with the last period of calm during which all the diverse elements of the Opposition had gathered around him. The career of Essex has a two-fold value in connection with the subjects of this study. In the first place he was the last Englishman of great political power on whom both the old Celtic influences played directly, as the two preceding chapters make clear, and at the same time his career reveals the extinction of the Spanish influence in England. As regards political effects Essex's final destruction had become, from the time that he came home from Ireland, an event almost inevitable and unimportant. But the very wide ramifications of his supporters gives a view of a complete cross-section of English life, which no other event of the time can provide. In particular the contrast is seen between the outlook of the younger generation, which the Italian influence and the new tradition of sword-manship had powerfully affected, and that of the older men, who had been youths when the Queen had succeeded and were now in bulk, ' official,' loyal, Cecilian and insular. The same contrast is found to a lesser degree among Catholics. This crisis also provides the materials for a study of the new Euphuistic literary influence, the fashion that it set up and the temperamental hostility that its adherents often aroused. The Celtic and especially the Welsh influence, which through Essex's supporters made itself felt in the capital, developed not only the normal English opposition, but also some strange affinities in the literary world.

Although his own temperament would always have stood in the way of any serious achievement, Essex's system of influence was built up on the old feudal lines, even though the upper regions were permeated with an Italianate air. It was this partly feudal and indeed almost viceregal character of his whole public life, which provided the last opportunity for the direct political exercise of the old Celtic influence. No later Viceroy was ever again to be converted by the O'Neill, nor was any aristocratic statesman to derive that degree of support which Essex obtained from the Welsh. As to the Spanish influence the change in England is now seen completed from the union of the Crowns Matrimonial, before the death of Queen Mary, to a mood of profound and almost universal hostility.

In this chapter the method now followed is to take a view of Essex and the various types of his followers, as they grouped about Essex House in January, 1601, before the Earl's Rising. A brief study of one member from each group, with his appropriate background, thus shows Essex's enemies as well as his friends. In this way the Manners influence is described, Lord Rutland at Essex House and the forces behind him. His mother provides in a sense a Protestant counterpart to the Duchess of Feria, while his tutor, Dr. Jegon, afterwards Bishop of Norwich, stands as a type of the mildly political clergyman in a still socially unrecognized Church. A consideration of the Manners uncles brings in an element profoundly hostile to Essex and the Court life of London, the great landed squires. The loyalty to the Government and to the Established Church, the distrust of foreigners, book learning and urban life, the acceptance of the duties of the new routine administration in the country and the devotion to an outdoor rural life, all play their part in building up that character from which the Cavaliers were to spring. The dislike of foreign-trained priests and the puzzled attitude, when faced by the firm nonconformity of the old Catholic squires, are as clear as the contempt with which they regarded Essex and the new literary elegance. A wide zone of the most prosperous side of English rural life is thus covered, forces which at the end of the century were closely connected with Essex, but hostile and menacing to him.

The next type to be considered is that of the heirs of the rich landed squires, and as an example Francis Tresham is chosen, partly because the strong Catholicism of his father, Sir Thomas, serves as a foil to the Manners tradition, and indicates the hopes and standpoint of that Catholic party for whom a change of Government might mean so much. The influence of the old Latin phrases and the example still followed of the house chaplain stand out plainly, manifested in the pious devices of Sir Thomas' building schemes, and in that constancy with which he suffered imprisonment rather than abandon the Old Religion. A firm devotion to the Queen's Government emerges, and an attitude of friendship towards those of the royal officials with whom he was brought in contact. His expenditure shows also how much the great Catholic landowners benefited by the prosperity of the times, a prosperity which alone enabled them to pay their fines. An impression of the internal feuds which rent the persecuted Recusants is provided by the numerous lawsuits in which he engaged. However much they might differ, both Sir Thomas Tresham and the elder Manners were opposed to the dangerous courses on which their son and nephew embarked, for they were united in their acceptance of Government and of the authority and power of the Prince.

Below these greater men in the Essex House circle there were the secretaries and the chaplains. Their influence at this time lay in their complete dependence upon their master, for men like Henry Cuffe had no prospects except at Essex House and in fact no separate and independent life outside it. Cuffe's status as the son of a yeoman deprived him of personal intimacy and raised a barrier between men of his station and the swordsmen. It was only in the very highest circles that his position as philosopher in ordinary gained him a name ; for most of the military followers he was always a butt. At the same time his personal contact with Essex was most confidential, part servant, part friend, a trust which he earned by his whole-hearted devotion. He was a man without inherited tradition and hampered by no prudent ties, with every interest centred upon Essex. It was just this lack of any tie, worldly or religious, which made him dangerous, a fatally devoted friend. In this circle William Barlow combines the position of a chaplain with the status of the old-established West Welsh dependents. A brief consideration of the religious and literary influences, in so far as they can be seen to affect Essex himself at this period, concludes the survey.

IF it is a characteristic of societies doomed to perish that, even in the last moments of their complete untempered life, they remain unaware of the dangers about them, this cannot describe the atmosphere of the fall of Essex House. It is frequently asserted that the closed Society which revolved around the Court of Russia was entirely unprepared for the catastrophe which overwhelmed it, that even in the March days of that last Imperial Year, its members were unaware of any danger and could not discern the changes on the Neva, that muffled distant thunder of the overburdened, breaking ice. But for the counsellors and the satellites who depended upon the Essex faction the thought of the great risks that they incurred was all part of the adventure, that somewhat conscious labour, the chosen background of a Hero's life.

Besides, when a whole society is involved, it is difficult to make danger seem real or for the members to obtain a conception of the still fettered rivals who are soon to supplant them ; so that, just as in certain mythologies, it is in fact by the unimaginable that their way of life is destroyed. For in 1787 how incredible the Jacobins of the Mountain would seem and how impossible ever to fit into any edge of the picture of that eighteenth-century manner, the mouldings and the ornament, the elegance and stiffness, as the sundial lines at Marly closed a finely balanced day. On the other hand, when there are two factions around the centre of power, the very social equality that they possess gives a wider scope for the exaggerated belief in the successfully evil designs of the rival. Thus, while the *Sans culottes* did not seem a menace at all in an earlier epoch, the image of the Great Cardinal rose threatening and dominant in his adversaries' minds in the years when Richelieu held power. And it was in just this same way that Essex's following would picture the dangers that they ran from the influence of Cecil on the now aged Queen. But then in the late sixteenth century, when the cult of a rather obvious form of courage ran high, this was a great inducement to the young courtiers who had decided to gamble on Essex's fortune, the sense that so much was at stake. Cecil had in fact become exalted into a bogey. And there is this quality in a bogey that the resulting dangers can in the last resort never be serious. Thus, for the young supporters of Essex there was all the pleasure of danger with an interior assurance of safety, so delightful a combination and one which the leaders of that fantastic, high-spirited and ironical fashion were well equipped to enjoy. What was it then that went wrong ? To indulge their speech and their frank and almost rebellious customs quite fully it was inevitable for these courtiers to run certain risks, from which they could always disentangle themselves in necessity, although the sum that this immunity would cost might prove heavy. It was a part of the *insouciance* and detachment of Essex that he would not take this trouble, so that a constant disregard of all warnings brought him in the end to disaster. There hovered close in his wake the attendants of such a career who moved on with his movement. They, too near to their leader, were destroyed with him also and were drawn down when the great ship of Essex's fortune had foundered ; but the rest remained free, surviving the storm, the fragments of what had once been the fleet of that great treasure hunting.

In this question it is important to note that the whole of the Essex House movement was a frame of mind and not a conspiracy. It was on the one hand, in the narrow sense, fashionable [1] and under another aspect it was the unquiet mood of the late Elizabethan *littérateurs* who desired a wider, more sceptical freedom. Yet again, for all those younger sons from the country, who had neither claims to fashion, nor to any literary sense, Essex would seem the precursor of a quite different freedom, that power of extravagant action, the freedom of swordsmen, which the staid rule of the Cecils denied them. The Queen was so old and, although Robert Cecil possessed the talents of the Renaissance, he had nothing of the new Heroic Manner, imperious and flamboyant, such as the age of Marlowe loved. And, for all these men, Essex satisfied a necessity of the mind and a craving. Then beyond these groups, which although so divergent had at least some direct personal contact with their patron, there were the other, very various men who found it so easy to think of Essex as their ally, the ribald London crowds and their opposites the new Puritan preachers. Yet even if all those who were connected with Essex however remotely should be considered, this would be far from indicating completely the value for an understanding of the whole cross-section of the life of the country which the events of the fall of Essex can bring us. For, as the description of the Welsh affairs of the Devereux has already made clear, it was the violent destruction of the Earl which has preserved for us the details ; as the lives of those around him stand sharp in that light, sudden and harsh, by which the catastrophe now had made clear the whole of the nation's political landscape.

All the troubles of the last years had made him fevered with an

---

[1] A letter from William Bonnington at Brill to John Coke either at Deptford or else at Mr. Greville's chamber in Essex House indicates that at this date, 15th July, 1600, both these men who were to become famous as Sir John Coke and Fulke Greville, Lord Brooke, belonged to this circle. Cal. Coke MSS., Report xii, i, p. 26.

activity in turning from resource to resource, which the secretive calm of Cecil bred in him. It was not in Essex's nature to concern himself with the past or with the effect produced [1] by his actions. Besides, in the months since his return from Ireland, and especially since his release in August, 1600, from the confinement into which that disastrous action had led him, he was wearied by the advice of his friends. His own household supporters were loyal, but these were the careful and elderly men who had presumed too far on a friendship with his father, Earl Walter, and now begged the son to have care. To Essex their prudence seemed merely a cloak to conceal that lack of a strong resolution which he prided himself he possessed ; yet this resolution was hardly a courage arising from a calm judgment of facts, but rather a fruit of indifference, careless and free. The coldness of the Queen, as it increased, thus seemed to him merely a reason for the more firm independence, so that as he was kept remote from all power his spirit only rose higher ; for this was no confidence, well based and secure, but the mounting heat of a fever patient. And in the closed and fire-warmed rooms of Essex House, that rambling palace, this mood set the tone, the servants following their master and the lords imitating their friend.

The long cold of that January in 1601 thus witnessed the climax of unreality in that dreaming and phantom-like life, for that winter had brought to the Master, much wine, some ague and unending talk. Through the long hours together, which Essex had once passed at the Court, the lords sat in their state with the delicate glasses and the spiced ' comfits ' before them, while their leader planned high. Beside him in the great chamber sat his friend Southampton, almost a brother, and the young Rutland, little more than a boy, with his pleasant and simple not over-intelligent face. It was wonderful for Rutland to sit and to listen to these heart-stirring plans, and it would soon be his privilege to be one of the rulers, when his magnificent friend was successful. To others it might have seemed an ill-omened association, but the wine had not quickened his wits, and it did not occur to him to consider his friend's exhausted strained pallor, and then beyond Essex there was Southampton also to rely on, that patron of muses. He, too, was a wonderful man, with that elaborate conversation he

---

[1] A passage from Bacon describes this admirably. ' And all the time aforesaid the re was " altum silentium " from her (the Queen) to me concerning the Earl of Essex his causes.' *Apology concerning the Earl of Essex*, p. 141.

affected so well, and certainly a soldier of spirit, for had he not lost in Paris three thousand crowns at *paulone?* This was a companion of whom everyone would be proud, and then as Southampton began a ' conceit,' phrased with smoothness and wit, he would raise his head, after settling the gold and silver-worked lace of his collar, which he wore so as to allow his hair to fall down to the shoulders, and would display the firm strong-columned neck, the full-flushed prominent nose and the heavy lids sinking. Their happy judgment did not lead Essex and Rutland to consider how it would do to rely on Southampton. His hair, though still long, was not so golden, high living had told a little rapidly upon my Lord.[1] (It is a commentary on this association that the succeeding Earls of Essex, Rutland and Southampton are found a generation later, fully fledged as Puritans within the Godly camp.) [2] This intimacy of the leaders, to which others were seldom admitted, is a mark of the strength of that union, which family connection and still more an identity of exalted rank brought at this period.

These three leaders were of course all relations, for Elizabeth Vernon, whom Southampton had married, was a cousin of Essex, and Frances Sidney, that girl of sixteen who had just become Rutland's bride, was a daughter of Lady Essex by her former husband, Sir Philip. But much more than this it was equality in rank that counted, so that Essex's own stepfather, Sir Christopher Blount, remained outside this innermost circle, just as did the three Manners brothers who had followed young Rutland. The careful manner in which while writing freely to one another they call the elder brother My Lord is typical of this comparative restraint and exclusion. It was the very real prestige of the wealth and political power of the great Earls under Elizabeth that kept them apart,[3] while throughout Essex's household the life of the friends appears thus divided into overlapping, but none the less well-defined, circles. One instance from each of these groups will suffice to give an impression of the background and life of the

[1] The contrast between the easy grace of the Welbeck portrait and the features of the Mireveldt head of Southampton in the National Portrait Gallery shows a very striking change.

[2] Thus the third Earl of Essex and the eighth Earl of Rutland were solemn Parliamentarians, while, in the ' character ' of the fourth Earl of Southampton, Clarendon has stated, ' He was of a nature somewhat inclined to melancholy. . . . He had never any conversation with the Court nor obligation to it. . . . He had a great dislike of the High Courses.' *History of the Great Rebellion*, Book vi. How completely the reaction had set in ?

[3] Their real connection with the urban communities was purely munificent. Thus Pembroke gave a golden bell to the City of Salisbury and Essex a golden snaffle in memory of the pleasures of Wilton and the races. Cal. Salisbury Corporation MSS., p. 233.

time and in the closest circle of all the case of Rutland and his brothers will suggest the varied reactions which the long reign had produced.

Roger Manners, fifth Earl of Rutland, was typical of the education and outlook which the end of that century made common among the great lords of the Court. He was now just twenty-four years of age and had received, when a boy of eleven, his immense and characteristically embarrassed inheritance. Irreproachable in their ancestry, it has not been the custom of the House of Manners to produce great leaders, and throughout English history they followed most closely the fashion, as it prevailed among their equals in rank, and have thus entered, as in the case of their dukedom, almost unawares on success. In this way at the Reformation they had gone with the tide and had amassed, without energy and almost without discredit, a very large fortune. Charley and Garradon, Beverley, Croxton, Warter and Rievaulx made a good list of fine property to obtain from the monks ; while with this as a background it is not surprising that the young Rutland's upbringing had pursued the conventional lines, quite remote from all contact with the ancient religion. There his guardians stood over the boy, stolid, with that Mid-Elizabethan reason and sense, the Mother and the Tutor, the Reverend Jegon, stuggy and fierce, and in the background the Uncles. Reason and loyalty and in Burghley's phrase ' this huntyng tyme at Belvoir '[1] and the field sports of the Fens, these words conjure a life which is left unaltered through change. In the depths of the country Rutland's Uncle Roger, lamenting that there were ' so few partridges,'[2] spans the literary centuries with a hardly voiced protest, the airlessness of London and the rapid, heated talk. While the literary fashions have changed, this attitude alone remains firm, there are still ' so few partridges ' in autumn in the Uffington woods.

All the characteristic ingredients were present through the course of this boyhood, even those long-recurrent lawsuits for land, which only served to show in their mutual conflict how strong were the great landed squires ; while behind the mother and tutor there was that dominant influence of the widespread Manners possessions, encumbered yet strong. Elizabeth, Countess of Rutland, by birth a

---

[1] Letter of Burghley to Rutland dated 12th August, 1590. Cal. Rutland MSS., i, p. 283.
[2] Letter of Roger Manners to his brother John, written at Uffington. ' We have great store of hawks, but so few partridges that I am angry and ashamed. If I were at Court again I would not come hither until ducking time.' Cal. Rutland MSS., i, pp. 121–2.

Charlton from Shropshire, was a woman whose determination was strengthened and her agitations smoothed down by her son's tutor and chaplain; thus standing almost at the head of that long line of great ladies who have received assistance from the doctrines of Divine Right and Obedience, as filtered by that well poised influence, the English Cloth. There were innumerable quarrels, and in each it was to Doctor Jegon that she turned, in the dissensions about her brother-in-law's will and the fight for the £4,000 out of settlement that she waged with his widow, and finally in that last losing struggle for the tithe corn on the lands about Newark, so petty a gain. Lord Burghley was more than kind in this trouble, standing almost *in loco parentis*,[1] a *rôle* which with the older nobility he was always prepared to adopt. And then the Queen, whom as a mere younger son's wife she had never yet known, also sent messages, but best of all there was good Doctor Jegon to whom she had entrusted her son. Here was a man who would never fail to show deference and to mark in her presence his sense of his own humble birth, so reasonable and wise about money, writing that 'good ling and haberdine will (at this time) be dear' and yet such a man. 'There is daily speech of nominating bishops,' he had written from Cambridge where he was tutoring her son, 'but yet no certainty. Do not let any bad dealing of your enemies disquiet you. You have the better end of the staff and scourges enough to ship them withal.'[2] She was so fortunate in having such a learned preceptor to bring up her son away from his father's interfering relations, and then the thought came of her troubles and of bills for the Earls' funerals, two years old and unpaid.

To John Jegon in his obscure position at Queen's it had long been even more reciprocally clear that Lady Rutland was also a godsend. Self-fulfilment was not even possible without a rich patron, and there hovered before him ' the nomination of bishops, but yet no certainty.' However, he had done what he could and had placed Tom Jegon, his brother, as steward in the dower house at Winkburne, so as always to

---

[1] The position had been a little delicate for Burghley, since he had just completed a marriage alliance between his grandson, William Cecil, and Lady de Ros, the daughter of the third Earl of Rutland and heiress general of the family, whose mother, the Dowager Countess, was the protagonist in this dispute; for Elizabeth, Lady Rutland's husband, the fourth Earl, had only held the title for a few months on the death of his brother. Nevertheless, it pleased Burghley to act as an universal providence if the parties concerned were of rank. Correspondence in Cal. Rutland MSS., i, pp. 250–300, *passim*.
[2] Letter from Dr. John Jegon to Lady Rutland, dated 3rd December, 1588. Cal. Rutland MSS., i, p. 266.

be close to my Lady. There was certainly no doubt whatever that she had ' the better end of the staff,' and then he would sit down to console her about the bills for the funeral. That had been a truly magnificent affair, and it was no wonder that there were suits of mourning unpaid for, since there had been eleven knights and six esquires and sixteen gentlemen retainers and twenty-four gentlemen in ordinary, all of the household. Mr. Jegon, as he then was, had watched the display from the background, as was proper and fitting, with five others of his own doubtful status, just before the sixty dressed yeomen. My Lady had provided it all, every inch of the hose and the doublets of elegant black bombazine. From these details one fact now emerges, that in spite of the contrast between Lady Rutland, a woman rather disturbed and provincial, and this capable clergyman, they were both united in regarding such funeral display as inevitable, the black hung escutcheons and the shrouded horses ambling and each mercenary movement of this carefully darkened band. Such things were of the essence of rank, fixed like the heavenly bodies, secure from all fall.

In such a way was young Rutland moulded, as a letter, which his tutor permitted him to write at fifteen to his mother in answer to a rebuke, fully shows. ' I give your Ladyship humble thanks,' wrote this carefully trained boy, ' for your honourable direction in your letters for my good. I do asseure your ladyship that the cariage of myselfe both towardes God and my booke, my comelinesse in diet and gesture shall be such as your Ladyship shall hear and like well of.'[1] ' God and my booke,' the libertines and Essex were not five years away.

Then, after these years at Cambridge, and the migration from Queen's to Corpus in the wake of his tutor, who had been forced as Master of Corpus against the Common Room's wish, there came the inheritance at last and full independence, and it was here that the Manners uncles came increasingly into his life. They were so different from Jegon whose intention to teach was subordinate to his constant strong-minded purpose to obtain a hold,[2] lasting and firm, on this

---

[1] Letter of Rutland to his mother, dated Corpus Christi College, Cambridge, 21st October, 1591. Cal. Rutland MSS., i, p. 297.

[2] An instance of this changed and now obsequious relation is furnished by a letter of the Master of Corpus to Rutland, dated 23rd May, 1597. ' I will make no doubt,' wrote Dr. Jegon merrily, ' that the Tallivero, for so he calleth himselfe, will and can presente my duetie to your Lordship in good congies and bad Englishe.' *Ibid.*, p. 339.

pupil of rank. But the uncles were such a relief, sincerely revering the Queen with the single hope that their nephew with £3,000 [1] a year and the prestige [2] of his earldom would rise to high favour. Yet this was an outlook of an old calm generation, for ahead lay Essex and his followers, the unquiet spirits of the storm.

Roger and John Manners, for their younger brother, poor George, who suffered so severely from ague was dead by this time, can in fact stand as types of that secure mental attitude, which the long Elizabethan successes had ripened. They had their position, representing the Rutland interest of the minor, safeguarded from any ambitious desires by the long line of their nephew's child brothers and utterly secure and at ease in their station. Their brother-in-law, Shrewsbury, that good Elizabethan, was the closest of friends, while Burghley's son, Robert Cecil would not fail to treat their age with respect. Although devoted to one another, there was a pleasant difference between them, Roger disinclined for much action, living chiefly for sport, something of a *gourmet* also and with a reputation as a man of the world, and John busy in local affairs, performing the routine duties in the Forest of Sherwood which the long minority brought him, a little self-important in manner and very much married. Roger had the tastes of a bachelor, but Sir John, as he fittingly became in the end, was the husband of the heiress of Haddon, that celebrated and legendary Dorothy Vernon. Their lives passed in the country were now drawing on to a close, for they were younger sons of the first Earl of Rutland and had been grown youths when the present Queen had succeeded. They were in all things perfectly loyal, with a distrust of the Foreigners which a home-grown education had fostered; while, in their county, swashbucklers and literary men were unknown and, like all the solid country life of their time, they were equally remote from adventurers, whether Catholic or Godly. The more intricate side of careers, such as those of Hawkins or Raleigh, were as unknown as the Jesuit or Seminary systems, for the ethics of

---

[1] In 1601 his revenues amounted to £3,194, while annuities to his two unmarried sisters, which had only now become payable, took away £791, both figures referring to the actual money. Cal. Salisbury MSS., xi, p. 141.

[2] The prestige and power, with their feudal origin and the new patronage value, were quite independent of the revenue, which in Rutland's case was not large for an earldom, since the income of Lord Wharton a quite ordinary peer was then (1605) £2,107, while Essex's mother possessed, as the widow of Lords Essex and Leicester, a jointure of £3,000 a year.

the sword are not needed by those who possess their own acres.[1] And this brings in their standpoint on religion. Against the foreign trained priests they were prejudiced, for the whole business smacked of book learning and no one could tell what strange notions they had picked up abroad. They did not share with their less prosperous friends that long and deep-rooted Catholicism, which the small, lost manors possessed, for Lord Rutland, their father, had been so close to the Court, that they had received all the benefit of each prayer book revision and doctrine, as the tutors had mildly endeavoured to engage their wandering attention, while their thoughts were fixed on the chase. As a result in religion they had deep devotion to their Natural Sovereign and a serene unstudied acceptance of those not too much precised doctrines which were sanctified by the Crown; while their remoteness from books gave to their religious expressions an archaic simplicity, which the then rising age would deride.

Life was so pleasant and tempered with England victorious. ' I feare your over travaill,' wrote [2] Roger to his brother, ' and you fere my ydelnes,' reposeful fear. And then Roger would turn philosophically serious. ' O Brother, what in this world or who shold man account of worldly welth. You know that the late Erl of Shrewsburie was accounted for cattell, corne, woll, leade, yorne, landes revenew and of redy money the greatest and only rych subject of England. Yet now he is ded, he was so poore as no executor will take upon him to performe his will. . . . God be mersefull unto us and deliver all our man frendes of the danger of the furnyce.' [3] They were happily not greatly concerned with the ' furnyce,' but perhaps those long dead procurators, whose rent rolls of their monasteries were now so well guarded at Belvoir, could suggest whom they ' wold account of worldly welth.' How united were these brothers together is shown by another letter of assured and calm piety. ' I desire no worldly thing more than that I may end my days with you in contemplation.' [4] But soon the note is changing, for ' Sir John

---

[1] It was thirty years since Roger Manners had been in attendance as one of the Queen's Esquires of the Body, for on 4th July, 1571, he had written to his nephew Edward, Earl of Rutland, ' I will leave the Court to younger folks and learn to keep your plough.' Cal. Rutland MSS., i, p. 94.
[2] Letter from Roger to John Manners, dated 10th February, 1591. Cal. Rutland MSS., i, p. 287.
[3] Letter from the same to the same, dated 21st December, 1591, sent on the occasion of the death of their brother-in-law. Ibid., pp. 285–6.
[4] Letter from the same to the same dated 25th February, 1601. Ibid., p. 367.

Byron,' wrote [1] Roger once more, ' sent me four pies of a dainty roe, but your fat hind,' he continued to his brother, ' will be very welcome when it comes.' The piety has gone, the calm remains. It was an age of peaceful conquest of nature over grace.

These lives thus suggest that contented and unruffled ease of the background of England. Against the scene of these fortunate harvests and the peace of the woods, the priests and their helpers, who regarded life with anxiety for the bringing back of religion, seemed at the least rather extreme, men who insisted even against opposition on a belief now becoming less common. To the Manners and all their wide circle, the great landed squires in the country, it seemed a mistake not to follow Her Majesty's wishes, and the sight of a man of good standing, a gentleman, going to prison, as Sir Thomas Tresham had done, was painful, embarrassing, in a sense a humiliation for the whole of their order. Really the Recusants would be wise not to continue to trouble the waters. The sense of visible age as a main test of worth, so essentially English, appears here again in the value that was set on the Queen. All the notions of Essex and his supporters seemed to the great part of the nation unpleasant and foolish; for there was no rural reflection of his elaborate, theatrical hopes; although he might perhaps dazzle young Rutland with the ideas that the uncles despised. To them the law gave protection and the age brought prosperity. They were plain, sensible men and, as they considered briefly the reign and its glories, this alone was enough to convince them and to strengthen their contempt for the boys who would willingly idle in London. No one need bother with politics when there was the right sort of Government and all knew Her Majesty's wisdom, for the Spaniards had been finely defeated. The crops now gave excellent promise and, dismissing all tedious matters, Roger Manners, in this a type of the rural and undying England, called his servant to bring round his horse.

Thus behind the elegant life which Rutland led with Essex, moody and splendid, and Southampton, always deploring the absence of exercise for his fine ear for Italian on which he dwelt with such pride, there moved the slow and undisturbed life of the country. To old Roger Manners, as he sat in the evening with his riding boots stretched out to the blaze and his gauntlets thrown on the table by his

---

[1] Letter from Roger to John Manners, dated 29th December, 1595. *Ibid.*, p. 329.

wet stained hat with its hardy feather, there was certainly matter for merriment, amusing and rather disgusting, a fine ear for Italian indeed, and, as for young Southampton's *protégé*, the very name was enough, Florio, he would soon pack that ruffian back home. It is a mark of the life of the period that in the mind of the Philistines there was always a sinister suggestion in waiting.

It is clear that in all his relations it never occurred to Essex, who exacted a profound deference to his rank, that he was not extremely broadminded and that a wider basis could be found than his system of friendship. All his supporters in Essex House, gentle birth being presumed, seemed Knights of the Round Table together ; for it was perfectly clear that he was cast for the part of an Arthur. But it was the misfortune of the Essex House group that, although there was clearly an Arthur and every *purlieu* was swarming with Knights, each group lived in separate apartments, carefully graded according to rank, and there could be no Round Table. And, if Rutland can stand as example of the company of the Earl's private lodging, Francis Tresham can well represent the men of that chamber, next below him in honour, to which the pages returning would carry the dishes. The name, with all that it implies of the Monteagle Letter and the Gunpowder Plot, comes from the centre of that caste below Manners, the families just under a peerage, very prosperous, knights of the shire.

Francis Tresham had much in his favour, a familiarity with the French Embassy Staff, a merry, strong spirit and an ample allowance ; while the fact that he was thought ' unstayed and wild ' was not in Essex's eyes a disfavour. At home he had tried to persuade the land steward to falsify his accounts to cover his borrowings, which will introduce the necessary fact, that, although a Catholic, he could not be considered a good one. This last essential detail in particular was an advantage, and behind him was the solid prestige of that ingenuous and estimable gentleman, his father Sir Thomas. The little rooms in Essex House looked down on the inner courts of this palace ; but the men who sat over these tables had their interests deep in the soil. Behind them, and by attraction or repulsion always affecting their moves, was their fathers' grouping, the squires, disturbed, though the land was their own, for the sons were its pledges. The contrast between Father and Son was in this case most definite, and Sir Thomas Tresham is paralleled, as a Catholic supporting the Queen and her

Government, by Roger Manners who stands as a type of her loyal and simple adherent.

Few episodes can indicate better how far removed was the Catholicism of the old English squires from any pro-Spanish sympathies than a consideration of the calm outlook at Rushton ; so typical of those wide reaches of the life of the country where the Old Faith still survived. Yet while Rushton and its household could be multiplied through all the lands of the great Catholic squires, its owner was apart and remarkable, with his wide ramshackle knowledge and his firm yet strangely cast mind. Nevertheless, just as Jerningham or Cornwallis, he stands as a symbol for the close of that epoch, which they were beginning. The religious sympathies acting upon a cultivated spirit and a mind, ingenious in the Elizabethan sense of the term, result in a certain atmosphere where Latin allusions are common. Yet this is no foreign learning, nor phrases gained in travel, but only the old use of the Latin of the Mass in the English churches and the memory of such classical tales as might furnish a rural retreat ; the Latin of the old house chaplain at his prayer and his study, that scene which Tresham remembered while the Manners forgot.

The catastrophe in which Rutland and Francis Tresham were involved was to come to these elders and, however divergent their sympathies, it was that common acceptance of Government by which they were saved. Yet in place of the rustic customs at Uffington, there was a very different *ménage* around the young Francis Tresham as he would pace with his father in the gallery chamber at Rushton to try the effect of the new window carvings. The free masons brought up on the property, old Tyrrell and his sons from the cottage, had laboured with cunning and skill and the monograms on the window shaft ends showed a clean cut, delicate work. Every mathematical and astrological problem was a joy to Sir Thomas, and Francis, in spite of his own sole absorption in the life of the sword, could now, from a long experience, trace the plan of his riddles in stone. On every part of the house he had set the seal of his curious spirit and the stonework at the end of the gallery and the staircases and the hall were all marked with his emblems, either the secret monograms ' in laud of the Mother of God ' or those triangles which brought back his thought to the Trinity and the Treshams, while everywhere in wood or stone the ' 25 ' was found intertwined, the quadrate of Jesus and Maria, that fortunate number. Hastily cast into a cupboard there lay the large cosmographical atlas and Clavius' arithmetic studies, which led to those conversational gambits with which Francis was by now so familiar and to the discussion of the effect of the triangular Warryners Lodge and the elevations and plans for the garden house out at Lyveden, which was only now rising. Behind all this and giving such fancies a chance to develop there was the strong income of that prosperous countryside [1] from the rich Northamptonshire fields and the market town tenements and then the London houses, so useful to Francis, the house in the orchard at Hogsden, which his father preferred, and the noisier lodging in Westminster, close to the river.[2]

Quaint if expensive ' conceits ' with a well filled chest to rely on ; this has proved the traditional recipe and many a gentleman in the centuries which followed was to show self-reliance of mind in cultivated, yet rural, retreat ; but Sir Thomas was different. Across the whole of the background there lay the threat of that prison, which he had already suffered for years, and if he possessed at the moment freedom, which he had but recently gained, he could not finger his drawings or consider the arrangement of roses, damask and red, without the thought of a new search party, the hoof beats of pursuivants on the gravel, the sheriff standing courteous, yet, once again, arrest. With this background Francis had been familiar since childhood, and he had seen, as a boy of fifteen, his father first go away captive, but there was no use in discussion, for Sir Thomas was always looked on in the light of a hostage and none could tell when a political change of the weather would make the Government wish to ' restrain ' him again. The ministrations of priests, long so familiar, continued ; but Sir Thomas would remember, as the nut trees in the avenue under the gallery windows now darkened with the loss of the light, that as far as search parties were concerned the evening brought freedom. Priests could so easily escape in the shadow of darkness, and it was always wiser to hunt them in the full light of the day

[1] A letter from the Board of Green Cloth to the Justices of Northamptonshire dated 9th February, 1598, indicated that Francis Tresham took some part in local life. Cal. Buccleugh MSS., iii, pp. 54-5.

[2] The second town house was in Tuthill Fields, Westminster, and the first stood ' in a little orchard and less garden ' at Hogsden, now Hoxton. These details, as well as the reference to Sir Thomas' interest in cosmographical maps, Calvius' arithmetic, the freemasons of the Tyrrell family and the arrangement of red and damask roses, are scattered through Sir Thomas' papers, which were discovered in 1828 at Rushton, walled up in a chest and were known from their later owner as the Clarke Thornhill MSS. The details of the houses the nut avenue and the building plans come also from this source.

And under his surface interests and that underlying fear of arrest, which all men could so well understand, there ran a strong vein of piety, which made the squires of the opposite party, like Manners, uneasy and seriously embarrassed his son. To the Essex House group an honest swordsman's belief, like that of Sir Christopher Blount, was quite natural, but there were some details of Sir Thomas' behaviour which struck them as old-fashioned and fervent, his references to himself, for instance, as suffering for Rachel, as he now termed the Church, ' for Rachel, beautiful and devoted and graceful.' Yet there is in the life of this persecuted squire no suggestion of forced virtue, for, if it would seem the characteristic of English and Continental Puritans that their lives often fitted into an ordered framework, some discreet portrait of a God-fearing gentleman whose white starched lace fell soberly on a coat of untrimmed black, there was on the contrary the widest freedom for the supporters of a Universal Church.

Even the fierce attacks of the Government could not temper their standing quarrels and their arduous, lengthy disputes, and the career of Tresham shows clearly how fully they played their part in the life of the period.[1] As for Sir Thomas, he had himself been brought back to the practice of the ancient religion by the Jesuit Fathers, and he remained a steadfast adherent with a profound attachment to England and the life of the fields. It was indeed an existence bound up with the spirit of the Elizabethan English, building and litigation and the riding through his own country, but different in that every pursuit in his case was lit by an ardour of Faith. A certain impetuousness had gathered his troubles together, the reverse side of that strong-willed endeavour which had caused him to suffer his confinements so staunchly. In early life he had undertaken a trusteeship in respect to a settlement on the daughters whom an earlier marriage had left to Lord Vaux,[2] before the latter had married Mary Tresham of Rushton.

[1] A letter from Sir Nicholas Poyntz to his sister Lady Heneage, dated 19th May, 1575, provides a contrast with the epistolary style of the earlier Catholic generation. ' I do not care,' wrote Sir Nicholas, ' the value of your stinkinst weed in your garden for the greatest personage living that intendeth to do me wrong. And all the harm I wyshe any of them ys that yff they be wyckid they may be yet afor they dy made sayncts.' Cal. Finch MSS., i, p. 21.
[2] The complex situation is explained by the two marriages of William, third Lord Vaux of Harrowden (1542–1595), first to Elizabeth Beaumont of Grace Dieu and secondly to Mary Tresham. The three daughters of the first marriage, Anne Vaux, Eleanor Brooksby and Elizabeth Vaux considered that their trustee Sir Thomas attempted to favour their stepbrothers, his nephews. He had, however, separate quarrels with one of these nephews, George Vaux and with his niece Muriel.

This trusteeship and the manner in which he championed his brother-in-law's cause, when he became prematurely decrepit, led to labyrinthine disputes, and in addition there were feuds with Lord Morley, whose son Monteagle had married his daughter Elizabeth.

Yet again there was trouble ' in the thwart and variable dealing in my cousin Tufton,' [1] whose daughter Francis Tresham had married, while the dispute appears suddenly clear in a letter attacking Lord Morley. ' I justly may grieve,' wrote [2] Sir Thomas to his son-in-law Lord Monteagle, ' at this his ingrate using me unparently prejudicing your lordship and violent wronging my poor daughter your wife.' At the same time there was all the Vaux tribe in the feud, beginning with old Lord Vaux, whom he assisted and pitied, just come up to town, ' raggedly suited and clothed unfittedest to give dutiful attendance on royal presence . . . moneyless and creditless, the unfortunatest peer of parliament that ever was.' This poor man was the feeble and yielding figurehead around whom raged the storm. The daughters claimed that his moneys were being misused by their stepmother's brother, Sir Thomas, while George Vaux and his father-in-law Roper had another side of dispute and behind them ranged Tufton and Morley, who were also hostile to Tresham, and finally far in the background was the easy figure of Fitton. ' A Fourth,' wrote [3] Sir Thomas in his anxiety, ' who for this four years hath troubled me most of all the rest is Sir Edward Phitton. He oweth me four hundred pounds, never fingered I penny of the money.' Then, to add to the difficulties, it was admitted by Sir Thomas that he had had financial transactions as a result of which he was bond for £2,400 for Lord Vaux and £1,500 for himself ' unto a merciless griping usurer.' [4] Meanwhile Anne Vaux was claiming £500 for her jointure and the Widow Vaux had brought an action against him and Sir John Arundell ' and others of reverent worth for cozening of the Lord Vaux of very great sums of money.' [5] ' Smally to my profit,' wrote [6] Sir Thomas

[1] Letter of Sir T. Tresham to Mistress Sedley, dated 16th May, 1592. Cal. Clarke Thornhill MSS., p. 63.
[2] Letter of Sir T. Tresham to Lord Monteagle, dated 2nd February, 1593. *Ibid.*, p. 65.
[3] Letter of Sir T. Tresham.
[4] Letter of Sir T. Tresham to the Bishop of Lincoln, dated 6th May, 1593. *Ibid.*, p. 74.
[5] Statement of Sir Thomas Tresham's Case, dated Summer, 1599. *Ibid.*, p. 102.
[6] Letter of Sir T. Tresham to George Vaux, dated 18th February, 1593. Another letter also bears this out. ' Aptly might I say,' wrote Sir Thomas, ' that Acteon's dogs he fostereth who while he mindfully feedeth them, they monstrously mercilessly would devour him.' *Ibid.*, p. 103.

at one stage of the struggle, ' prove I the words of the prophet most true. Inimici hominis domestici ejus.' A saying that in this case cannot be contested. There was also trouble in his own household as well, since Muriel Vaux, another of these recalcitrant wards, eloped with George Foulshurst, the steward at Rushton, which involved Sir Thomas Tresham in rising circles of anger. ' This witless casting herself away on a landlopper,' he wrote [1] with his vigour of phrase, ' a very beggar and bankroot base fellow.' Here is the mounting Henrican wrath which formed that tremendous background which older men still admired ; for as long as the Queen's reign endured they were careful to live in the shadow which her royal father had cast.

It is one of the contrasts between the late Elizabethans like Essex and his supporters and the generation before them that while the latter thought King Henry heroic, the former touched by the Renaissance outlook had lost the old sense of reverence for the huge preposterous King. Yet with his untrammelled strength there is no question of regarding Sir Thomas as quarrelsome, but rather as a man who would translate into action each impulse as it came. Thus he was devoted to Muriel Throckmorton, whom he had married when still quite a boy, and his letters to her throw shadows of his fantasy and piety, each quick exuberant view. The end of one round of his struggle with his eldest Vaux niece, Mrs. Brooksby, is in this way faithfully reflected. Sir Thomas had come to London in autumn and the household was settling down quietly now that his steward Foulshurst ' that arrant varlet ' had gone. ' Jesus Maria,' he begins,[2] ' this present weeping All Souls Day (which exceedeth all the extreme wet days of this long matchless wettest season) have arrived (as my petty Hogsden Common was coming for my dinner) my now kind former unkind cousin accompanied with old Broksbie and a pettifogging formal solicitor of hers with a retinue of many servants, I having then none here but Hilkton and my trusty cook. Justice Beawmont groweth weary of it . . . now they depend on me to solicit her father. My greatest adversaries rely much of my good nature. They term me Machivelian, but they seem to trust me as reformedst Christian,

---

[1] Statement of Sir Thomas Tresham's Case, dated Summer, 1599. Cal. Clarke Thornhill MSS., p. 102.
[2] Letter from Sir Thomas to Lady Tresham, dated Hogsden or Hoxton, 2nd November, 1594. Cal. Clarke Thornhill MSS., p. 84.

devoid of spleen and fraught with charity. . . . Farewell Tres, Almighty God bless all ours.' [1]

It is the interest of this correspondence that it gives an impression of the life of the wealthy Catholics at the end of the reign, and shows that the Government's action might cripple but could not debar them from the common round of their day. The custom of reading into the sixteenth-century conditions that partial ostracism of Papists, which the eighteenth century brought forth, is nowhere more firmly corrected. All Tresham's divided opponents were Catholics, but this was a natural state of affairs, since Tudor litigation arose from disputed views upon contracts, a bond which in those social conditions would normally concern a close kindred. Besides, they only quarrelled within their own kindred because at that time the ties of mere friendship were still seldom sufficiently close to involve a business relation.

Again, it is curious to note with what friendship this devoted Catholic regarded the new Anglican Bishops who were so closely concerned with the laws from which he now suffered. This is a point which throws light on the outlook of those great Catholic squires who supported the Queen. It would seem to result from the fact that in so far as they were gaolers, as the Bishop of Lincoln had been to Sir Thomas, the Anglican prelates acted as servants of the State, a purely official function to which the Authoritarian thought of the Catholics could not attach blame. Then in the second place the high offices of State were still often granted to bishops, and they received in regard to their duties all that prestige which still followed the Crown's representative. Thus, for instance, Archbishop Mathew of York would receive in his secular and official capacity letters of effusive respect written with a quite sufficient sincerity by the northern Catholics of influence, whose Ancient Faith he opposed. However much they might differ, Sir Thomas Tresham and Manners were united in their acceptance of Government, the authority and power of the Prince. Yet it might be considered that the names of this group were ill-omened for a peaceful Catholicism, Tresham and his son-in-law Monteagle and Robert Catesby his nephew and his friend Digby's

---

[1] As a letter heading ' Jesus ' alone was not, although an old custom, exclusively Catholic. ' Maria ' was the test of one party, ' Emmanuel ' of the other. *Cf.* Trevelyan Papers, iii, *passim.* Lord William Howard always began his letters, when writing to his co-religionists, with the sign of the Cross. Household Books of Naworth, 1612–40, *passim*, Surtees Society.

D D 2

son at Stoke Dry, the young gallant Everard. But here again there is contrast between the older staid men, Roger Manners and Tresham, and the young and riotous crew who now followed Essex so bravely and were later to prove the nucleus of the Gunpowder Plot. It is a mark of that foolishly desperate affair that, however much it affected the public opinion in England, it could gather hardly a trace of sympathy among the contemporary Catholics. It was in fact not even a movement of the Catesbys or Treshams, but in each family the effort of ' one wylde and unstayed man.' The Civil Wars and the Recusants' action, all the lives that they gave and the money poured out for the King would surely in time have come to satisfy Tresham. For beyond his imprisonments and lawsuits and the building plans and Latin lay an abiding deep content ; a peace to which the ending of a letter to his wife would seem clearly to provide us with the key. ' God turn all to good,' Sir Thomas wrote, ' who grant us of his grace and bless all ours. Farewell Tresse.'

Thus behind Rutland and Tresham there lay the great influence of the rural landowners, conforming or Catholic, prosperous or half crippled ; [1] but in each case giving a value and substance to the actions of those who in the young Earl's service in London could speak for these acres. Yet the same power of the land which gave them meaning, that heavy influence of their fathers' shires, acted upon their freedom like a brake. The Queen now stood for all the solid things. But in Essex House, beyond Rutland and Tresham and the groups of the lesser landed squires, below the Gelli Meyricks and the Davys, men who gained a stake, if only by marriage, in the land, there came my Lord's literary followers, who had carefully forgotten their past and no longer retained an existence separate from their functions in that miniature court. It was one of the chief weaknesses of Essex House and a flaw which helped to bring about disaster that there were some within its inner circle who had no independent life outside its walls. The secretaries of the Earl had this position, and no one was so closely bound up with Essex, nor on his chief's admission more disastrous than the principal secretary, Henry Cuffe, a man whose every prospect

---

[1] In regard to the incidence of the Recusancy Laws, a careful assessment has been made in *Timperley of Hintlesham* by Miss L. J. Redstone, to whom acknowledgment is due for much courteous assistance. Convictions were recorded in Quarter Sessions all over England, at the Assizes and in the Court of King's Bench ; extracts of conviction being returned by the judges to the Clerk of the Estreats, who issued corresponding ' summons of the greenwax ' to the sheriff of the county concerned.

was bounded by the limits of this one patron's fortune. Rash counsels would thrive in such a case, for ahead lay the success of Cuffe's ambition, even in failure his patron would maintain him; but it was his error that he forgot the block.

It was partly the depressed condition of such dependents which urged them forward; for a transition from contract to status was the goal of every man's desire. It was characteristic of the age that status was considered solely in regard to landed wealth, accompanied inevitably by the field sports which were its life and the heraldic emblems which were its badges very ruthlessly displayed. Academic distinction and even the political posts, short of the highest, conveyed no such status; but the friendly condescension of these relations could be terminated instantly at will.[1] Meanwhile an attitude composed of indifferent friendliness and horseplay rewarded those obsequious efforts which were not refused. The very fact that contract governed the relations also involved the happy consciousness of the Earl's gentlemen that it was no part of their duty to make welcome ' those gents of the first head ' whom their Maecenas had the folly to receive.

It was a mark of this curious situation that only those near to Essex in rank could understand the motives of his action. To Rutland therefore the introduction of a philosopher in ordinary into the household was merely another proof of his friend's wonderful mind, and Sir Charles Danvers too, as his letters still prove, considered it a nicely distinctive action, but as the gentlemen drew further from this centre their comments were each louder and more coarse; nor did Henry Cuffe lack the qualities for their enjoyment. The memories of his youth were precious to them with their barbarian distaste for rising talent which no civilization had yet come to quell. They did not permit him to be unconscious of the heavy farmer's stock from which he sprung, his own weak incapacity in the harvest, the long hours of waiting for his patron, standing bareheaded on the terrace front at Hinton, while old Lady Elizabeth held sway. It was not the scholars on the free school benches who pleased the gallants most among their men. They could perceive the pride of intellect and sharpness; but it was hardly to be expected they should consider that

---

[1] Blackmail, of course, remained a possibility, as most of the political patronage passed through the secretaries. *Cf.* Essex's decisions as to burgesses for Parliament. Cal. Hereford Corporation MSS., p. 338, Cal. Shrewsbury Corporation MSS., p. 57, Cal. Dunwich Corporation MSS., p. 85.

the farmer's son from Donyatt, with the Somerset 'burr' upon his careful wisdom, would ever meet them upon equal terms. Down in the country all their clanship of the masters moved forward, a slowly balanced lifetime of receipt; but even now, while Mr. Cuffe was summoned to delight my Lord, they were conscious of the character of his brother's labour, that he was doing not his own but Powlett's work. This was a factor which embittered all Cuffe's memories, the rich harvests of the West Country, the apple orchards by the lanes to Combe St. Nicholas, the rising skyline of the Dorset hills; for he had seen these lovely and quiet seasons in their changes from the driver's seat behind the plough.

He provides an instance therefore of a type, later to be so much more common; that of a man whose every spoken utterance reflects the University contacts of his youth. Trinity gave the basis for him to build on, since Hinton St. George, lying in the sunlight with its outbuildings and courts and around it the widening circles of the manor, was an impression securely locked away. Henceforward he was to be a learned scholar with pleasant relaxations into wit success-fully forming against setbacks that composite character the Grecian Cuffe. But a certain lack of proportion in the outlook of this philo-sopher of the opposition gave his opponents every chance which they could wish. To Tresham and his companions dicing away the boredom of the wearisome evenings in the winter, every foible was to prove a godsend; for the apparatus of learning struck their humour, the massive knowledge which Cuffe marshalled so precisely, the little Italian phrases when he was happy, and from time to time the weighed severe remarks. It is not surprising that in the days of waiting the learned Hotomanxus his correspondent and the translation of Gelasius the Cyzicene were gambits which yielded up their prey. For now six years that deeply obscene scurrility, which was then the hall-mark of a gentleman of breeding, had played upon him without ceasing; but in the seventh came destruction and Cuffe in a measure brought about the fall.

Their worlds in fact at no point touched, and it was not safe to keep within this company a spirit, at once so vaulting and remote. There are several instances of conflict, and especially the letter sent [1]

[1] Letter of Sir Anthony Standen to Edward Reynolds, dated from Dublin 27th April, 1599. Cal. Salisbury MSS., ix, p. 144.
    In regard to his patron's favour this would not seem to have proved constant. 'After this sentence,' Wotton wrote of Essex's confinement on his return from Ireland, 'Cuffe, his Secre-

from Ireland that ' Mr. Cuffe's brain pan be wonderfully shaken by the importunity, or rather sauciness, of the undiscreet martial sort.' His brain pan might indeed be shaken, but it would have proved much wiser for those captains to have cast him off entirely from their circle, but that, so long as he retained his patron's favour, it was entirely beyond their power to do. Meanwhile, his ideas developed as unofficial agent for his master, first in Paris and then in Italy, and he took a hand in foreign politics and even in a military design.[1] The despatches he sent surely called for caution, the details of the ' bagascia who is infinitely potent '[2] as he dwelt on his fortunate relations with the King's mistress, the Duchesse de Beaufort, the ' vilcacheria ' of the King of France and then, when the scene shifts again to Florence, the complacent account of his admission to the Accademia della Crusca, all this is hardly serious diplomacy. A letter from Florence clearly shows his quality, the dilettante, but the rather unsophisticated dilettante of affairs. ' The Scommunica against Don Cesare I enclose,' he wrote[3] in reference to the Ferrara Excommunication, ' the Mother Church which has been long with child of Ferrara begins now to fall in labour and, as you may gather by these her cries, she stands in fear of a sore travail.' Self-assurance by now was well established, for the days of his early secretaryship were far behind him, the humble cabin of the *Due Repulse*. And yet he had always a firm devotion to his patron. ' The times are so bad,' he wrote[4] from Ireland to his fellow-secretary, good honest Ned, ' and the surly humours with you there (in England), that I fear rather than wish this journey. Notwithstanding " jacta est alea." I would rather lose with him (Essex) than gain with his opposites.' He was a man without inherited tradition, devoid of independent experience, unhampered by any vested wealth, his every interest centred upon Essex, an embarrassing, a fatally devoted friend.

tary who always persuaded the Earl to stand stoutly in his own defence, began plainly to tax him with cowardice and pusillanimity, which so angered the Earl that he ordered him to be put out of the roll of his servants ; yet Merrick, the Steward, forbore though he was of Cuffe's mind.' *Memoirs of the Earl of Essex*, p. 17.

[1] A proposal was sent to Henry Savile from Paris on 14th June, 1597, in favour of a design against Havana ; ' the emprise of the Terceraes is less feasible and less important.' Cal. Salisbury MSS., vii, p. 234.

[2] According to despatches of the summer and autumn of 1597. *Ibid.*, vii, pp. 234 and 424.

[3] Letter of Henry Cuffe to Henry Savile, dated from Florence 27th December, 1597. *Ibid.*, vii, p. 525.

[4] Letter of Henry Cuffe to Edward Reynolds, dated at Dublin 4th August, 1599. It is interesting that even in this devoted letter Cuffe's over-subtle character is clear. ' I used a little cunning,' he wrote, ' in getting a copy of the Council's letter.' Cal. Salisbury MSS., ix, p. 270.

THE CELTIC PEOPLES & RENAISSANCE EUROPE

This was the world of the secretaries, and there also moved in the same social half-light my Lord's chaplains, for, as Sir Thomas Tresham would put it, they were bound closely together, ' the Atheists and the Heretikes ' in ' this dampnable crew.' There had first been the jovial and insincere Alabaster; but he had gone over to Rome and was now confined in the Tower. They could well remember his tragedy on *Roxana* and his manuscript poems, the studies in the Cabala and his magical signs. These last had brought him to favour and the lords would graciously summon him after their dinner, so that, as they sat fingering their sweet comfits, he could give out his discourse on horoscopes and the black arts, very diverting. But now his place had been taken by Abdie Ashton the Puritan, and when Alabaster returned to resume his Anglican ministry he found that his patron was dead.

More significant than either of these men was the portentous figure of Barlow, the Bishop of Chichester's son. Among all the Anglican clergy Lord Essex affected him most, for he had been brought up to know so well that lumbering figure at Lamphey, when he lived there as a boy. He was very loyal to the Devereux, as was his Catholic cousin at Slebech, and for the last thirty-five years, ever since he had gone down from Balliol, he had been as far as preferment was concerned on the market. Essex had done what he could for him and Barlow's four episcopal brothers-in-law had not been unwilling; but he was not easy to help. Yet it was just those characteristics which made it difficult to accommodate him with an income that led to the strong sympathy of Essex's curious mind. Now that he was close upon sixty, with Antonia's husband at Winchester, he had been established there with a stall and Essex and Mary Barlow between them had made him Treasurer up at Lichfield, where his brother-in-law held the see, and he was also Rector of Easton with valuable parsonage lands. It was a suitable enough provision for a bachelor of certain pretensions, and meanwhile his great work, *The Navigator's Supply*, was completed and he was secure in harbour at last, and this was fortunate since he was not in any sense adventurous and ' by natural constitution of body,' as he wrote in his preface, ' even when I was young and strongest I altogether abhorred the sea.' At Essex House he was hardly at ease, for he could feel that in those circles he was not completely accepted,[1] and the Catholics were stiff with him as the son of a monk, but the condescension with which Essex treated him made up for all slights. There at last in the private cabinet he was sure of a welcome, for he was always received with graciousness and his patron would pay as much attention to his exposition as could be expected from a man of rank, nor would he ever leave without his fee. 'May it please you,' he wrote [2] in the course of this last winter to his protector, 'not to defer your conference with Mr. Wright concerning the use of the celestial and terrestrial globe. I earnestly desire that you would give me leave to confer with you about the nature of the magnet, a thing of most admirable effects and use. I do not doubt but to resolve many questions without flying into " Sympathia," "Antipathia" or "Occulta Proprietas," the usual refuges of ignorance in this argument. I very earnestly wish that you would assay to provide you of 3 or 4 excellent good loadstones.[3] They be rare jewels and very hard for any mean man to attain to.' 'For any mean man to attain to,' a lifetime of precarious flattery had taught him when to slip the needed phrase.

These men then, added to the Welsh soldiers like Meyrick and that general military following, already discussed, represent the variety of the types about Essex, all dependent upon his bounty or fixed to his friendship, most urging him forward, meeting and caballing in the little rooms of this rambling palace, always close about him and anxious. In those last months if the Earl with his changing will had any hope of peace he was deceived, however calm he might sit in his privy chamber alone with Southampton and Rutland as the pages stirred the fire and drew the hangings against the rain with its sharp patter. Outside, the lighted rooms around the courtyard were filled with the gentlemen whom he had chosen, dicing and grumbling with the hand on the chased sword hilt ; while beyond the farthest kitchen buildings the inns and stables in the streets around were crowded

---

[1] The determined action of the Bishop of London in the later crisis seems to reflect a somewhat anti-episcopal trend at Essex House. This is borne out by an account of the conversation of Thomas Overbury, who belonged to this group. ' Mr. Thomas Overbury,' so runs the entry, ' spake much against the Lord Buckhurst as a very corrupt and unhonest person of body. He spake bitterly against the Bishop of London, that darling convict for a counterfaiture of passes was a better scholler ; that the Bishop was a very knave.' 11th April, 1603, John Manningham's *Diary*, 1602–3, Camden Society, pp. 168–9.

[2] Letter from William Barlow to the Earl of Essex, dated at Easton on 5th January, 1601. Cal. Salisbury MSS., xi, p. 4.

[3] Essex kept *The Bibill of Geomancye* in his library. Cal. Northumberland MSS., Third Report, Appendix ix, p. 113.

with their serving men and horses. All the household, men of letters as of the sword, were pressing forward. Only Essex remained untouched and aloof, while the tide swept about him seething and dangerous.

*   *   *   *   *

It was towards the end of January that the details of the Rising began to clear. Yet, until the end and that last abortive ride, the ordinary round at Essex House continued, for, since it was essential to avoid suspicion, there must be no ceasing of that streaming life. A general desire for some action and a sense of all the armed men who stood waiting for orders increased that inner tension, which the wide ramifications of that following and the multitudinous over-coloured action did so much to conceal. The absence of any controlling order and the profound detachment of the guiding spirit [1] only increased the luxuriance of the growth. It is this supreme indifference in Essex which accounts for so much. Now that the different groups have been considered, an impression of the confusing conflict which their close association produced will lead to an understanding of Essex and the springs of his conduct in the last and crucial days of his liberty.

The temporary freedom which marked this gathering of all who opposed the Queen's old and staid Government emphasizes the contrasted elements which a long reign had subdued and, if it was the carefully controlled Government of the Cecils which had roused such diverse opposition, it was the compound of a remoteness of spirit and an outward magnificence which had focussed them about this leader. There was something very near to tolerance in Essex House. Secretaries of a somewhat conventional mould, like the young Henry

[1] A remark of Bacon's after the return from Ireland typifies Essex's own spirit. ' I told him (Essex) My Lord, " nubecula est, cito transibit." ' *Apology for the Earl of Essex*, p. 148.

Wotton, might feel ill at ease in the writhing 'tabacca' smoke of the new kingdom of Euphues; but this did not for a moment hinder the freedom of the swordsmen and literary gallants, just as the scepticism of Cuffe in no way affected the fervent if hot-house Catholicism which honeycombed the whole movement. At a time when religious feeling ran high, there was not only a Puritan section, but there were men in the innermost circle both passing away from and into the proscribed Catholic Church. Southampton, for instance, was slowly abandoning the Faith of his childhood, turning as John Donne had turned from the old, sober, exacting religion; while another tide had carried Sir Charles Danvers and Davys into the Catholic fold in its least homely aspect. Sir Christopher Blount, Essex's stepfather, was a Catholic from birth [1] and represented another type, good natured and artless, the 'Good Mr. Kyt' [2] of Leicester's contemptuous affection. And then to crown this diversity there was Essex's sister, the now shrill and desperate Penelope with her hectic courtesan's vision of that haven of peace, and everywhere the religions were criss-crossed. Thus Christopher Blount was married, when hardly out of his boyhood, to the ageing Countess of Leicester, Essex's mother, who was as fervent a Protestant as her hatred of the Queen would allow. On the other hand, Penelope Rich had surrendered, with her husband's connivance, to Christopher's brother Mountjoy, the father of her children, a defender of the Pure Gospel, a worthy, godly peer. [3] Yet from all these diverging opinions Essex kept himself free. [4] This was not an age when the ideas of the women folk counted, and he was hardly likely to consider Penelope's standpoint [5] or the restrained Catholic

---

[1] According to a letter from Thomas Morgan to the Queen of Scots, dated 10th July, 1585, 'Mr. Christopher Blunt . . . is a tall gentleman and valiant and has been well brought up by his careful and devout parents who are Catholics.' Cal. State Papers, Scottish, 1585–6, p. 13. At the same time his career resembled Sir William Stanley's, for as late as 28th May, 1600, Sir Geoffrey Fenton was writing to Sir Robert Cecil to express his disbelief in Udall's statement that 'Sir Chris Blount was reconciled to Popery at his last being in Ireland.' Cal. S.P. Irel., 1600, p. 209.

[2] Letter of Leicester to Mr. C. Blount dated 7th June, 1587, 'I am sorry Mr. Kyte for your hurt.' Cal. Pepys MSS., pp. 180–1.

[3] 'Being in his youth addicted to Popery he began to be confirmed in the Reformed Doctrine, which I am confident he professed and believed with his Heart. He never used Swearing and rather Hated it.' Description of Lord Mountjoy, Fynes Moryson, History of Ireland, i, pp. 107 and 113.

[4] As an instance of how early Essex had suffered from misrepresentation on this point, Crispin Norrys reported in August, 1596, that one Brown declared that Essex was a Catholic. Cal. Somerset MSS., p. 15.

[5] Lady Penelope's early inclinations, her proposal to return to Catholicism and her deathbed reception 'by one of ours' are described by Fr. John Gerard, S.J., in his autobiographical fragment, ed. Morris, pp. 100–2.

tendencies of his own calm and virtuous wife; while, as to Sir Christopher, he was perfectly and serenely conscious of his stepfather's limited mind. In so far as he was affected, Essex followed the Sidney tradition with a still stronger Italianate influence which led from the definite cults.

The Renaissance, in its later Italian conceptions, had only impinged so recently on the ideas of the great English lords that they were still bewildered by phrases, captivating and vague. The visit of Giordano Bruno, that contemptuous reference to Oxford as ' la vedova delle buone lettere ' formed the background of Essex's youth and of the high intellect of the time. Fulke Greville was always ready to discuss the great master who had made the most wise concession to the taste of his time by mingling erotic suggestions with his metaphysical talk. That move at any rate had attracted the gallants as they met ' to discuss matters of a nice and delicate nature behind the closed doors ' ; a link which running through the coteries would unite so many sections,[1] until it reached the most thick-headed swordsmen for whom the coarse jest was too subtle, however much they might desire it. But it was another aspect of Bruno and *Gli Eroici* which appealed now to Essex, the great ringing phrases and the shadow of destiny. For an impression was given of victims lost in a maze of unreality, struggling futilely ' de Umbris Idearum ' in the infinite space that was God. Then how transient was each human activity, for Alberico Gentile had maintained that it was as easy to take oaths as to take soup,[2] and that mankind was tormented by incomprehensible scruples. The coincidence of contraries and the plurality of worlds, such phrases from this new thought sounded so fine. ' Con questa filosofia l'anima mi s'aggrandisce, mi se magnifica l'intelletto.' It was not necessary to have complete understanding or even very arduous consideration ; but all these theories contributed to foster that sense of magnificence. There was much in this Italianate influence to suggest a boundless

---

[1] Although the Nolan's attitude towards the ' common people ' of England was hardly likely to be shared, it is worth noting in relation to the remoteness of this court life. ' When they (the common people) see a foreigner,' declared Bruno, ' they become so many wolves and bears . . . they put on the malevolent look of a pig when you take away his trough.' *Cena dell Cenere*, Dialogo ii.

[2] ' He said,' runs Sir Tobie Mathew's account of his interview with Dr. Gentile, ' I should do discreetly to take it (the Oath of Supremacy) in such sort as had taken his oath of believing the Council of Trent before he came out of Italy in his youth. I asked him how that was ; and he made this answer in direct words (for we spake Italian) : ' Giusto come pigliarei un scudello di brodetto.' *The Conversion of Sir Tobie Mathew*, p. 89.

horizon, and every manifestation Essex gathered to himself.[1] Equally with the swordsmen with their Milanese blades, he cherished the young gallants from Drury House eager to play Philautus to a Southampton Euphues ' enamling with pied flowers their thoughts of gold.' All the pleasures of that day stretched out towards him, the romantic friendships of the Italian fashion, the coming of the new stressed metres, the half lights of the *Pastor Fido*, all confused and mingling, yet each emphasizing for Essex his intellectual remoteness and his power. He would welcome Harrington and Henry Constable with ' his excellent conceitful sonnetts ' and his verses ' unto Her Majesty's sacred honourable maids ' equally with the brawling and drink-laden soldiers; while in a further sphere ' the Vulgar,' to quote Fynes Moryson, ' gave ominous Acclamations.' It was indeed an excess of support and favour, ' l'anima mi s'aggrandisce, mi se magnifica l'intelletto.'

[1] In this connection Essex's sonnet, *The fable of the Bees*, is interesting, and especially that line, so artificial, yet expressive, ' Tis only I must drain Egyptian flowers.'

CHAPTER XXI

THE FINDING OF THE RAYNED DEER

The survey once completed, the actual episodes of the Essex Conspiracy are now considered. Granted his complete absence of actual political power, the problem before Essex and his supporters was how to obtain control of the great posts in the State. There were two possible courses of action, either to determine to obtain control of the Queen or to concentrate on ruling her successor. The achievement of the first objective would result in the success of the second, provided that James VI of Scotland should come to the throne. The three directions from which aid could come are detailed, Scotland, Ireland and Wales, and Essex's negotiations during the winter are examined. As regards King James' assistance, the most that he could obtain was the promise that the Earl of Mar, who was being sent into England as Ambassador, should be instructed to give him a strong diplomatic support. In Ireland the factor of importance was the character of Mountjoy, the Lord Deputy, who was the only one of the high State officials who had been Essex's dependent and friend. The nature of this relationship, the part played by Lady Rich, who was Essex's sister and Mountjoy's mistress, the entanglements which the military supporters of Essex House had introduced, all affected these negotiations which had a crucial share in the disaster. Nothing shows the unreality of Essex's political outlook more clearly than the hopes which he formed of serious military aid from this Government servant. The agents whom he employed with their personal and anti-national loyalties and their outmoded chivalry reveal how the whole Essex House system was passing away, no more than the attitude of the *Guisards* and the League was it capable of sustaining itself in the seventeenth century.

At this point the plans which Sir Gelli Meyrick had formed and now put into practice for obtaining military aid from Wales are considered. The situation created by the death of the President of the Marches, Lord Pembroke, and the consequent vacancy of all his offices is noticed, together with that advantage, more apparent than real, which this factor gave to disorder. The various movements in Wales and the concentration of Essex's Welsh supporters on London and in particular the events following Pembroke's death on 19th January are traced when this is possible. The pressure of the swordsmen on Essex is thus clearly seen, and those factors which now made inevitable some armed display against Cecil and his faction at Court.

There remain to be considered those two sections of opinion in London on which Essex in these last days relied and his confidence, so completely misplaced, that he could obtain support from the City and from the Puritan group. The relations with these two bodies make clear a central weakness in Essex, his intention vaguely to collect every group of the nation round him, although he was never able to move beyond the small circle of the ideas of his *coterie*. The summons to attend the Council, which proved the occasion for the Rising, the hurried consultations and the events of Saturday and Sunday, 7th and 8th February, are then described in detail, a minuteness justified by the fact that this pitiful and haphazard failure marked the last influence of so many movements.

THE FINDING OF THE RAYNED DEER

THE political situation at this period is easily described. Around the ageing Queen there stood a circle of Councillors, the great public servants of the reign, men like the Earl of Nottingham, who had commanded against the Armada. Occupying the key position of Secretary of State, Sir Robert Cecil was now firmly established, supported by Lord Treasurer Buckhurst. The Government was now stable and experienced in power. The war with Spain still lingered on, although the heart had gone from it with the death of Philip II in 1598. France under Henry IV was definitely a friendly power and relations with Scotland were satisfactory, but guarded. The Queen always refused to discuss the Succession.

Essex had held no political power since his disastrous return from Ireland, and he had passed many months in an honourable confinement, now relaxed. His lack of influence had been painfully emphasized in the winter by his failure to obtain from the Queen the renewal of the lease of sweet wines,[1] a source of income which had hitherto proved [2] a mercifully stable asset in his very disordered finance. As to the greater ministerial figures, they regarded Essex with disapproval in varying degrees. Sir Walter Raleigh was an open enemy; nor could it be doubted that Sir Robert Cecil cherished enmity in secret. Lord Nottingham and many of the elder courtiers had suffered from Essex's arrogance in the days of his power. He had, however, one intimate friend in high office, the Lord Deputy Mountjoy. Considered broadly, there were two possible courses of action for Essex, either to determine to obtain control of the Queen or to concentrate on ruling her successor. It was held that the achievement of the first objective would result in gaining the second. It had been wisely decided by Essex's friends, in the course of their changing manoeuvres, which as a rule gave small sign of wisdom, that James VI of Scotland was destined to succeed to the Throne.[3] The question of military action became urgent at this stage, and could be used in two ways.

---

[1] That his interest in this subject was of long standing is shown by a letter from the Lord Admiral to the Mayor of Southampton, dated August, 1589. ' But whereas I finde by my Lord of Essex (whom I accompte of and love as my dearest friend) that the said lease (of sweet wines) would greatly pleasure him, so do I surrender over my said Lease.' Cal. Southampton Corporation MSS., Report II, i, p. 127.

[2] According to John Chamberlain, ' the Erle of Essex kepes much here in towne fed with hope that somewhat will follow, but the licence for sweet wines lies at anchor aloofe and will not come in.' Chamberlain Letters, pp. 92–3.

[3] A correspondence with Lord Chancellor Maitland of Thirlestane was carried on as far back as July, 1595, but at that date Essex had written ' I receive nothing but by my soveraynes privitie.' Cal. Mar and Kellie MSS., Supplement, pp. 36–7.

A direct attempt might be made to overthrow Cecil's Government and force the Queen to accept more noble advisers; or the threat of military action could be kept in reserve, so that, should the Queen die, Essex could act with decision and seize the key positions in the name of King James. It was clear that either plan, if successful, would usher in a long period when Essex would be the chief minister. The continual, although secret, recruiting which Meyrick had practised in Wales and the armed gentlemen gathered in London were both concerned with these plans. It is difficult to resist the impression that Essex believed that fortune would surely favour him and that, if he could only keep his men in control, the Government would fall into his hands through the natural death of the Queen. At sixty-eight and ailing, it was not unreasonable to imagine that her constitution would not in fact carry her through the two years which she had still to live. Yet, even for a leader much more prudent than Essex, it would not have been possible to keep his armed men in check for so long.

As to practical details, there were three sources of aid, the King of Scotland, who would bring Essex's hopes into the European political sphere, the Lord Deputy Mountjoy, who could provide, if he was willing, an army of five thousand men, and the mass of gentry in Wales, which formed his chief ground for recruits. It was now a question of who should be used in these matters. The men whose loyalty had been proved in Ireland were marked out for the trust, and at this time Francis Bacon, who had been so close to Essex's fortunes, was beginning to keep more aloof. Finally, the Scottish negotiations were left in the charge of Mr. Cuffe,[1] the Irish were supervised by Sir Charles Danvers and the Welsh were in Sir Gelli Meyrick's care. The obvious ' impasse ' which had been reached in Essex's affairs made it essential for him to sound the possibilities of the situation. About him in the fevered atmosphere of Essex House there was a sense of impending danger, while he was told so often that Sir Robert Cecil would undo him that he was prevailed upon to set his levers moving. Even so, he made no plans, merely reserving to himself the decision as to

---

[1] According to the examination of Henry Cuffe, dated 2nd March, 1601, ' he confesseth that the matter concerning the Earle of Essex writing to Scotland was debated about Christmas last by the Earle of Essex, the Earle of Southampton, Sir Charles Danvers and this examinate and that the miniute of the lettre was agreed on between them.' *Correspondence of James VI with England*, Appendix, p. 90.

whether or not he should take action. These three negotiations each interlocked and affecting the issue were all concerned in his fall.

Communications with Scotland had been established for more than two [1] years, and the King had even been pressed to make a demonstration on the Border in Essex's favour. The reply from King James was, within the limits of his defective information, careful and prudent. Any armed action would of course be ridiculous ; but Essex was a powerful noble with that handsome presence which King James prized so highly, and the prestige of a popular hero. The fact of his difficulties under the present *régime* only showed that he would have proved loyal to a more generous sovereign. The King therefore was gracious and promised that the Ambassador, whom he was sending, would receive special instructions to give Essex assistance. The choice of envoy, however, shows how little understanding of Essex King James ever possessed. A very noble personage was chosen, the Earl of Mar, a close friend of the Sovereign, and Essex awaited his arrival with that intermittent eagerness which was the only substitute in his temperament for any constant political aim. They were not destined to meet, for Essex was dead before the Scottish Envoy reached London. He was a cautious acquisitive nobleman of middle age, great master of the royal household and known to the King as ' Jock a' sclaitis,' [2] John of the Slates. In Scotland he had arranged the diet of the Court. ' On the flesch day,' he had ordered,[3] ' to the first service ane peis beiff, twa peis sotten muttoun, ane builyeit foull, with sex disch of pottage.' It was as well perhaps that he did not arrive for the inevitable and contemptuous quarrel when Essex would put forth his nebulous argument, strengthened by the new foreign phrases, as he sat at his delicate meat.

The second negotiations, those with Ireland, possess a crucial importance and show how Essex's chances were viewed in his day. The Lord Deputy had been his constant follower, and he felt that he could count on assistance when his peril was grave. The relationship between them was strange. Its beginning was very romantic, reconciliation and friendship following a duel at the Court when Essex

---

[1] ' Concerning the intelligence of my Lord of Essex with that King (James VI), I cannot certainly affirme howe longe it hath continued, but sure I am that it hath benn for at least these two yeares.' Letter of Henry Cuffe to the Council, February, 1601, *Correspondence of James VI with England*, Appendix, p. 86.
[2] Letter from the King. Cal. Mar and Kellie MSS., p. 37.
[3] Memorandum dated 4th February, 1594. *Ibid.*, p. 41.

was the youthful Favourite and Mountjoy a lesser rival[1] for the Queen's good regard. They had fought about a gold enamelled chessman that the latter had received from Her Majesty and wore bound to his arm.[2] Essex had first taunted and then vanquished him, and after this shown forgiveness and taken him to favour, how heedless and arrogant a basis for friendship.

The continuance of the alliance depended on more tangible facts. Charles Blount, who had inherited the ancient barony of Mountjoy, had been for a number of years the acknowledged lover of Essex's sister Penelope. She was approaching forty and the tie was most binding, for her husband, Lord Rich, had withdrawn entirely in deference to his patron, Lord Essex, and the situation was complicated by her twelve little children. Rich had accepted the paternity of the first seven infants, but the last five, born since he had retired from the scene, were Mountjoy's undisputed possession. In the background of this life there was this persistent entanglement which finally led to his ruin when Rich had brought a divorce and King James disgraced the Lord Deputy on account of his marriage. Meanwhile the presence of this mistress, whose high rank gave her a constant claim upon him which her five children did so much to reinforce, must have infused a bitterness at times into Mountjoy's relations with his powerful friend. He was finally to be disgraced through Penelope, but he was all the more determined that he would not die for Penelope's brother. In addition, Essex had opposed his Irish appointment asserting that ' he was too bookish and had small experience in martial affairs.' But how careless Essex remained of these matters, when he sent to ask for his aid.

Nevertheless, Mountjoy had run far in Essex's courses, the first passion for Lady Rich perhaps blinding his judgment, that close appreciation of facts which was to give him all his successes. He had even engaged in that first correspondence with Scotland and would apparently have seemed to have promised to lead over his troops into England, a quite impossible plan. It is difficult to suppose that a politician of Mountjoy's prudence ever intended to carry out such a promise; but the mere fact of toying with the suggestion, with however little sincerity, exposed him to grave danger. But he had

---

[1] Sir Robert Naunton describes Lord Mountjoy as being at this period ' of a brown hair, a sweet face, a most neat composure and tall in his person.' *Fragmenta Regalia*, p. 57.
[2] Description of the duel in Marylebone Park. *Ibid.*, p. 53.

now been eighteen months in Ireland, the successful campaign was developing, Lady Rich was with her brother in London and Mountjoy's judgment was clear. The industry of his secretary, the traveller Fynes Moryson, has provided minute details of Mountjoy's appearance and habits, which simplify considerably the tortuous negotiations of this part of the Essex Conspiracy. Every phrase serves its purpose, the impression so well conveyed of an exquisite now past his prime, whose idiosyncracies made him a butt for the gallants. Every point in the description goes to explain the ill ease that he felt in the company of those who, like Essex, were successfully *mondain*. And then, after the faintly ridiculous picture is clear, those characteristics are mentioned which helped his cool judgment. The preface to this description is admirable. ' I must acknowledge my Weakness,' begins [1] Moryson, ' such as I cannot fully apprehend his compleat Worthiness.' And then the smooth phrasing continues. ' He was of stature tall and of very comely Proportion, his skin fair, with little hair . . . on his Head, where it was short, except a lock under his left Ear, which he nourished the time of this War, and being woven up hid it in his Neck under his Ruff.' It appeared that ' for some two or three years before his Death he nourished a sharp and short Pikedevant on the chin. His Forehead was broad and high, his eyes great, black and lovely ; his Nose something low and short and a little blunt in the End.' It is almost superfluous to add that in Mr. Moryson's opinion, ' his countenance was cheerful and as aimable as ever I beheld in any man.'

The account of his apparel is also revealing, for, after mentioning the black or white taffetas and satins and the plain black beaver hats, which were the commonplace of his age and rank, Mr. Moryson continues. ' He wore two (yea sometimes three) Pairs of silk stockings, with black Silk grogram Cloakes guarded and Ruffs of Comely Depth and Thickness, a Taffeta quilted Wastecoat on Summer, a Scarlet Wastecoat and sometimes both in Winter. In Ireland in the Field, yea three Wastecoats in cold Weather, and a thick Ruff, besides a Russet Scarff about his Neck, thrice folded under it.' The picture presented is that of a quiet, sedate gentleman, just a little eccentric. ' He delighted in Study, in Gardens, an House richly furnished and delectable for Rooms of Retreat, in riding on a Pad to take the air,

[1] Fynes Moryson, *History of Ireland*, ed. 1735, i, p. 104.

in playing at Shuffle board or at cards.'[1] A certain care and a realization that he did not maintain the intellectual ferment of the Essex
House group is evident. ' He understood but did not venture to
speak French and Italian.' So much for the outer aspect of the man
but it is the last few isolated sentences which deserve to be weighed
with greater care. ' And as he had that Commendable yea Necessary
Ability of a good Captain, not only to fight and manage the War well
abroad, but to write and set forth his actions to the full at home. He
was also frugal and saving. He was a close concealer of his secrets,
a free Speaker or a Popular Man could not long continue his Favourite.
A Friend, if not cold, yet not to be used much out of the Highway
and something too much reserved towards his dearest Minions. In
all events he was not without evasion.'[2] In these few sentences the
ruin of Essex is made clear.

And, at this crisis in his affairs, Essex had sent to gain so astute a
leader, not a prudent diplomat, nor even a man of guile like Cuffe,
but young Charles Danvers. This friend had all the qualities of Essex
House and had conceived the opinion[3] that the army should come
from Ireland to his patron's aid. He had a deep loyalty and courage.
' I loved him best,' he declared[4] later in reference to Essex, ' and
did confese myselfe to be most behowlding to him of any man living.
He had saved my life[5] and that after a very noble fashion. He had
suffred for me, and made me by as many means bownde to him, as
on man could be bownde unto an other. The lyfe he saved, and my
estate and means whatsoever, he should ever dispose of. . . . I knew
his Lordship was to noble, howsoever he might enterprise unlawfull
things, to attempt anything fowle or ignominious.' The great estate
of Seven Downs[6] in Wiltshire, the parks at Cornbury, the art collection and that jewellery, which his generation prized, were sacrificed.
It was the last victory of the Philip Sidney standards.

[1] Description, Fynes Moryson's *History*, i, pp. 106–8.
[2] Description in Fynes Moryson's *History of Ireland*, i, pp. 108–12.
[3] ' It beginge thought by Sir Charles Danvers that the army of Ireland would suffice alone.'
Confession of the Earl of Southampton, March, 1601, Appendix to the Camden Society's *Correspondence of James VI with England*, p. 97
[4] Declaration of Sir Charles Danvers, dated 1st March, 1601. *Ibid.*, p. 101.
[5] His pardon after the killing of Henry Long in a fray is also attributed to his mother's
efforts, who ' married Sir Edmund Carey, cousin german to Queen Elizabeth, but kepte him to
harde meate. Aubrey, *Lives*, i, p. 193.
[6] Under his brother, Lord Danby, the estate was worth £11,000 a year in Stuart values,
according to Aubrey, and, although this is presumably an exaggeration, it shows the general
opinion of their wealth. *Lives*, i, p. 194.

THE FINDING OF THE RAYNED DEER

It is no wonder that this meeting proved unfruitful. But Danvers made the Deputy a second proposal, and this he appeared to accept: ' for in all events he was not without evasion.' Essex had proposed that Mountjoy should write a letter to the Queen urging her to abandon her corrupt advisers. It was useless to argue with such a mood, but to the proposer of this dangerous treason he gave a soothing answer, as to a madman or a child. ' Sir Charles,' as Cuffe subsequently declared,[1] ' founde him very affectionate to the Earle, as thinckinge the public to suffer with his private, and consequently that his retourne to her Majesties former grace would tourne to the good of thousands.' Quite so : Mountjoy, at any rate, was determined that his head should not fall upon the block.

It is an interesting study ; Mountjoy, confident in the success of his Irish Government, listening to these ridiculous proposals. ' Sir Charles Danvers,' Southampton wrote [2] in his confession, ' was sent . . . to perswade my Lord Mountjoy to write a letter to him wherin he should complaine of ill gouerment of the state and to wish that some course might be taken to remove from about her Majesties person those which weare bad instrumentes.' He might not be a match for the wits of Essex House, he might be ill-educated and fussy ; but in diplomacy Mountjoy was on his ground. The fact of the first letter to the King of Scots was kept by Essex as a guarantee, according to the polite and almost chivalrous blackmail of the day, and it had been necessary to explain this move away before he could make his new position clear. ' My Lord Mountjoye imparted to myselfe,' wrote [3] Danvers, ' that . . . he had written to the King of Scotts. . . . The cause that mouved my Lord Montioye to enter into this course with Scotlande, and to procede therin afterwards, was, as he protested, his duty to her Majesty and his contry : for he could not thinke his contrye safe, unless by the declaration of the successor it were strengthed agaynst th'assaults of our most potent enemyes, who pretended a title thereunto : nor he coulde not thinke her Majesty so safe by any meane as by making her owne kingdom safe by that union agaynste theyre attempts now.' In this one sentence is embodied all that was to conquer in the Elizabethan system, the courageous mind,

---

[1] Letter of Henry Cuffe to the Council, dated February, 1601. *Correspondence of James VI*, p. 88.
[2] Confession of the Earl of Southampton. *Ibid.*, p. 98.
[3] Declaration of Sir Charles Danvers. *Correspondence of James VI*, p. 102.

the pure expediency, the resolute and labyrinthine thought. It is not surprising that, when compared to the replies from Scotland and Ireland, Essex must have found a strong encouragement in the Welsh outlook and in Sir Gelli Meyrick's simple, feudal mind.

To Sir Gelli it seemed so straightforward, a clear call to vengeance after his master's harsh treatment when he came back from Ireland and then these hesitations and pinpricks. It was only a greater incitement to show that at least his Welsh friends were loyal. He took his orders from Essex direct and was not concerned with the others, so that his plans in that ill-balanced confederacy suffered no hindrance. For some time past now, the friends upon the Welsh border were stirring. ' The summer is half over,' Sir Henry Bromley had written [1] in the previous July, ' time is precious. Let us not lose the start that we have gotten, but bethink of some means either to be winners or savers.' Besides, if the ultimate impracticability of any Welsh military scheme is left out of the question, circumstances seemed favourable ; for the administration of the Marches, which had been running slowly for years was now at the moment held up by the death of the President.

The long period of life as an invalid,[2] tenaciously clinging to office, had robbed the Earl of Pembroke's Presidency of its early success. From Wilton he still attempted to control [3] the orders at Ludlow and the somewhat unruly Councillors, with whom his constant embarrassments had lately become very sharp. There had apparently been attempts by the legal section of the Court of the Marches to obtain his removal and Pembroke had written of his ' causeless crosses ' [4] and that Mr. Townshend ' because I was not willing to forego the Presidentship of Wales, therefore to weary me out of it . . . plotted to diminish the authority which I now have.' [5] This was the same Earl, that friend of Cecil and Burghley, who had earlier shown his contempt for Sir Gelli, so that such a gradual loosening of control was most welcome. All through the last winter he had been sinking,

[1] Letter from Sir Henry Bromley to Henry Cuffe, dated from Holt Castle on 29th July, 1600. Cal. Salisbury MSS., x, p. 250.

[2] A letter of the Queen to Henry, Earl of Pembroke, dated 21st June, 1590, excuses him ' considering his indisposition of health and inability to repair to Wales to hold the session.' Cal. Dovaston MSS., Report xiii, p. 247.

[3] Letter from the Earl of Pembroke to the Queen, dated from Wilton 18th June, 1598, ' his infirmities force him to retire to Wiltshire from service in the Marches of Wales.' Cal. Salisbury MSS., viii, p. 220.

[4] Letter dated 20th December, 1599. Cal. Salisbury, ix, p. 415.

[5] Letter dated 4th April, 1600. *Ibid.*, x, p. 98.

and on 19th January he died. It was an event which could not have failed to affect Sir Gelli's endeavours, for it was not only the Presidency of the Marches which fell vacant, but also those innumerable offices in the West Country and Wales, which had drifted in on that great household at Wilton.[1] In that winter afternoon Her Majesty was deprived of her Constable of Bristol and Brecknock, her Steward of Brecon and Dinas, her Porter of Brecon, such a curious title, the steward of her three castles of the Monmouthshire Trilateral, her Custos Rotulorum of Monmouth and Glamorgan, and finally her Vice-Admiral of South Wales. And at this point an added difficulty arose. These offices were to some extent dependent upon the choice of a President, and it would be likely to be some months before that much contested post was allotted. At the same time, Pembroke's son was in extremely bad odour at Court, for he had seduced a Maid of Honour and was on the point of committal,[2] so that it was certain that not even the most trivial appointment would pass in succession.[3] It was not that these offices had great importance, but in case of any military movement their vacancy would prove useful; while the absence of the Lord President was of considerable value, for until a new appointment was made there was no official of rank. The standing of the acting President, Sir Richard Lewkenor, was quite insufficient to keep the greater gentry quiet in their counties. This should not be forgotten as a spur to the action and a letter sent a week later marks the effect very clearly. 'The news here,' wrote [4] Sir Gelli, 'not being answerable to my desire (concerning my Lord) I have had no great desire to trouble you with them; only this, his Lordship is in health and we expect better news, which God send.'

The difference made by the Lord President's death was of course more apparent than real, the judicial system and all the organized work of the Council of the Marches went on as before and there was also the direct and unimpaired action of the Privy Council in London. Yet there was just this difference that, if a mere change of ministers

---

[1] An account of their wealth is provided in the elaborate *Survey of Wilton*, Roxburgh Society.
[2] 'You see,' wrote Lord Herbert with justice, 'both the shelfs I am like to suffer shipwreck on.' Letter to Sir R. Cecil, dated 5th January, 1601. Cal. Salisbury, xi, p. 4.
[3] The day *before* his father died Lord Herbert wrote fruitlessly to Cecil, 'You know there be some offices now fallen into the Queen's hands which my lord in his lifetime held and though of small commodity etc.' A letter which mirrors faithfully the sentiment of that age. *Ibid.*, p. 13.
[4] Letter of Sir Gelli Meyrick to Sir Arthur Chichester, dated 26th January, 1601. Cal. Salisbury MSS., xi, p. 19.

THE CELTIC PEOPLES & RENAISSANCE EUROPE

was in prospect, it would be easier for Essex to lead the Welsh gentry to support his claim to assist their own high-descended Welsh Queen now that there was no leader in Wales to rally them to the Queen's present Government. Nevertheless, it was along simpler lines that Sir Gelli and his supporters in Wales regarded the temporary eclipse of the Presidency of the Council. Now that there was no Pembroke left to mask such activities, they could see the proclamations sent forth in the name of the lawyers, Lewkenor and Townshend, and there rose starkly at Ludlow the gaunt framework of the Tudor law system, coercive and curbing. There was no incentive more powerful to set the ancient Welsh forces in motion.

It is difficult to reconstruct, at this date, these intricate movements. Sir Gelli was able to act alone as regards Essex's interests in Wales, and he was in many cases the only link between the Welsh gentry and his master. It would also seem that there was a dispute [1] at this time between his son-in-law, Sir John Vaughan, and the Countess of Essex, a factor which would tend to increase the isolation of these squires from Essex's personal circle in London.

After Christmas Sir Gelli had gone down into Radnorshire, and it was reported [2] that 'Sir Guylliame, doubting what might ensue, conveyed his goods to one Roger Vaughan, Esq., his inward and familiar friend.' The statements of Sir Richard Lewkenor make it clear that there had been some shifting of Sir Gelli's 'treasure' in Wales, and he refers [3] to Sir John Vaughan 'that married Sir Gelly Meyrick his daughter, to whose house Sir Gelly his wife removed and carried her plate and principal stuff[4] (as it is informed) a fortnight or three weeks before (the eighth of February).' It was in Pembroke-shire that these activities were supposed to have centred, in that region where the Essex influence was aided by those local gentry with Devereux connections, led by the Recusant John Barlow of Slebech.

[1] Letter from Sir Gelli Meyrick to Sir Arthur Chichester, dated 26th January, 1601. 'Concerning the questions in dispute between my Lady and Sir John Vaughan.' The editors accept this as a reference to Lady Essex, a point which might be disputed. Cal. Salisbury MSS., xi, p. 19.
[2] Report of Trollope from Sir Gelli's servant, Prise, obtained on 12th February, 1601, an unsatisfactory source. Ibid., p. 43.
[3] Letter of Sir Richard Lewkenor to Sir Robert Cecil, dated 25th February, 1601. Cal. Salisbury MSS., xi, p. 83, supported by further information, Acts of the Privy Council, 1600-8, p. 208.
[4] A statement, valueless except perhaps for local rumour, declares that 'about Allhallow-tide, there was conveyed and carried many great trunks suspected to contain much treasure from Glairstree (Gladestry) and other places into Carmarthenshire.' Cal. Salisbury MSS., xi, p. 135.

424

THE FINDING OF THE RAYNED DEER

Behind them was that shadowy figure, the old Sir George Devereux [1] and Essex's untenanted palace of Lamphey. ' Sir George Devereux, knt, uncle to the Earl of Essex,' so ran the charge,[2] ' being in the commission of the peace in cos. Pembroke and Cardigan in South Wales, came down upon the sudden, with one man only attending him, at Christmas last, and did ever since (as yet he doth) sojourn at the house of John Barlow in Slebech or Mynwere, which houses are on both sides of Milford Haven in co. Pembroke : which John Barlow is and hath been of long time an obstinate notorious recusant, being a man of greatest living and power in that shire. By whose greatness the Judges of assize of that circuit could not as yet at any time get him indicted albeit they endeavoured their uttermost, in such awefulness he holdeth the people, and so strongly was he countenanced by the Earl of Essex, through the means of Sir Gelly Merrick, who (as is supposed) made his gain of £100 a year of him.

' George Barlow,[3] eldest son of the said John, having been married to one of the Vernons, cousin german to the Earl of Essex and sister to the Countess of Southampton (by whom he hath two sons), liveth there with his father and Sir Geo. Devereux in house all together at Mynwere, by the side of Milford Haven, where a ship of 400 tons may come to the house. . . . This Barlow, anno '88, and in all times of foreign invasion, hath been greatly suspected of the better sort knowing him. Also it is to be considered that one Devereux Barrett (so christened by the old Earl of Essex, Walter) now being sheriff of Pembrokeshire, is of alliance to the Earl of Essex, now being, and is his known professed follower, and most familiar and inward with Sir George Devereux and Barlow ; in regard whereof and of a piece of money, for which Sir Gelly Merrick made him registrar for the diocese of St. David's (consisting of 7 counties, for his life and two sons in law of the said Barrett named Meade) he is the more to be suspected for the execution of such services as may concern any of their traitorous confederates, or persons before named.' It was a strange, remote group, entirely dependent on Essex, Sir George Devereux,

---

[1] Sir George Devereux had held a command in the Earl of Sussex's army in Scotland as far back as 1571.   Cal. Savile Foljambe MSS., p. 8.

[2] Information of John Bird, dated February, 1601.   Cal. Salisbury MSS., pp. 92–3.

[3] From details of benefactions to his parish church, recorded in an article on ' The Barlows of Slebech ' by Francis Greene, George Barlow would seem to have conformed although he was still suspected of recusant leanings in 1627. *Historical Society of West Wales Transactions*, iii, pp. 138–40.

ancient and shifty and always penurious,[1] the Meyricks first and unfortunate patron, John Barlow of Slebech, a man now past seventy, a widower and fervently Catholic, and his more prudent son George, just into the thirties, with the young and fashionable bride, whom his father's wealth [2] had secured. All represented the old Essex tradition and the days when the Devereux had been great in West Wales and around them grouped the young Meyricks,[3] who had remained in the County,[4] Sir Francis of Monckton, Harry of Rosetown and John. It was upon Essex House that their interest was centred and every indication would show that the gathering in Wales was inspired by Sir Gelli, while the informations received, when the Rising had failed and Essex's friends were in prison, reflect his wide influence throughout the whole country. All the characters whose connections with Essex have been considered in the account of his relations with Wales are revealed in the light of this final disaster.

'One James Price,' so ran another charge,[5] 'now or late keeping about the Strand (servant to Sir Gelly Meyrick . . .) long before said he knew much of the Earl's intentions and his master's, and that great matters were in handling which would shortly break into action. . . . Mr. Broughton, of the Council of Wales, held for a great politician and lawyer and most inward with the Earl (to whose government he was left in his minority) cannot be thought ignorant of the Earl's intentions by many secret consultations together in Essex House a little before Christmas and being of his counsel for conveying his lands to others, best knew the considerations him thereunto moving. Price can discover one Owen James in Wales, who was used by Sir Gelly Meyrick and his brother, Sir Francis for a bad instrument in sundry unsound actions, and therefore meet to be sought out. Sir Gelly was as stirring a rebel, as well of the Earl to break out as many gentlemen in Wales.'

---

[1] 'All the annual means I had to help me are dead . . . and my years and sickness keep me from employment,' wrote Sir George Devereux on 4th June, 1601. Letter to Sir R. Cecil, Cal. Salisbury MSS., xi, p. 217.
[2] Details of the Inq. Post Mortem of John Barlow of Slebech, October, 1613, are printed in *Historical Society of West Wales, Transactions*, iii, pp. 131-7.
[3] The pedigree of the Barlows is contained in the Book of Golden Grove and there are descents of the Barlows and Meyricks given in Lewys Dwnn. *Visitation of Wales*, i, pp. 117-8 and 137.
[4] Descriptions of the lawsuits of the Meyricks with the Owens of Orielton show that their relations with their neighbours were not always peaceable. Cal. Star Chamber Proceedings relating to Wales, p. 133.
[5] Informations taken by John Bird, notary public, dated 4th March, 1601. Cal. Salisbury MSS., xi, pp. 106-8.

THE FINDING OF THE RAYNED DEER

' By Price's report,' the accusation then continued, ' the Welshmen had common knowledge near to Christmas of this intended rebellion. Price being a man of 100 marks lands concluded to pass a mortgage thereof unto Sir Gelly his master and received beforehand in part of a greater sum £150 and no assurances are thereof as yet passed. . . . The presumption is great that Roger Vaughan, lieutenant of Radnorshire and a justice of the peace, of lands £1000 by year, cannot be ignorant of this rebellion and a favourer thereof. For Sir Gelly and he not a fortnight past before (the eighth of February) came together from Wales, where Sir Gelly " estated " his lands upon him in trust and conveyed from his own house much of his own goods, yet remaining with Vaughan, and continued bedfellows in Essex House until this broil began.

' Neither may Sir Gelly's sons-in-law,[1] David and William Gwyn, be thought clear . . . , for they (accompanied with others at the time of the Earl's apprehension) were at Colbroke coming to him, but thereupon were discomforted and returned to Wales, sending their minds by James Price to Sir Gelly. The like did Sir John Vaughan., Then references are made to the messengers employed and especially to ' one Piers Edmondes . . . whom Sir Gelly sent, as it is said, with messages into Wales, as before he had been with secret instructions into Ireland, to such as the Earl there best reckoned of.' Again, the specific accusations against the Barlows and the Meyricks are repeated, and finally suspicion is cast upon ' the sheriff of Pembrokeshire, Devereux Barrett, and the sheriff of Denbighshire, being the Earl's followers, and another brother of Sir Gelly's, a customer for Cardigan and Pembrokeshires and justice in commission.' Although the authority of this accuser, from too long employment in ' the public service,' is not of the best,[2] there is no doubt of the sympathy for Essex felt by these men and of the constant stirring of the pot by Sir Gelli. For again in North Wales we find a gathering of friends. ' Sir John

---

[1] In reality stepsons, children of Lady Meyrick by her first husband, Mr. Gwyn of Llanelwed. Lewys Dwnn, *op. cit.*, i, p. 137.
[2] The following statement may suggest prejudice to an impartial mind. ' And as Cerberus, Herberus and Sphinx, are said to be a triplicity of heads of Hydra's kind, from whom many other prodigious monsters increased for Lucifer's kingdom and were alluded unto such damnable vices as most reign over voluptuous and mortal men ; so from them and others of their hellish Romish rebellious rout of Jesuits and Seminaries many libertines of this age have so much surfeited their poisonous bulls and Romish drugs etc., etc.' Letter from Mr. Registrar Byrde to Sir R. Cecil. Cal. Salisbury MSS., pp. 363–4.

Lloyde,' so ran this further report,[1] 'lately knighted in Ireland by the Earl of Essex, whom he followed in the late service there . . . did harbour and entertain in his house . . . John Salusbury, his brother in law, Owen Salusbury and Peter Wynn, all three captains and followers of the Earl of Essex and the two last formerly pardoned for treason and so known unto him. Those three were the greatest friends and the inwardest that the said knight had. They had his house at their command and his purse and some of them had most of their means from him. There has been of late divers meetings and private conferences between them, as namely in Christmas last in the town of Wrexham, Denbigshire, they all met there, and there Sir John Lloyde became bound for Captain John Salusbury for money he received for his journey to London. He was likewise bound in divers great sums of money for him. Captain John Salusbury, being in Sir John Lloyde's house, received a letter from the Earl of Essex a fortnight before Christmas or thereabouts and the next day he took his journey towards London. . . . The said John Salusbury, captain, came immediately after his coming to London to Essex House.' Thus Essex had received a promise of aid from a Scottish Ambassador and a temporizing letter from Ireland. These things were not dangerous; it was rather Sir Gelli Meyrick's management, the influx of swords-men from Wales that brought him his peril. For these only came to swell the already large company of his armed and im-provident courtiers, but they were soldiers of fortune and had come for a purpose.

To them it seemed a straightforward matter that an armed manœuvre was planned. And all the time Essex and those using his name were encouraging the most incompatible friends, the Puritans and the City. As he brooded carelessly on his wrongs, Essex saw himself as a Patriot, barely reached by Plebeian applause, against that literary background on which his actions were shadowed. He would save the Island City, still remaining remote and Athenian. Thus he contented himself with a contact with those representatives of these alien parties, who, appearing to have some semblance of culture, could surely speak for their more uncouth fellows. In connection with the mercantile community he relied upon the Sheriff of London, a gentle-man of restrained martial tastes, colonel of 1000 men, 'and,' as

---

[1] Information, dated February, 1601. Cal. Salisbury MSS., xi, p. 96.

THE FINDING OF THE RAYNED DEER

Essex would say with complacence,[1] ' at his command.' And this same trait, the absence of a sense of reality, shows forth still more clearly in his dealings with Puritans. He stood for a ' religion of the purer sort,' a phrase which must have sounded curious to those who knew Essex House inside the gates ; but the Puritans had no right of entry and were only aware of my Lord as a strong fighter against the great Babylon. Yet they must have had lingering doubts, and it was perhaps with a sense that only their emissary need bow so low before Rimmon, that their leading divine Mr. Egerton was allowed to go to the Earl. To the Bishop of London this preacher proved a serious trial and his crowded congregations [2] at St. Ann's in Blackfriars, a standing insult in one who had ' approved the practice of the pretended Presbyteral discipline.' [3] ' The ministers of London,' to use the Bishop's phrase for his own clergy, ' did greatly complain ' and ' all within my jurisdiction have conformed themselves,' the prelate continued on a rising note, ' save Mr. Egerton on whose behalf the Earl of Essex was earnest.' Abdie Ashton, the Earl's chaplain, a clergyman of well modulated Puritan ideals,[4] had perhaps secured the introduction, but a letter of Mr. Egerton's throws most welcome light upon the reasons for which Essex found him sufficiently congenial.

' Plato (in some things divine),' wrote [5] Stephen Egerton, ' hath said (as Tully relates) neque parenti neque patriæ vim afferre oportere. As to the other imputation about the authority of the ministry in making laws for church matters, in my opinion they may devise rules and orders for the government of the church and tender the same to the Christian magistrate, but to put them in practice without his approbation, I have never maintained or imagined.' This is a contrast to the great stern generation and, to those Puritans who looked for a City of Refuge west of Jordan, such phrases would surely seem strange ; less fitting for the Pure Evangel than for the Secretary of

[1] Evidence of Sir Christopher Blount, dated February, 1601. Cal. Salisbury MSS. xi, p. 98.
[2] The following entry dated 19th October, 1600, shows his popularity in extreme Protestant circles. ' After prairs I went to Mr. Egerton's sermon . . . after (dinner) I went againe to his exercise and thence home to my lodginge wher I wrett some of his in my testament.' *Diary of Lady Margaret Hoby*, ed. by Dr. D. Meads, p. 150.
[3] Letter of Richard Bancroft, Bishop of London, to Sir Robert Cecil, dated 2nd April, 1601. Cal. Salisbury MSS., xi, p. 154.
[4] It appeared that ' Mr. Ashton . . . desired me to ask that your Honour would procure him an advowson of a prebend at Windsor . . . with this clause, proximam vacationem non obstante alique priori concessione.' Letter of William Cooke to Sir Robert Cecil, dated 17th April, 1601, Cal. Salisbury MSS., xi, p. 169.
[5] Letter of Stephen Egerton to Sir R. Cecil, dated 8th April, 1601. *Ibid.*, xi, p. 161.

429

THE CELTIC PEOPLES & RENAISSANCE EUROPE

State's polite archives. Yet it enables us to see Essex successful again, for the leader of these strange men was his henchman. But, although he intended vaguely to collect every group of the nation round him, this shows how little Essex really moved from his orbit. The preacher's visit left a pleasant flavour, there was a suggestion, very civilized, in his phrasing, Plato in some things divine.

There was no real effort to simplify the interlocked play of these interests [1]; but the gathering forces made conflict inevitable. It is therefore no longer a question of discerning the causes of the explosion, that slow accumulation of years, but rather to discover the occasion of the outbreak and the hot and tangled aims which then swayed them. The Court and the City had passed in comparative calm through the last days of January and on the Continent there was undisturbed peace. Henry IV of France had just completed his stupendous Rubens marriage and in the circles about the Court the rumours ran as to the identity of the Ambassador, who would be chosen to bring to Marie de Medici the well-turned compliments of the English Queen. It is significant that as late as 4th February John Chamberlain records [2] that the Earl of Rutland and the Earl of Hertford were the two rivals for that honourable post; so late as that the Essex faction could still maintain apparent favour. In the Secretary's private correspondence all was peace, the offers coming from Carew Raleigh to send pheasants up from Wiltshire, the repairs needed in the Chase at Cranborne, the desire of some country neighbour to obtain a good price for Cranborne Alderholt [3] by playing on the Cecil love of land, the quiet movement of a shrewdly rural idyll. And then on Sunday, 8th February the conflict came.

It was on the evening of 7th February that Secretary Herbert was sent to request Essex's presence at a Council which was to be held in the house of the Lord Treasurer, who was sick. But Essex excused himself, while his followers asserted that his enemies Raleigh, Cobham and Cecil were intent on his murder. There was this slight justifica-

[1] Lady Hoby who had married Walter Devereux, Essex's brother, may have provided a link with the Puritans. 'I went,' she records under the entry of 8th January, 1601, 'to Walsingham house wher I saw my Lady Rich, my Lady Rutland and my Lady Walsingham.' *Diary of Lady Margaret Hoby*, p. 161.
[2] 'The Erle of Rutland and the Erle of Hertford,' wrote Chamberlain to Dudley Carleton, 'stand in election whether they shall be sent into Fraunce to congratulate with the new quene.' Chamberlain's Letters, Camden Society, p. 102.
[3] Letter of Sir Edmund Uvedale to Sir Robert Cecil, dated 26th January, 1601, from Hoult lodge. Cal. Salisbury MSS., xi, p. 19.

430

tion for their alarm that it would seem to have been the concourse at Essex House which had led to this summons. Already the Welsh supporters were riding to join them, and the same evening Sir Christopher Blount came up from the country, stabling his horses at the *White Hart* in the Strand.[1] The names of the supper party, which Essex and his wife entertained in the great chamber, have still been preserved, that family group which alone held this privilege, Southampton and his brother-in-law Vernon, Lady Rich, Sir Charles Danvers and the newly come Christopher Blount. According to Danvers' account,[2] as soon as the talk had turned on the question of surprising the Court and gaining control of the City, he had ' persuaded (the Earl) to fly with some hundred gentlemen to the seaside or into Wales, where he might command some ports.' It is very characteristic of Essex that ' the Earl gave no answer ' as he rose for the last time in peace from his table and went down to converse with the gentlemen.

At Gunter's in Temple Bar a noisier group was at table, Sir Gelli entertaining his Welsh supporters, the Salusburys and Peter Wynne and Warburton from the edge of the Marches, with that now silent and doubtful spirit, the uneasy Secretary Cuffe. Then there came in from Essex House Sir Christopher Blount, the *liaison* between the Earl and the military men, Sir William Constable and a number of gentlemen. Blount departed again, and Sir Charles Percy proposed that they should adjourn to the Globe playhouse at the Bankside over the water, and, with one significant exception, they all left on this riotous errand. Cuffe alone remained in the house with that disgust for the exuberant gentry which came so easily to him. His cultivated perceptions were most sensitive to this crudeness, and he saw that his bold diplomacy had now gone to the winds and that his master's affairs were slipping into the hands of the swordsmen with their unintelligent minds. At the theatre in Southwark, Sir Gelli gave forty shillings to the players to act *Richard II* and hurried back to the gathering, where he was seen ' in the gallery at Essex House . . . and much more bustling than it was his wont to be.'[3] It would

---

[1] All these minor details are to be found in the examinations of prisoners in Cal. S.P. Dom., 1598–1601, pp. 547–90, and Cal. Salisbury MSS., xi, pp. 30–183, *passim.*
[2] Examination of Sir Charles Danvers, dated 18th February, 1601. Cal. S.P. Dom., 1598–1601, p. 580.
[3] Examination of Thomas Lea, dated 14th February, 1601. Cal. S.P. Dom., 1598–1601, p. 565.

be interesting to fathom the reason for his choice of this play, but the title perhaps made some appeal. Like all those men of his time, to whom reading was painful, his remote historical knowledge was sprung from ancestral tradition and in Wales the sympathy for Richard II, aided by the strong Glendower tradition, had never quite vanished and the memories of Bolingbroke's plotting still lingered. It was about the question of plots by the Cecil faction that he wished to arouse curiosity ; when he ferried across for this interview, before he settled down to that sending of messengers, which was to prove the night's business. It was not that the Welshmen conceived for a moment the possibility of dethroning their own Tudor Queen ; but that they were ready for action and for that well-organized bloodshed which would lead Essex, their chief, to the highest posts in the State. In such an outlook, Wales seemed a source of supplies, and Sir Gelli could think of the gentlemen who were even now riding through the Marches to join him ; but, for the more sophisticated among the Essex House circle, Wales was at best a place of safe refuge.

Thus, to Sir Christopher Blount, the possibility presented itself of freeing Essex from his enemies and carrying him away with some sixty horse into Wales,[1] a plan which could be compared with Sir Charles Danvers' later remedy of a break through to the North. Yet, it was not for such a poor climax that the swordsmen had gathered. The impossibility of surprising the Court was soon clear, and on the Sunday morning the followers of Essex streamed into his courtyard from the Strand and the alleyways of their lodgings. The night had been passed in excitement, and they were all imprudently gathered, not only the immediate circle, but also all my Lord's friends, Lords Cromwell and Monteagle and the melancholy Lord Sandys of the Vyne, Grey Brydges and Sir Edward Baynham of the Forest of Dean and to represent Northumberland, Sir Charles Percy and his brother Sir Josceline, besides the crowds of the gentry. Obscure among them were three names which the Gunpowder Plot would bring to fame, John Wright, John Grant and Robert Catesby.[2] Lady Rich went in her own coach for the Earl of Bedford, for even the most distant of the friends must be brought in.

---

[1] Examination of Sir Christopher Blount, dated 13th February, 1601.   Cal. Salisbury MSS., xi, p. 47.
[2] Sir Charles Danvers subsequently supplied a list of names, which can be checked by the table of those indicted. *Ibid.*, pp. 86 and 102–3.

THE FINDING OF THE RAYNED DEER

Meanwhile the Court had taken action and four emissaries came from the Queen to demand the meaning of this assembly. It was an impressive embassy, the Lord Keeper, the Lord Chief Justice, the Comptroller of the Household, and to give them further ranking in view of the jealousies of the peerage, the Earl of Worcester. With this arrival, the excitement mounted steadily, and Essex, taking these guests to his private library, declared that he would soon be ready to go with them to the Queen. His intimates were with him, Sir Ferdinando Gorges boldly guarding the safety of these ancient men, and it would seem to have been at this moment that Sir Charles Danvers gave the advice [1] that Essex should either treat with the Queen through these hostages or make his way out through Highgate and then ride away northwards and over the Border. Essex refused to do anything so decisive. As he came down the stairs to his men in the courtyard, he possessed his last moment of freedom. But he had always gone with the tide and he made no attempt to resist that current which swept round him so strongly. All the friends were assembled, Rutland come up from Walsingham House and Southampton and the Secretaries with all the dependents and the military men, well over two hundred. Amid the din he could distinguish the encouragements of Penelope and young Lord Bedford's hesitant misery and Sir Gelli Meyrick's loud courage, for his day had now come at last. As they crowded through the Essex House gates and out on to the cobbled lanes, which led east to the City, their day indeed had come surely, for they had crossed with sword in hand that barrier which divides mere foolishness from high treason.

Eye witnesses describe the further scene, making so clear the contrast between the Earl's confused intentions, the ill-considered suggestions that Cecil was in league with Spain and the Infanta, and the determined action of the Court, for whom Essex's armed progress to the City was a sign for his proclamation as a traitor. The first account deals with the haphazard movements of the force. ' But Orrell, before mentioned, who holds his neck awry,' wrote [2] William

---

[1] According to Aubrey who quotes the authority of Viscountess Purbeck, Sir Charles Danvers' niece, *Lives*, i, p. 192.

[2] Letter from William Reynolds to Sir Robert Cecil, dated 13th February, 1601. The writer describes himself as ' bold to write simply without flattery, being a poor distressed man.' In a second letter he becomes more explicit. After referring to the Anglican formulas, he concludes : ' This faith I do stedfastly believe according to the truth of the Scriptures and Athanasius his creed. I pray a letter or warrant for £20 pension yearly out of London and Middlesex.' Cal. Salisbury MSS., xi., pp. 46–94.

Reynolds of a private enemy [1] among the Essex captains, 'did run and leap in the forefront with Sir Christopher Blunt and Mr. Bushell, their weapons drawn, crying " Saw, Saw, Saw, Saw, tray, tray," where I saw Sir Christopher Blunt run a man into the face that his rapier bowed and Bushell run at my Lord Burghley's footman and the rest in like manner at divers others who were hurt. I came first (from) the sermon and service in her Majesty's chapel and I went out of the Court gate with my Lord Admiral and your Honour (Sir R. Cecil) and so with the proclamation into London. I ran to my Lord Bishop of London and told him of the rumour and proclamation. I had no weapon, nor I could get none when I saw time to use one ; and when I cried " Down with Essex the traitor " divers rebuked me and had some of his followers seen me, I am sure they would have done their best to kill me ; which made me not dare look openly amongst them whom I knew. But divers serving men put up their swords, whispering in their masters' ears the proclamation, which made some slip away and others swore " Wounds and blood " with " Tush, they cared not." I heard say that Norris was amongst them, little Captain Norris' brother, a drunken desperate fellow ; which Norris and one Captain Devorax, spake once very unreverent words of her Majesty in my company . . . I returning to Ludgate, the cry and 'larm came with people running that Essex was coming again, whereupon I desired a weapon of the Bishop's men who are all well acquainted with me.'

After an atmosphere has been conveyed by this first letter, an account written by one of Essex's supporters will give an accurate impression of his movements. ' I must confess,' began [2] John Bargar, ' that I loved my Lord of Essex. I had reason to do so. I served Her Majesty as a voluntary in four actions under him, which had cost me well near a brace of thousand pounds. His smiles only promised me recompense, the which I had almost forgot, I have so seldom seen him since I came out of Ireland. He seemed to be a religious, honest gent ; now he is found otherwise, I will never trust precisian for his sake. The circumstances was (as I shall be saved) thus. Having been at the sermon at Paul's Cross and coming into the body of the Church, I heard a confused noise, crying Murder, murder, God save

---

[1] He describes him as ' a follower of the Lord Montegle, a most desperate rakehell as lives.' He asserts that Captain Green is ' a cutpurse, picklock and thief and lives by consuming shifts, and makes the customary attack upon Lord Southampton's moral character.' *Ibid.*, pp. 93–4.
[2] Letter of John Bargar to his patron, Lord Cobham. Cal. Salisbury MSS., xi, pp. 30–2.

the Queen. My Lord of Essex should have been murdered in his bed by Sir Walter Rawleigh and his confederates, that they had gotten a strong troop of horse and that they were ready to charge them in the rear and that he sought nothing but a sudden defence till her Majesty might be better informed of it. The voice of so many earls, barons, knights and gent made me believe it. Afterwards, it was renewed and confirmed by the entertainment of the Sheriff and Alderman Martin, for he was kindly welcomed to the Sheriff's House, had been sent out to his company and armourers sent thither, that promised him arms to furnish his company. I imagined that they knew it to be true, for I presumed they would not have promised aid to the Queen's enemy ; but it appears that their promises were but delays to make him lose time. It was said that my Lord Burlye had some bickering with the head of my Lord of Essex's company, but he was soon gone and I saw him not, being in the rear.'

It had indeed fallen out as might have been foreseen. Essex had gone to the City to the house of his friend Sheriff Smith and expected, in his remote and impersonal way, assistance in what was now treason. ' The next that came to us,' John Bargar continued, ' was my Lord Mayor with a herald, who dealt not as if he would have his company forsake him, for then he would have him proclaimed traitor in the head of his troops, but he desired rather to single him from his company to the Sheriff's house. I having had some little acquaintance with the Lord Mayor and beginning to suspect my Lord of Essex his cause not to be so honest as it should be, I stepped to the Lord Mayor and desired him that he would take me to go at his stirrup and employ me as he pleased. My drift on this was to get myself free from my Lord of Essex to the Lord Mayor, for then I did not care how I got home, but I was far from my lodging and had no cloak and to go in that fashion through the streets would have bred me many inconveniences. After this, my Lord Mayor sent me three or four times to my Lord of Essex to the end to draw him from his company into some house, which he by no means would hearken to. After this I heard the Sheriff persuade my Lord of Essex that he should go down to Cheapside and so to Ludgate and Newgate, that he might possess them and hold that side of the city secure and he himself would go and provide armour in the mean time, both for himself and his company. Upon this my Lord of Essex took down Lombard Street, where I met with a friend, to whom I disclosed my opinion of the matter. I desired him to help me to my cloak that I might me gone, which he promised me to do, and so parted from me beside the stocks. We met again with my Lord Mayor, my Lord of Essex being past by him; he called me to him by name and told me that my Lord of Essex took a very ill course, which would undo him. I told him I thought so. He entreated me to very earnest with my Lord of Essex to go home with him to his house and promised him that he should have a good guard of his own followers with him and he would warrant him to save him harmless from any of those his adversaries which he said he feared, and withal told (him) that if he would not do it, it should be the worse for him. I overtook my Lord of Essex and forced those reasons my Lord Mayor willed me to him, so far that he grew offended with me and said I knew not what I did.

'My Lord then went down towards Ludgate, where below Paul's stood Sir John Lewson with a certain guard and the street chained up before him. My Lord of Essex had made an approach before I came in; but Sir John denying him passage, he retired a small distance from them and so stood close with his company about him, in the end, looking towards Sir John and spying me between them both, he willed me to tell Sir John that the sheriff of the city willed him to go (to) Ludgate and make that good, that he would send him arms thither, that pass he would and for my Lord of Cumberland, who had set him there, he knew if he were there himself he would not deny his passage, in regard that there were so many of his kinsmen, earls, barons and gent., which being naked, only with their rapiers, must enter upon armed pikes and shot. Sir John's answer was that if the Sheriff would come himself he would give way as to the Queen, otherwise there he must stand. This speech was seconded by Bushell, my Lord of Essex' gent. usher, from my Lord. In the meantime my Lord came on crying " God save the Queen " and although Sir John made me wish myself away, yet my Lord of Essex' approach was so sudden that back I could not go, till the throng behind me was some-what broken, but as soon as ever I could get back I hurled away my weapon and went to a house hard by and borrowed a cloak and got me home to my lodging.' Although a constant desire to minimize his share in the tumult is clear, this writer gives an impression more clearly conveyed than any other account of that ride into the City to

Gracechurch Street and then the slow return and the embarrassments of the merchants. And in his sentences some of the confusion of Essex's mind seems reflected.

Already, in that journey westward, after he had failed to gain aid and when he could merely hope to return to his house once again, the failure and dangers stand clear. It is at this point, when Essex approached the barrier at Ludgate, that Sir John Leveson, the most reliable of the three witnesses takes up his account of the day. 'I John Leveson, knight,' begins [1] the pompous but circumstantial detail of the report, ' coming from the house of Lord Cobham in the Blackfriars towards Ludgate the said day in the afternoon, met with the Earl of Cumberland, the Lord Bishop of London and others to me unknown, all on horseback; and, at my coming under the vault of the said gate, I was spoken to by the said Earl or Lord (Bishop) of London, that it should be well done by me, having heretofore served her Majesty in the wars, to put the company there in some order. . . . Resolving to do my endeavour, I spake to one whom I found there with a halberd in his hand, a man to me unknown, but by his personage a tall man and, as it proved after, one Waight, who died of hurt received there, that he would bring up such pikes as were there to me to the posts and chain above the said two lanes; which he did accordingly and after this I prayed him to bring up the shot which stood under the gate. Then did I pray him to put the shot next the chain and to place the pikes behind them. Which done, I placed 12 halberdiers, 6 at the end of the lane leading to Burgavenny House and other 6 at the end of the other lane leading to Carter Lane. I also moved the Lord of London to cause the chain to be drawn cross the street and to be fixed to the posts. This done, my Lord Bishop of London gave order to free the street of idle gazers, wherewith it was much pestered, and rode up and down encouraging the company which were there (being for the most part his own servants and armed with his armour) to stand to it like men.

' Within half an hour and less after we were thus assembled at the chain my Lord of Essex came with his company from Powles churchyard towards us and when he approached within 4 pikes' length of the chain he made a halt and asked who commanded there, to which answer

---

[1] Declaration of Sir John Leveson, dated 16th February, 1601. Cal. Salisbury MSS., xi, pp. 59–61.

was made that the Earl of Cumberland was there. Then his lordship commanded that one should go to him to pray him to suffer him to pass ; to which answer was made that he had commanded that none should pass there. Then said the Earl, " Oh I have wounded him " ; and the Earl, approaching nearer said, " I see Sir John Leveson, go to him, for I am assured that he will not deny me passage."

‘ Then came Sir Ferdinando Gorge to me and told me the Earl prayed me he might pass to his lodging, protesting he would pass peaceably without offering offence to any : to which I replied that I was commanded by the Earl of Cumberland and my Lord of London that none should pass that way and that I had so undertaken and, God willing, would perform it ; and with this answer Sir Ferdinando departed.

‘ Then the Earl sent Capt. Bushell to me to require the like passage, saying that he had departed with the Lord Mayor and Sheriffs in good terms and that they had given him full liberty.’ After this details are related of Sir Ferdinando Gorges’ second message. ‘ To which I answered as before and told him that Ludgate was locked and that I neither had the keys, nor could tell who had them.’ This was followed by the message by John Bargar, whose evidence has been described, and by a second and final entreaty through Captain Bushell. ‘ He said,’ continues Sir John in reference to the Captain, ‘ that I would be the cause of the effusion of more blood of the nobility and gentry of England than any man born within mine age, for, said he, here be earls, barons, knights and the flower of the nobility and gentry of England. To this I answered that I was sorry for their being there and that, if there should be that effusion of blood he spake of, the fault would prove theirs and not mine. Then said he, " I will tell you that my lord saith that he will and must pass and that he will pass by you as a true subject to Her Majesty and a friend to the State and that he only seeketh to suppress the tyranny of those who have sold and betrayed the State to the Spaniard."

‘ Whereto I answered that it was above my capacity to understand the designs of his lordship ; and for his passage that way, I must and would deny it.

‘ Presently upon this one of the Earl’s side cried " Shoot, Shoot " and then the pistols were discharged at us within a three quarters pike’s length of us and they were answered again by such shot as we had and forthwith Sir Christopher Blunt charged with his sword and target and came close to the chain and cut off the head of sundry the pikes, and with him divers other of the Earl's company, of which some got between the post and the chain and let drive among our pikes and halberts : and in this encounter Sir Chr. Blunt was hurt, first by a thrust in the face and then felled by a knock on the head. Upon the sight whereof and of the fall of young Mr. Tracy, the Earl's page, our company coming upon them put them back, which the Earl perceiving called them off and so departed from us.'

It is not surprising that Essex was seized by that quick despair which Mr. Edwards, a draper, well describes.[1] ' I could not,' declared Richard Edwards, ' certainly hear every word that the Earl of Essex did speak, but saw him and heard him speak with a " gast " countenance and like a man forlorn, and said with a loud voice, " You should not be cosined so or conicatched so," and then spake of Sir Walter Raleigh I could not certainly understand what, the confusion of the noise was so great ; but heard him say that the Crown of England was sold to the Infanta or King of Spain, or words to that effect and that they should believe honest and religious men and not be " conicatched." ' And then, checked at Ludgate and deserted by the citizens, Essex hurried down to the first watersteps and, accompanied by fifty of his bodyguard, took boat in haste upstream to Essex House.

The plot had failed most completely, for the Government was not even shaken ; but, as the clumsy strokes of the hired boatmen hastened them forward, Essex remembered that the presence of the distinguished hostages, locked in his library, would enable him to negotiate and to secure a promise of pardon, so that all concerned might forget the miseries of this nightmare. Yet even so, he had hardly power to arrange this fortunate issue. In the first place he would never consent to murder and a mere threat to detain his guests longer was valueless, and then he had nothing really to use as a basis. The Queen valued her dignity and the manner in which her envoys were treated, but she had no particular concern for her safety. They were among the old and tried servants on whom the reign had reposed, the now withered stalks from whose earlier sap was to spring the great ducal families.

---

[1] Examination of Richard Edwards, dated 18th February, 1601. Cal. Salisbury MSS., xi, p. 67.

How richly they were to be rewarded for those political loyalties, which they had chosen so wisely; for already those eighteenth-century glories of the great households of Bridgwater and Beaufort lay implicit. Nevertheless, the Queen's affections were not here engaged : it was no question of her ' dearest minions ' and the news of their massacre would have resulted first in a well staged explosion and then in a stoical calm.

This was the situation to which Essex returned, as he sat in the sternsheets with the wounded Lord Sandys of the Vyne at his side, while behind them came the others, John Salusbury's boat with Monteagle, and then those with the swordsmen, full laden and deep at the gunwales, lost and diminishing round the sweep of the Thames. It was less than an hour before sunset when they came over the dull February water to the river steps which the Earl's men guarded.

It had been a time of great anxiety for the Queen's envoys, since, on their first arrival, the infuriated threats of ' Kill them,' ' Cast the great seal out of the window ' and ' let us shop them up ' [1] had come up confusedly from the men in the courts. The shouting had greatly alarmed them, with Owen Salusbury crying out after Mr. Francis Bacon, as he passed outside the gates, ' there is one of them let us pull him in to the doing withal,' [2] and Sir Gelli and Francis Tresham stamping below in the courtyard. There was a prudence in my Lord Chandos' conduct, who, finding himself in such a company ' said nothing,[3] but went out . . . with his black cloak cast about his face and went another way.'

Yet the calm which succeeded when Essex and his supporters had poured out to the City was more dangerous still. Outside the door of their chamber, musketeers under Captain Salusbury [4] were posted and Sir Ferdinando Gorges had charge of their safety ; but the excitement soon drew him away to the City and the suave Sir John Davies succeeded him in this trust. Half an hour after Essex was gone, Sir John brought down Lady Essex and Lady Rich to their chamber, ' the better to pass the time ' for the Lords. At any moment the mob of Essex's supporters might come homeward again and then, in the

[1] Declaration of Lord Keeper Egerton, dated 18th February, 1601. Cal. S.P. Dom., 1598–1601, p. 586.
[2] Examination of Sir William Constable, dated 16th February, 1601. Ibid., p. 573.
[3] Evidence of Sir John Davies. Cal. S.P. Dom., 1598–1601, p. 549.
[4] ' Three musketeers and a caliver with matches ready and fire in their hands and the pieces charged.' Evidence of Ellis Jones, Cal. S.P. Dom., 1598–1601, p. 549.

disorganized rout, it was painfully clear how small was their chance of survival, unless the master was there to protect them. It seemed so likely in case of a check that the Earl's infuriated adherents would come tumbling back to their stronghold before him. In point of fact it was the check at Ludgate which saved them and the fortunate prudence of their guardian, Sir Ferdinando, all of whose resourcefulness was called forth by the military failure.

Sir Ferdinando Gorges was, in all matters save his perspicacity, typical of that generation which the spirit of the times, rather than any personal affection for Essex, had drawn into this faction. He was a young man, reasonably adventurous, but more seriously attracted by the happy commercial flavour which colonial adventures possessed. It was an interest and a success which was always increasing, couched in a sufficiently poetical manner, as in that pride in ' the Great Neptune,' which his prosperous pilchard fishing suggested. And then his curious knowledge, the hospitality which he extended to the three ' Penobscots,' those unfortunate natives whom Captain Weymouth brought home, every detail in fact was now concentrated on that attainment of fortune which was at last to be realized when the Lord Proprietorship of Maine had come into his grasp. At this moment he had come up from his governorship at Plymouth to assist his old patron and among the Essex supporters after that fatal check at Ludgate, his mind alone could work clearly. His own subsequent letter expresses his attitude very precisely. ' I utterly dislike that course,' he wrote [1] later about the Essex Rising, ' as besides the horror I felt at it, I saw it was impossible to be accomplished.' Meanwhile at Ludgate Essex had ruined him by his folly, but his own resource was equal to his desperate plight. A newsletter of the day describes his plan. ' Sir Ferdinando Gorges,' so runs [2] this document, ' of his own head either from remorse or cunning came back and ordered (the lords) in the Earl's name to be discharged a quarter of an hour before his return. He (Essex) was wonderfully discontent and with good reason. . . .'

As the boats came alongside the water-steps Essex learned that his last hope of earning a pardon was destroyed. It is not surprising that of all the prisoners who were so soon taken Sir Ferdinando alone went

[1] Declaration of Sir Ferdinando Gorges, dated 18th February, 1601. Cal. S.P. Dom., 1598–1601, p. 577.
[2] Letter of Sir Robert Cecil to the Lord Deputy. *Ibid.*, p. 547.

happily to the Tower. Two hours after the release of the hostages, the Lord Admiral came with his troops; for the Court had received the satisfying intelligence, first of Sir John Leveson's engagement and the loyalty of the City and then of the return of the Earl to Essex House. It was now only a question of the wise deployment of force. 'Towards six o'clock,' wrote Sir Robert Cecil in his first despatch, 'the Lord Admiral threatened to blow up the house, which he had foreborne to do because my Ladies Essex and Rich were within. Thereupon, notwithstanding their bravery they yielded to Her Majesty's mercy.'

*   *   *   *   *

The manner in which the disaster was received shows how suddenly the shooting star had fallen and with what completeness it had dissolved. There was no longer any bond [1] to hold the faction together with Essex in the Tower as a traitor and all his adherents arrested. Few episodes show more clearly the power of the idea of the Prince. Common rumour singled out some names as those of ringleaders. 'Sir Christopher Blunt was proved the chiefe agent,' so the stories ran,[2] ' Mr. Caff was the greate dealer to perswade, Sir Charles Davers a forward plotter, Sir Gilly Merrick for barricadoing his master's house.'

Roger Manners echoes again the heavy voice of the country.

---

[1] An instance of the persistent belief on the Continent in Essex's strong Protestantism is seen in a letter from the Fugger correspondent at Cologne, dated 4th March, 1601. ' Great sorrow has been excited . . not only in England, but also in Holland and Zeeland among the common people, for the said Earl (of Essex) was greatly devoted and attached to his religion.' *Fugger News Letters*, No. 222, ed. Viktor von Klarwill, p. 238. Compare the statement of Thomas Wright, priest, on 16th February, 1601, that ' he thought the Earl of Essex was a Catholic but concealed it from policy.' Cal. S.P. Dom., 1598–1601.

[2] Narrative, Cal. Rutland MSS., i, p. 370. It is notable that Cuffe is often singled out for most blame. ' Essex suffered at the last,' wrote Sir Robert Naunton, ' from desperate advice. . . . Among whom Sir Henry Wotton notes his Secretary Cuffe a vile man and of a perverse nature.' *Fragmenta Regalia*, p. 54.

THE FINDING OF THE RAYNED DEER

Good Brother,' he wrote [1] to John Manners at Haddon immediately upon this catastrophe, ' of this tumult this berer can tell you more than I have will to write. I wold my three nephewes had never byn borne then by so horrible offence offende so gratius a sufferan, to the overthrow of ther howse and name for ever, alwais befire loyall. And a few days later Screven, the steward in London, continues in a similar if less vehement strain. ' The matter most ymportant to me,' he declared,[2] ' the preservation of your most noble howse and bloodde, never yet spotted since it tooke beinge. It is taken and so fully interpreted that my Lord (Rutland) came sodenly and rawly into the action in that dismall day in the morning and that he was not any of the complotters nor any pryvy thereunto . . . save to a feare that the Earle of Essex had . . . and so thorowgh love and affection was lyke a lambe drawen along among them.' There was no doubt that Rutland was not a match for the intelligence of the other partners of this disastrous friendship, but nevertheless, as his letter of penitence from the Tower makes clear, Essex had not been without his influence and he was rather a sophisticated lamb.

A fine of £20,000 had been levied which provided occasion for this note. 'I am now by Her Majesty's divine mercy,' Rutland wrote [3] after this favour, ' heartened to bring my humble offer to her Highness of a small sacrifice for so great an offence. All that I have I hold by her Majesty's grace and ever shining mercy with livelihood and being. . . . My living is but little, being but £2700 (of which also I pay yearly to her Majesty for ever above £400) and my debts for myself and my sisters' portions are £10,000. But if every tree on my land was Indian gold I would lay all at her Majesty's feet.' It is a melancholy letter, inspired in all its phrasing by Essex, now lying dead within the Tower. Yet even so it serves to suggest how rapidly the Essex influence waned.

In the Tresham household, where Francis at last had escaped with a mere 400 marks fine, the dangers also issued in relief. ' Jesus Maria,' wrote [4] Sir Thomas to his daughter, Lady Stourton, ' After a sudden

---

[1] Letter from Roger Manners to John Manners, dated at the Savoy 16th February, 1601. Cal. Rutland MSS., i, p. 366.
[2] Letter from Thomas Screven to John Manners, dated 23rd February. *Ibid.*, p. 366.
[3] Letter from Rutland to Sir Robert Cecil, dated 13th June, 1601, from the Tower. Cal. Salisbury MSS., xi, p. 230.
[4] Letter of Sir Thomas Tresham from Rushton, dated 2nd June, 1601. Cal. Clarke Thornhill MSS., p. 110.

and unexpected desperate danger you behold no unspeedy delivery thence of your brother (Francis) and here you should have been an eyewitness of not only my wedging in myself deeper and faster by easing of your brother, but also otherwise, I drenched up (as it were) in a world of adversities. . . . Nevertheless I have more left to maintain me and mine (in some poor plight) than I can challenge of due, or would, without offence to God. He who hath give all may take away, His holy will be done.' The round of country life continued, and a few weeks later we find Sir Thomas writing [1] from Hogsden that he daily wishes himself in the country and means to come down for the sheep clipping, even if he has to return again to town. This was a point of view which Roger Manners would echo, the life of the countryside now victorious over the weak glitter of London, a happy and, except for the Recusants, a peaceful time, with little boys growing up on the old manors who would live to be the Cavaliers.

[1] Letter of Sir Thomas Tresham, dated 27th June, 1601. Cal. Salisbury MSS., xi, p. 230.

CHAPTER XXII

AFTERMATH

This brief epilogue deals with the changed situation which was revealed once Essex, and with him the late Elizabethan fashions, had gone from the foreground. The state of the governing party in Ireland, then under the rule of Mountjoy, is considered and then the condition of Tyrone and the Irish. The situation in Wales is described and the increasing Anglicization of the politically significant elements. The chapter concludes with an account of the Spanish tendencies under Philip III. Each portion of the survey emphasizes most strongly the end of the spiritual unity and the break with the old Celtic past.

THE changes, in themselves so many and varied, which resulted from this disaster mark the Essex Conspiracy as the end of a period. It was the last chance of direct political influence for so many movements; for there was never another occasion on which the old Celtic and feudal forces approached so close to the Throne of what had now been established as a bureaucratic and national Power. A consideration of the effects of the failure makes this point stand forth clear.

In Ireland the effect of Essex's fall was prodigious and none was more affected than his friend the Lord Deputy. Mountjoy was at the moment engaged on a progress through the provinces at the slow rate of his rather valetudinarian fashion and had reached Trim in Meath on the day of the Rising. The general situation in Ireland was not without its embarrassments, for after all he had only entered into Essex's wasted inheritance. 'The frame of that business,' as he truthfully observed[1] to Cecil, 'hath been none of mine. That which I proposed I am confident may be better, but it cannot be worse. The Muster master of this kingdom is one whom, out of my particular affection and charity, I cannot but commend to Her Majesty's favour; but not for this place, in the which he is only a bare cipher, and whose extreme weakness doth multiply the corruption of all the ministers of that office. The Controller upon my knowledge, how sufficient however he may be, is corrupt and a traitor to the Queen's profit.

[1] Letter of Lord Mountjoy to Sir Robert Cecil, dated 4th February, 1601. Cal. S.P. Irel., 1600–1, p. 175.

445

The twenty Commissaries were (such as they were chosen) a course which the captains could not have desired better to colour their deceit.' This picture at first sight may suggest depression, but it is to be noted how carefully his loyalty is stressed and that he was not without ' The Necessary Ability of a good Captain ' is soon apparent. With what a fine staunchness did his rule appear in these troubles, as he turned the following day with none of the roughness of Perrot or the impetuosity of Essex to the very necessary exercise of the literary art ?

'I therefore will repose,' he wrote [1] to the Privy Council, ' my confidence and comfort in the justice of your Lordships' judgements and the sincerity of my own conscience and the consideration of my poor estate unto Her Majesty's best pleasure, unto whom I do owe myself and it ; with this humble desire unto your Lordships to consider that the more I do launch the impostumes of the rebel or subject in this generally infected state, the more likely are your Lordships to be troubled with the clamours of such as feel the present smart.' It was a neat riposte against the slanderers. ' I (as I look for health or help to my soul),' he continued manfully, ' do only faithfully intend their cure and proceed in it sincerely with the best of my discretion and the uttermost of my labours, wherein I am so far from not acknowledging what sound assistance I may receive from your reverent directions and what good fruit I may reap by your favourable admonitions that I desire continually to read them and respect them above any human precepts.' Such a correspondence was an effort and a satisfaction ; but he could hardly realize how soon ' the sincerity of my conscience ' was to be tried.

From Trim he had moved on 11th February by leisured stages, spending a night at Westmeath with Lord Delvin, that peer now grown sobered and careful, since the doubtful adventures of twenty years back, the Nugent and Baltinglas Risings. Then he had gone on by gentle journeys across ' a Country of Champion and nearly waste ' [2] to Mullingar and so by Sir Francis Shane's castle and Sir Tibbot Dillon's, a quiet progress, ten miles in the day, to the provincial capital Athlone. It was a calm ten days before the news from England reached him, for even in these official correspondences there

[1] Letter of Lord Mountjoy to the Privy Council, dated 6th February, 1601. Cal. S.P. Irel., 1600–1, p. 176.
[2] See Fynes Moryson's *History*, i, pp. 200–2 for the details of this itinerary.

was often considerable delay. The letter describing the Essex Rising, which Cecil had written on 10th February, did not reach Sir George Carew until 28th February,[1] while a despatch sent to Sir Geoffrey Fenton on 13th January only arrived on 20th February at Dublin Castle.[2] The Lord Deputy had begun his homeward journey and had reached McGeoghegan's Castle in Westmeath when the blow fell. No comment is needed to Moryson's description of the scene.

'The same 22nd of February,' began [3] the faithful Secretary, 'his Lordship received a Packet out of England, by which he understood that the Earl of Essex was committed to the Tower for Treason, which much dismayed him and his nearest Friends and wrought strange in him; for whereas before he stood upon terms of honour with the Secretary (Cecil), now he fell flat to the Ground, and insinuated himself into inward love and to an absolute dependency upon the Secretary so as for a time he estranged himself from two of his nearest Friends for open Declaration they had made of Dependency on the Earl of Essex; yea rather covering than extinguishing his good Affection to them. It is not credible that the Influence of the Earl's malignant Star should work upon so poor a Snake as myself, being almost a Stranger to him, yet my nearness in Blood to one of his Lordships above named Friends made it seem to his Lordship improper to use my Services in such nearness, as his Lordship had promised and begun to do. So as the next Day he took his most secret Papers out of my Hand, yet giving them to no other, but keeping them in his own Cabinet. . . . In truth his Lordship had good cause to be wary on his Words and Actions, since by some Confessions in England himself was tainted with Privity to the Earl's Practices, so that howsoever he continued still to importune leave to come over; yet no doubt he meant nothing less, but rather (if he had been sent for) was purposed with his said Friends to sail into France, they having privately fitted themselves with Money and Necessaries thereunto. For howsoever his Lordship were not dangerously engaged therein; yet he was (as he privately professed) fully resolved not to put his Neck the Fyle of the Queen's Attorney's Tongue.' The contrast between this

---

[1] The letter in question is endorsed by Carew, 'received the last of Feb. 1600.' Cal. Carew MSS., 1601-3, p. 22.
[2] Letter of Sir Geoffrey Fenton in reply to Sir Robert Cecil, dated 20th February, 1601. Cal. S.P. Irel., 1600-1.
[3] Fynes Moryson, *op. cit.*, p. 205.

account and the preceding correspondence is most interesting, and it should be stressed that, throughout, Fynes Moryson admired the prudence of this statesman of whom he had earlier declared that he could not ' fully apprehend his compleat Worthiness.'[1]

Nothing appears more plainly than the entire difference of outlook between the Lord Deputy and his patron. To Mountjoy, in the midst of his laborious and difficult task, the memories, not only of the charms, but also of the folly of the Essex House circle were faint. He had never imagined that they would deliver themselves in this manner to a crazy adventure which would rock his foundations, but rather congratulated himself on the calculated, temporizing reply he had given to Danvers. The English Government were happily placed, for the wise policy on which they decided, that determination not to inculpate either Mountjoy or King James, had left them the widest liberty to apply the spur to their servant. It would be well that Mountjoy should prove himself more faithful in future.

Yet, it was not only these English embarrassments which had caused Mountjoy to cut loose from his former associates, but also the curious contacts which Essex had made with the Irish. It was hardly a conscious support and never appears in the detailed confessions of prisoners, which mention the various sources of aid which Essex explored, but the imagination of the Irish had been fired by this hero, and not only Tyrone and his henchmen, but all the priests of the West regarded him as an ally. This was a curious instance of that too-widely cast sympathy, contradictory and facile, for Essex was the chief opponent of Spain, while Tyrone was the strongest supporter. But for Mountjoy, whose mind never harboured the Elizabethan knight-errantry, the chief need was to dissociate himself from the man whose name now sounded heroic to the ecclesiastical rabble, the term with which he dismissed Tyrone's priestly supporters.

This was a prudent decision, for soon the repercussions of Essex's Rising reached him from Ulster. In April Moriertagh McDermott McShee, a pledge from the White Knight who had been with Tyrone, returned to the South ready to report his late doings. ' He said,' so ran [2] the official report, ' that when he came with the Irish forces into O'Rourke's country, they heard that the Earl of Essex was entered

[1] Fynes Moryson, *op. cit.*, p. 104.
[2] Examination of Dermott McShee at Limerick on 21st April, 1601. Cal. S.P. Irel., 1600-1, pp. 281-2.

into open action of rebellion in England and that Tyrone was ready to send him any aid, whereof they were glad, which when they came into Clanrickarde they heard the contrary, which made them very sorrowful.'

'He saith,' the deposition continued, 'that, at his first coming prisoner into Ulster, Tyrone speaking of the Earl of Essex(s) troubles in England, he heard him wish that Essex had been with him there. He saith that he, being admitted after to play at tables with Tyrone's lady, heard her say "I would to God that Essex would stir trouble in England, for then would we not care for the aid of any other prince."'

'From Tyrone,' he concluded, 'many of his people daily slip away . . . , notwithstanding he and they (the rebels) are there very bragging and merry among themselves.' This was a problem to Mountjoy, however repellent, and a second examination of a traveller only served to emphasize this side of the question.

'First he saith,' began [1] this longer account, 'that on St. Patrick's day last he left Munster and went over the Shannon into Thomond; from thence to the Country of Clanrickarde to Kilcoligin. The next night he lay at the abbey of Rossirrill [2] with the Friars. From thence in two days he came to the Bishop O'Hart's town, dwelling in the county of Sligo, who after ordinary conference told to this examinate that he had lately been at Sligo, [3] where O'Donnell and the rest of the Lords of those parts as O'Rourke, McWilliam, O'Connor Sligo and the rest, had a parly upon the receipt of certain letters from O'Neill.

'This Bishop told him further that he saw a letter written from the Earl of Essex to O'Neill. The superscription was to the General of Ireland and the effect was that he and the rest of his confederates should be of good comfort, for that he would shortly draw the English forces from Ireland into England, whereby he should with better ease obtain his purpose there, and desired O'Neill to send him a thousand light men to play withal in England; for the letter was received of O'Donnell the beginning of Lent. [4] About this letter and O'Neil's

---

[1] Examination of Dermod McMorris before Sir Francis Barkley on 29th April, 1601. *Ibid.*, pp. 296–7.

[2] These details of the friaries show that remote civilization where Essex's name was invoked; for Ros Irial was in the midst of marshes and bogs, only approached by a causeway two hundred paces in length, and so little effect did the Law have on these friars that the enclosure was only completed in 1572, long after the house's nominal extinction. Franciscan MSS. at Dublin, Printed in C. P. Meehan's *Franciscan History*, pp. 63–93.

[3] According to a letter from Lord Justice Pelham to the Council, dated 15th December, 1579, 'all the Irish save Maguires are at the devotion of O'Neill from Dundalk to Sligo,' the same unchanged boundaries. Cal. Carew MSS., 1575–88, p. 184.

[4] In this connection Ash Wednesday fell in 1601 as late as 7th March.

other directions, O'Donnell and the rest held consultation three weeks at Sligo. From the Bishop's he (the examinate) went to Ballymote, O'Connor Sligo's house, where he heard the former news confirmed. From Ballymote he went into O'Rourke's country and to McGlanckie's, where he heard nothing but general news of their preparation for Connaught. From thence he went to Termon McGraffe, where St. Patrick's purgatory is, which place was the colour of his journey. . . . From thence he went to the Abbey of Donegal, where he found O'Donnell which was their Easter even. Tyrrell (another rebel) being before O'Donnell told him the cause of his coming out of Leinster was the coming in (of) almost all Leinster to the Lord Deputy. . . . He told O'Donnell the first news that the Earl of Essex had lost his head, for which they were all very sorrowful.' This same impression of a hope that Essex would aid them is found in another examination to test the ideas of the Irish.

'In November last,' so ran[1] the account of Donell Kavanagh, 'as I was in Upper Ossorie, in a town called Garran McCouley, I met with a priest called Farrell Magoghegan, who was inquisitist for news out of England, and I no less desirous to hear from the North. He told me that he was five days before with Tyrone in an island near Donganyn, where Tyrone showed to a multitude of his own men a handful of letters, which he said came lately to him from his friends in England and that one of them was from the Earl of Essex and read to the priest and to some few that spoke English wishing him to be of good comfort and to persist in his wars and that he should shortly have relief and assistance to his content. The priest did not tell the name of any of the rest that saw those letters . . . and I durst not then ask more particularly, lest I should be suspected to be an intelligencer for the Queen's Majesty.' However vague are these suggestions, and in especial this last, they suffice to show that the name of Essex had power among the 'Wild Irish.' These messages may have been merely a flourish at the Court of Tyrone, but they greatly contributed to the hardening of Mountjoy's new opinion.

The very idea of these friars and kernes, the details of such vagabonds, repelled the Lord Deputy. He had seen these Ulstermen and had passed with his well-ordered bodyguard through the wretched

---

[1] Examination before Sir George Carew on 9th March, 1601. Cal. Carew MSS., 1601–3, p. 27.

AFTERMATH

villages that they had ravaged. Everywhere he heard the same story
of their barbarous lives. ' At this time,' so it appeared,[1] ' they offered
and sold at their camp, a stripper, or cow in calf, for sixpence, a brood
mare for three pence and the best hog for a penny.' And then tattered
and bare-legged they would go out to canvass these bargains. By
contrast, it is only necessary to recall the Lord Deputy's habits as he
gravely used his tobacco and praised the herb's virtue and, adjusting
his bands, ate with care the bonadoes that he took with his breakfast.
He could reflect in this liberty, in that quasi-philosophical manner
which the new century loved, that, with Essex vanished, all contact
with this wilder life was now gone and his fastidious peace
undisturbed.[2]

The thought of Tyrone, too, was displeasing. The story, which
Moryson repeats [3] with such confidence, was very familiar, that
Tyrone's father, Dungannon, was brought up as a blacksmith's [4]
son at Dundalk and was given at the age of fifteen to old Con O'Neill,
who would generously accept the paternity of a stalwart young bastard.
These were not antecedents to whose possessor a nobleman of nice
judgment would give the title of friend. Not only Tyrone's magnificence but his fern tables [5] under the trees might appeal to Essex
and Harington, to those sophisticated Arcadian sympathies which
Mountjoy could never quite understand, but there was no room for
them in this present common-sense century. The Lord Deputy's
sense of values in this world of reality caused him acute irritation that
Essex's ill-judged favour seemed to engage such men as allies.

For Mountjoy, the fall of Essex meant that all danger of irresponsible adventures was over. The system of the Castle government
was smoothly established and the official class, which was to be of
such crucial importance in the Ascendancy period, had now developed.
The accord between the new settlers and the governors was strong and
complete ; a compact which, save under Wentworth's rule, was to

---

[1] Annals of the Four Masters, 1598, p. 2079.
[2] Bacon dedicated his ' Apology concerning the Earl of Essex ' to Mountjoy, ' first because
you loved the Earl of Essex.'
[3] Fynes Moryson, op. cit., i, p. 14.
[4] A Speech of Secretary Cecil before the Star Chamber shows how seriously this alleged
paternity was regarded. ' There is such a pride and confidence of his own greatness put into,
Tyrone the Rebell that he thinketh of the forme of a black smithe to be king of Ireland forsooth.'
Farmer Chetham MSS., i, p. 31, Surtees Society.
[5] ' His fern table,' Harington declared of Tyrone, ' (was) four forms spread under the stately
canopy of Heaven. His guard for the most part were beardless boys without shirts ; who in
the frost wade as familiarly through rivers as water spaniels.' Nugæ Antiquæ, 11, p. 6.

grow constantly firmer. The predominance in the Administration of those resident officials, who were all permanently loyal to the Crown, was a solid achievement, which Mountjoy had helped to cement. The efforts of the Confederates in the Civil War and of the seventeenth-century Jacobites would break against this system; for it was built upon the ruin of that older Ireland, whose foundations the Tudor policy undermined and whose destruction the capitulation of Limerick completed. It is not surprising that the ' Boyne Water ' should fall so harshly upon Irish ears.

*   *   *   *   *

The effect upon Tyrone of the destruction of Essex as a political power was more complex. Yet, it has its importance, since his House was the spearhead of the old Celtic movement and his contacts with the outer world were reflected, as these reports of travellers show, right down through the different stages of Gaeldom. In order to gauge Tyrone's attitude, the simplest test is to construct, in so far as the sources allow, an account of his interests and immediate background at the time Essex fell and this accumulation of detail, which may in part seem irrelevant, will all contribute to place the part Essex played. Tyrone could hardly have hoped for much aid, and there is only weak evidence to support the idea that he had received in the winter even a letter of friendship. But the gift of the ' Penna Phœnicis ' had heightened his pride and the coming of Mateo de Oviedo, the presence of the Spanish Archbishop of Dublin on the quays of his harbour, had heartened him and it seemed that the mastheads of the ships from Spain for that Kinsale expedition, which was to prove so abortive, would soon rise over the sea line. As he held high court the recent events passed before him, the plan of the Clanricarde

452

AFTERMATH

Burkes at their Easter hosting ' to march directly eastwards along the straight roads of Machaire-Chonnacht until they arrived at Elphin of Moylurg ' [1] and the means which his friends had taken to defeat them ; and then the news of the death of the Lord Mac I Brien Ara, which the runners had brought in from Baile an Chaislen, a cause for great keening. He had been a strong defender of his country, and ' there was no other lord of a territory in Ireland, so old as he on the night that he died.' [2]

In the evenings when Tyrone sat with the lords, while they, distinguished yet admiring, attempted to remember the ritual of the courtesy fingers, as their host waited gravely, the talk would turn upon Essex and his sudden disaster. All that they knew were the details of his Irish adventure, a magnificent lord, and the story of his lengthy march to the South. ' The Gaels of Ireland were wont to say,' it is recorded,[3] ' that it would have been better for him (Essex) that he had not gone on this expedition to Hy Connell Gaura, as he returned back after the first conflict that was maintained against him without (having received) submission or respect . . . and without having achieved any exploit worth boasting of, except only the taking of Cathair Duine [4] Iasgaigh.' But conversation about foreigners flagged, and the guests would return to the themes of their country, while the host listened with courtesy to the praises of Donegal and his ally and those religious emotions, to which Essex was stranger, would stir. ' The Sons of Life and the psalm singing elders of the Order of Francis,' so the ' ollamhs ' of O'Donnell declared,[5] ' used to offer Mass without leaving it (the House of Donegal) ever, either for English or Irish, and moreover they had never,' so the mounting praises would continue, ' been driven from that dwelling, from the first moment that blessed conical roof had been given by that royal star that was prophesied, Hugh Roe, son of Niall son of Turlough of the Wine.' They were well launched, and Essex was forgotten and then they would come to the battle of the Curlews and the protection of the Queen of Heaven in that fight upon her feast and to the description of O'Donnell's charge. ' Mariæ Deiparæ Virginis sacrosanctæ

[1] Annals of the Four Masters, 1601 .pp. 2249–51.
[2] He died in February, 1601, a few days after the Essex Rising. *Ibid.*, p. 2241.
[3] Annals of the Four Masters, 1599, pp. 2119–21.
[4] Cahir-on-Suir.
[5] Extract from Lughaidh O'Clery, *Life of Hugh Roe O'Donnell*, pp. 282–3, expressive of the official sentiments of their adherents in the last days of O'Donnell and O'Neill.

ope hostem Hæreticum cum antea semper vicimus ' ; [1] how fine the Latin sounded for a high supreme lord, phrases as strong and unyielding as the terrible showers of the beautiful ash-handled javelins. But for himself, Tyrone's thoughts would come back to his own high victory, to Beal an atha buidhe and the coarse bog grass and the whitethorn bushes. Essex was now very far away.

Nevertheless, the death of Essex marked a change, for, if he seemed to the Irish a remote but favourable figure, there was no other leader in England who was to come so close again. He had been a rival for the control of the Government and the old Celtic forces were ready to support this endeavour, a phenomenon which was never to recur. Besides, there was an essential difference in outlook between Tyrone as the Aodh O'Neill and Owen Roe, forty years later, with his strict Spanish military code. Essex, as a legend, affected the Irish and in turn Tyrone at Anagh Clint had changed his career ; but the Flight of the Earls overshadowed these matters. It was only six years later that O'Neill and O'Donnell sailed away to Spain and the power in Ireland vanished and, in this event, the sentence of the Masters, that ' they entered the ship on the festival of the Holy Cross in autumn,' [2] reflects the last falling of the leaves.

*   *   *   *   *

The end of the sixteenth century witnessed the close of a period in Wales, as in Ireland. Here there was the same sense of the gradually withdrawing influence of the old-fashioned life, as of an ebbing tide which had come in for the last time to the walls of political England and now slowly drew out again to the westward. Sir Gelli Meyrick had brought the ancient forms into contact with the new England, and,

[1] Philip O'Sullivan Beare, *Historiæ Catholicæ Iberniæ Compendium*, 1621, tom. 3, lib. 5, c. x.
[2] Annals of the Four Masters, 1607, p. 2359.

when he fell, they had lost their solitary spokesman. Besides, there was little doubt, even from the moment of the arrest, that it was the Earl's household which would suffer; unless the Queen should show mercy. As far as the old Welsh-speaking gentry and their ideas were concerned, all hope of influence vanished, for, if Essex were to die, there was little hope that his intimates, Sir Charles Danvers, Secretary Cuffe, Sir Gelli and Christopher Blount, would possess a chance of escape. The Queen, in fact, remained firm, and a painful series of accusations developed. Essex, even now light-headed in ruin, repeated a declaration that Danvers and Cuffe had misled him; but Sir Gelli remained undisturbed, stubborn and loyal.[1] In the end Essex, Danvers and Blount were beheaded, while the privilege of the axe was denied to the others and Cuffe and Sir Gelli were hanged. The rest of the Welshmen were fortunate, especially the group under Vaughan, which was riding to London, but returned on hearing at Colebrook that the Earl was arrested. The matter was rapidly settled and the Welsh squires up from Radnor vanished to return to their sheep and their small stone houses. This was for them the end of adventure, and they would never ride again with hope into London. The stables would no longer echo with the quick Welsh speech of the grooms, nor would the voice of the Great Vaughan be heard in the inns by the Strand.

Sir Gelli received the sentence of death with calm fortitude and not a great deal of surprise. As Steward, he had been efficient and regular, while his deep-rooted [2] and feudal devotion to the great noble house of the Devrasaid had carried him fairly smoothly through these uncongenial affairs, but it was the military support of his patron which was really his province. The contrast between his own calm and the extreme agitation of so many of Essex's friends is partly explained by this fact; for, while they were discussing 'nice matters'

---

[1] A detailed account of the Essex Trial recorded by an eye witness is preserved in Farmer Chetham MSS., i, pp. 1-24. In regard to Cuffe's attitude the words of a hostile witness may be quoted. 'There was amongst his nearest attendants,' wrote Wotton, 'one Henry Cuffe, a man of secret ambitious ends of his own and of proportionate counsels, smothered under the habit of a scholar and slubbered over with a certain rude and clownish fashion that had the semblance of integrity.' Memoirs of the Earl of Essex, pp. 57-8. Few passages express more clearly the lasting hatred of the gentry towards the successful *parvenu*.

[2] A letter from the Earl of Essex then aged thirteen to his agent, Richard Broughton, dated at Cambridge 19th October, 1579, records their first meeting. 'Mr. Broughton,' the Earl begins, 'my countryman Meryck now wayeteth on me I pray you let my L. Treasurer understand of it that I maye knowe by you howe he is affected, for myself I have good liking of the man.' Devereux Papers in Camden Miscellany, xiii, p. 21.

with freedom over the wine, Sir Gelli, the Guy Fawkes of the circle, was standing down in the basement with the match and the powder. Even this present predicament seemed in the line with great attempts in the past, like that effort which Henry of Buckingham had based upon Wales. It was part of the old Welsh outlook to regard Essex almost as royal, an idea which perpetually grated on the sensitive and exquisite young men in London. But for gentlemen so imbued with a sense of their own high descent, as were the Central Welsh squires, it was essential to attribute great rank to one who accepted so carelessly their own noble service. Then the spirit of nationalism entered, and for the last time, into their fervent support. Never again would the Welsh squires unite to support a private citizen to assist their own nation with arms, and, in the deep quiet of their thin mountain pastures, the sons of these men would wonder how their fathers could ever have dreamed of embarking on such an adventure or have hoped to influence London with their heavy and cumbersome swords.

Two quotations from the same source will serve to point out this change in the life of the people. The place chosen is Montgomeryshire, ancient Powys, those lands which lie at the core of the Welsh central ' Massif.' The family concerned is the younger branch of the Herberts and the dates considered are 1590 and 1620, years marking a period during which the Anglicized influence saturated those ancient families of good political standing whose resistance to outside forces had been so firm and prolonged. Edward Herbert, later Lord Herbert of Cherbury, was a boy of seventeen, wealthy and married, at the time of Essex's Rising. The life in Wales in his childhood and the very different social customs with which his mature years were familiar are described in his autobiography in passages which illuminate sharply the contrast and changes. ' My grandfather,' began Lord Herbert,[1] in reference to the years before 1590, ' was noted to be a great enemy to the outlaws and thieves of his time, who robbed in great numbers in the mountains of Montgomeryshire. . . . Some outlaws being lodged in an ale house upon the hills of Llandinam, . . . the principal outlaw shot an arrow against my grandfather which stuck in the pummel of his saddle. My grandfather . . . delighted much in hospitality as having a very long table twice covered every meal

---

[1] Autobiography of Lord Herbert of Cherbury, pp. 4–6.

with the best meats that could be gotten. It was an ordinary saying in the county at that time, when they saw any fowl rise, "Fly where thou wilt, thou wilt light at Blackhall," which was a low building, but of great capacity, my grandfather erected in his age.'

' My father, whom I remember to have been black haired and bearded (was) of a manly and somewhat stern look, but withal very handsome and well compact in his limbs and of great courage, whereof he gave proof, when he was so barbarously assaulted by many men in the churchyard of Llanerfyl . . . defending himself against them all . . . until a villain coming behind did wound him in the head with a forest bill.' This picture in its brevity and clear outline suggests all those ancient Welsh manors, patriarchal in character, at war to protect their own power from the landless men on their borders ; houses, independent as social units, self-contained and remote, where a generous hospitality fostered the old national speech and the bards.

The second description will show how completely this state of affairs passed away from the gentry. ' I spent much time also,' Lord Herbert continues,[1] ' in learning to ride the great horse, that creature being made above all others for the service of man.' Here a transitional frame of mind is apparent, but the next paragraph carries us into a far different period. ' To make a horse fit for the wars,' declared the author, ' and embolden him against all terrors, these inventions are useful ; to beat a drum out of stable first and then give him his provender, to beat the drum in the stable by degrees and then give him his provender upon the drum. . . . When he is acquainted herewith sufficiently you must shoot off a pistol out of the stable . . . then you may shoot off a pistol in the stable and so by degrees bring it as near to him as you can, till he be acquainted with the pistol, likewise remembering still after every shot to give him more provender.' Welsh as the sole everyday speech and the idea of a Cymric nobility, distant and almost self-governing, seemed as remote as the bows and the arrows and the Civil Wars were now close. The rule from England was perfectly effective at last and amid the changing of the stirrup leathers and the strapping of horse pistols, the Welsh squirearchy, accepting the English system and the State Church of that country, rode out in vain to save the English King.

---

[1] Autobiography of Lord Herbert of Cherbury, p. 76.

THE CELTIC PEOPLES & RENAISSANCE EUROPE

If the Celtic influences were withdrawing, they were not spiritually more remote from opinion in England than the ideas of the Court of Spain had now become, a divergence all the more striking when the traditional alliance and the broken unity of their religious Faith is considered. Even Philip II had remained throughout life in close, though hostile, contact with England, but now the last link between the countries was broken.

The new King Philip III was leaving Valladolid for the spring palace at Aranjuez when the news of Essex's execution arrived. As far as Spain was concerned, the man had always proved himself hostile and the event passed without comment, while the beginnings of an inertia had already seized on the King. Young and devout, home-keeping, no traveller, Philip III moved uncertainly through his reign, the thin blood of his Austrian mother's family depriving him of his father's vitality and his military carriage. Gentle and peaceful, his whole intention was centred on preserving the full Christian Faith, that precious and heavy burden which Providence had placed upon his frail shoulders. The questions of England and Holland were very disturbing, whether or not he was bound to continue the war. Even now he was sending a small expedition to assist O'Neill and the Irish, but the result of all his heavy expenses was small; yet could he in conscience give up? It was fortunate that he had the sons of St. Dominic to assist him and especially his own wise confessor to encourage him on the hard path of his duty. He was grateful that the Divine Mercy had granted him the great blessing of fruitful, chaste marriage; but he knew his frivolous nature, against which he struggled, and that tendency to disembarrass himself of his cares. The case of Holland was particularly difficult. God had entrusted him with the care of these peoples and, if he abandoned them now and formally admitted the rights of their new plebeian rulers, would not the immense weight of the sacrilege bear on his conscience? He knew already the Dead Sea fruit of the spirit which had sprung from that nation, since the teachings of Christ were defied, and he thought of the stripped, bare churches and the host of desecrate shrines. It seemed indeed his duty to struggle that the full revelation of Christian Faith might one day be restored. For, if he was weak, he was none the less the King of Spain and Providence might use him.

THE DREAM OF PHILIP II.
El Greco.   From the Salas Capitulares in the Escorial.
Photo: Anderson.

AFTERMATH

Then he would go out to rejoice, childlike, in his splendours, beside him the Grand Equerry Lerma, his good, trusted friend and all the lords of the Court and the Chivalrous Orders, the knights of Alcantara in their spotless silk cloaks and the Calatrava cross flory, a brief vision as he sat beneath the white and gold of his canopy. He could not think of the oppression of the taxes draining the country, nor of the burden of the ' Alcabala ' levied when commodities passed, for he had not been trained in such matters ; but they were in capable hands and there appeared among the crowds in this movement, the cunning and strong face of Siete Iglesias. And then the King would rise to go to the hunting, to that ' Battue ' of the driven deer in his avenues at Aranjuez, which formed his chief pleasure. As he rose from granting his audience and played with the sprays of diamonds in the feathered plumes of his hat and thought of the new custom of crimson silk ribs in the ruff,[1] he would accuse himself of frivolity ; but he would pray to God for amendment and he would never omit his nine rosaries when the day's pleasure was done. ' Lerma and the woods rule all ' [2] ran the common saying. At the close of the day's hunting the King would ride home to his country palace through the sycamore groves and past the dark elms by the river, which his father had brought from England and planted. The sun set beyond the western reaches of the Tagus, which with the approach of summer already flowed less strongly, a movement that reflected the retarded pulsation of the life of Spain, the river and the country slowly draining towards that far gold-laden mirage, the Indian waters, a treacherous sea.

*   *   *   *   *

With London as its strong centre, a great modern state, bureaucratic and national had now come into being. This national consciousness, so much increased, gave a definitely insular impress to all parts of this organism in which the strength of an hereditary monarchy had been augmented during the long and stable rule of a sovereign

[1] For these details ,see Egerton MSS., 367.
[2] Letter from Francesco Soranzo, Venetian Ambassador to Spain, to the Doge and Senate, dated 15th July, 1602, at Valladolid. ' Every one complains of the Duke of Lerma who manages the whole machine as he chooses.' Cal. S.P. Venetian, 1592–1603, p. 467.

who, with her advisers, was well fitted to adapt to such conditions the Renaissance Italian theories of the State. The religious changes had made the English Channel a spiritual barrier, a dividing line which influenced to a marked degree the country's life. In religion the new form of worship, which the State's authority had imposed, balanced the insular tone of trade conditions. An English mould would come in time to recommend the novel doctrines both to the rising merchants and the squires, whom the absence even of such travel as their forefathers were forced to experience in the foreign wars had tied more surely to their native soil.

In the politics of the country this peculiarly national character also entered. There was no direct counterpart abroad to the Cavalier and Puritan positions, nor to the manner in which these parties held their religious and political beliefs. It was upon the ideal of a purely national unity, aimed at but not achieved, that the life of seventeenth-century England turned. In opposition and within the circle of the English law there had stood the remains of an earlier civilization, based in some of its aspects upon feudalism, but in part pre-feudal in its structure. At every point this ancient system showed weakness, in those ties of personal loyalty upon which so much depended, where the detached machinery of the English State could work such havoc, in the lack of political unity and intention.

Circumstances, which were in great part irrelevant and accidental, had brought the English and Spanish monarchies, distant but fairly permanent allies, into close contact. The religious changes drove them apart and the threatened civilization of the Celtic fringe appealed for aid to that great, once friendly power, which now represented the spiritual unity that formed their only bond. It has been the object of this study to piece together and reassemble the different links in these two movements. The failing Celtic remnants, strangled by the strong power of England to the East, yet influenced her in turn in their death struggles; while in the background the Spanish policy made constant effort to make use of the desires for a restoration of the Celtic past, which was outside their comprehension. The desire for a return to the ancient spiritual unity, now broken, alone held them together; but there was no basis for concerted worldly action. The memory of an united Christendom grew faint: slowly the vision passed away.

APPENDIX OF DOCUMENTS

THE series of documents which follow are included for the light which they throw upon the subject of this study. They are divided according to the country with which they deal and are numbered consecutively, the subjects being dealt with in the following order :—

A. Documents relating to Wales.

B. Documents relating to Scotland.

C. Documents relating to Ireland.

D. Documents relating to England and Spain.

A. DOCUMENTS RELATING TO WALES

THE documents in this series form part of the State Papers Domestic for the reign of Elizabeth and are preserved at the Public Record Office. The reference marks given refer therefore to these papers. The three documents are published in chronological order.

I. Notes concerning Sheriffs for Wales, Vol. CCXXXV, 18. 1572.
II. Analysis of the Council of Wales, Vol. CVII, 11. 1576.
III. Notes of such as desire to be placed Justices in Wales, Vol. CX, 13. 1576.

The lists which are here printed throw a light on the social and administrative history of Wales. The first, which clearly appears from internal evidence to belong to 1572, contains a series of notes for the pricking of Sheriffs, three names being submitted for each county. Certain annotations are made in Lord Burghley's hand and a note, obviously intended in a hostile sense, has been placed against those men who are said to have obtained the favour of Sir Henry Sidney, then Lord President. A brief explanation is needed to make clear the significance of this point. Sir Henry had only recently returned to Ludlow and to his work on the Council of the Marches after a prolonged absence. On 17th November, 1572, he had written to Lord Burghley from Ludlow in reply to a statement of the criticisms urged by the Justices against his selections. It was maintained that he appointed as sheriffs even those of his favourites who lacked the qualification of landholding in the shire. The details given on this subject and the particular cases cited in Brecknockshire throw a light on the relations existing between the Lord President and the more Anglicized sections of the Central Welsh gentry. A letter from Walter, Earl of Essex to Lord Burghley, dated 2nd December following, indicates that even at that date the Devereux were prepared to regard themselves as defenders of the liberties of the Welsh squires against all intruders.

The two documents which conclude this series and are attributed to the year 1576 are concerned with an analysis of the composition of the Council of Wales and a note of such as desire to be placed as justices. Both of these papers indicate the contrast between the two elements on the Council, the lawyer class and the squires and the influence of the Old Religion is shown very clearly. A general impression of the social conditions can thus be obtained, and the encroachment of the power of the law upon the wilder districts in Wales is most evident. When studied in conjunction with the other documents printed by the author in *The Bulletin of the Board of Celtic Studies* for November, 1931 and May, 1932, an impression is provided of the conditions existing in Wales and the Marches in the last decade of the sixteenth century.

STATE PAPERS, DOMESTIC, ELIZABETH, BOOK 235, NO. 18

I. NOTES CONCERNING SHERIFFS FOR WALES

Calendared as ' 1590 '? but with an MS. note affixed, suggesting the date as ' apparently 1572.' The two subsequent letters dealing with the same subject and written to Lord Burghley show the accuracy of this attribution. It is clear that

462

DOCUMENTS RELATING TO WALES

the mark placed opposite one of the three candidates in each of the counties does not always indicate the name of the sheriff pricked, but would seem to be merely a tentative suggestion. The list deals with the appointments for the ensuing year and would have seemed to have reached Lord Burghley about the beginning of November, 1572.

Denbighe	Elice price Legum Doctor. Sir John Salesburye. Peers Holland.
Flynt	Hugo Puleston, (The presidentes man) [1] dwelles in Carnervonshire and hathe no Landes in this shire (he hath suff. in Wales).[2] Henrie ap Harry. Peers moston Junior.
Montgomery	John Trevor of Trevallin (my Lord Buckhurstes man) [1] and hathe no Landes in the shire and dwelles in denbigheshire (as pulston).[2] Richard Herberte. David lloid blayney.
Anglesey	(Richard owen Teddir).[3] Owen Wood. Thomas moston.
Carnervon	Ricardus Vaughan de lloynederies (The presidentes man and) [5] a unquiet person (not ye presid. man he hath sufficient).[4] Griffythe Davies. Thomas Wynne ap William.
Merronethe	Rowland Puleston, he hathe no Landes in the shire and dwelles in Carnervon shire (and is the presidentes man).[5] (as pulston).[4] John Lewes owen. Rice Hughes.
Glamorgan	William Herberte de Swansey. William Herberte de Coganpill. Ricardus Gw . . . e [6]
Breknocke	Charles Awbrey, an Attorney in the marches and a common dronkerd (A Just. of peace not drunk).[4] Charles Walcote a man of no credit hathe no Landes in this shire, dwelles in Salop, and was under porter in the marches. (he hath sufic. frehold).[4] Thomas Lewes, honest and good in religion (it is sayd yt he is a papist).[4]
Radnor	John price of pillethe. John price of whitton. Jeun. Lewes a vearie honest and upright dealer.

[1] These words are struck through.
[2] Annotation in Burghley's hand, placed in the margin of the original.
[3] Altered by Burghley from ' John Wynne of Trevarreg.'
[4] Annotations in Burghley's hand, placed in the margin of the original.
[5] These words are struck through.
[6] Torn.

APPENDIX OF DOCUMENTS

Carmarthen   Henrie Jones miles pp.
David Philippes of Kilsayne a briber and a lewd person.
Rotherche dd ap Rotherche alias Gwyn.
(Thomas Wyllyans an honeste man of good relygyon and good abylytye and serves no man).[1]

Pembroke   Ricardus Vaughan, an honest man, but was Shiref the Laste yere of Carmarthen shire to his great chardge.
Alban Stepnethe.
George Wyriot.

Cardigan   Peers Salisburye, (The presidentes man) [2] hathe no Landes in the Shire and dwelles in denbighe shire (he hath landes suffic. in wales).[3]
James Lewes.
Morgan Gwyn, (The presidentes man) [2] hathe no Land in the shire and dwelles in mountgomerye shire (as Salisbury).[3]

(Endorsed)   18 for ye sheriffs of wales (Unmet mens names).[1]

The use hathe byn to make strangers, that hathe neither Landes nor goodes in the countrie shireffes in Wales, and they lie in alehouses and lives of the spoile of the contrey, or els takes C li. of a polling undershiref for the office and never Comes there, and if none weare appointed Shireffes but those that dwelle in the shires the Quene and countrey shuld be well serued for althoughe their be many evill, yet is there sufficient choise of them that be good to serue this torne,

STATE PAPERS, DOMESTIC, ELIZABETH, BOOK 107, NO. 11

II. Names of Officers in the Welsh Council (extracts)

Firste to consider the Counsell there at this daie. The vice president a verie sicklie man not able to take the toyle of yt sevice.

The Justice of xviij[en] yeres contynuance, well knowen.

Seborne of xxij yeres contynuance, lerned, a sober, a Councellor in his Countrie of good experience in that service, suspected of papistrie yett observe the order in repairinge to the Churche and receivinge.

Price after vj or vij yeres contynuance was displaced nowe by lettres made of the Counsell againe of small lerninge and lesse etc.

Pates of xij or xiij yeres contynuance well knowen to yo[r]sellf.

Doctor Ellis of xij or xiij yeres contynuance a good Mountaigne doctor and seldome called to attendaunce there.

Secretary Foxe of xx[tie] yeres contynuance appliethe more his office then comen cause, of good experience in the service of yt howse.

Leighton of Plasshe, lerned a greate Counsellor in his Countrie and at tymes maie serve.

Powell of Oswaldestre newlie placed well seene in Welshe Stories, in that srvice sittethe like a zipher.

Jerom Corbette a yonge man an utter barrester Court but so slowe of dispatche as not meete for that Court.

Fabyan Phes [4] a yonge man, an utter barrester of small experience at the barre or banche of noe knowen lyvynge savinge a baliwicke or Stuardshippe.

---

[1] Annotations in Burghley's hand, inserted in the text.
[2] These words are struck through.
[3] Annotations in Burghley's hand, placed in the margin of the original.
[4] An abbreviated form of Phillippes.

DOCUMENTS RELATING TO WALES

George Bromley   twoe of the Justices thone of Sowthwales thother
and Phetiplace   of Northwales whoe serve not.

These be the lerned persouns that attende the Counsell. The reste of the
Counsell besides Bushoppes are Sir John Perrot, Sir John Lyttleton, Sir Nicholas
Arnolde, Sir John Hubaud, (blank) Throckmerton, Leighton of Wattlesboroughe,
Townshend, Smythe of Cambden etc.

STATE PAPERS DOMESTIC, ELIZABETH, BOOK 110, NO. 13

III. Note on Justices of the Peace

(Endorsed) A note of suche as desyre to be placed Justices in Wales by the new
statute,[1] with their qualities and conditions etc., 1576.

Hierome Corbett brother to Sir Andrew Corbett the vice president an honest
sober gent well learnyd and of good livinge zelous in religion and very well
enclyned to Justice.

Henry Townshend of Lincolns Inne an honest gent of good learninge and
substncyll lyvinge he was borne in Noffolke and by reson his Father was Justyce
in Chester and of this counsell he draweth towarde these partes and is a Counsellor
at Assuses and sessyons in the marches and well lyked of all men and zelous in
religion I knowe not a man of better dispocicion.

Richard Pates of Glocester one of this counsell an auncyent sober gent of good
wealthe and lyvinge and an auncyent professor of the gospell.

Richard Seborne one of this counsell dwelling besides herefors an auncyent
sober gent of good wealthe and lyving, he is thoughte not to be sounde of religion.

William Leighton of the Countie of Salop a proper man of good wealthe and
lyving, yet as Sir Andrew Corbett the vice president his kynsman and very freende
tolde me, he is yll affectyd to religyon.

James Boyle of hereford an honest learnyd gent, very sober and modest and
being a Counsellor at the barre, had euer the best lyking of the benche, he hath
great wealth and faire lyving, he hath both lyving and freendes kn the countie of
Radnor, and therefore meeter for another circuite then there.

James Warnecombe of Lempster an auncient gent well learnyd honest and
faire lyving and great wealthe, and hath servyd heretofore as depute to Sir Robert
Townshend with great comendacion, he is nowe growen corpulent and hevye,
and somewhat gyven to surfeyt with drincke in thafter none.

Mr. Wetherall of Lyncolns Inne   both light headyd of smalle discrecyon
accomptyd to be very covetous and dealers
for interest, yll of religion, I knowe and
Mr. Kerle of Grays Inne   am privy to it that these twoo are desirous
to be made Justyces in Wales.

Fabian Philips a yonge man lately (as I doo heare) a common solycytor of
causes, poore, of smalle or no sufficient staye of living, yet by means preferryd to
be one of this counsell, And nowe in servyce here, sheweth himself (as is reportyd)
more presumptuous and affectionat then wise and meaneth to make this servyce a
staye of his lyvinge.

Mr. Stevens of the temple lately preferryd to be one of this counsell, as I heare
reportyd (for I knowe him not) a playne softe man, of no great wealthe and sickely
dwelling in Glocester shere.

Edmond Walter a man full of passyon and rancour, a common drunkerd and
poore he hath bene a practizer at the barre for these many yeres in the marches of

---

[1] 18 Eliz., c. 8. See Bowen, *Statutes of Wales*, pp. 152–6.

Wales, I have hearde the counsell sondrie tymes of opinion to sequester him the barre for his intemperance.

Edward Davyes a poore man and not well learnyd.

Robert Barton of Grays Inne one of this counsell brother in lawe to Mr. William Gerrard who though he be a reader of Grays Inne, is in my opinyon to be accomptyd with the aforenamyd Wetherall and Kerle, worthie of no servyce in the common wealthe and hathe his chief grace in scoffinge.

Thomas Spencer a proper yonge student latelie growen to be a practizer, alied by mariage in a stocke of the busyest people in these partes.

There be dyvers others that be practizers at the lawe here that I thinke neither themselfes nor no man els thinke Fytt for that servyce, as Thelwall, Bowen, Prynce, and Jones, with some others whose names I knowe not.

B. DOCUMENTS RELATING TO SCOTLAND

THE first two documents in this series are taken from the collection of State Papers, Scotland, preserved at the Public Record Office. They have not been published hitherto. The third paper is contained among the MSS. in the archives of the Scots College at Valladolid. A grateful acknowledgment must be made to the Rector of the College for permission to transcribe and to the Editor of the *English Historical Review* for permission to reprint it.

IV. State of the Nobility in Scotland, Vol. XIX, 38. 18th September, 1570.
V. Memoranda of the Western Isles of Scotland, Vol. XVII, 44; Vol. LI, 86.
VI. Colonel Semple's Report on Scotland, Legajo I, Coronel Semple, 1610. Fragment of an earlier report. *Ibid.*

The three papers relating to Scottish affairs consist of lists of lords and chiefs and their possessions, notes which derive a great part of their value from the conflicting points of view from which these forces are assessed. Thus the State of the Nobility in Scotland in 1570 is a document drawn up in the interests of the existing Government, which was friendly to England, anti-Marian and anti-Catholic. Dealing with the same subject of the state of the Scottish peers, but taking the opposite standpoint, the much later Report on Scotland by Colonel Semple gives an impression of the result of the changes; linking up, as it does, Scotland with Spain. The document relating to the Western Isles gives an excellent impression of their military strength and the divisions of clans, those two controlling factors which have been discussed in the chapter on the Out Isles of Scotland.

STATE PAPERS SCOTLAND, ELIZABETH, BOOK 19, NO. 39

STATE OF THE NOBILITY IN SCOTLAND ON 18TH SEPTEMBER, 1570

(Calendared as ' probably sent by Lennox to the Countess his wife to be delivered to Sir William Cecil ')

Thir noblemen and yair freindis ar presentlie obedient to the Kingis Majestie and his auctoritie.
The erle of Lennax lord Regent his allia, notor
The erle of angus, unmareit
The erle of Mortonn mareit ane of the dochters of the last erle of Mortonn.
The erle of Mar mareit the dochter of the laird of Tullybardin
The erle of Glencarms present wiff is dochter to the laird of Capringtoun.
The erle of Menteith unmareit
The erle of Erroll auld his sone the Maister quha dois the service mareit the heritoice of Lyne of yat hous' quha was My Lord Regentis sistar dochter
The erle of Montrois auld, his oy the Maister of gr'hame that matris the service hes mareit the lord Drummondis dochter.
The erle Marschall auld, his sone the Maister mareit the erle of Errolis dochter.
The erle of Buchane mareit the heritrice of Buchane

467   H H 2

APPENDIX OF DOCUMENTS

The erle of Caithnes mareit the erle of Montrois' dochter.

The erle of Sutherland mareit ye erle of Caithnes Dochter and is sistar sone to my lord Regent, he hes laitlie left the erle of huntley.

The erle of Cassillis hes diuers tymes subsciuit the kingis obedience and now offeris his obedience, he mareit the lord glammis sistar.

The erle of eglintoun hes not accumpanyet the adversares and now offers his obedience, mareit ye lard of Innerpeffriis Dochter, drummond eftir he was divorcit frome the duikis dochter.

The erle of Athole, howbeit he haif kepit cumpany with the adversares, yit he avowes the kingis auctoritie, and departit crabitlie frome the remanent at the first conventioun, and he hes offert to cum and serve the king as he had wont to do. his wiff is the lord flemyngis sistar.

The erle of Rothes obeyis the kingis proclamationis, and at na tyme hes accumpanyet the adversares sen he returnit in Scotland, he is wedo.

The erle of Craufurde albeit he has bene agains the king, yit he hes of new maid offer for obedience, he mareit the cardinall betonis dochter.

The lord simple, wedo

The lord Ruthven mareit the lord Methvennis sister

The lord lindesay mareit the lard of Lochlevennis sister

The lord Methven mareit the lord Ruthvennis sister

The lord glammis mareit the lord Saltonis sister

The lord uchiltre wedo

The lord Cathcart wedo

The lord crychtoun of Sanquhair ane pule his haill freindis obedient to the king

The lord Yester mareit the lard of farnyhirstis sister

The lord Borthwik mareit the laird of Bukclewchis fader sister

The lord gray mareit the lord ogiluyis fader sister

The lord Sinclair mareit the lord forbes Dochter

The lord Lovatt mareit the erle of Atholis Dochter

The lord Saltoun wedo

The lord forbes auld, his sone ye Maister quha hes to wiff the erle of huntleyis Is obedient to the king and hes not taken parte with huntley sen his lait Defectioun.

The lord of Sanct Johnis mareit the laird of Polmais dochter

The lord Drummond hes obeyit and neuir bene agains theking, his wiff Is the Lord Ruthvennis fader sister

The lord Maxwell hes also obeyit and neuir bene agains the king, unmareit.

The lord Elphinstoun his wiff Is the lairde of Innerpeffreis Dochter Drummons, and he hes laitlie offerit his obedience

The lord hwme hes accumpanyet the adversares and yit seamys still to profes the kingis auctoritie, his haill freindis ar with the king, and he has maid offers of lait be messingers for his obedience, his wiff is the lord grayis Dochter.

The lord Ros' hes not accumpanyet the adversares and is beeinn obedient, maried the lord simple's dochter

The lord olyphant sicklie, quha hes mareit the erle of errolis dochter

The lord somerwell sicklie, quha hes mareit the lord seytonis Dochter

The lord Ogiluy mareit the lord forbes Dochter and hes maid offers for obedience,

Thie noblemen pretendit thair obedience to the Quene.

The duke of Chastallarault mareit ane of the auld erle of Mortonis dochter's

The erle of Huntley mareit the duikis dochter

The erle of Ergile mareit lady Jane king James the fyft base dochter

The lord Boyde mareit the dochter of a gentleman named Colquhoun

468

DOCUMENTS RELATING TO SCOTLAND

The lord flemyng mareit ye lord Ross' brother dochter
The lord levinstoun mareit the lord flemyngis sister
The lord hereyis mareit ane of the last lord hereys Dochters
The lord seytoun mareit Sir Williame hammiltonis dochter.
(Endorsed in the hand of Sir William Cecil) 18th September, 1570.
The state of ye Nobillite in Scotland.

STATE PAPERS SCOTLAND, ELIZABETH, BOOK 51, NO. 86

MEMORANDA OF THE WESTERN ISLES OF SCOTLAND

The West Ilis of Scotland ar dividit in foure partes euery part haueing in it a principall Ile with a number of smaller Ilis about the same, Twa lyis northward, The Lewis and Sky and twa southward. Illay and moll.

Lewes hes Joyned with it be a small gripp of twa or thre pair buttes Length the harreich, Lewes is xxxij myles of Length and harrich viij myles, Lewes perteynes to *Mccloyd of* the lewes wha being an ould man, famous for the massacring of his awen kinesmen, his bastard sonne called corquill (sic) oig usurpes now the rowme. This Ile will make vij C men to the weirs besydes them which occupyes the ground which neyther in that nor na other of the Iles ar charged to the weirs but suffers to remayne at hame for labouring of the ground.

The uther part of this Ile Called *harreich perteynes to M^cloyd* of herreich, wha is presentlye a chylde and hes sundrye other Landes. On this land of harreich he will rayse vij^{xx} men able for the weirs.

Ewist is ane yle of xl myles of Length but of small breadth the north part therof perteynes to the clandonalld in ye north to whom donald *gormson* is chiftain wha will rayse on their part iij C men.

Barra perteines to Macneill of Barrey, wha may rayse theron and some little Iles adiacent ij C able men.

Rona perteining to M^cloyd of the Lewes lx men.

Pabba perteining to M^cloyd of harreich xl men.

Helsker perteining to murray ycolmkyll xx men.

Colsman not inhabited.

Irt or hirtha perteines to M^cloyd of Harreich. The inhabitantes rude and simple sendes na men to the weir.

Skye is ane large Ile of xl myles of length and also mokle of Breadth perteineth of auld to the Lords of the yles, whais Bastard posteritye now brookes sundrye partes, and uther partes ar possest by diuerse inferior clanes, Trontyrnes and slait possest be donald *gormeson*, Trontirnes will raise VC men, and slait vij^c men. Watternes perteyning to Mcloyd of the Lewes wheron he wil. rayse ij^c men.

Durenes pracadaill and Meynes perteyning to Mccloyd of Harrich, wheron he will rayse v^c men.

Raarasy possest be Macgllicallum of Raarsaye of the clanlewyd of the Lewes will rayse lxxx ¹ men.

Eg perteining to the clanrannald will rayse lx men.

Romb possest be the clanrannald will rayse x men.

Canna possest be the clanrannald will rayse xx men.

Ellan a mok possest be Macane of ardnamurchan will rayse xvj men.

Scalpa perteining to M^claine of Dowart will rayse xx men.

Mull is xxiiij myles of length in some partes xvj myles braid, in some partes but xij myles. And will rayse to the wears ix^c men.

---

¹ This figure is altered from ' viij^{xx}.'

APPENDIX OF DOCUMENTS

Lismoir perteining to the erle of Argile, & glenurquhy will rayse ij^c men.

The twa hwnais pertaining to M cowll of lorne and John Stewart of the appin will rayse lx men.

Ullowaye perteines to M^{c}cowler & will rayse lx men.

Comantra perteins to M^{c}clane of dowart & will rayse xx men.

Inchenyt perteining to M^{c}clane of dowart & wil rayse xx men.

ycolmekill is the Bishopes seat of the Iles and the buriall place of the auld kings of scotland.

Coill perteyning to the lard of Coill of the Clanlane will rayse vij^{xx} men.

Tierhie very fertyle will rayse iij^c men.

Ilaye is xxiiij myle lang & xx myle braid the ane half possest be M'clane of Dowart, & the other be anguse M^{c}cowll. The great massacre and blude shed that hes bene betwixt them was for the proffite & comandment of this Ile. The haill Ile will rayse viij^c men.

Iura xxiiij myles of length narrow & for the maist part wildernesse. It is possest equallye be clandonnald & clanlane, & will rayse j^c men.

Collonȝa and Orronȝa ar baith in effect but ane Ile, possest be ane called M'cafie depender upon the Clandonnald & will rayse j^c men.

Seill perteins to the erle of Argile & will rayse vj^{xx} men.

Loing possest be M^{c}clane of Dowart of therle of argyll and wyll rayse xx men.

Scarba perteins to M^{c}clane of Lochbuye & will rayse xx men.

Geygha possest be the Clandonnald will rayse j^c men.

Rauchlin on the cost of Ireland possest be the clandonnald althoughe perteininge heritable to the Lard of barsky'men in Kyle.

Arrane and bute ar not numbered amongst the other Iles abouewritten but lyes in the firsth of Clyde toward kintyre and Argyle on the south syde thereof.

Thes Iles gif they wer on ane end ar estemed to be xiiij^{xx} & xij myles in length. It is halden that they may rayse gif they wer all under ane comandement vj^m men to the weir besydes the Laboures of the ground, Theirof ij^m with acebous habershonis & knapscalles, the remnant bowmen and many of them now become hacquebusters.

Besydes the inhabitantes of the Iles their is many in scotland that speiks the Iresh toung as namely the *brayes* of Cathnes and Sut'land haill scrathnaber the bray and norh cost of ros lovet glengarry knoydert and moydert Petty brachley scratherne badzenoch and lochquhaber. The bray of Murray, strathspay scraithowin. The brayes of Mar Atholl braidalbane buchquhidder Monteith and the Lennox. Thir dependes upon the erle of Argile diuerse in braidalbaine menteith snd the Lennox, besides Colball ergyle knapdaill and clorne and besyd sundrye his freindes & tennantes in the Lawlandes, kintyre, although for the maist part the Kinges proper land, be the forfalter of the Lordes of the Iles which were alswa erlis of Ross, yet haill kintyre is presentlie possest be Anguse M^{c}coull and others the clandonnald of the south. His princepall bowndes ar kintyre in the maynland, Ila, Iura, Collonza, gighey, his princepall dependers in his weirs against M^{c}clane wer they of the clandonald, in south, donnald gormsonn & his Clandonnald in the north, the Clanrannald & McIane of ardnamurthy.

the princepall bowndes of M^{c}clane ar the Iles of *mull coill* and *tierhie*. And in the mainland morverne & som partes in lochquhair, his princepale dependers in his weirs against M^{c}coull wer they of the clanlane M^{c}cloyd of harrich Macky'nnon of Strathoradell Macneill of barrey. Their concords & discordes are difficille & almaist impossible to declair for sen their reconsiliacion after the barbarous weirs the tutor of harrich is Joyned with donnald gormson, and as some sayes also torquill usurpit of the Lewes.

In Straith naver and the brayes of Cathnes and sut'land makky hes dominion, torquill the eldest sonne of M^{c}cloyd of the Lewes, pure unable and opprest be his bastard brother the usurper romains in coigheanch on the mayn land.

Then Mackenzie occupyes kintaill lochbeny & in effect the haill north part of ros. And the bray of the south part thereof & all ardmanoch to cromarty.

The Lovet possesses the lord lovit frashr & be north him lyes the boundes of knoydert moydert and glengarry perteining to the clanlannald which rekkins them selues of the clandonnald and ar freindes and assisters to them.

Glengarry hes assisted the erle of Huntlye against Macyntocsh and sa hes allen M^{c}coull alby chiftane of the clanchadronn in lochquhaber and alister Macrannald chiftane of ane other branch their.

The clanquhattane wherof Macyntoshe is chiftane dwelles in badzenoch therle of Huntlyes Land, and about inernes in petty brachley stratherne & straithnerne therle of morayes land.

The Lard of grant occupyes streathspay straithowin urquhart glenmornestonn.

The erle of Athole occupyes Athole stratherdill genshe apuadaill and straithtat.

The Lardes of glenurquhy laweris glenlyony and others therle of Argiles frendes occupyes braidalbaine, glenlyon glendochert glenfalluch and uther within perthshire.

The clangregors dependers on the erle of Ergile dwelles on the maist part of all menis land betwixt Dunbartan and Dunkeld.

The Macfarlanes buchannains M^{c}cawlais culquhonnis galbrayth and others within the Lennox under the Duke therof althoughe devyded amanges them selfes.

(Endorsed) The note of the weste Isles of Scotland for the L(ord) Threasurer.

COLONEL SEMPLE'S REPORT ON SCOTLAND, 1619

In the archives of the Scots College of San Ambrosio at Valladolid there is a report on the state of Scotland drawn up for the Spanish Government in 1610. The document is in Italian and is written by Colonel William Semple, who was at that time sixty-three years of age and resident in the Calle de Chinchilla at Madrid as gentleman-in-waiting to the King. He was wealthy, related to many of the southern lords and had visited Scotland in 1604; for twenty years he had been the representative of the Scottish party in Scotland at the Court of Spain and he was in communication with King James. A number of Presbyterian peers are omitted from his list as he was chiefly concerned with possible supporters of the Spanish policy, but apart from this it seems that his report suffers rather from an undue reliance on the somewhat decrepit supporters of his cause than from any wilful perversion of the facts. The manuscript is written on seven separate sheets and is contained in a volume described as Legajo I ' Coronel Semple.'

Della nobilita o nobilj de Regno de Scotia

Le forze del Regno de Scotia consistana nella nobilita come in Ingliterra nel populo, perose il populo d'Ingliterra e molto richo et de Scotia e molto povero. Laltra cause delle forze della nobilta de Scotia e la conservetione del medisimi nome delle case, et quilli del medisimi nome seguitare il capo del nome et se defendano l'un l'altro in ogni causa, et seguitarano lor capo senza risguardar se la cusa e giusta o ingiusta, o contra il principe o altro qual si voglia, come il capo del nome de Hamylton o di Gordon s'hanesse de fare, tutti de qual nome le seguitariano et spendariano le vita per luj senza l'apertegn'a al capo per alsi ma altra ragione se no se siano del medesimi nome et questi fariano all gli suoi prossimj parei d'altro nome. La nobilta consiste in Marchesi, Conti, Lords o Viceconti et Baroni, ma perch gli Baroni per la mayor parta seguitano gli Marchesi Conti o Lords, o per causa de vassalayia o de ensanguinta, o per esser del medesimi nome,

APPENDIX OF DOCUMENTS

o per amicitia qui no si fara mentione delle Barroni. Il regno di Scotia e divisa per quattro finimi grossi, fortha Taw, dia et speia, a talche si sappia in che parte del regno habitano gli nobili, sarano dist'e per gli detti finimis.

Tra il fiume de fortha et l'Ingliterra habitano Catholici

' Il Marchese de Hamylton, capo de nome molto numeroso delli Hamyltonj de sangue regia, et heride del Regno di Scotia manchando questo Re colla sua prole. Come che fra sei et fatte catholico, non se ancora scoperto per Catholico,[1] per buene ragioni. Le conte de Abircuen suo cognato, de nome de Hamylton. Tutti del nome de Hamylton tanti gentii de Catholici seguiterani questi Dmi Sigri, gli fariano mille cavelli et piu, 50 lanceati del nome del Hamylton.

Il conte de Angus capo del nome numerosissimo del Douglas sta in Francia [2] sbandito per la fede.

Il conte de Hume capo del valoroso nome de Hume.

Il conte de Venton [3] capo del nome grande de Seton.

' Il conte de Lithco capo del nome de Livingstone non se scopto Catholico, la contessa [4] sua moglie e manifestamete Catholico et la defende il marito lui hanuto l'educatione delle figluole del Re.

Il conte de Bothuol [5] valoroso sigre sta in Spagna.

Il lord o viceconte de Maxuel [6] capo de nome grande de Maxuel sta in Francia.

Il lord o viceconte de Herys del nome de Maxuel.

Il lord o viceconte de Semple [7] capo del nome de Semple.

Il lord o viceconte de Sanchar [8] capo del nome de Critton.

Il lord o viceconte de Boyd [9] capo del nome de Boyd.

Il lord o viceconte de Elphynston [10] giovane capo del nome de

' Il lord o viceconte de Rosbraugh capo de grande nome de Car, per ancora non se scuperto per Catholico ma si sa et se tale.

' Il lord o viceconte de Bulclouch[11] capo del nome de Scot, valoroso signore fu convertate a Roma per el pre Tyrie ma l'retornato all eserciteso delle heretici per de cura e castello.

Tra il detto fiume de fortha et l'Ingliterra habitano questi heretici

Il conte de Glencarne capo del nome de Cuningham fornese et assaj potente heretico.

Il conte de Montgomery capo del nome de Montgomery freddo heretico et nemico capitale del sopra deto Conte de Glencarne contra il gli jungeria s'c alli Catholici.

Il conte de Cassile capo del nome de Kenedy mezzo heretico. Il tutore [12] era Catholico.

---

[1] The note book of Dr. John Southcote states that the Marquis of Hamilton died a Catholic.
[2] The Earl of Antus was living at Saint Germain des Pres.
[3] This was presumably George, Earl of Winton. His elder brother was still living but insane.
[4] Lady Helen Hay sister to the Earl of Errol.
[5] Francis Earl of Bothwell is said to have supported himself by necromancy at Naples at this date.
[6] Lord Maxwell was living in Paris and was executed for treasonable fire raising and murder on his return.
[7] Lord Semple had made a fortune by piracy with the laird of Ladyland.
[8] Lord Crichton of Sanquhar was hanged for murder in 1612.
[9] Lord Boyd spent much of his life on the Continent, being troubled by a vehement dolour in his head.
[10] Lord Elphinstone's brother had served the Spaniards in Sicily.
[11] Better known as Sir Walter Scott, a stepson of Lord Bothwell.
[12] Sir Thomas Kennedy of Culzean who was killed in 1602.

DOCUMENTS RELATING TO SCOTLAND

Il conte de Mar capo del nome de Erskyn fermato heretico de poco de forze o seguita.

Il sig*r* Georgio Hume conte de Dunbar et sig*r* de Berwico, per il solo favore et liberalita del re rivolissimo, ma de la piu bassa nobilta, figliolo sedo o terzo genito de sua familia, da molti odiato, fermato heretico, in la sua seguita depo' de suoi denari.

Il lord o viceconte de Leslie seguitara il conte d'Errol capo de sui nome.

Gli lorde o viceconte Borthik[1] d'Ochiltre de Ross de Carnart[2] de poco de forze.

Tra il finimi de Fortha et il fiume de Tayo Catholici

' Il conte de Rothes il giovane capo del nome de Leslie il pr*e* e vecchio inutile.

' Il conte de Pertha capo del nome de Dru'mond valoroso.

' Il conte d'Argil capo del nome de Campbel, non se mo'strato publica'te Catholico[3] fiu co'vertito alla fede a Roma per un padre Jesesuita, confessato el evisato se maritato alla figliola del Marquesi de Huntly molto Catholico.

Il conte de Domfirmeling Cancellario del regno, de grand' authorita et prudentia.

' Il conte de Tulibarn capo del nome numeroso de Murray.

' Il lord o viceconte Innerpofray.

Il lord o viceconte de Oliphant,[4] capo del nome de Oliphant

Heretici tra gli detti finimi

Il conte de Menteith de perf''issme forze.

Lord o viceconte de Lyndesay de poco destina o seguita.

Tra il fiume de Tayo et il fiume de Dia Catholici

Il conte de Errol[5] capo del nome de Hay et conestablio del regno, valoroso.

Il conte de Craford[6] vecchio capo del nome de Lindsay sui fratelli sono Catholici.

Lord o viceconte d'Ogilby capo del nome numeroso Ogilby.

Lord Gray[7] capo del nome de Gray gub'nator hereditario della pri'tia d'Angus.

Heretici

Il conte de Athol[8] povero indubitato, de vassali razzi senza cavalaria.

Il conte de Monterosa capo del nome de Grame, amico de Catholici, et dire de la sua espada e molto Catholica.

Il conte de Marischal capo del nome de Keith gli sono pocchi lo governa il congnato. Thomaso O'Gilby molto Catholico et valoroso fratello della Co'tessa[9] sua moglie Catholica.

Il lord de Glamis capo del nome de Lyon il suo zio[10] e Catholico et lo governa.

---

[1] Lord Borthwick is supposed to have been murdered by the Galloway witches in 1623.

[2] This was presumably the laird of Carnwath, Sir Robert Dalzell.

[3] The Earl of Argyll kept this a secret until 1618.

[4] His father, the Master of Oliphant, who had disappeared, is said to have been living in Algiers as a slave.

[5] There was madness in this family and his two brothers were insane.

[6] Lord Crawford died soon after in the debtors prison at Edinburgh.

[7] Lord Gray had lived in Italy for several years.

[8] Lord Atholl had been imprisoned for misrule in his country and was confined to the capital at this time.

[9] Margaret Ogilvie of Airlie, her brother was a ' resetter ' of Jesuits.

[10] Sir Thomas Lyon, Master of Glamis.

APPENDIX OF DOCUMENTS

Tra il fiume de Dia et il fiume de Spes Catholici

Il marquesi de Huntly capo del nome numerosisso de Gordon governa quasi tutti les provincie tra questi duoi fiume molto Catholico valoroso et fortunata in guerra.

Heretici

Il lord o viceconte de Forbes [1] capo del nome de Forbes.

Tra il fiume de Speia et il mare Settentrionane Catholici

Il conte de Suderlanda domino quasi a tutta la cuntra de Suderlande.
Il conte de Caitness[2] capo del nome de Sinclair domino a tutta la Cathanesia.
Gli segri MacIgny [3] et Mackey sono potenti segri Catholici

Heretici

Il conte de Murray seguitara il marquese de Huntly suo socero Lord o viceconte de Lovat capo del nome de Fraser, se rendo al obsequio del marquese de Huntly et per questo si li paglia ogni anno un stipendio assai bueno.

De questi nobili heretici sono molti gli end'agli [4] nel cuore sono Catholici, et al tempo seguitariano gli Catholici. Li forze precipue delli heretici cu'sistono nelle terre grosse et baroni delli gli non si fa mensione de questa numerasione si vede che le forze delle Catholicii sono dieci molte piu grande che quelle delle heretici de che un solo et medessimo giorno li Catholici possono occuparate tutti le terre Grosse et porti del mare de Tutti il Regno de Scotia.

(Endorsed) Guillermo Semple 1610

There is also a fragment of a report written in Spanish by Colonel Semple. It contains notes on the characters of various Scottish leaders and a list of peers, and it seems to date from the time of his visit to Scotland in 1588.

Los qui seguiran el rey de Escotia en qualquere casisa y sus poderes
El duque de Lenos de menor edad y por cor lo no se meneban sus parientes y vassales.
El conde de Murray su poder de conte es legos.
El conde de Athol su poder es legos.
El conde de Merchal de buen seguito mas pobre de hasienda.
El conde de Mar por un cor valeroso de persono h'm'o la nasion requere no tene mucha seguito.
Mi lord Hamilton de grandes tierras mas il mayor parte segur su hermano menor por cor valleroso y as muy buen Catholico.
El conde de bothwel almirante de la mar valleroso de su persona de muy gran seguito mas facil de condision y no Catholico.
El conde de Craufurd resoluta de su persona mas pobre.
El conde de Montrois su poder es legos.
Mi lord Ogilbie de buen seguito y en buena parte Seton, Semple y Lord John Hamilton, Libiston,[5] herries de buen gente y un buena parte.
My lordis de Hume, de enchafesa,[6] de Flemyng de amicos y mas muchos barones de gran poder y por no cor large se escuse escribir.

[1] His brother was a Capuchin under the name of ' Archangel of Scotland ' at Tourni.
[2] It is curious that Patrick, Earl of Orkney is not mentioned in this list, as he was beheaded for rebellion in 1614 and had been a prominent pirate for some years.
[3] This name seems to have been a version of Mackenzie.
[4] There are several instances in this report of Colonel Semple's curious Italian.
The mark [1] which he placed before the names of several peers seems to indicate that these men were not openly on the side of Spain.
[5] Lord Livingstone.
[6] This was probably the laird of Enchaffray.

DOCUMENTS RELATING TO SCOTLAND

Las calidades de los que governen al rey de Escosia

Mi Lord Cansallii del reyno hijo segundo de un pequino barron que par autoridad de su ofisio es segunda persona al rey de Escosia.

El senor de Henelndan hijo segundo de un baron.

El barron de condonknows de mas poderosos que ay entre estos.

El barron de carmichel valleroso de su persona mas pobre.

El senor de glamas thesorero del rey hombre valleroso y prudente mas poco seguito por cer hijo segundo.

Todos estes son del consejo y governa al rey de Escosia a desguito de todo el reyno.

Ser seros catolicos de Escosia	Politicos	Herejes
los condes de Huntle	el conde de Rothes	el rey de escosia
„ Morton	Conde de bothvel	Conde de Atholl
„ Cathnes	que es almirante	Conde de Mershel
Conde Sutherland	Conde de Muray	el duque de lenos
Conde de arrel	Conde de Argyl	Conde de anguis
Conestable de Escosia	Conde de Glencarno	Conde de Mar
Conde de craufurd	Conde de Casilli	Conde de aran
mi lords ogilbie	Conde de Montetha	mi lord linsay
„ hume	mi lord enermethe	mi lord sumervail
„ seton	„ enchafray	„ hamilton
„ semple	„ doune	„ ochiltre
„ gray	„ cathcart	
„ lebinston	„ ros	
„ heris	„ borthik	
„ Yland	„ yester	
„ flemyng	„ boyd	
	„ lovat	
	„ glamis	
	„ creichton	

C. DOCUMENTS RELATING TO IRELAND

The following documents relating to Irish affairs form part of the State Papers Ireland for the reign of Elizabeth and are preserved in the Public Record Office. They have not been published hitherto. The first two papers are produced in full but in the case of the lengthy political enquiries which form the subject-matter of the second series only a summarized abstract has been included. This accounts for the fact that the spelling is modernized in this section.

VII. Argument against granting a pardon to the Countess of Desmond, Vol. LXXXIII, 7. 12th May? 1581.

VIII. Examination of Sir James of Desmond, Vol. LXXVI, 25, i. 25th August, 1580.

IX. Summarized abstract of interrogatories administered to the Earl of Kildare and Lord Delvin and of the confessions and examinations relating to the Nugent Rising, Vols. LXXXIV, 36 and 38 and Vol. LXXXVI, 19, i, Vol. LXXXVIII, 47, i. 19th July, 1581–21st January, 1582.

The first two papers throw a vivid light upon the state of affairs in Desmond, the Earl's physical weakness and paralysis, his way of life and relations with the Countess, the contact of the Desmond brothers with O'Rourke and Baltinglas and the details of the sack of the settled towns by the Geraldine horsemen. The last section describes the material upon which a great part of the account of the Baltinglas and Nugent Risings is based. It should be noted that the long interrogatories, with which these papers begin, in reality contain the whole case for the Crown against Lords Delvin and Kildare. The confessions and examinations which follow, give an impression of the social life of the Pale and of the meetings and habits of the Anglicized gentry. The connection with the septs and the vague background of rebellion in Ulster and Desmond is always apparent.

STATE PAPERS IRELAND, ELIZABETH, BOOK 83, NO. 7

ARGUMENTS AGAINST GRANTING A PARDON TO THE COUNTESS OF DESMOND
DATED C. 12TH MAY, 1581, COPY

A note shewinge the inconveniences that shall ensue (*by*) [1] the pardoning of the Comitise of Desmound.

Firste if she be pardonned or protected she shall seame to by asubiecte (nomine & non rei) to heunder the service upon the traytour her husbaund as in sendinge him warninge of all the iourneys that shalbe made upon him by the Lord gennerall, & freindinge hym to her uttermoste that others shuld take his parte so that the Lord gennerall shall not be able to do no service but she or some of her frendes aboute the Lord gennerall by her procurment shall prevent it in giving her or him notice thereof so that the Lord gennerall shall never go without fire in his bossome unknowen to himsellfe.

Secound if ye meane (to procead) [2] the service to proceed & the rebellion

---
[1] Interlineated.
[2] Struck through.

DOCUMENTS RELATING TO IRELAND

ended shortlie, ye are not to pardon the said Contise, for that if the said traytour be pursued he hathe more care for the said Contise and her traine to kepe them, then he hathe of himself, for if were not for for her & her traine he might be in adefians with 5 m. men if they were in the contrey for as long as the force is togider he (may)[1] go with as fewe company as please him from wood to wood & from bogg to bogge or to Spaine scotland ulster or elswher to wourcke further mischieve, but having her in his traine he cannot chuse with the Leave of god being well pursued & spied but by over threwen or taken for the traytour is ympottent and hathe but one quicke side. he cannot mount a horsbacke of himselfe nor light from his horse without the help of men. he hath the palsy also, so that by all reasoun the traytour being well stricken in yeares cannot live long, nor hathe but fewe cossins lineall or collaterall to succide him in this accion of rebellion.

Thyrd whate derogacion & disabilities were it for the crowne of England to pardon the like traytour or traytores, & an encouradgment to others to play the like trayterous parte, as they have doun, viz. howe the said Comitise have mainteined & sett forward the traytour to clayme the regall Jurisdiction of her majesties towne of youghull, & also howe she sett the traytour forward in this accion of rebellion in retaininge horsmen before the rebellion begann, as in giving of horsses to gentlemen to take the traytour is parte the which might be proved, and further when the said traytour came to youghull at the sacking therof wente to the tollcell Courte of the said towne & seeing her majesties armes there in the saide courte as it ought to by, caused the said armes to be pulled downe brocken to peces & trodden under foote, seing his owne armes ought to by there & no other armes, & having assimbled his rabble of traytours aboute him (in)[1] the said courte, tooke Consell whether he would put the twonesmen bothe man woman & child to the swerd or not, & being put backe thereof by his brother John the traytour who said who said (sic) it was ynoghe to burne the towne banishe the people take awaye ther goods & brecke the walles & so ther shalbe no passadge nor no intertaunment for englishemen to travayll from Waterford to corcke & in that there assimblie the said traytour in derision & mockerie of her Majesties auctoritie Crowne & dignitie have made one nyclas power maior & (two) galliglasses balliffes who went in there gownes & typpettes & made proclamacion uppon the markett crosse to make havocke of all the goodes in towne & proclaimed the gallon of aquavita for a penny the gallonn of wynne of a halffpenny the barr of Ironn for a fardding & dayes of paiment for ever.

(Endorsed in Burghley's hand) Against ye Contise of Desmonds pardoun.

STATE PAPERS IRELAND, ELIZABETH, BOOK 76, NO. 25, I

THE EXAMINATION OF SIR JAMES FITZGERALD KNIGHT, DATED 25TH AUGUST, 1580

Thexaminacion of Sir James fitz Gerald knyght, brother to therle of Desmound taken on the xxv[th] of August 1580 before the Right honourable the Lord generall and others her Majesties Comysyoners whose names ar subscribed.

He sayeth that about half a yeare past one Hiffeniane brought a Lettre directed to therle, Sir John and to this examinate, subscribed (to) with thandes of the vycount of Baltinglas and feaghe m'c Hewghe, declaring how they intended to ioyne with them in deffence of the popes cawse and requeiring the promyse and assurance of therle and his bretherne unto them and that they shold be sure to enioye their owne landes when the popes forces shold come, Unto which Lettre therle Sir John and he, retourned aunswere graunting that request in everie poynt,

---

[1] Interlineated.

APPENDIX OF DOCUMENTS

Item in May last therle his brother tould him that he was assured of good assistance and that but few daies before one Robert fitz Morris fitz James of Osberston brought him a Lettre from the vyvount of baltinglasse promysyng his redie ioynynge wyth them.

Item he sayethe that therle his brother sent a messenger to Anele O'Donell Sowrloy boy and other gentlemen of the North requiering them to move warr in those partes, which messenger he sawe, retourne to his brother therle who tould that both they and Orowrke haue undertaken to do so.

Item being demaunded whether anie the Lord of Upper Ossories bretherne weare combyned with therle his brother and Sir John, he saithe he knoweth not moche thereof, and that frere James Toraghe was more privie to the demges of Sir John then he, yet he sayeth a monthe or more past the Lord Justice and the Lord generall beeng in the countye of Corke he hard Sir John beeng then at the Clealishe neere the great wood say that abowte that tyme kalloghe keaghe the baron of upper ossories brother was spoyling of the Countye of kilkenny.

Item he sayethe that therle his brother told him that Piers Grace was ioyned unto him with greate assurance.

Item he sawe John bourke fitz William late of Suerfyane in thereles companye who desyered this examynate to accompanie him to Arloghe to spoyle therle of Ormondes countreys.

Item he saieth that there were long since moore messengers come unto therle his brother from Spayne, the contentes of those messengers he knowethe not more, then that they promysed present ayde, therle sent over (one Christofer Lombard) [1] of whome there is nothing hard, yet do they daylye expect to heare of him.

> Thomas ormounde
> Warrham Sentleger
> Nicholas Walshe
> John Myaghe

(Addition in Jeffrey Fenton's hand) [2] yt weare good her Majesties Agents in Spaine weare aduertised to espye this Christofer lombard and to Apprehend hym. Jeff. fenton,

(Addressed) [3] To the right honorable Sir fräuncis walsingham knight, principall secretarie to her Majesty and of her highnes pryvy Councell.

(Endorsed in a modern hand) 10th September, 1580.
> From m^r Gefray Fenton.

STATE PAPERS IRELAND, ELIZABETH

The paper described as Book 84, No. 36 and dated 19th July, 1581, contains a list of thirty-seven interrogatories administered to the Earl of Kildare, then detained in Dublin Castle. The principal questions which he had to answer were whether he had ever received any letter from James Fitzmaurice after his last entry into rebellion or from any other rebel touching the aid which the Earl should give to them, whether he had informed the Archbishop of Dublin on 4th July at the musters upon the hill of Tara that he understood that the Viscount Baltinglas meant to rebel and whether he had later countenanced the Viscount's rebellion. The Government version of the Earl's action in regard to Lord Baltinglas' apprehension is given in

---

[1] Underlined.
[2] The rest of the document including the signatures is in a secretarial hand.
[3] The address serving also as the outer cover for Fenton's letter, No. 25.

the interrogatories 11–29. It is suggested that he wilfully concealed from the Archbishop the fact of Lord Baltinglas' presence among a troop of horsemen at Killeen and that he refused the Archbishop's advice to take Sir Thomas Harrington's horsemen for his capture. On the Wednesday following this meeting it was stated that a conference had taken place at which the Earl had deceived the Archbishop by offering to ride to Maynooth to meet the Viscount, thus providing the Government with an opportunity for his capture. It was further stated that such promise, if made, had not been carried out and it was suggested that another scheme for apprehending the Viscount at Monckton was proposed by the Earl to the Archbishop at a second conference on the following day. It is implied that Lady Baltinglas and Lady Upper Ossory acted as go-betweens at this time and that a third conference, when the Archbishop came to the Earl's Dublin lodging, likewise proved abortive. The name of Thomas Meaghe was brought up as that of a messenger from the Earl to the rebels and it was queried as to whether Baltinglas had brought to him a book from Rochforde, a priest, containing contrition, remission and satisfaction. It appeared from the eighteenth question that the Archbishop had deposed that the Earl had said that Lord Baltinglas was his kinsman and that his country would hate him and that it would be a perpetual reproach to his house if he should take him.

Two days later twenty-two interrogatories (Vol. LXXXIV, 38) were prepared to be administered to Lord Delvin, who was also in Dublin Castle a prisoner. Several of these, including those referring to Rochforde whom Lord Delvin was accused of concealing, were identical with the earlier questions to which his father-in-law, Lord Kildare, was subjected. In addition it was implied that Lord Delvin had taken an oath to the Viscount promising to join in his rebellion. It was suggested that he had spoken to the Viscount at Tara on 4th July and that Lord Kildare had told him of his privy conferences with the Archbishop.

The report of examinations dealing with the Nugent Rising opens with two confessions taken on 6th October, 1581, Vol. LXXXVI, 19, i. The admissions of William Clinkle are confined to the statement that William Nugent endeavoured to induce various gentlemen of the Pale to join William Nugent on the preceding 27th September, but those of Patrick Cusacke enter into considerable detail. According to this examinate Richard Cusacke, bastard son to Christopher Cusacke of Rothes, came to him in the fields of Ardmolghan ' about a sevennight before the fifteenth of August ' and entreated him very earnestly to go with him and all the rest of the Cusackes to Clancyhely to make prey to avenge the death of his father. They met John Cusacke of Ellistonreede ' by his harvest folk in the fields ' and were told that the Cusackes were for the most part determined to go to William Nugent to aid him. Patrick Cusacke admitted that he went down to Delvin with his kinsmen Richard and John and met William Nugent in a grove called the Dyrrys below Castleton Delvin, Lord Delvin's house. At this time William Nugent was accompanied by thirty kernes of the Nugents and O'Reillys. In addition Patrick Cusacke declared that he had heard John Cusacke of Ellistonreed tell William Nugent that he had received promises of support from the following gentlemen : John Cusacke of Cassington, George Netterville, George and Mark Clynes of Skreene, Richard Cusacke of the Grange of the Bertyffe and Phyrell M'Owen O'Reilly. The last named would bring one hundred men with him. Besides this, the Garlands, Drakes and Clintons, the Ferniants of Drom and the baron of O'Malie's band were prepared to assist him. As to their intentions Patrick Cusacke mentioned a plan to burn Athboy, Trim, Mullingar, Maynooth, Mellifont and Chyverston, to ravage the Plunkett's country and Sir Lucas Dillon's land at Rathrannan and to drive away the Bishop of Meath's kine from Ardbrackan. They hoped to be relieved by the gentlemen of Delvin, especially the Nugents,

APPENDIX OF DOCUMENTS

and reference was made to Laurence M'Craddery who had kept William Nugent in his barn for two nights in September. Piers Conagan, a servant of Lord Delvin, had also relieved them, giving them meat and drink at his master's houses at Clonin and Kiltorme.

Three days later on 9th October a confession, Vol. LXXXVI, 19, iii, was taken from John Cusacke of Cassington. He said that about three months past John Cusacke of Ellistonreede had met him at the Navan and had endeavoured to persuade him to join in rebellion with William Nugent. He, however, refused. John Cusacke then told him that one of the Baron of Dungannon's brothers 'called Arte (as he remembreth)' had promised to assist him, but that Lord Slane's son-in-law, William Fleming had refused to receive one of Nugent's letters urging him to rebel.

The examination of George Netterville taken the same day, *ibid.*, 19, iv, was however, more fruitful. He admitted to yielding to John Cusacke's suggestion that he should join William Nugent. The meeting with Cusacke took place at the Navan and at Garlandston and on one occasion when hunting near Irishtown. In addition to those previously implicated, he declared that he had heard that Robert Scurlocke, Nicholas Cusacke of Drakeston, Christopher Barnewall of Kilbride, James Tankerde of Castleton and Lord Louth's brother, John Plunket, had consented to join in rebellion. He admitted writing about this treasonable project to Christopher Bath of Rafeagh, Robert Scurlocke and John Cusacke of Ellistonreed. He said that 'the aforesaid iii consented to join with William Nugent for Religion.' It was agreed that they should assemble at the hill of Crankynege near Stemenston when John Cusacke sent them word. They had been assured that when they drew over old Turlough (O'Neill) many of the O'Reillys with the O'Mores and O'Rourkes and Viscount Baltinglas would join them.

The next series of papers dealing with this matter is an abstract of notes, Vol. LXXXVII, 1, i, dated 3rd December, 1581. Here it is stated that Nicholas Cusacke, Ferrell O'Reilly and John Scurlock who were executed for their share in this action confessed but would not accuse any other. A summary was made of the various other confessions. On 25th November John Cusacke of Cassington, who had by now confessed his share in the Rising, declared that their first purpose was to have released the Earl of Kildare and Lord Delvin. On 14th November Patrick Cusacke, who had referred to letters sent from Lord Delvin to William Nugent, charged Lord Delvin's uncles with being promoters of this rebellion. Similarly Robert Scurlocke charged Lady Delvin with relieving William Nugent since his entry into rebellion and Patrick Cusacke declared her responsible for conveying Nugent away. Finally on 25th November John Cusacke of Cassington declared that Ellistonreed had asserted that he had been with Turlough O'Neill to persuade him to assist them and had assured him that a great number of Spaniards would come into Ireland before Christmas.

A sheet of notes at this point, *ibid.*, 22, i, gives personal details of some of the rebels. 'George Netterville,' so the paper begins, 'son to Netterville of Dowth within 3 miles of Drogheda of the matter of xxxj years old, having neither land nor living. Robert Scurlocke son to old Scurlocke of Scurlocketown about xx years old, whose father is yet living. John Cusacke of Coshington related to the Baron of Delvin of xxij years. Ferrell O'Rely a young gentleman of the O'Relys bred and brought up in the Pale and served the Viscount of Gormanston against his own name having neither land, nor living. Eustace of Cardiston in the county of Kildare with his eldest son. David Sutton of Castleton, within 2 miles of Maynooth, a very young gentleman of xxii years who might dispose of £300 of good land. Morris Eustace of Castle Martyn in Kildare a young gentleman of xxiiij years old who might dispose of £100 in land. His father is dead lately.'

The examinations now recommenced. In a paper, *ibid.*, 44, i, dated 13th December, 1581, and containing the gist of a confession obtained from Thomas Eustace of Cardiston on 22nd November previous, the deponent declared that the Viscount (Baltinglas) told him that he had better helpers than he knew of and said that the Earl of Kildare would not bear arms against him. He said that the Viscount told him that the Earl never did him a better turn than when he did not arrest him at the meeting on the hill of Tara. On 30th December Sir Owen Hopton examined James FitzChristopher Nugent in a more serious manner, *ibid.*, 69. In the first place the examinate declared that he had never received any letter from James Fitzmaurice after his last entry into the realm and that he never knew him or had anything to do with him. Asked when his nephew William Nugent entered into virtual rebellion, he declared that the morning after Lord Delvin's committal at Dublin William Nugent ' ran to the farthest part of the country.' With the exception of an unsuccessful meeting at Ballynock he had not seen William Nugent since his entry into rebellion. He admitted that he had heard that William Nugent had spent Christmas Eve at Clonin, but that he had not been to this house since Lord Delvin's imprisonment.

Further information is contained in a document dated 23rd January, 1582 an abstract of a confession, Vol. LXXXVIII, 47, i, made by John Cusacke of Ellistonreed. Marginal notes, which are here indicated by brackets, are appended in the handwriting of Secretary Fenton. ' He imparted to the La. Dellfin,' the paper begins, ' the desire to surprise the Castle of Dublyn and willed her to relate it over to the Earle of Kildare and the Baron of Delvyn, which she promised she would. This is treason in the Lady of Delvyn. He imparted to Nic'las Nugent his intention to break out. (Nicholas Nugent is apprehended.) He broke with Edward Cusacke of Lismollin that he wold enter into rebellion. He mortgaged him his land to raise money to that end and the said Edward gave him a callyver. (Edward Cusacke is apprehended.) Ric. Cusacke, Plunkett of Belparc and Tho Plunkett son to Ollyver Plunkett of Cloanston consented to the conspiracy. He imparted the conspiracy to James Tankard who consented to do what Ric Cusacke would do. (He is apprehended.) . . . He saith that Willm Nugent met Pires boy Nugent at Mareston and John Nugent at Scurlocketon who gave to Willm Nugent a callyver. They met also at Ric Ceosses house at Chapelston to contrive about Wm Nugent's child. There was Nic'las Nugent's wife also. He confesseth that Richard Cusacke of the Grange consented to the conspiracy and promised to come to Willm Nugent. (Richard Cusacke is apprehended.) '

The final paper is the abstract of a document, *ibid.*, 44, iv, dated 21st January, 1582, and containing brief personal notes on the Nugents. Nicholas Nugent, late Justice of the Common Pleas, is described as a man well liked in the English Pale among his neighbours for that he did allways join with them in all their actions. His wife is a daughter to Sir John Plunket, Chief Justice of the King's Bench, and mother to William Nugent's wife and Niclas Nugent is uncle to the Baron of Delvin and Willm Nugent. James Nugent is uncle to William Nugent. He is a gentleman of great authority upon the borders where he dwelleth and may do great service there if he be so disposed . . . and if only he may keep those parts in quietness. Lavallyn Nugent is but a simple witted man and of no great living, a good man and well beloved among his neighbours.

D. DOCUMENTS RELATING TO ENGLAND AND SPAIN

THREE of the documents in this series are taken from the collection of State Papers Domestic for the reign of Elizabeth and are preserved at the Public Record Office, while the other two form part of the archives of the English College at Valladolid. A grateful acknowledgment must be made to the Rector for permission to transcribe these papers. None of these documents have been published hitherto.

X. List of English receiving pensions in Spain, Vol. CV, 9. 1575 ?
XI. Abstract of certain papers in the archives at Valladolid relating to Sir William Stanley and to benefactors of the English College.
XII. Certificate of Sheriff Massam's search, Vol. CLXXII, 103. 27th August, 1584.
XIII. List of ports used in Barbary, Vol. XVC, 9p. 1574.

The list of Spanish pensioners gives an impression of the Continental background to the life of the exiles, while the names of the benefactors to the College at Valladolid suggest some of the social contacts between the English and Spanish grandees. The extract from the certificate of Sheriff Massam's search for Recusants at the time of the Babington Plot is included for the detailed description which it gives of the way of life of middle-class families in London, with especial reference to those whose Catholic sympathies caused them to be suspected of opposition to the existing system. The different treatment meted out to Lord Kildare's household is worthy of note. The little paper with a list of Moroccan ports has an interest in connection with the gunrunning to Morocco, which formed the more patriotic alternative to the illicit trade with Spain.

STATE PAPERS DOMESTIC, ELIZABETH, BOOK 105, NO. 9

LIST OF ENGLISH RECEIVING PENSIONS IN SPAIN

Persons provyded for here

The Countess of Northumberland . .	200
The Erle of Westmorland . . .	200
The Lord Dacre	100
The Lady Hungerford	100
Sir Frauncis Englefyld	84
Mr Christofer Nevyll	60
Sir John Nevyll	60
Mr Doctor Parkar	50
Mr Richard Norton	56
Mr Copley	60
Mr Markenfyld	36
Mr Tempest	40
Mr Bulmer	30
Mr Danby	30

Mr Francis Norton	36
Mr Thwyng	30
Mr Chamberlen	60
Mr Lygons	40
Mr Standen	50
Mr Mockett	30
Mr Hughe Owen [1] . . .	40
Mr Nolworthe	40
Mr George Tyrrell . . .	30
Mr Jenny	30
Mr Tycheborne	30
Mr G. Smith	30
Mr Bache	30
Mr Robert Owen	30 not yet graunted
Mr Powell Priest	10
Mistress Storey wydowe . .	16 di.
Mr Olyver	8
Thomas Kynred	16 di.
Mr James Hamelton . . .	80
Mr John Hamelton . . .	60

Persons gone towardes Spayne to serve for pencyons

My Lord Edward Seymer
    Mr Southwell
    Mr Carewe
    Mr Harecourte
    Mr Francis Moore
    Mr Blackston
    Mr Predyaux
    Mr George More
    Mr Wyllyams
    John Storey
    Mr Denys [2]

14 Jan. 1574   Mr Eightington

6 July 1575 Hamelton Charles Browne like to be seruiceable when occasion shall
to ye Scott.   be offred

15 dec. 1573 Guer   Gylbart Curle
to ye duke d'Alua Mr Henton [3] promised to be a good & faithfull instru-
                ment for ye King.

22 Maij   Humfrey Cotterel a booke binder in pauls Churche yarde
             at ye golden angel a conveyer of letters.

(Directed) [4]   To the Duchesse of Ferya her good grace

(Endorsed)   persons prouided for (by) the King of Spaine.

---

[1] Interlineated.
[2] The rest from here is in another hand.
[3] Blotted out and ' P ' written above.
[4] The following note will assist in the dating of this document. ' And now the said Lord
Edward Seler (Seymour) pretends to be a Catholic and gives out that he desires to serve under
Don John of Austria.' News letter of 17th September, 1574, Cal. S.P. Rome, 1571–8.

APPENDIX OF DOCUMENTS

LIST OF SPANISH BENEFACTORS OF THE ENGLISH PRIESTS

The Duke of Medina Sidonia 1595–1604 a personal friend of Father Parsons and benefactor of the houses at San Lucar, Seville and Valladolid (Classe 1 Legajo 10).

Don Pedro de Toledo grants a pension of 120 ducats for English students (Classe 1 Legajo 15).

The Count of Villanova grants a pension of 160 ducats.
The Count of Ordenes gives 130 ducats.
The Duke of Medina Celi
The Duke of Alva
The Duke of Infantado
The Duke of Pastrana
The Duke of Zea
The Duchess of Terranova
The Count of Lemos
The Count of Alva Liste
and the Count of Chinchon give a yearly pension of 50 ducats each.
Among other benefactors are the Prince of Squillace,
The Archbishop of Toledo
The Bishop of Segorbe
The Bishop of Cuzco in Peru
The Inquisitor General
The Church of Toledo
The Church of Salamanca
The Church of Valladolid
The Church of Burgo de Osma
The Church of Oviedo
and the Council of the Indies and the various Royal Councils (Series 1 Legajo 1).

PAPERS OF CORONEL STANLEY AN ENGLISH KT.

List of those people who came over to the Duke of Parma.

Colonel Stanley	10 officers 52 soldiers
Captain Piers Fears	9 officers 46 soldiers
Major Thomas Roberton	8 officers 62 soldiers
Captain William Carre	9 officers 70 soldiers
Captain Martin Maynard	9 officers 61 soldiers
Captain George Throckmorton	10 officers 68 soldiers
Captain Robert Piers	8 officers 49 soldiers
Captain Henry Floyd	8 officers 62 soldiers
Henry Jervis	7 officers 67 soldiers
etc etc in All	90 officers 626 men.

(Note the English agents in Spain were often settled down in religious houses in their old age. This is shown in a document in the same legajo.)

16 October 1610   His Majesty having promised to Sir Hugh Owen, English Knight, 2300 scudos to be paid to him in Sicilian pounds in recompense for a

particular service which he did for him and because of the great necessities in which he was on account of the persecutions which he had suffered, he was also granted a corrody in the house of Hoskins father of the Company (of Jesus) in Madrid and in that of his successors Vice Prefects of the Mission.

STATE PAPERS, DOMESTIC, ELIZABETH, BOOK 172, NO. 103

A CERTIFICATE OF SHERIFF MASSAM'S SEARCH, DATED 27TH AUGUST, 1584

Theise places appoyntyd by the Lord Maior to bee serched by William Masham one of the Sheryves of London.

Aldgate i.   The Lord Mordantes howse therby, where the Lady Ratcliff lyeth, a pryvy vaut by a bedd syde there a back dore.
Leaden Hall 2.   One Fowler a Marchant, one Mathew White lodginge there.
Lumberdstrete 3.   The Horse shoe.
Minchingelane 4.   A hirer out of horses or a porter.

The certyficatt of the said William Masham Sheryve upon his searche made in three of these places etc.   As folowith . . .
i. First according to the direction . . . for the Lord Mordantes howse, I repayryd thether and callinge to me Roger Holland Constable & others of his watch as I thought meetest dmaunded of them in secrett maner of the same howse and they answeryd me that there was noe howse thereaboutes knowen by that name, whereupon I repayryd to thother places and havinge there made search I repayryd to little St Bartholomewes without Aldersgate aboute ij of the clock where I learnyd a howse was soe namyd And callinge to me some dwellinge therby I understoode that the Lady Ratcliff lay not there this half yere past and that there laye this last night the Earle of Kildare with his family whoe hath hadd the same howse about iij^{re} monthes last past And that noe other lay there (Excepte some gentlemen beinge come thither with the same Earle from huntinge).   And for that cause I thought good to forbeare to make searche in the same howse for this tyme untill I should haue further order therein.
2. Secondly . . . I entryd into the howse of Lancelott Ian a hacknyman dwellinge in Minchinge lane where I found these persons followinge . . .
Agnes his wife
Helen Coles his mayde servant aged aboute xxxvj yeres of a good stature & of a sanguyn complexcion whoe hath dwelte there aboute a yere.
Thomas Ledger unckle to the wife of the said Ian a man very aged belonginge to the buttry in the tower and hath dwelte in the same howse above xxx yeres past.
William Huckerby servant to the same Ian, a man of a lowe stature with a black head & bearde and hath dwelte there aboute half a yere past.

Margarett & ⎫ his children ⎧ of thage of xj yeres
Sara   ⎭   ⎩ of thage of iij yeres

And upon farther serche made in all the romes of the howse I found no (other) [1] person nor eny bookes or lettres suspicious in eny of the Chestes or cubberdes or suche lyke places of the same howse.
2. After that I entyrd into the howse of Thomas Frampton a Porter of the Wey Howse in London dwellinge in mynchinge lane aforesaid where I founde hym & these persons followinge . . .
Agnes his wife.

[1] Interlineated.

Jane Flood his mayde servant of thage of xxiij^{ty} yeres of a reasonable stature full facyd.

Elizabeth Jones of thage of ix yeres broad facyd & her nose somewhat flatt.

And upon farther serche made in all the romes of the same howse I found no other person nor eny bookes or lettres suspicious in eny chestes or cuberdes of the same howse.

3. Thirdly I entryd into the howse of Walter Bolton haberdasher dwellinge at the signe of the golden horseshoe in the parish of St Mary Wolners in Lumberdstrete where I found hym and the persons folowinge . . .

Helen wife of the same Bolton.

Cisley & Elizabeth } his children { of thage of v yeres / of thage of ij yeres

William Wilson a iournyman of thage of xxv yeres of a lowe stature somewhat fully facyd & a little bearde of a brownish colour.

Anthony Deatt his srvant of thage of xviij yeres leane visagyd whoe hathe bynne there sithence Shrofetyde last past.

Cisley Brumall Spinster sister to the wife of the same Bolton of thage of xviij yeres lowe & somewhat bigg of stature and servith as a servant in the same howse.

Avyce Homerstone Spinster of a mydle stature somewhat whitly coloryd havinge a longe bare crest on her forhed upwardes, whoe aboute a yere too Whitsontyde last was from thence and before that was iij yeres dwellinge there and came thither againe at Whitsontyde last and sithence hath dwelte there.

And upon full serch I found no lettres nor bookes suspicious nor eny other persons in the same howse which persones abouenamyd I didd comaund the same Bolton to haue forthcomynge according to the article in that behalf.

STATE PAPERS, DOMESTIC, ELIZABETH, BOOK 95, NO. 90

The paper relating to the ports in Barbary, which follows, is concerned with those harbours through which an intermittent trade in ordnance passed. This traffic caused great irritation to the Spaniards and is closely bound up with the question of gunrunning to Spain, since it served for the English merchants as a rightful and patriotic counterpart to that doubtful adventure. The despatches of Don Bernardino de Mendoza to the King of Spain throw light upon this subject. Five letters deal with the matter.

[1] On 21st May, 1580, Don Bernardino de Mendoza, the Spanish Ambassador, wrote to King Philip that he had been informed by Pedro de Zubiaur, a merchant established in Seville, that when the latter landed at Plymouth he learned that two English ships had arrived at places about four leagues from there. One of them had come from Algiers whither she had taken a cargo of munitions. These two ships had also stolen a ship of Martin Visante valued at 40,000 crowns.

[2] On 9th January a second despatch was sent by Don Bernardino. Here he asserted that the English employ their profit (made from the prohibited Spanish trade) in sending a multitude of vessels to Barbary with arms and munitions; while on 20th October following he sent a third [3] letter from London stating that ' some Englishmen have arrived in this country from Morocco having arranged with the King of that country to take him a great quantity of timber ready cut to build his galleys.' Throughout the winter he was still pursuing this subject ' some of the [4] timber,' the Ambassador wrote on 27th January, 1582, ' has been

[1] Cal. S.P. Spanish, 1580–6, p. 32.
[2] Ibid., p. 72.
[3] Ibid., p. 199.
[4] Ibid., p. 277.

DOCUMENTS RELATING TO ENGLAND AND SPAIN

sent to Barbary from Holland. One shipload bound for the port of Santa Cruz has arrived at the harbour of Larache according to the report written on 10 December.' Finally he turned to the question of secret official aid in this matter, asserting that, on hearing that the Duke of Medina Sidonia meditated an attack on Larache, the Queen had sent for Jan Sympcote an important Barbary merchant in London. ' He was sent,' declared [1] Don Bernardino, ' a week ago with letters to the Sheriff (of Morocco) offering him such aid and munitions as he might require. This Sympcote is a merchant, a man about 55, of good constitution and wears a grey beard. He takes in the ship a quantity of powder and some arms.'

STATE PAPERS, DOMESTIC, ELIZABETH, BOOK 95, NO. 90

(Endorsed)   Portes in Barbary which the Queens Subiects use to trafick 1574.

The Queenes Majestie subiectes doe trade to the places and portes followinge in the kingdom of Barbarie.

To sail to the port of *allarache* and other portes within the streates⎤ clothes
which serve for the trade of fesse for saill of   ⎦

To the porte of *saphia* and so to *morocus* for the sailles of our clothes⎤ Sows
and from thence to the countrie of   ⎦

To the porte of *capo de gerre* [2] to Rellade [3] our shippes for to retorne For england.

So the queens subiectes are content not to trade beyond the *cappe rioll* which is to the sowthewest of the kingdome of barbarie & not farre from the cannary.

---

[1] Letter dated 13th December, 1582, *ibid.*, p 424. An earlier letter from the Spanish agents had asserted in 1578 that the Sheriff of Morocco, who was supplied with iron cannon balls by John Williams and Hogan, paid for them in saltpetre and sugars. Other English merchants were said to have sent a hulk laden chiefly with oars for galleys and artillery into Barbary in the previous year. Cal. State Papers Foreign, 1577–8, p. 476.

[2] ' Gell ' is written above ' Gerre.'

[3] ' Rellade ' is struck through and   relade ' written above. The revisions are in Burghley's hand.

E. NOTES

Monastic Survivals in Wales
Personal Feuds in Dublin
Ordnance in Ireland

NOTES

NOTES ON MONASTIC SURVIVALS IN WALES

THERE is an accumulation of evidence that the monastic life lingered on for a time in Wales, although, by the laws of Henry VIII, the monasteries themselves had perished. The lawless condition of the interior of Wales made many strange survivals possible, for the English were seldom concerned with the doings of the remote Welsh in the forests and the Marcher administration hardly even attempted to control the wild districts, as long as the roads from the coast remained safe. In the Black Mountains and the high woods of Merioneth, but perhaps most of all in Arwystli, the tract of moorland covered with oakwoods and bogs which ran for twenty miles eastwards from Plynlimon, there was always a refuge from the English law. These wild districts were all connected and it was possible for outlaws to ride in safety from Arwystli by way of Gwerthrynion and the camps of the robbers in Elvael to the hiding-places above Glamorgan, or North through the country of the Cochion tribes in Mawddwy to the Caernarvon hills. In consequence when the monasteries had surrendered it was a simple matter to retreat into the woods. The monks took with them only their chalices and some-times their relics, for secrecy was essential, and it was always a question of evading the law, not of open defiance. The English communities in Pembrokeshire perished, but the great Welsh houses, which were often built at the gateway of the hills, reverted for a time to an earlier form of existence. It is very difficult to follow these movements in the forests, although the official records contain information about the beginning of pilgrimages with minute details of guest-houses and the supporters of monks. Messengers and pilgrims can often be traced coming up from the valleys, but when they have left the low country they vanish. Occasionally the changes of shrines or some archæological discovery makes it possible to trace the communities, although this is unusual. Most of the evidence for their later movements comes from the bards, and it is fitting that the chief supporters of Welsh patriotism should have used as their refuge those remote districts where the last remnants of Welsh independence still lingered.

On account of the varied nature of the evidence it is necessary to consider the cases in detail, for the fate of some monasteries is doubtful, although those pros-perous houses which drew their vigour from the soil nearly always survived in some measure. Among these native houses the most important survivor was the Cistercian Abbey of Strata Florida, the burial place of the Princes, which sur-rendered in 1539. It stood in a desolate and at times a treeless country in a gap of the hills towards Cwmwd Deuddwr. The abbey pastures stretched[1] for eight miles along the tracks to Rhayader and Llangurig and brigands had long been established[2] in the hills along the northern boundary of these lands. The English authority on this Cardiganshire borderland had always seemed remote, for the royal power had no strong defenders along the coast. There had been disorders in Strata Florida, false money had been coined in the abbey ale-houses and there

---

[1] For a description of the situation and lands of Strata Florida, see Leland's *Itinerary*, pp. 118 and 122. The bonds and indentures of the Vaughans of Trawscoed contain many details of the abbey lands. Cal. Crosswood MSS., 52–4 and 65–73.

[2] Stowe MSS., 1670, 141d, ff. 26–8.

NOTES

were furnaces hidden for this purpose beyond the gates. The abbot Richard Talley was a considerable landowner in the country, a man of middle age with little regard for English rule. His cousin, David Vaughan, lived as an outlaw in the woods by Machynlleth. The eleven years of Abbot Talley's rule were stormy; he had been accused [1] of clipping and coining by the monks, and after the Dissolution he retired to Ystrad and devoted himself to increasing his fortune for his son. It seems that the great relic of Strata Florida, the Holy Grail, was hidden, and the monks disappeared into the hills. Llangurig in Montgomeryshire, almost deserted in the fifteenth century, was their only cell in the great woods, situated in a district devoutly Catholic [2] and controlled by local nobles, who made a scanty livelihood out of robberies from the few travellers to the sea. [3] It was to this place in the South of Arwystli and on the track to Llanidloes that the monks came from Strata Florida, for the crozier of St. Paternus had been brought for safety from the church at Llanbadarn and the miraculous arm of St. Cyricius of Iconium was guarded [4] there.

During the last hundred years the nobles of Arwystli had conducted the local administration as receivers and agents for the Crown. There seems to have been little intercourse between the rest of Wales and these isolated lands behind Plynlimon; so that when the forests attracted the dispersed communities of Powys they depended for all record on the bards. Thus Huw Arwystli, writing in the last years of Henry VIII, refers [5] to the choir of monks which had come to Llangurig and in other poems there is reference to the monastic house at Llys Celyddon, while there was also a famous sanctuary at Carno, round the hospice of St. John of Jerusalem, which had remained undisturbed.[6] In addition to this, there were always some wandering friars looking for refuge on their way to the more dangerous zones in the North. Llys Celyddon was far from the tracks, an obscure grange on the slopes of Y Foel, and perhaps the monks from Strata Florida came there when Llangurig was dangerous, or religious may have come for sanctuary through the lands of the Cochion robbers from Cymmer Abbey, through Cydewain from Strata Marcella, or perhaps from Cwmhir. The monks seem to have followed their rule until all the survivors were dead, for there are several references, some possibly as late as 1580, to the sacred fire at Llys Celyddon [7] and there is ample evidence that Arwystli enjoyed ' the protection of saints.'

There were few religious houses of any importance in Brecknock at the time of the Dissolution and it seems very likely that the nearest group of monastic survivors were those hidden in the Black Mountains, a forty-mile ride to the South, where the monks from the Vale of Glamorgan sheltered. But about half the distance from Arwystli, there was a house of secular canons at Llandewi Brevi, some of whose members lived on in the district when their house was dissolved. Certain churches in the hill-country had been seized by the Catholics and when the

---

[1] Letters and Papers, Henry VIII, vii, pp. 477, 487.
[2] British Museum Add. MSS. 814, 972 and ' Ode to the Four Brothers in Llyfr Ceniarth.'
[3] British Museum Add. MSS. 14, 989.
[4] *Ibid.* A letter sent by Sir Richard Rich to the Abbot of Strata Florida on 10th April, 1537, shows how pictures and relics were removed from smaller monasteries to the great houses, when the former were suppressed. ' The bringer Edward Beawpe,' wrote Sir Richard, ' made suit to us for a picture of Jesus in your custody, lately belonging to the house of Combhyre, dissolved.' Cal. Letters and Papers Henry VIII, xxi, i, p. 397.
[5] British Museum Add. MSS. 14, 989, *Ode to the Choir of Heaven.*
[6] Ashmolean MSS. 1820a, printed in *Archæologia Cambrensis Parochialia*, 1909-11. A note written under Henry VIII states that ' the sanctuaries have lost their authority as places of refuge, except in the cases of the chance medley and the killing in self-defence.' Chronicle of Griffith Ellis, Mostyn MSS. 158, f. 509b.
[7] British Museum Add. MSS. 14, 949.

491

NOTES

priests of Llandewi died out (for there were only three survivors [1] in 1555) these were probably served by the monks. Services were conducted with the greatest secrecy and, according to the depositions of 1592, a deserted church was used for Popish practices [2] two days' journey from Llandeilo into the hills. There was a network of lonely churches in Cardigan used by the priests—Llanina, on the coast near Aberayron; Llanarth, which had been dependent on Llandewi; and Capel Llangrest, where Mass was said on Corpus Christi and the Epiphany.[3] It seems likely, at least in the earlier part of the period, that monks going between the Black Mountains and Arwystli served these shrines. The deserted state [4] of these old churches, which is specially vouched for in the depositions, would make such temporary occupation the more easy.

A similar character also marked the gatherings of the monks in Central and South Wales. To provide but one instance, the state of affairs at Abbey Cwmhir at the time of the Dissolution is very suggestive. Only three monks were returned as belonging to the monastery at that date; but a comparison with the Register [5] of the Bishops of Hereford shows a total of twenty-four ordinations *ad titulum* of that house between 1505–32. It seems not unreasonable to suggest that this disparity is caused by the high proportion of monks in Cwmhir, who had sacrificed their chances of a pension in order to follow their religious life in peace.

In South Wales the position of the pilgrimage centre of Penrhys, a dependency of Llantarnam Abbey, is curious; for it stood in the centre of that wild country which had so long provided a refuge for the outlaws from the seaport towns. Certain indications and in particular the poems of Lewis Morganwg would suggest that the pilgrimages continued [6] after the official suppression of the shrine; but owing to the difficulty of fixing precise dates to these allusions the suggestion must remain still tentative. It is at any rate clear that the Catholic influences in the neighbourhood were strong, as the fields about Penrhys passed with Llantarnam, the mother house in Monmouthshire, to the possession of the Morgans and there was a hunting lodge at Ystrad Dyfodwg belonging to the Mathews of Radyr, a family who were then turbulently Catholic [7] and who seem to have kept up an hereditary protection towards the shrine. It is not impossible that the Franciscans of Cardiff, who announced that they would die for the Pope and disappeared, may have retired here and some such remote grange was also likely to have supplied the refuge for the Benedictines of Ewenny Priory, who seem to have left that house before its fall. The position of Sir Edward Carne, who appears as a protector both of the exiled Benedictines and of the shrine at Penrhys, may have a significance in this connection. An argument against the survival of Penrhys is however

---

[1] Cardinal Pole's Pension Book in Miscellanea of the Exchequer, 31.

[2] 'The child has been taken two days' journey from the said house of Llandeilo to a deserted church by Gwenllyn Evor where it was baptized by Popish rites. Evor, the deponent, cannot say whether the service was in English or Latin, but the priest asked the name of the child in Welsh.' Deposition dated 4th September, 1591, Harleian MSS. 6998b, ff. 3–16b.

[3] Harleian MSS. 6990c f. 19 and 6995, f. 67.

[4] A controversy between the church building and the tavern in the 'Dream of Thomas Llewelyn of Rhygos,' Y tafarn yn traethu, a mid-Elizabethan poem, provides an instance of this condition. The translation of verses 95–100 runs, 'You have not in you, no people Except old, dead people. You have not in you neither Tapers, nor a pax, nor a pyx, Nor images, nor a comely Vestment, nor a cross of gold or silver, But you are like a barn without Rood loft and altar. There is no Pleasure in you or beauty. There is no need for any one to Frequent you often,' Printed in *Hen Gwndidau*, by Chancellor Hopkin-James, LL.D., to whose courtesy the author is indebted for this allusion.

[5] Register of the Bishops of Hereford, Henry VIII. For another explanation of the decrease see 'The Cistercian Abbey of Cwmhir,' by Rev. E. Hermitage Day, *Archæologia Cambrensis*, 1924, pp. 284–91.

[6] Llanstephan MSS. 47, ffff. 109 and 164, f. 166.

[7] Cal. Star Chamber Proceedings relating to Wales, p. 8.

NOTES

supplied by the use of the past tense by Leland,[1] when referring to the pilgrimages there.

Both the abbeys of Neath and Margam owned large sheep runs in this hill country and another possibility is represented by that persistent tradition which records the presence of monks at Llangynwyd, a monastic grange, near the southern border of the moors. It is to be noted that Neath seems to have been the most national of the southern houses, where bards were always supported and there was a prevailing dislike for the English.[2] The last year of Neath was troubled by charges of sedition, and there were quarrels with the Government because Abbot Leisan had sheltered a monk from the rebellious Cistercian abbey of Furness.[3] In the middle of these accusations of connection with the Bishop of Rome the abbey surrendered and the monks disappeared, but the chapels near the Brecknock-shire border remained undisturbed, although all the lands in the valleys were taken. The reports of the survival of the community at Llangynwyd may be unfounded, but it is probable that there was some kind of headquarters, for it is certain that the Cistercians supplied not only those old priests who served their chapels, but also many of the wandering monks who passed into North Wales along the hills, using a chain of desolate churches at the time of the feasts.

In the North the Cistercian Abbey of Valle Crucis had always been the chief modern house of the white monks. The Government had recognized this to some extent, and, under the Tudors, Valle Crucis had become a stepping-stone to bishoprics, while remaining a centre of pilgrimage with its treasured statue of the Risen Christ. These pilgrimages continued until the end and the life of the community was only interrupted by troubles with the Royal Commissioners of this time. The abbey seems to have fallen into debt and in May, 1535, the abbot, Robert Salisbury, was accused [4] of highway robbery near Oxford, while staying at the Bell Inn at Kidlington with several accomplished coiners in his train. This accusation, together with a charge of coining was repeated three months later, and the abbot was imprisoned and deposed. The Abbot of Cymmer seems to have been concerned in some way in this affair, for he was intriguing for the reversion of the abbacy, had recently won the favour of the Royal Commissioners and had offered [5] £20 to Cromwell as a bribe. The Commissioners described the whole community, with the exception of the prior, as being very evilly disposed and the next year the house was broken up. There stood on the abbey lands close to the Dee and about four miles to the East an old house called Plas yn y Pentre. A stone altar was carried there. The lands passed to the recusant family of Edwards of Plas Newydd, who contrived hiding-places in the house, so that it was only in the nineteenth century that various relics were discovered, and these included a broken statue of the Risen Christ. The treasures of the abbey seem to have been

---

[1] 'To Penrise village, wher the pilgrimage was, a mile.' Leland's *Itinerary*, p. 16. An indication of the strength of this countryside as a refuge is indicated by this author. 'To go from est to west yn the highest part of Glamorganshir toward the rootes of the Blak Montayne is a xvi miles of wild ground almost all.' *Ibid.*

[2] Letter of Henry VIII to Sussex, dated 27th March, 1537, to inquire into the use of the disloyal monks of Furness and retain John Estgate who would go to Nethe till the King knows why he prefers that place. Letters and Papers of Henry VIII, xii, i, p. 315.

[3] The Abbot's relations with the English Cistercians were strained and when coming to London he refused to visit the house of his Order, but stayed at the *White Hynd* Inn, a common resort of poor Welshmen in Cripplegate, Stowe MSS., 1670, 141e, f. 24.

[4] Letter of Sir Walter Stonor to Cromwell, dated May, 1535. Letters and Papers, Henry VIII, viii, p. 295.

[5] Report of Adam Beckanshaw and Dr. John Vaughan sent to Cromwell on 1st September, 1535, 'we intend to deprive the abbot on 4 or 5 September and wish to know your pleasure for a new election. The Abbot of Kymmer, who is a good husband, would fain have it and would give £20 towards your duty, but no more.' *Ibid*, ix, p. 83.

dispersed, for the last official notice of these relics was the discovery of the Book of the Sangrael, which was kept secretly by Mr. Bostock, a gentleman with 'a rolling eye,' who lived at the Red House in Chester in 1582. But pilgrimages still continued, perhaps to the statue at Plas yn y Pentre and monks remained in the countryside for many years.

The old mountain road which led from Llangollen past Valle Circus to Bangor seems to have been a centre of some activity. Ten miles along this road there was a cell of Strata Marcella at Llangor and a few miles further on a chapel at Cerrig y Drudion on the land of the Aberconway monks. For twenty miles the way bordered the monastic lands in Hiraethog, where the monks went in November for St. Winefred's pilgrimage at Gwytherin, before reaching the hospital of Yspitty Ifan across the mountains from Bangor. This house, which the Knights of St. John had long abandoned, had in the fifteenth century become a haunt of brigands,[1] and, although the first band was exterminated by the Wynnes of Gwydir, it was again recaptured by other outlaws, perhaps recruited from the robbers of Dolwyddelan and the neighbouring hills. This second band, which held the hospital until the middle of the Elizabethan period, had definite affiliations with the dispossessed religious and the monks could always find a refuge in such haunts after going out to prophesy rebellion on the hillsides along the northern coast.

The general effects of such action are described in a report made by the Royal Commissioners in 1595, which gives an impression of those gatherings, organized during so many years by the dispossessed monks and friars in the North. ' The people,' so runs [2] the document, ' utterly ignorant of God or their salvation do still in heaps go in pilgrimage to their wonted wells and places of superstition, and in the night after the old offerings are kept at any idol's chapel. Albeit the church be pulled down, yet do they come to the place where the church or chapel was, by great journeys barefoot very superstitiously. The move for the meeting and know-ledge of the place pilgrims shall come is chiefly wrought by their " pencars "or head minstrels at the direction of some old gentlewoman, so do they ordinarily give summons for such meetings. Upon Sundays and holidays the multitude of all sorts, men, women and children of every parish, do use to meet in sundry places either on some hill or on the side of some mountain. . . . Here it is to be noted that when they lie idly on the mountain sides, how then they talk of the fastness and natural strength of every way, place and hill of their country. Truly at this day if you look throwlie at the whole number of the gentlemen and others of all sorts in North Wales, ye shall find scarce any, the Bishops and some few others excepted, yet in any sort instructed in the faith of Christ. For the whole multi-tude, that which is under thirty years of age hath no show of any religion, the others nearly all generally dare to profess and to maintain the absurdest points of Popish heresy, according to which knowledge most lamentable to be spoken, the greatest number of them do frame their lives.' This paper of itself serves to show the tenacity with which the monks clung to their shrines and how the Catholic Religion declined as they died. But in any case they could not have maintained their gatherings for long, since these depended on a background of disorder.[3]

It was this absence of calm, ordered rule which marks the distinction between

[1] ' There was contynually fostered,' wrote Sir John Wynn, ' a wasps nest whic trowbled the wholle countrey. I mean a Lo : belonginge to St. Johns of Jerusalem called Spytty Evan, a lardge thinge w'ch had priviledge of sanctuarie . . . a receptacle of thieves and murtherers.' History of the Gwydir Family, p. 53.

[2] Lansdowne MSS. 60, 140, ff. 103–12.

[3] Mostyn MSS. 144, the White Book of Cors y Gedol, throws light on the relations of the robbers with the religious offenders.

NOTES

Central Wales and the country to the East of the March.[1] A special reason operated in the one district in which it would seem that the monastic life lingered. A cell and various chapels of Abbey Dore formed a nucleus around which the religious life gathered and their relics became objects of pilgrimage. The wild country along the borders of Monmouth and Hereford, in which the cell of Llangua stood, was their centre and the arm of St. Thomas de Cantelupe was carried through it in secret. To the West this district merged into the Black Mountains along the Welsh border. The old monastic chapels at Llanfair Cilgoed and Blackbrook were untouched and the Darren was the headquarters where there were armed processions on Corpus Christi and Mass on the hills. Throughout the reign of Elizabeth these conditions were never disturbed, while the state of affairs was unchanged in 1605 when Bishop Bennet sent in his report. 'The Justices,' wrote [2] the Bishop, 'went unto ye Darren and did make diligent search from village to village, from house to house, about thirtie miles compasse neere ye confines of Monmouthshire, where they found houses full of altars, images, bookes of superstition, reliques of idolatry, but left desolate of men and women, except here and there an aged woman, or a child, all were fled into Wales, and but one man apprehended.' By this date the monks had died out, but here was the reason for the survival of the relics and shrines; it was always possible to retreat to the lawless districts of Wales.

NOTE ON THE PERSONAL FEUDS IN DUBLIN

Since the number and intricacy of the personal feuds among the Government officials in Ireland influenced the development of Irish politics directly, the following notes are appended. They bear chiefly upon the situation described in the chapters on the Risings in the Pale and Lord Deputy Perrot; but had they been included under these headings they would caused too great congestion. In order to save space the entries are made very brief and only those are included which refer to personal enmity, official feud or ill health, the three drags on the progress of government.

On 11th February, 1581, Lord Chancellor Gerard complained [3] of the evil doings of the Chamberlain of Chester, Mr. Glaseour. The Chancellor had been ill with sciatica [4] since the previous October and had been forced to go to take the bath at Buxton, since he asserted [5] that there was no physician in Dublin. On 23rd February Sir William Morgan wrote [6] to Burghley of his long service without reward and declared that his legs had swelled through lying on the ground. On 20th July Auditor Jenyson wrote [7] of the ill desert of Lord Chancellor Gerard who had recently died, and referred to his own gout. Nevertheless, in a letter of

---

[1] Nevertheless, although the monastic communities in the settled lands seem to have vanished completely, it is remarkable how many monastic buildings on the East of the March passed into Catholic hands and were used by visiting priests. Thus Lilleshall Abbey was held by the Lawsons, Wormesley Priory by the Charltons, Wormbridge Priory by Sylvanus Scory, Whiteladies by the Giffards, Halesowen by the Littletons, Gracedieu in Monmouthshire by the Milbornes and the Priory at Abergavenny by the Gunters, all families whose chiefs figure in the Recusant Lists. Among smaller monastic buildings more certainly used for the Mass were the Grange of Penrhos, belonging to Gracedieu, held by the Powells of Llantilio, the chapel at Blackbrook, owned by the Bodenhams, and the chapel and grange of Llanfair Cilgoed held by the Morgans, where Mass was said until 1691.
[2] Report of the Bishop of Hereford, printed from the State Papers in Catholic Record Society.
[3] Cal. S.P. Irel., 1574–85, p. 285.
[4] Ibid., p. 266.
[5] Ibid., p. 280.
[6] Ibid., p. 288.
[7] Ibid., p. 312.

NOTES

10th January, 1582, Sir Henry Wallop objected [1] to Mr. Jenyson's large pays and ingratitude. On 6th December following another report came [2] from Wallop accusing the Master of the Rolls (Nicholas Whyte) of being a solicitor for all traitors; while a letter to Walsingham of 17th March, 1583, makes the situation still clearer. In this paper Wallop complains [3] of Burghley's continued dislike for him and declares that Auditor Jenyson is ' a great Papist, his cunning great and conscience little.' He had heard that Her Majesty had been moved to bestow Baltinglas on Sir Henry Harrington in respect of his hurts, but he makes clear his opinion of the latter's folly and unfitness to govern. In connection with these accusations, Sir Nicholas Malby had written [4] in the previous September that Wallop was ' of nature and condition somewhat sour.'

A sign of an alliance appears when the Lords Justices commend [5] Sir William St. Leger's character. On 8th August, 1583, Waterhouse wrote [6] to Burghley as to the hard opinion conceived against him touching the boats at Athlone and two months later Sir Nicholas Whyte reported [7] that the favour shown to the Countess of Kildare was well bestowed, and that the Justice Dillon continued his evil doing. In the following month Archbishop Loftus wrote [8] in favour of Sir Robert Dillon maliciously traduced; but the latter had already involved himself in another feud by writing [9] a week earlier against Geoffrey Fenton declaring that his office of General Collector was useless and complaining of his choleric speech.

In November, 1583, John Brown declared [10] that Sir Nicholas Malby was sad and sick. The disgrace he had at his last being in England and his debts would cause his death. At this point Lord Deputy Perrot appears and begins by complaining[11] of Auditor Jenyson's sickness and slackness, Sir Henry Wallop referred[12] to Mr. Fenton as ' a most apparent bribe taker ' and described Marshal Bagenall's greedy course. The feuds, which followed, have been described[13] in the book in some detail.

Meanwhile in an account of his service Lord Deputy Sidney had declared[14] that ' the Earl of Ormonde (my professed foe) sometime with clamour, but oftener with whispering did bitterly backbite me.' Six years earlier Sidney had been forced to defend himself against complaints[15] of his hard dealing with Sir William Drury in Munster. On 7th June, 1581, Lord Upper Ossory appealed[16] to Leicester against the ' malice and hate of my great enemy the Earl of Ormonde,' both of them being Governmental and Protestant Lords; while Sir Nicholas Malby, also, was Ormonde's consistent enemy.[17]

Complaints of ill health seem to have been constant. The medical history of Lord Deputy Perrot is recorded in detail elsewhere; but the references to Auditor Jenyson's gout, for instance, are perpetual. Sir Edward Waterhouse refers[18] in

[1] Cal. S.P. Irel., 1574–85, p. 340.
[2] Ibid., p. 415.
[3] Ibid., p. 434.
[4] Ibid., p. 398.
[5] Ibid., p. 460.
[6] Ibid., p. 462.
[7] Ibid., p. 473.
[8] Ibid., p. 479.
[9] Ibid., p. 479.
[10] Ibid., p. 482.
[11] Ibid., p. 535.
[12] Ibid., p. 403.
[13] See Chapter XI, passim.
[14] Cal. Carew MSS., 1575–88, p. 350.
[15] Ibid., p. 81.
[16] Ibid., p. 321.
[17] Ibid., p. 327.
[18] Cal. S.P. Irel., 1574–85, p. 340.

NOTES

January, 1582, to his own weak body, and Sir Warham St. Leger complained [1] of his long sickness. Archbishop Loftus wrote [2] that his body was weak and diseased; while in the summer of 1584 it appeared that Sir Henry Wallop still remained [3] very weak in the hot weather on account of his illness and that Geoffrey Fenton was recovering [4] from the ague; nor were these isolated cases but a series of continual complaint. A light is thrown on the official life in Ireland by these difficulties and these feuds.

NOTE ON THE ORDNANCE IN IRELAND

As far as corruption in the Ordnance Office in Ireland during the Wingfield period is concerned, it appears evident that the policy which aroused so much complaint was one of economising on the upkeep of Her Majesty's store. Later direct traffic with the rebels developed. In July, 1583, a petition was sent [5] to England by the Master Smith against the bringing in of sword blades, armour and munition to the strengthening of the rebels.

At the same time the old policy still seems to have continued as evidenced by the complaint [6] of Lord Justice Wallop giving details of the lewd dealings and forgeries of John Shereff, late Clerk of the Ordnance, in counterfeiting bills in the names of sundry captains and officers who are dead. In the next summer, 1586, this subject was pursued by Auditor Jenyson. 'The office of the Ordnance here,' he wrote [7] to Burghley, ' is far out of order, wanting so sufficient and diligent ministers as thereto doth appertain. And Jaques Wingfield, master thereof, having remained there (in England) these four years come Bartholomew tide, will not upon any persuasion come to account, either for his band and ministers of the ordnance, or the great mass of munitions, habiliments for the wars and other provisions and furnitures for that office, for which he hath yielded none account for these ten years past, nor yet for his disbursements concerning that office.' Lord Deputy Perrot on this subject was explicit. ' The Master of the Ordnance,' he had written [8] in the previous January in reference to Jacques Wingfield, ' is absent and old and I wish there were a more sufficient man in his place.' In the following year Mr. Wingfield died in England very much in debt to the Crown, although he still retained [9] the parsonage of Dunboyne and the keepership of Dublin Castle, as well as his Ordnance Office. A brief ' résumé ' of his career is necessary for an understanding of the position of affairs.

On 13th July, 1558, a letter from Queen Mary had directed[10] that Sir John Travers and Jaques Wingfield, who had led over 300 men from Milford Haven, should have the office of the Ordnance. Sir John Travers, who had been Master of the Ordnance as early as 10th March, 1540, died in Ireland on 25th May, 1562, and was generally reputed a very honest man. It was from this moment that Mr. Wingfield's difficulties began. He was well known in Ireland, having served in subordinate capacities since 1534 and he had incurred the hostility of Lord Deputy

---

[1] *Ibid.*, p. 361.
[2] *Ibid.*, p. 398.
[3] *Ibid.*, p. 513.
[4] *Ibid.*, p. 523.
[5] Petition of John Morgin, Master Smith of Ireland to the Privy Council, dated July, 1583. Cal. S.P. Irel., 1574–85, p. 482.
[6] Letter of Lord Justice Wallop, dated 2nd January, 1585. *Ibid.*, p. 545.
[7] Letter of Auditor Jenyson to Burghley, dated 17th June, 1586. Cal. S.P. Irel., 1586–88, p. 79.
[8] Letter from Lord Deputy Perrot to the Privy Council, dated 31st January, 1586. Cal. S.P. Irel., 1586–8, p. 16.
[9] Note dated 10th September, 1587. State Papers, Elizabeth, Ireland, Vol. CXXXI, No. 11.
[10] Cal. S.P. Irel., 1509–73, p. 147.

NOTES

Sussex. Only a month later Lord Sussex sent [1] home a memorial. ' Jaques Wing-field to have his course ordered in Ireland, to be punished and to resign his patent.' This seems to have been approved ; for in July the instruction came [2] back that Jaques Wingfield was to be discharged from the office of Master of the Ordnance and from all other offices and places on account of his untoward conduct in the field towards Shane. However, he survived this setback and appears to have gained his pardon in the following year, perhaps through the influence of Sir Henry Sidney who was always his friend.[3] A few years later he was in trouble with the succeeding lord deputy, Sir William Fitzwilliam. On 25th September, 1572, the Master wrote [4] to Burghley that the Lord Deputy had received him unfavourably and had refused his request to lodge in the Castle. Fitzwilliam himself was more explicit. ' Jaques Wingfield,' he wrote [5] on 13th June, 1573, ' treads the same cross paths.' At this point another effort was made to remove Mr. Wingfield, who retorted by a relation [6] of his forty years service. In this paper, which he sent over to Burghley, he laments to be discharged unheard and to be condemned as unworthy to live and explains that he flies to his patron in aid of his innocency. The appeal was successful and he remained at his post.

The later years of his tenure were disturbed by his creditors [7] and by the appearance of a fresh set of enemies. In a series of notes from Lord Justice Wallop to Walsingham the following entry occurs [8] : ' The Master of the Ordnance not to be paid his reckoning till his account be taken.' The *riposte* took the form of laying thirty-four charges, ' the sinister information ' to which reference has already been made [9] and which was the immediate prelude to his final departure for England.

Nevertheless under his successors matters did not improve and, after the brief tenure of office by Sir William Stanley had ended with his treason in Holland, the control of the Ordnance in Ireland became a pawn in the Perrot dispute. The Queen intervened to command that Sir Thomas Perrot, the Deputy's son, should be summarily dismissed [10] from this charge and Sir George Carew was granted the office of Master. A memorial sent to Burghley shortly before will show the state of affairs at this date. ' That your Lordship,' the request to the Secretary began,[11] ' will take order that a Master of the Ordnance may be sent to reside upon his office, because there is neither clerk nor other accountant in that office, and the Master Gunner old and impotent and thereby not able to look to that charge.' Later papers hardly show much change. On 21st July, 1589, Thomas Chapman wrote [12] home to Burghley in reference to the accounts of the Master of the Ordnance and prayed for some means to check the deceits used in that office. Seven years later these difficulties are again referred to in a letter to Burghley, this time from Lord Deputy Burgh and his Council. They recommend [13] to his favour-able consideration John Allen, Clerk of the Ordnance, who had complained of his ' small entertainment which was only 15*d*. per diem ' for himself and a man and had not been paid for four years. They add significantly that they have ' No

[1] Memorial of the Earl of Sussex. *Ibid.*, p. 196.
[2] Instruction for the Earl of Sussex, dated 3rd July, 1562. *Ibid.*, p. 197.
[3] Sidney Papers, i, p. 282.
[4] Cal. S.P. Irel., 1509–73, p. 484.
[5] Cal. S.P. Irel., 1509–73, p. 511.
[6] Cal. S.P. Irel., 1574–85, p. 27.
[7] Letter dated 20th November, 1579. *Ibid.*, p. 195.
[8] Letter dated 11th October, 1582. *Ibid.*, p. 403.
[9] See Chapter XI, ' The fall of Lord Deputy Perrot.'
[10] Carew MSS., 1575–88, p. 460.
[11] Cal. S.P. Irel., 1586–88, p. 432.
[12] Cal. S.P. Irel., 1588–89, p. 221.
[13] Cal. S.P. Irel., 1595–8, p. 212.

498

NOTES

present means ' to relieve him. The explosion of six lasts of gunpowder on Dublin Quay in the following Spring caused Mr. Allen's imprisonment and at the enquiry which was held in the Castle a number of porters deposed [1] that they had worked for whole days for the Clerk of the Ordnance and had not received pay. On 6th November, 1597, Sir George Bourchier, Carew's successor, appealed [2] to England for instructions as to how he should deal with the defalcations of munitions and arms; while the investigation made by Lord Deputy Mountjoy shows that this condition was chronic. ' The bearer Mr. Ersfield,' [3] wrote the new Governor to Cecil, ' can give an honest relation of the state of the munition. There have been great abuses in that kind and they are likely to continue. Sir George Bourchier has such mean entertainment for his under officers that they cannot be of any sufficiency or of any great sincerity : himself doth not so thoroughly understand that business, as so great a charge requireth.' After detailing the necessity for some under officer with a greater fee as a Surveyor of the Ordnance in Ireland, he recommends Ersfield for the post; but as long as the Irish war continued there was no great improvement.

One outstanding question remains to be decided, the extent of the traffic between the officers of the Ordnance and the Irish and the quantity of munition which found its way to the enemy. In this matter it is only possible to gain vague impressions from the series of increasing complaints, and it is of interest to observe that these only begin to be serious several years after the loss of the Armada. After the explosion in Dublin an accusation was launched [4] against Allen of selling munitions secretly to John Shelton and Alexander Palles, Sheriffs of the city of Dublin, for transmission into the West.[5] This had been foreshadowed by the report sent over in 1596 by Sir John Dowdall to Burghley. ' In any wise,' he had written,[6] ' restrain them (the Irish) from powder. It will be said they make powder ; assure yourself it is a very small quantity and Ireland yieldeth no brimstone . . . such . . . as oppose themselves against God and his word what will they leave undone for gain and what will they leave undiscovered under confession.' The evidence of Sir Henry Docwra can also be adduced in support. ' The Scottish galleys,' he had reported [7] in 1599, ' bring powder to the rebels and natives of the northern parts. The munitions embezzled in the royal forces are underhand sold to traitors by the ministers of the Master of the Ordnance.' As a corollary to this accusation there appears a statement [8] of the following year that ' the Clerk of the Munition had writ in the accounts that he had sixty barrels of powder and sixty of match, but that he had but six and they short and the rest . . . missing or rotten.' A few details should now be given of the salvage from the Armada, which would seem to explain both the comparative calm of the period of the earlier Risings, as far as treasonable sale is concerned, and also the desire for fresh cannon set up once the Irish could play with this fire.

In the first place some guns had been carried ashore in the various landings. Thus, according to the statement [9] of Juan de Nova, the men in landing from the *Rata* had taken such small stores as they could, some munitions and a field

[1] State Papers Ireland, Elizabeth, cxcviii, No. 26, iv.
[2] *Ibid.*, cci, No. 59.
[3] *Ibid.*, ccvii, No. 21.
[4] State Papers Ireland, Elizabeth cxcviii, No. 26, iv.
[5] One aspect of the Irish attitude should be noticed. ' One hundred and forty four barrels of powder,' wrote the Annalist, ' sent from England destroy Wine Street in Dublin and a quarter of the city and a multitude of honourable persons.' Annals of the Four Masters, 1597, p. 2013.
[6] State Papers Ireland, Elizabeth clxxxvii, No. 39.
[7] Report of Sir Henry Docwra. Lambeth MSS. 632.
[8] Sir Henry Docwra's ' Relation,' printed in *Miscellanea Celtica*, p. 234.
[9] Statement of Juan de Nova, dated 21st January, 1589. Cal. S.P. Spanish, iv, p. 509.

NOTES

piece. In other cases they rescued some guns when the ships themselves were cast on the shore. George Woodlock, for instance, when writing [1] of the galleon wrecked upon Borris, referred to ' the ship cast up on the shore. She had in her 50 pieces of brass, beside four great cannon, so as the ship is past recovery.' After the landing in the McSweeney's country it was soon reported [2] that the Irish chiefs and their followers ' have gotten great store of the Spanish calivers and muskets.' Similarly in the rebellion of Sir Murrough O'Flaherty in the spring of 1589 it was asserted [3] by the Mayor of Galway that ' the rebels are upon two thousand men and have much furniture out of the Spanish wrecks with the great ordnance of three ships and about twenty Spaniards.' It is not surprising that very soon orders were given [4] that ' straight dealings and tortures were to be used to recover from the Irish the treasure taken from the Spanish wrecks.'

The Government were not slow in this vital matter and as early as October, 1588, steps had been taken to salve the Spanish ordnance for the Crown. ' And touching the ordnance and other munition lost here,' the Lord Deputy had written, [5] ' all diligence should be used to save as much as may be for Her Majesty's use, but the great ship at Bellicro and the rest cast away about those islands, are now all broken in pieces and the ordnance and everything else utterly lost I fear me.' Geoffrey Fenton was sent [6] down to Sligo on behalf of the Government, but was soon obliged to report [7] his ill success in digging out the Spanish ordnance. As the Winter progressed the Lord Deputy forced a hopeful spirit. ' Of the Spanish munition,' he wrote [8] to the Privy Council, ' there is saved upon Connaught side but three small pieces, but it is thought by Mr. Secretary (Fenton) that next summer there will be some others worth the labour gotten. The like opinion hath also Sir George Carew, the Master of the Ordnance, for some on Munster side. And further I hear that three fair pieces of brass, which lie within view between rocks at Bunboys, where Don Alonzo was drowned, will also be recovered.' One comment on these activities may be noted, the statement, [9] admittedly the report of an interested witness, that Sir Geoffrey Fenton lost £5,000 worth of artillery from the Spanish wrecks. The whole question is difficult and has not yet been entirely cleared up.

[1] Letter of George Woodlock forwarded to Walsingham 12th September, 1588. Cal. S.P. Ireland, 1588–89, p. 136.
[2] Advertisement from Henry Duke, dated 26 October 1588, *ibid*, p. 65.
[3] Letter of the Mayor of Galway to the Lord Deputy, dated 5 April 1589 *ibid*, p. 148.
[4] Sir Richard Bingham's orders reported to Burghley on 27th July, 1589. *Ibid.*, p. 223.
[5] Letter of Lord Deputy to Burghley, dated 1st October, 1588. Cal. S.P. Ireland, 1588–9, p. 48.
[6] Letter of Geoffrey Fenton to the Lord Deputy, dated 7th October, 1588. *Ibid.*, p. 53.
[7] Letter of Geoffrey Fenton, dated at Ballymote, 9th October, 1588. *Ibid.*, p. 54.
[8] Letter of Lord Deputy to the Privy Council, dated 31st December, 1588. *Ibid.*, p. 97.
[9] Letter of Sir Richard Bingham to Walsingham, dated 14th September, 1589. *Ibid.*, p. 237.

BIBLIOGRAPHICAL NOTE

BIBLIOGRAPHICAL NOTE

A list is appended of a number of primary authorities which bear on the subject of this study. In order to reduce space the list is confined to British sources and only those papers are mentioned to which reference has already been made at some point in the text or the footnotes. All Continental authorities, whether printed or in manuscript, as in the case of the important Valladolid MSS., are left unmentioned. This list is therefore not intended to be in any way exhaustive, and even in regard to English and Celtic affairs it only indicates a portion of the sources used.

I. GENERAL STATE PAPERS

Acts of the Privy Council.
State Papers among the Record·Office MSS.
Calendar of State Papers, Domestic.
Calendar of State Papers, Foreign and Spanish.
Calendar of State Papers, Ireland.
Calendar of Carew MSS.
Calendar of State Papers, Rome.
Calendar of State Papers, Scottish.
Calendar of Hamilton Papers.
Calendar of State Papers, Venetian.
State Trials.

II. HISTORICAL MANUSCRIPTS' COMMISSION REPORTS

Calendar of Ancaster MSS.
Calendar of Bagot MSS.
Calendar of Buccleugh MSS.
Calendar of Coke MSS.
Calendar of Clarke Thornhill MSS.
Calendar of De Lisle and Dudley MSS.
Calendar of Dovaston MSS.
Calendar of Drummond Moray MSS.
Calendar of Egmont MSS.
Calendar of Essex MSS.
Calendar of Finch MSS.
Calendar of Gawdy MSS.
Calendar of Mar and Kellie MSS.
Calendar of Molyneux MSS.
Calendar of Montagu of Beaulieu MSS.
Calendar of Northumberland MSS.
Calendar of Pepys MSS.
Calendar of Rutland MSS.
Calendar of Salisbury MSS., i–xv.
Calendar of Savile Foljambe MSS.
Calendar of Somerset MSS.
Calendar of Stafford MSS.

NOTES

Calendar of Burford Corporation MSS.
Calendar of Dunwich Corporation MSS.
Calendar of Hereford Corporation MSS.
Calendar of Salisbury Corporation MSS.
Calendar of Shrewsbury Corporation MSS.
Calendar of Southampton Corporation MSS.

III. MISCELLANEOUS ECCLESIASTICAL AND LEGAL PAPERS

Calendar of Fiants, Ireland.
Calendar of Patent Rolls, Ireland.
Calendar of Registrum Magni Sigilli Regnum Scotorum.
Calendar of Star Chamber Proceedings relating to Wales.
Entry Book of Orders and Decrees of the Court of Castle Chamber, Ireland,
    see Cal. Egmont MSS.
Pension Book of Cardinal Pole.
Register of the Chapter Acts, St. David's.
Register of Cardinal Bainbridge, Surtees Society.
Register of the Bishops of Hereford.
Register of Sir Thomas Butler, Cambrian Journal iv.
Register of the English College, Valladolid, C.R.S., xxx.
Records of the Society of Jesus (ed. H. Foley S.J.).
Douai Diaries.
Franciscan MSS. (ed. C. P. Meehan).
Blairs Papers (ed. M. V. Hay).
Burghley Papers, C.R.S.
Churchwardens' Accounts of Ludlow, Camden Society.

IV. VARIOUS DOMESTIC PAPERS

Household Books of Naworth, Surtees Society.
Household Books of the Earl of Northumberland.
Household Books of the Earl of Derby.
Calendar of Coleman Deeds.
Calendar of Crosswood Deeds.
Calendar of Hawarden Deeds.
Farmer Chetham MSS., Surtees Society.
Survey of Wilton, Roxburgh Society.

V. LETTERS, DIARIES AND CORRESPONDENCE

John Chamberlain *Letters*, Camden Society.
John Leland *Itinerary*.
Fynes Moryson *Itinerary*.
Henry Machyn *Diary*.
Richard Symonds *Diary*.
John Manningham *Diary*.
Lady Margaret Hoby *Diary* (ed. D. Meads).
Leycester Correspondence, Camden Society.
Plumpton Correspondence.
Stradling Correspondence.
Correspondence of James VI with England, Camden Society.
Fugger News Letters (ed. V. von Klarwill).
Devereux Papers, Camden Misc. xiii.

BIBLIOGRAPHICAL NOTE

Sydney Papers, i. and ii.
Trevelyan Papers.
Warrender Papers.
Calendar of Wynn Papers.
Yelverton Papers.

VI. Annals, Histories and Biographies

Annals of the Four Masters.
Annals of Loch Cé.
Annals of Ulster.
Thadeus Dowling *Annales Hiberniæ.*
Spicilegium Ossoriense (P. F. Moran).
Nicholas Sander *De Schismate Anglicano* (ed. D. Lewis).
John Foxe *Actes and Monuments.*
Sir John Wynn *History of Gwydir.*
Sir John Dodridge *History . . . of the Principality of Wales* (1630).
Thomas Russell *Relation of the fitz Geralds of Ireland* (1638).
Geraldine Documents (ed. Hayman and Graves).
Fynes Moryson *History of Ireland.*
Philip O'Sullevan Beare *Historiæ Catholicæ Iberniæ Compendium.*
John Spottiswood, *History.*
John Aubrey, *Brief Lives.*
Henry Clifford, *Life of Jane, Duchess of Feria.*
R. Smith *Life of the Lady Magdalen, Viscomtesse Montague* (1627).
The Conversion of Sir Tobie Mathew (ed. A. H. Mathew).
John Gerard, S.J., *Autobiography* (ed. J. Morris, S.J.).
Lord Herbert of Cherbury *Autobiography.*
Lughaidh O'Clery *Life of Hugh Roe O'Donnell.*
George Owen *Dialogue of Wales ; Description of Pembrokeshire.*
John Stowe *Survey of London.*
Sir John Harington *Nugæ Antiquæ.*
Sir Robert Naunton *Fragmenta Regalia.*
Sir Nicholas Lestrange *The Merry Passages.*
Anthony Munday *The English Romayne Life.*
James Wadsworth *The English Spanish Pilgrim* (1629).
Sir Henry Wotton *Memoirs of the Earl of Essex ; A Parallel between the Earl of Essex and the Duke of Buckingham.*
Francis Bacon *Apology concerning the Earl of Essex.*
Sir Henry Docwra *Report*, Misc. Celtica.
William Maitland *Apologie of Williame Maitland.*
Richard Bannatyne *Journal of the Transactions in Scotland.*
William Allen *Defence of Stanley*, Chetham Society.

INDEX

INDEX

In the case where several members of one family are mentioned, these are grouped around a chief to whom their relationship is shown. Dates of death are given to distinguish peers bearing the same title. Slight variations of spelling, due to quotation from contemporary sources, are given in brackets. The documents printed on pp. 462–87 are not included in this index since they consist of lists of names already arranged under headings.

INDEX

INDEX

INDEX

INDEX

INDEX

INDEX

INDEX

INDEX

INDEX

INDEX

INDEX

Meyrick, Elizabeth (Gwyn), his dau.-in-law,
    Lady 345, 427
    Sir Francis of Monckton, his son, 342, 426
    Henry of Roasetown, his son, 426
    Simon, his son, 341
    John, his son, 341, 426
    Lewis 73
Mhic an Toisich, 287
Michelgrove, 14
Michell, John 297
Middelburg, 245, 313, 315
    Lange Jan Toren at 245
    Lange Delft in 245
Middleham, 4
Middleton, Captain 259
    a merchant, 314
Middleton Keynes, 23
Midletons, 40
Milan, 2, 76, 78, 83–6, 90, 272, 326–7
Milford Haven, 29, 226, 297, 302, 425, 497
Mochnant, 32
Monarchia Sicula, 134
Monasternenagh, 134, 174
Monckton, 426
Monkstown, 199, 202
Montagu, Anthony (Browne), d. 1592, first
    Viscount 27, 61, 234
    Magdalen (Dacre), his wife, Viscountess 61
    Mabel, his sister. *See* Kildare, Countess of.
    Mary, his daughter. *See* Southampton,
        Countess of.
Monteagle, William (Stanley), d. 1581, third
    Lord 7, 256
    William (Parker), his gd.son, d. 1622,
        fourth Lord 376, 401–3, 432–4, 440
    Elizabeth (Tresham), his gd.dau.-in-law,
        Lady 401
Moore, Sir Garret 205
    a priest, 22
Moray, Lord James (Stewart), d. 1570, Earl
    of 96, 101–6
Mordaunt, John, d. 1572, second Lord 23
More, Sir Thomas 8, 9, 15, 18, 127
Morgan, Henry, Bishop of St. David's, 32
    Sir Mathew 369, 376
    Thomas 83, 89, 90, 252–4, 316, 411
    Sir William 301, 495
    of Llanfair Cilgoed, 495
    of Machen, 89
    of Tredegar, 252
Morley, Henry (Parker), d. 1556, eighth Lord
    7, 12
    Henry, his gd.son, d. 1577, ninth Lord 28,
        136
    Edward, d. 1618, tenth Lord 401
Morocco, gunrunning to 323, 486–7
Morone, Cardinal Giovanni 121, 177
Morra, Mgr. Bernardino 84
Morris, Robert 194
Morton, James (Douglas), d. 1581, fourth
    Earl of 107, 300
Morven, 285
Moryson, Fynes 189, 415, 418–9, 446–8
Mospatrickhope, 102
Mostyn, Sir Thomas 61
    Captain Hugh 258, 369

Mostyn of Mostyn, 38
    of Talacre, 51, 74
Moulsoe, 23
Moyn, 184
Moythe, David 47
Mountgarret, Edmund (Butler), d. 1602,
    second Viscount 191, 364–5, 373
    Richard, his son, d. 1651, third Viscount 365
    Margaret (O'Neill), his dau.-in-law, Vis-
        countess 365
    Eleanor, his sister. *See* Cahir, Lady.
Mountjoy, Charles (Blount), d. 1606, eighth
    Lord 320, 360, 411, 414–22, 445–52, 499
Much Wenlock, 19
Muinter Eolais, 265, 267, 275
Mull, 277, 281, 285, 289
Mullingar, 205, 446
Multifarnham, 184
Munday, Anthony 82
Murloch, 283
Murrish, 270
Musgrave, Sir William 5
Mynachdy, 353, 356
Mynwere, 425
'Mytchell Wylie.' *See* Maitland, William.
Mytton, Sir Piers 74

Nabs, Cornelius 313
Nantconway, 343
Naples, 134, 140–2, 273
Naunton, Sir Robert 71, 211, 418
Navarre, Court of 94
Navestock, 12
Navigator's Supply, 408
Naworth, 5, 7
    Household books of 5
Neath, Abbey of 493
    Abbot Leisan of 493
Neri, St. Philip 144
Netterville, George 205
Neuenaar, Count Adolf Moers 242, 247
Neville. *See* Westmoreland, Earl of.
    Sir John 177, 234
Nevski, Pan Alexander 84
Newark, 392
Newborough, 47
Newcastle-upon-Tyne, 17, 215, 309, 312
Newdigate, Dom Sebastian 234
Newfoundland, 295
Newport (Bucks), 15, 22–3
    (Mon.), 295
New Radnor, 354
Newry, 222, 363, 369
Newton in Makerfield, 256
Nolan, Thady 225, 227–8
Nombre de Dios, 140
Nonsuch, Palace of 383
Norfolk, Thomas (Howard), d. 1554, third
    Duke of 4
    Elizabeth (Stafford), his wife, Duchess of
        3, 4, 13
    Agnes (Tilney), his stepmother, Duchess of
        1, 4
    Anne, his sister. *See* Oxford, Countess of.

INDEX

INDEX

INDEX

INDEX

INDEX

INDEX

INDEX